DESIGNING WITH COLOUR

HOAKI

Hoaki Books, S. L.
C/ Ausiàs March, 128
08013 Barcelona, Spain
T. 0034 935 952 283
F. 0034 932 654 883
info@hoaki.com
www.hoaki.com
hoakibooks

Designing with Colour
The Use of Gradients in Graphic Design

ISBN: 978-84-1065-008-4

Author: Amy Guanghui Niu
Editor: Sam Wu
Proofreader: Kevin Krell
Designers: Pan Yuhua, spread: David Lorente
Cover design: Claudia Martínez Alonso

DL: B 19125-2025
Printed in China

DESIGNING WITH COLOUR

THE USE OF GRADIENTS IN GRAPHIC DESIGN

Amy Guanghui Niu (ed.)

HOAKI

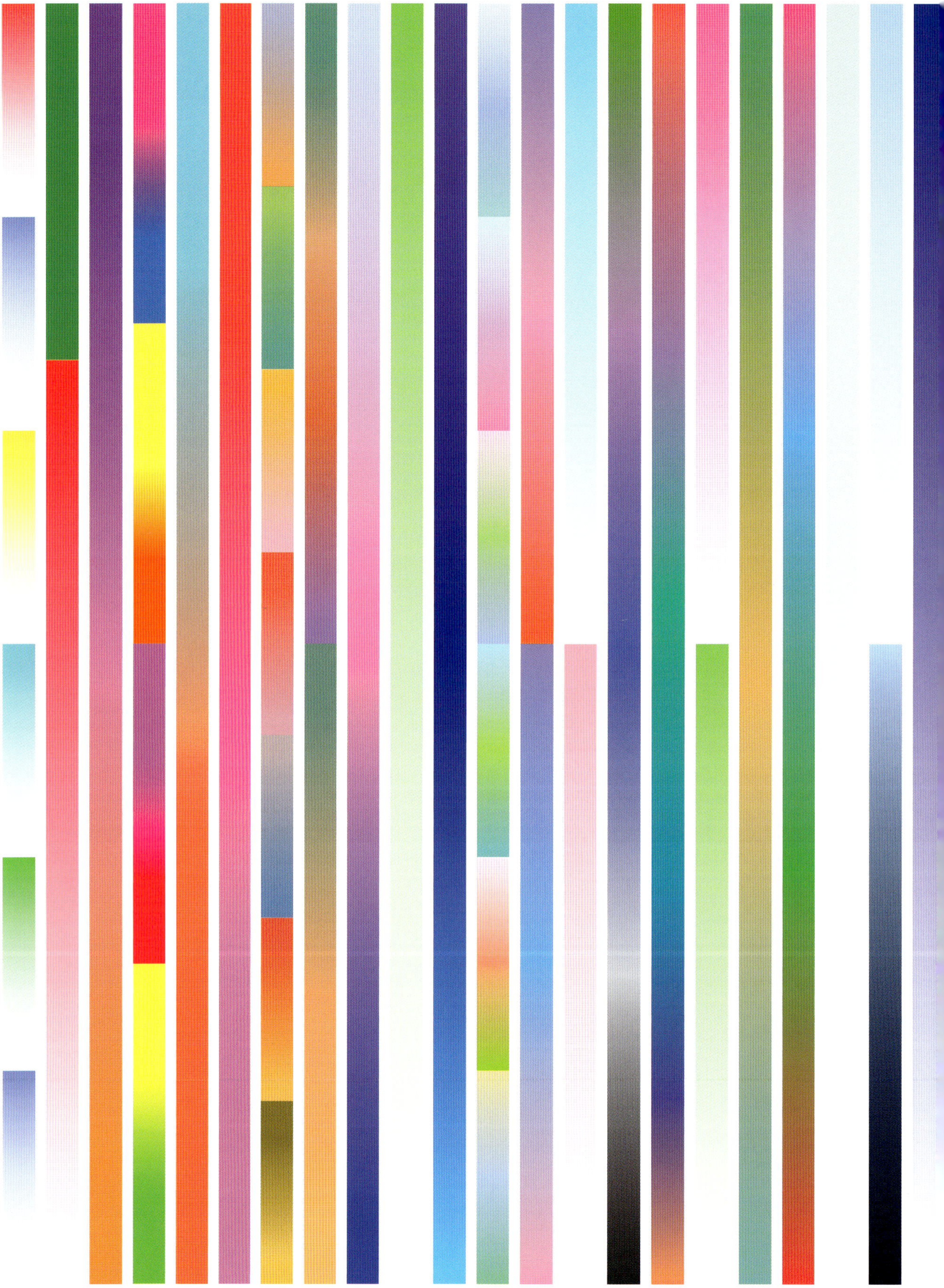

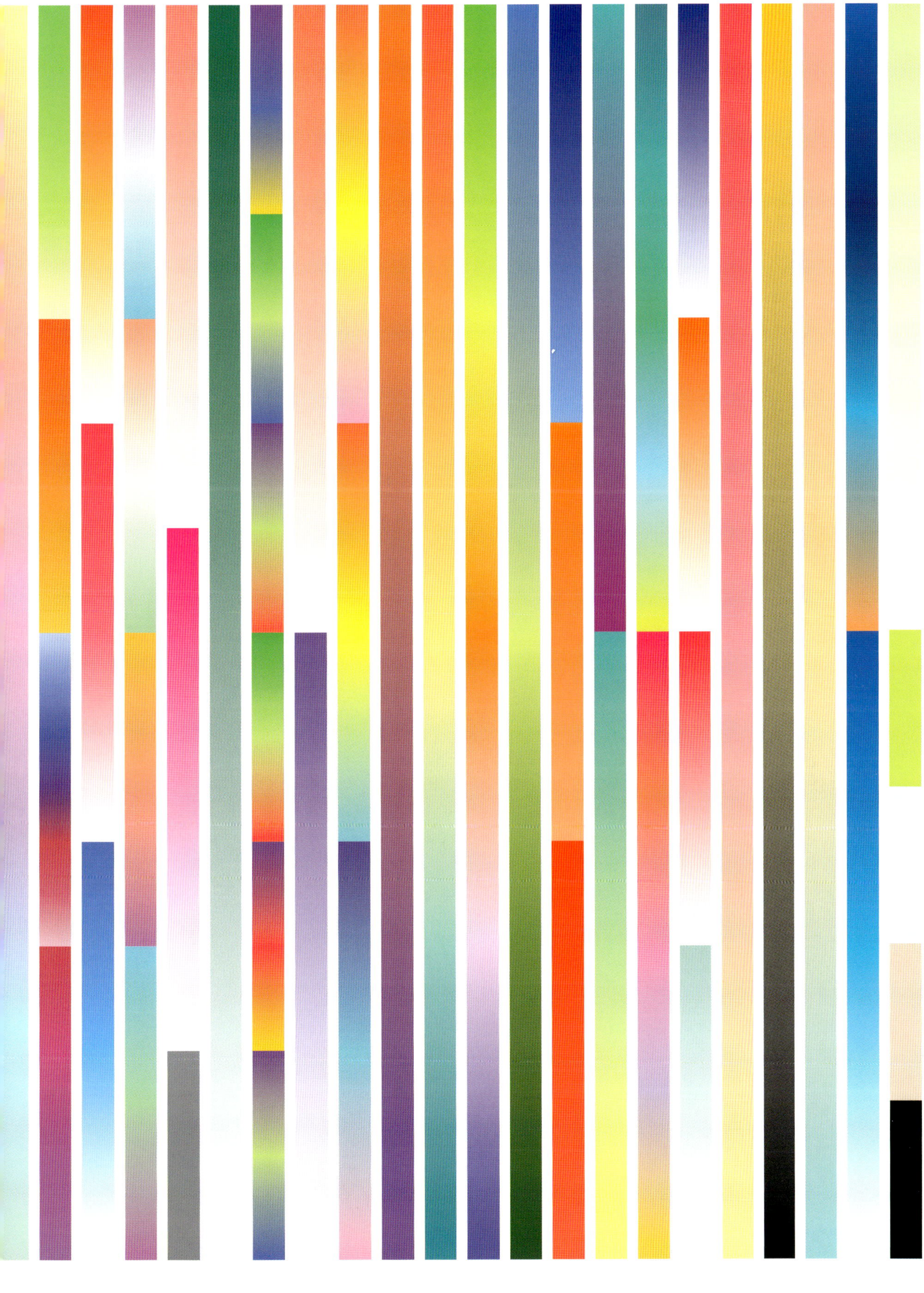

CONTENTS

INTRO

FROM THE GRADIENT TO MULTIGRADIENT

Gradient design has always been a dynamic and expressive form in the world of design, captivating audiences with its seamless transitions and rich depth. Gradient design was initially used in graphic design to simulate three-dimensional effects. In 2013, Apple launched the IOS 7 interface, adding a gradient effect of similar colours in flat colour blocks. Gradient colour gradually becomes a design element that breaks through the previous role of creating a sense of three-dimensional space. It enriches the way of visual presentation in colour. In 2016, PANTONE first chose two colours as representative colour, and used the mixed gradient of the two colours for colour presentation. From then on, gradient colours started to become a new trend in design.

The power of colour blending lies in its straightforward yet profound ability to evoke emotions and create immersive visual experiences. When used appropriately, gradient design can transform a simple piece of work into a compelling and enchanting atmosphere that draws viewers in and leaves a lasting impression.

This book aims to be the definitive guide for mastering the art of gradient design, offering both essential knowledge and a wealth of inspiration. We begin our journey by delving into the fundamentals of gradient design, starting with an exploration of the principles of colour theory. Understanding how colours interact and blend is crucial for creating harmonious and impactful gradients. By grasping these basics, you will be equipped to make informed design choices that enhance the overall aesthetic of your work.

In the next chapter, we shift from theory to practice by showcasing a variety of design projects that utilize different gradient techniques and colour combinations. These projects are intended to spark your imagination and demonstrate the versatility of gradient design. From subtle, monochromatic shifts to bold, multi-coloured transitions, you will see how gradients can be applied across various mediums and styles. Each featured project will include an introduction to the design inspiration and the colour values used to achieve the desired effect.

Blending theoretical knowledge with practical inspiration, this book is designed to be your comprehensive resource for gradient design. Whether you are a seasoned designer looking to refine your skills or a novice eager to learn, you will find valuable information and inspiration within these pages. By the end of this book, you will not only understand the principles of gradient design but also be able to apply them creatively and effectively in your own projects.

DESIGN WITH C

NG
OLOUR

C0 · M84 · Y51 · K0

UNVEILING THE SPECTRUM OF GRADIENT DESIGN

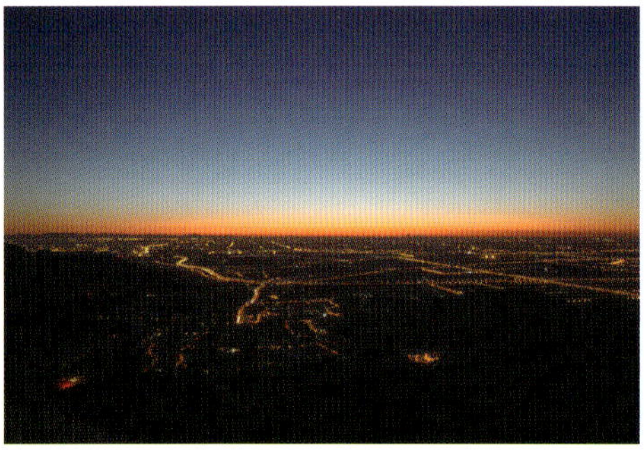

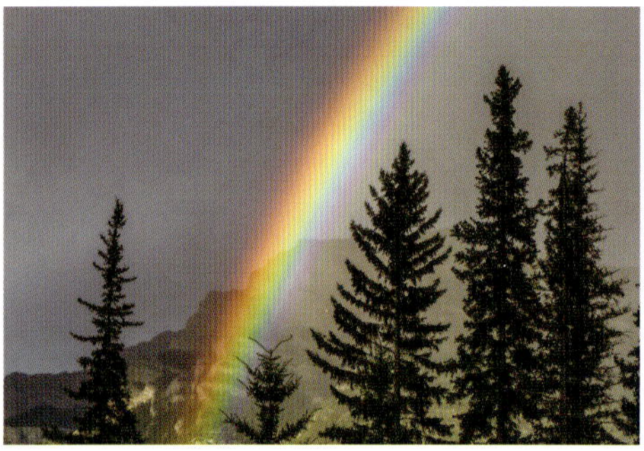

1 COLOUR GRADIENTS ALL AROUND US

Picture a beautiful sunset. As the sun begins to set, the sky near the horizon might be a deep, rich orange. As you look higher, that orange smoothly transitions into a softer pink, and higher still, the pink fades into a light blue, and finally, the blue deepens into the darkening night sky. This smooth, gradual change from one colour to another is a perfect example of a colour gradient.

In more technical terms, a colour gradient is a gradual blend between colours. It's not a sudden change where one colour ends and another begins, but rather a smooth and continuous transition.

Colour gradients are everywhere! You can see gradients in other parts of nature too, like in a rainbow where colours transition seamlessly from red to violet, or in the way the ocean changes colour from the shore to the deep sea. Artists and designers often use gradients to add depth and interest to their work because gradients can make a flat image look more dynamic and alive.

Nowadays, colour gradients are widely used in digital design, art, and various visual applications to create depth, interest, and beautiful visual effects.

Gradients offer a range of visual and psychological benefits that can enhance the appeal, functionality, and emotional impact of a design.

Attracting viewers

Gradients can add a sense of depth and three-dimensionality to otherwise flat designs. This helps elements stand out and makes the design more engaging. Gradients introduce a dynamic visual element that can capture attention and hold the viewer's interest. The smooth transition of colours is more intriguing than a single flat colour.

Guiding Attention

Designers can use gradients to guide the viewer's eye to specific parts of the design, creating a visual hierarchy. A gradient that transitions

LINEAR GRADIENT

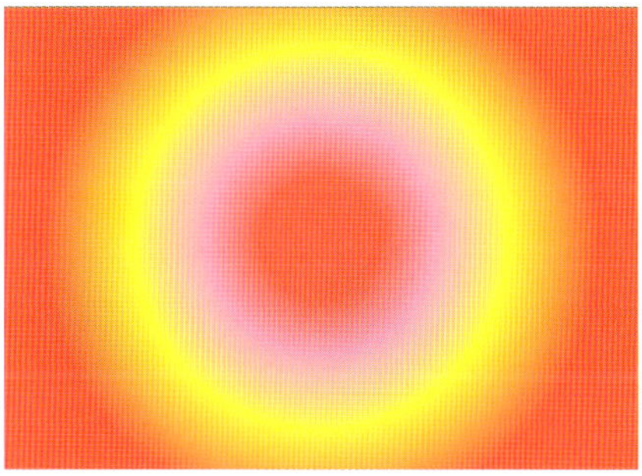

RADIAL GRADIENT

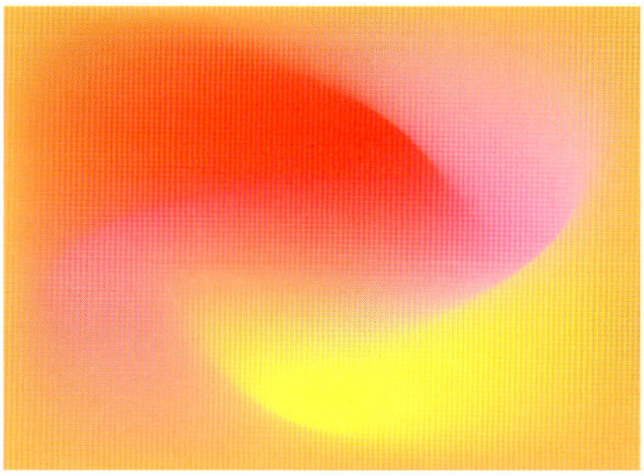

MESH GRADIENT

from light to dark can lead the eye towards a central element or focal point in the design. This is useful for highlighting important information or calls to action.

Branding and Identity

The limited number of distinct colours can make it challenging for brands to create unique identities. Traditional solid colours, while effective, are finite and often overused, leading to a saturated market where many brands begin to look similar. However, the introduction and popularity of gradients allows designers to craft unique and recognizable brand identities that are not easily replicated with standard solid colours.

2 CATEGORY OF COLOUR GRADIENTS

Colour gradients can be categorized based on how the colours transition and the pattern they follow.

Linear Gradient:

Think about a sunrise where the colours of the sky transition from deep blue to pink to orange in a straight line as you look from the horizon up to the sky.

In a linear gradient, the colours change along a straight line. You define two or more colours, and the gradient smoothly transitions between them from one end of the line to the other.

Radial Gradient

Consider the way the light radiates out from the sun. The colours might start very bright and intense in the centre and gradually fade out to a softer glow. A radial gradient starts from a central point and moves outward in a circular pattern. The colours transition from the centre to the outer edge, creating a radiating effect.

Mesh Gradient

Imagine the iridescent colours on the surface of a soap bubble, where different colours blend and shift smoothly in a complex pattern.

A mesh gradient is a more complex pattern where colours can transition in multiple directions, not just along a line or radius. It's like a patchwork of gradients blending smoothly into each other.

3
HOW TO APPLY AN EFFECTIVE GRADIENT COLOUR SCHEME

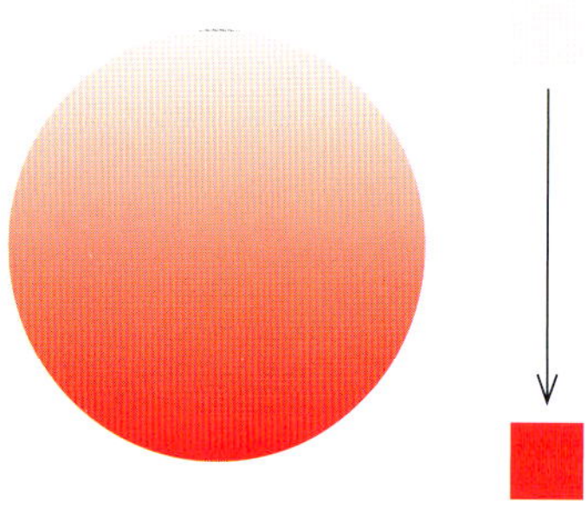

SAME COLOUR WITH DIFFERENT TINS AND SHADES

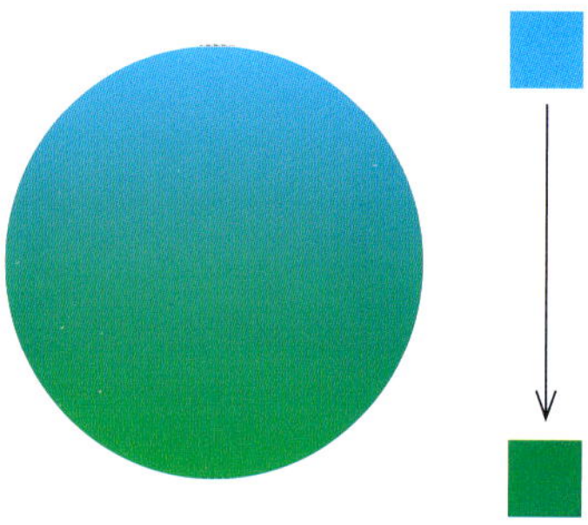

CHOOSE ANALOGOUS COLOURS

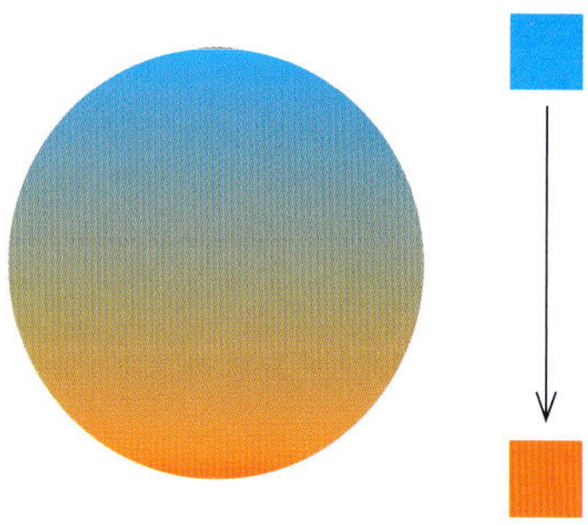

CHOOSE COMPLEMENTARY COLOURS

Applying an effective gradient colour scheme involves several key considerations to ensure that the gradient enhances the design rather than overwhelming or detracting from it.

Same colour with different tints and shades

Using tints and shades of the same colour creates a unified look that ties different elements of the design together. This cohesiveness is pleasing to the eye and helps convey a sense of balance and harmony. Also, variations in tints and shades add depth and dimension to the design which can make flat designs appear more dynamic and three-dimensional.

Choose analogous colours

Analogous colours are naturally harmonious because they share a common hue and are close in wavelength. This closeness creates a soothing and pleasant visual experience for the viewer. Since the colours are closely related, they blend well and create a cohesive look across a design. This unity is particularly beneficial in designs where you want to avoid jarring transitions and maintain a consistent mood.

Choose complementary colours

Complementary colours contain vibrant elements. These colours stand on opposite sides of the colour wheel and produce a sharp contrast when used together. Start with your brand's primary colours and then expand to gradient combinations that complement them.

4 TIPS ON USING GRADIENT COLOURS

ADD A THIRD COLOUR

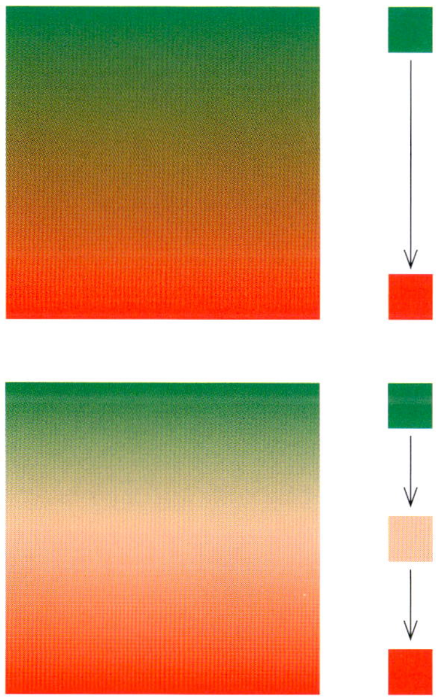

GRADIENTS WITH TRANSPARENCY

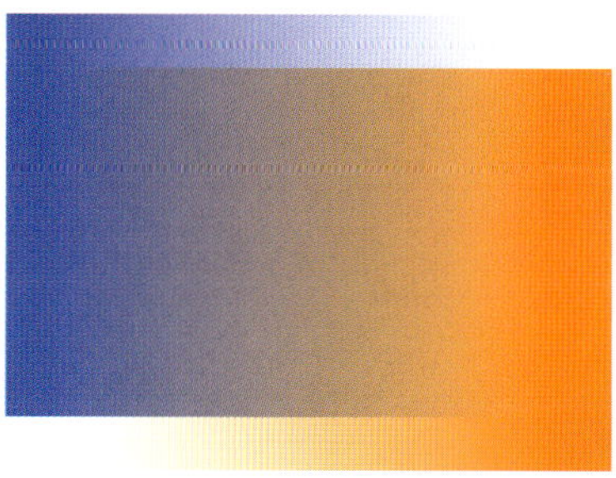

1
Add a third colour to the gradient to avoid a greyish centre. If you don't set a transition colour in the middle, the gradient may not make a smooth transition and you will end up with grey in between.

2
Be careful about banding. Bandings are the lines that appear in a colour gradient. So, the viewers will see a subtle demarcation between colour values instead of a smooth transition from one colour to the next. Using gradients with transparency can create a rich overlay effect, which works well on photographs and background images. Transparency can help gradients blend more smoothly with adjacent colours or elements.

3
It's important to try, and don't refuse to do additional testing to determine if the colour scheme you've chosen is optimal. Gradients of different colour depths give subtle effects, so several trials must be made to find the best one.

4
Test on multiple devices. Different devices and screens display colours differently. Check your gradient on multiple screens to ensure it looks good on mobiles, tablets, and monitors.

5
Make a moodboard. A gradient design moodboard not only serves as a source of inspiration but also acts as a practical guide for maintaining visual consistency throughout a project. By systematically collecting and organizing gradients and related design elements, you ensure that the final outcome resonates with the intended aesthetic and emotional goals of your project.

MONO-
CHROM
GRADIE

ATIC
NT

C0 · M100 · Y0 · K0

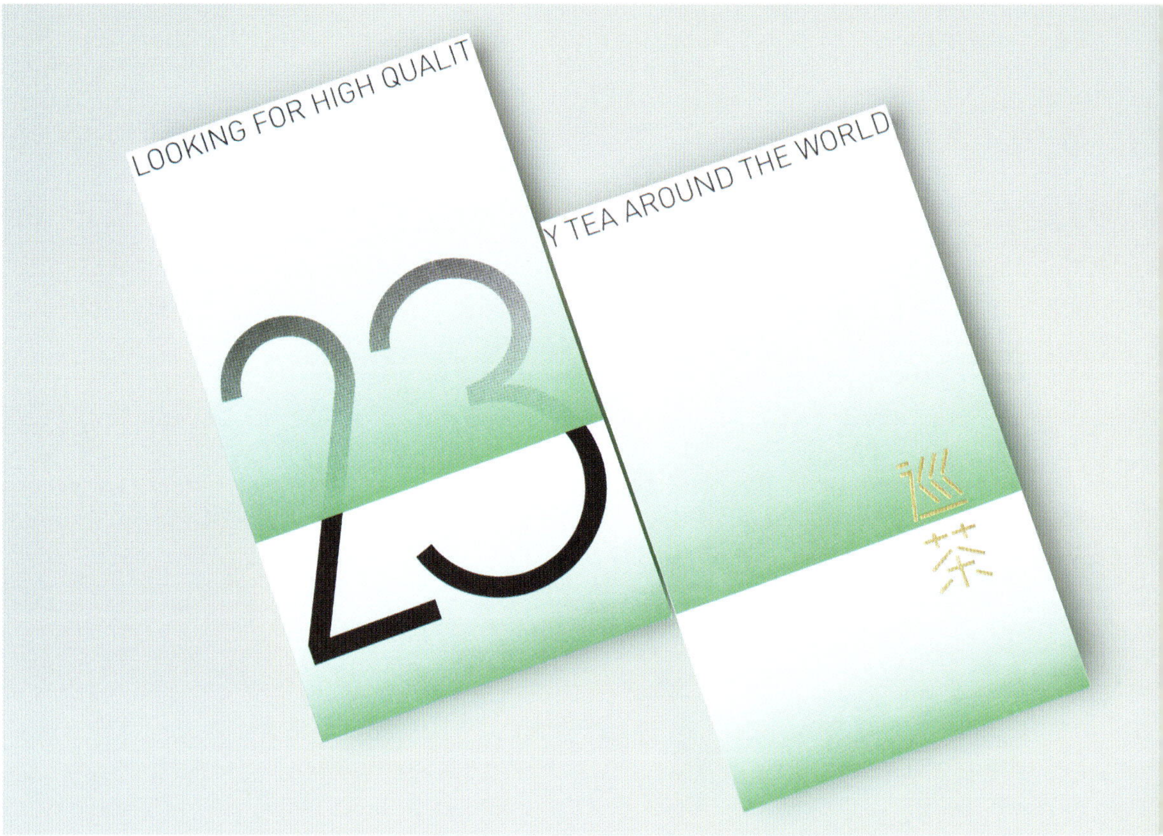
LOOKING FOR HIGH QUALIT
Y TEA AROUND THE WORLD
23
巡
茶

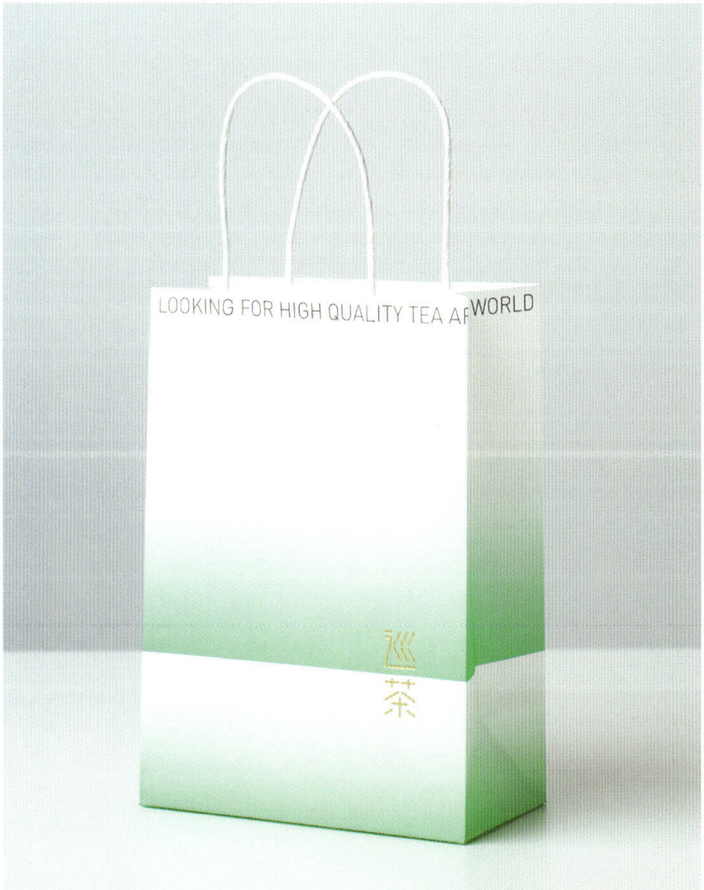
LOOKING FOR HIGH QUALITY TEA AR
WORLD
巡
茶

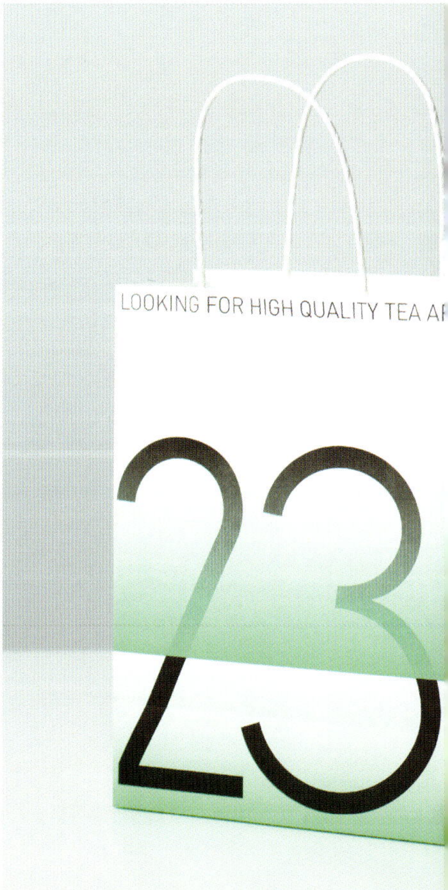
LOOKING FOR HIGH QUALITY TEA AR
23

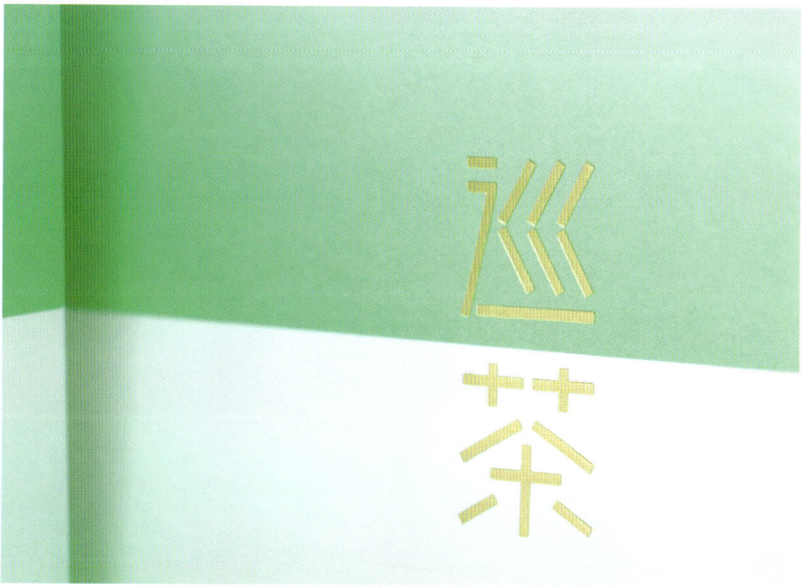

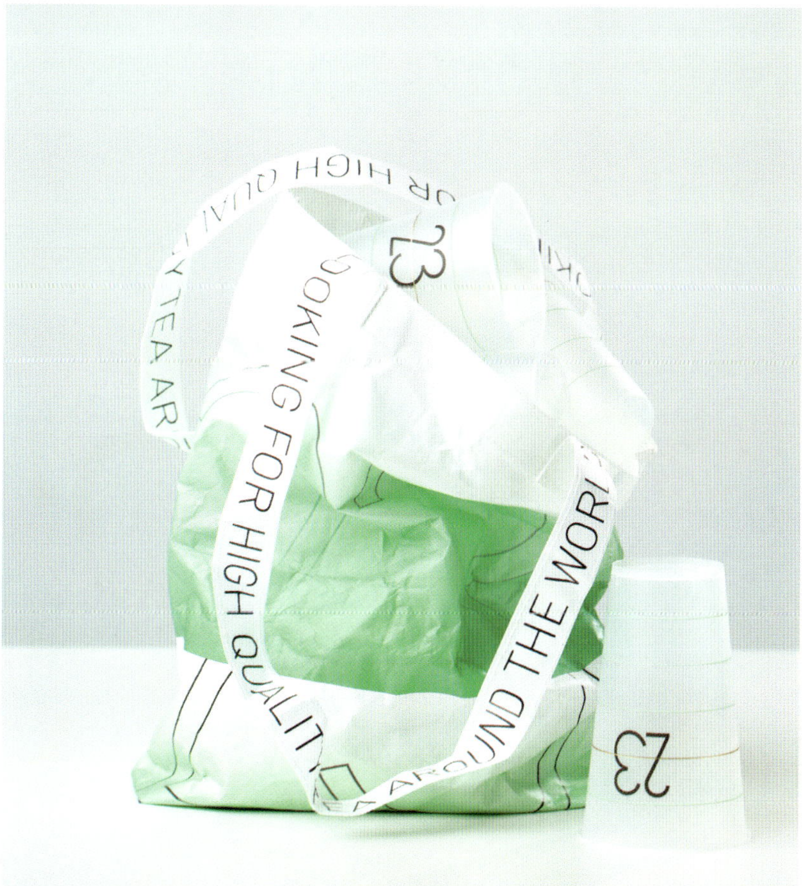

23 TEA-XUNCHA

23 tea is a selected brand series by *Xuncha*. 23 represents that the tea is selected from the growing area located at 23 degrees north latitude. At the same time, this series blends a variety of teas in different proportions to make tea bottoms. In our design, we make strict selection and blending the core of the two product highlights, visualize the concept, and apply it to typography. It looks delicate and quiet, intended to convey the pure craftsman spirit of the brand and products.

Creative Director
Vincent

Art Director & Designer
Alex

PANTONE 801

PANTONE 806

PANTONE 803

PANTONE RED WARM

PANTONE 803 100% + PANTONE 801 80%

PANTONE 801 60% + PANTONE 806 60%

PANTONE 801 100% + PANTONE 806 50%

PANTONE WARM RED 50% + PANTONE 803 100%

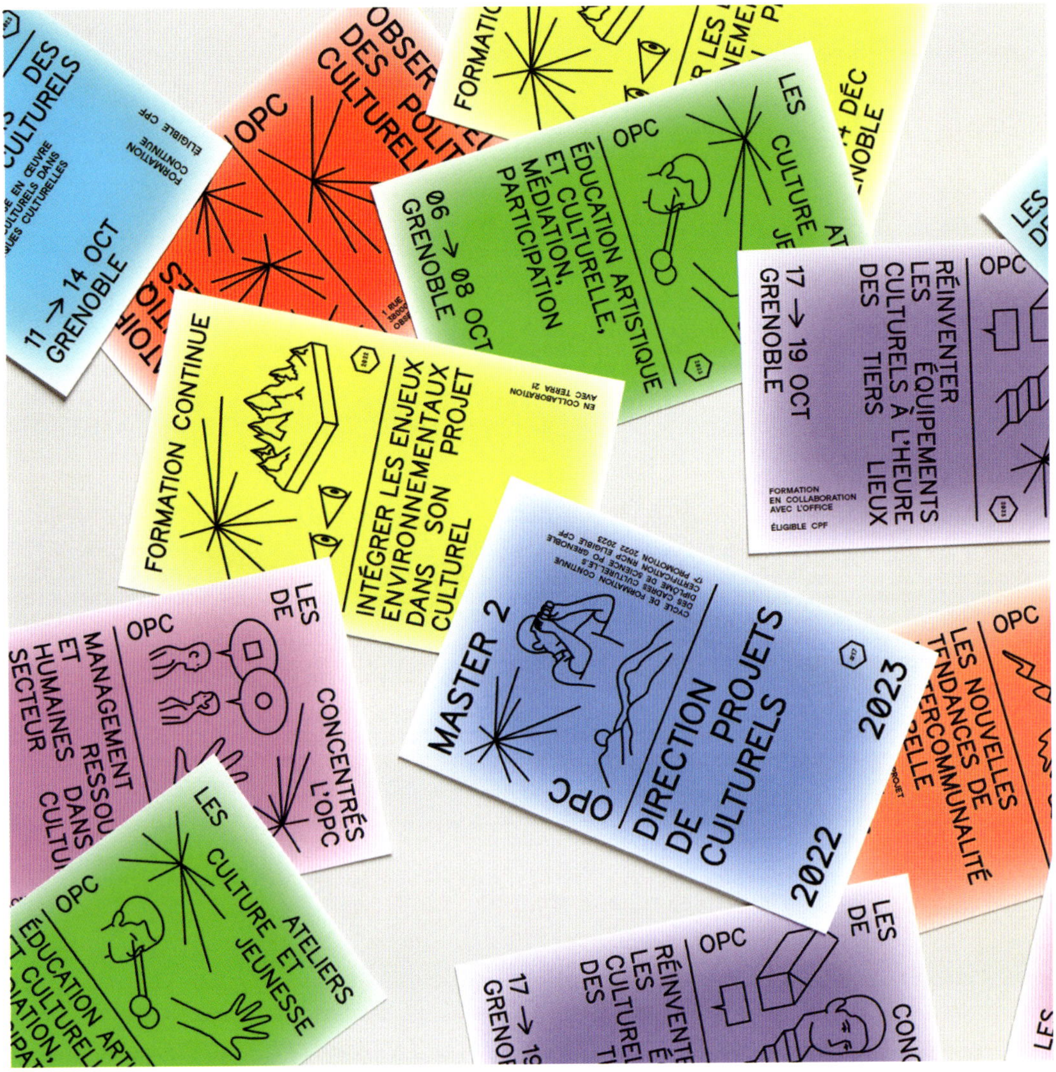

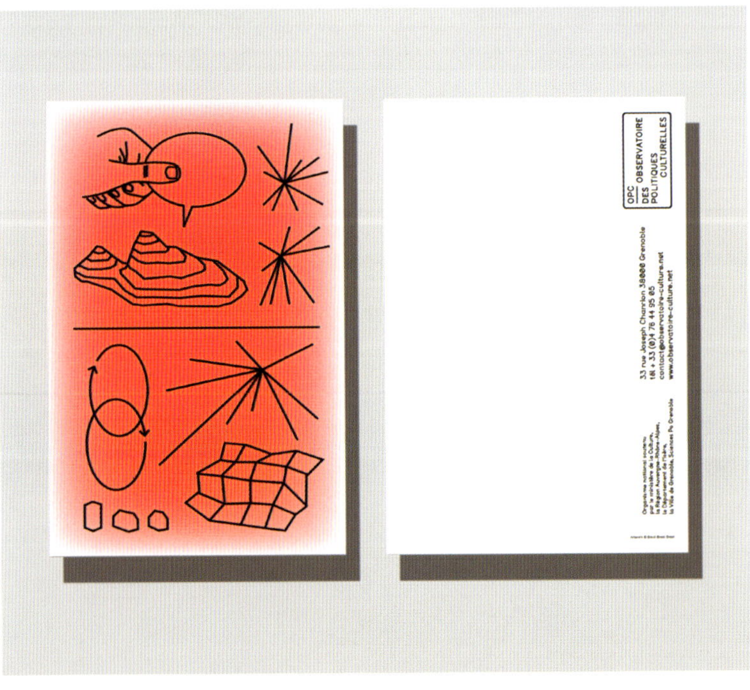

OPC— OBSERVATOIRES DES POLITIQUES CULTURELLES

Visual identity of the Observatory of Cultural Policies in Grenoble (FR).

Design Studio
Brest Brest Brest

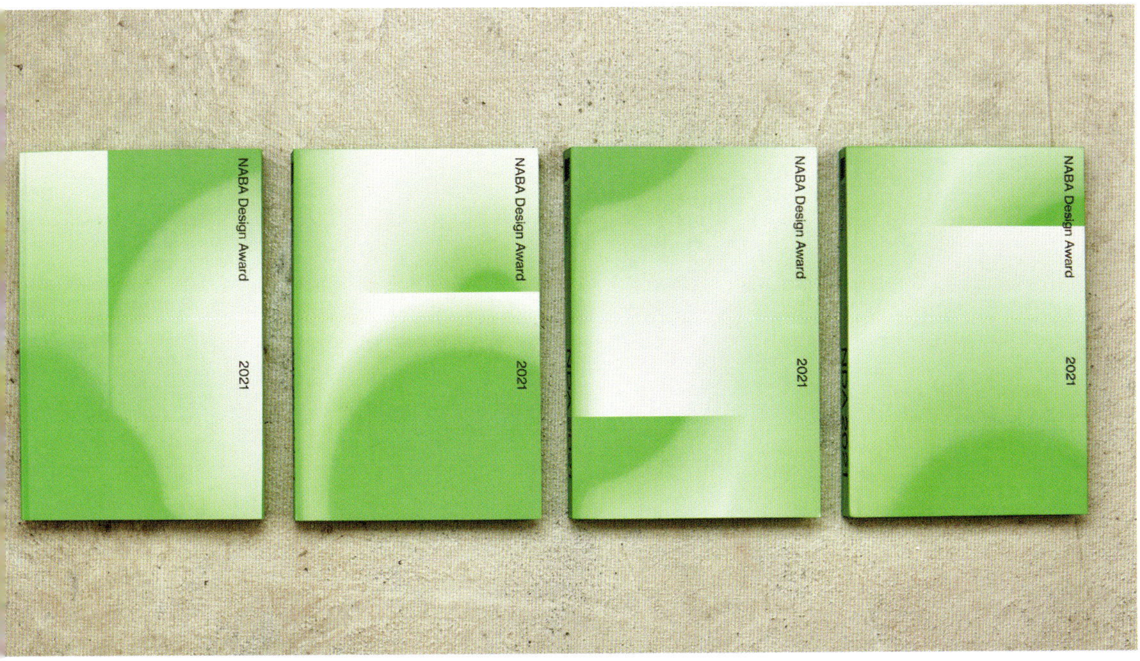

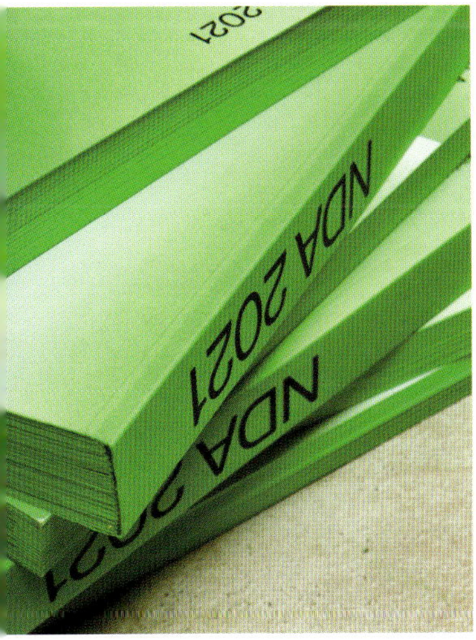

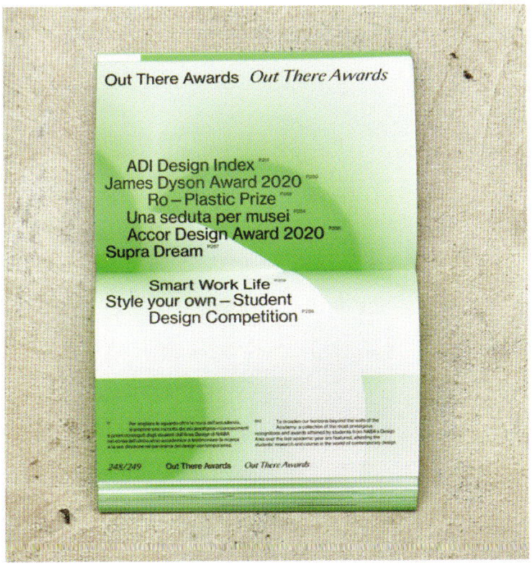

NABA DESIGN AWARD 2021

The *NABA Design Award* is an event that honours the best projects from the students of the Nuova Accademia di Belle Arti in Milan. Traditional offset printing is thoughtfully augmented by the use of Pantone fluorescent green that extends to the external page edges of the book.

Art Direction
Atto

Designer
Irene Pinatto

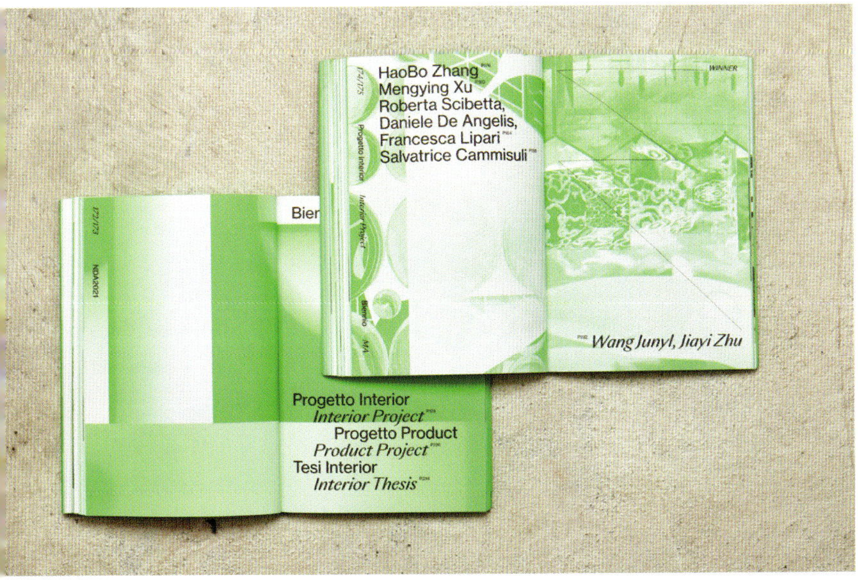

C26 · M37 · Y0 · K0

C0 · M81 · Y80 · K10

C98 · M23 · Y66 · K0

C95 · M65 · Y11 · K1

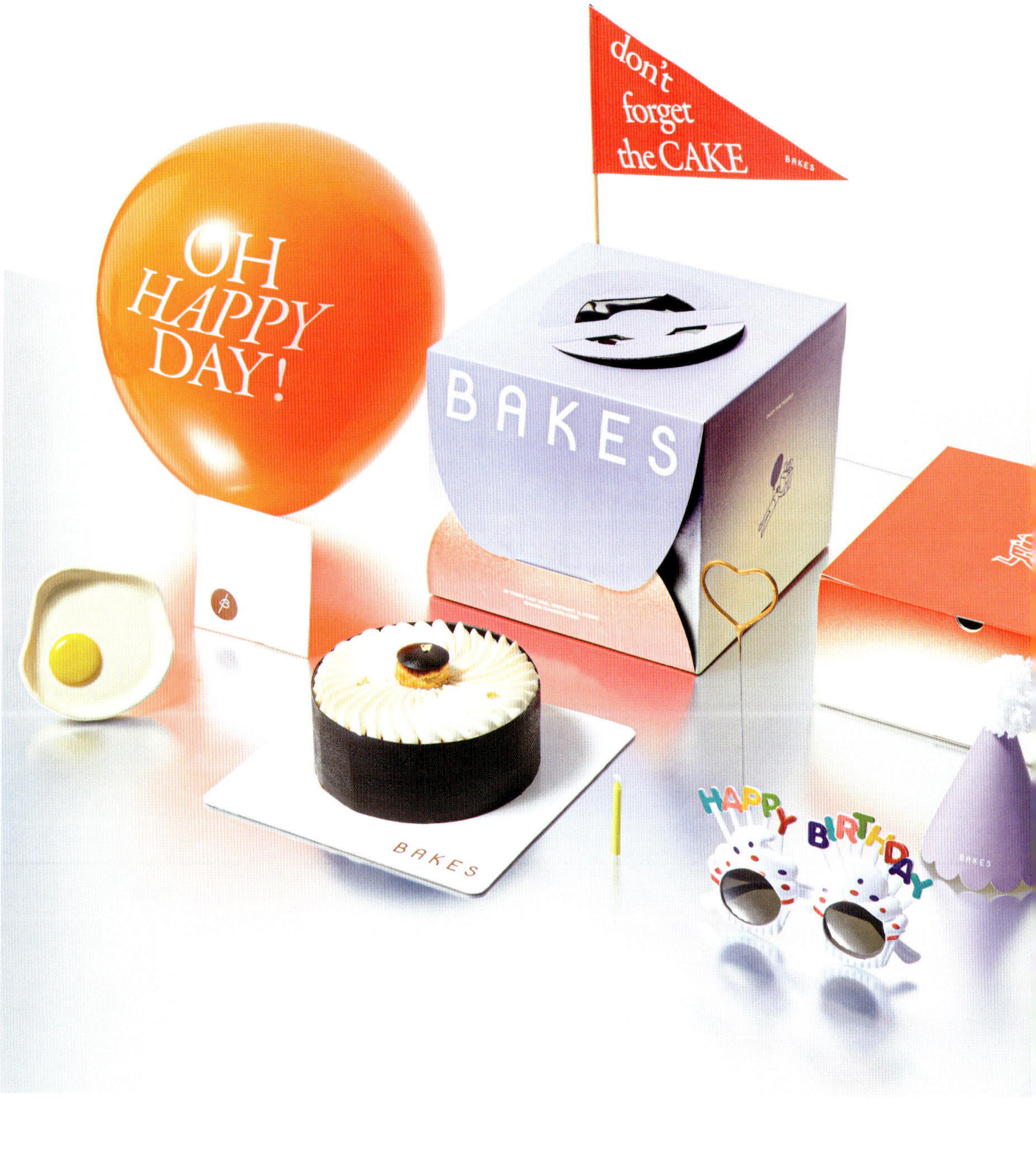

BAKES FLAGSHIP

Bakes, a French patisserie and bakery, recently opened a flagship store in Thao Dien, a neighbourhood in Ho Chi Minh City with a growing local population which is also a popular weekend destination. The designer created a design system that balances the everyday (like bread) and special occasions (like birthdays), from branding to packaging.

Creative Director
Tuan Le

Designer
Nghi Tran, Jun Kohmura & Trang Dinh

Draftman
Hiep Tran

Graphic Support
Xuan Phan

Illustrator
Huong Ngo, Reo Le

Production
Kai Le

Procurement
Hanh Le, Tam Chau, Hai Nguyen, Hai Uyen Huynh & Huyen Huynh

Strategic Partnership
Phuong Anh, Duy Lam

Business Support
Bryan Doan, Lab HR

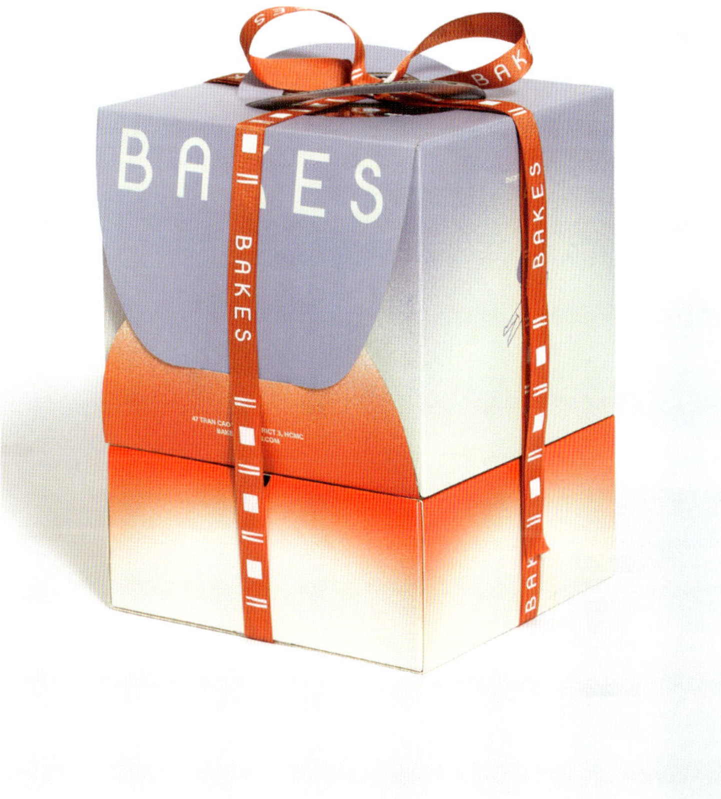

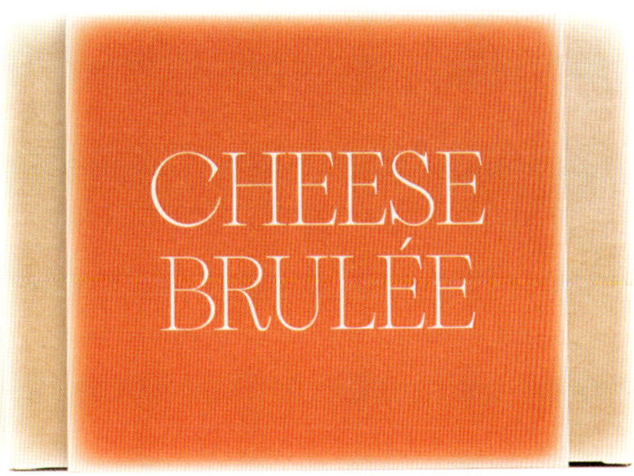

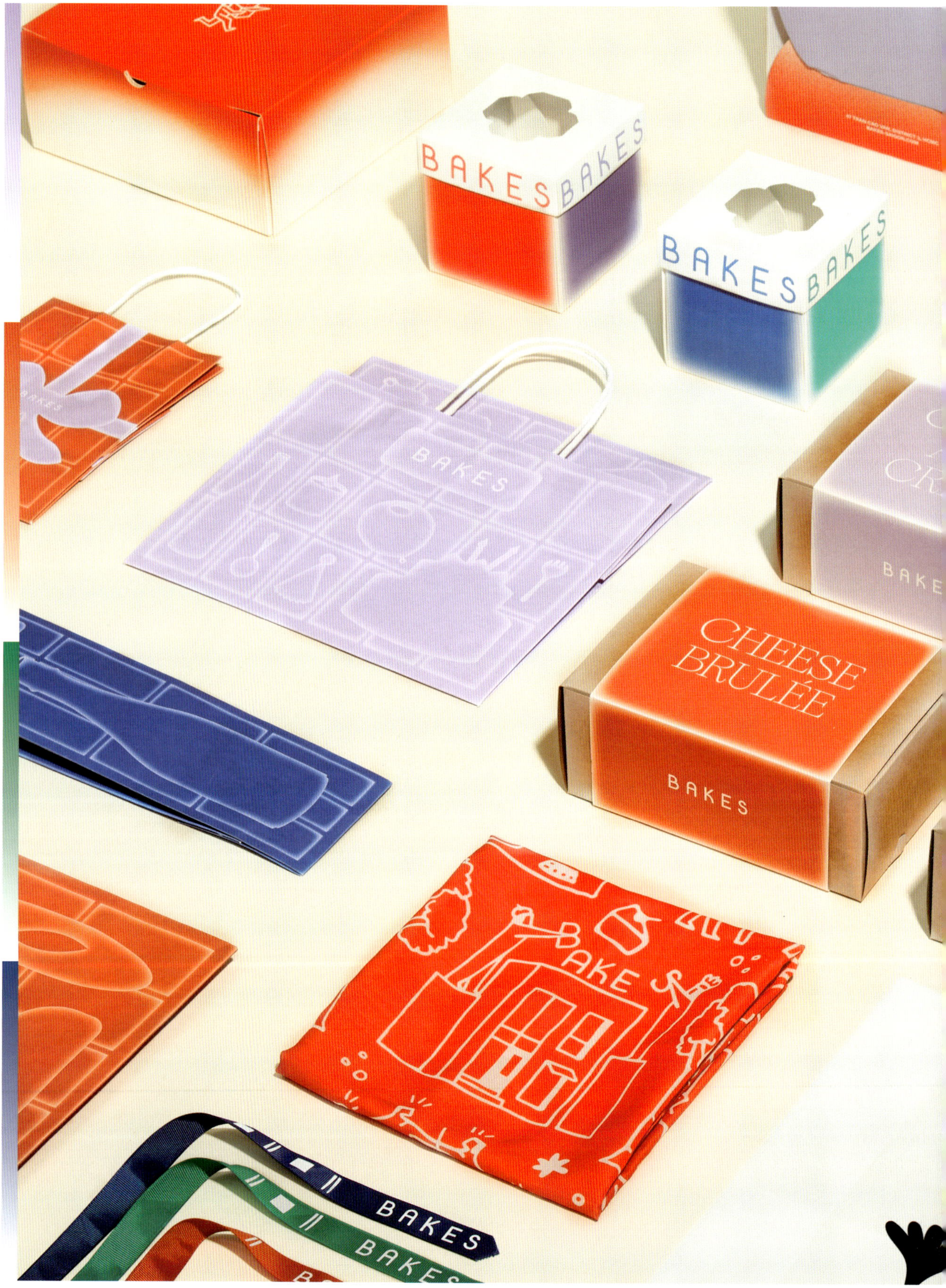
BAKES
BAKES
BAKES
BAKES
BAKES
CHEESE
BRULÉE
BAKES
BAKES
BAKES

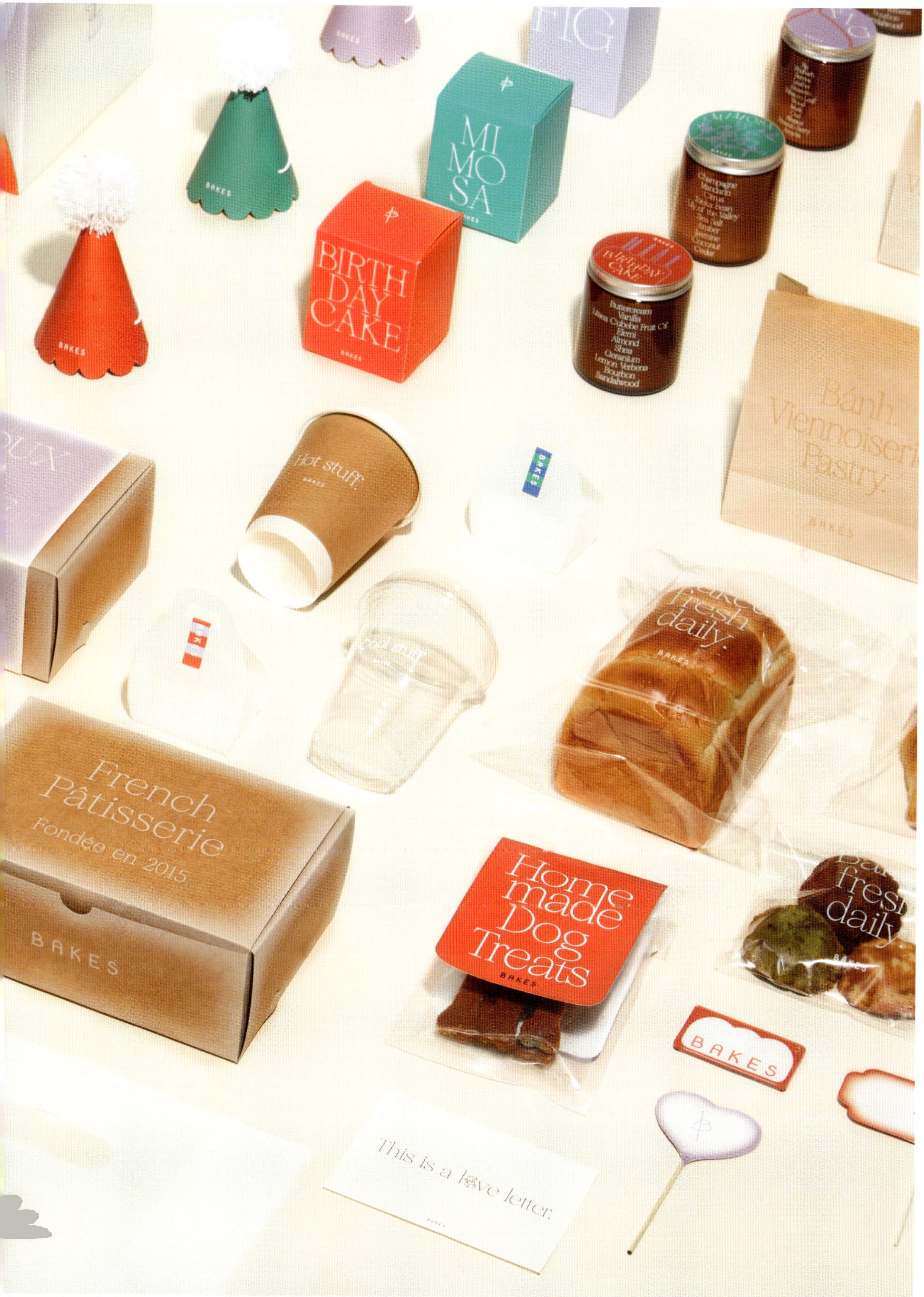
FIG
MI
MO
SA
BIRTH
DAY
CAKE
Champagne
Mandarin
Citrus
Tonka Bean
Lily of the Valley
Sea Salt
Amber
Jasmine
Coconut
Cedar
Buttercream
Vanilla
Litsea Cubebe Fruit Oil
Elemi
Almond
Shea
Geranium
Lemon Verbena
Bourbon
Sandalwood
Hot stuff.
BAKES
Bánh.
Viennoiseri
Pastry.
fresh
daily.
French
Pâtisserie
Fondée en 2015
Home
made
Dog
Treats
This is a love letter.

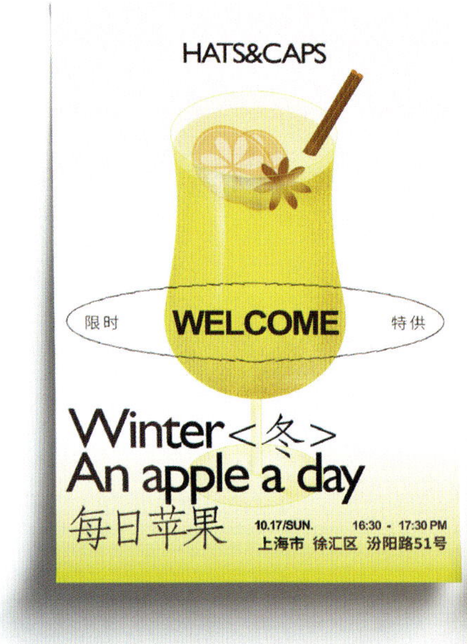

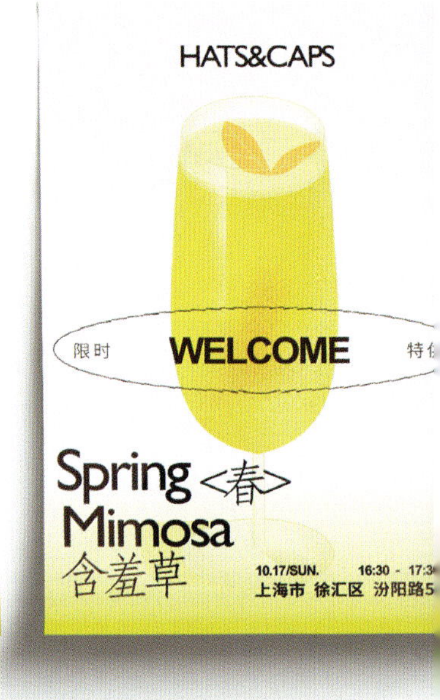

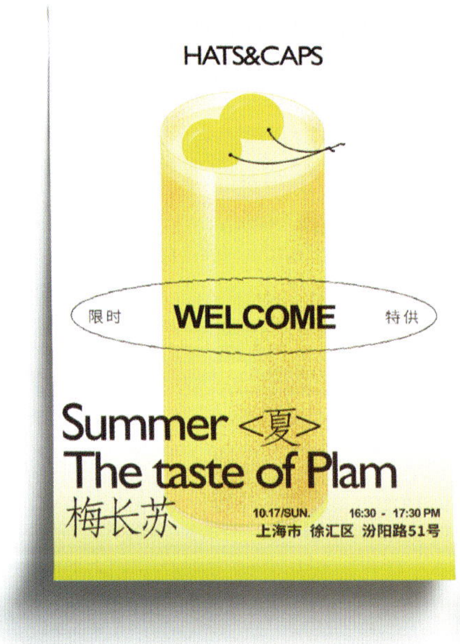

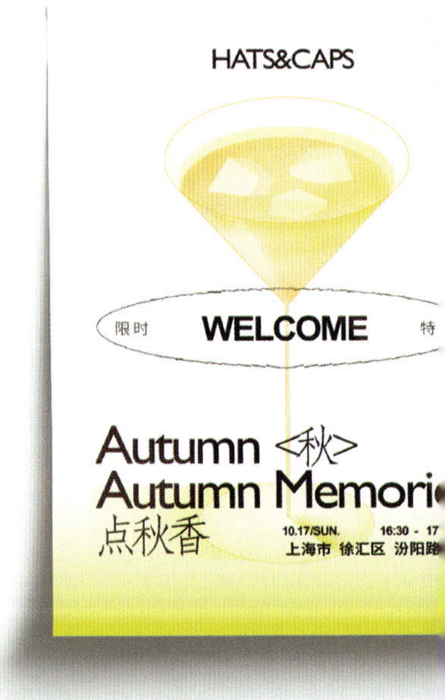

THE WIND OF THE FOUR SEASONS

"The Wind of the Four Seasons" theme concert was held for the musician's book. In the warm and stylish bar *Hats & Caps*,, in Shanghai, in autumn, the city is full of the fragrancy of osmanthus flowers, and the colour of osmanthus flowers was selected as the visual. The words and colours were broken and cut to suggest the state of the wind.

Designer
Hongrui Shen & Fan Cao

Design Studio
Hoooly Design

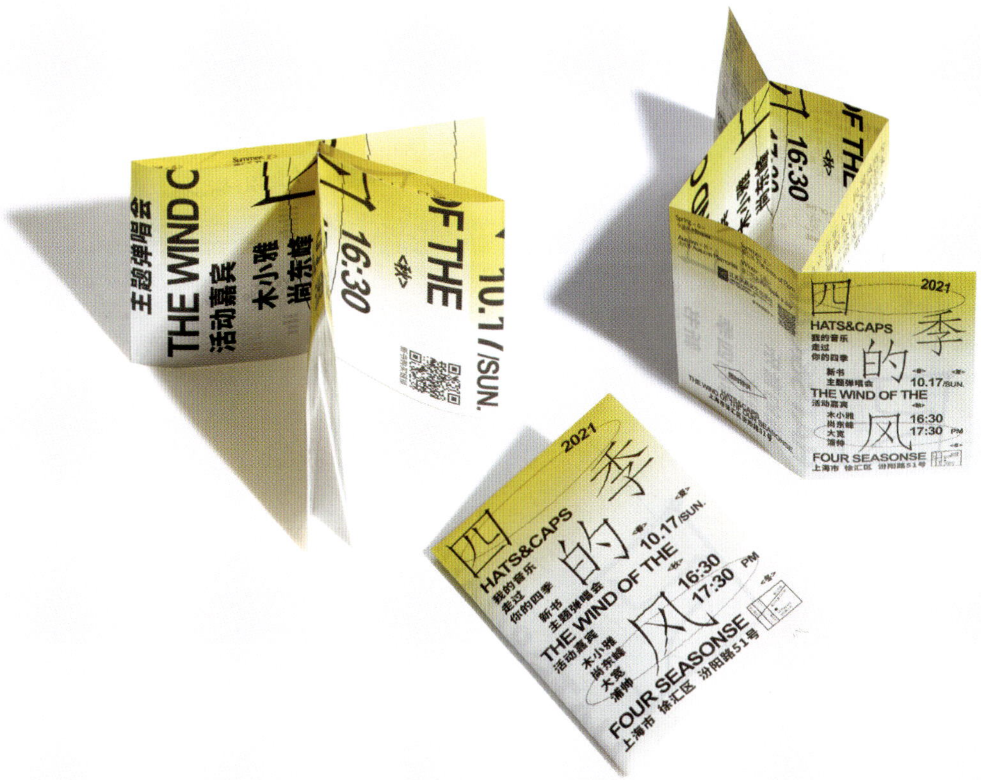
2021
四
季
的
风
HATS&CAPS
我的音乐
走过
你的四季
新书
主题弹唱会
THE WIND OF THE
活动嘉宾
木小雅
尚东峰
大宽
浦帅
10.17/SUN.
16:30
17:30 PM
FOUR SEASONSE
上海市 徐汇区 汾阳路51号

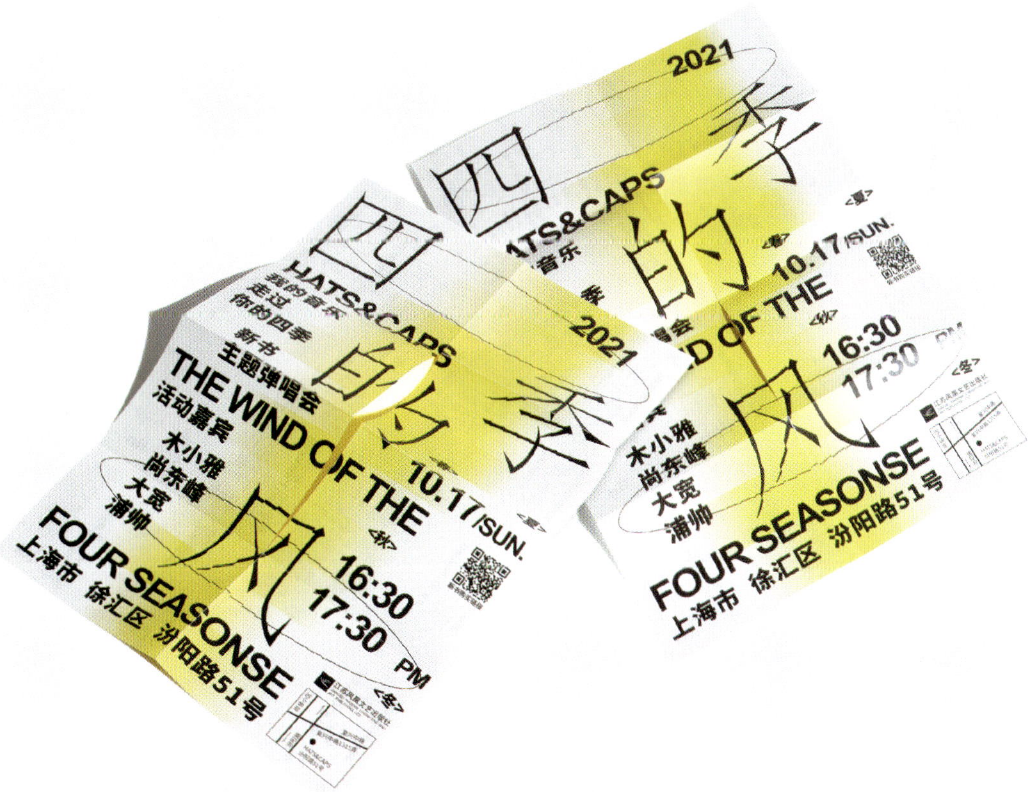
2021
四
季
的
风
HATS&CAPS
我的音乐
走过
你的四季
新书
主题弹唱会
THE WIND OF THE
活动嘉宾
木小雅
尚东峰
大宽
浦帅
10.17/SUN.
16:30
17:30 PM
FOUR SEASONSE
上海市 徐汇区 汾阳路51号

C0 · M84 · Y51 · K0

C0 · M30 · Y84 · K0

C9 · M11 · Y87 · K0

C60 · M0 · Y95 · K0

C75 · M0 · Y23 · K0

C77 · M48 · Y0 · K0

C35 · M86 · Y0 · K0

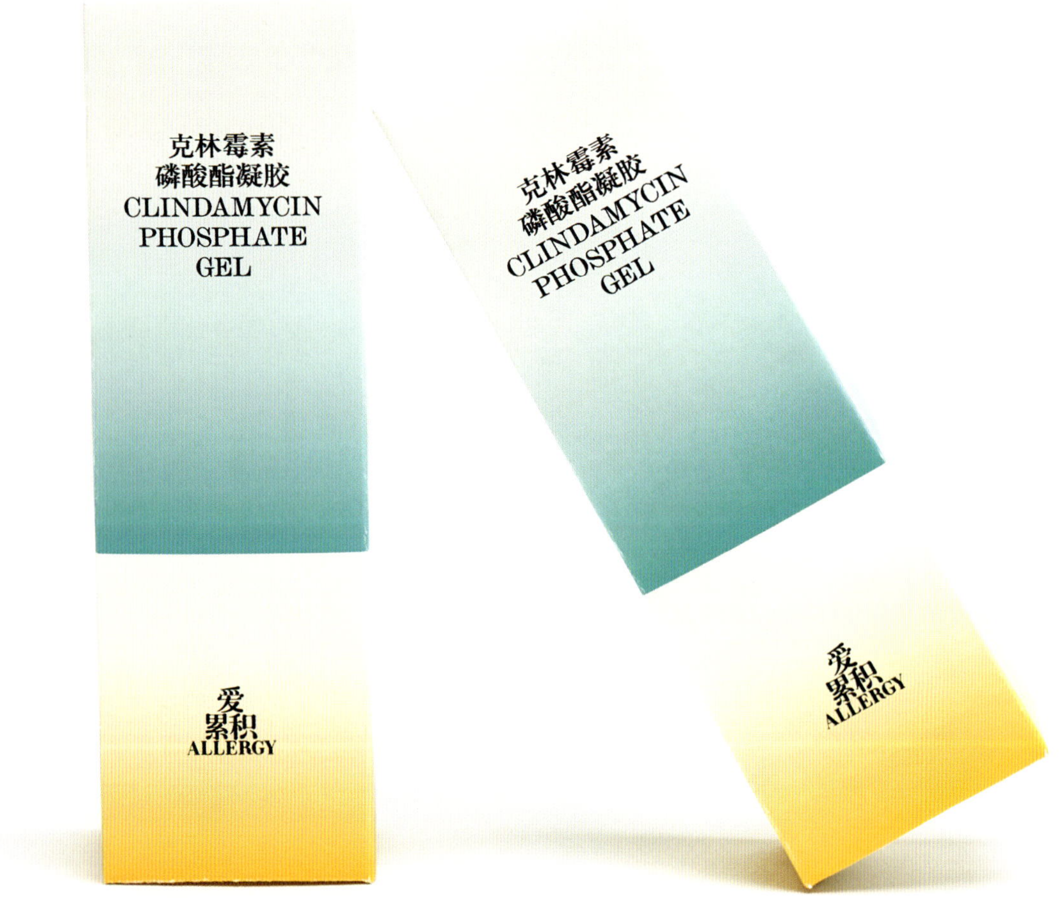

ALLERGY

Allergy is an internet medical brand specializing in infant allergy prevention and protection.
The visual system of *Allergy* is constructed based on grid systems. Adopting 15% as the gradient level, the system simulates the degree of allergic symptoms by controlling the rhythms and pad of the gradual changes: for example, using gradient red to signify the degree of skin redness and swelling.

Art Director & Designer
Feng Lei

Design Studio
One By One Lab

Photographer
Yuanzi

Client
Halolab

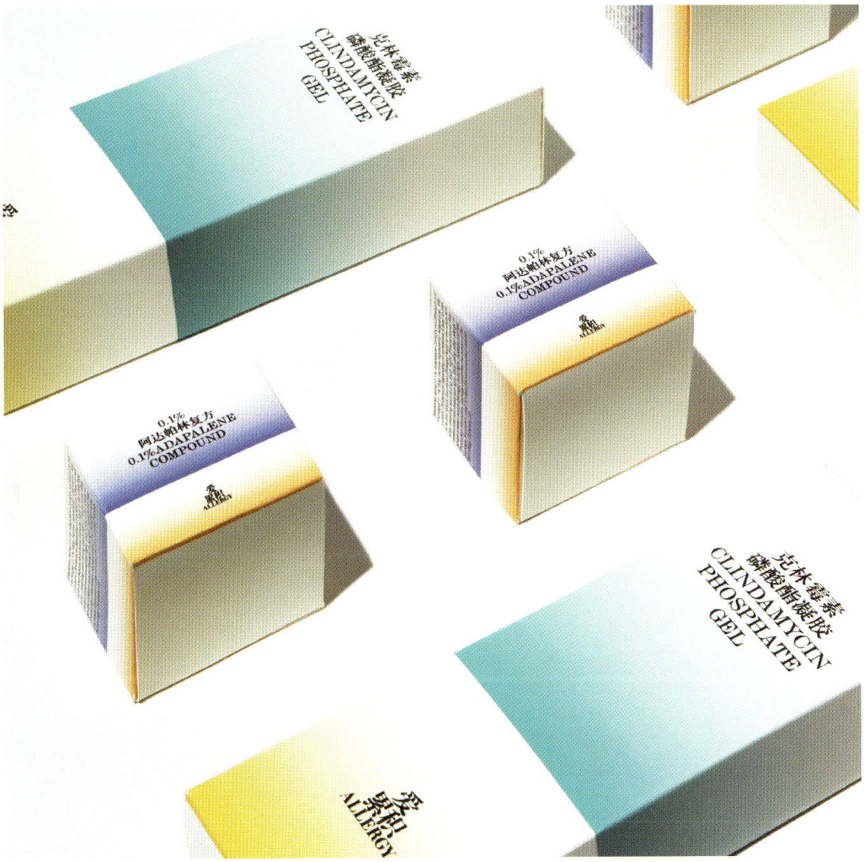

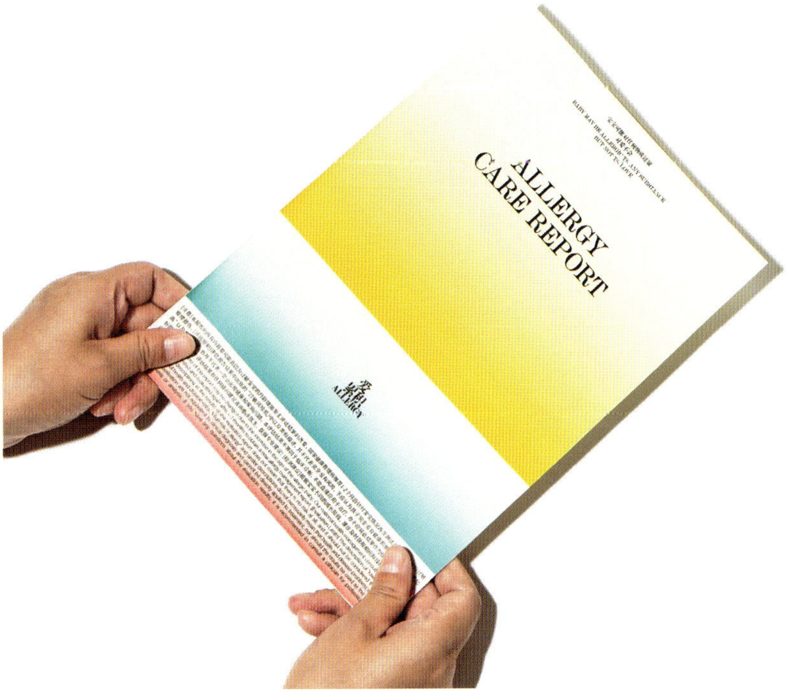

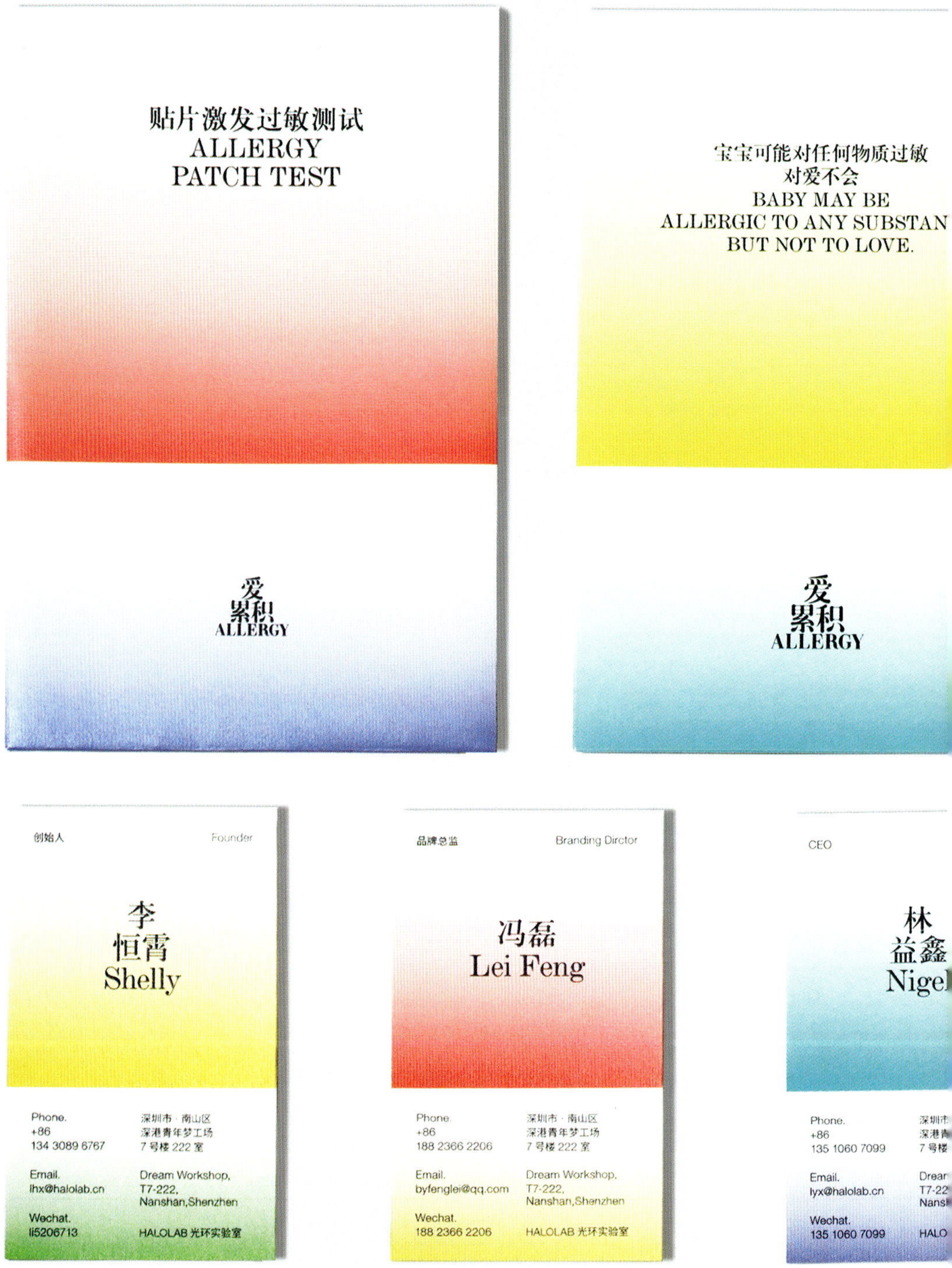
贴片激发过敏测试
ALLERGY
PATCH TEST
爱
累积
ALLERGY
宝宝可能对任何物质过敏
对爱不会
BABY MAY BE
ALLERGIC TO ANY SUBSTAN
BUT NOT TO LOVE.
爱
累积
ALLERGY
创始人
Founder
李
恒霄
Shelly
Phone.
+86
134 3089 6767
深圳市 · 南山区
深港青年梦工场
7 号楼 222 室
Email.
lhx@halolab.cn
Dream Workshop,
T7-222,
Nanshan,Shenzhen
Wechat.
li5206713
HALOLAB 光环实验室
品牌总监
Branding Dirctor
冯磊
Lei Feng
Phone.
+86
188 2366 2206
深圳市 · 南山区
深港青年梦工场
7 号楼 222 室
Email.
byfenglei@qq.com
Dream Workshop,
T7-222,
Nanshan,Shenzhen
Wechat.
188 2366 2206
HALOLAB 光环实验室
CEO
林
益鑫
Phone.
+86
135 1060 7099
Email.
lyx@halolab.cn
Wechat.
135 1060 7099

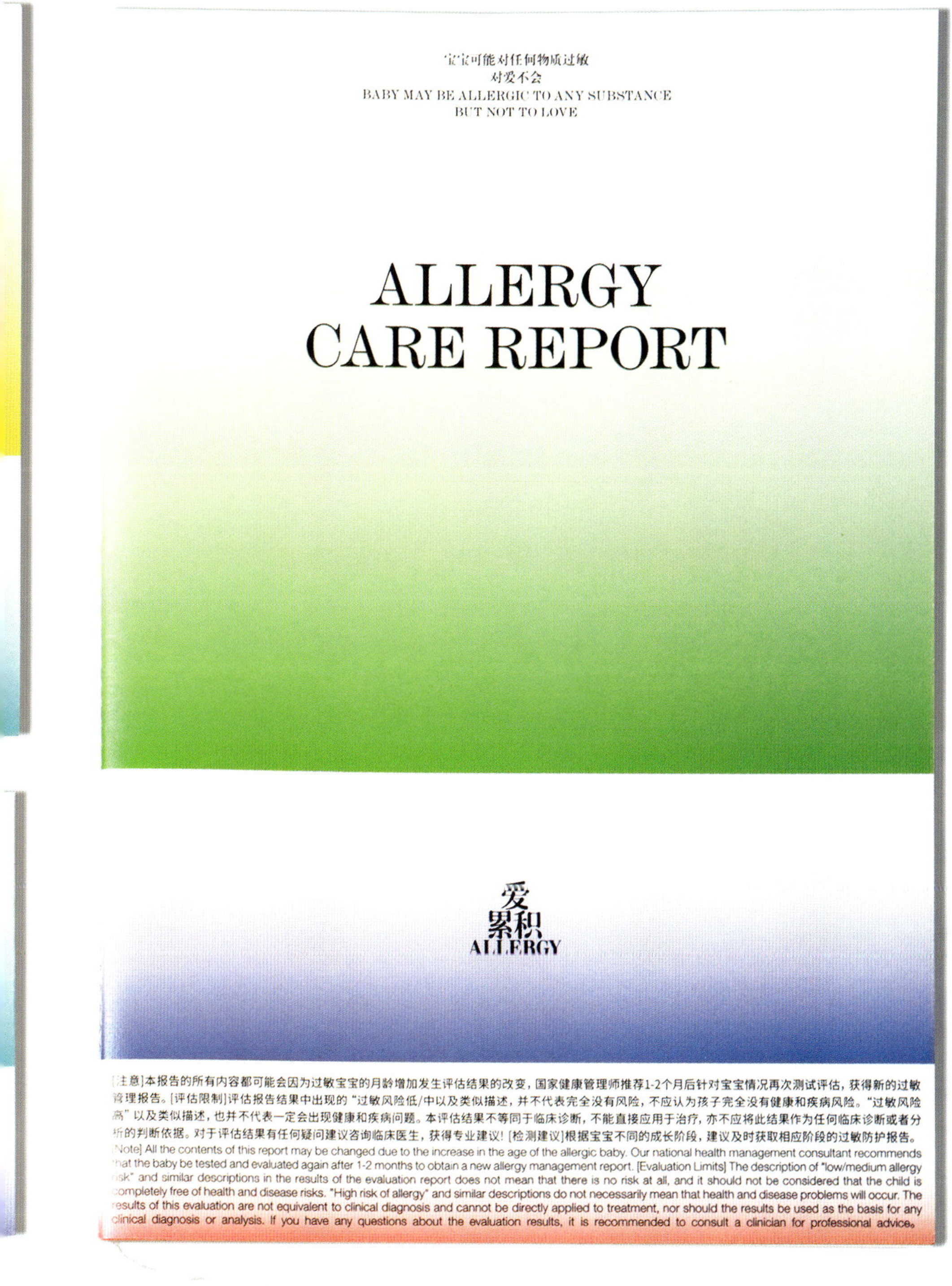
宝宝可能对任何物质过敏
对爱不会
BABY MAY BE ALLERGIC TO ANY SUBSTANCE
BUT NOT TO LOVE
ALLERGY
CARE REPORT
爱
累积
ALLERGY
注意]本报告的所有内容都可能会因为过敏宝宝的月龄增加发生评估结果的改变，国家健康管理师推荐1-2个月后针对宝宝情况再次测试评估，获得新的过敏管理报告。[评估限制]评估报告结果中出现的“过敏风险低/中以及类似描述，并不代表完全没有风险，不应认为孩子完全没有健康和疾病风险。“过敏风险高”以及类似描述，也并不代表一定会出现健康和疾病问题。本评估结果不等同于临床诊断，不能直接应用于治疗，亦不应将此结果作为任何临床诊断或者分析的判断依据。对于评估结果有任何疑问建议咨询临床医生，获得专业建议! [检测建议]根据宝宝不同的成长阶段，建议及时获取相应阶段的过敏防护报告。
Note] All the contents of this report may be changed due to the increase in the age of the allergic baby. Our national health management consultant recommends that the baby be tested and evaluated again after 1-2 months to obtain a new allergy management report. [Evaluation Limits] The description of "low/medium allergy risk" and similar descriptions in the results of the evaluation report does not mean that there is no risk at all, and it should not be considered that the child is completely free of health and disease risks. "High risk of allergy" and similar descriptions do not necessarily mean that health and disease problems will occur. The results of this evaluation are not equivalent to clinical diagnosis and cannot be directly applied to treatment, nor should the results be used as the basis for any clinical diagnosis or analysis. If you have any questions about the evaluation results, it is recommended to consult a clinician for professional advice。

C6 · M16 · Y13 · K0
C0 · M7 · Y8 · K0

C21 · M2 · Y23 · K0
C10 · M1 · Y12 · K0

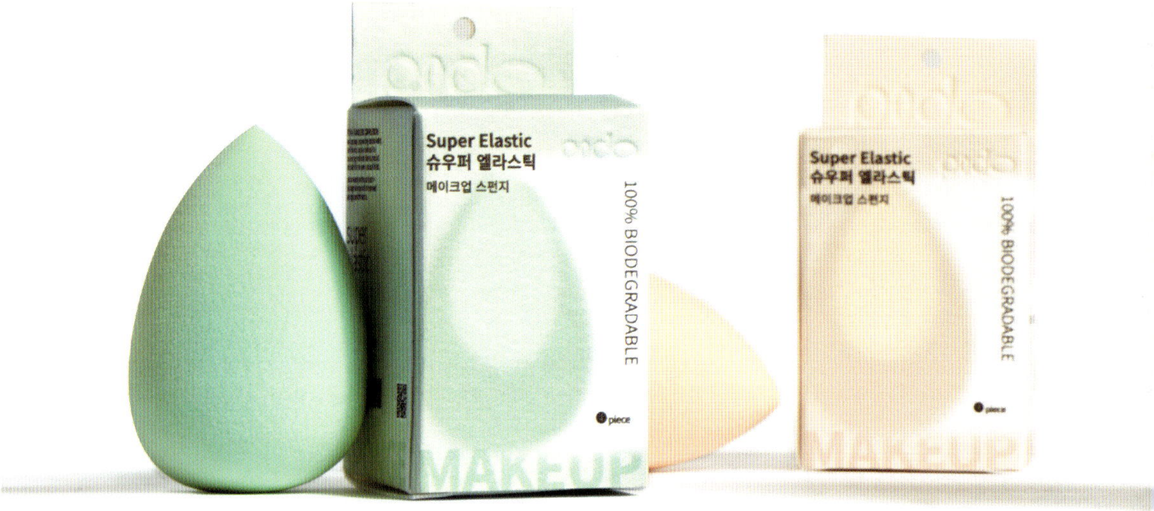

C10 · M25 · Y2 · K0
C5 · M11 · Y0 · K0

C29 · M2 · Y7 · K0
C18 · M2 · Y4 · K0

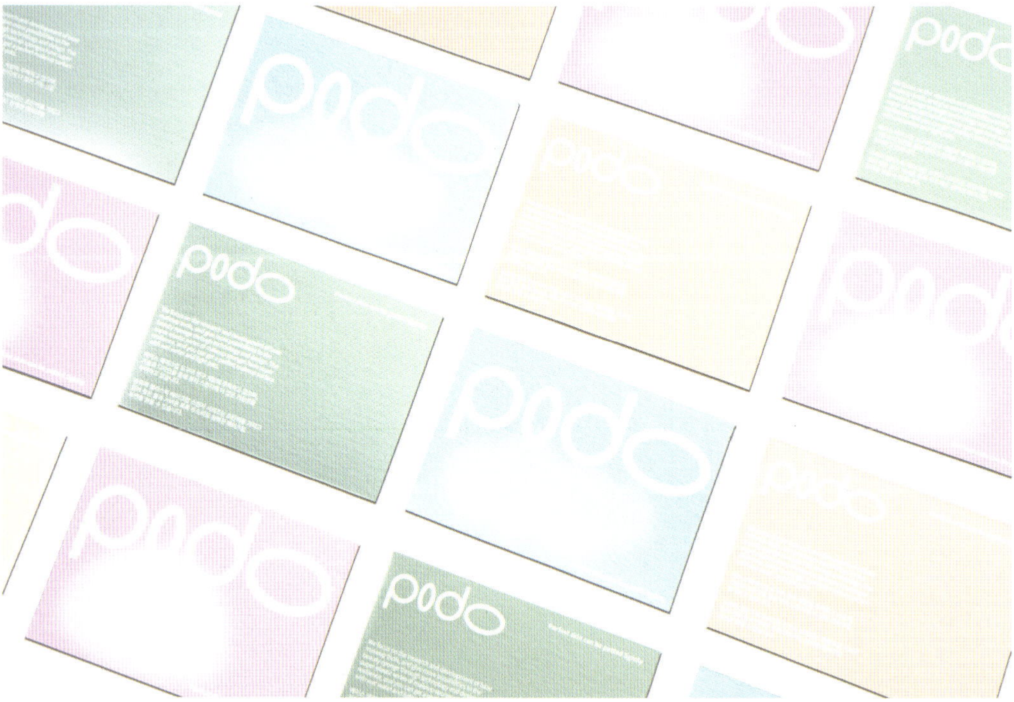

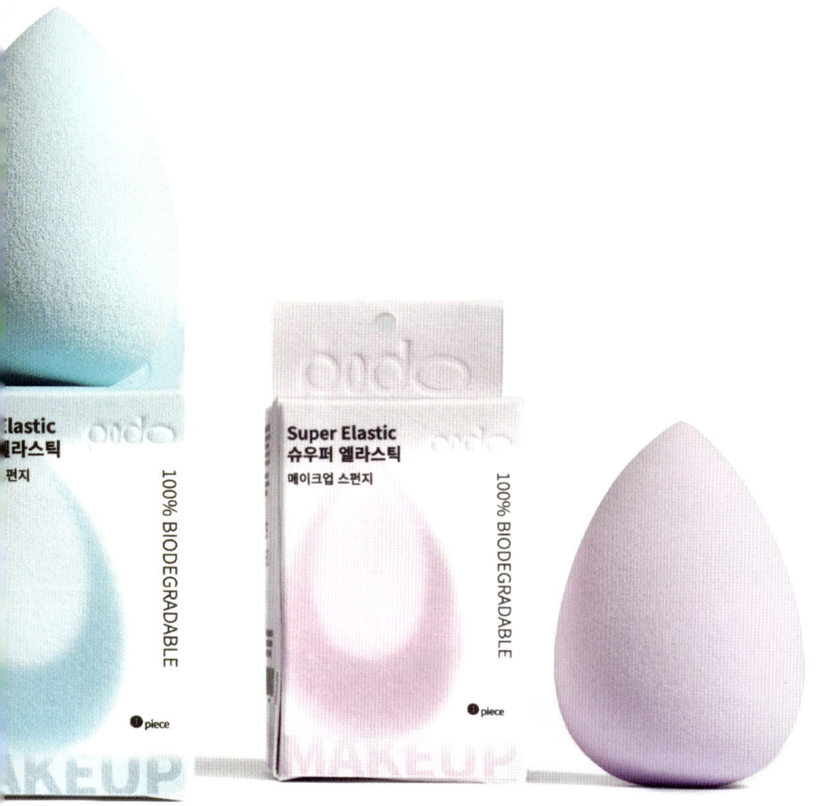

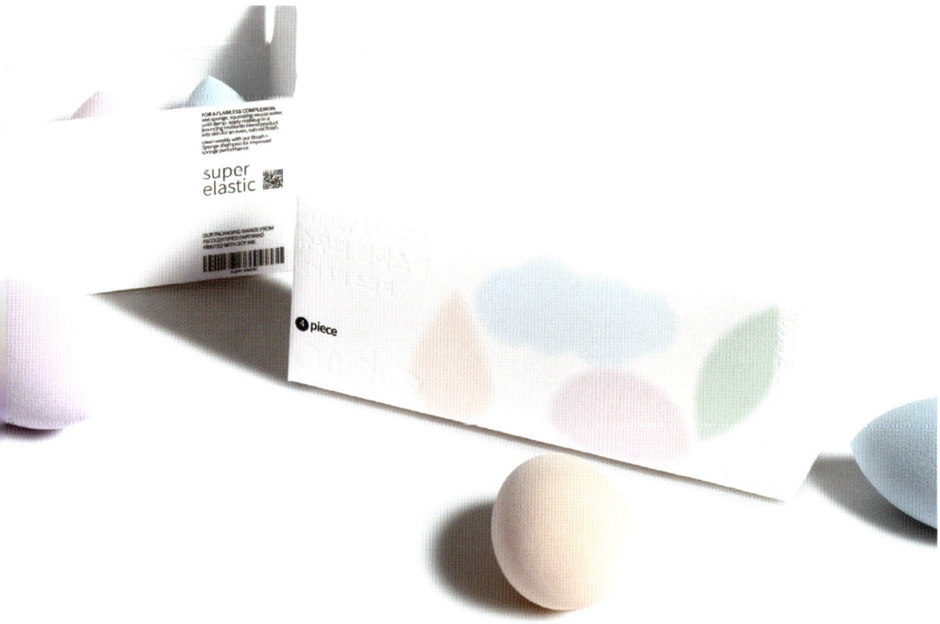

PODO MAKEUP SPONGE

Podo advocates the use of natural sponges. The designer disassembled the English font of "podo", and the circle in the text was depicted with a sense of rhythmic expansion and contraction, which is an interesting echo of the product's high elasticity. The package was designed with edge blurring and gradation to express comfort, and the graphics on the front and back were made in pure white to emphasize the product concept.

Design Studio
XXD Design

Art Director & Designer
Xu Yuqing, Xiao Qiyuan

Client
Podopodo Co., Ltd

PANTONE 811

C0 · M100 · Y0 · K0

PANTONE 877

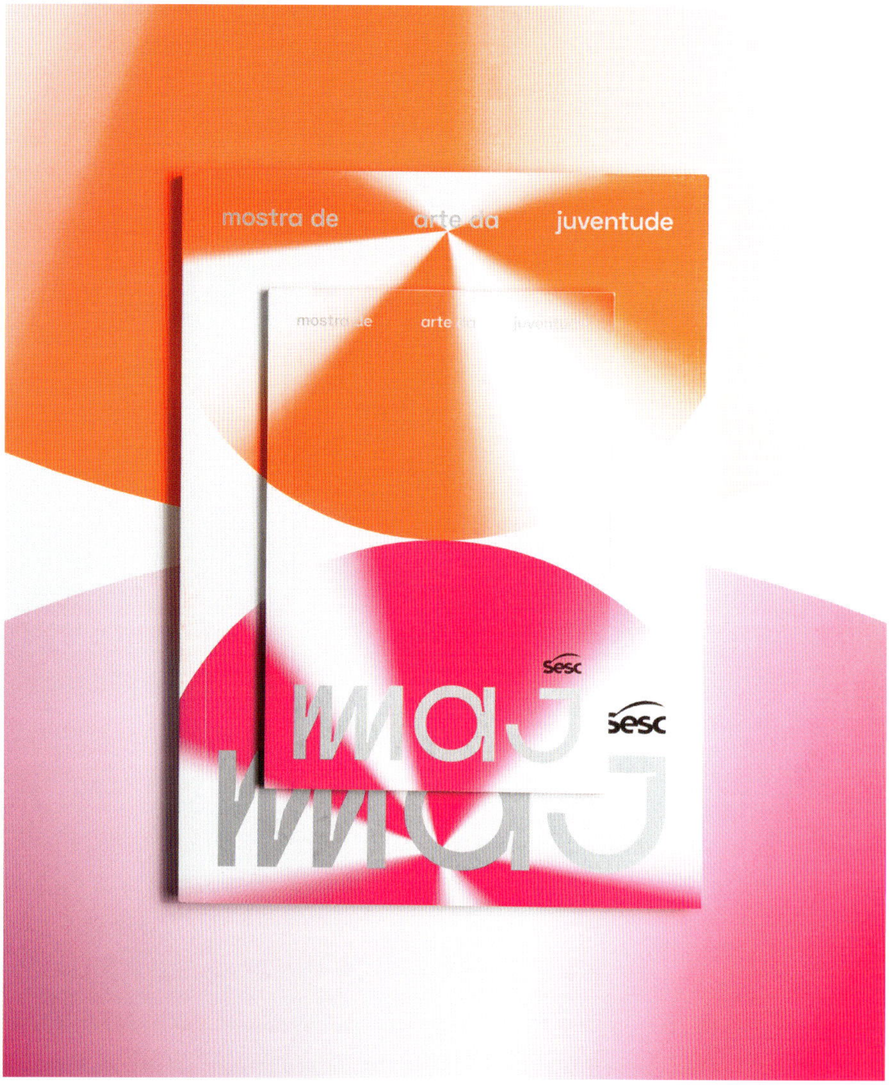

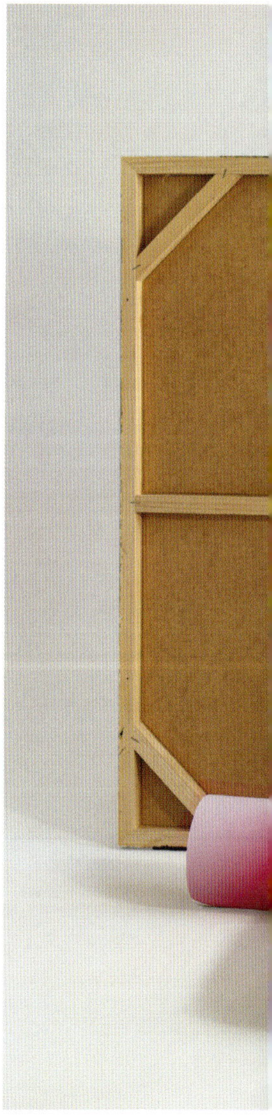

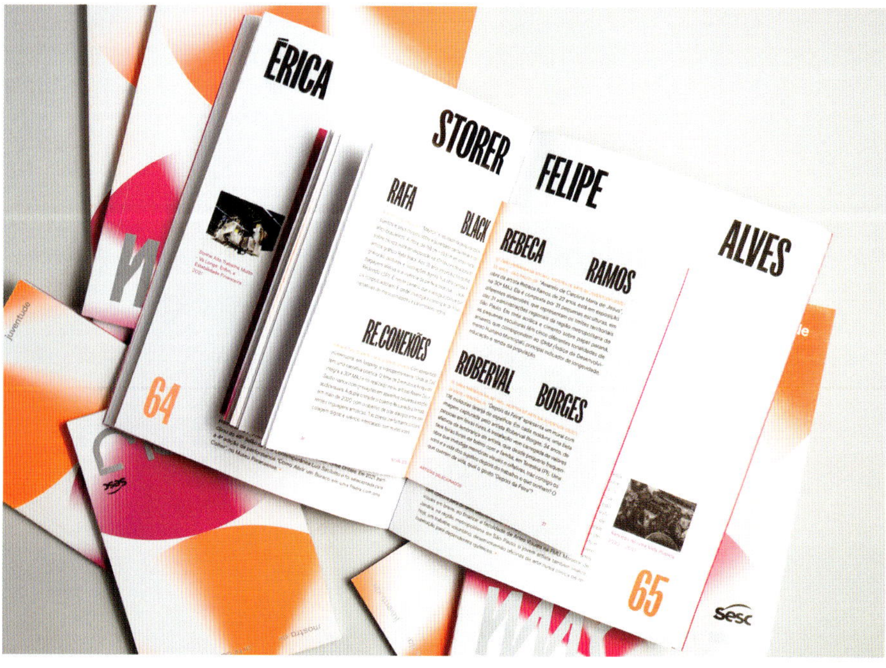

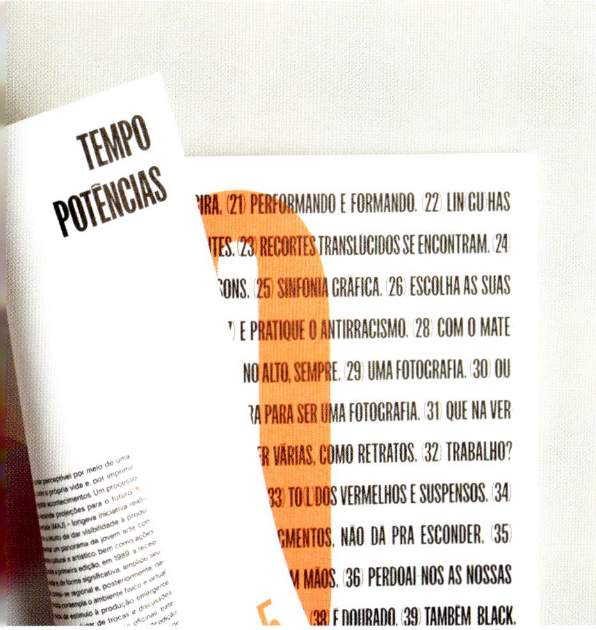

30TH MOSTRA DE ARTE DA JUVENTUDE

Mostra de Arte da Juventude—freely translated as Youth Art Exhibition—was created in 1989 to provide visibility to the production of emerging artists. In 2022, Polar was invited by Sesc to create the visual identity of the 30th edition of MAJ, in addition to developing the materials for its communication.

Design Studio
Polar, Ltda.

Creative Director & Designer
Lais Ikoma, Ralph Mayer

Motion Designer
Lais Ikoma, Luciana Mayume

Photographer
Lais Ikoma, Ronaldo Arthur Vidal

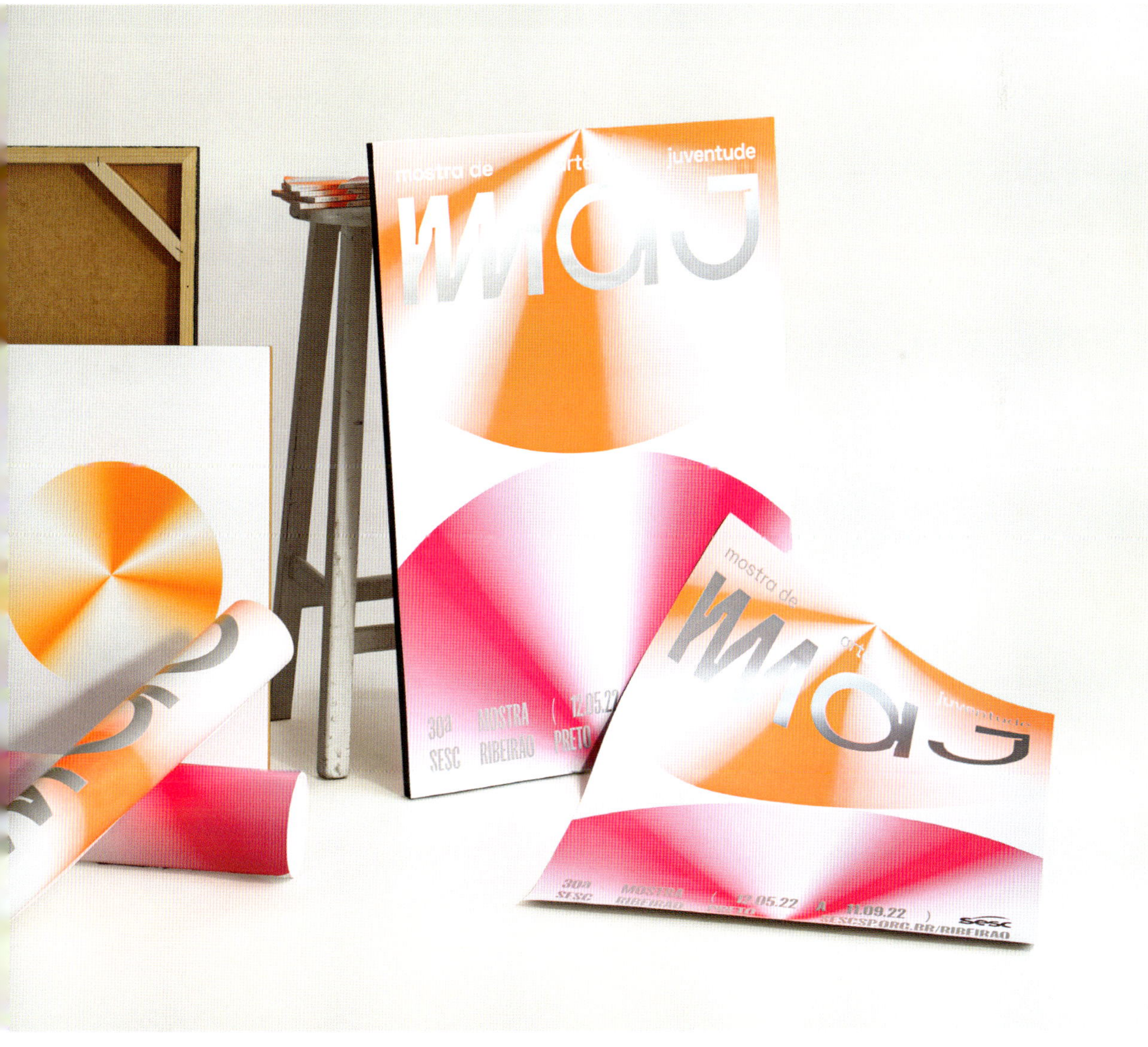

R84 · G0 · B0

R253 · G52 · B2

R209 · G210 · B210

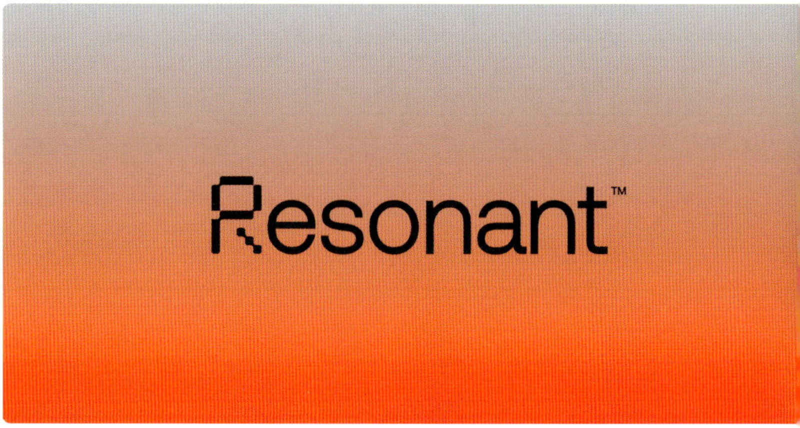

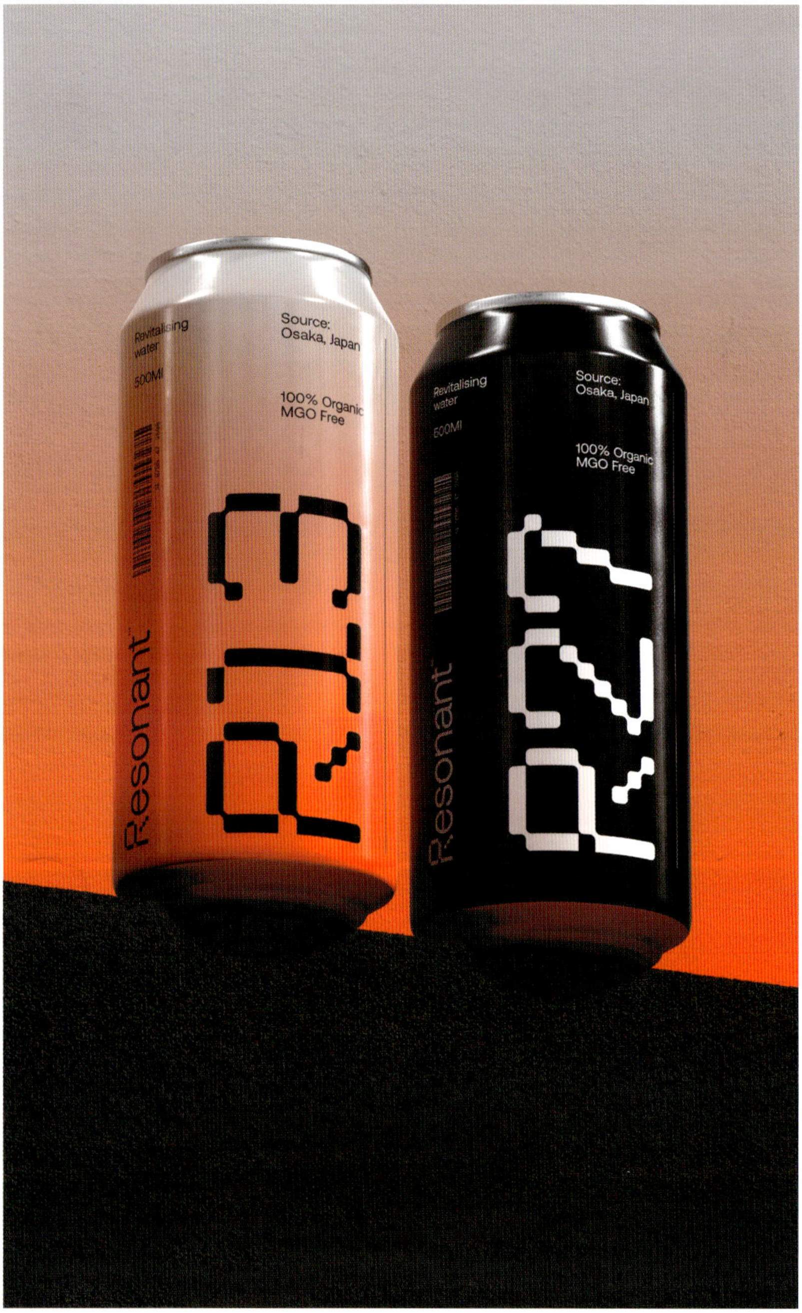

RESONANT

Resonant stands as a vitamin water brand with an unwavering commitment to 100% natural ingredients, rejuvenating your body while promoting detoxification. Sourced from a spring nestled in Osaka, Japan—renowned for its health-conscious inhabitants—*Resonant's* water embodies purity. The designer meticulously crafted a brand that aligns seamlessly with *Resonant's* values and individuality, featuring vibrant colours and an innovative brand system that sets us apart in a fiercely competitive market. As a final touch, we designed a fully custom-made typeface, culminating in a truly distinctive identity that resonates with our discerning audience.

Designer
Olivier Segers

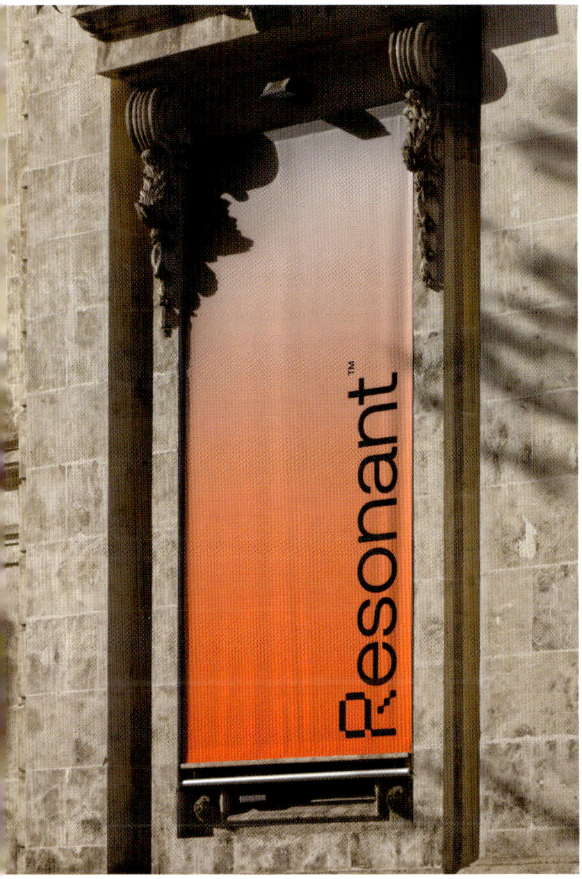
Resonant™

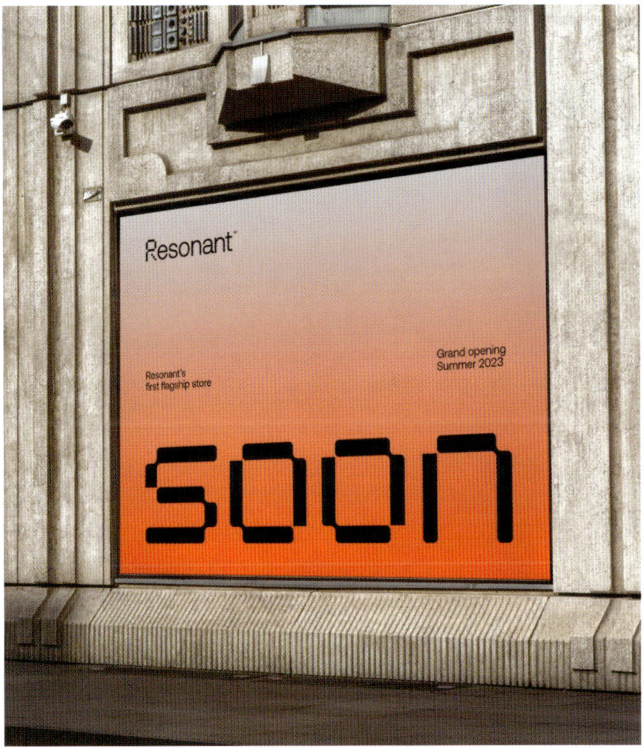
Resonant™
Resonant's
first flagship store
Grand opening
Summer 2023
soon

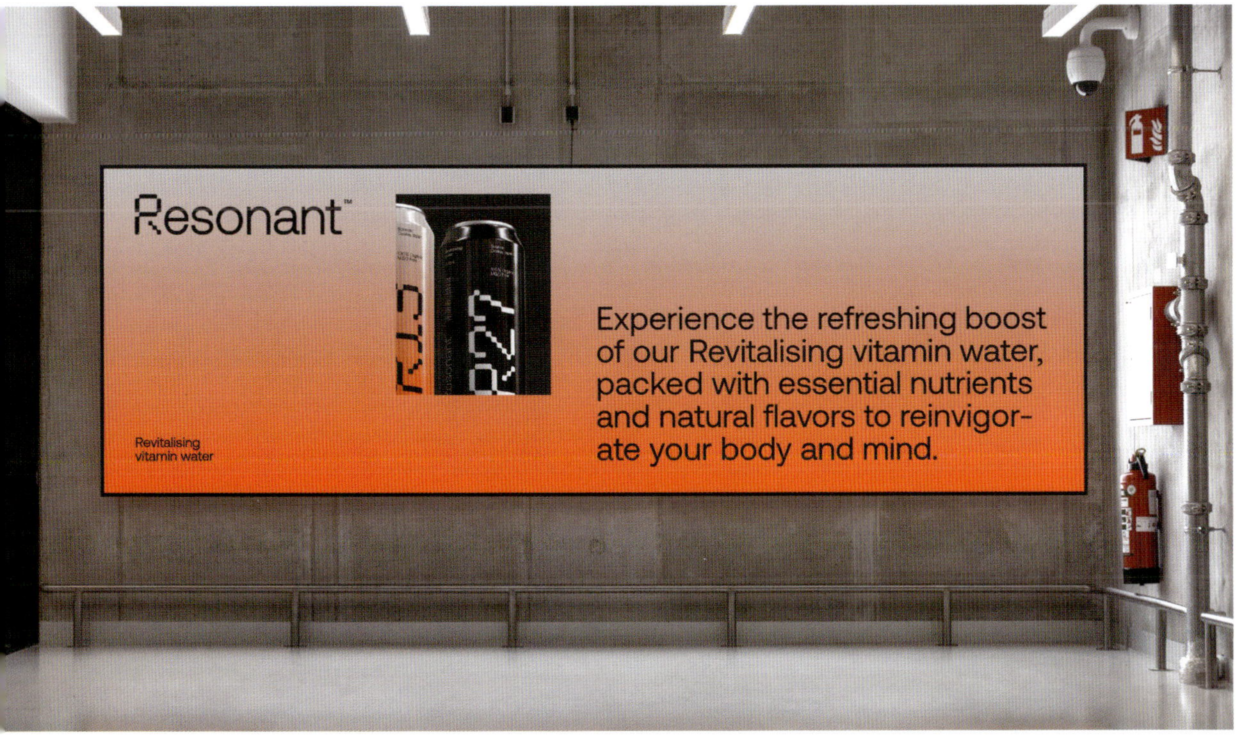
Resonant™
Revitalising
vitamin water
Experience the refreshing boost
of our Revitalising vitamin water,
packed with essential nutrients
and natural flavors to reinvigor-
ate your body and mind.

PANTONE 212 C

PANTONE 7487 C

PANTONE 7441 C

PANTONE 610 C

PANTONE 7579 C

PANTONE 7455 C

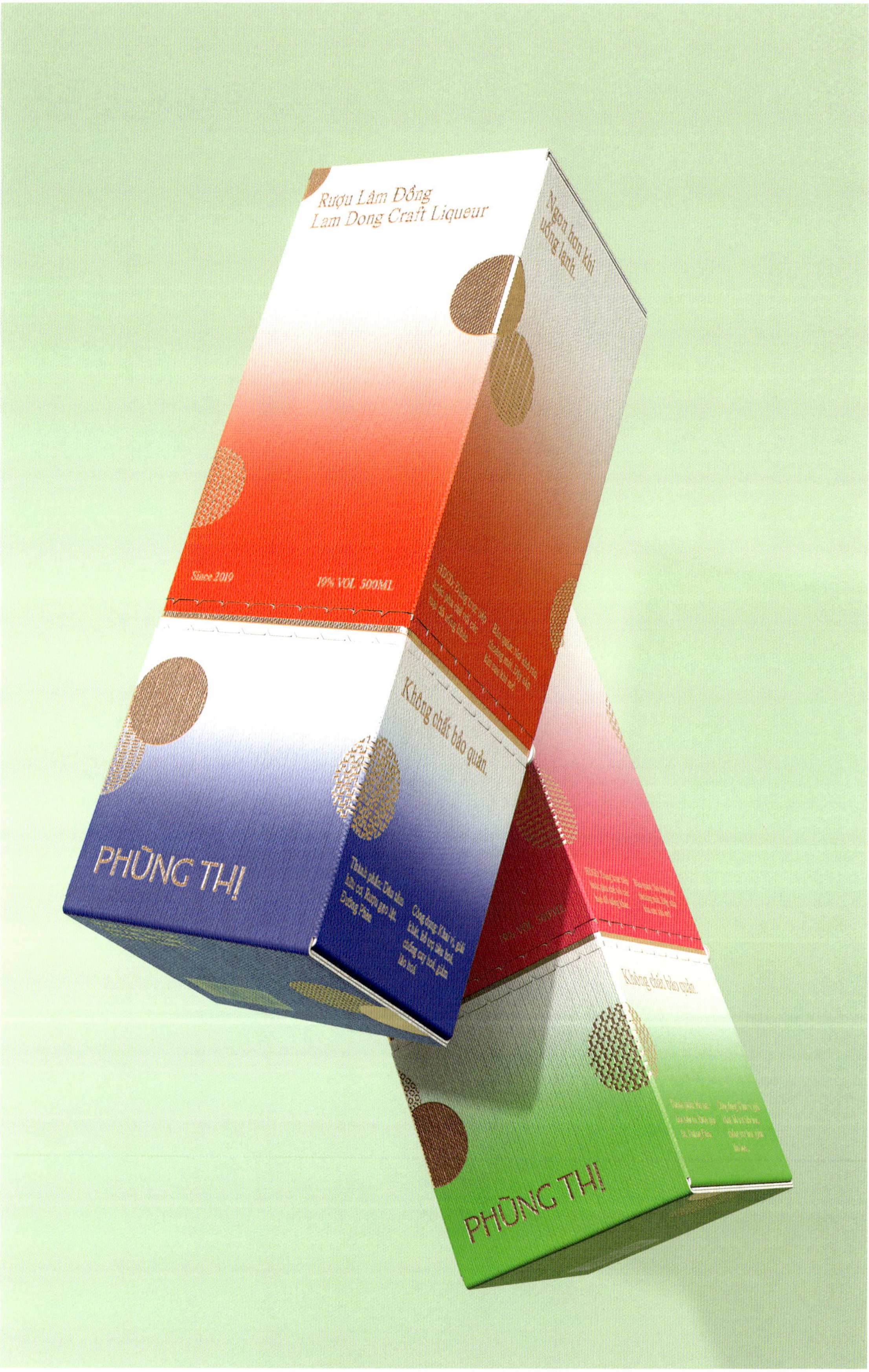

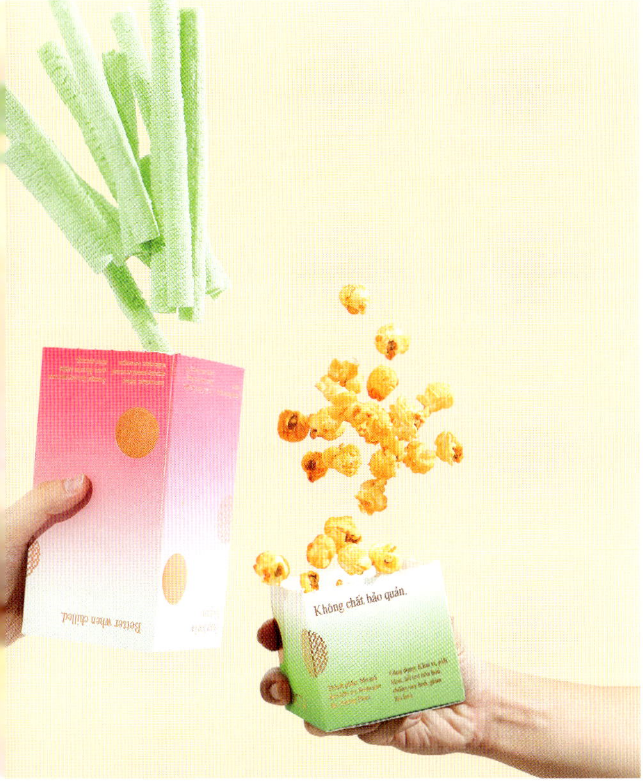

PHÙNG THỊ APRICOT

Phùng Thị offers exquisite Vietnamese specialties, including the standout "Apricot Craft Liquor", made from rare, 30-year-old apricots. The meticulous two-year fermentation process creates a unique flavour profile, emphasizing a smooth, fragrant character. The packaging reflects the northwest region's captivating landscape, blending traditional patterns and local imagery. A contemporary colour palette, elegant typography, and unique linen paper enhance the modern aesthetic. The "perforation" technique adds to the unboxing experience, promoting sustainability.

Design Studio
Layơ Lab

Creative Director
Alex Dang

Client
Phùng Thị

3D Visualization
Duy Tran

Photographer
anchoicreative, h.tungf & Ngo Thanh Huu

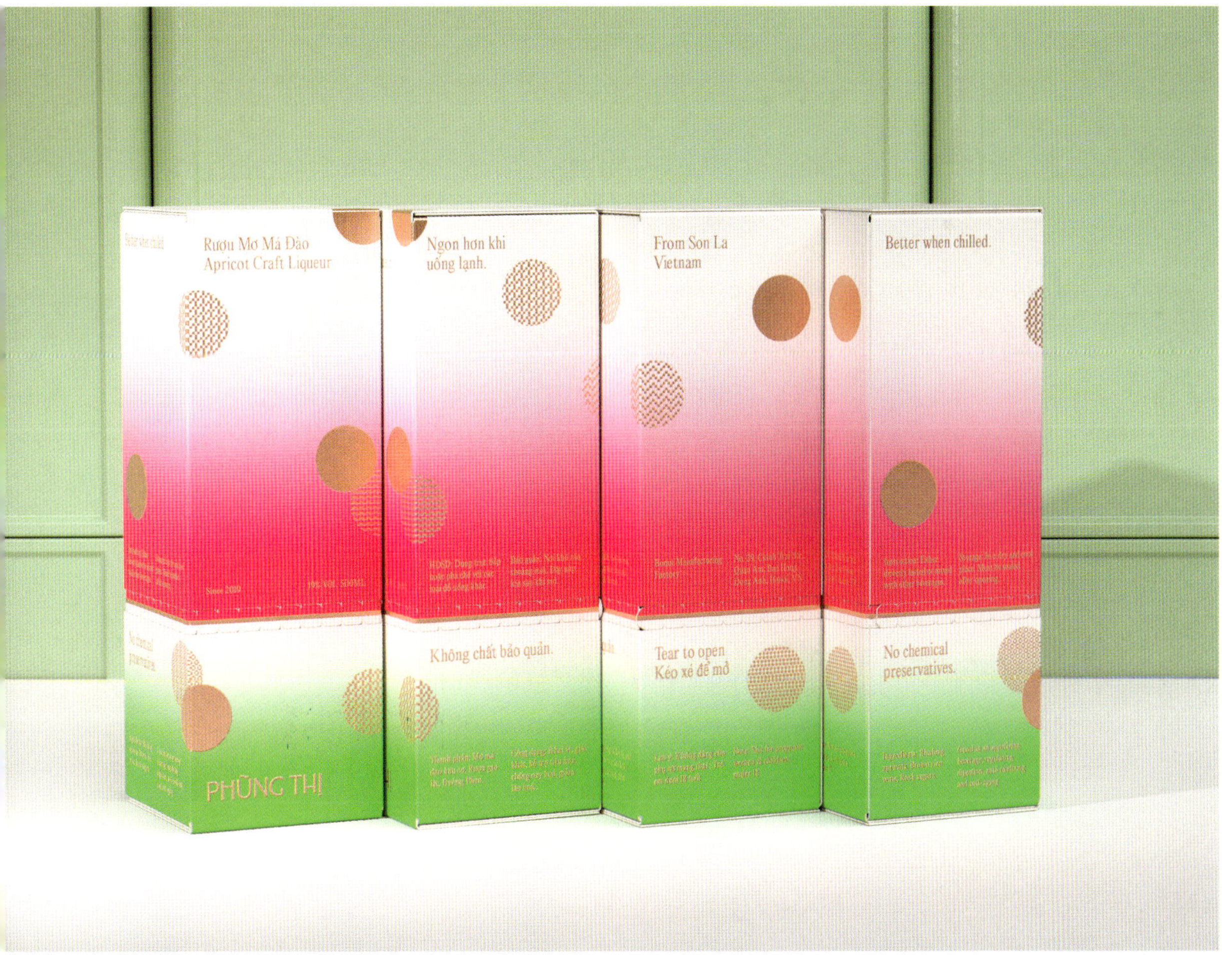

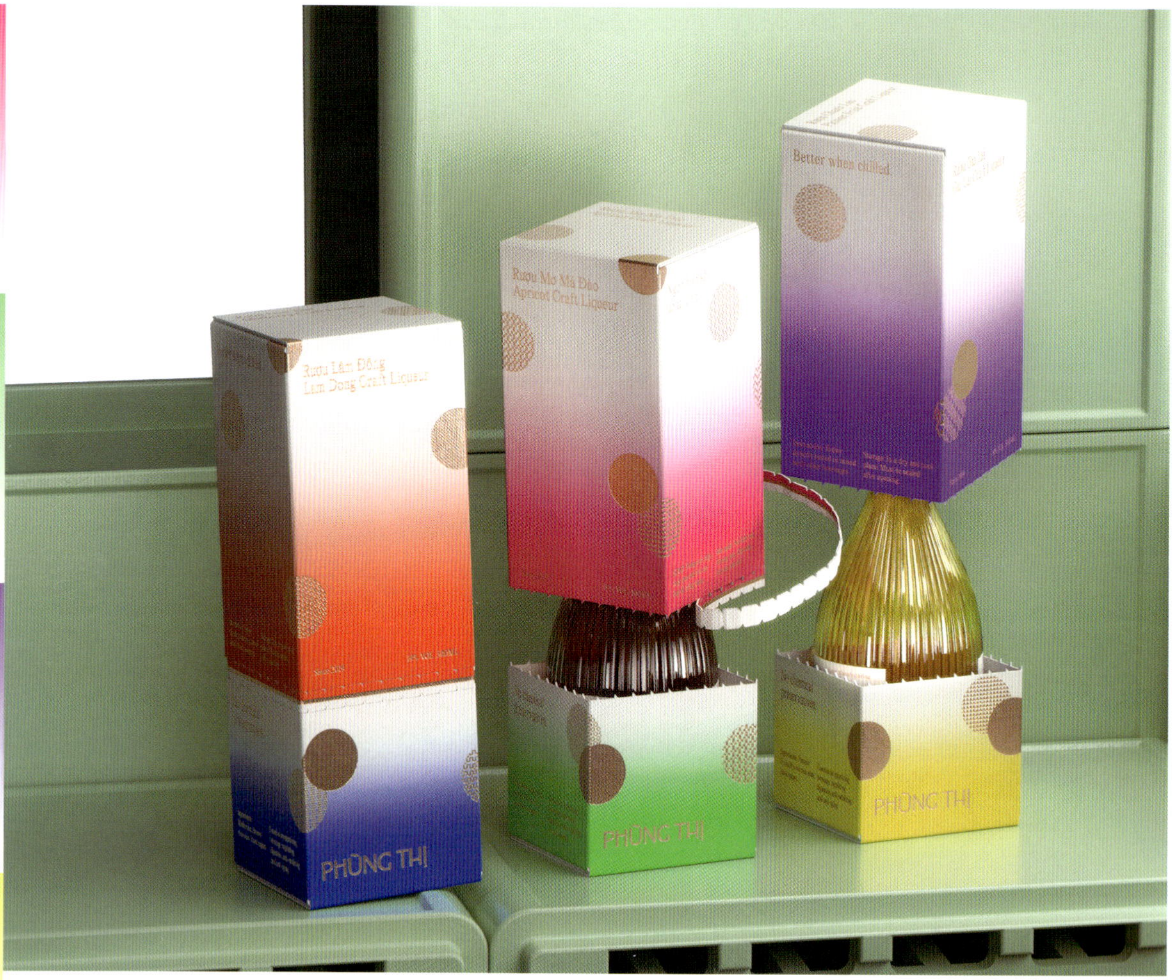
Better when chilled
Rượu Mơ Mã Đào
Apricot Craft Liqueur
Rượu Lâm Đồng
Lâm Dong Craft Liqueur
PHÙNG THỊ
PHÙNG THỊ
PHÙNG THỊ

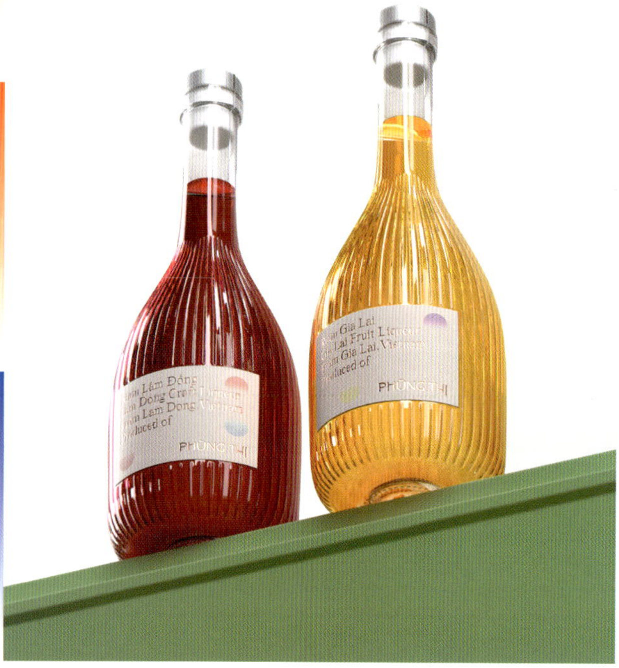
PHÙNG THỊ
PHÙNG THỊ

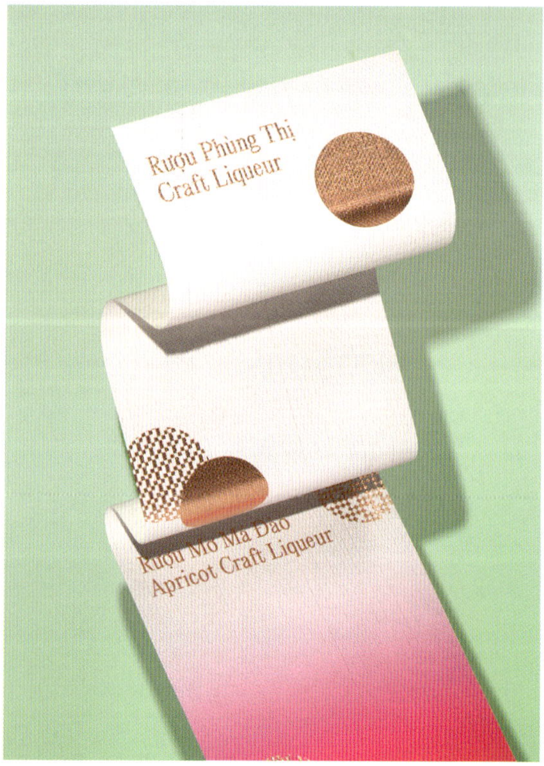
Rượu Phùng Thị
Craft Liqueur
Rượu Mơ Mã Đào
Apricot Craft Liqueur

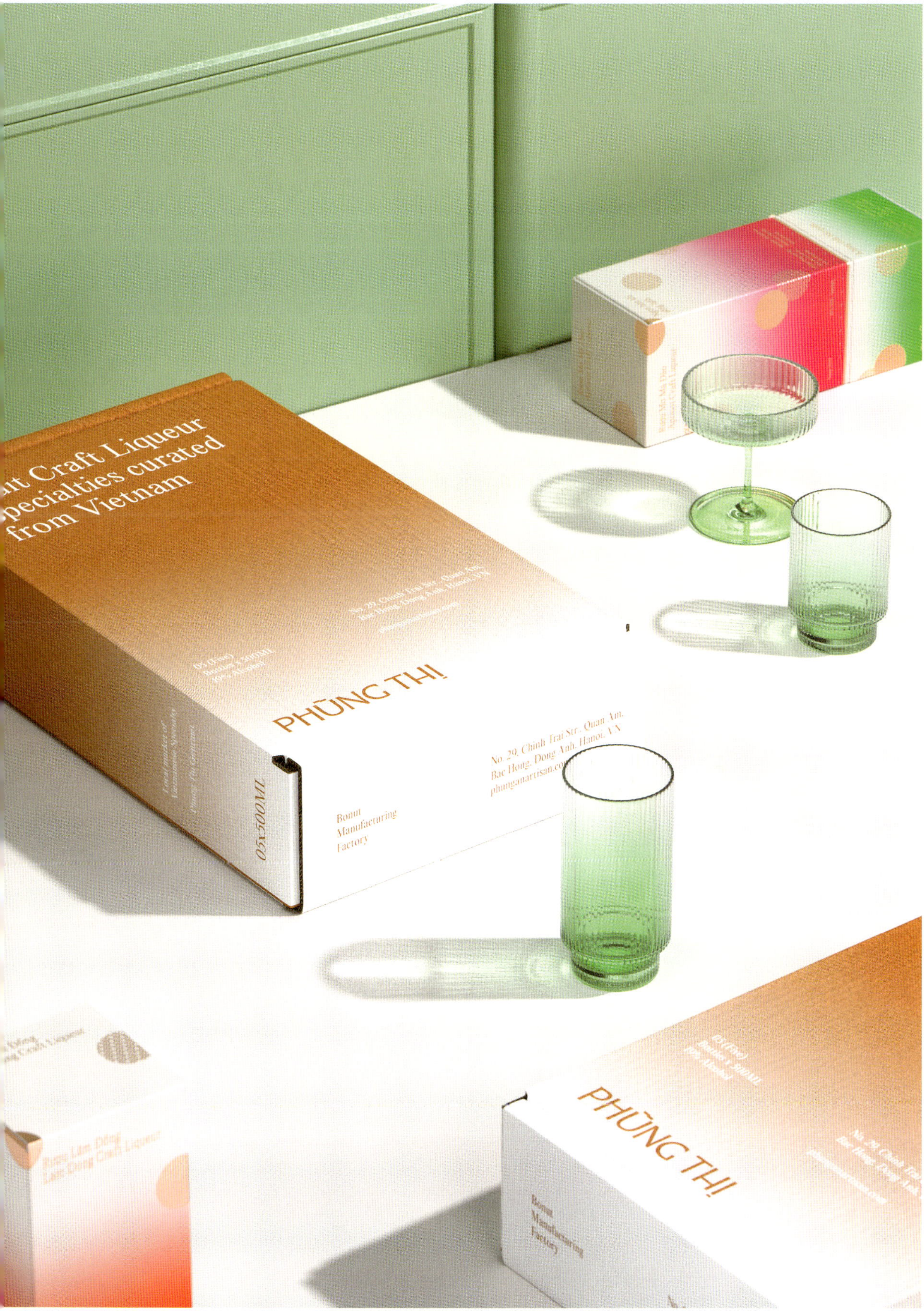
ut Craft Liqueur
pecialties curated
from Vietnam
PHŨNG THỊ
No. 29, Chinh Trai Str., Quan Ant,
Bac Hong, Dong Anh, Hanoi, VN
Bonut
Manufacturing
Factory
05x500ML
PHŨNG THỊ
Bonut
Manufacturing
Factory

PANTONE 354 U

PANTONE WARM RED U

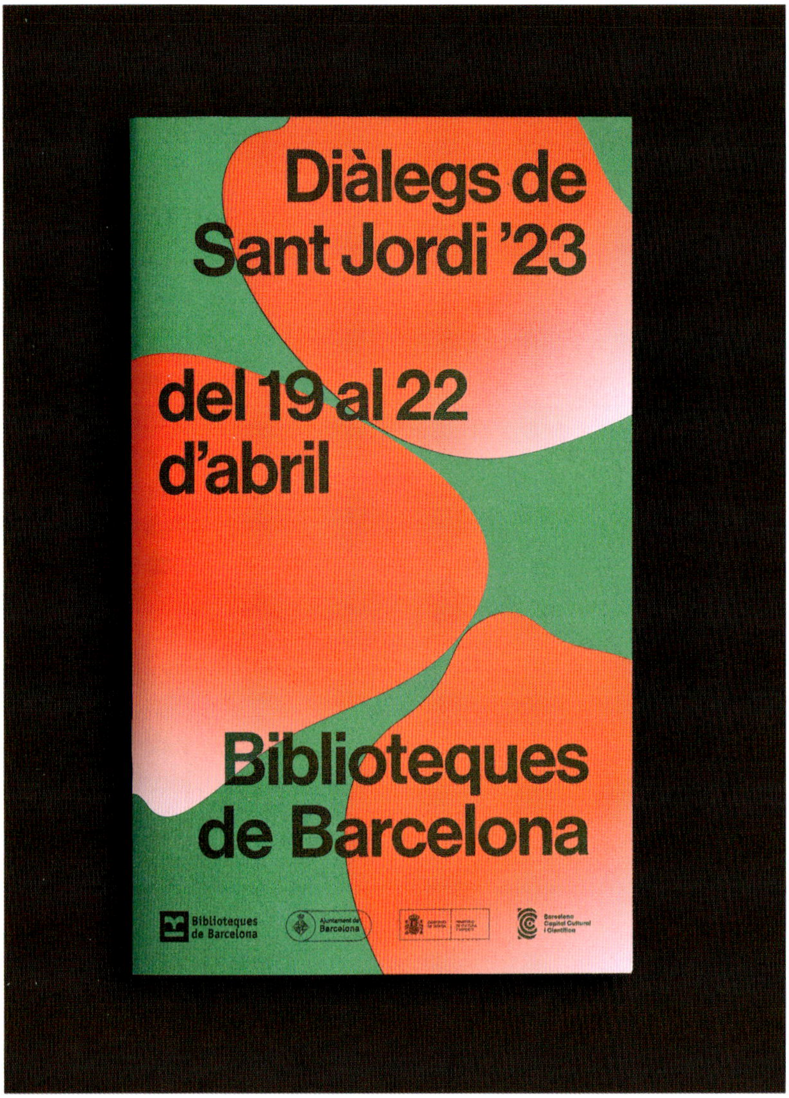

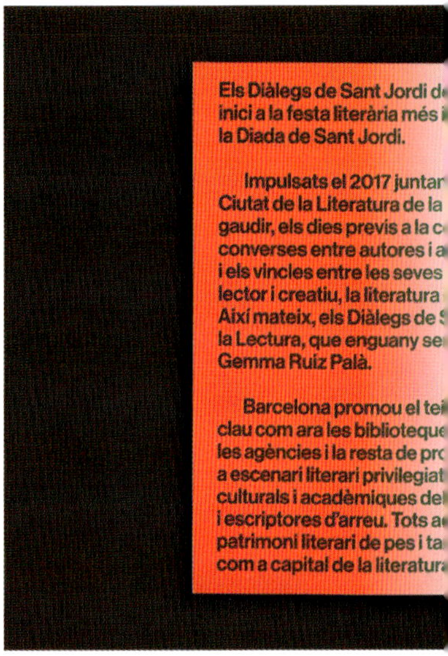

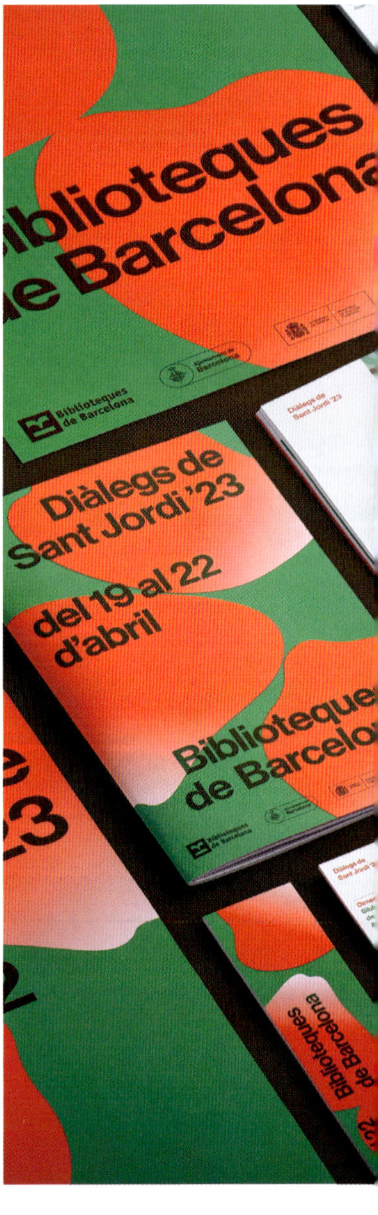

DIÀLEGS DE SANT JORDI '23

Organized by Biblioteques de Barcelona, *Diàlegs de Sant Jordi* is an event consisting of three days of conversations and talks between writers from all over the world based on similarities in their latest works. Forma was commissioned to design the campaign for the 2023 edition.

Design Studio
Forma

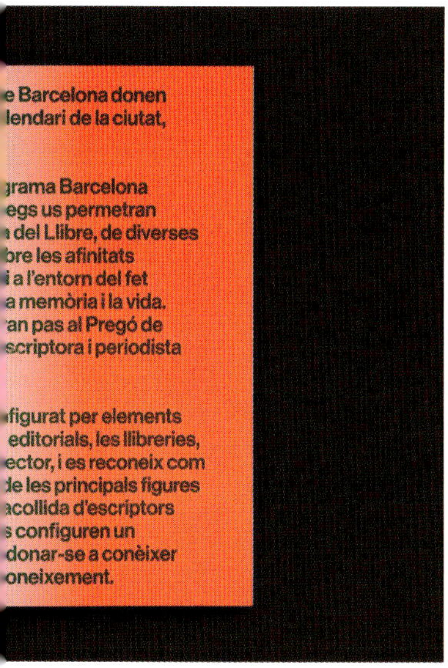

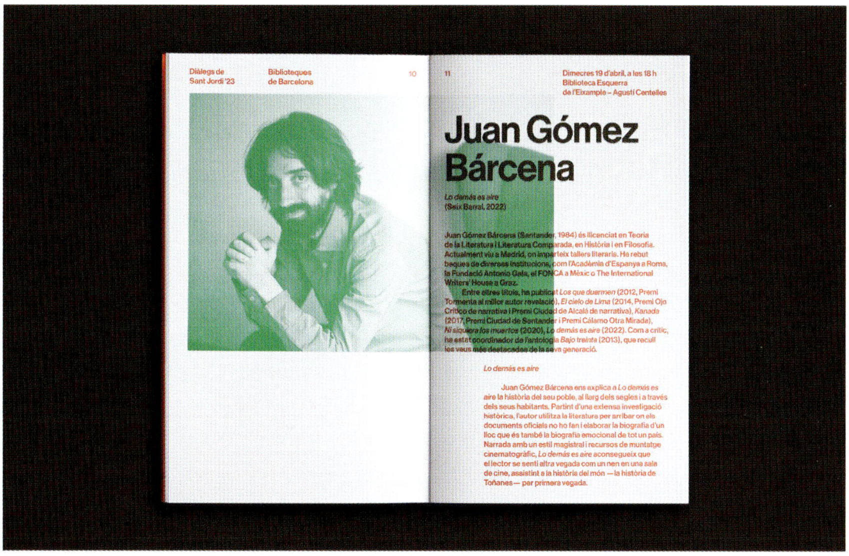
Diàlegs de Sant Jordi '23
Biblioteques de Barcelona
10
11
Dimecres 19 d'abril, a les 18 h
Biblioteca Esquerra de l'Eixample – Agustí Centelles
Juan Gómez Bárcena
Lo demés es aire
(Seix Barral, 2022)
Lo demés es aire

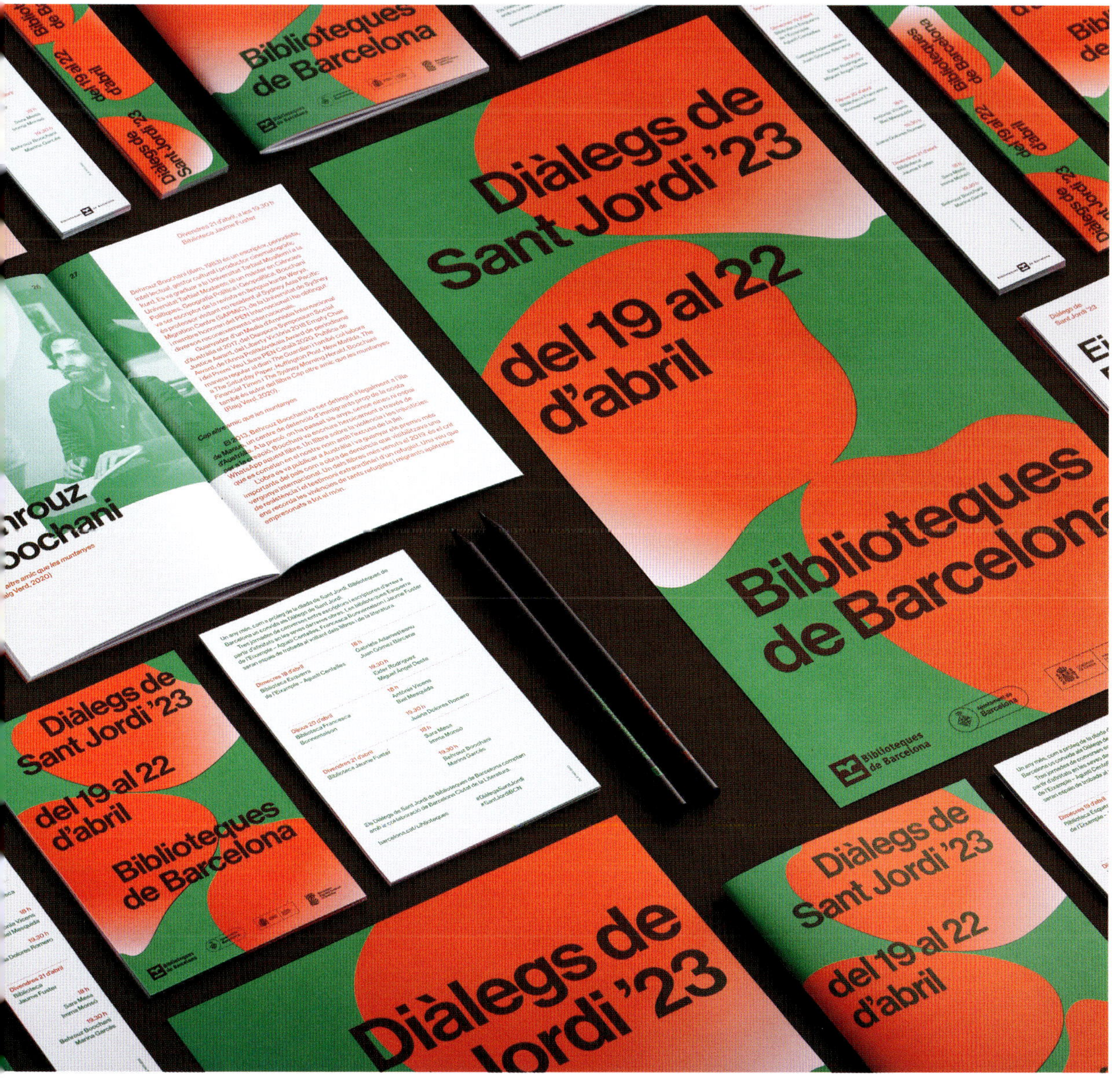
Diàlegs de Sant Jordi '23
del 19 al 22 d'abril
Biblioteques de Barcelona
Biblioteques de Barcelona

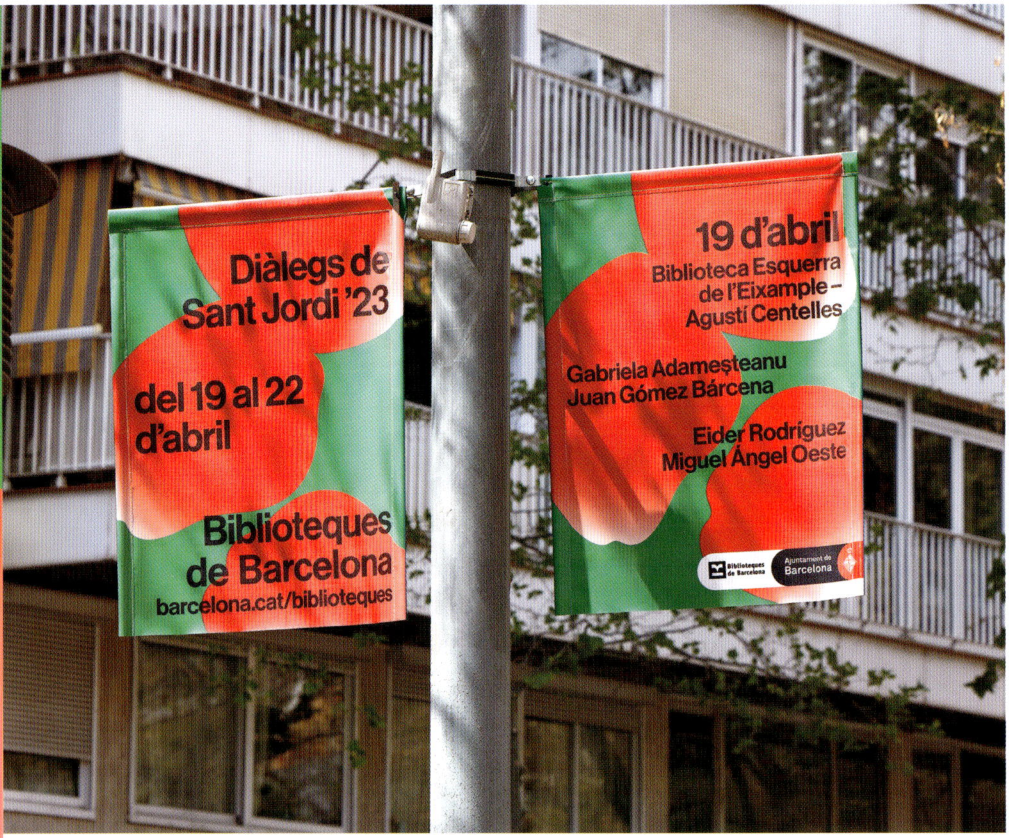
Diàlegs de Sant Jordi '23
del 19 al 22 d'abril
Biblioteques de Barcelona
barcelona.cat/biblioteques
19 d'abril
Biblioteca Esquerra de l'Eixample – Agustí Centelles
Gabriela Adameşteanu
Juan Gómez Bárcena
Eider Rodríguez
Miguel Ángel Oeste

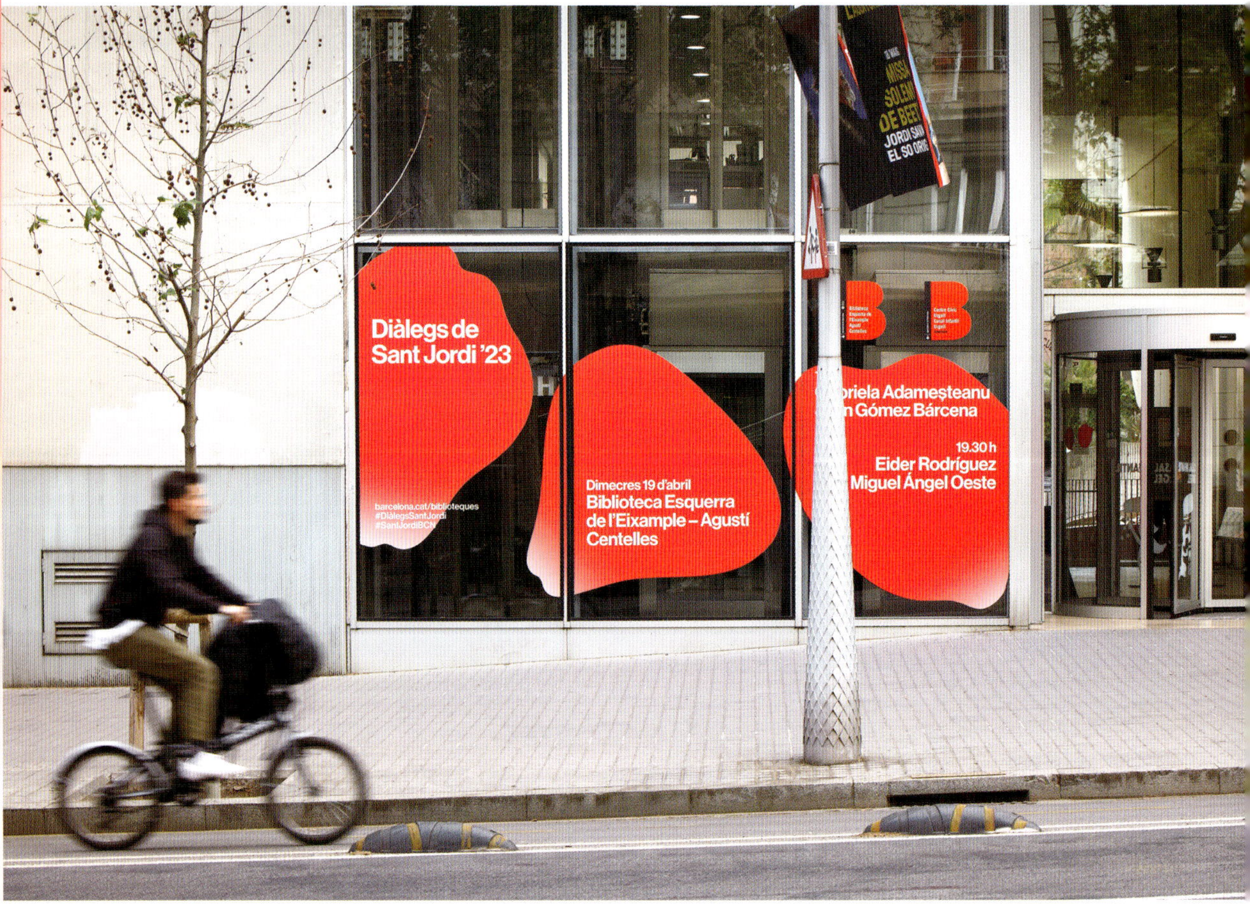
Diàlegs de Sant Jordi '23
barcelona.cat/biblioteques
#DiàlegsSantJordi
#SantJordiBCN
Dimecres 19 d'abril
Biblioteca Esquerra de l'Eixample – Agustí Centelles
19.30 h
Eider Rodríguez
Miguel Ángel Oeste

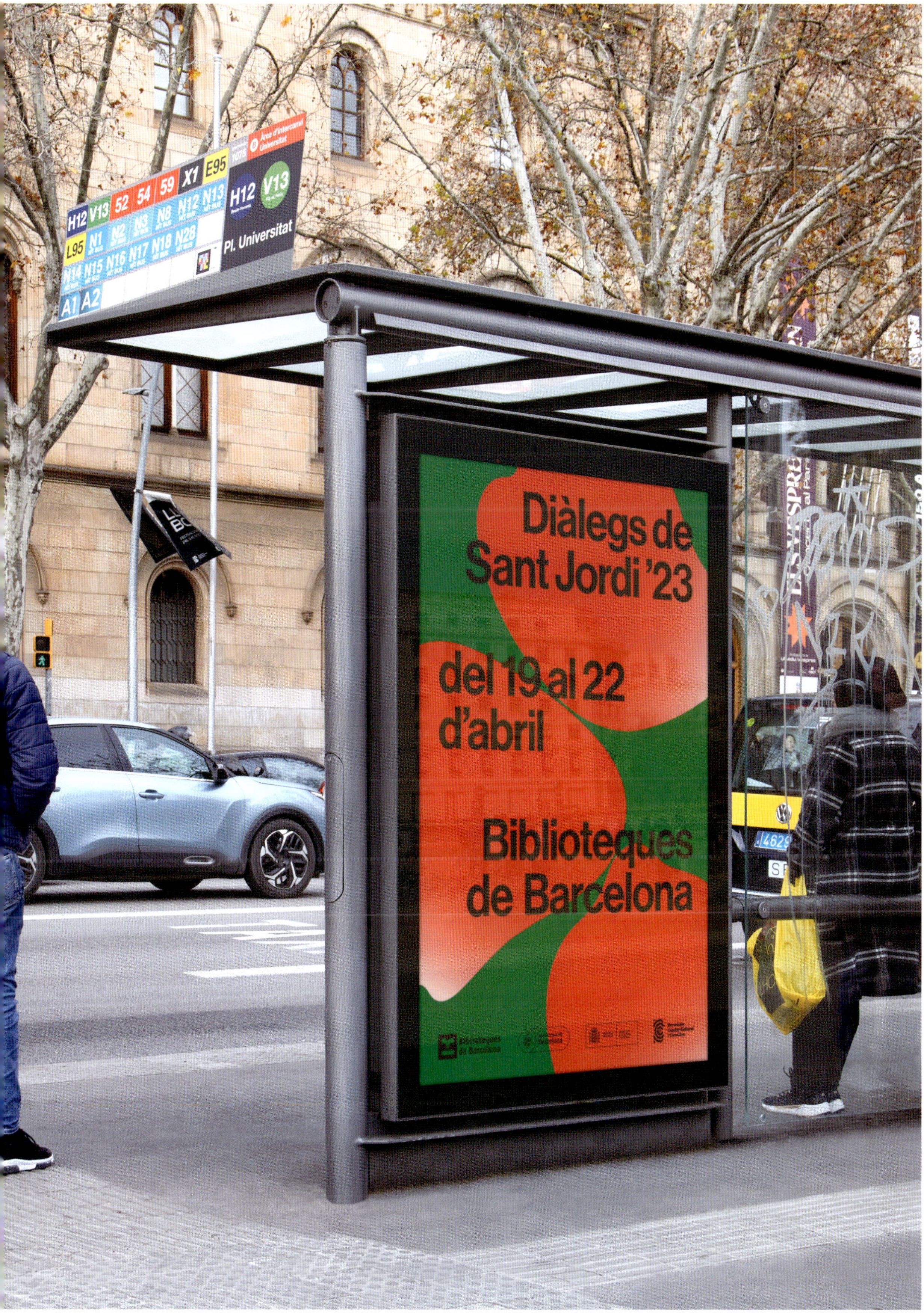
Diàlegs de
Sant Jordi '23
del 19 al 22
d'abril
Biblioteques
de Barcelona
Pl. Universitat

PANTONE 2296 C

PANTONE 809 C

PANTONE 649 C

PANTONE 2310 C

PANTONE BLACK 3 C

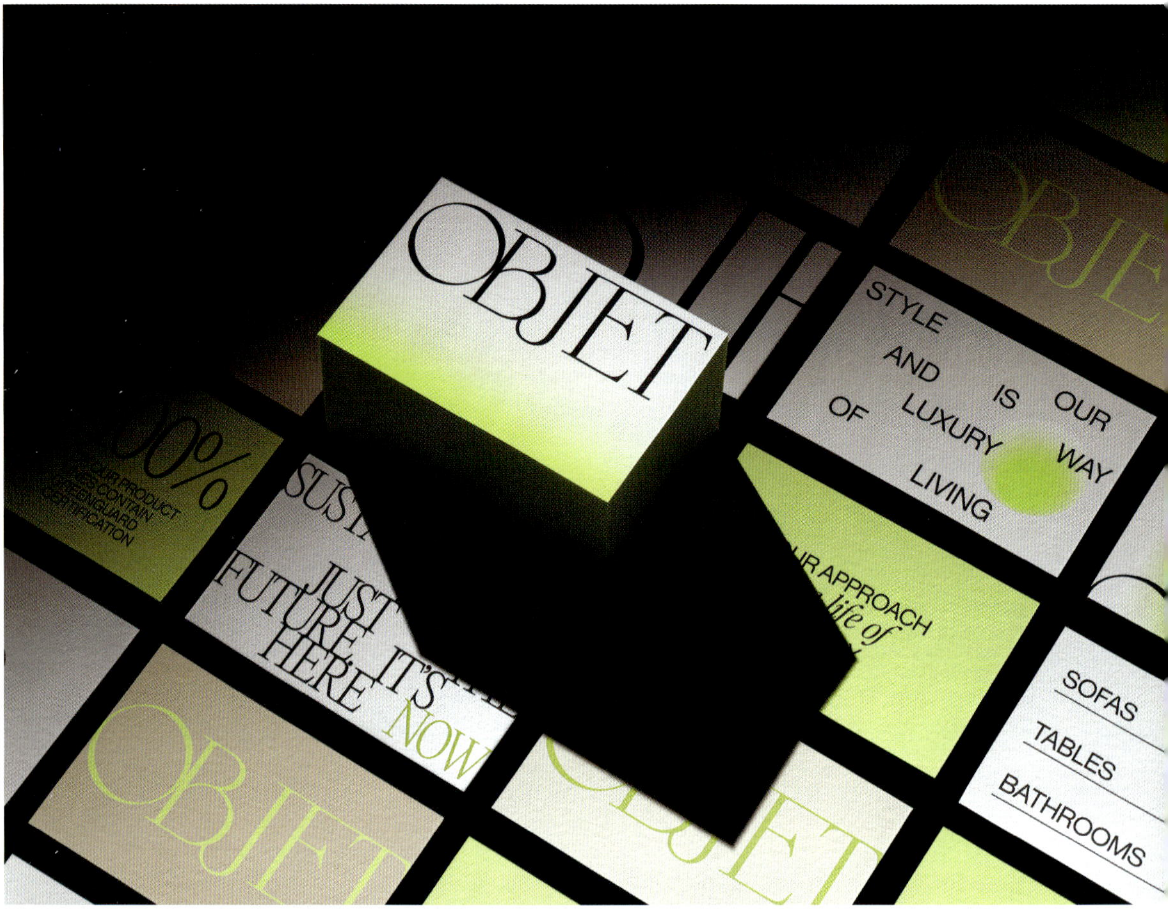

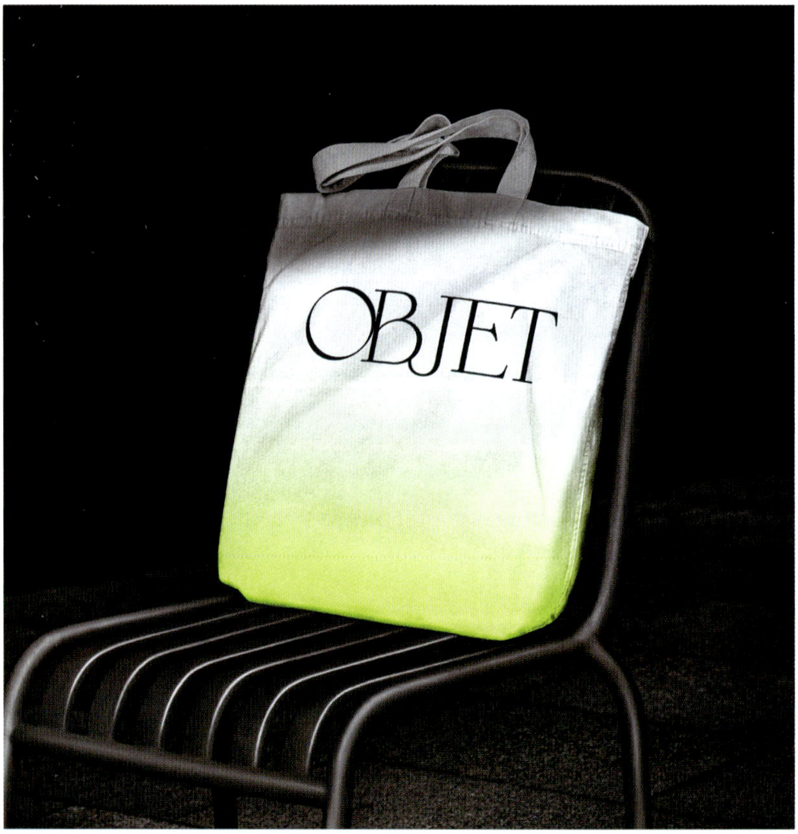

OBJET

As an e-commerce platform curating high-end interior design brands, *Objet* boasts a vibrant visual identity embodying “modern & cool” luxury. With a bold gradient and elegant typography, Objet seamlessly blends these two worlds into one.

Design Studio
Mirela Melo Design

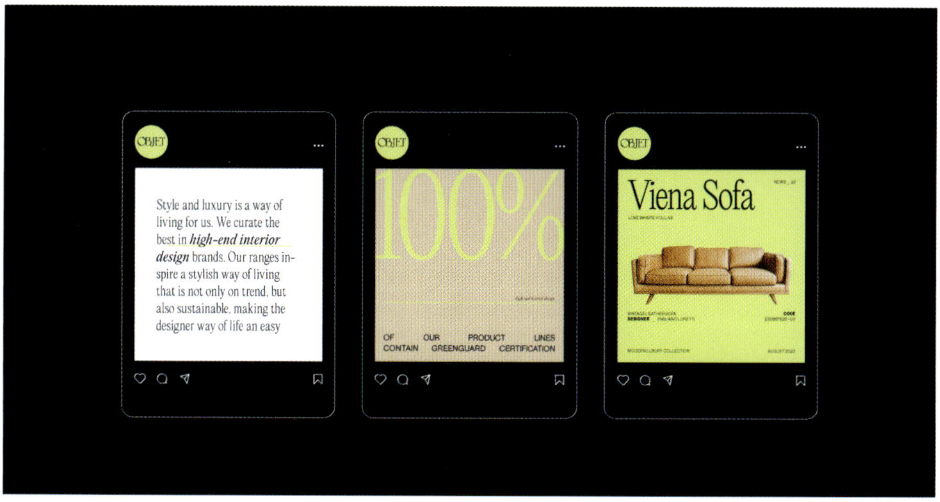
OBJET
Style and luxury is a way of living for us. We curate the best in high-end interior design brands. Our ranges inspire a stylish way of living that is not only on trend, but also sustainable, making the designer way of life an easy
100%
OF OUR PRODUCT LINES CONTAIN GREENGUARD CERTIFICATION
Viena Sofa

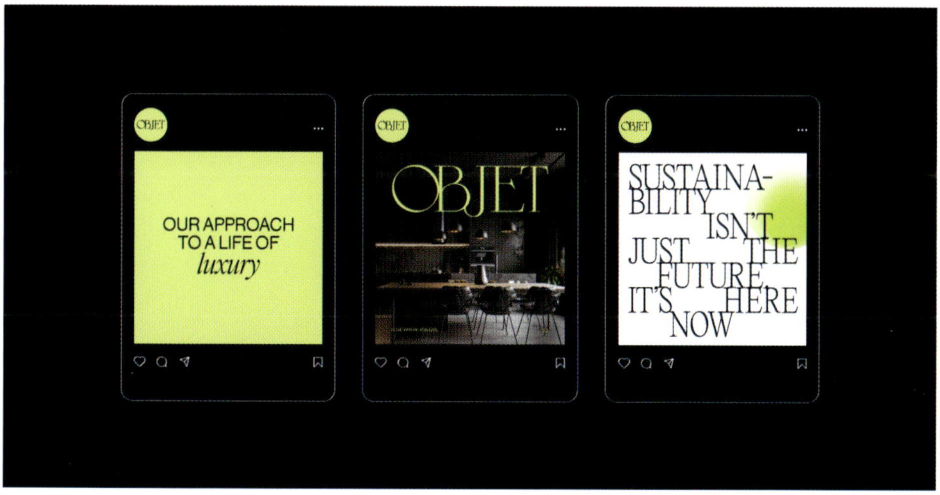
OBJET
OUR APPROACH TO A LIFE OF luxury
OBJET
SUSTAINABILITY ISN'T JUST THE FUTURE, IT'S HERE NOW

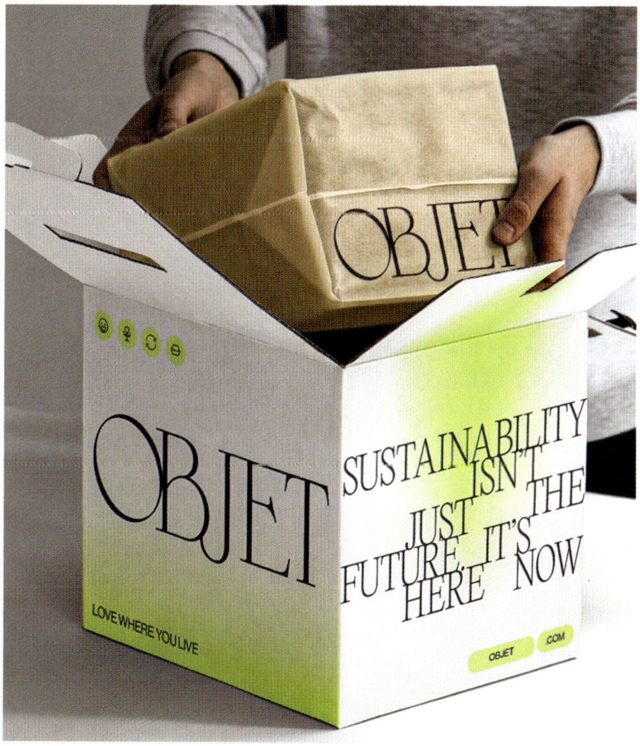
OBJET
OBJET
SUSTAINABILITY ISN'T JUST THE FUTURE, IT'S HERE NOW
LOVE WHERE YOU LIVE
OBJET .COM

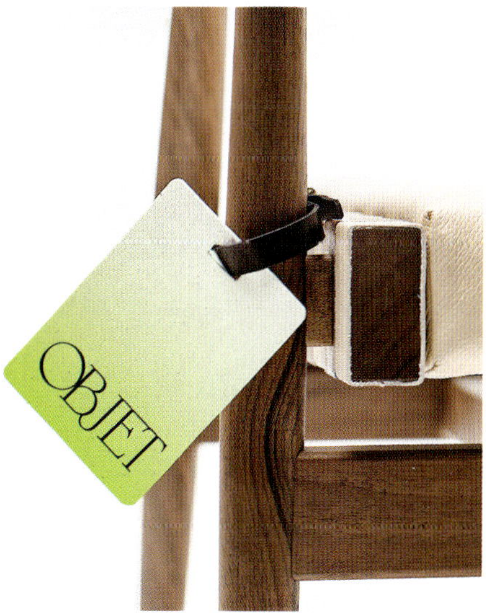
OBJET

R200 · G162 · B80
R26 · G26 · B26

R122 · G103 · B198

R0 · G170 · B117

R212 · G77 · B0

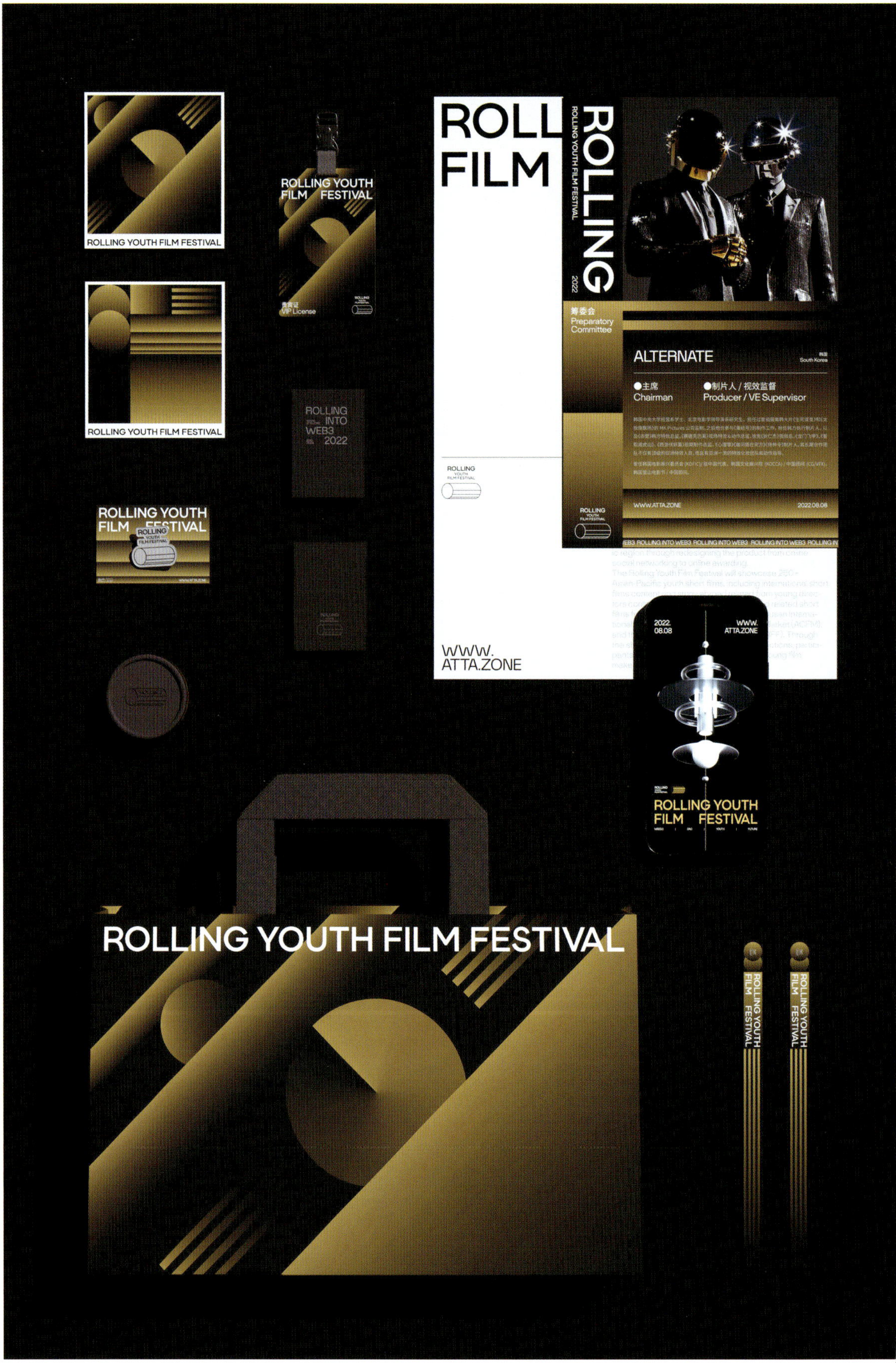

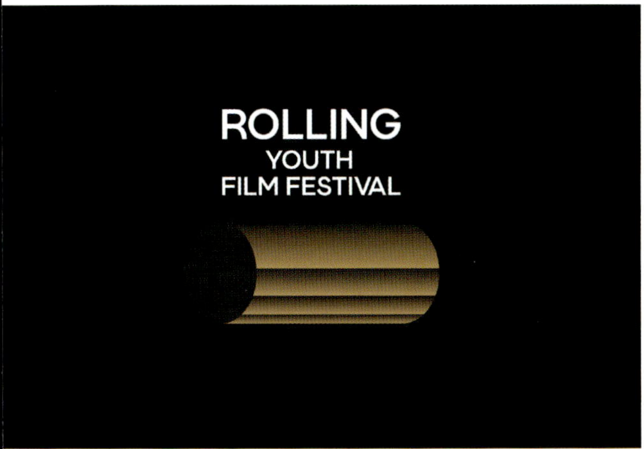

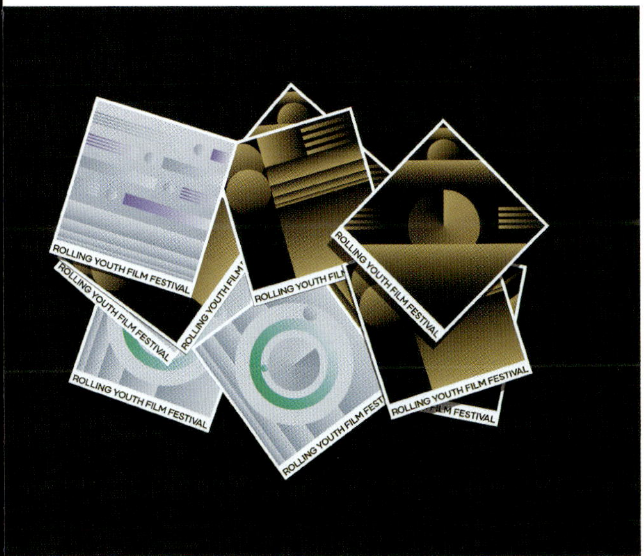

ROLLING YOUTH FILM FESTIVAL

"Rolling" originates from the the film age and indicates that film has rotated in the camera. ODL took a cinema scene as a starting point, explored the world of Web3.0 from the perspective of film, and expressed features of "Always Rolling On". Based on Web3.0 | Film Art of "Rolling Youth Film Festival, ODL", imported the characteristics of Testbild into a vision system, which reflects the pioneering quality of "Rolling Youth Film Festival" as a Web3.0 film festival, and then established the avant-garde identity of Web3.0 and narrative nature of the film festival.

Design Studio
ODL

Art Director
Jiahao Qin

Creative Director
Yan Wang

Motion Designer
Jian Liu

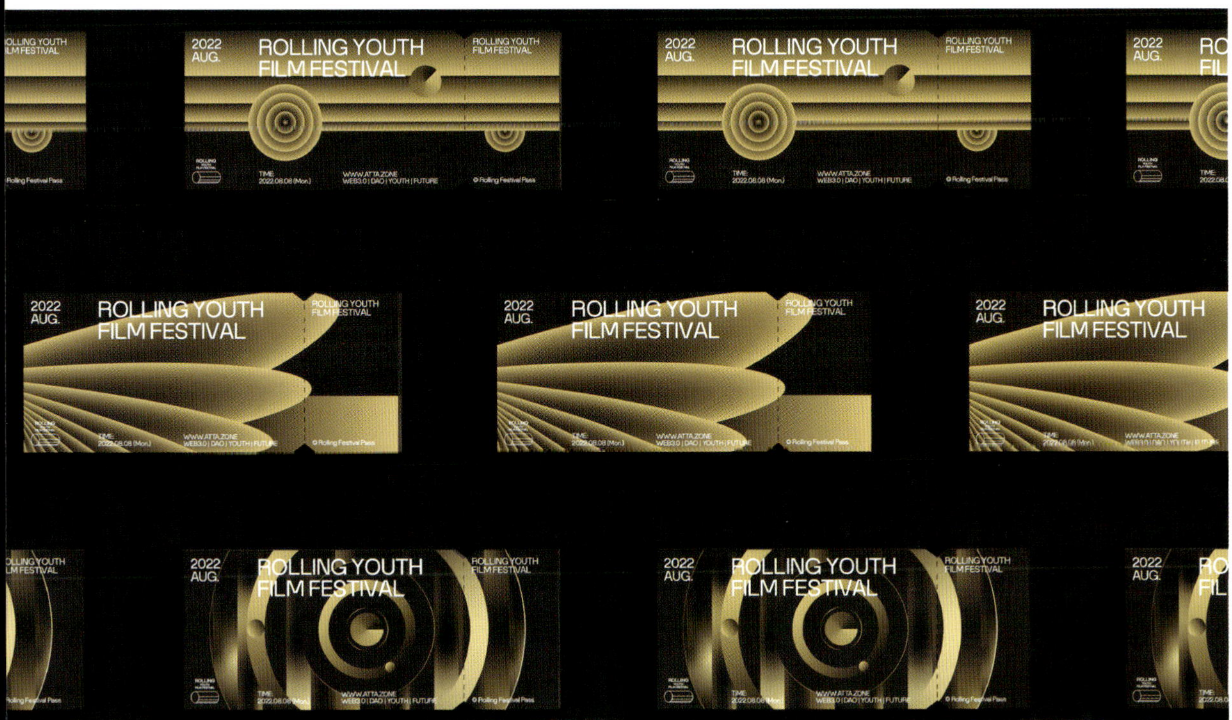

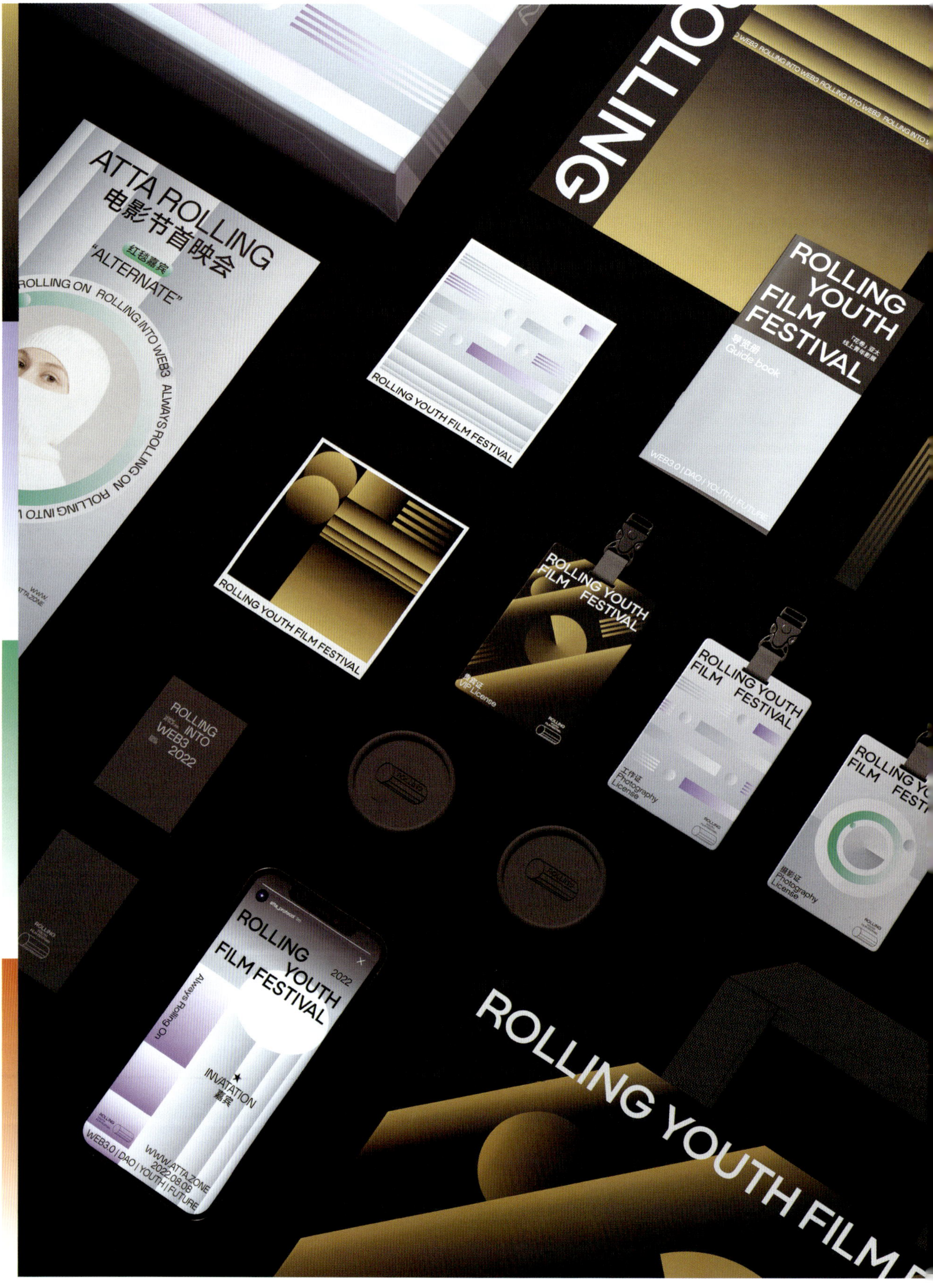
ATTA ROLLING
电影节首映会
红毯嘉宾
"ALTERNATE"
ROLLING ON ROLLING INTO WEB3 ALWAYS ROLLING ON ROLLING INTO
ROLLING YOUTH FILM FESTIVAL
Guide book
WEB3.0 | DAO | YOUTH | FUTURE
ROLLING INTO WEB3 2022
VIP License
Photography License
ROLLING YOUTH FILM FESTIVAL 2022
Always Rolling On
INVATATION
嘉宾
WWW.ATTA.ZONE
2022.08.08
WEB3.0 | DAO | YOUTH | FUTURE
ROLLING YOUTH FILM

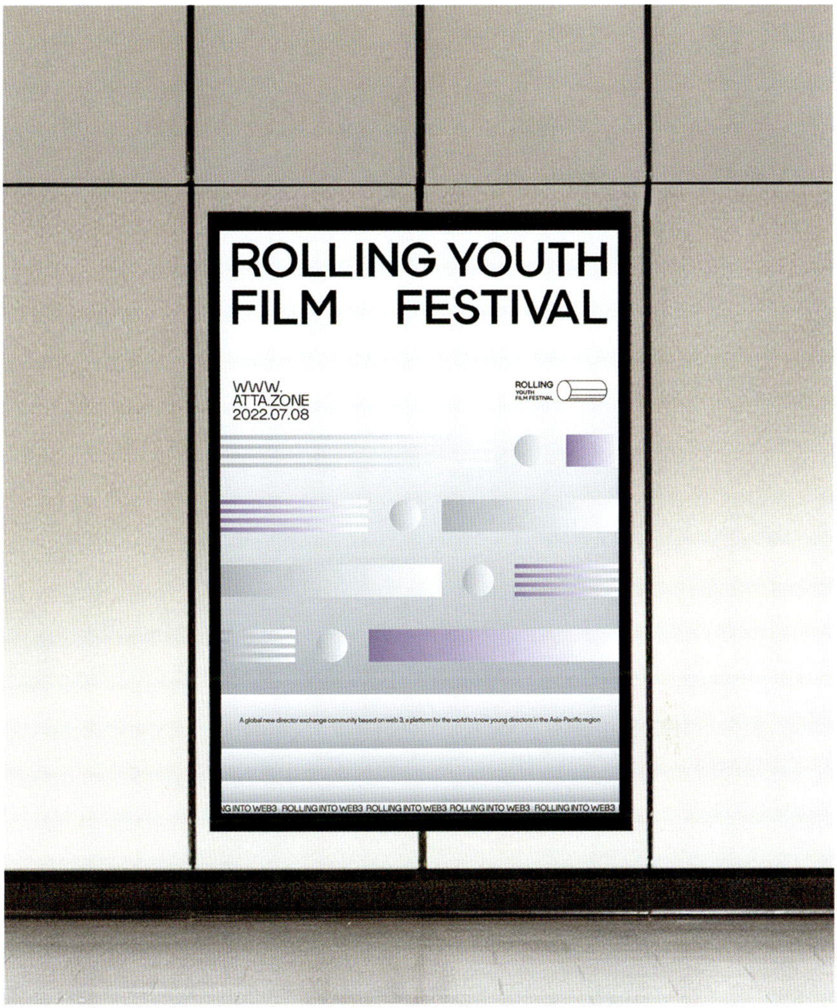
ROLLING YOUTH
FILM FESTIVAL
WWW.
ATTA.ZONE
2022.07.08
ROLLING
YOUTH
FILM FESTIVAL
A global new director exchange community based on web 3, a platform for the world to know young directors in the Asia-Pacific region
ROLLING INTO WEB3 ROLLING INTO WEB3 ROLLING INTO WEB3 ROLLING INTO WEB3

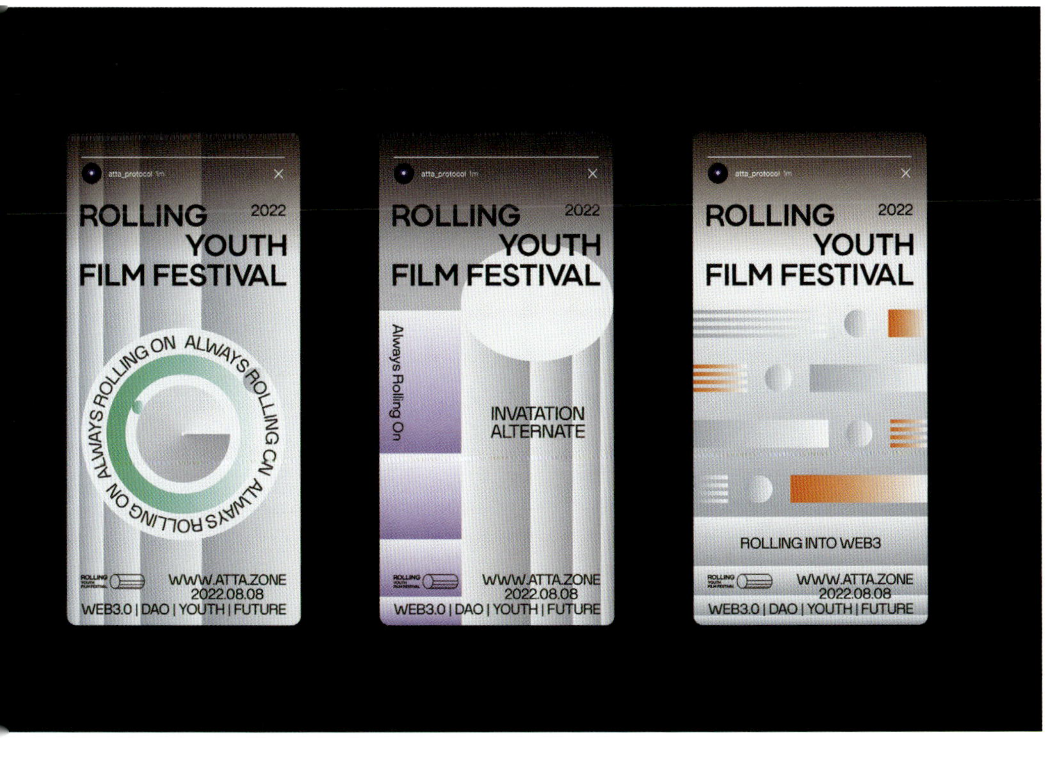
ROLLING
2022
YOUTH
FILM FESTIVAL
ALWAYS ROLLING ON ALWAYS ROLLING ON ALWAYS ROLLING ON
WWW.ATTA.ZONE
2022.08.08
WEB3.0 | DAO | YOUTH | FUTURE
Always Rolling On
INVATATION
ALTERNATE
ROLLING INTO WEB3

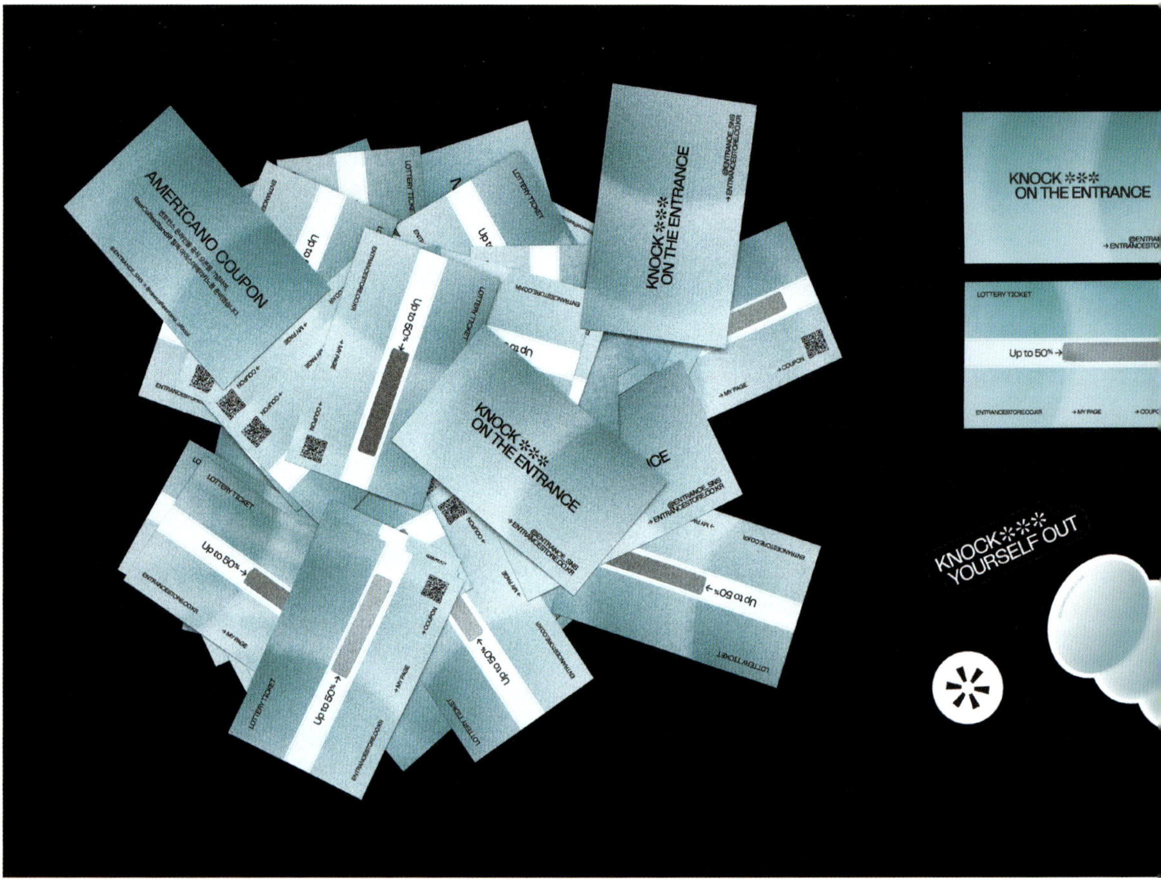

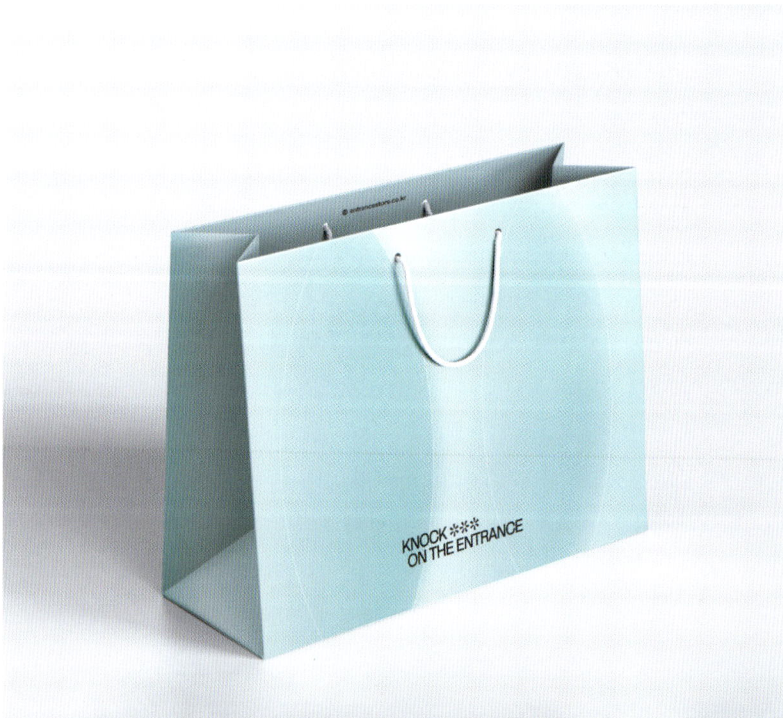

KNOCK ON THE ENTRANCE

This is a short-term marketing project created to commemorate the opening ofthe online store "Entrance" ("Entrance" is a men's clothing multi-brands store in South Korea.) We have created graphics that visualize the sound effects produced when knocking on a door.

Designer
Minkyun Seo

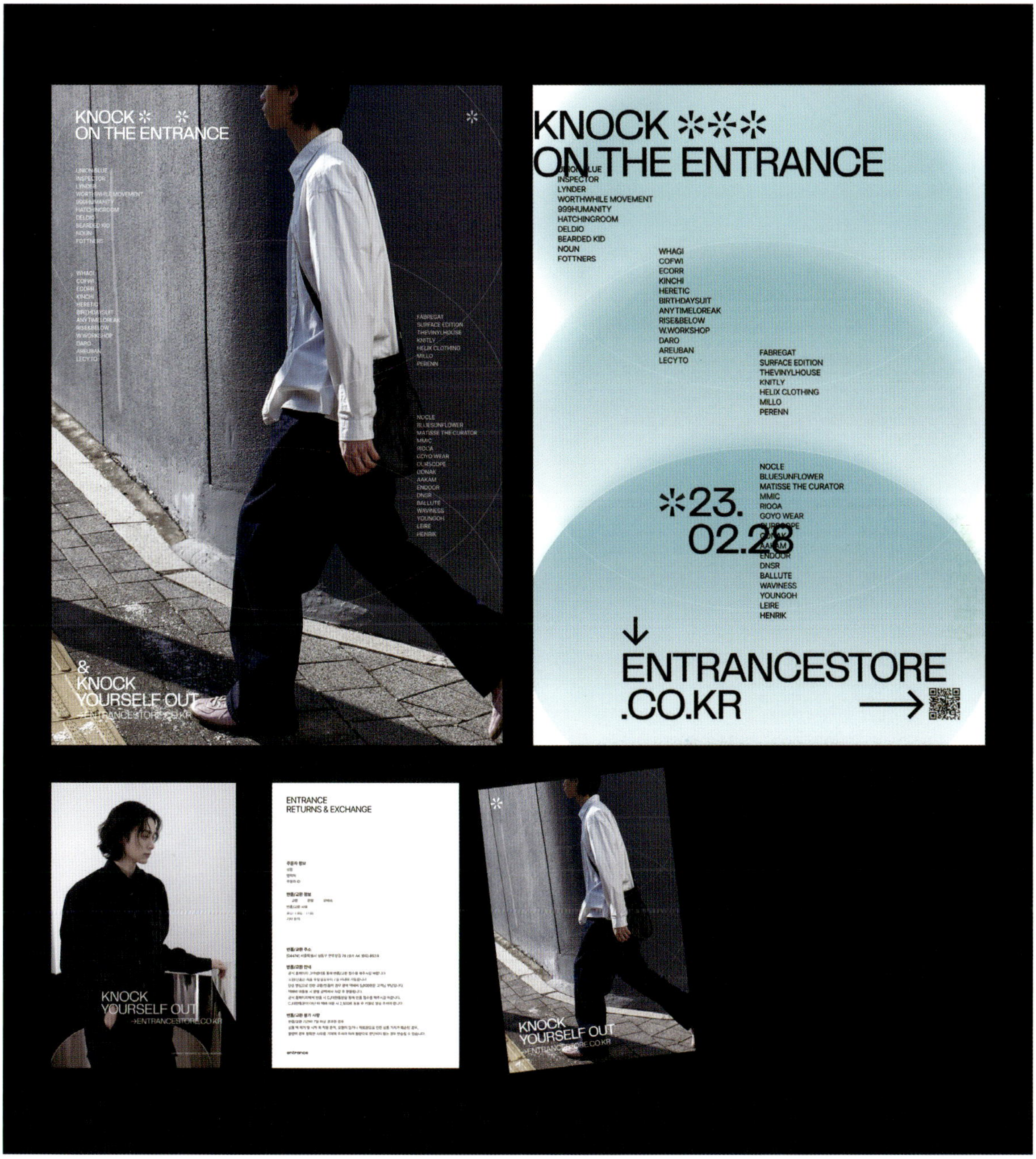
KNOCK
ON THE ENTRANCE
& KNOCK
YOURSELF OUT
KNOCK
ON THE ENTRANCE
INSPECTOR
LYNDER
WORTHWHILE MOVEMENT
999HUMANITY
HATCHINGROOM
DELDIO
BEARDED KID
NOUN
FOTTNERS
WHAGI
COFWI
ECORR
KINCHI
HERETIC
BIRTHDAYSUIT
ANYTIMELOREAK
RISE&BELOW
W.WORKSHOP
DARO
AREUBAN
LECYTO
FABREGAT
SURFACE EDITION
THEVINYLHOUSE
KNITLY
HELIX CLOTHING
MILLO
PERENN
NOCLE
BLUESUNFLOWER
MATISSE THE CURATOR
MMIC
RIOOA
GOYO WEAR
ENDOOR
DNSR
BALLUTE
WAVINESS
YOUNGOH
LEIRE
HENRIK
23.
02.28
ENTRANCESTORE
.CO.KR
KNOCK
YOURSELF OUT
→ENTRANCESTORE.CO.KR
ENTRANCE
RETURNS & EXCHANGE
KNOCK
YOURSELF OUT
→ENTRANCESTORE.CO.KR

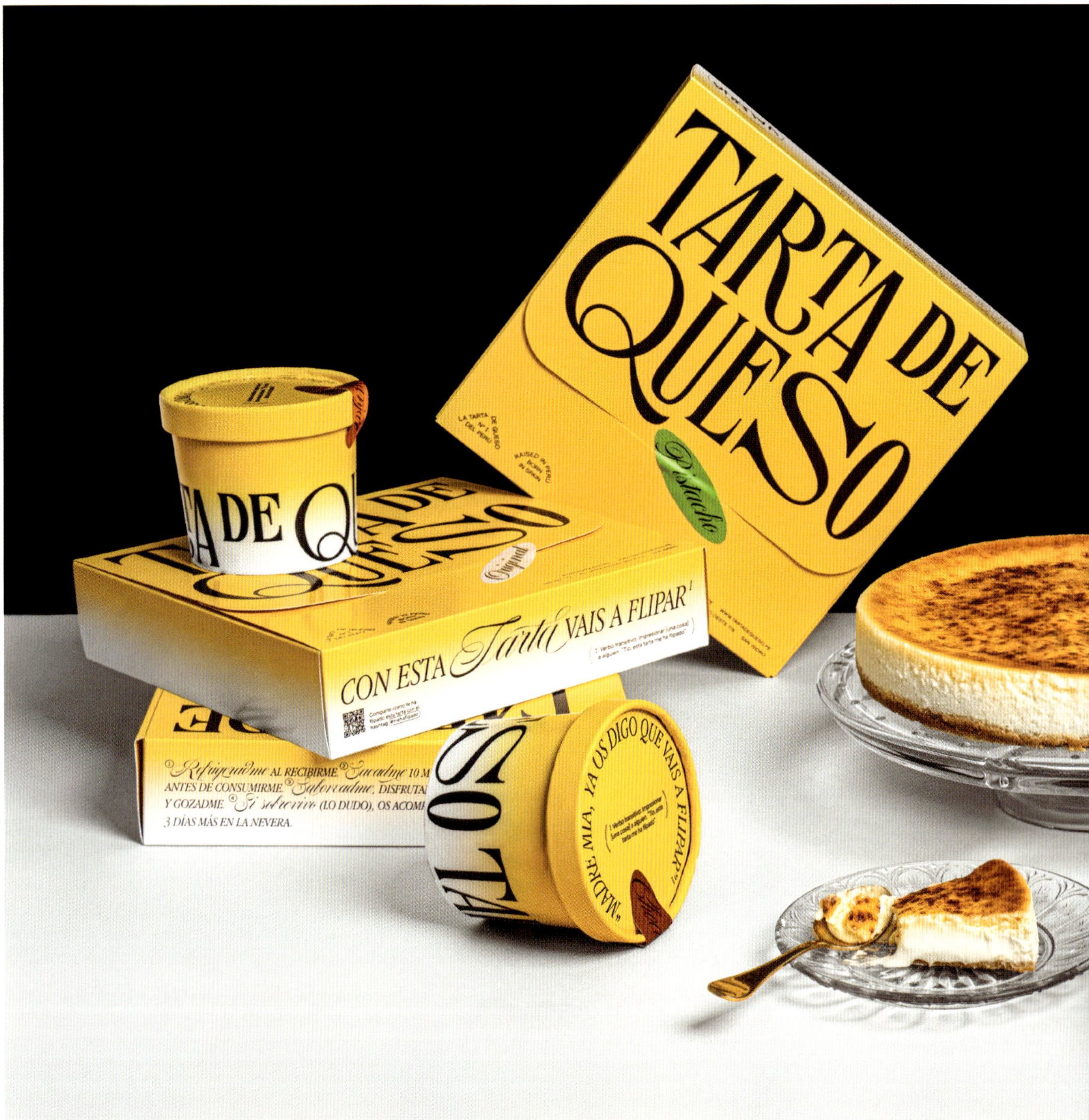
TARTA DE QUESO
Pistacho
Original
CON ESTA Tarta VAIS A FLIPAR¹
"MADRE MIA, YA OS DIGO QUE VAIS A FLIPAR"¹
Refrigeradme AL RECIBIRME.
ANTES DE CONSUMIRME.
Y GOZADME.
(LO DUDO),
3 DÍAS MÁS EN LA NEVERA.

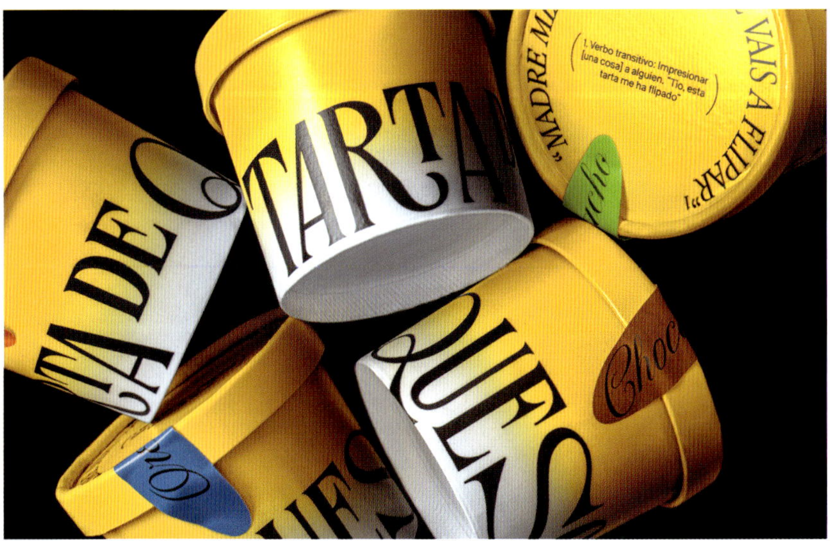
TARTA DE QUESO
"MADRE MI
VAIS A FLIPAR"¹
1. Verbo transitivo: Impresionar [una cosa] a alguien. "Tío, esta tarta me ha flipado"

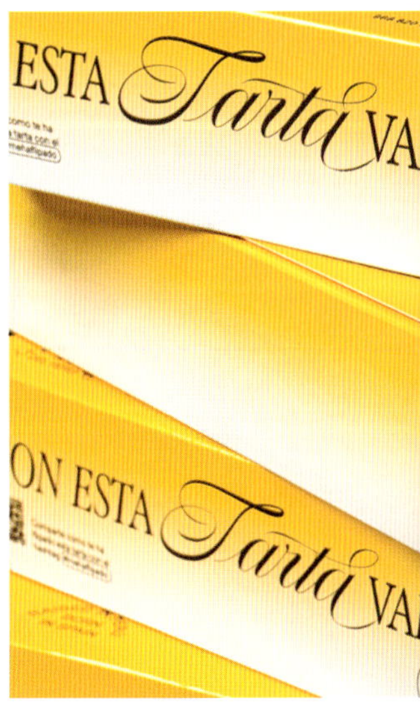
ESTA Tarta VA
ON ESTA Tarta VA

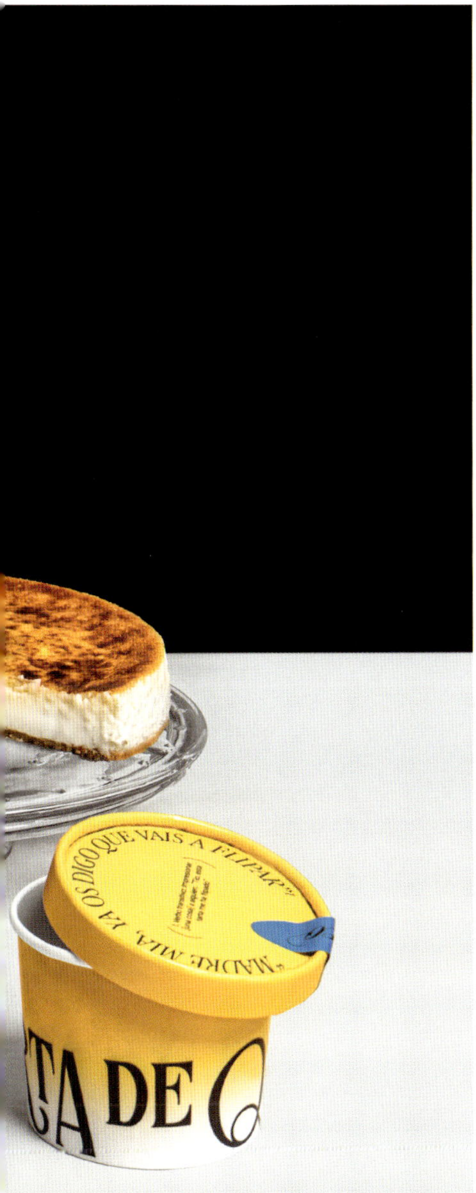

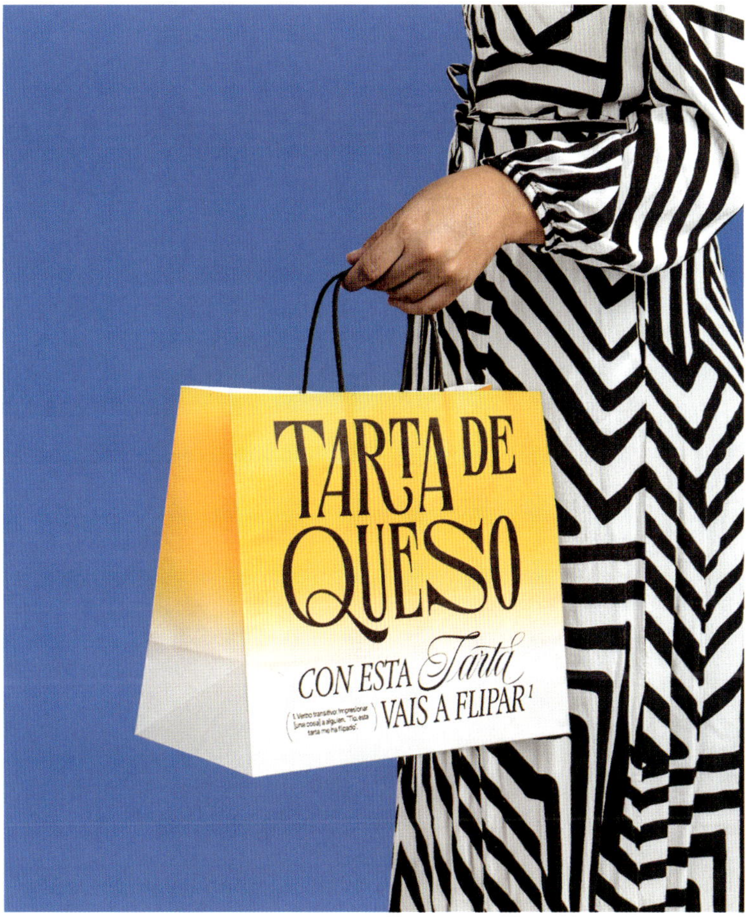

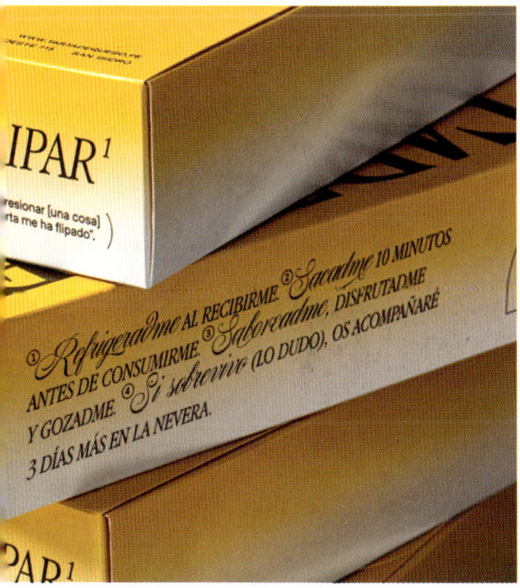

TARTA DE QUESO

The dessert that has taken Spain by storm has arrived in Peru. As ambassadors of Basque cheesecake, the designer aimed to incorporate certain visual elements, such as the vibrant yellow gradient of the cheese, and of course, the unique way Spanish people speak. They created typographic compositions that visualize the poetic nuances of their speech, always maintaining an elegant yet playful tone in their communication.

Art Director
Paloma Nieri

Designer
Belen Diaz

Project Manager
Valeria Tizon

Lettering
Paola Vecco

Photographer
Jimena Agois

C55 · M0 · Y5 · K0

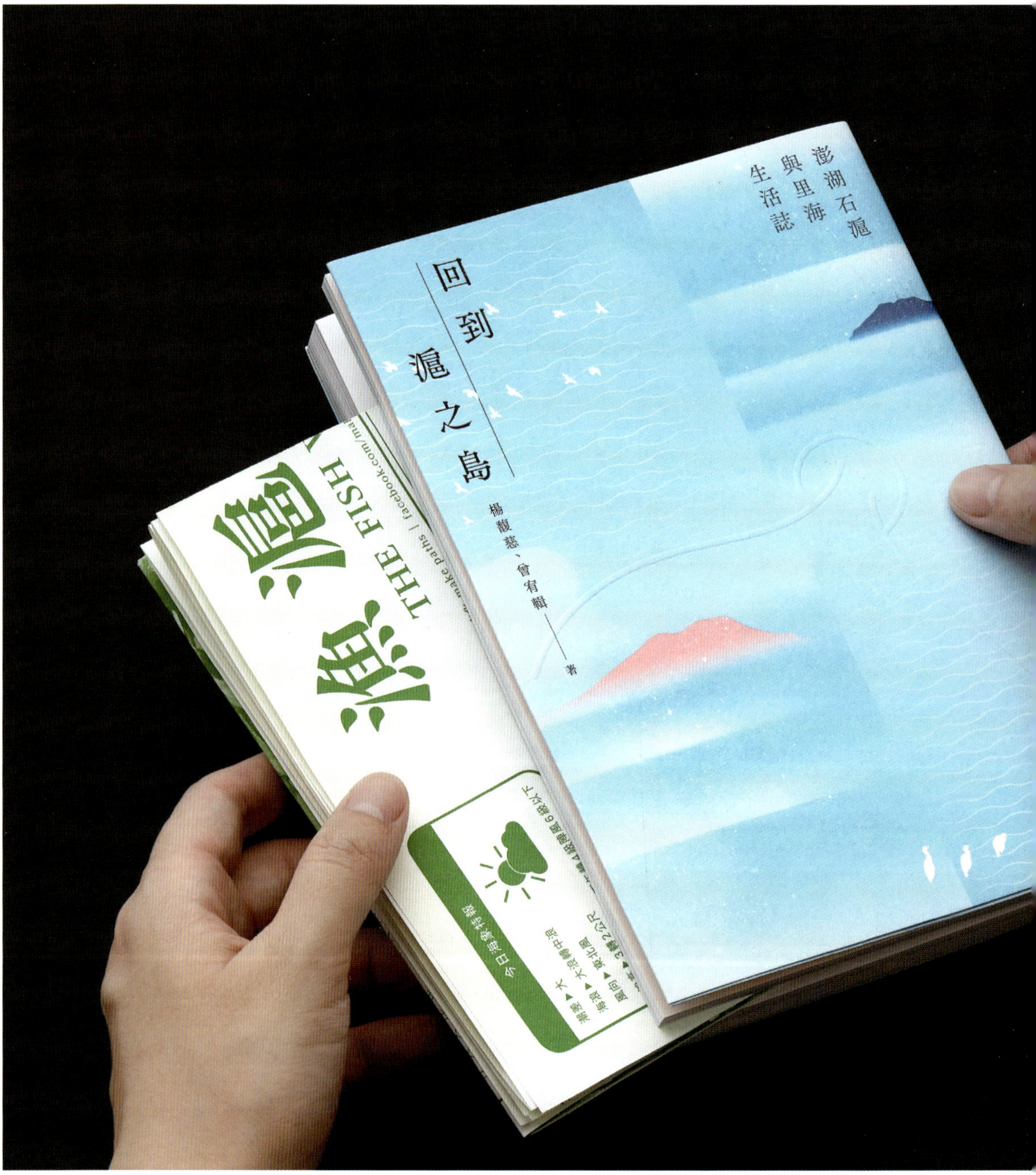

C0 · M45 · Y15 · K0

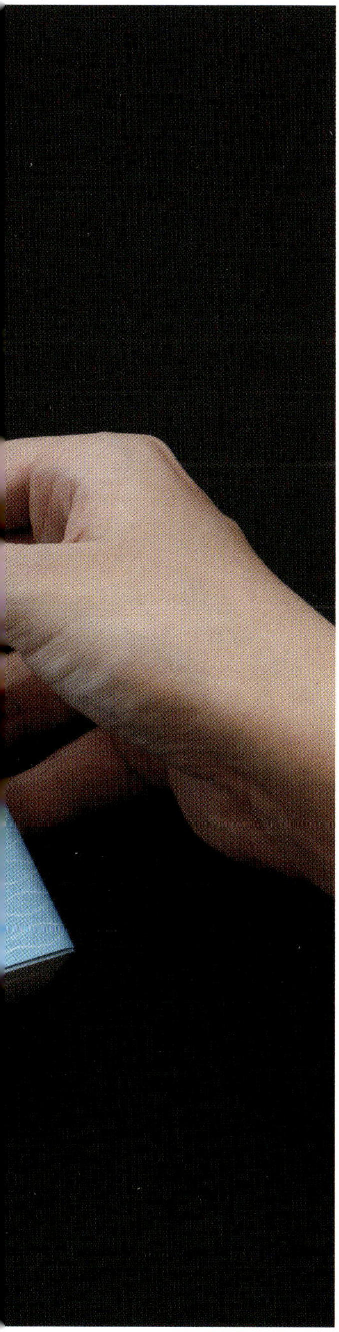

RETURNING TO THE ISLAND OF STONE WEIR

The gradation of the staircases symbolizes the change of tides, and the ancient marine techniques and way back home are paved by this progressive wave to the boundless ocean again. The pattern of stone weir is presented in a convex way and spans between the two districts. The different colours of the islands represent different cultures and people of different districts, talking about the common memories of the Caspian Sea that are linked together by the stone tidal weir.

Designer
Chia-Lin Wu

Illustrator
Whitebirdingrass

Client
Make Paths

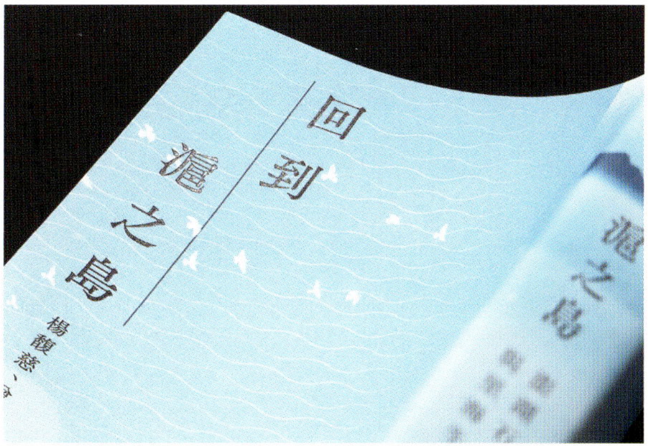

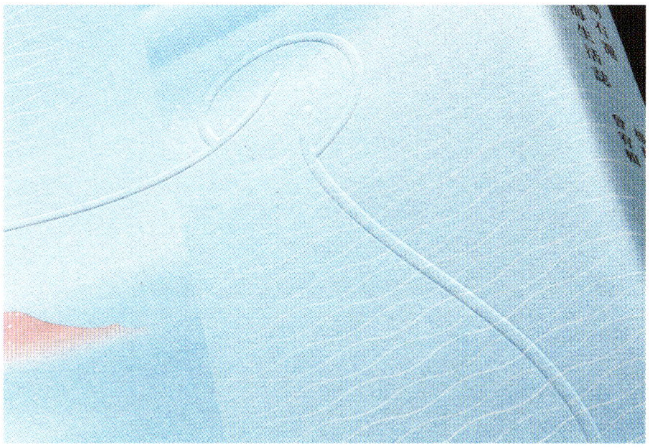

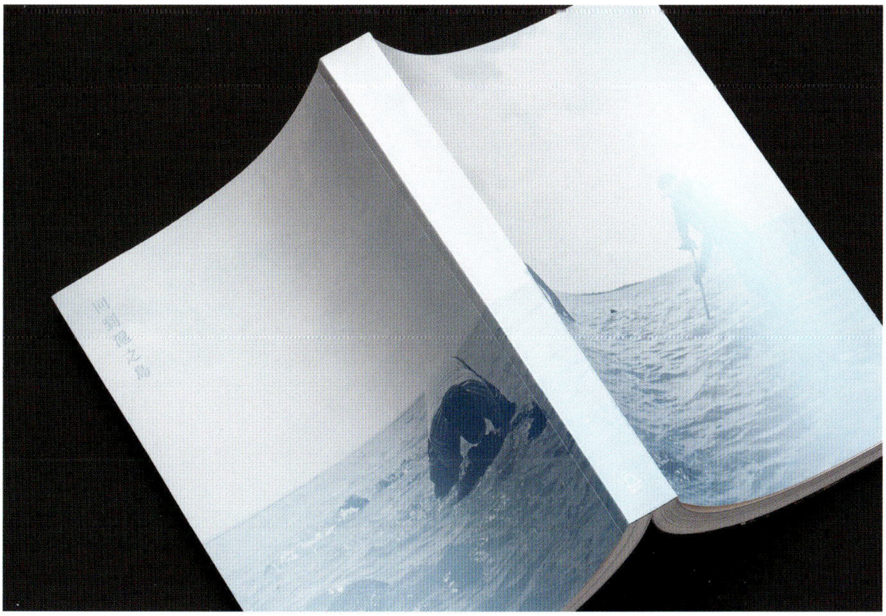

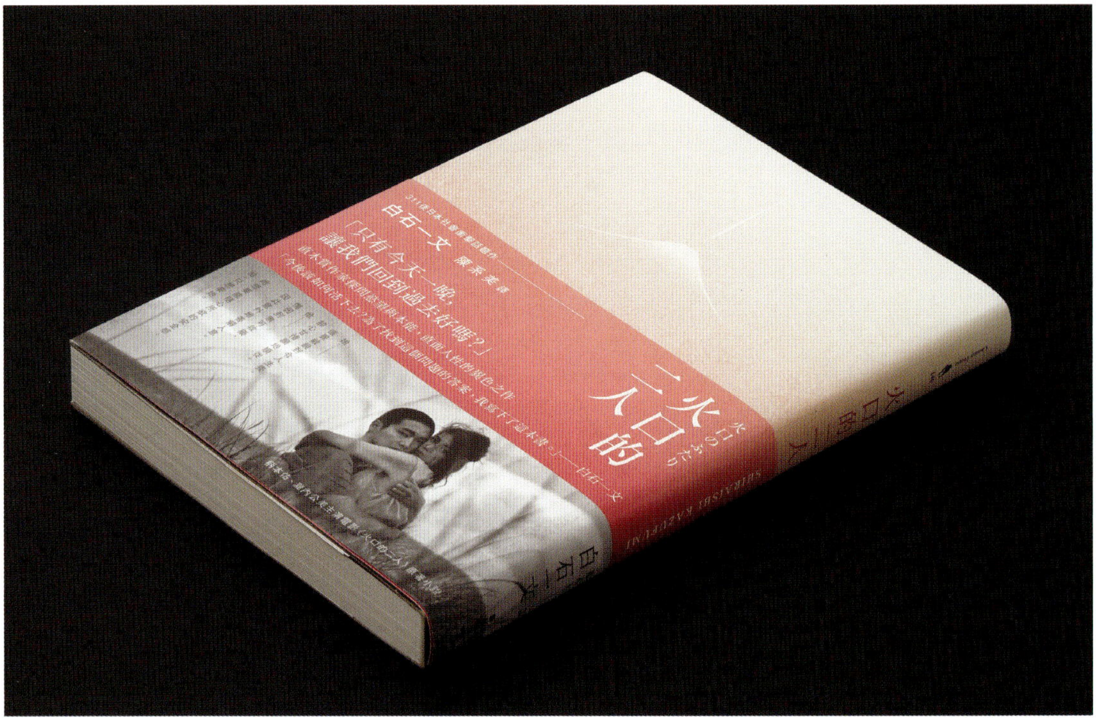

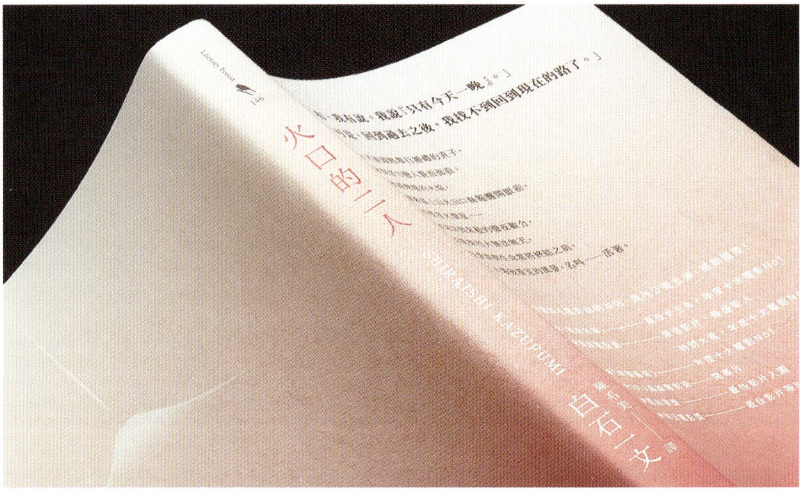

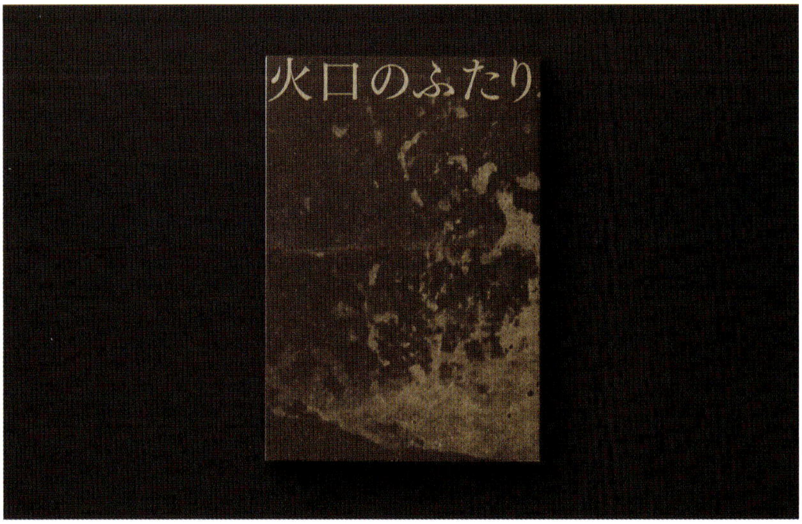

IT FEELS SO GOOD

This book is the original novel of the movie of the same name. The cover design uses the erupting Mount Fuji as a symbol, which is reversed to show the private parts of a woman's body. It seems to imply their emotional state, forbidden but hard to suppress, letting their bodies be occupied by restlessness and desire before the great destruction comes and becomes their salvation.

Designer
Chia-Lin Wu

Client
Thinkingdom Media

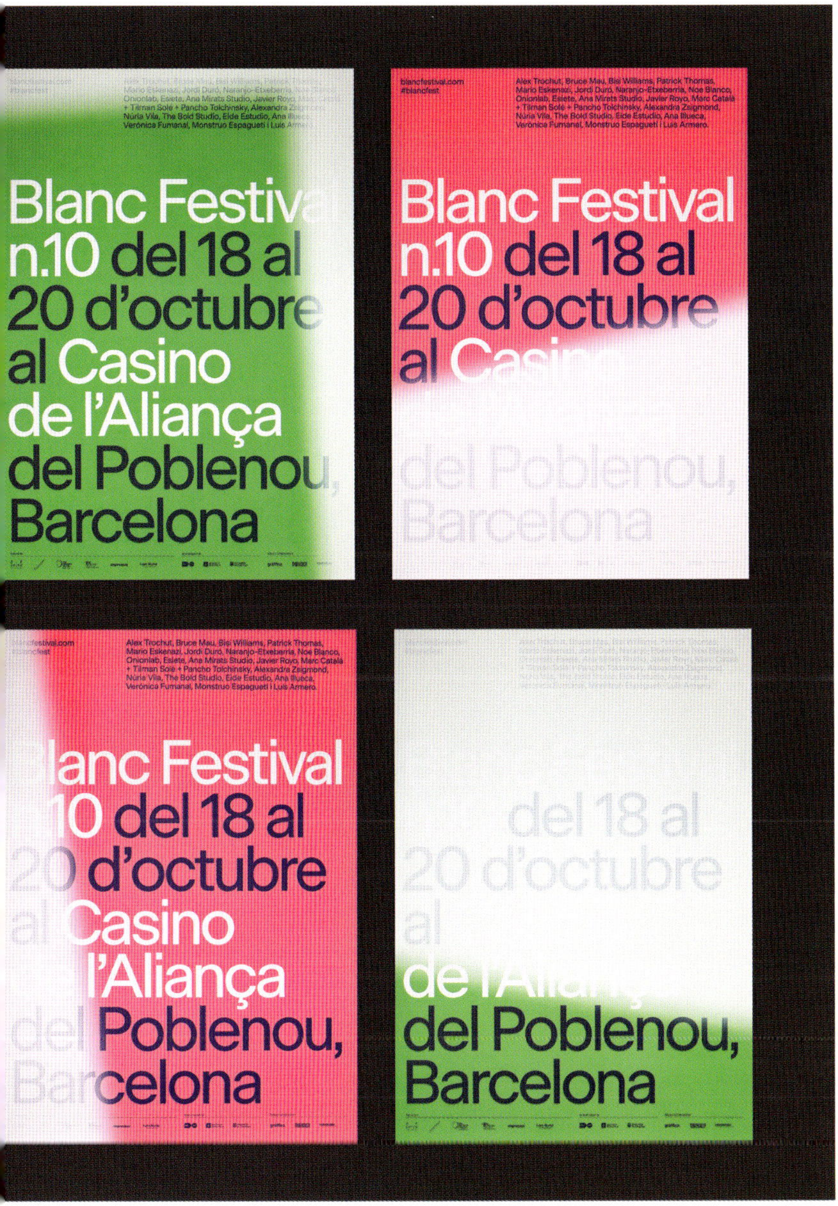

BLANC FESTIVAL NO.10

Born in 2009, Blanc Festival is one of the most important graphic design festivals in our country. The winning combination of a familiar approach with a high-level lineup has made Blanc a must-go event for designers from Catalonia and Spain. Forma was commissioned to design the visual identity and the opening credits for its 10th edition. The identity is based on the fact that all inks (design) tend to white (blanc, in Catalan) with the effect of time (10th anniversary).

Design Studio
Forma

PANTONE 806 C

PANTONE 802 C

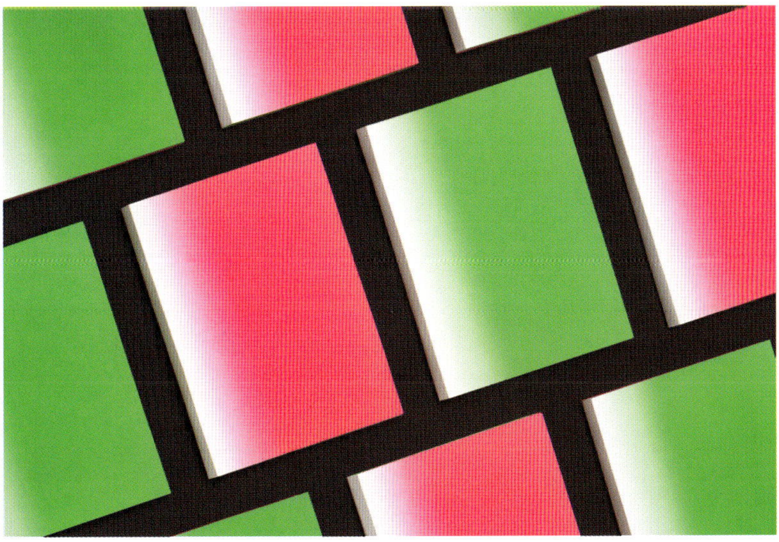

PANTONE 286 U

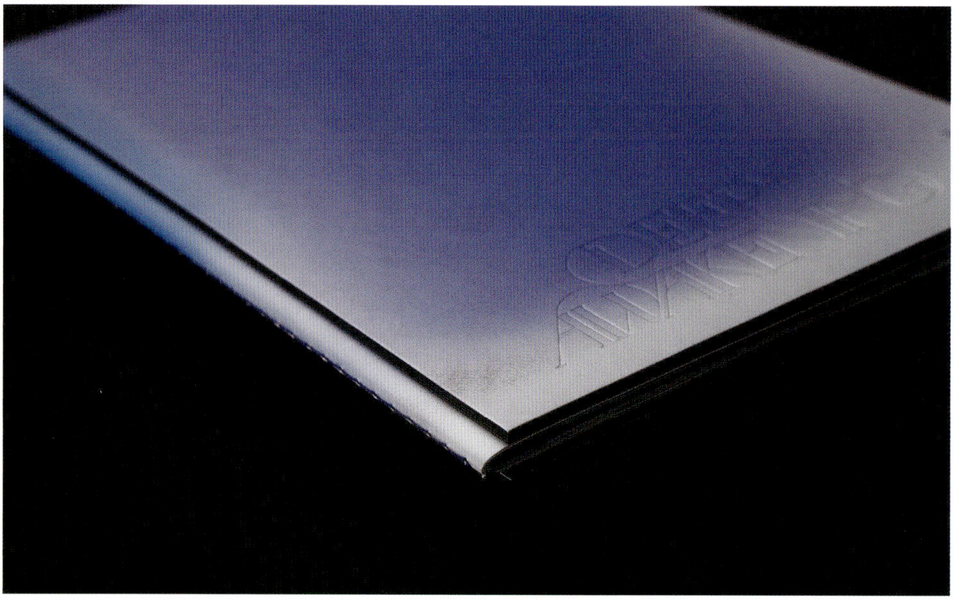

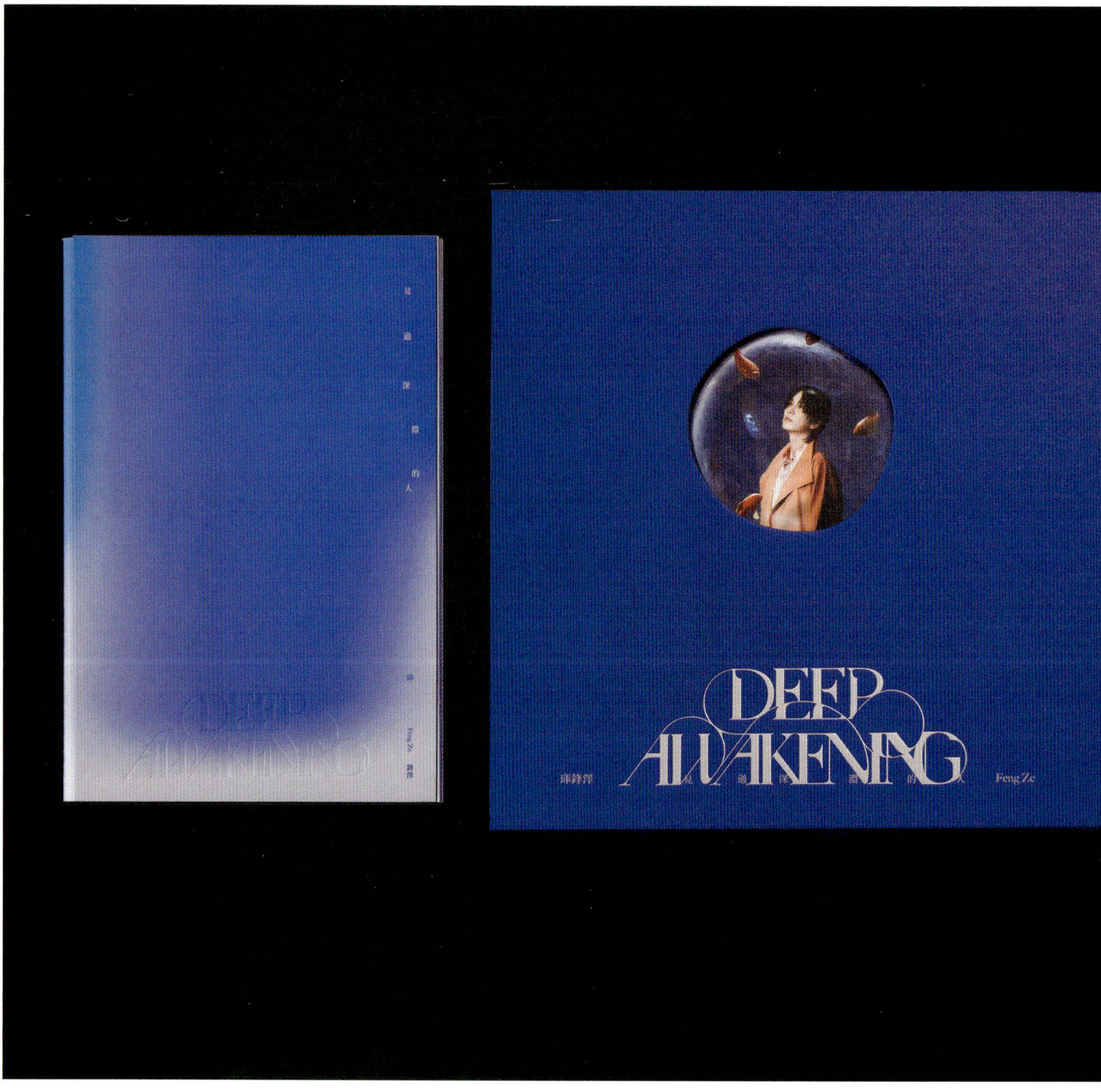

PANTONE 877 C

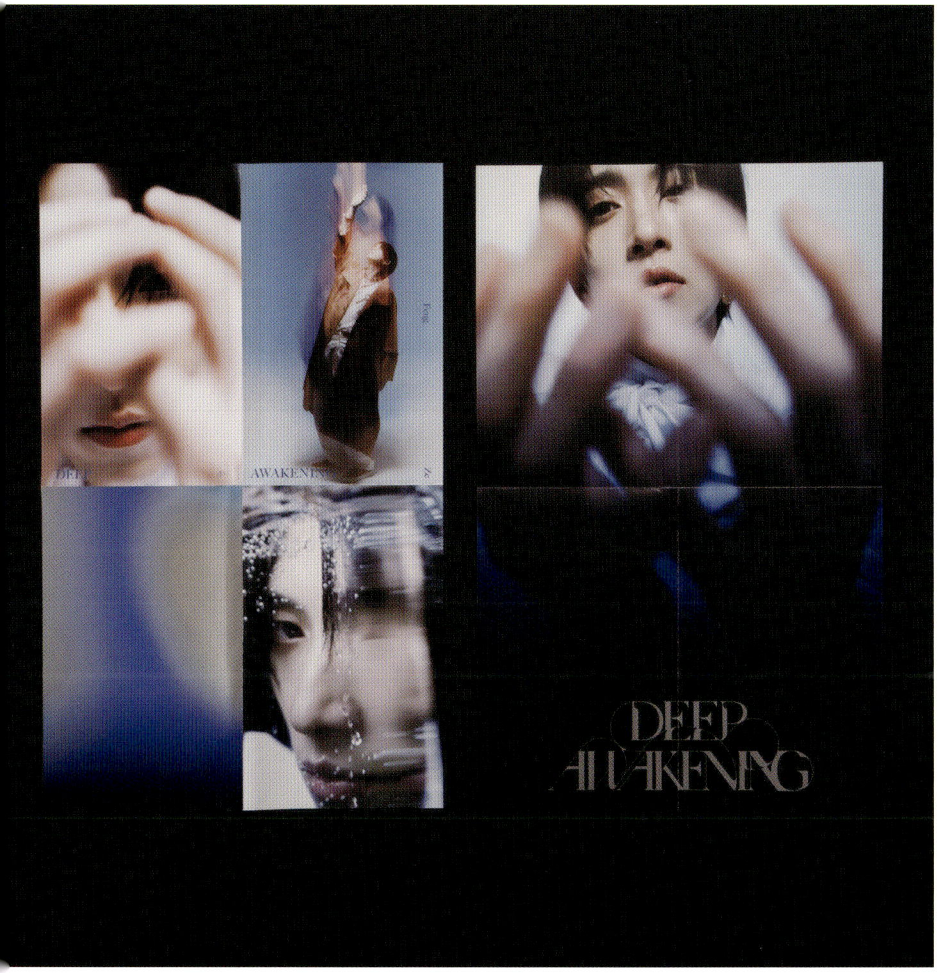

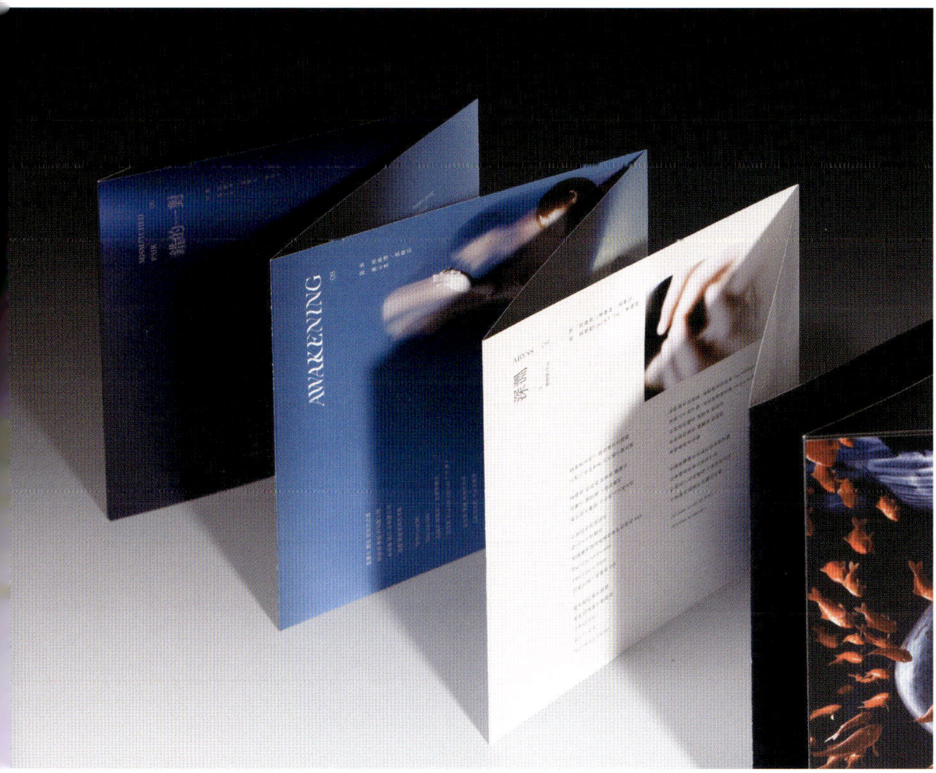

DEEP AWAKENING

The album *Deep Awakening* was for the singer Feng Ze in both hardcover and paperback versions. When diving, you need to struggle until sinking down to the bottom. Then you start to float, and only then can you begin to transform. Through the design, the designer hope to guide the audience to feel the storytelling of the music in the process of dismantling and reading, which is the journey of breaking through the comfort zone.

Client
Reason Brothers Ltd.

Publisher
Rock Records Co.,Ltd

Art Director
Yaga.studio

Content Creator & Planner
Yafay

Project Manager
Mebo

Graphic Designer
Nayu

Photographer
Chou mo

CGI
Garting , Yafay

Printing
Jiushui

Photographer
Lin Chun Teng

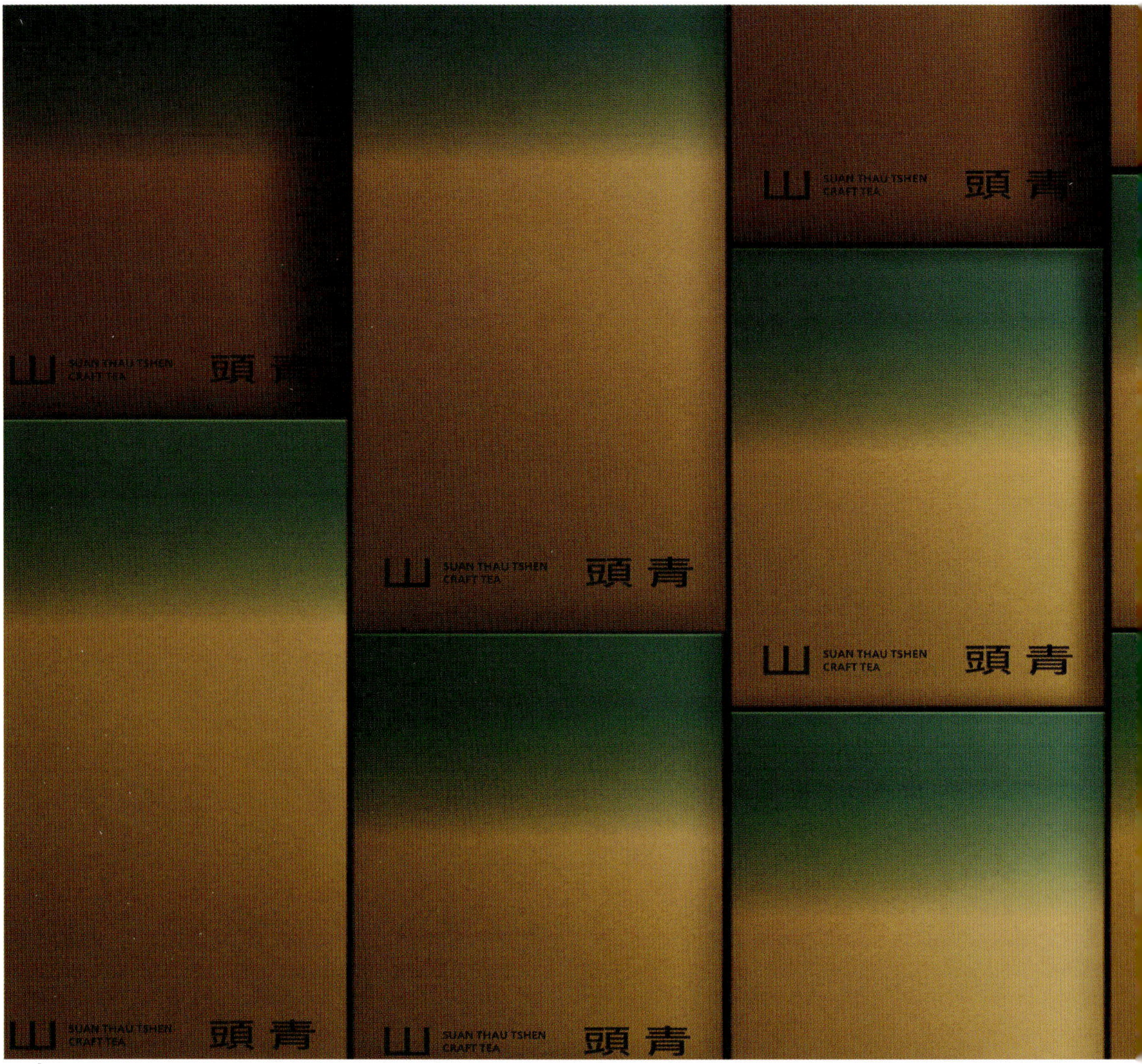
SUAN THAU TSHEN
CRAFT TEA
頭青

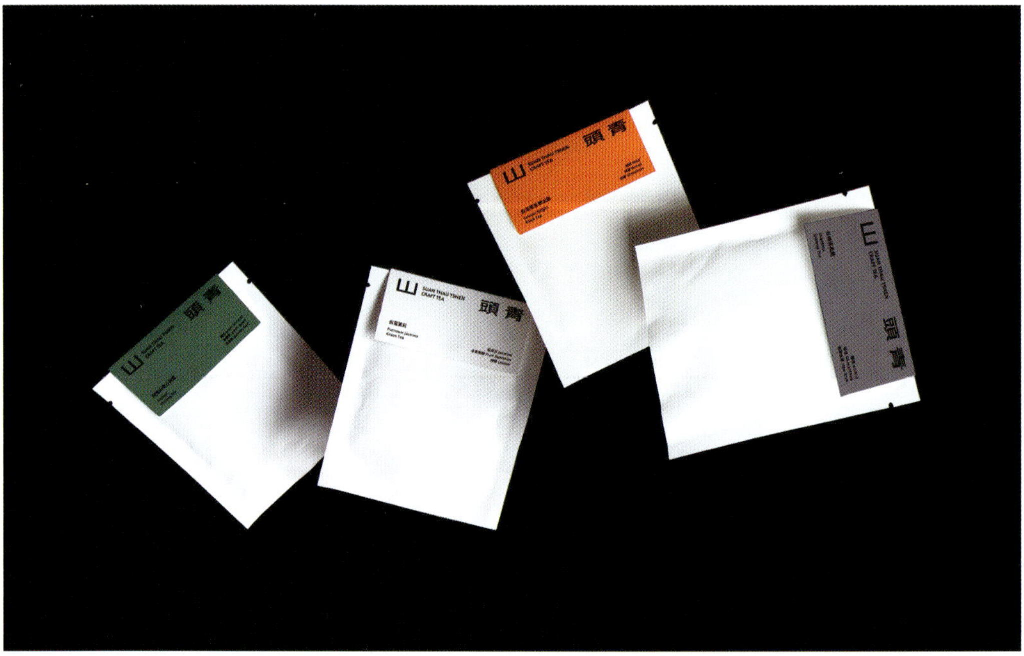

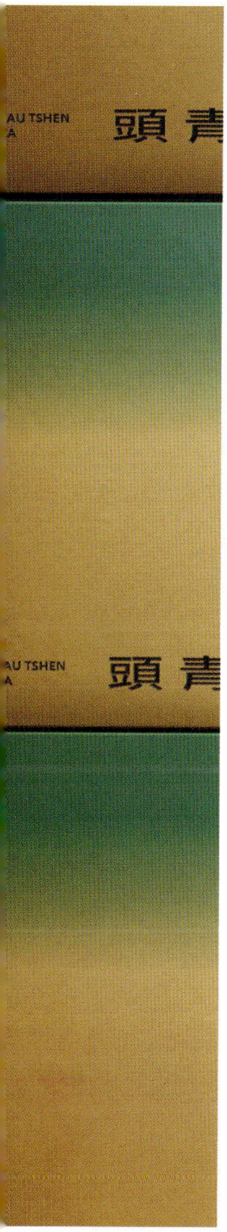

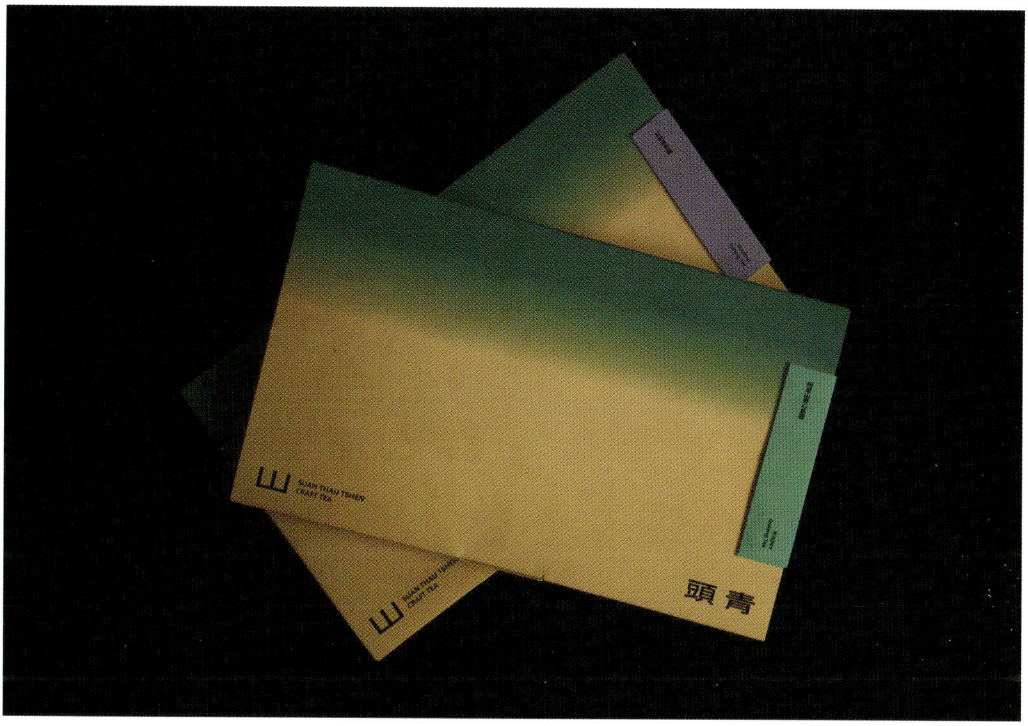

SUAN THAU TSHEN

Suan Thau Qi (vibe of the mountain) refers to the microclimate of tea gardens, nurturing unique tea qualities. Even the same tea variety yields different flavours in different regions. Drawing inspiration from traditional Chinese landscape paintings, our packaging creatively showcases mountain and river imagery. The touch of green in our branding echoes the name *Suan Thau Tshen.*

Designer
Lung-Hao Chiang

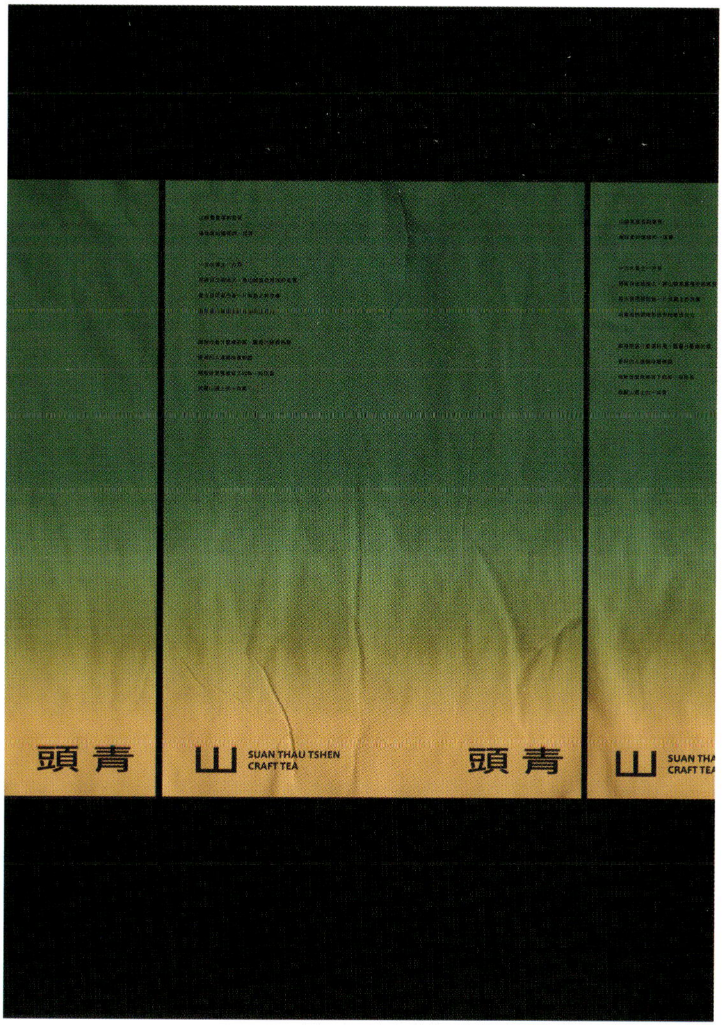

EVA EXHIBITION

In an era when virtual selves mirror physical selves, "Eva" champions virtual freedom of expression. This immersive exhibit delves into the impact of technology on digital presentation, leading visitors through encounters which advocate for the sanctity of anonymity. "Eva", which stands for Exposed Virtual Anonymity, is an art project founded in 2023 by Tra Giang Nguyen (Gydient).

Design Studio
The Lab Saigon

EVA Founder
Tra Giang Nguyen (Gydient)

Creative Director
Tra Giang Nguyen (Gydient) & Tuan Le

Manager
Thao Ngoc, Huong Uyen, Duy Lam, Anh Nguyen & Mei

Graphic Designer
Tra Giang Nguyen (Gydient), Xuan Phan, Ven Bui & Thinh Tran

Spatial Designer
Hung Le & Tess Ngo

Print Producer
Kai Le & ItIt company (expo producer)

Studio Team
Tuan Le, Truc, Loc Huynh, Chuong & Trinh

Support Artist
Nghi Tran, Hieu Vu, Huong Ngo

PANTONE 658 C

PANTONE 658 C

PANTONE 7547 C

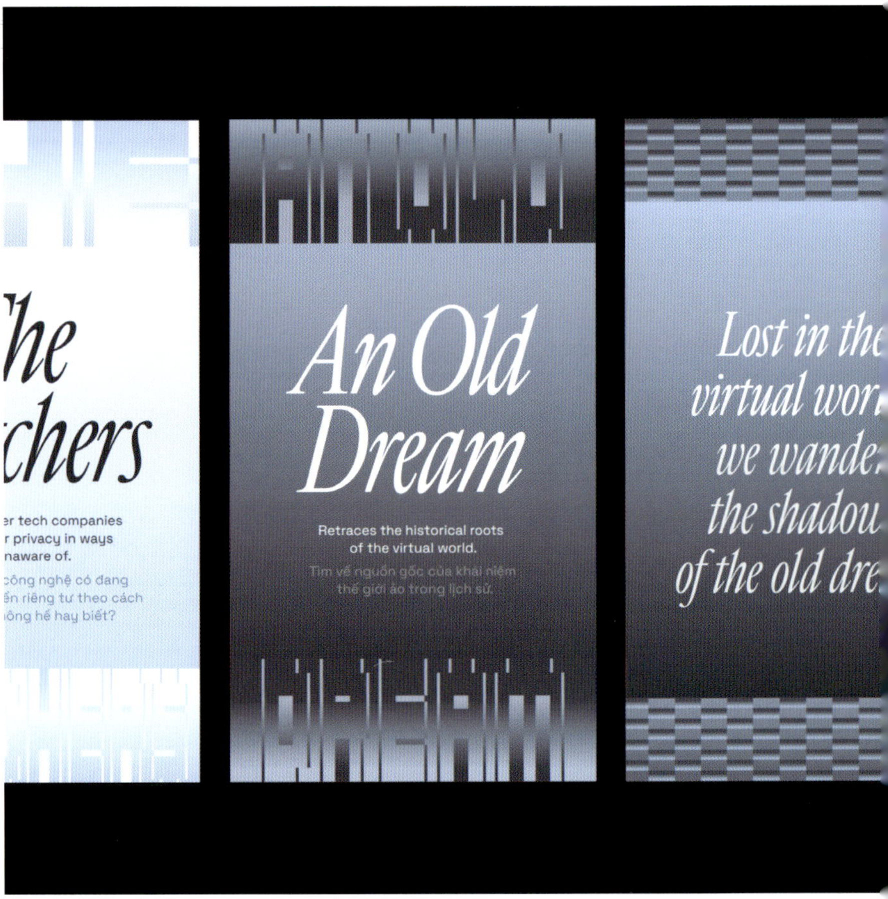

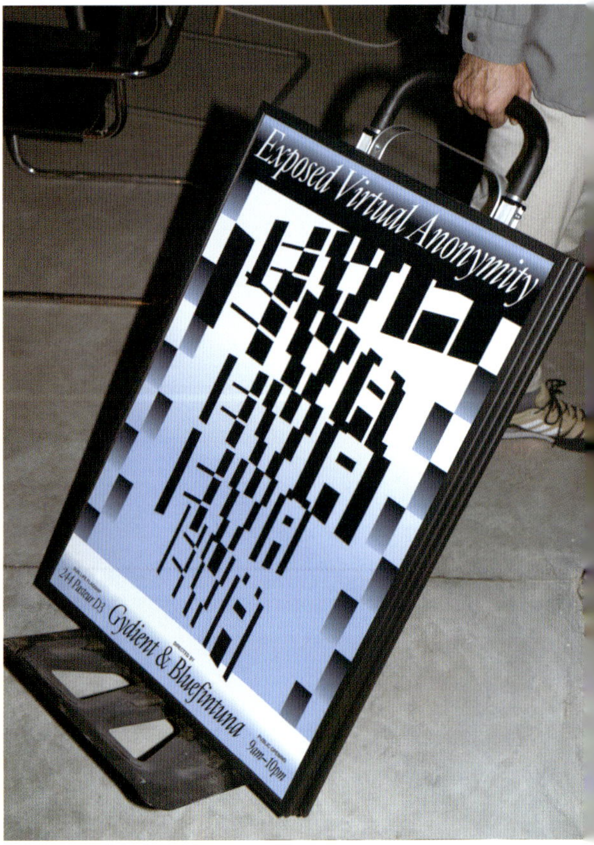

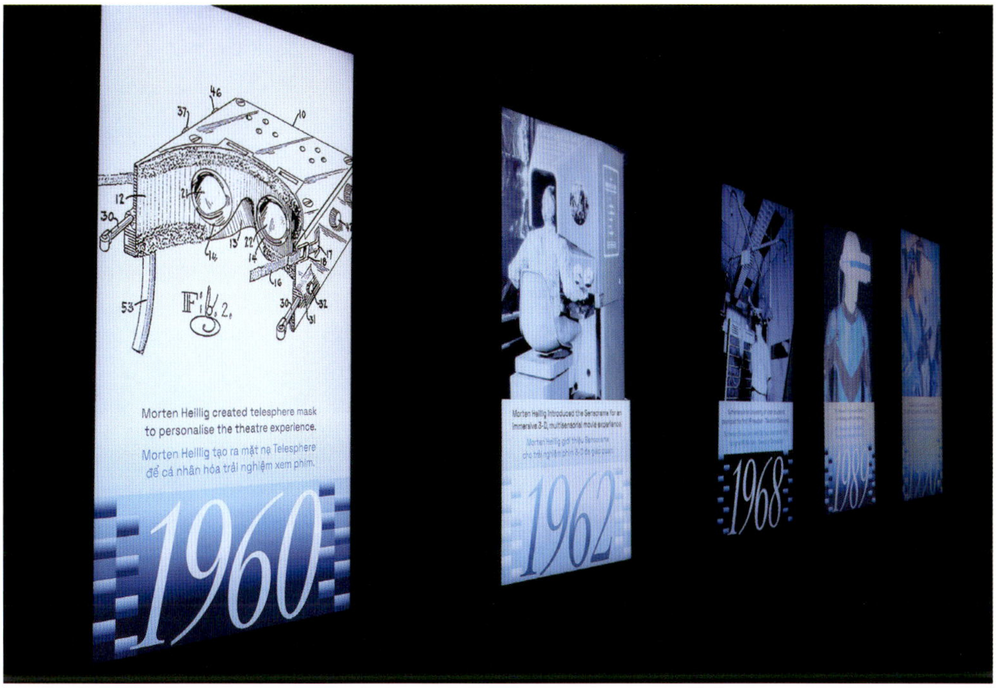
Morten Heillig created telesphere mask
to personalise the theatre experience.
Morten Heillig tạo ra mặt nạ Telesphere
để cá nhân hóa trải nghiệm xem phim.
1960
1962
1968
1989

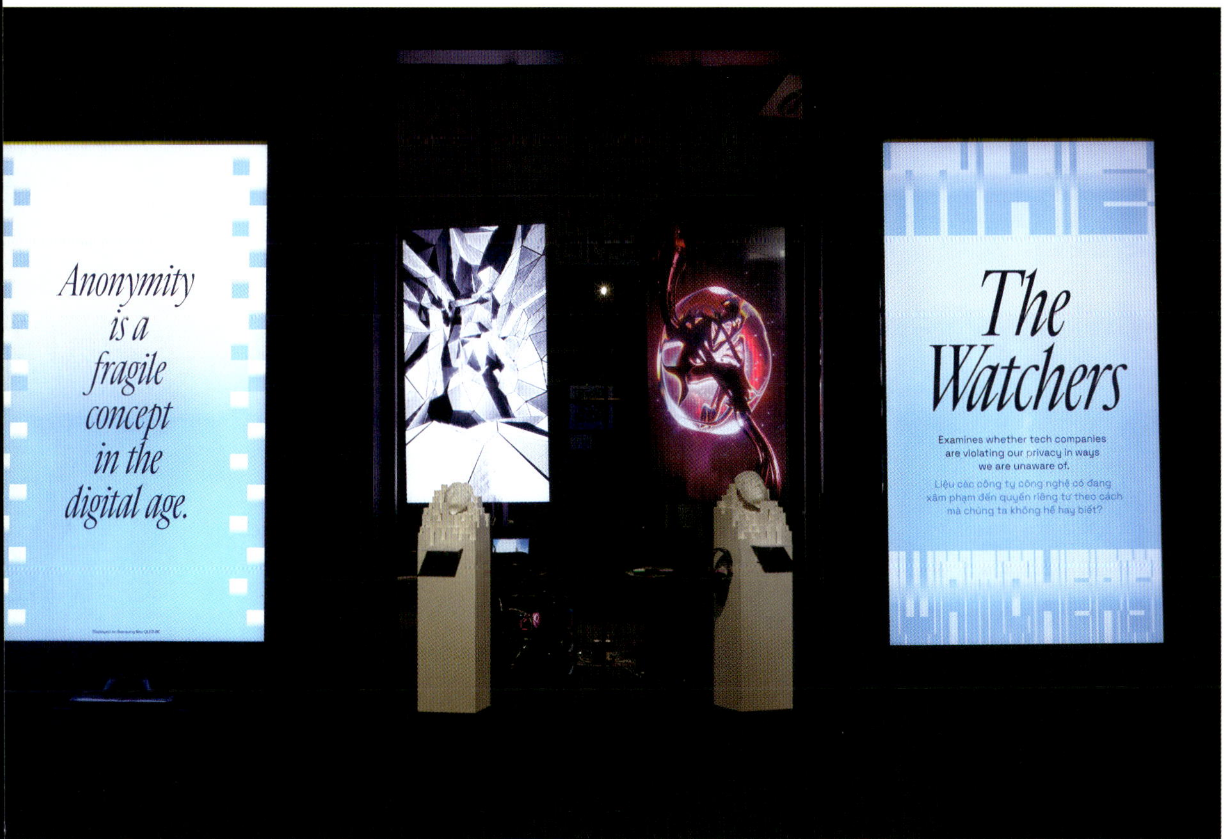
Anonymity is a fragile concept in the digital age.
The Watchers
Examines whether tech companies are violating our privacy in ways we are unaware of.
Liệu các công ty công nghệ có đang xâm phạm đến quyền riêng tư theo cách mà chúng ta không hề hay biết?

PANTONE 129 UP

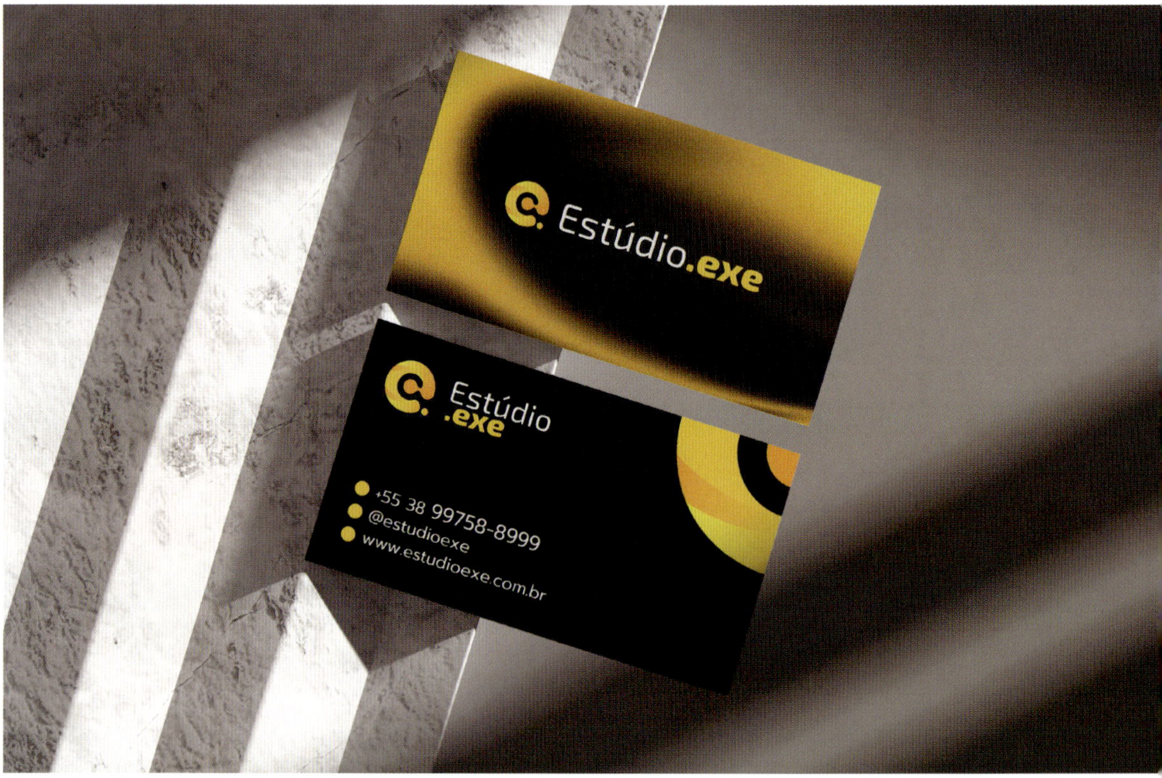

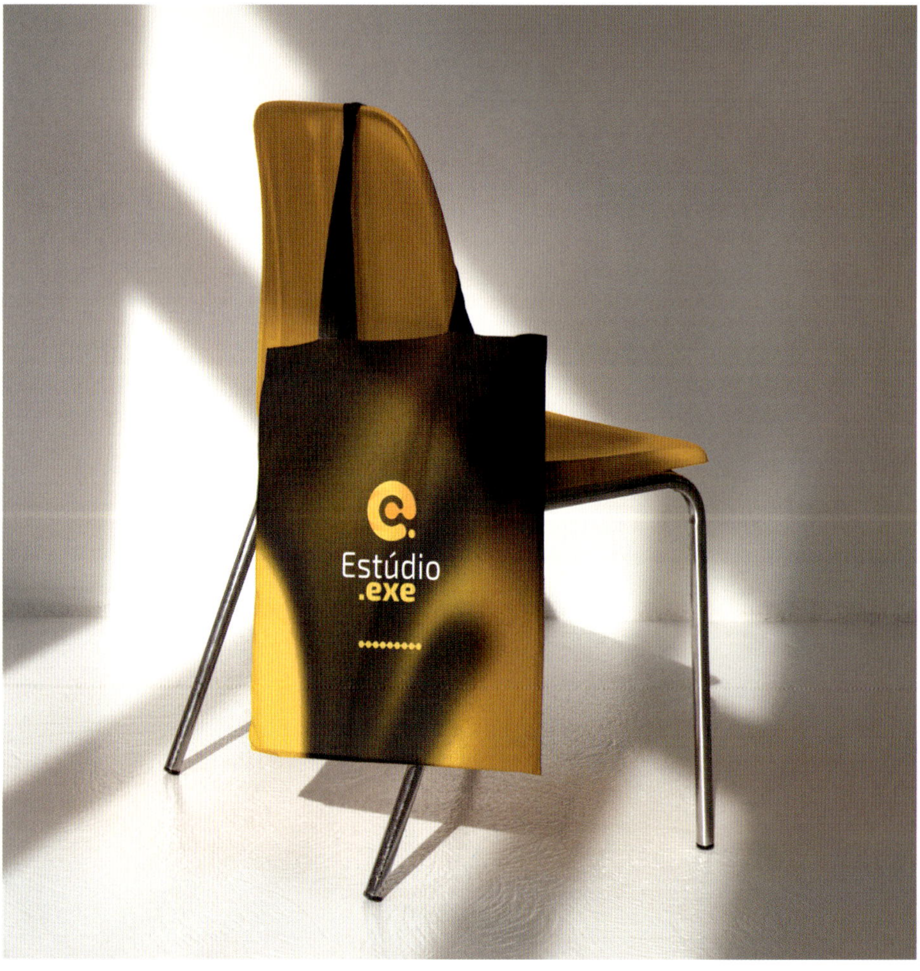

CO · MO · YO · K100

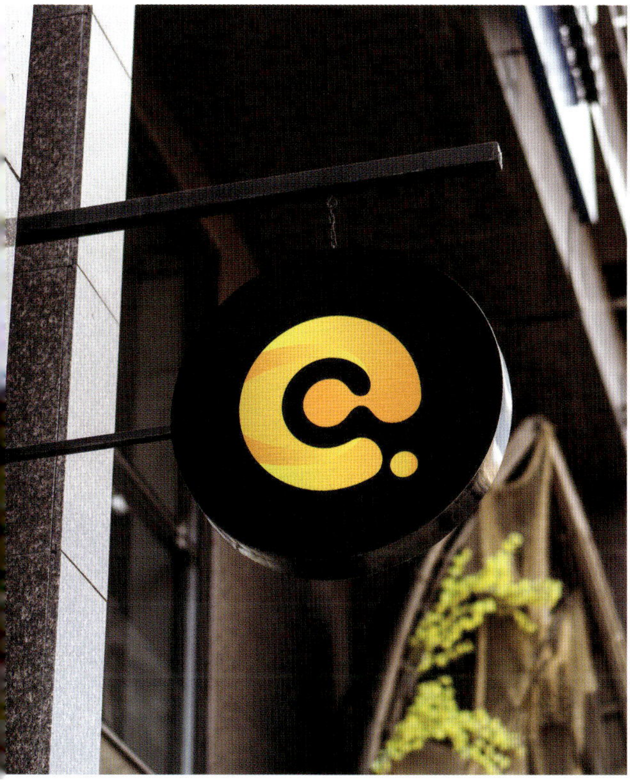

ESTÚDIO EXE

Estúdio.exe is a design studio from Brazil dedicated to transforming companies' digital presence, significantly increasing engagement on social media with high-converting creatives. The designer used a colour gradient that goes from black to yellow. The gradient creates a sense of movement and evolution, symbolizing the transition from obscurity to clarity and prominence. In addition to being visually attractive, this gradient strengthens the brand by capturing the essence of transformation and growth, fundamental elements for Estúdio. exe's mission to elevate its clients' digital presence.

Designer
Ianca Alves

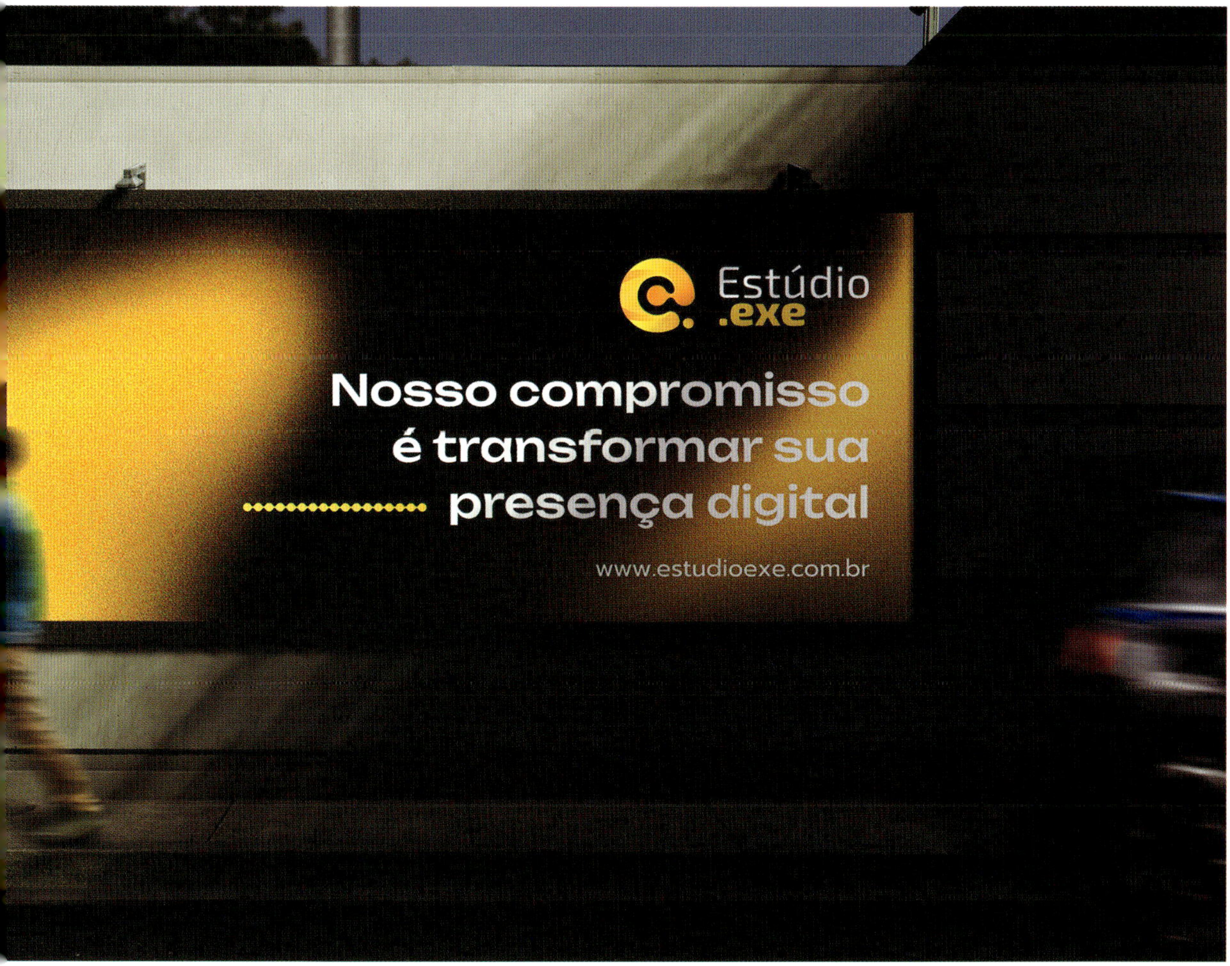

C0 · M95 · Y91 · K0

C0 · M43 · Y93 · K0

C95 · M80 · Y0 · K0

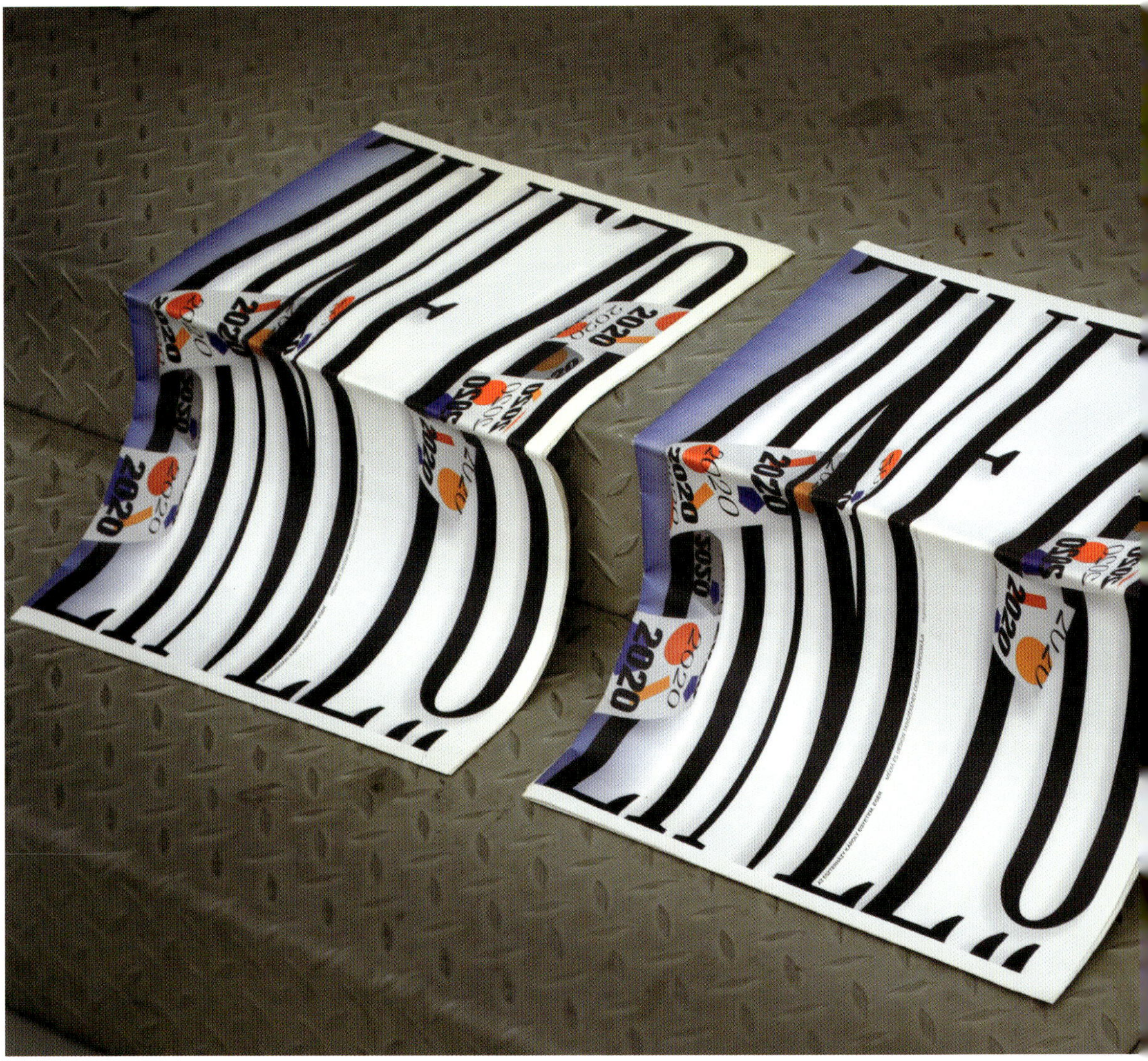

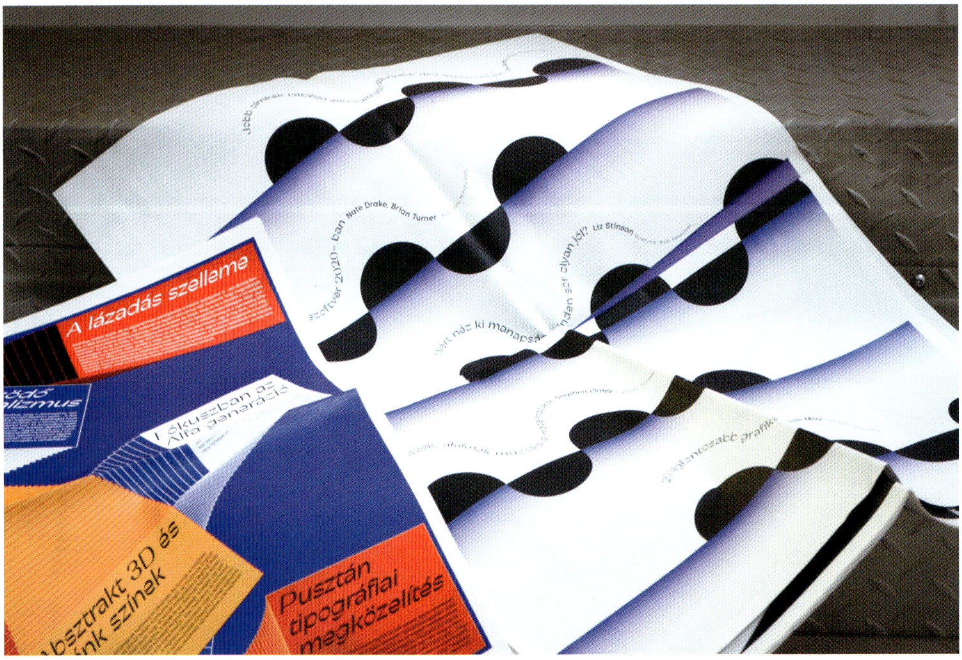

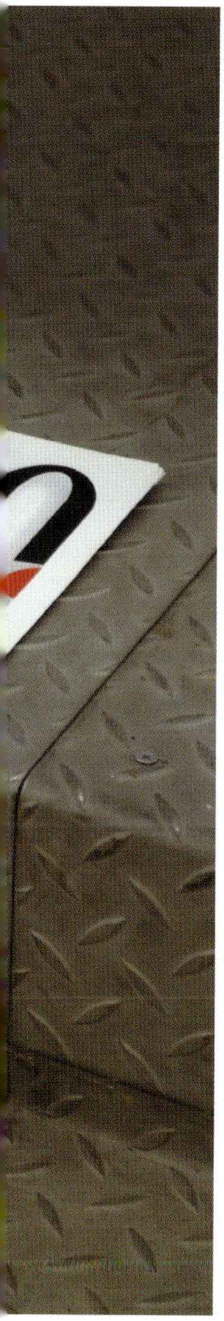

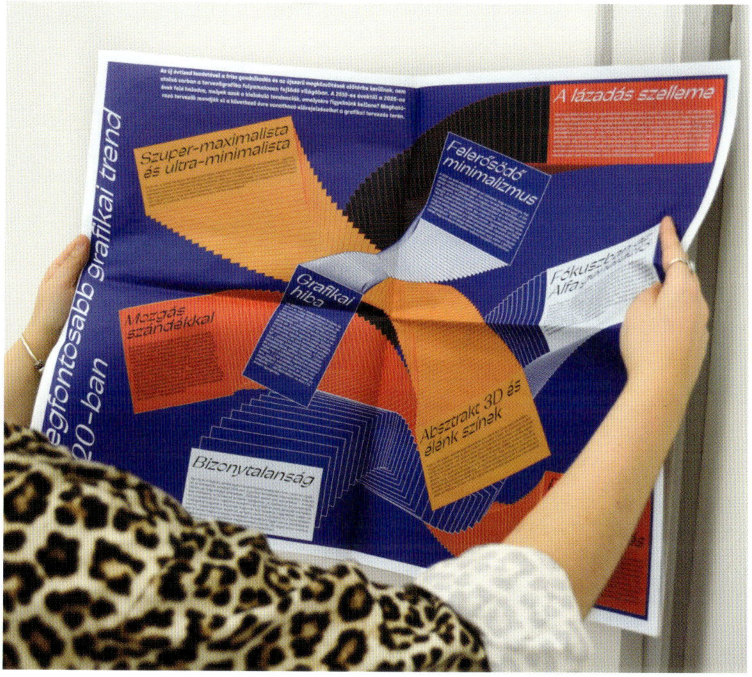

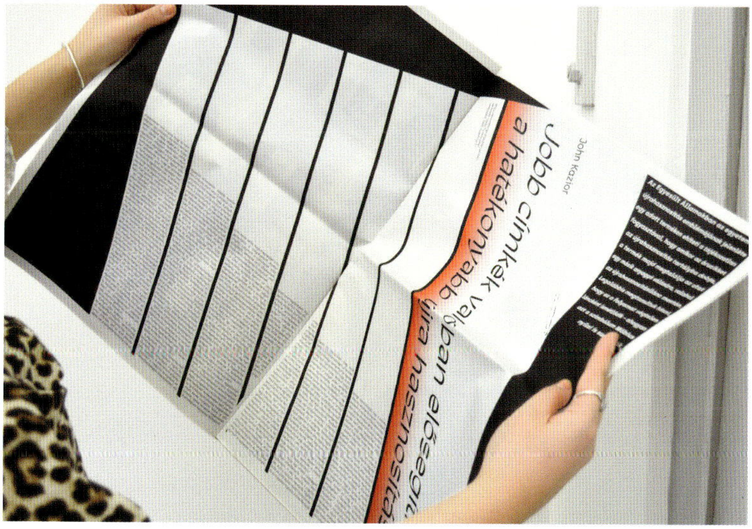

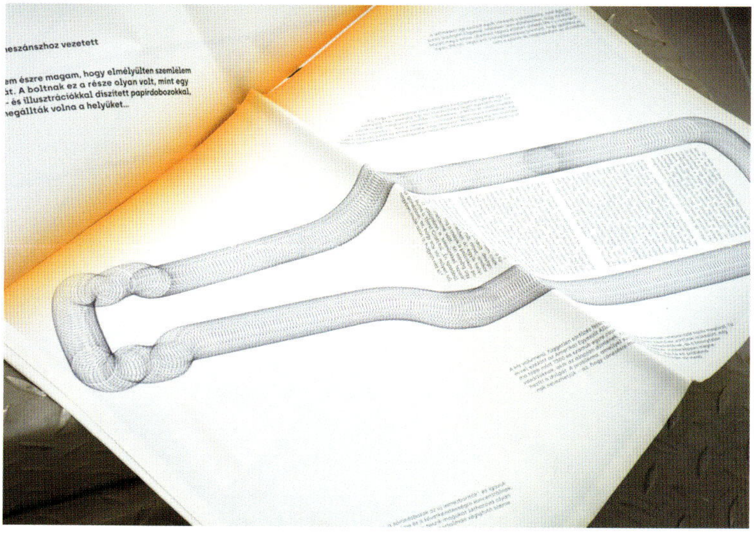

ZINEZŐ I.

Zinező is a periodical broadsheet-sized zine containing articles about the latest design trends translated into Hungarian. The designer put a lot of emphasis on keeping the old-style, in many places now forgotten, broadsheet-size newspaper strict layout and text wrapping. The concept was based on elements of Brutalist design and the use of 4 colours, as well as experimenting with gradients in such a large format on thin paper.

Designer
Keresztény Lilla

Made at
Media and Design Institute, EKKE, Eger, Hungary

Print Studio
Newspaper Club

PANTONE P 102-8 C

PANTONE 1585 CP

PANTONE P 62-7 U

PANTONE P 133-12 C

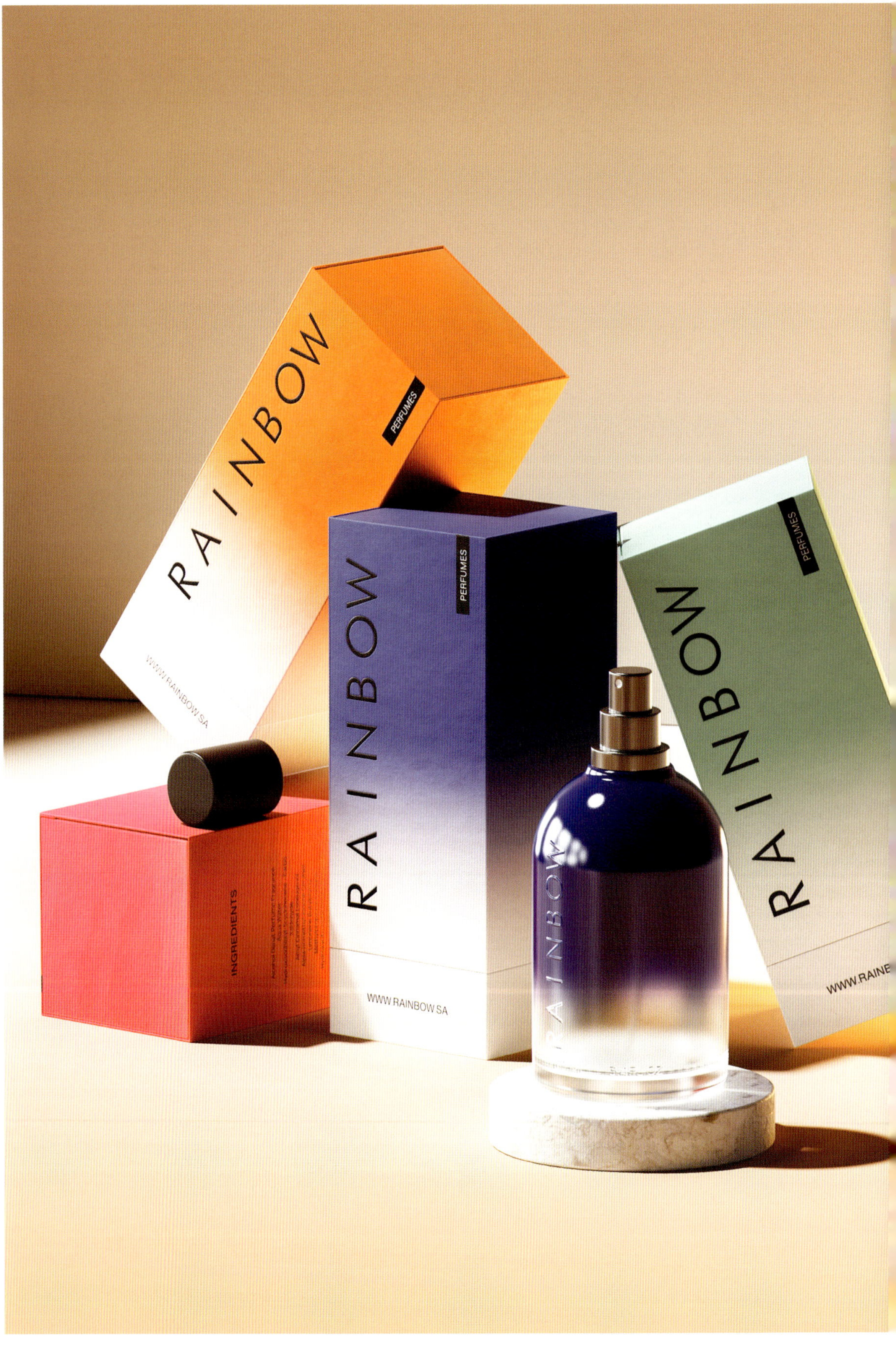

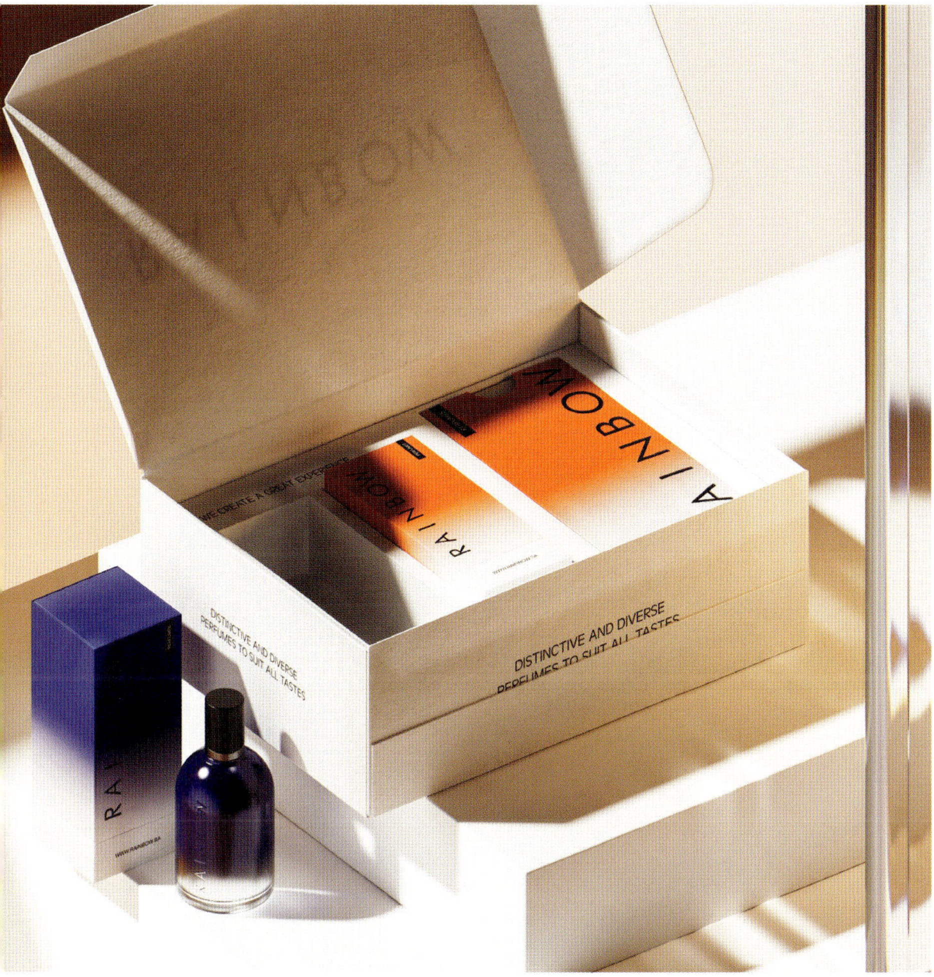

RAINBOW PERFUMES

Embark on a journey through the vibrant world of *Rainbow* perfumes, where creativity intertwines with vision to create an unparalleled aromatic experience. This case study delves into the intricate process of designing and developing the identity of *Rainbow* perfumes, a journey filled with inspiration, creativity, and innovation.

With the vision set in motion, the design team meticulously curated the visual elements that would define the identity of *Rainbow* perfumes. Through a careful selection of colours, lines, and shapes, the team sought to strike a harmonious balance between elegance, modernity, and luxury. Each element was thoughtfully chosen to embody the essence of *Rainbow*, ensuring a cohesive and captivating visual representation.

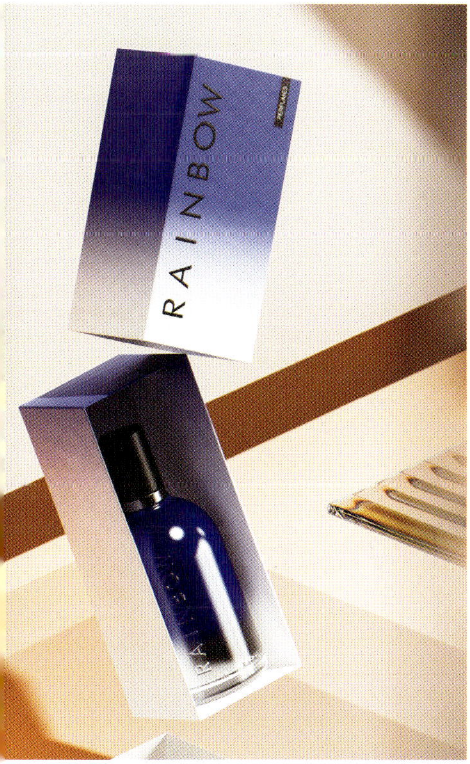

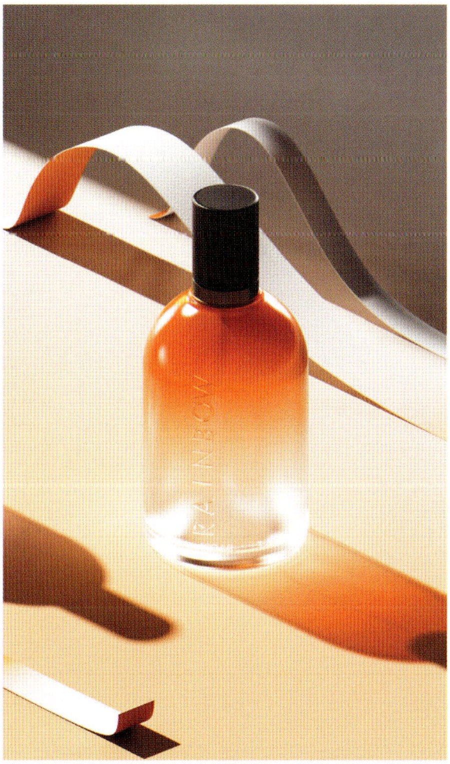

Agency
Mr.Studio Co.

Creative Director
Mashari Alazizi

3D Designer
Luã Matos

Graphic Designer
Adnan Ali

Packaging Designer
Gina

C9 · M40 · Y98 · K1

C7 · M33 · Y82 · K1

C6 · M27 · Y65 · K1

C4 · M20 · Y49 · K0

C3 · M13 · Y33 · K0

C1 · M7 · Y16 · K0

ZIJA

Zija, also known as "Malvazija" in Slovenian, celebrates ancient fermentation techniques without filtering in a contemporary way. This process is expressed by a label that guides the viewer on a journey through a series of doors, imparting a sense of materiality and three-dimensionality. Thanks to a particular process of blind debossing on 7 levels, the design invites the viewer to explore and fully immerse themselves in the sensory experience offered by *Zija* wine.

Creative Director
Paolo Vendramini

Art Director & Designer
Andrea Flemma

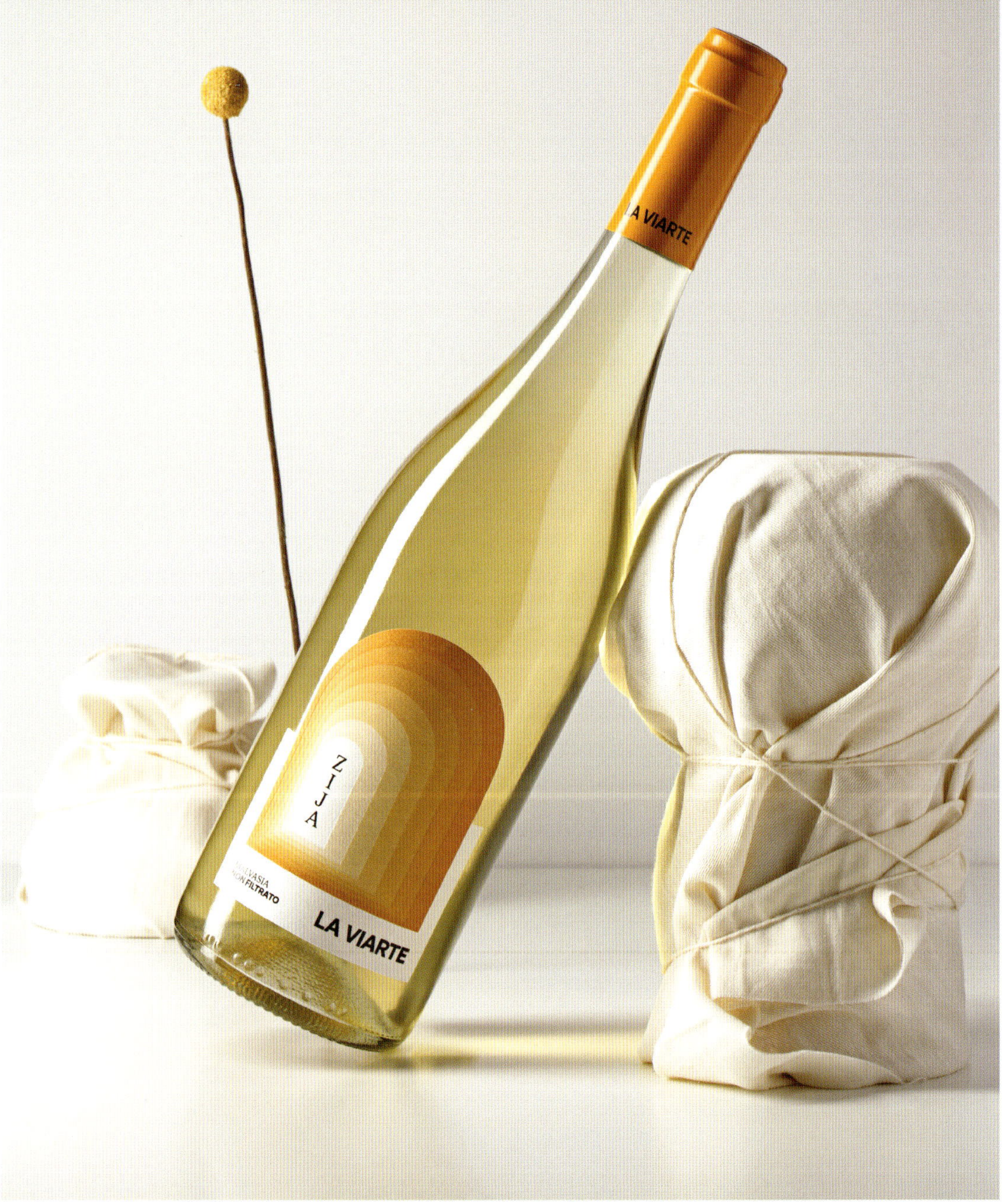

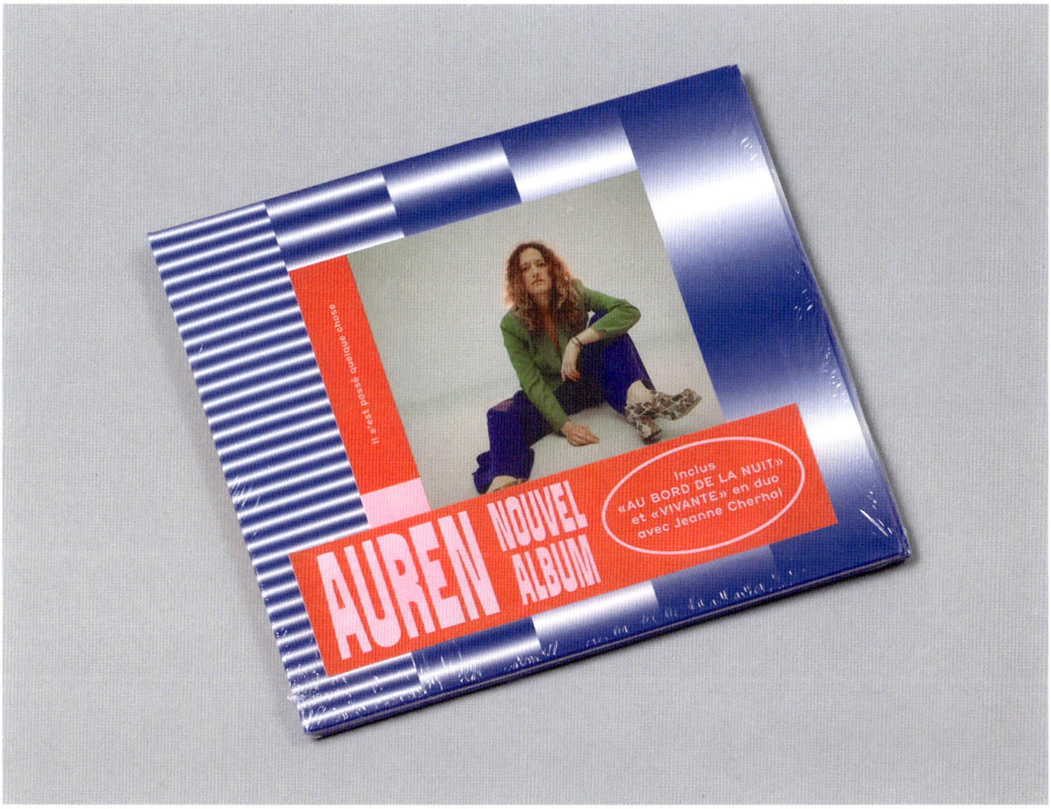

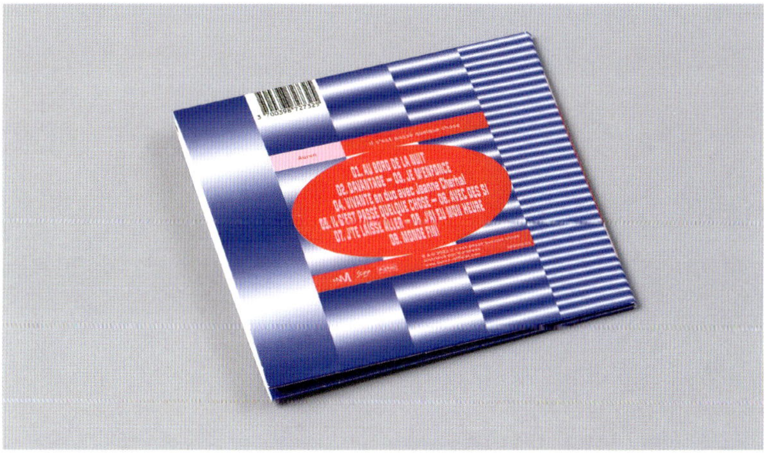

AUREN-IL S'EST PASSÉ QUELQUE CHOSE

Album cover design for French musician Auren.

Design Studio
Brest Brest Brest

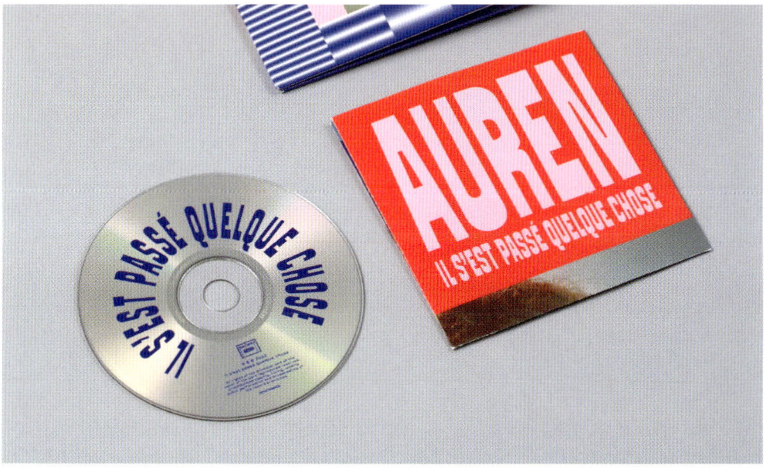

PANTONE 185 U

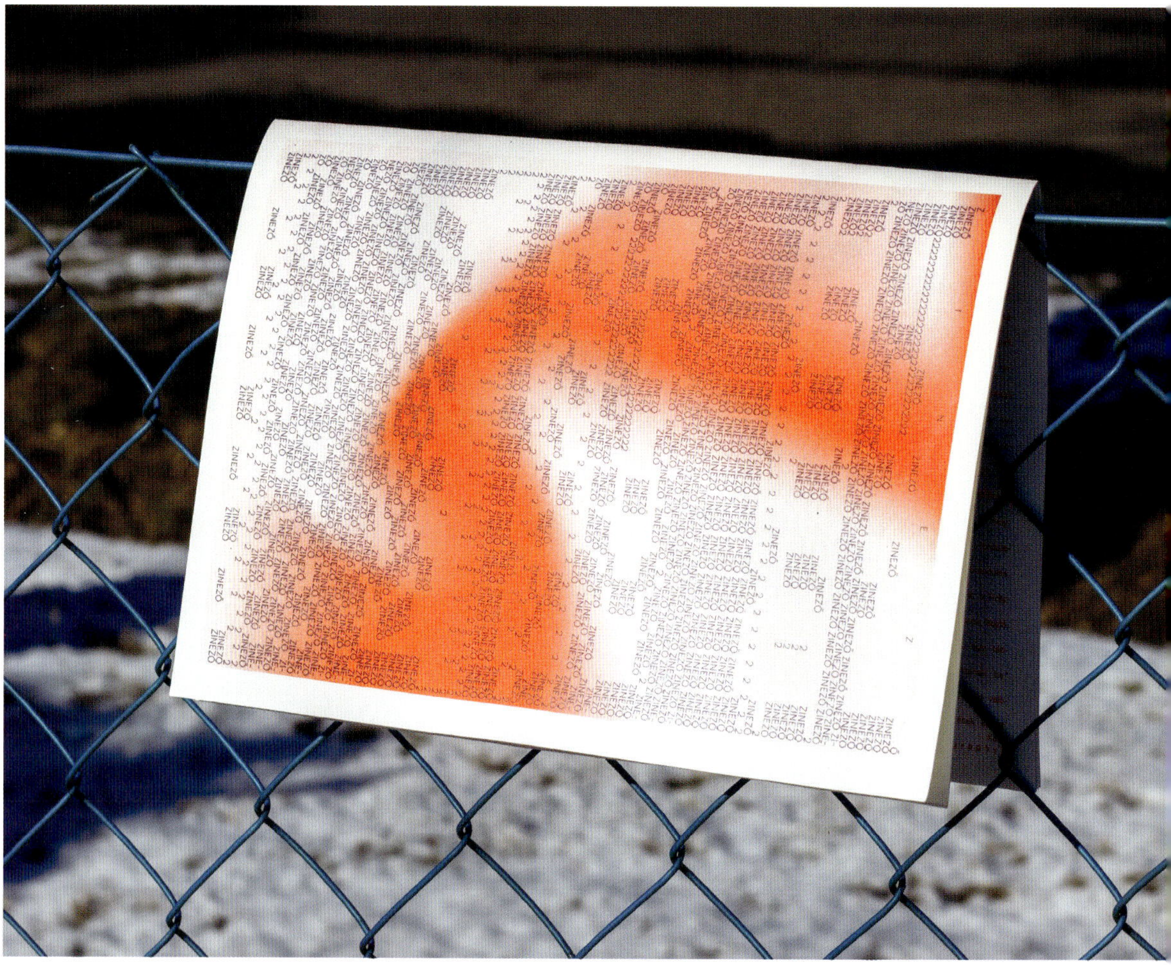

PANTONE 2685 U

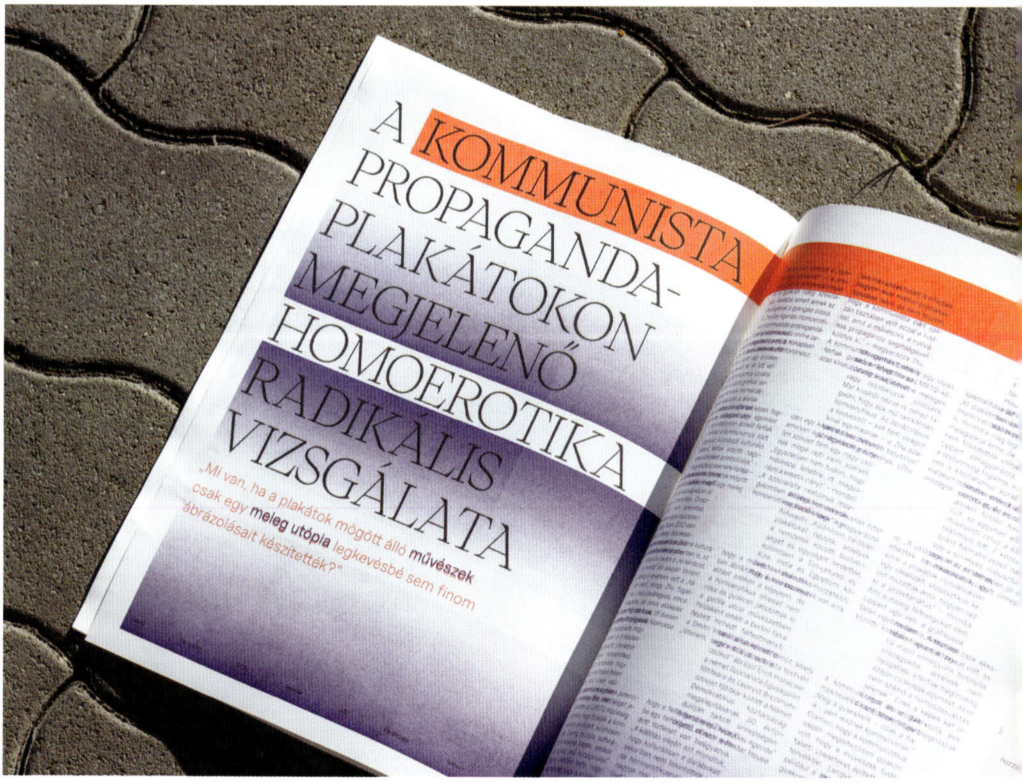

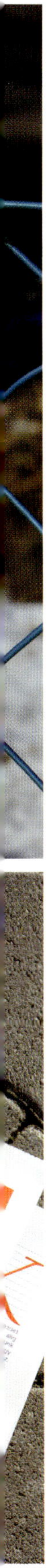

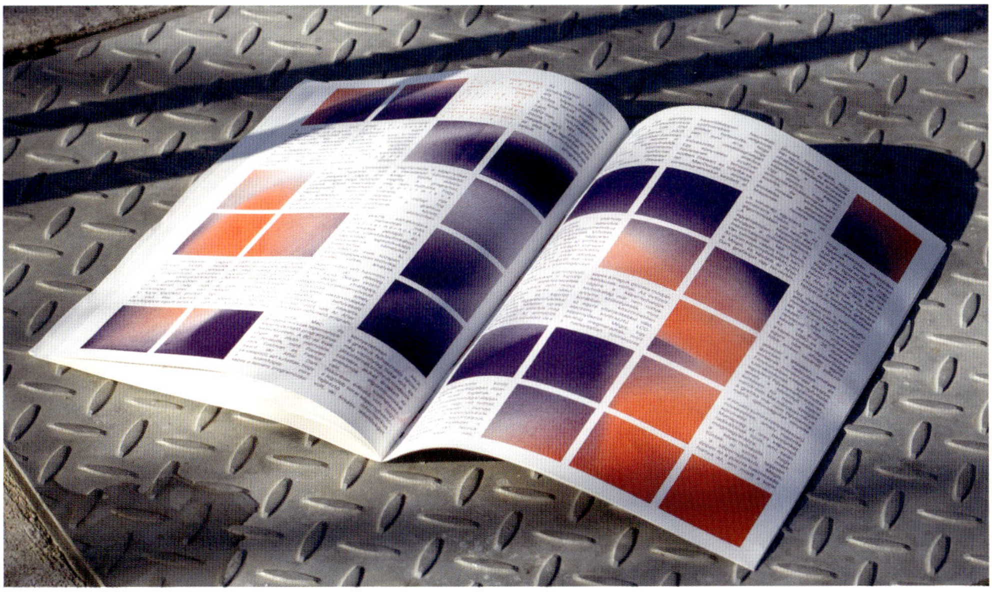

ZINEZŐ II.

Zinező is a design periodical full of articles about graphic design and digital art over 20 pages. This is the second edition in the Zinező series and is printed using the risograph technique. The designer used three colours during the printing and tried to understand the bread text units as graphic elements, creating layouts and compositions in an exciting way.

Designer
Panna Eszenyi

Consultant
Szabolcs Süli-Zakar

Made at
Media and Design Institute, *Ekke*, Eger, Hungary

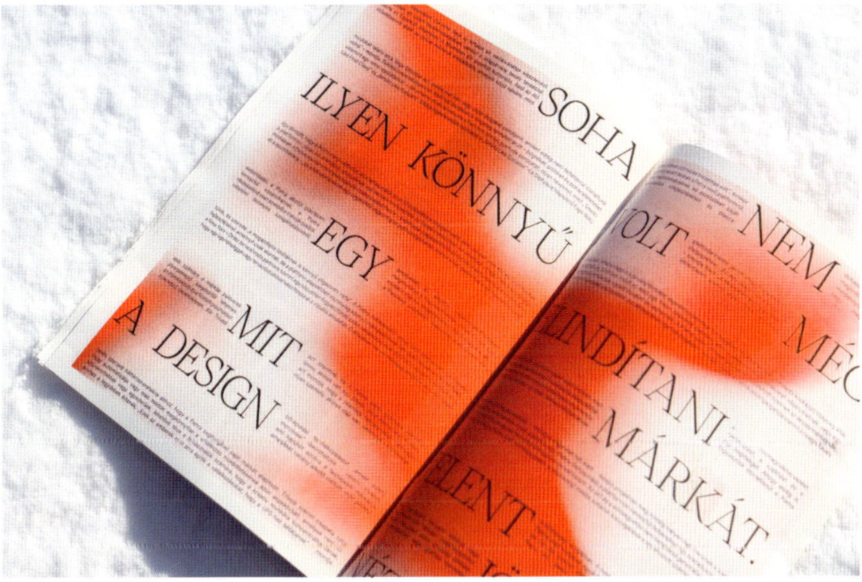

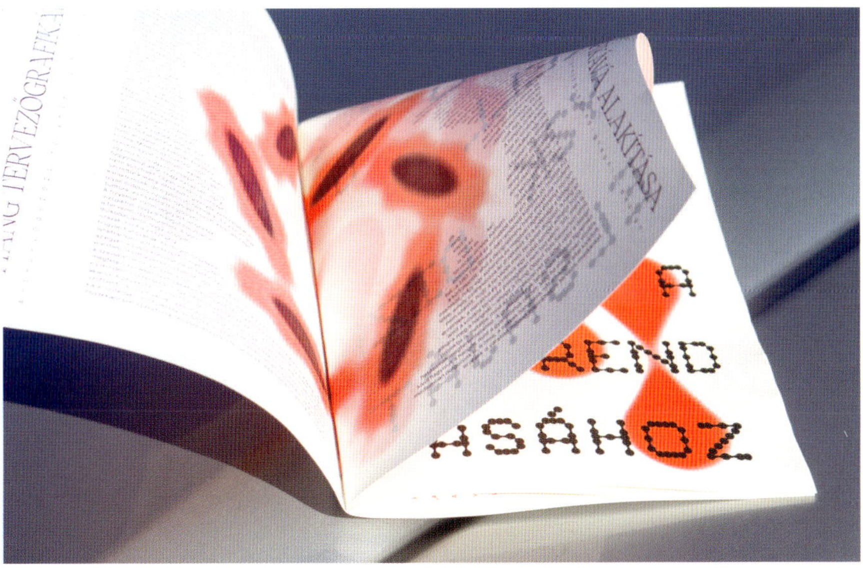

BICOLO
GRADIE

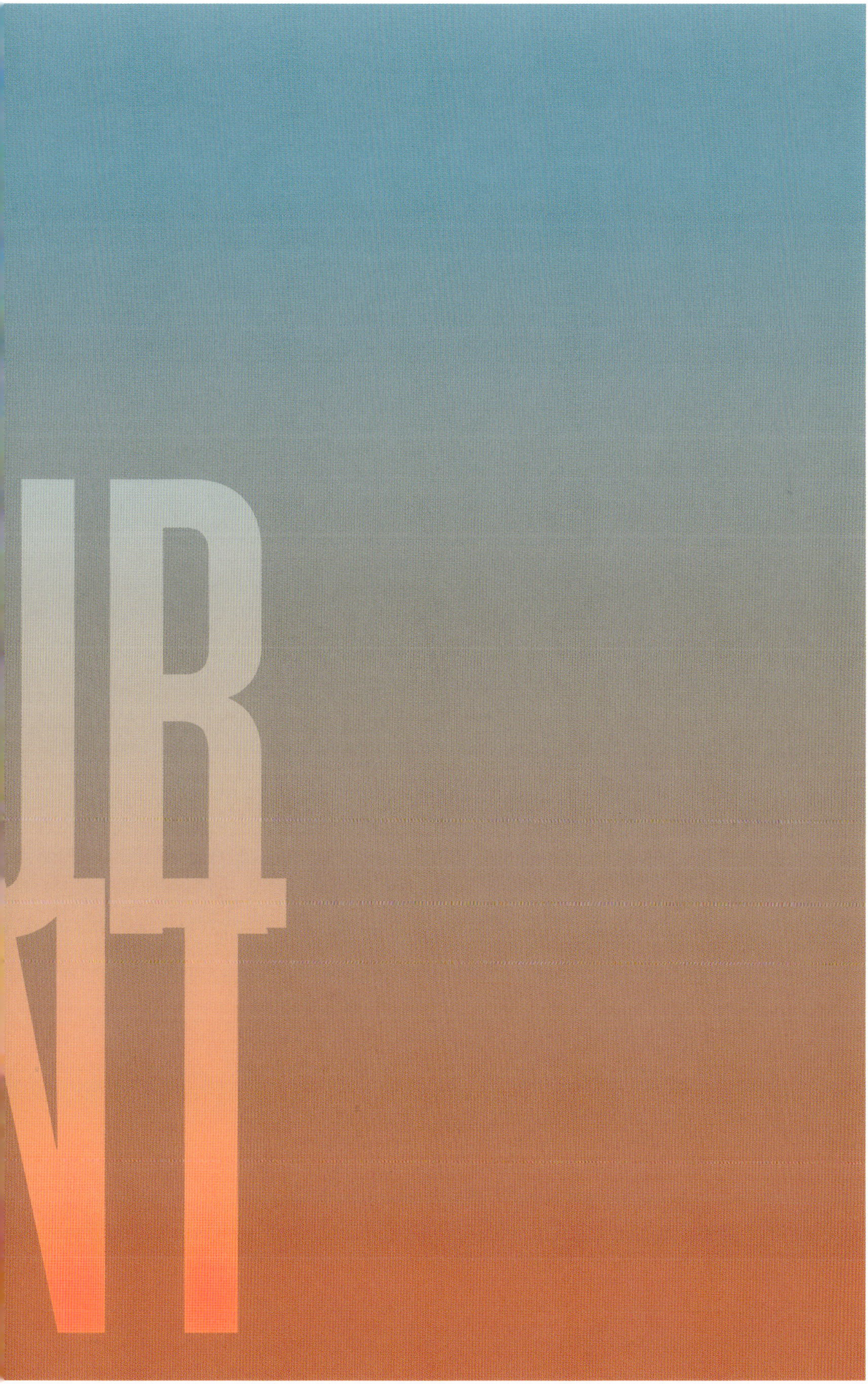

C59 · M0 · Y19 · K0

C0 · M68 · Y67 · K0

AURA FESTIVAL

R255 · G135 · B27

The identity was created for a fictional Art & Sound Design Festival.

Designer
Anaïs Vidal (anaisvidal.ch) & Irini Gleglakou (irinigleglakou.ch)

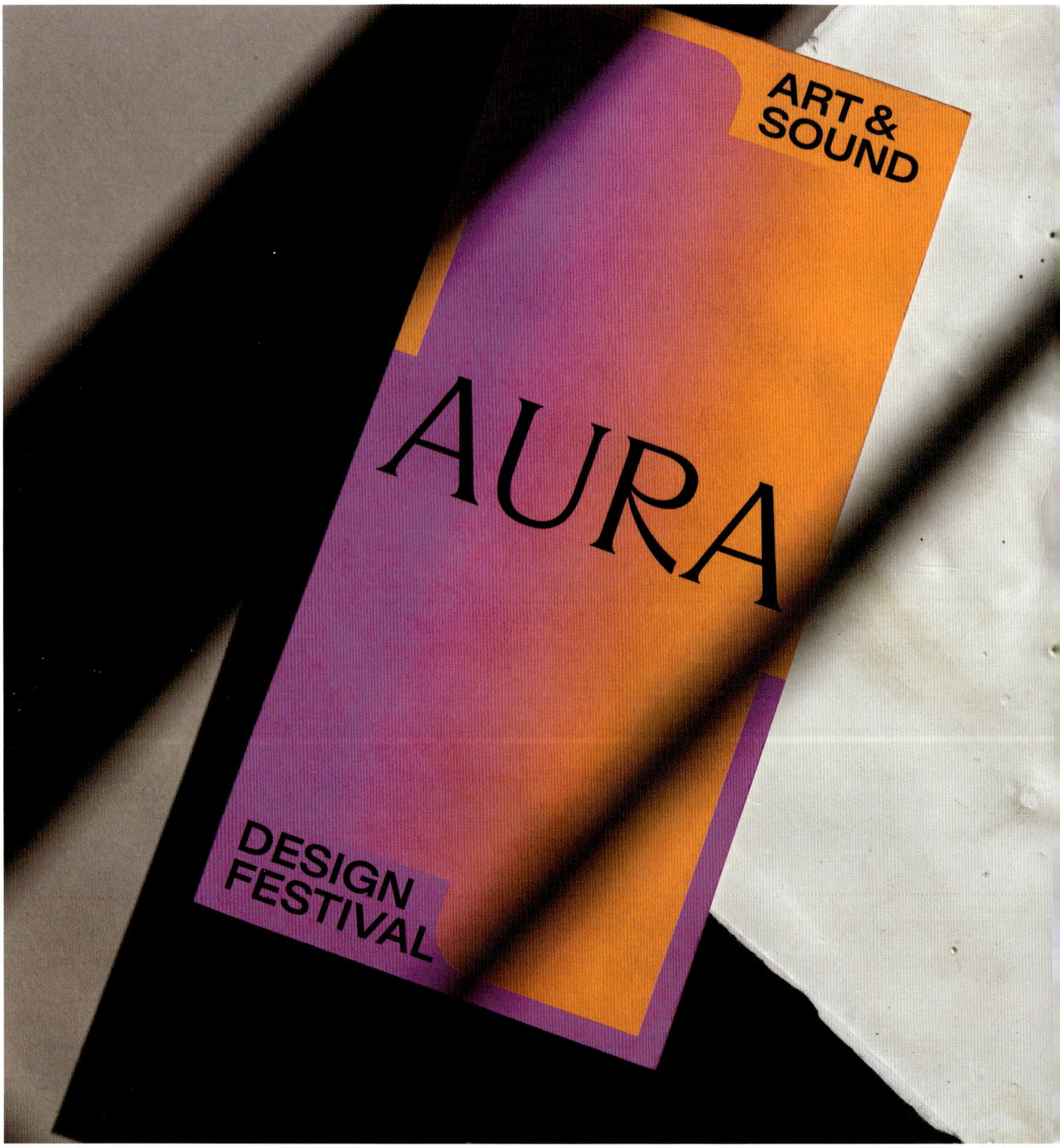

R197 · G70 · B255

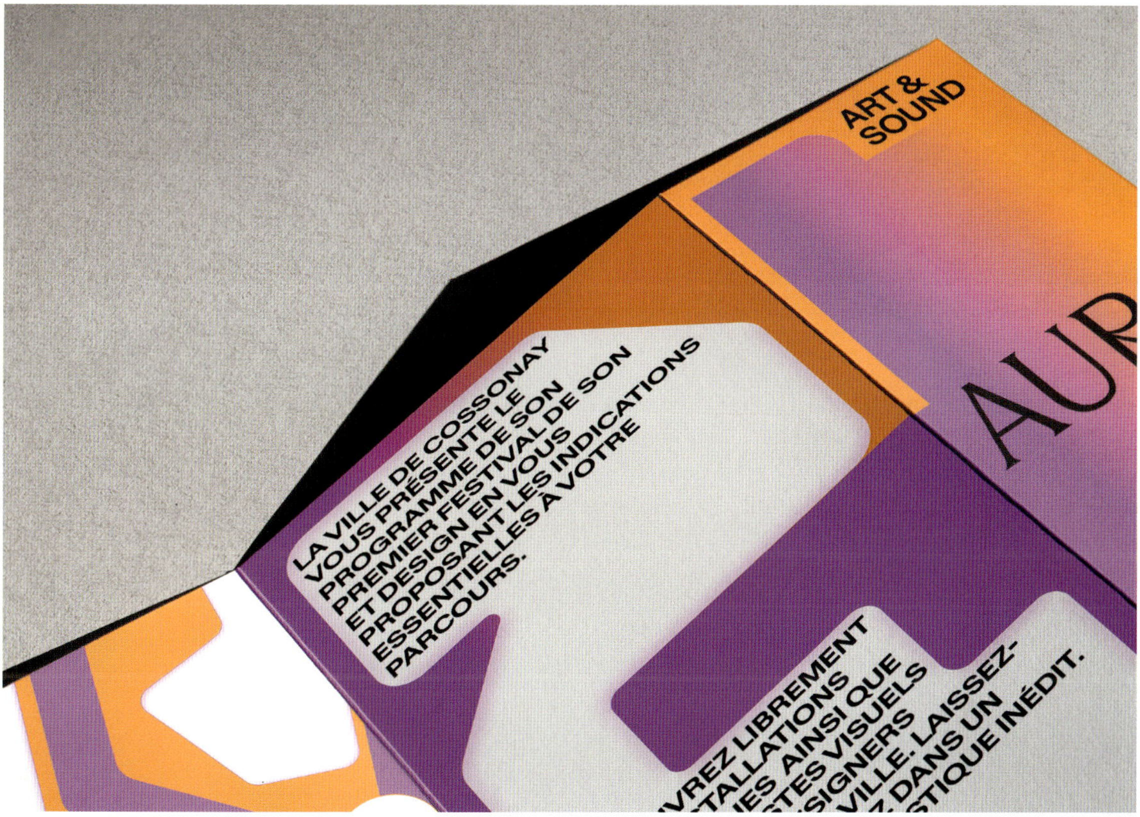
ART & SOUND
LA VILLE DE COSSONAY VOUS PRÉSENTE LE PROGRAMME DE SON PREMIER FESTIVAL DE SON ET DESIGN EN VOUS PROPOSANT LES INDICATIONS ESSENTIELLES À VOTRE PARCOURS.

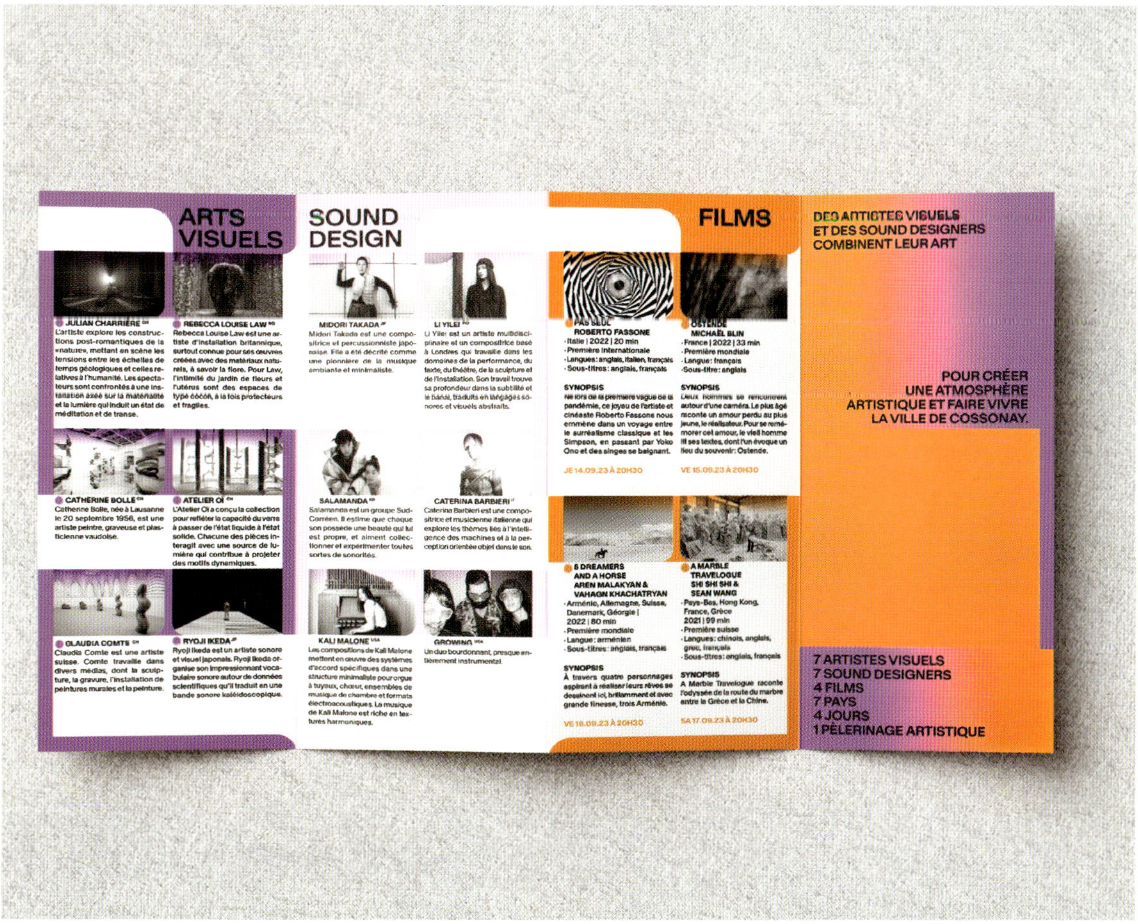
ARTS VISUELS
SOUND DESIGN
FILMS
DES ARTISTES VISUELS ET DES SOUND DESIGNERS COMBINENT LEUR ART
POUR CRÉER UNE ATMOSPHÈRE ARTISTIQUE ET FAIRE VIVRE LA VILLE DE COSSONAY.
7 ARTISTES VISUELS
7 SOUND DESIGNERS
4 FILMS
7 PAYS
4 JOURS
1 PÈLERINAGE ARTISTIQUE

C69 · M97 · Y51 · K42

C0 · M98 · Y78 · K0
C85 · M70 · Y0 · K0

C69 · M0 · Y100 · K0
C85 · M70 · Y0 · K0

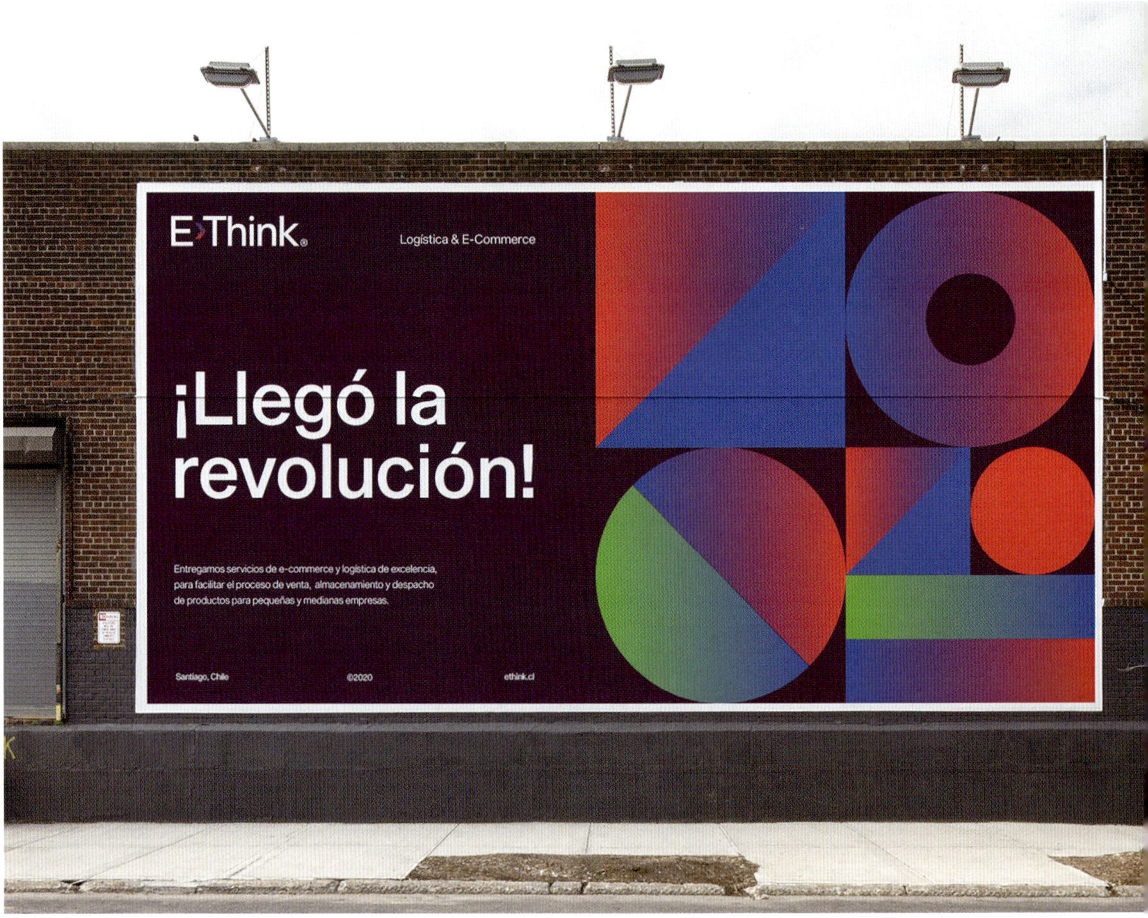

E-THINK

A brand that seeks to bring companies closer to their customers through an e-commerce and logistics service that allows people to access their products easily and quickly. In this way, they facilitate the process of sale, storage and dispatch of products for small and medium-sized companies. An identity was created that uses geometric shapes as the main visual element and that seek to represent the order of storage of products. In addition, the shapes are complemented with a palette of vibrant colours that add warmth and dynamism.

Design Studio
Brandtown Studio

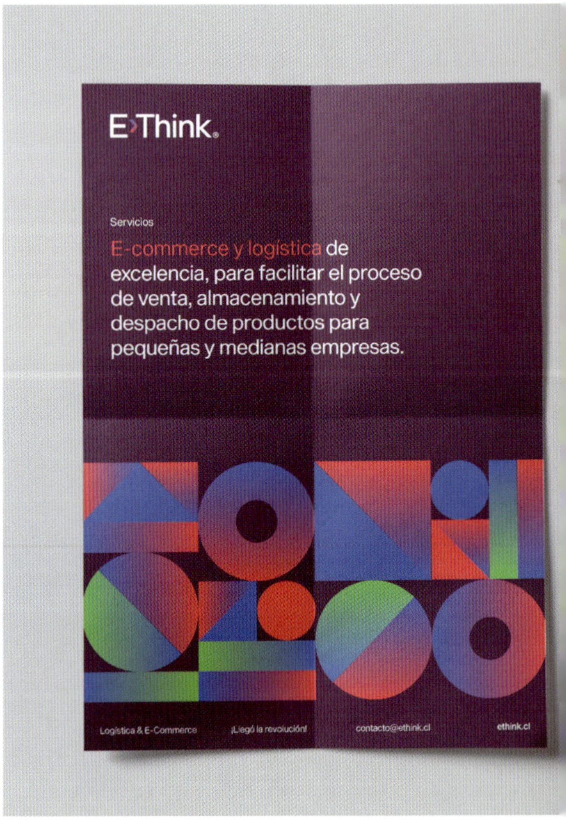

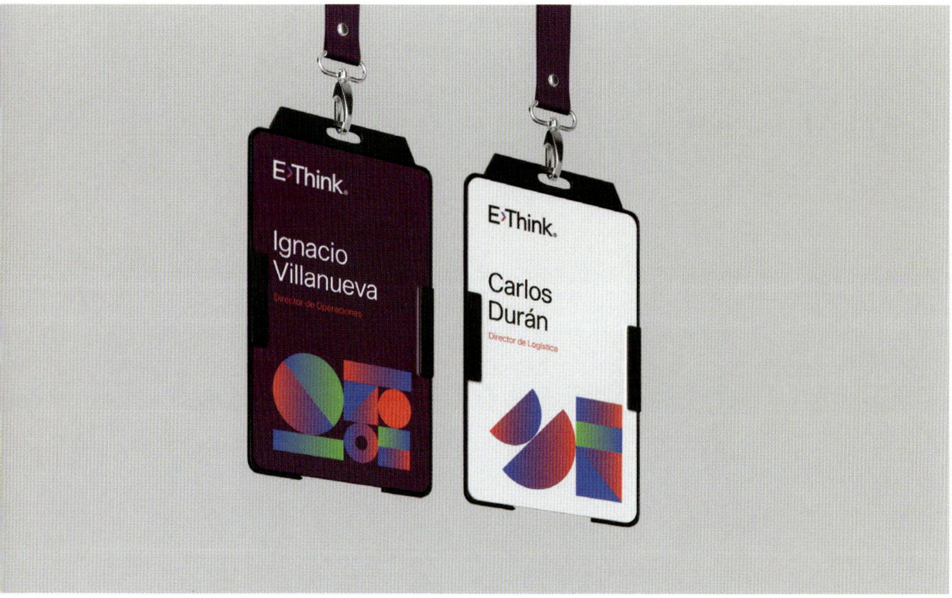
E›Think.
Ignacio Villanueva
Carlos Durán
Director de Logística

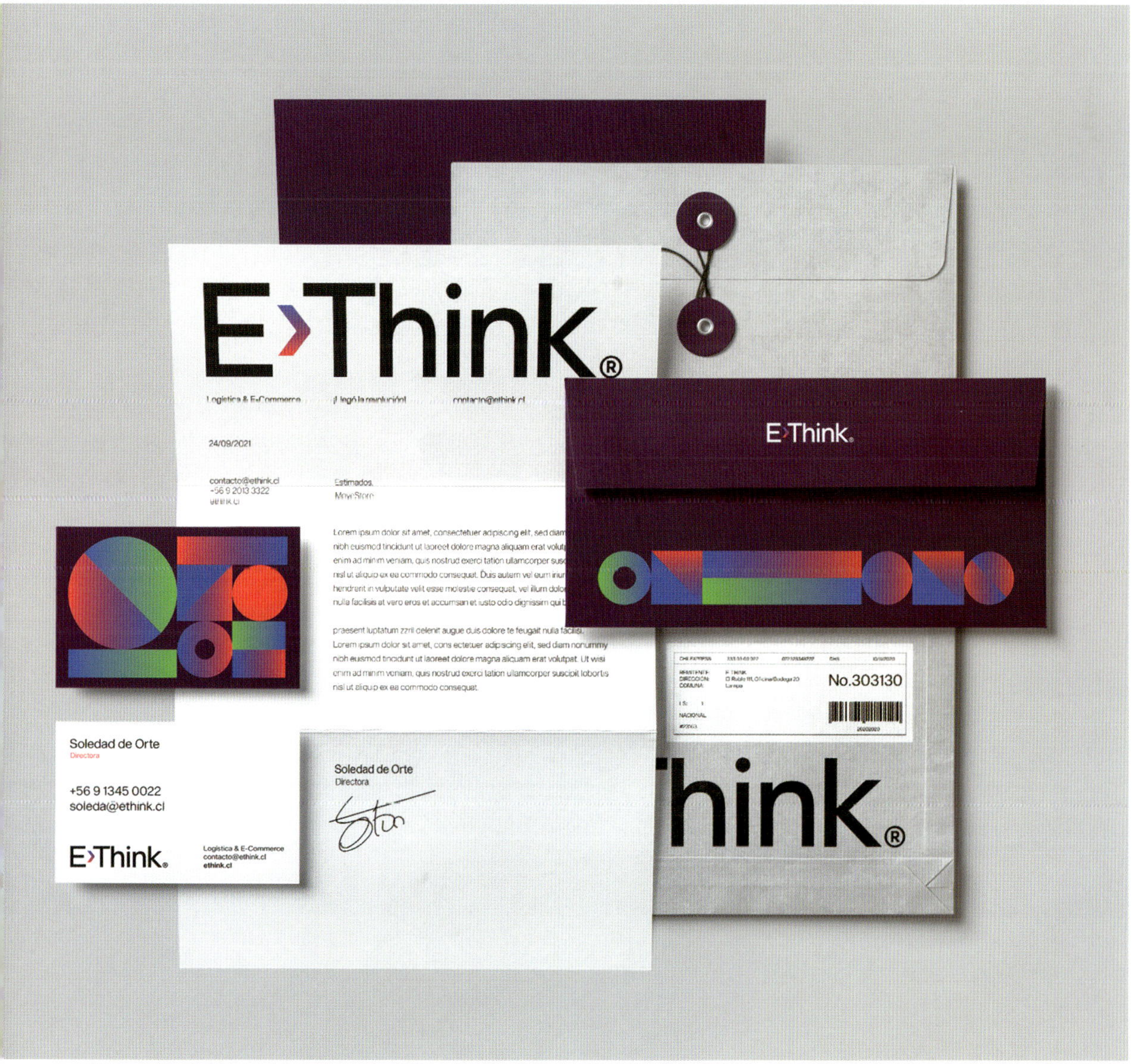
E›Think®
24/09/2021
contacto@ethink.cl
Estimados,
Soledad de Orte
Directora
+56 9 1345 0022
soleda@ethink.cl
E›Think.
Logística & E-Commerce
contacto@ethink.cl
ethink.cl
No.303130
hink®

PANTONE BLUE 072 C
PANTONE 284 C

PANTONE 716 C
PANTONE 714 C

PANTONE BRIGHT RED C
PANTONE 7416C

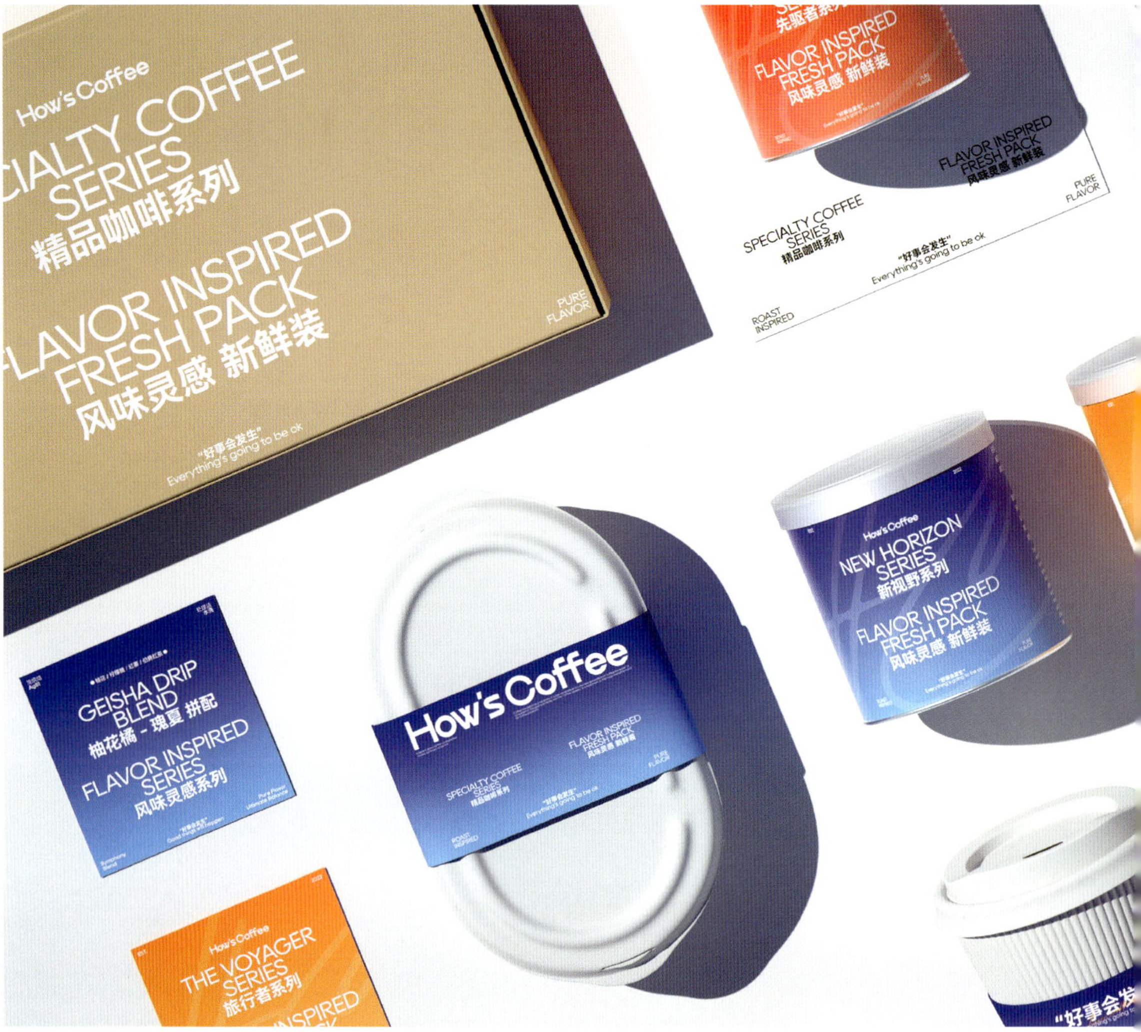

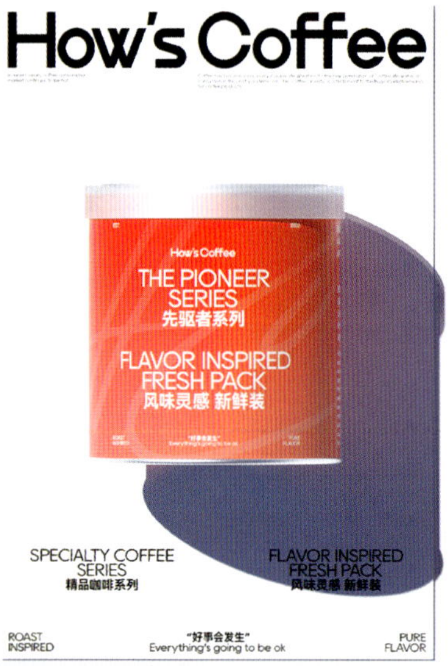

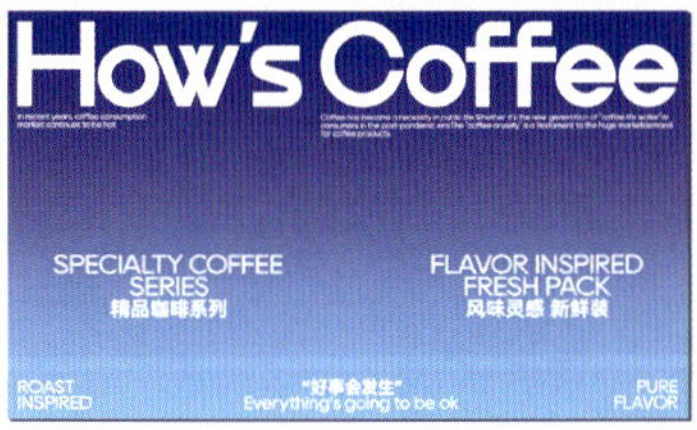

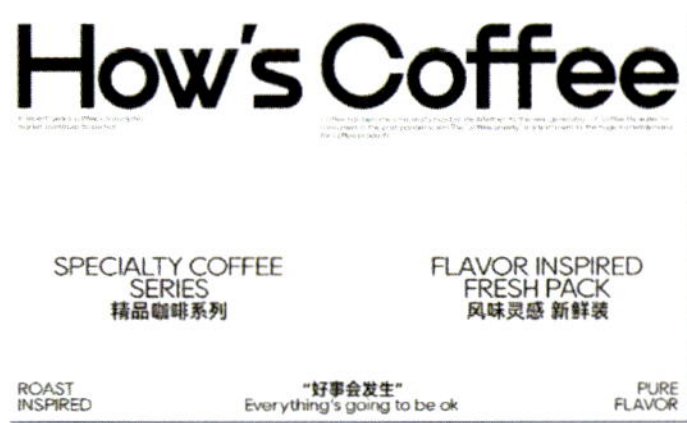

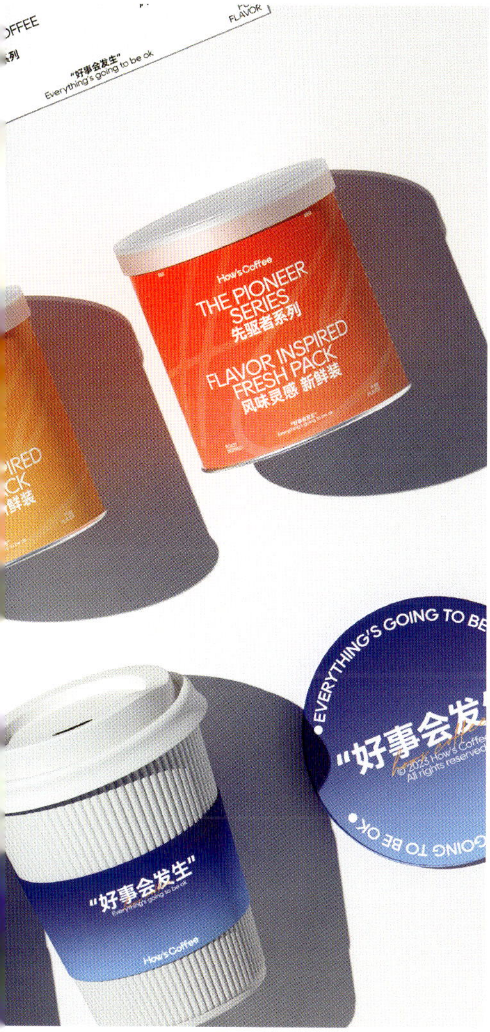

HOW'S COFFEE

The philosophy of *How's Coffee* is to take life seriously and embrace life warmly. Therefore, visually, the designer brings a strong sense of order, a clear typography style, and a rational exterior to convey the emotional interior. Products are based on high-quality coffee beans, while divided into "daily, advanced, professional" three-product lines. Through the layout and very bright colours, how's brand image and product packaging have established a strong association, in line with young brand positioning at the same time to bring different added value to the brand.

Design Studio
Guangzhou Sense Design

Designer
Zhenglin Wang, Hui Wei

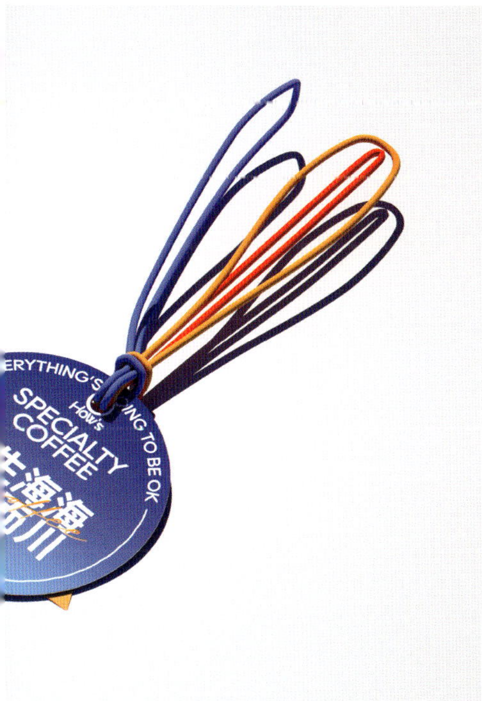

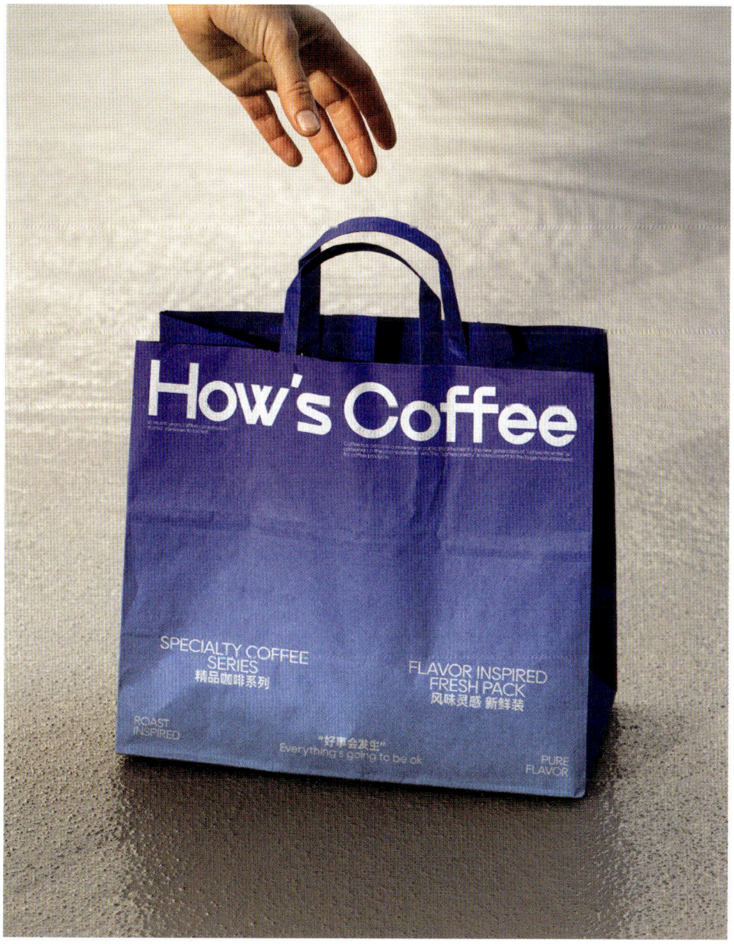

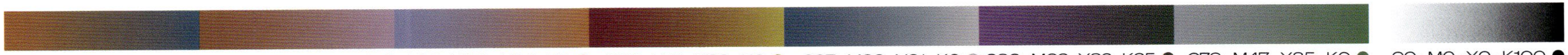

C84 · M59 · Y49 · K4 C40 · M70 · Y86 · K2
C39 · M52 · Y23 · K0 C44 · M73 · Y80 · K6
C38 · M68 · Y84 · K0 C56 · M50 · Y15 · K0
C38 · M41 · Y89 · K0 C53 · M94 · Y72 · K25
C37 · M33 · Y31 · K0 C84 · M63 · Y49 · K6
C80 · M63 · Y82 · K35 C60 · M80 · Y25 · K0
C79 · M47 · Y85 · K0 C49 · M41 · Y35 · K0
C0 · M0 · Y0 · K100 C0 · M0 · Y0 · K0

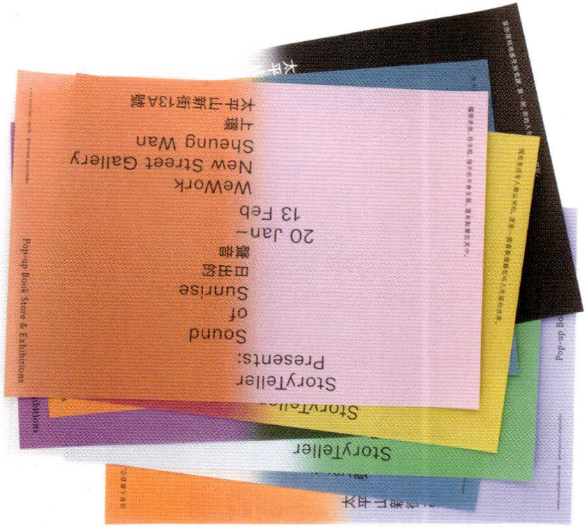

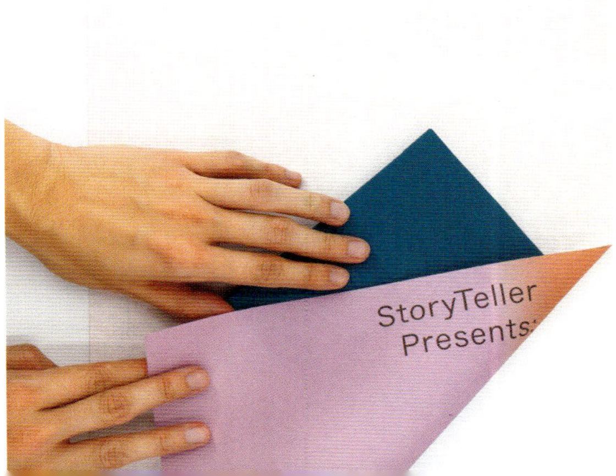

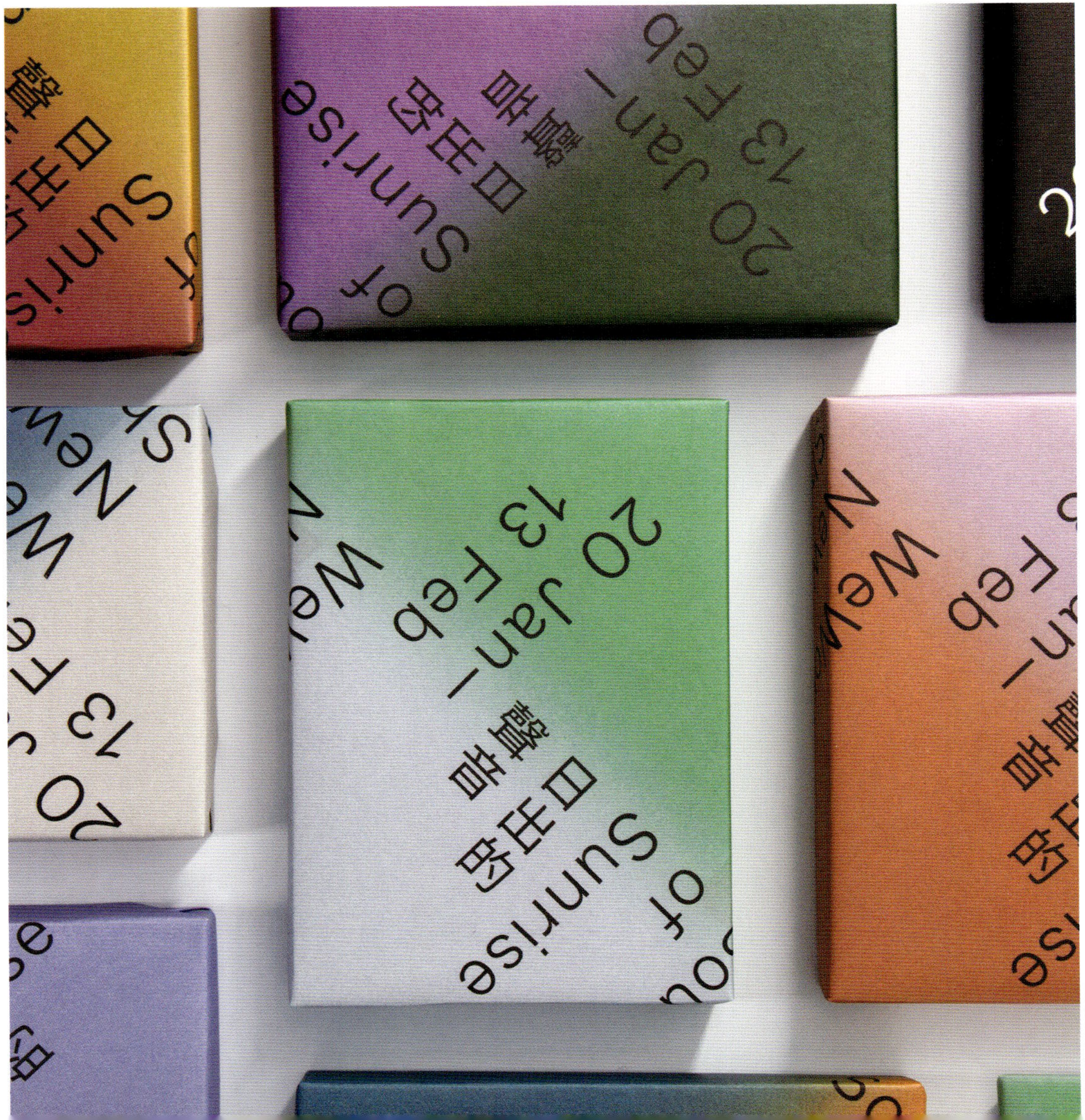

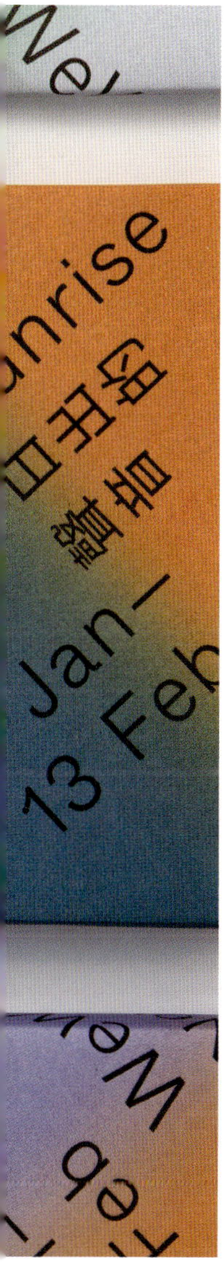

SOUND OF SUNRISE

"Sound of Sunrise" is the pop-up exhibition for new launches from small Hong Kong publisher. The different tones of gradient depict the colour of the sunrise that echoes the stories in the two books; readers can engage with the authors at the pop-up and the exhibition poster that also can be used as wrapping paper for the reader to bring home. The gradients with different tones also preview the upcoming series of the book.

Creative Director
William Tsao

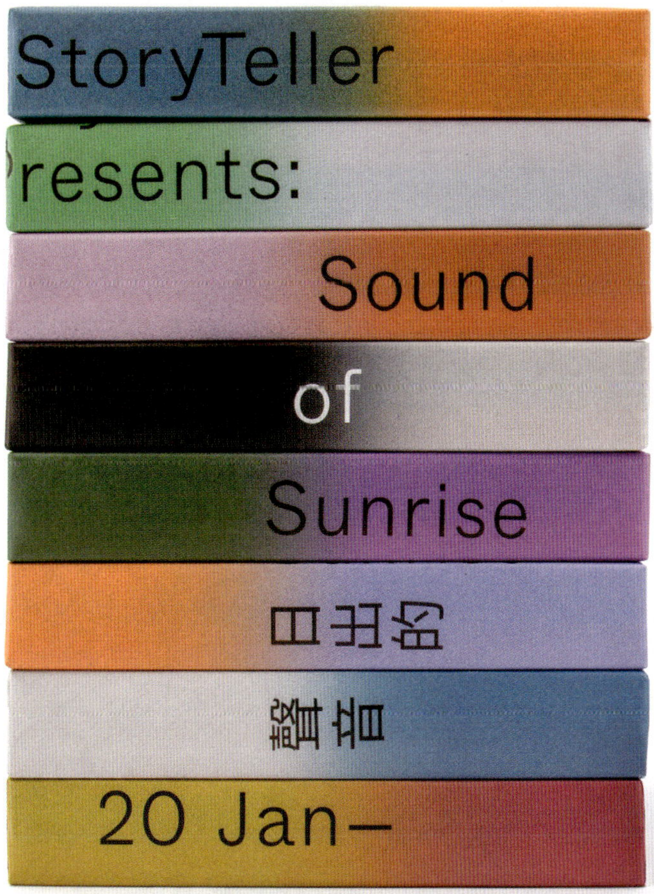

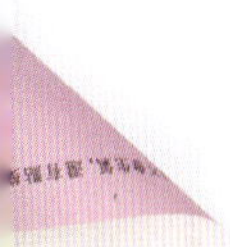

PANTONE 326 C
PANTONE 101 C

PANTONE 326 C
PANTONE 247 C

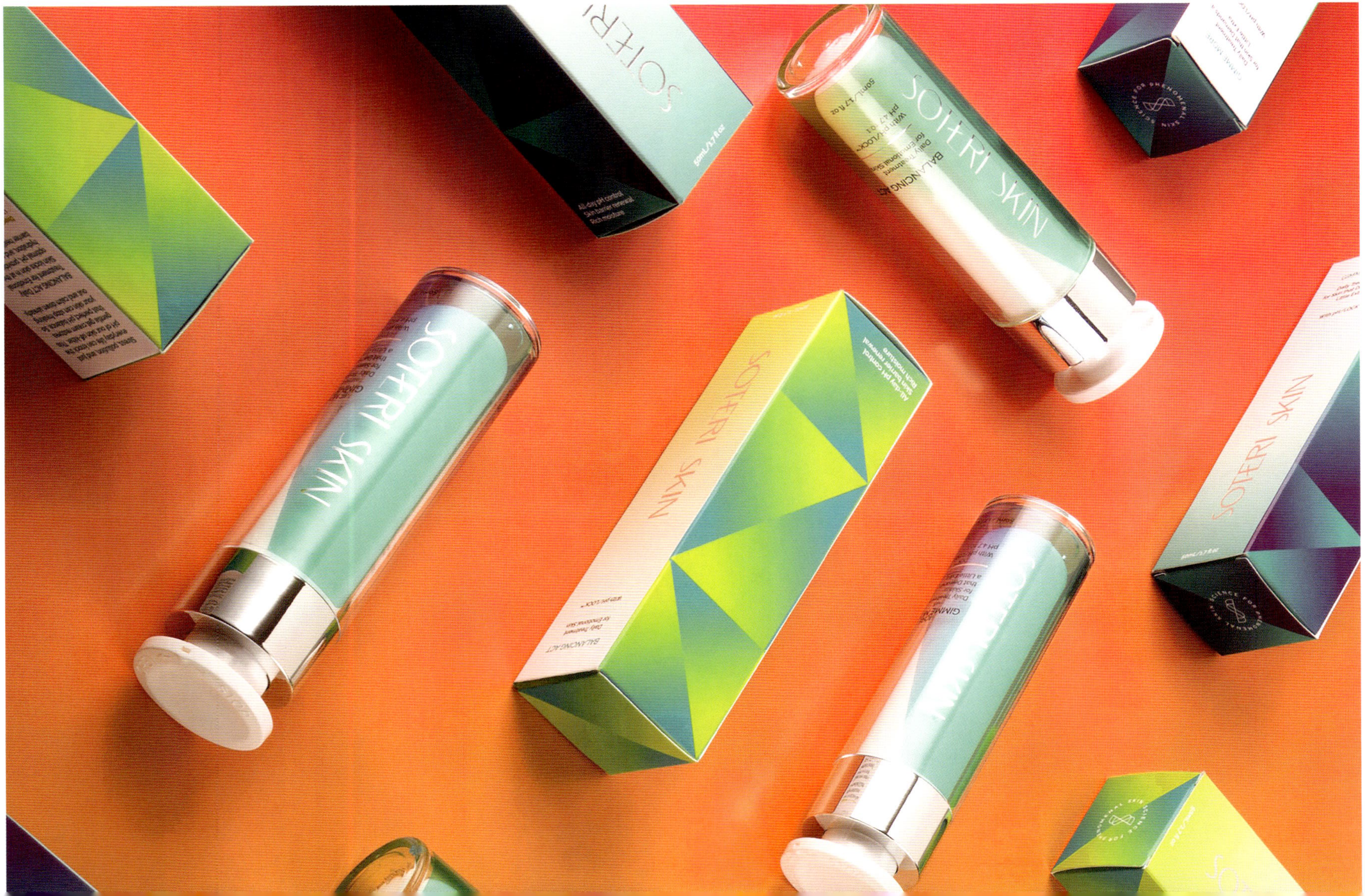

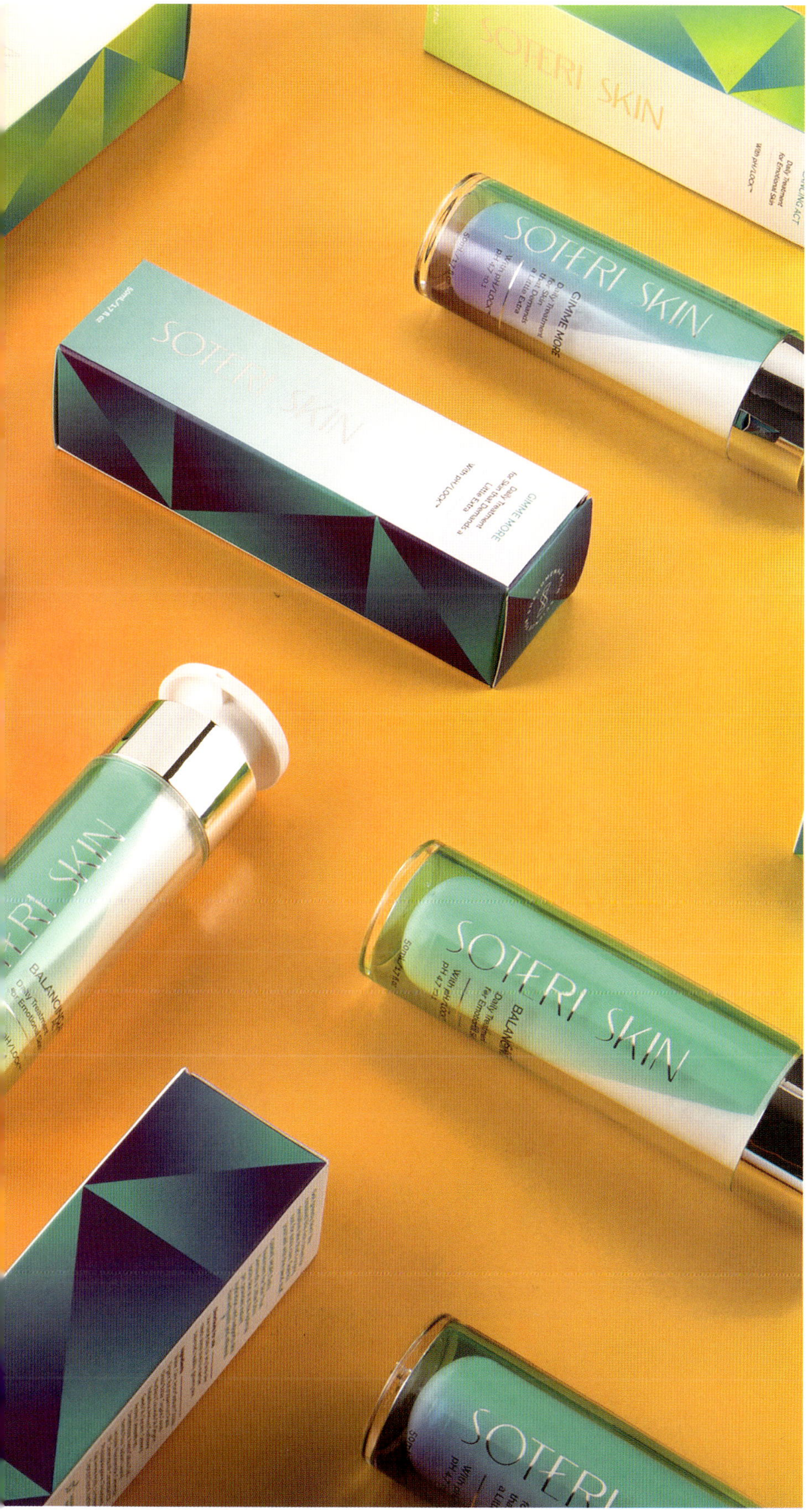

SOTERI SKIN

Soteri Skin is a brand that knows beauty is balance, especially when it comes to skin; because the skin reflects security and confidence when facing the challenges of a fast-paced and stress-filled world. *Soteri* is a healing and safe place that seeks harmony between protection, science and beauty for skin care.

Design Studio
Estudio Albino

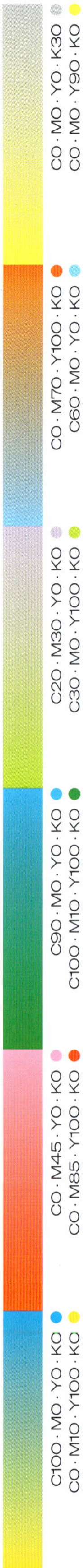
C0 · M0 · Y0 · K30
C0 · M0 · Y90 · K0
C0 · M70 · Y100 · K0
C60 · M0 · Y0 · K0
C20 · M30 · Y0 · K0
C30 · M0 · Y100 · K0
C90 · M0 · Y0 · K0
C100 · M10 · Y100 · K0
C0 · M45 · Y0 · K0
C0 · M85 · Y100 · K0
C100 · M0 · Y0 · K0
C0 · M10 · Y100 · K0

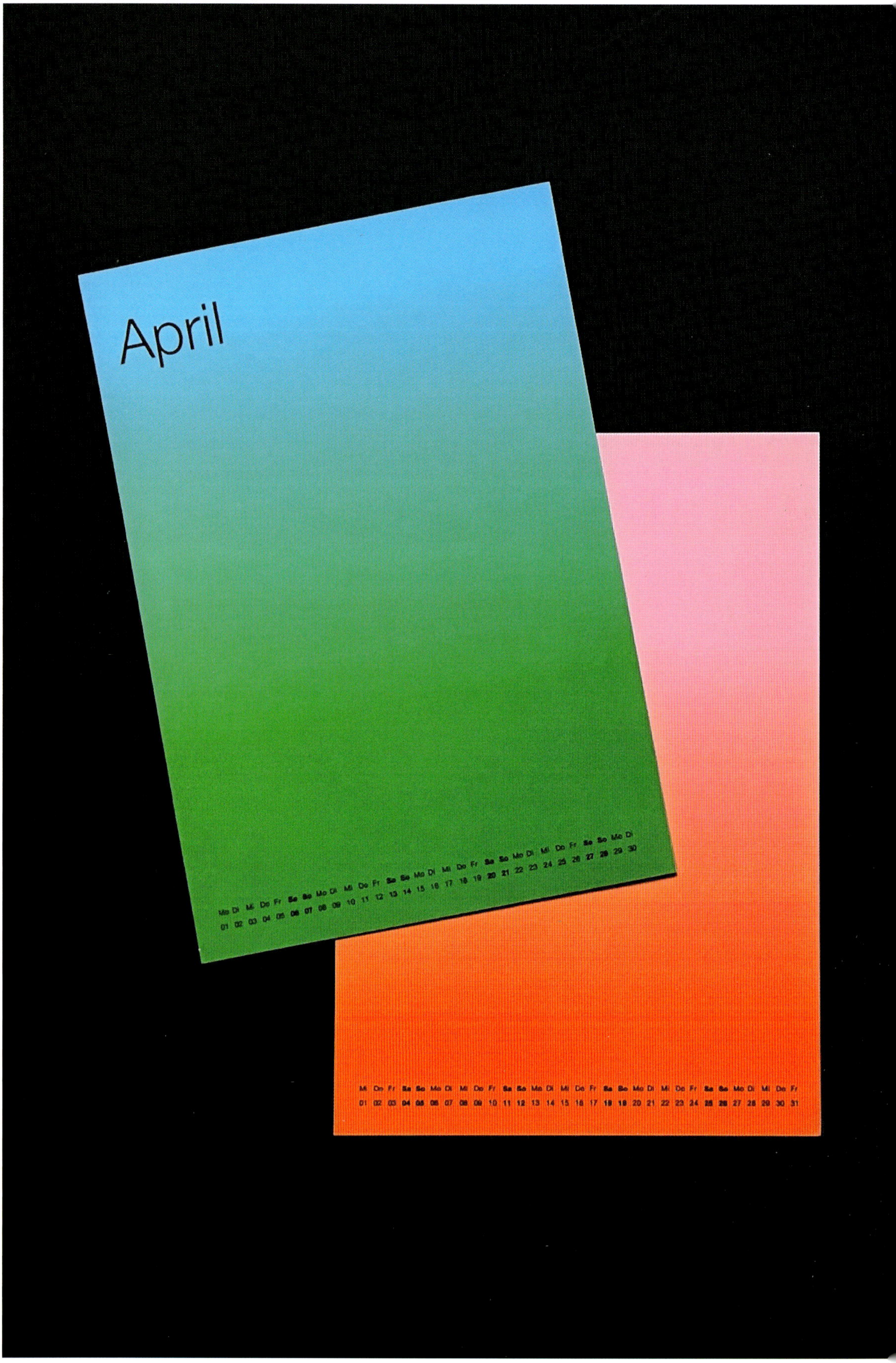
April

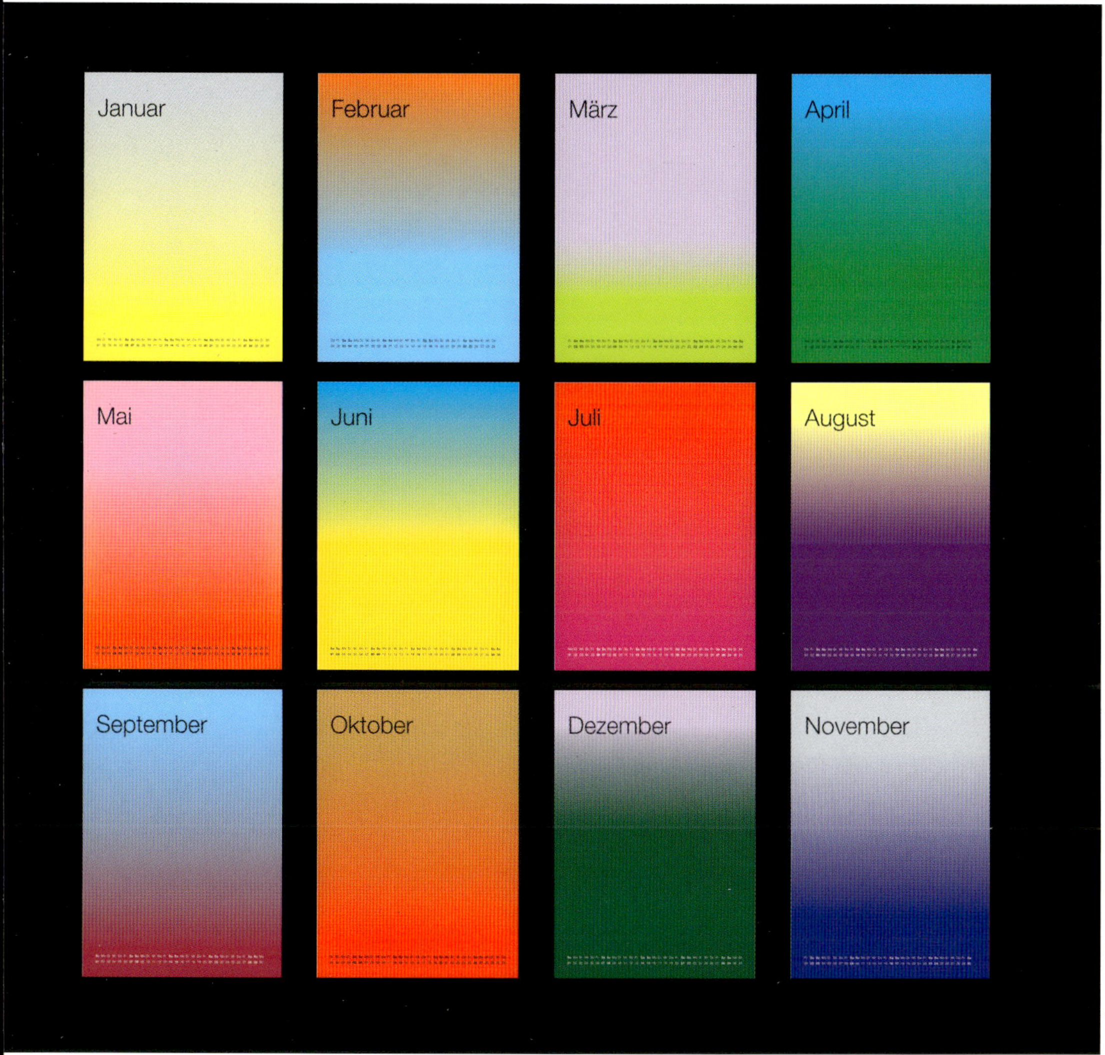

GRADIENT CALENDAR

2024 *Gradient Calendar* is a calendar consisting of 12 monthly pages, each with a seasonal colour combination. It was designed as a New Year's greeting for all clients, partners and companions.

Designer & Photographer
Luzia Hein

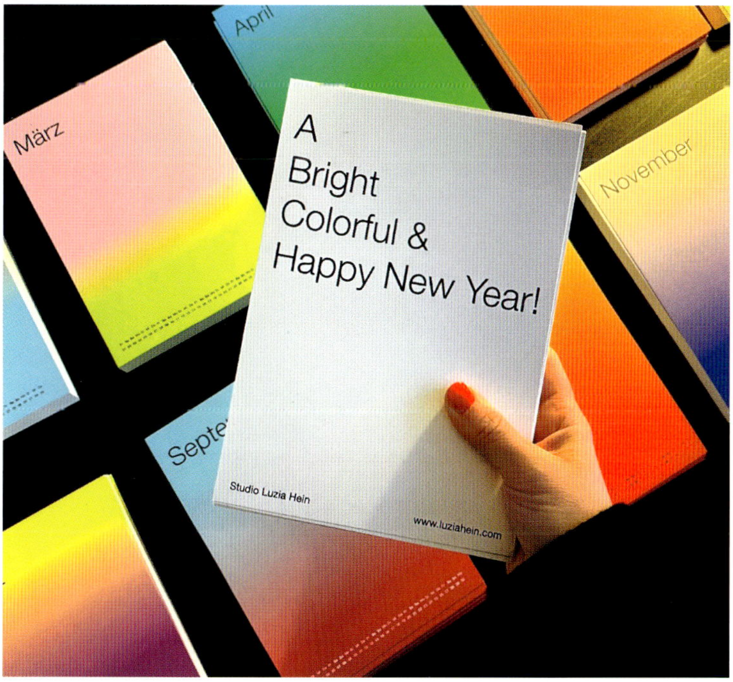

C0 · M100 · Y100 · K0
C15 · M100 · Y0 · K0

C0 · M65 · Y0 · K0
C70 · M100 · Y0 · K0

C60 · M0 · Y0 · K0
C35 · M10 · Y50 · K0

C0 · M35 · Y75 · K25
C0 · M100 · Y100 · K0

C0 · M0 · Y0 · K30
C0 · M100 · Y90 · K0

C20 · M30 · Y0 · K0
C100 · M30 · Y85 · K35

PANTONE 2738 C

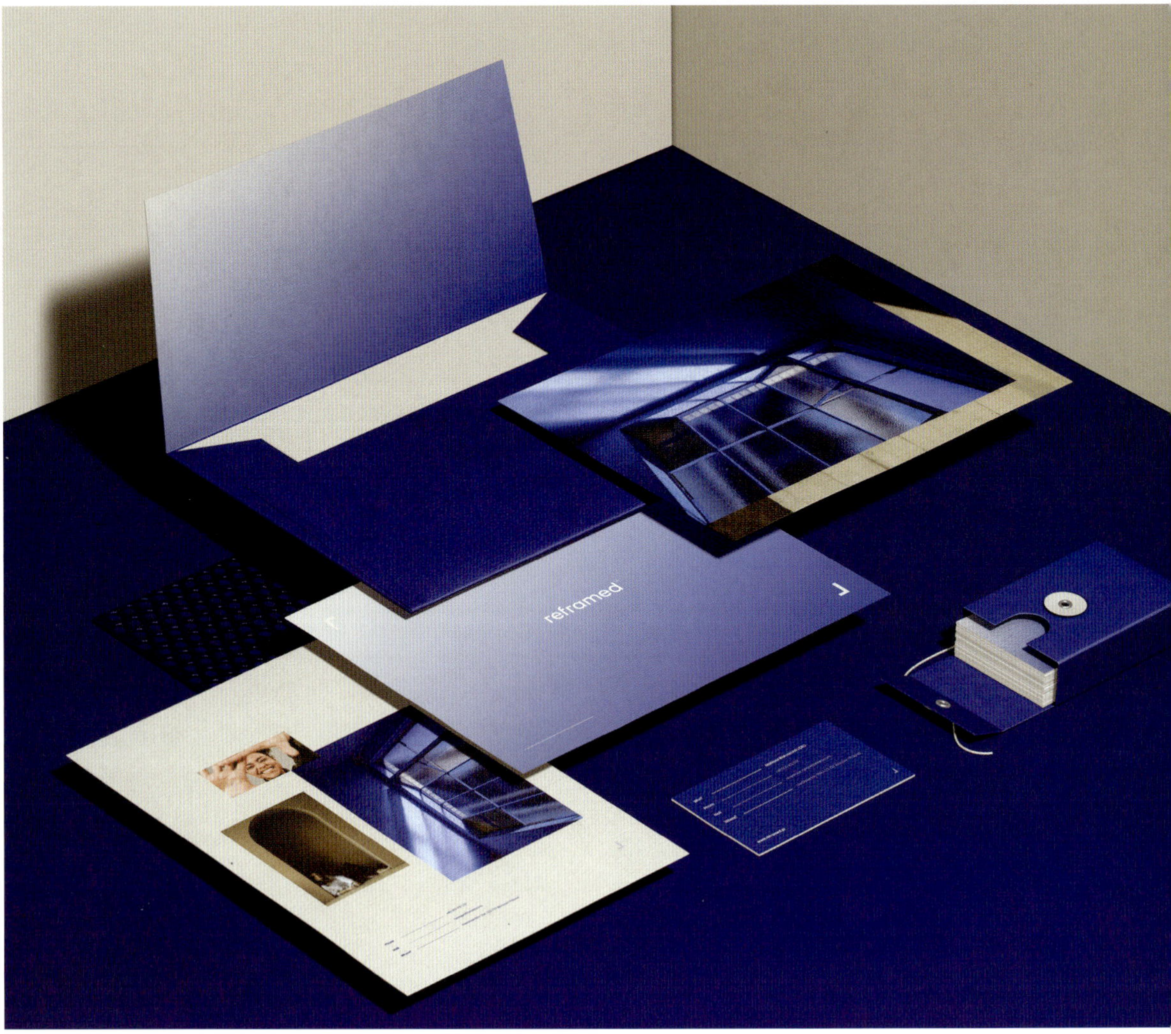

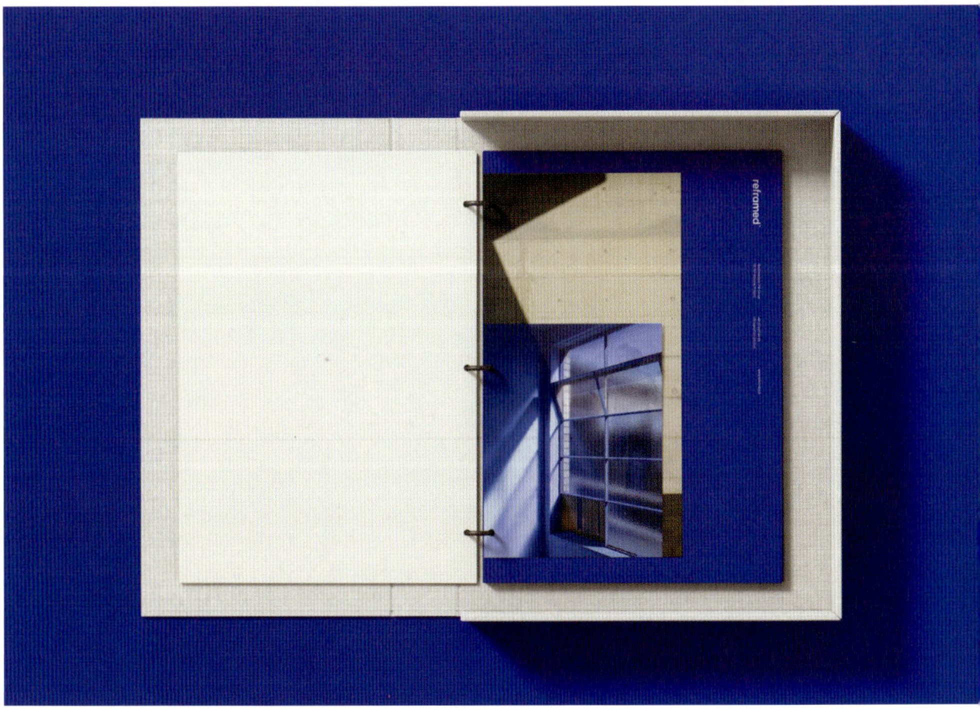

PANTONE 9226 C

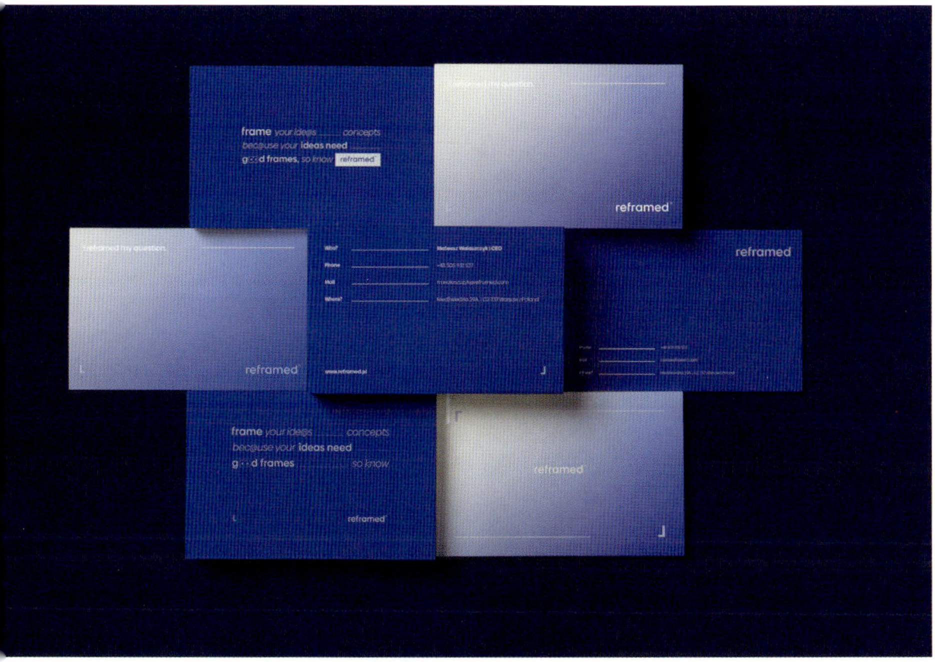

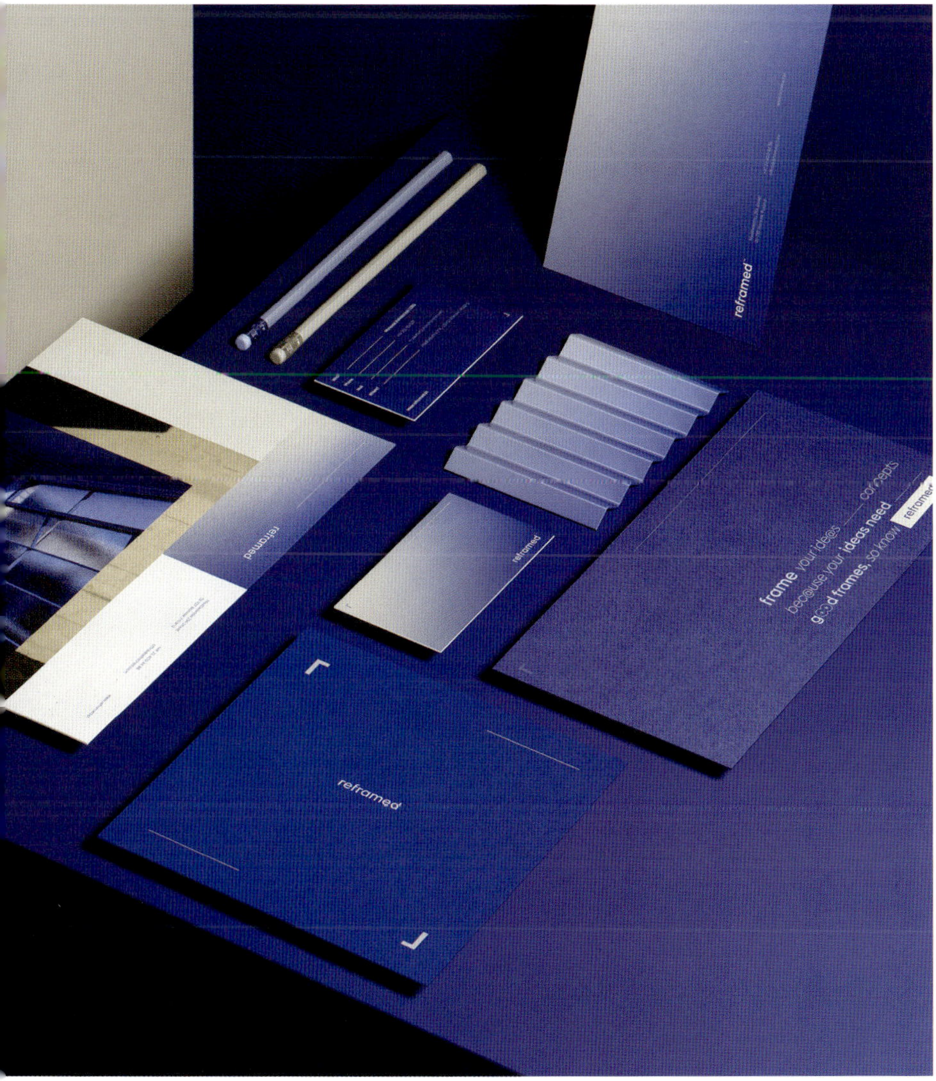

REFRAMED

The name *Reframed* carries a signifcant meaning as it refers to the act of reinterpreting or restructuring perspectives. In English, "reframed" embodies the essence of looking at things from a new and fresh perspective, which served as the inspiration for the creative direction in developing the brand identity. The brand is based on the meaning of the word "reframed" — focusing on changing frames, perspectives, and forms. A distinctive feature is the unconventional combination of cobalt and a warm ecru beige hue. The gradient transition and the fusion of these two colours serve as a strong brand identifer. The typographic logo, where the letter R has been reformatted, provides a solid foundation for the design of other materials.

Designer
Teresa Chylińska-Kur

Photographer
Stocksy photo bank (Rowena Naylor, Marko, W2 Photography, Oleksii Syrotkin)

AMARILLO ZINC #FB102
TELEMAGENTA #FB402

LIGHT BLUE #FB508
RED ORANGE #FB214

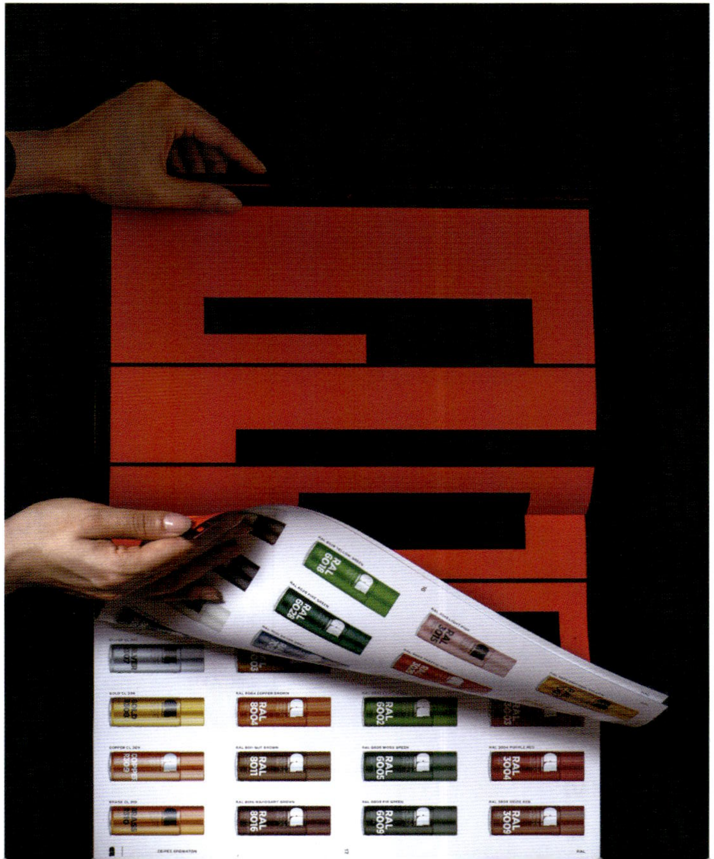

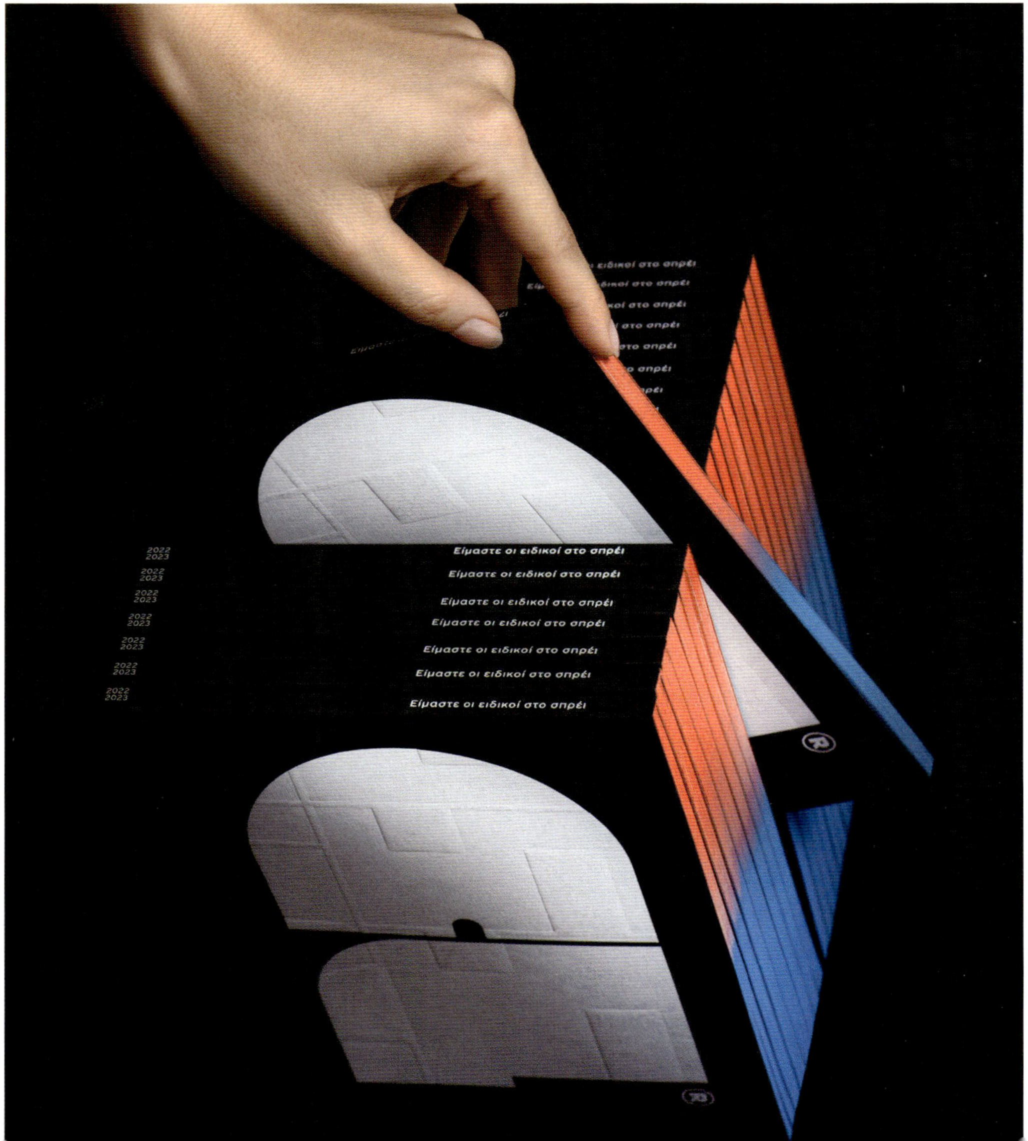

CL PRODUCT CATALOGUE 2022-2023

CL Product Catalogue 2022-2023 is all about colour. Emphasizing the products' substance, *Cosmos Lac* products become the focus of this year's catalogue. A gradient book-edge, spray-painted with *Cosmos Lac* spray paints, is the first thing that captures the eye in a black and white cover. The direction is bold and fresh with use of intense typography, custom titles for each finish category (gloss, satin and matt). A catalogue inspired by the big and full forms of *Cosmos Lac's* identity.

Creative Director & Designer
Veronika Design Studio (Veronika Papadopoulou)

Print Producer
Kostopoulos Printing House

Spray Paint
Jola818

Photographer
Athina Souli

Client
Cosmos Lac

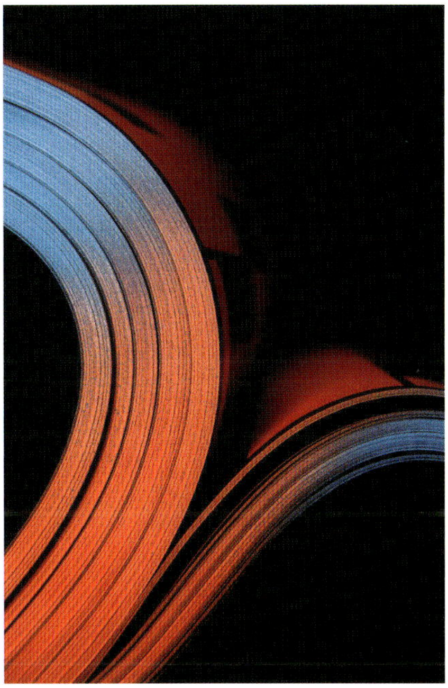

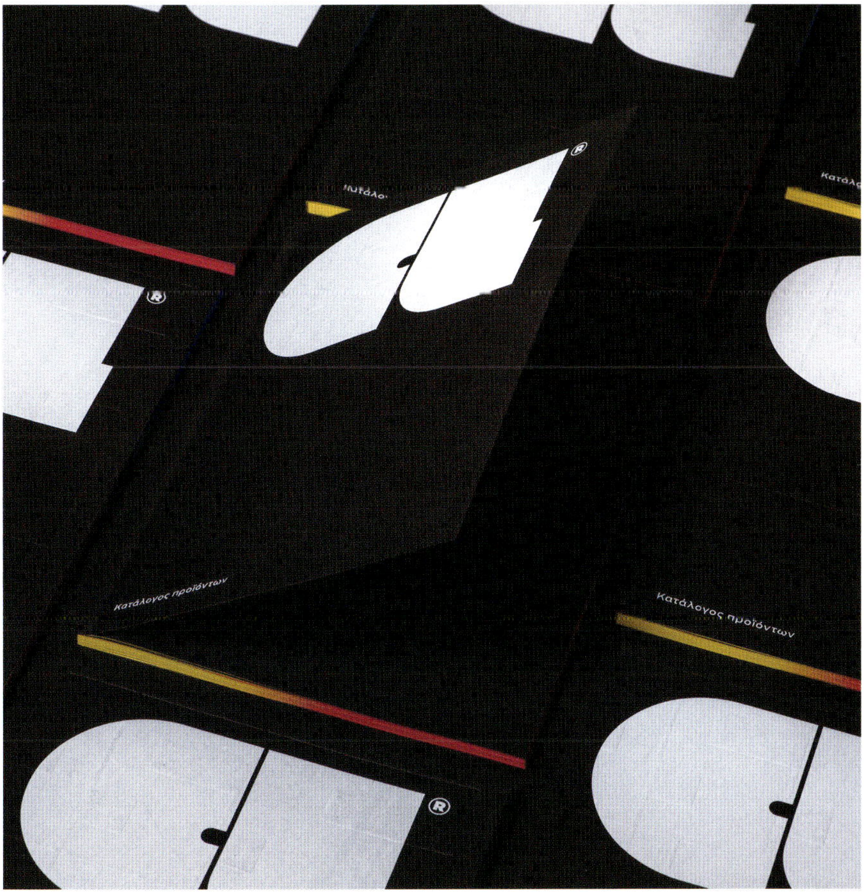

PANTONE 252 C
PANTONE 2198 C

PANTONE 170 C
PANTONE 2268 C

PANTONE 136 C
PANTONE 170 C

PANTONE 252 C

PANTONE 2198 C
PANTONE 2268 C

PANTONE 252 C

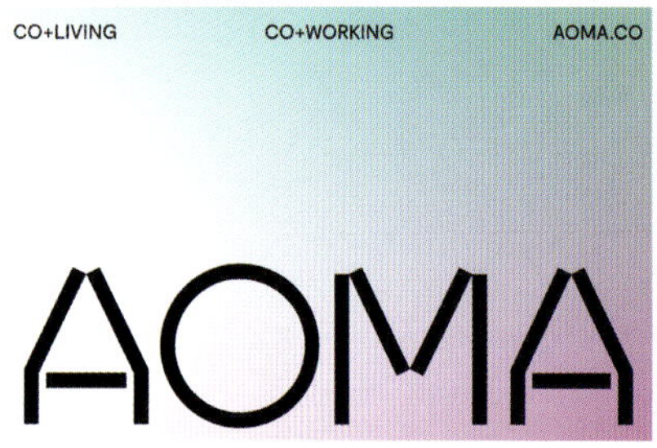

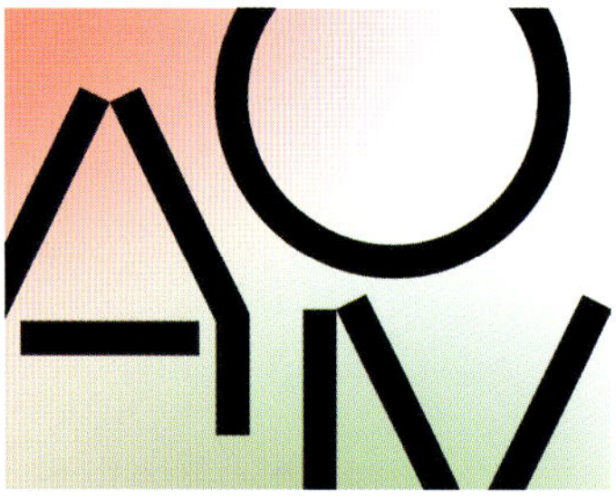

AOMA. CO+LIVING & CO+WORKING

Aoma is a co-living and co-working project in Ericeira, Portugal. Both the architectural project and the visual identity are inspired by the Japanese concept "Ma". Font (Studio) seeks to convey the idea of light, complete experience and fullness through colour and gradients. The brand conveys the modularity of the architecture, and enhances the points of contact between modules to also convey the *Aoma's* philosophy.

Designer
Manel Font

Design Studio
Font (Studio)

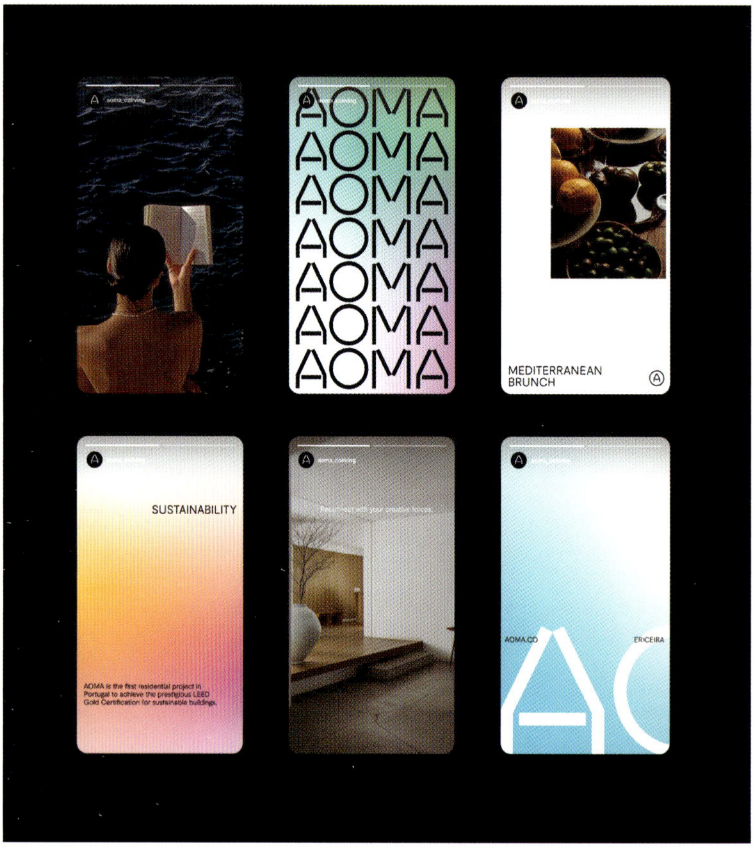

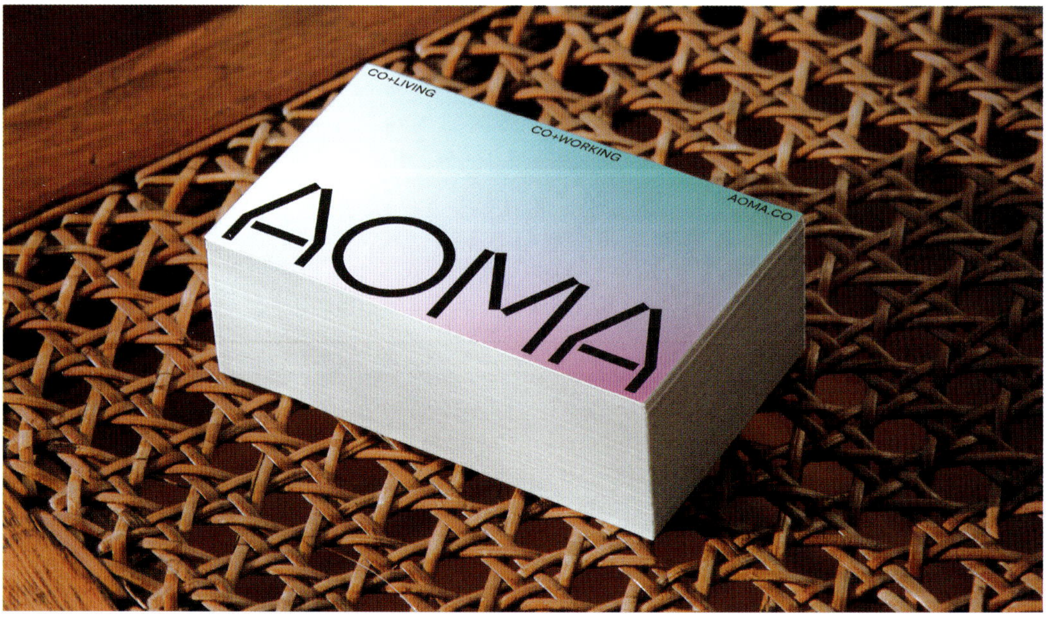

PANTONE 906

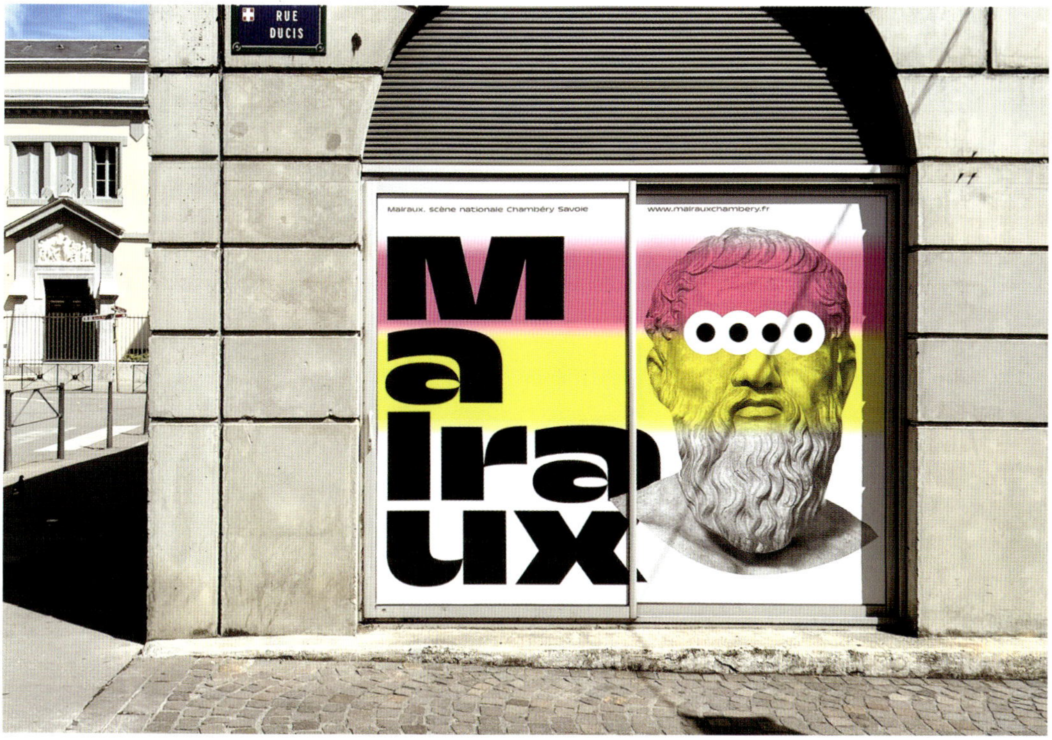

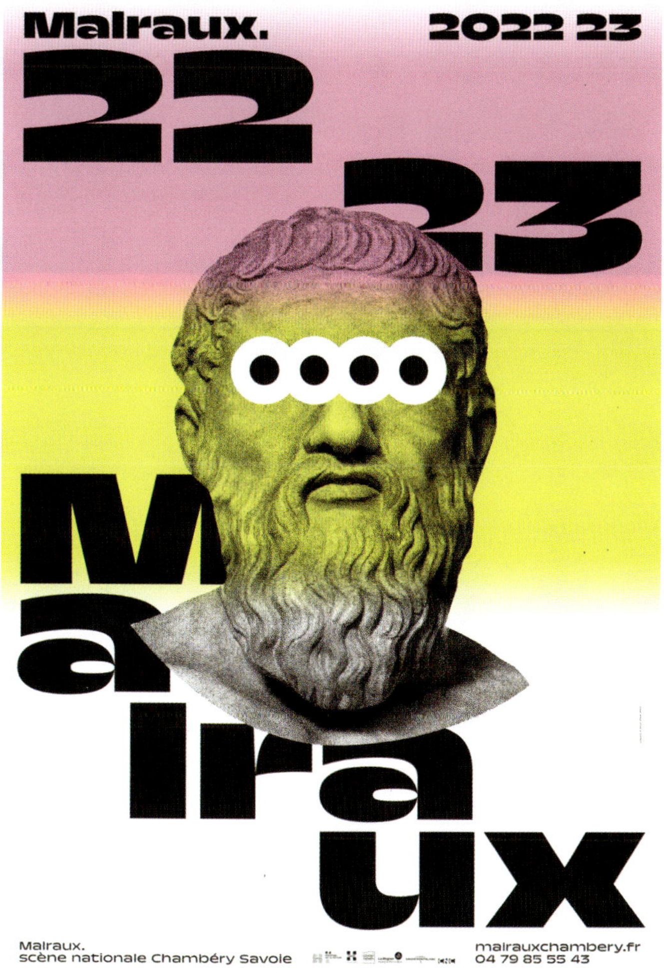

MALRAUX-SCÈNE NATIONALE CHAMBÉRY SAVOIE 2022-2023

Visual identity for the 2022–2023 season of Malraux—National Stage of Chambéry (FR).

Design Studio
Brest Brest Brest

FLOUSAMRT JAUNE CHARTREUSE

C14 · M0 · Y0 · K0
C0 · M6 · Y33 · K0

C0 · M37 · Y30 · K0
C0 · M6 · Y33 · K0

C0 · M37 · Y30 · K0
C6 · M80 · Y68 · K0

C50 · M5 · Y22 · K0
C6 · M80 · Y68 · K0

C50 · M5 · Y22 · K0
C0 · M20 · Y17 · K0

C8 · M43 · Y16 · K0
C0 · M20 · Y17 · K0

C8 · M43 · Y16 · K0
C60 · M42 · Y20 · K0

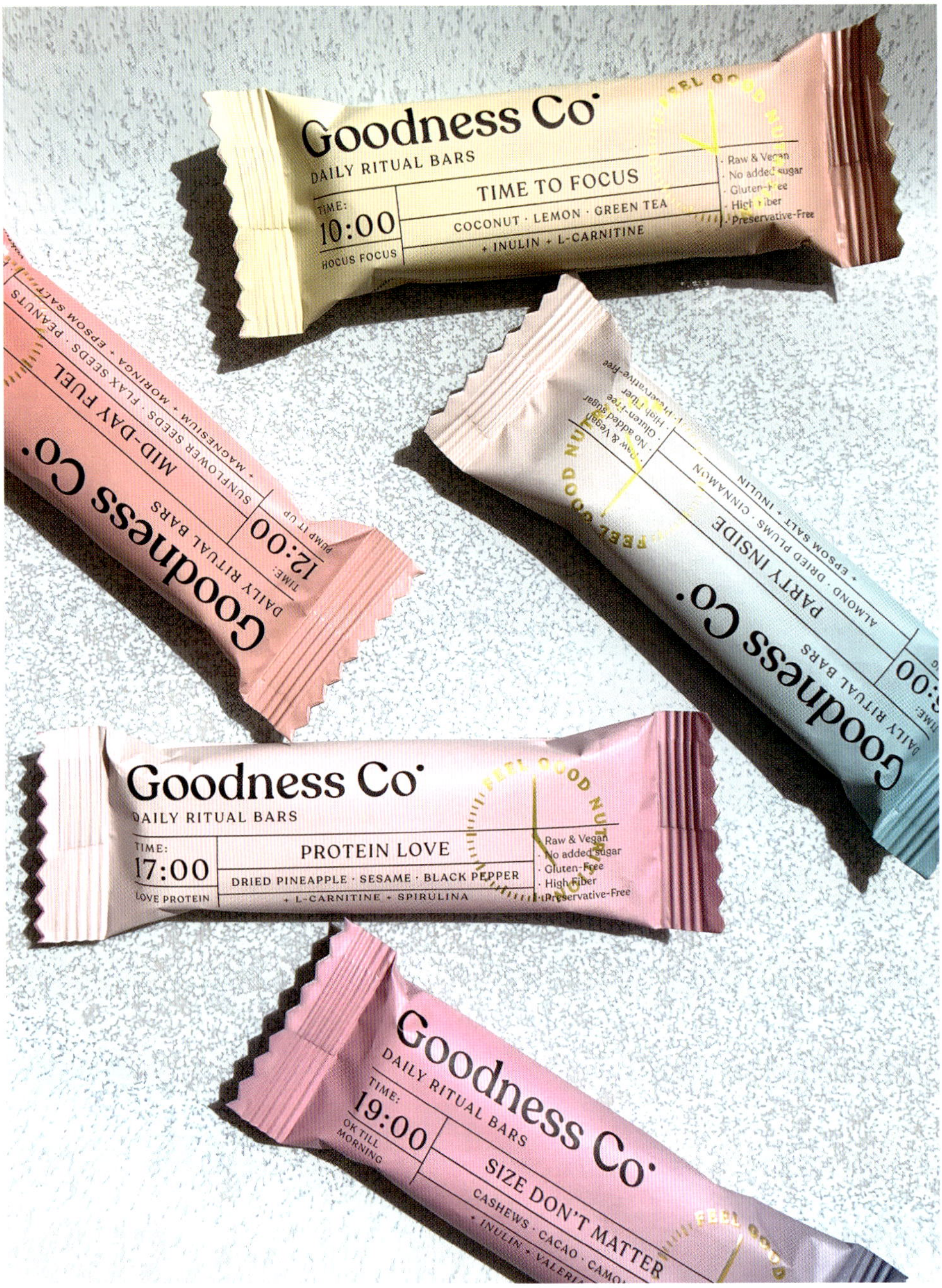

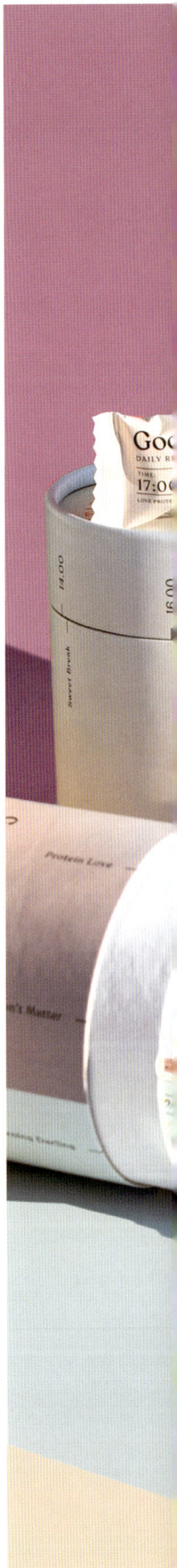

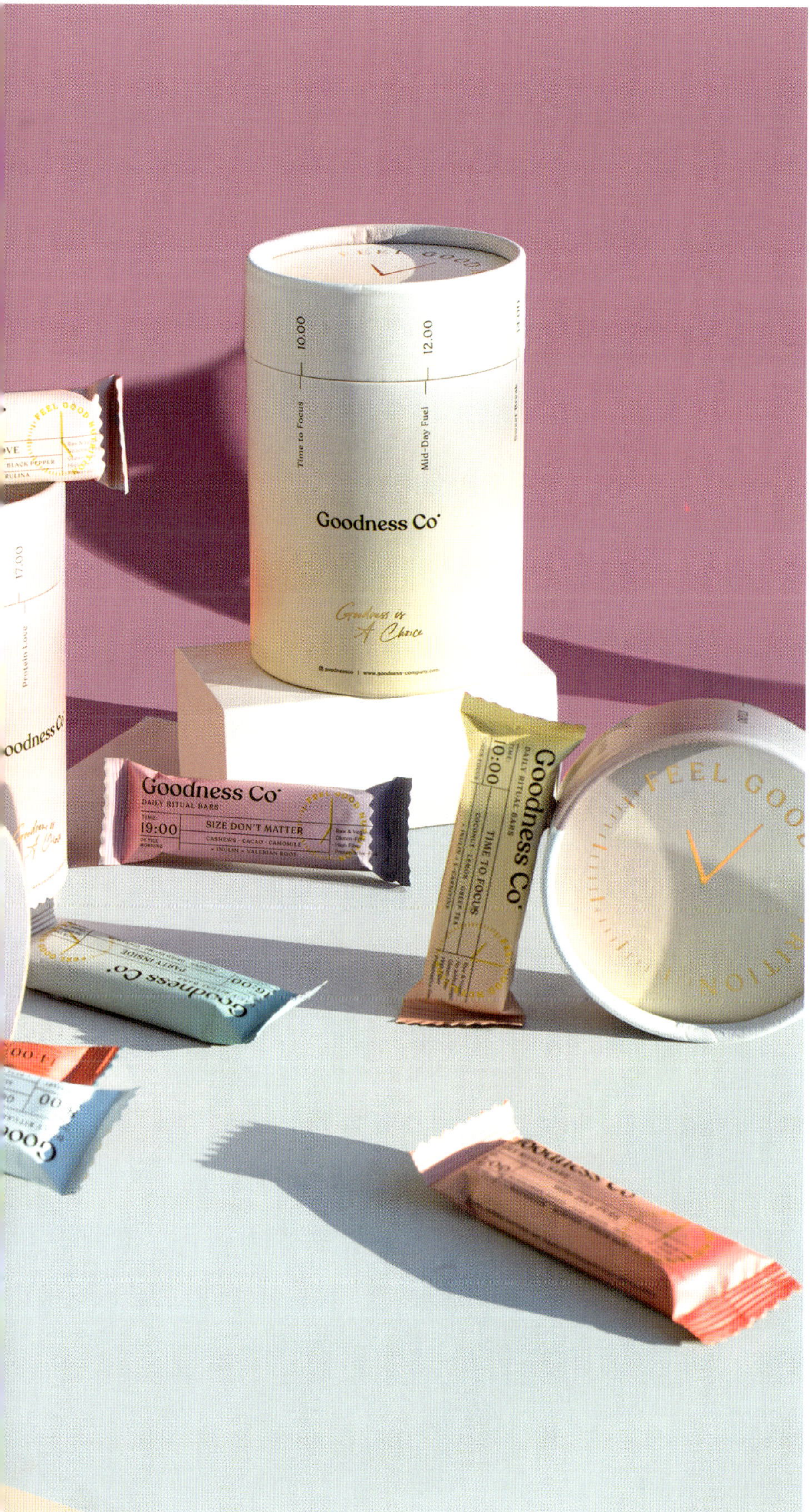

GOODNESS CO.

Goodness Bars, an innovative snack based on the body's natural circadian cycle, are full of healthy supplements and nutritious foods your body needs to complete its daily routine. Studio Born named their creation *Goodness Co.* to reflect the wholesome and beneficial nature of their bars. With playful text, informative typography, and a soft transitioning colour palette inspired by the gradient sky throughout the day, they set the tone for the branding, starting with a soft pale blue and yellow, and ending with a deep purple. Each bar completes the other when put side by side. The tiny touch of gold foil on the clock logo determines the consumption time for each bar along with the cylinder box that's meant to be your daily snack.

Creative Director
Ebru Sile Goksel &
Ipek Eris Ugurlu

Designer
Ebru Sile Goksel,
Ipek Eris Ugurlu &
Alara Murkozoglu

Design Studio
Studio Born

#A2D7F6

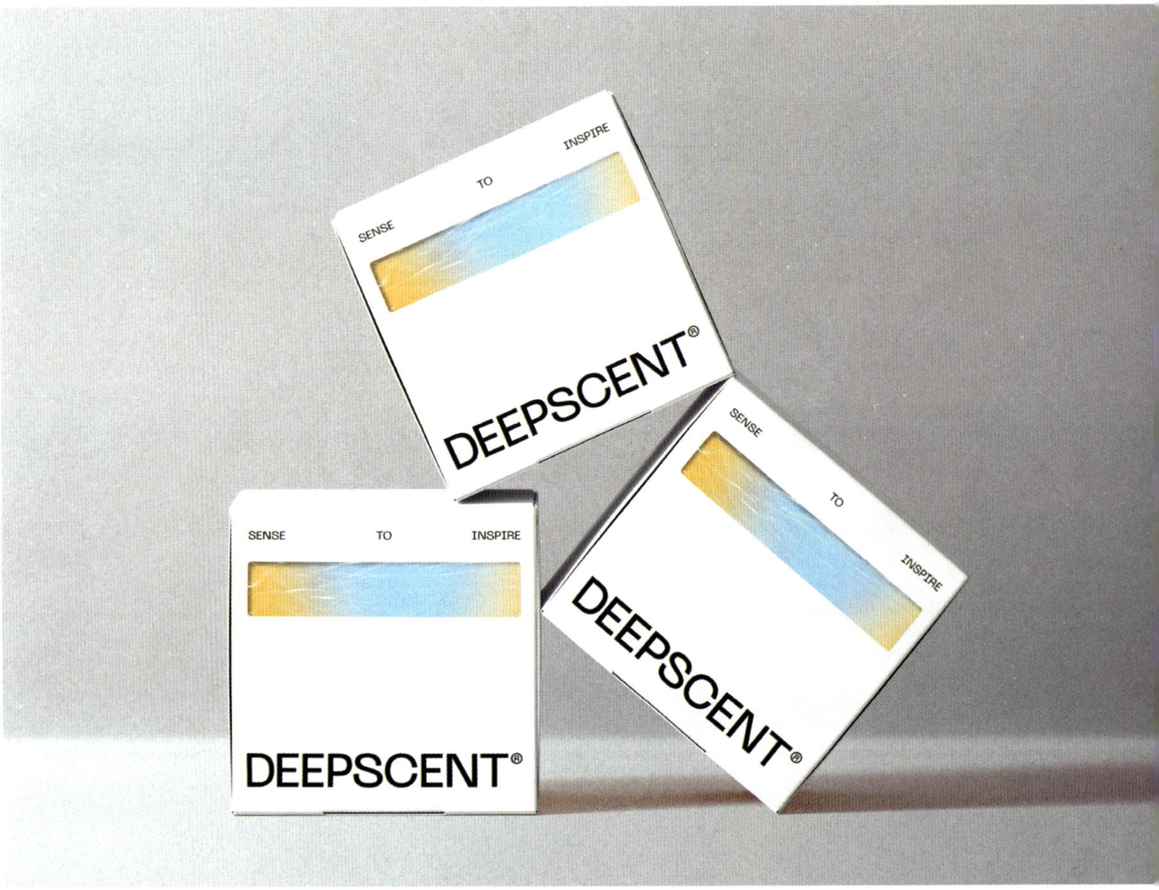

DEEEPSCENT

Deepscent is a Korean company that leads the digital transformation of the fragrance industry. After an in-depth interview with their client, VIW Design redefined their meaning of work, pointing out the exact spot between fragrance and technology, and reset *Deepscent's* values to consolidate their goal, arranging several visual assets to deliver the image and mood to make it more effective to appeal to their users.

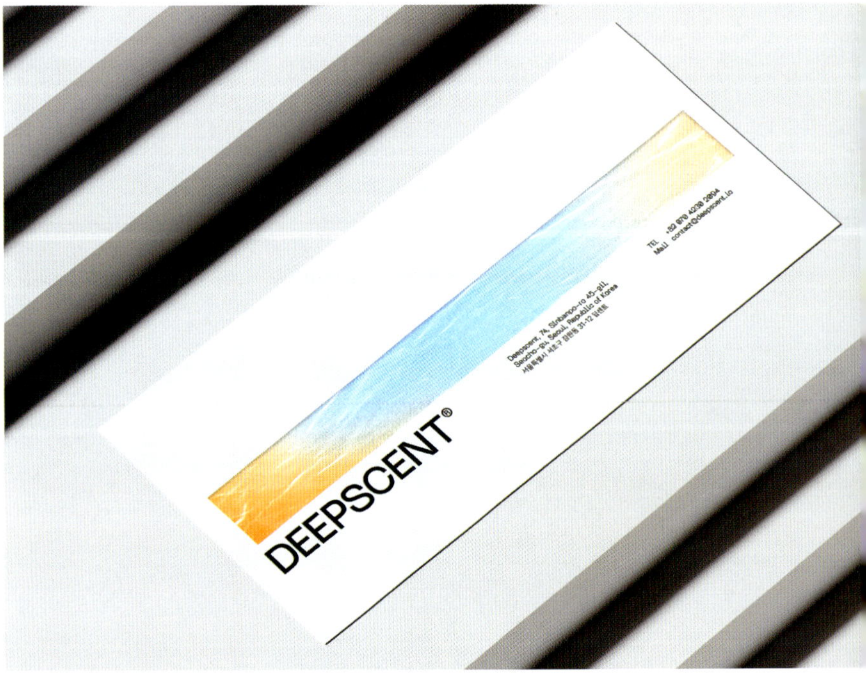

Creative Director
Daniel Kim

BX Designer
Han Gyeol Kim,
Woong Kang

#FFBD4C

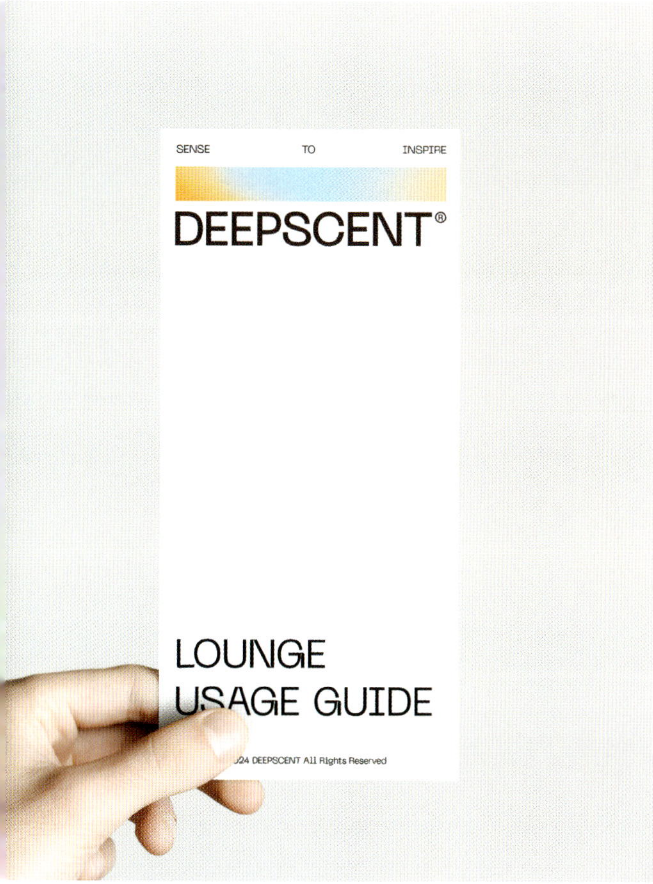
SENSE
TO
INSPIRE
DEEPSCENT®
LOUNGE
USAGE GUIDE
…24 DEEPSCENT All Rights Reserved

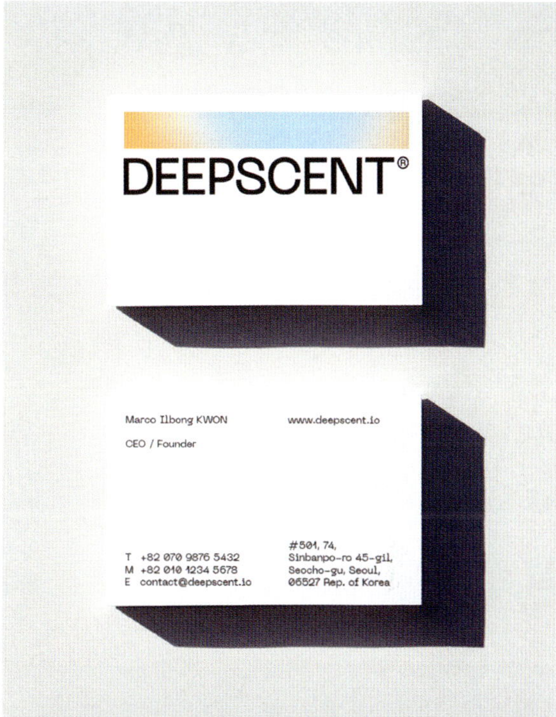
DEEPSCENT®
Marco Ilbong KWON
CEO / Founder
www.deepscent.io
T +82 070 9876 5432
M +82 010 1234 5678
E contact@deepscent.io
#501, 74,
Sinbanpo-ro 45-gil,
Seocho-gu, Seoul,
06527 Rep. of Korea

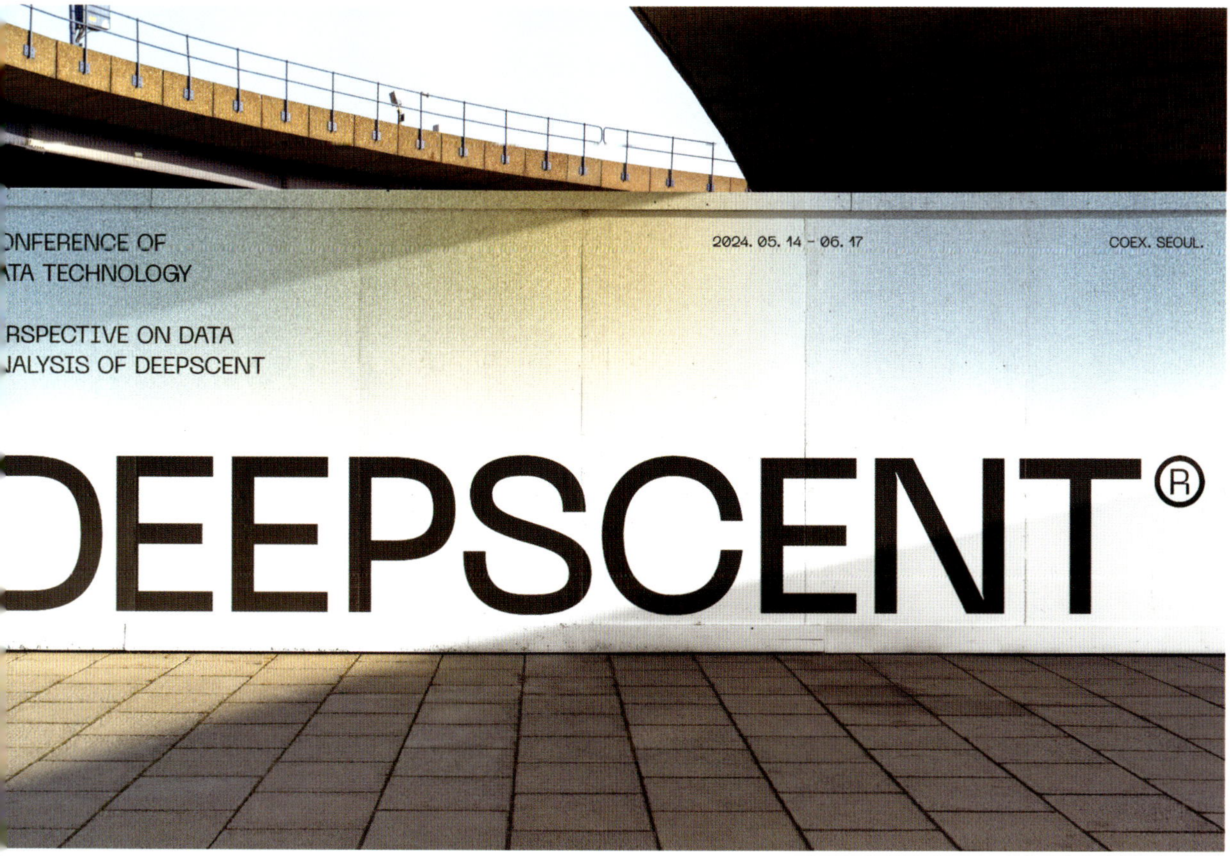
…NFERENCE OF
…TA TECHNOLOGY
…RSPECTIVE ON DATA
…ALYSIS OF DEEPSCENT
2024. 05. 14 - 06. 17
COEX. SEOUL.
…EEPSCENT®

#D4145A
#DA288D
#E03DBF
#E651F2

#D4145A
#DB487F
#E9BACB

#B0D1F6
#5F9CFB
#2C6CFF
#813FAB

#F15A24
#F68118
#FAA70C
#FFCE00

#8CC63F
#B0D741
#D5E844
#9F946

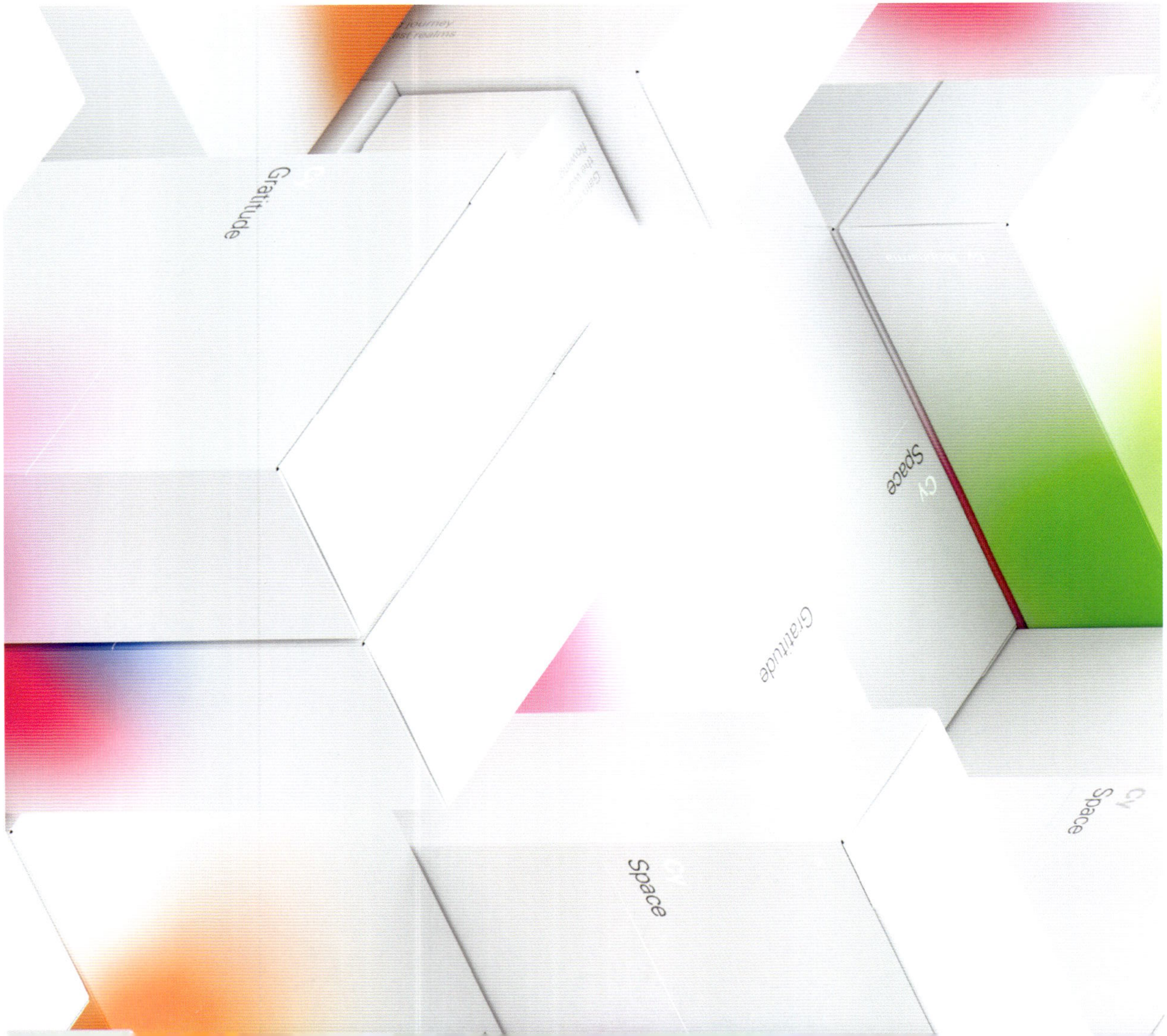

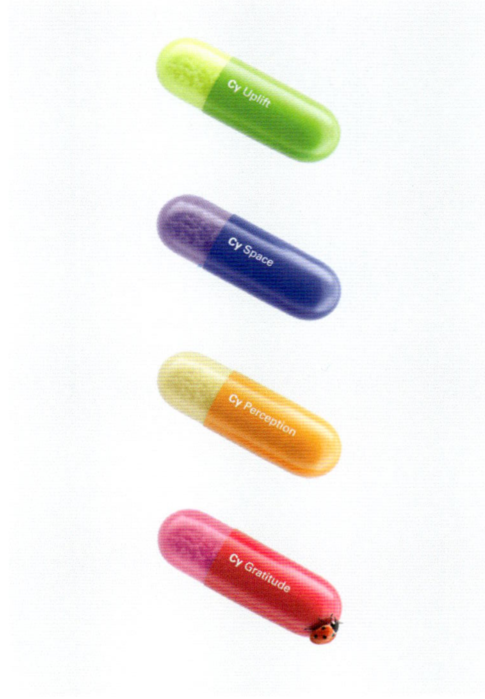

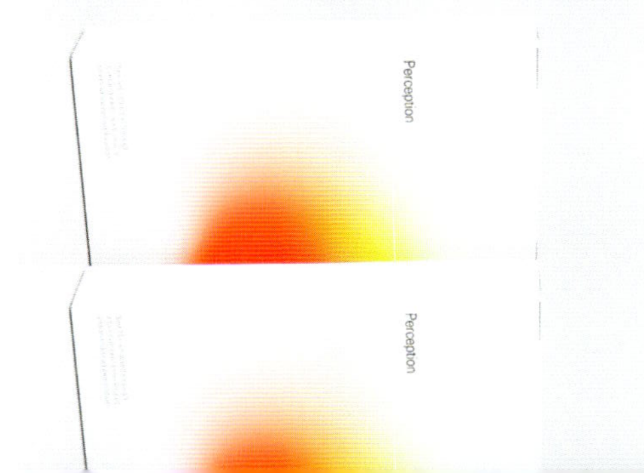

CY BIOPHARMA

Cy Biopharma develops breakthrough drug therapies for treating chronic pain. Vibrantly fuzzy, neon-tinged, amorphous shapes are grounded by Swiss design grids and sharp, clean typography. Colourful and serene nature imagery echoes *Cy's* vision—"working with nature to enhance nature".

The website design reflects the scientific and transcendental qualities of the *Cy* brand. Swirling gradients invite visitors to scroll and explore. Generous space throughout fosters a sense of freedom and openness.

Executive Creative Director
Casey Martin

Creative Director
Kyle Lee Beck
& Mathew Foster

Operations Director
Lindsay McMenamin

Design Director
Kelly Scheurich,
Ellis Latham-Brown,
Rosie Manning
& Owen Cramp

Senior Interaction Designer
Jaime Patino-Calvo

Senior Designers
Simon Blackensee
& Claire Whitman

Designer
Chandler Reed
& Dylan Wells

3D Artist
Marcio Flausino

Motion Designer
David Kopidlansky
& Xiaoxue Meng

Copywriter
David Schermer

Web Developers
Ottofeller

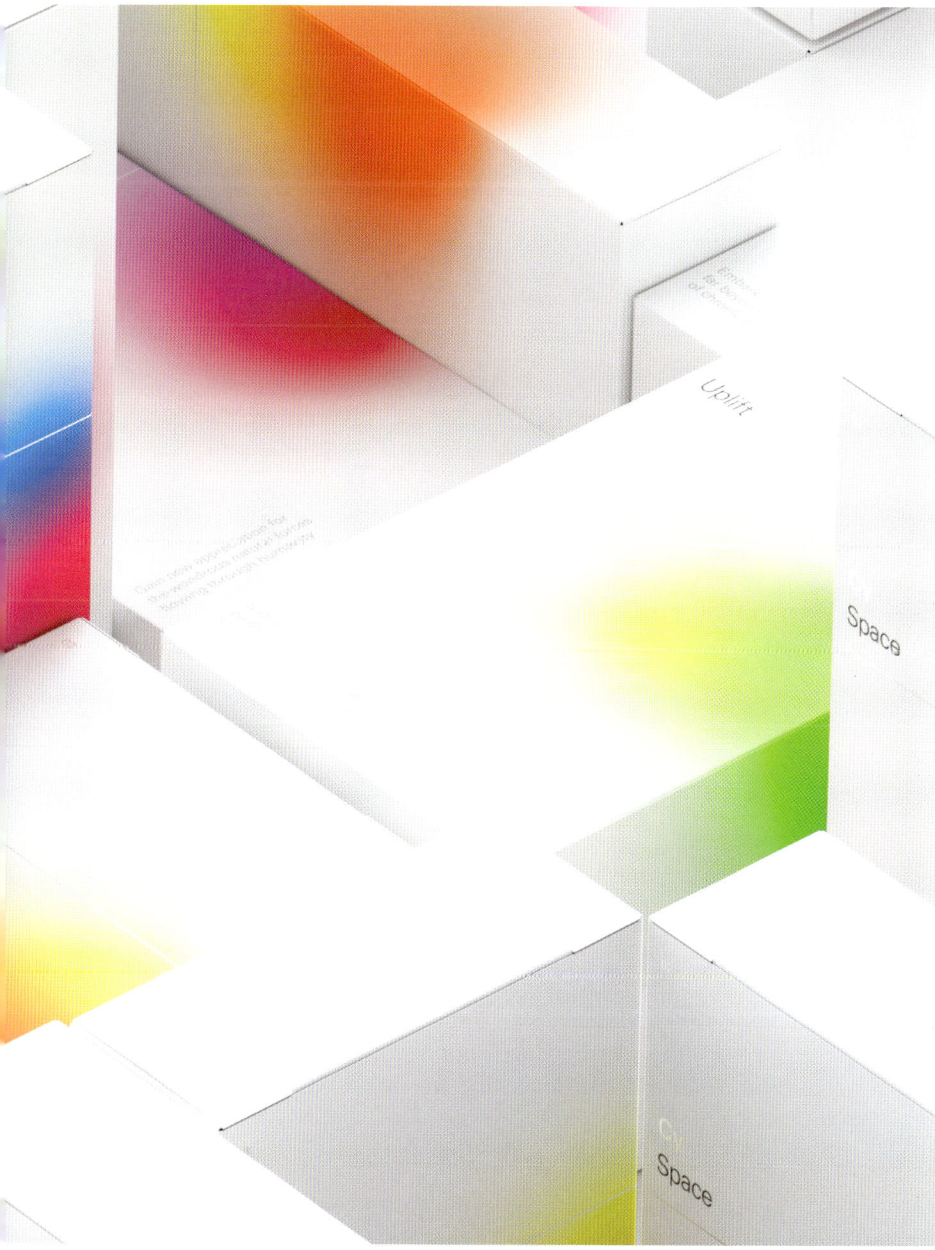

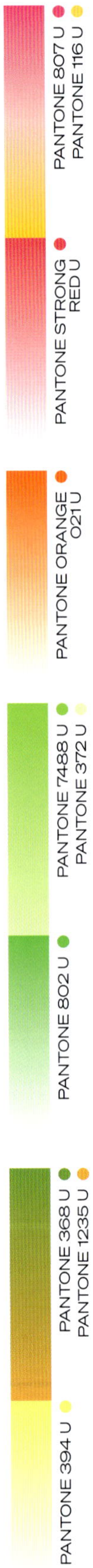

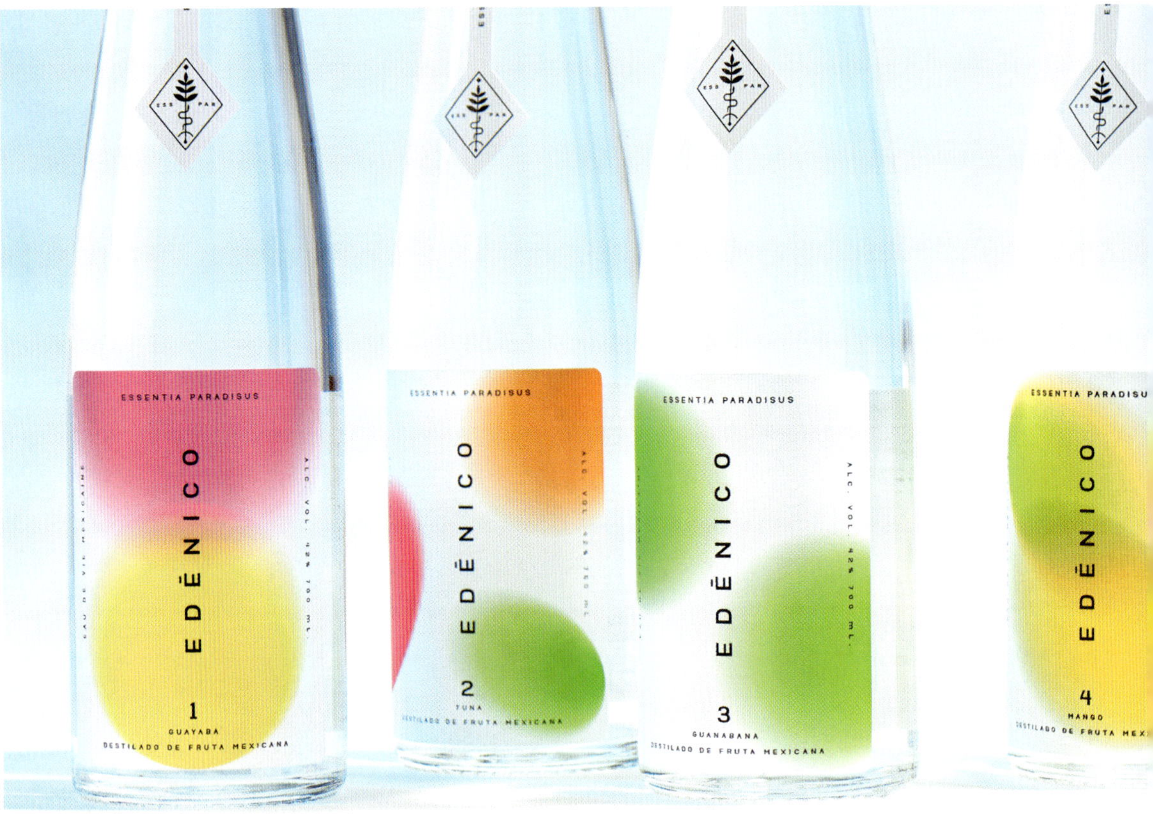

EDÉNICO

Edénico is a distilled spirit that unites the European tradition of "Eau de Vie" and the diversity of Mexican fruits. The brand takes inspiration from the story of Eden and its richness of fruits and vegetation, while the symbol takes elements of this and shows them in an abstract way. A set of labels were designed to represent through bright colours and ethereal forms each one of the fruits that make up the *Edénico* collection. The packaging label represents the main idea of distillation: to take the purest part of something and transform it while preserving its essence.

Design Studio
Monograf Studio

Creative Director
Ramsés Lecourtois

Photographer
Liliana Barraza

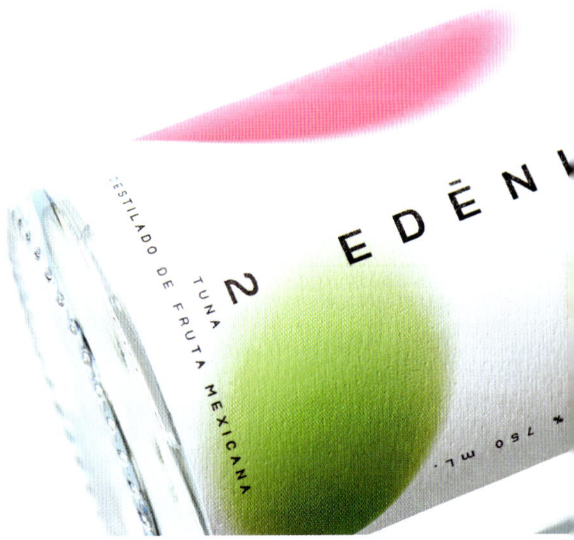

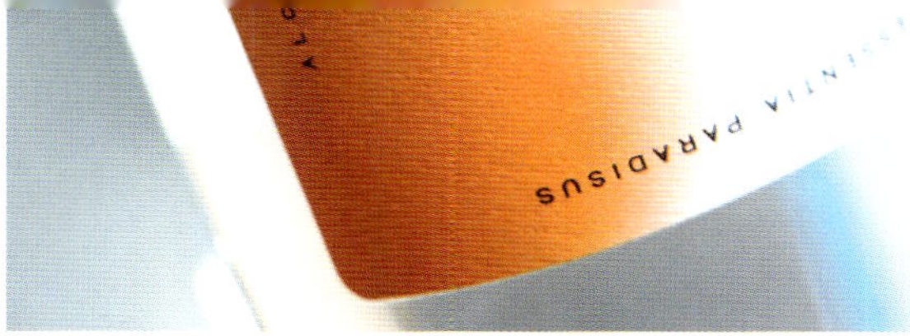
ESSENTIA PARADISUS

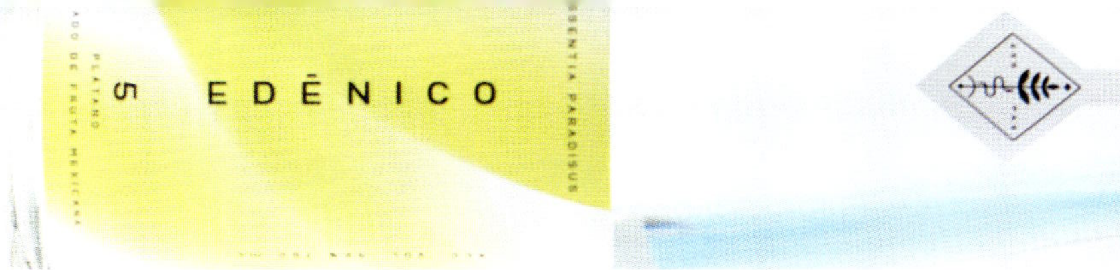
ESSENTIA PARADISUS
EDĒNICO
5
PLATANO

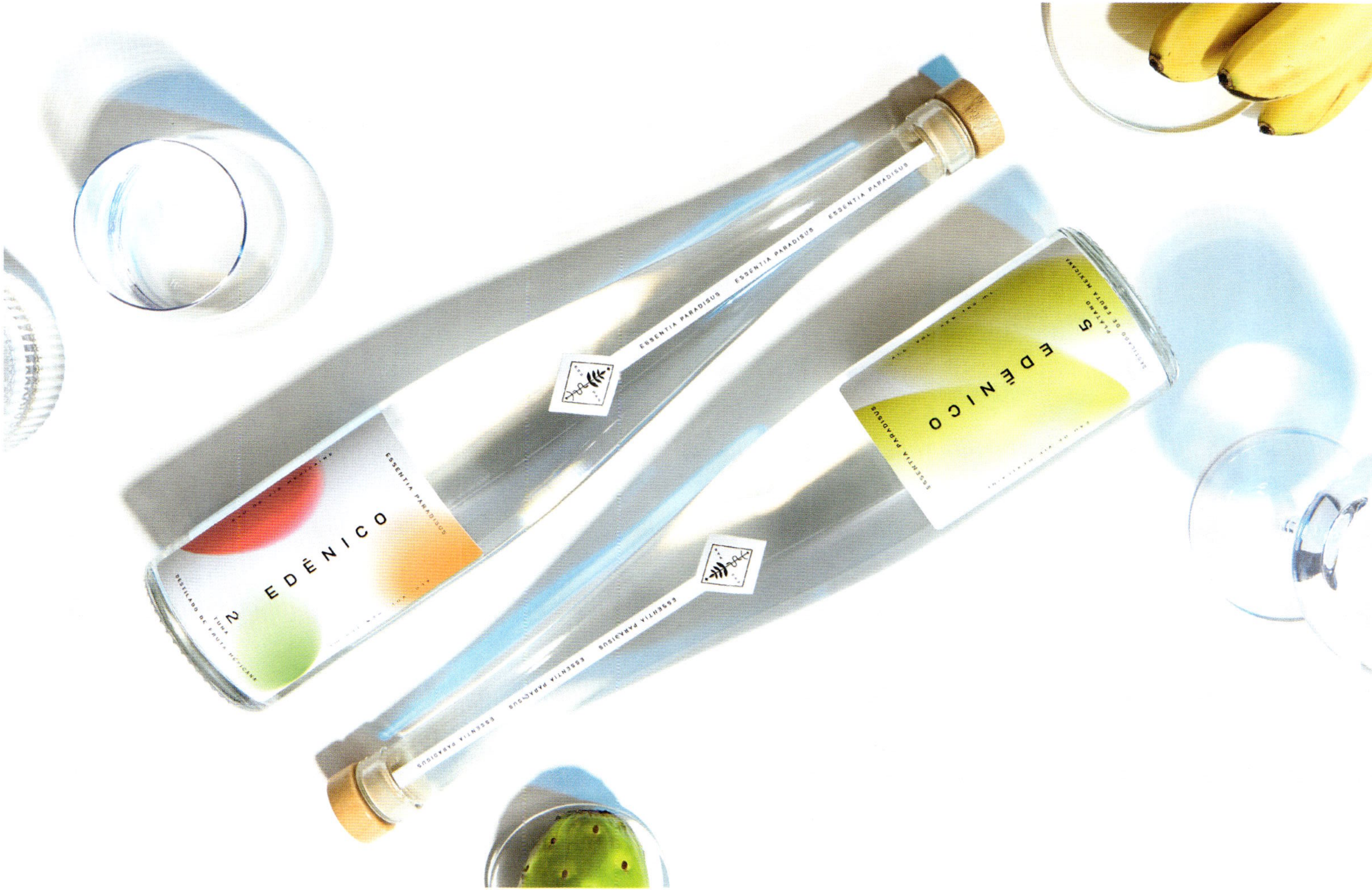
EDĒNICO
2
ESSENTIA PARADISUS
EDĒNICO
5
ESSENTIA PARADISUS

C47 · M0 · Y18 · K0

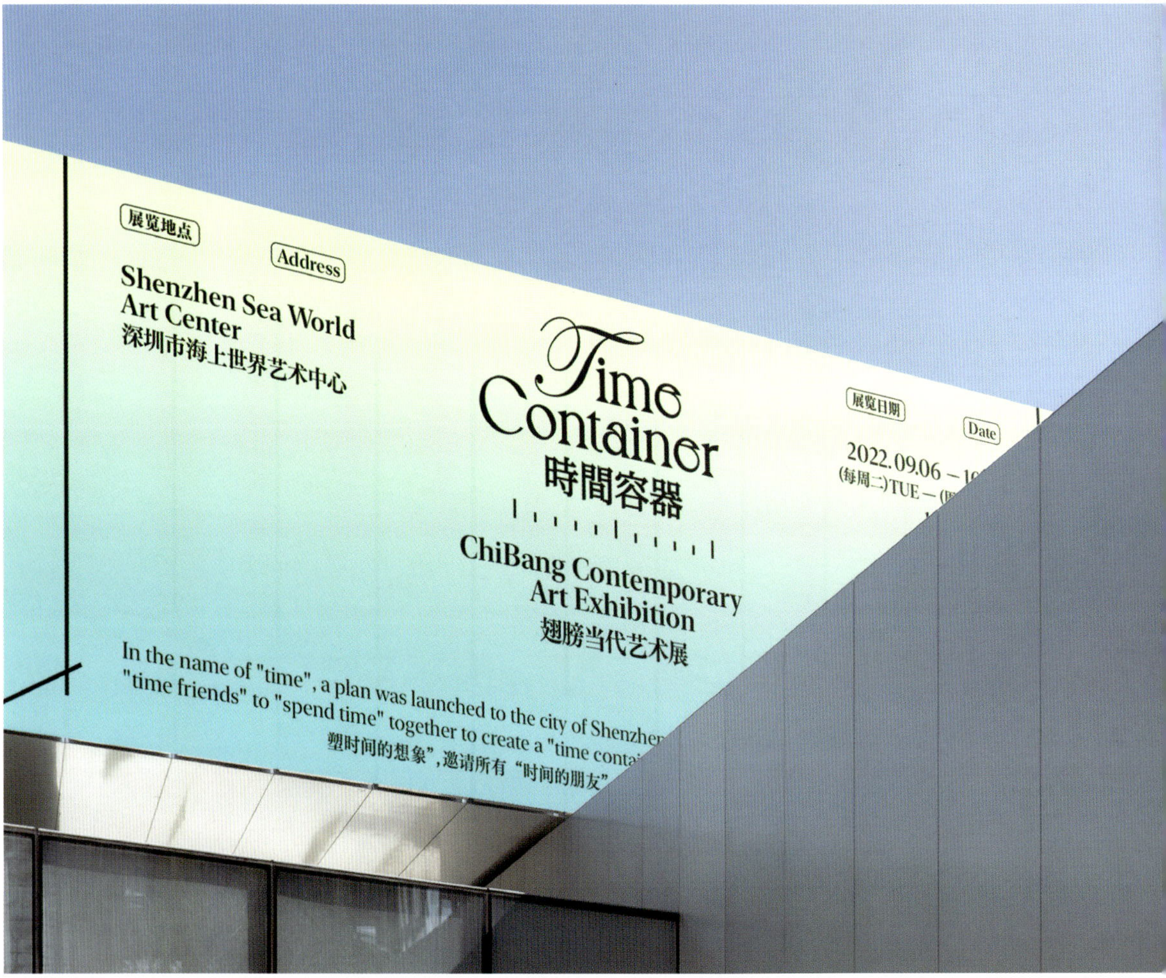

TIME CONTAINER

In the name of "time", a campaign was launched for the city of Shenzhen: "Reshape the imagination of time", inviting all "time friends" to "spend time" together and create a "time container". Considering the structure of analogue clock hands, they respectively set exhibition opening and finishing time as cyan and yellow to display time even without numbers.

When the two colour blend together, they have a nice gradient colour palette to express the spirit of *Time Container* in an abstract way.

Art Director
Jackie Price

Design Studio
CB Design

Lead Designer
BBlue CCat

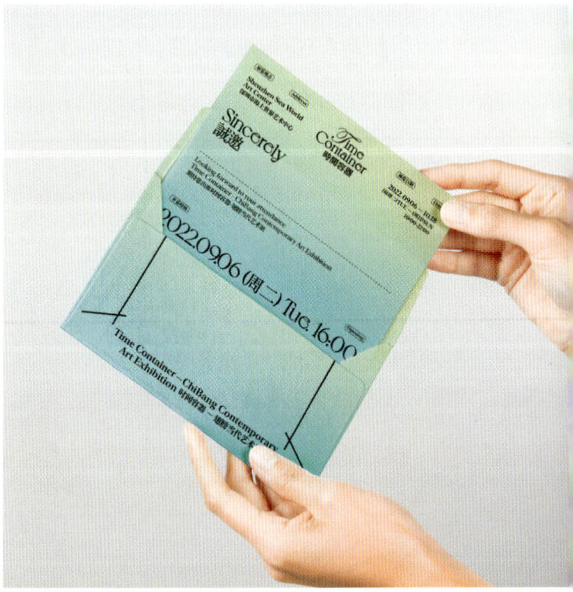

C12 · M0 · Y29 · K0

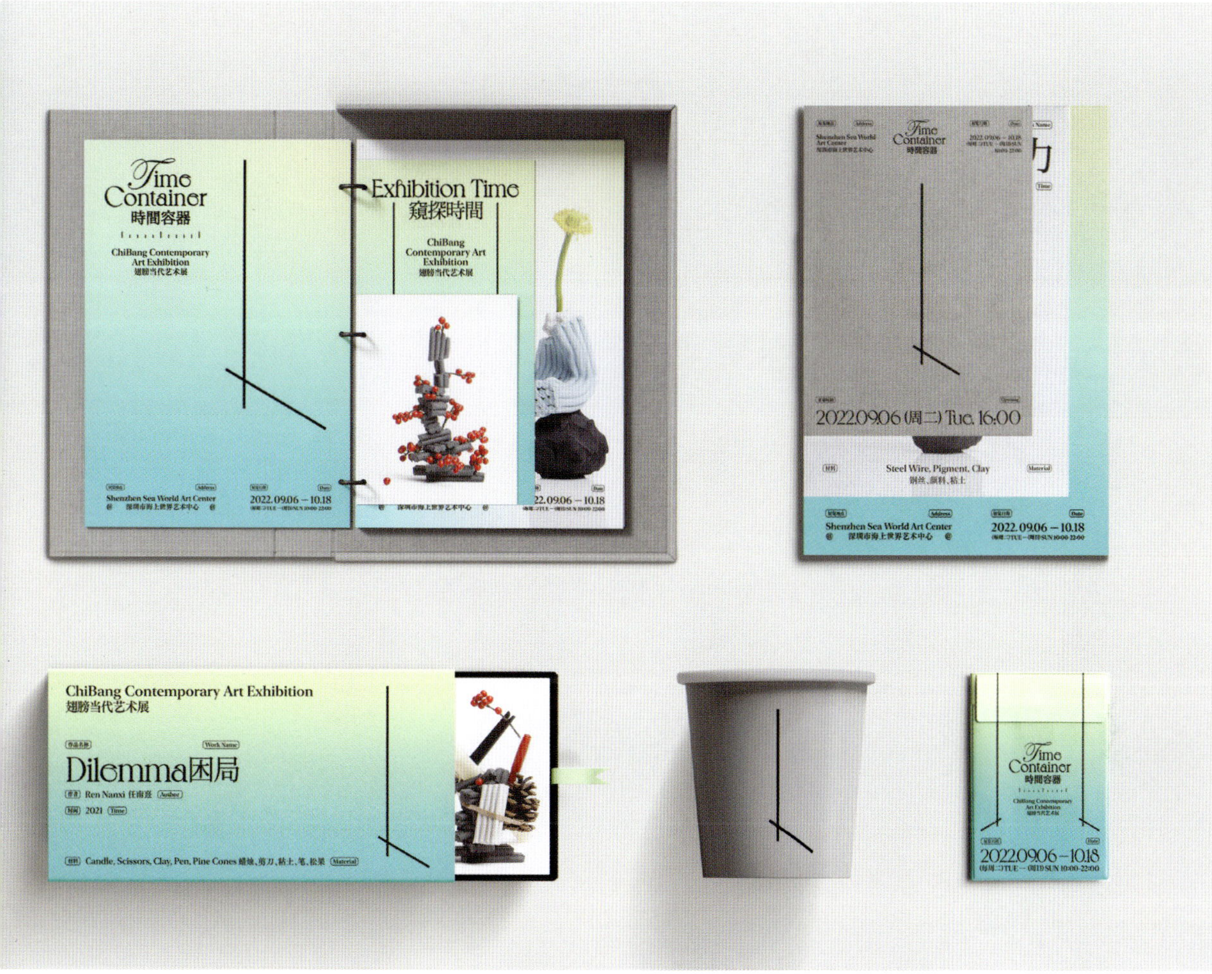

Time Container 時間容器
ChiBang Contemporary Art Exhibition 翅膀当代艺术展
Exhibition Time 窺探時間
Shenzhen Sea World Art Center 深圳市海上世界艺术中心
2022.09.06 – 10.18
2022.09.06 (周二) Tue. 16:00
Steel Wire, Pigment, Clay 钢丝、颜料、粘土
Dilemma困局
Ren Nanxi 任南熙
2021
Candle, Scissors, Clay, Pen, Pine Cones 蜡烛、剪刀、粘土、笔、松果

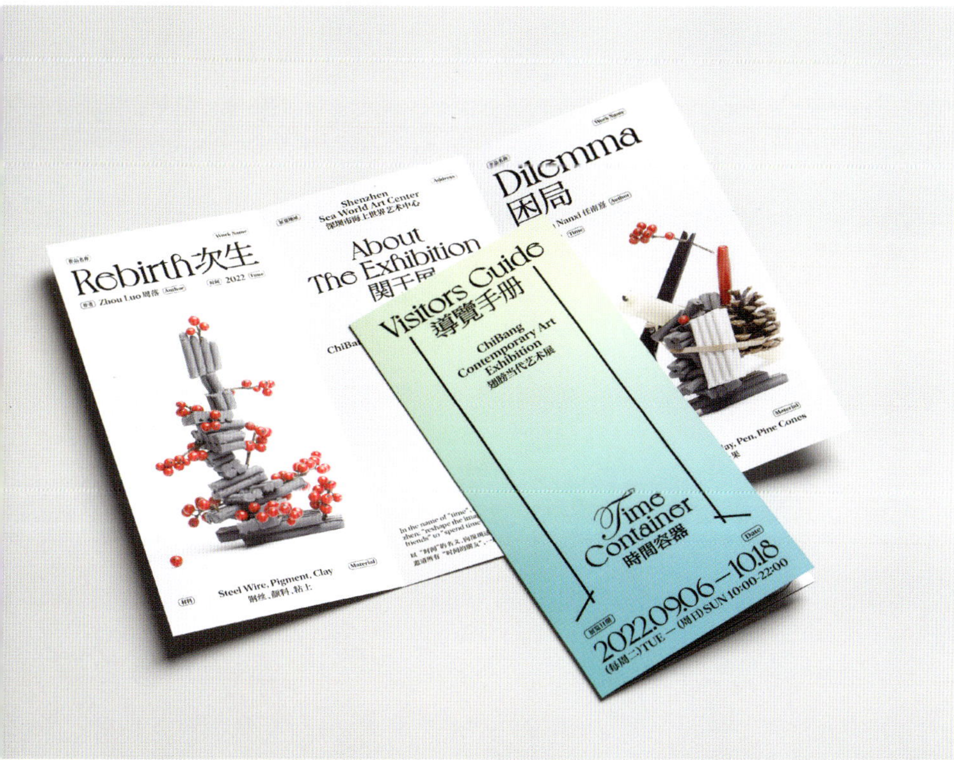

Rebirth次生
2022
Shenzhen Sea World Art Center 深圳市海上世界艺术中心
About The Exhibition
Dilemma 困局
Visitors Guide 導覽手冊
ChiBang Contemporary Art Exhibition 翅膀当代艺术展
Steel Wire, Pigment, Clay 钢丝、颜料、粘土
Time Container 時間容器
2022.09.06–10.18
(每周二)TUE – (周日)SUN 10:00-22:00

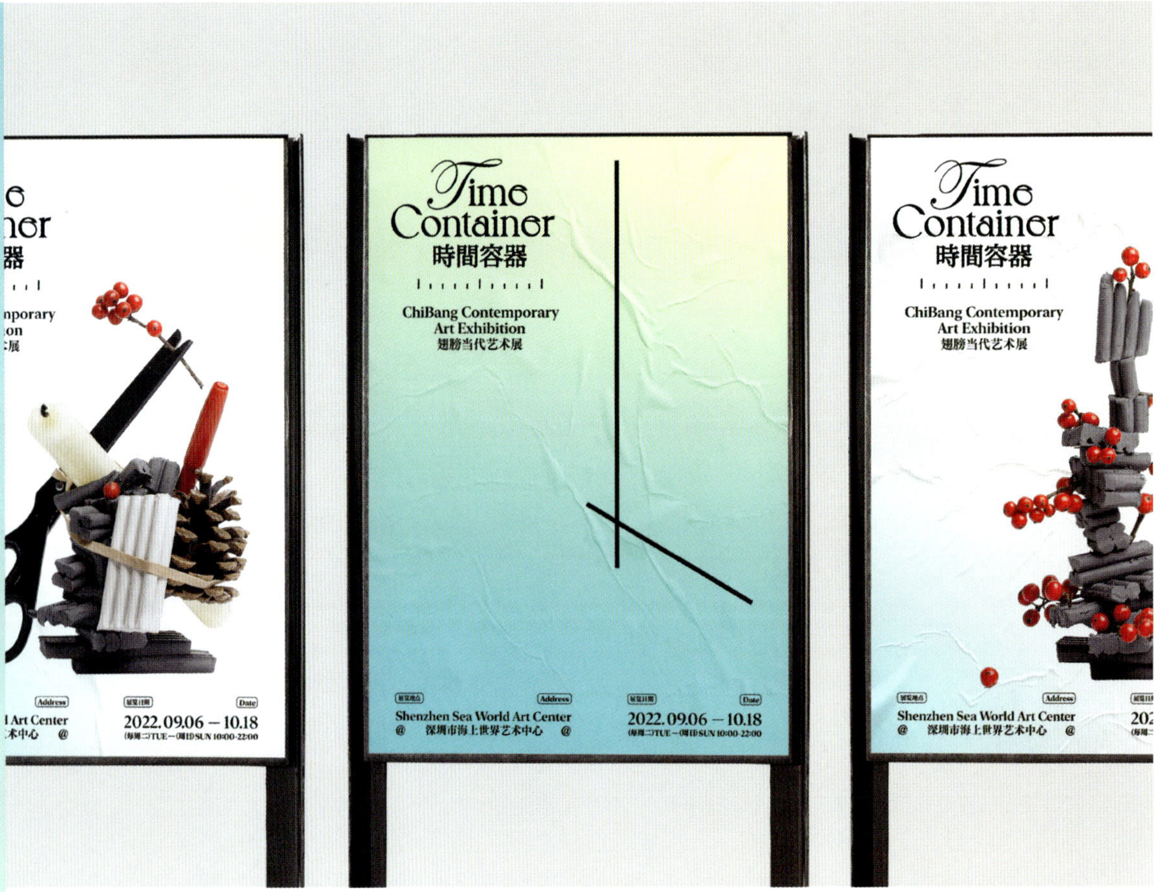
Time
Container
時間容器
ChiBang Contemporary
Art Exhibition
翅膀当代艺术展
Address
Shenzhen Sea World Art Center
深圳市海上世界艺术中心
Date
2022.09.06 – 10.18

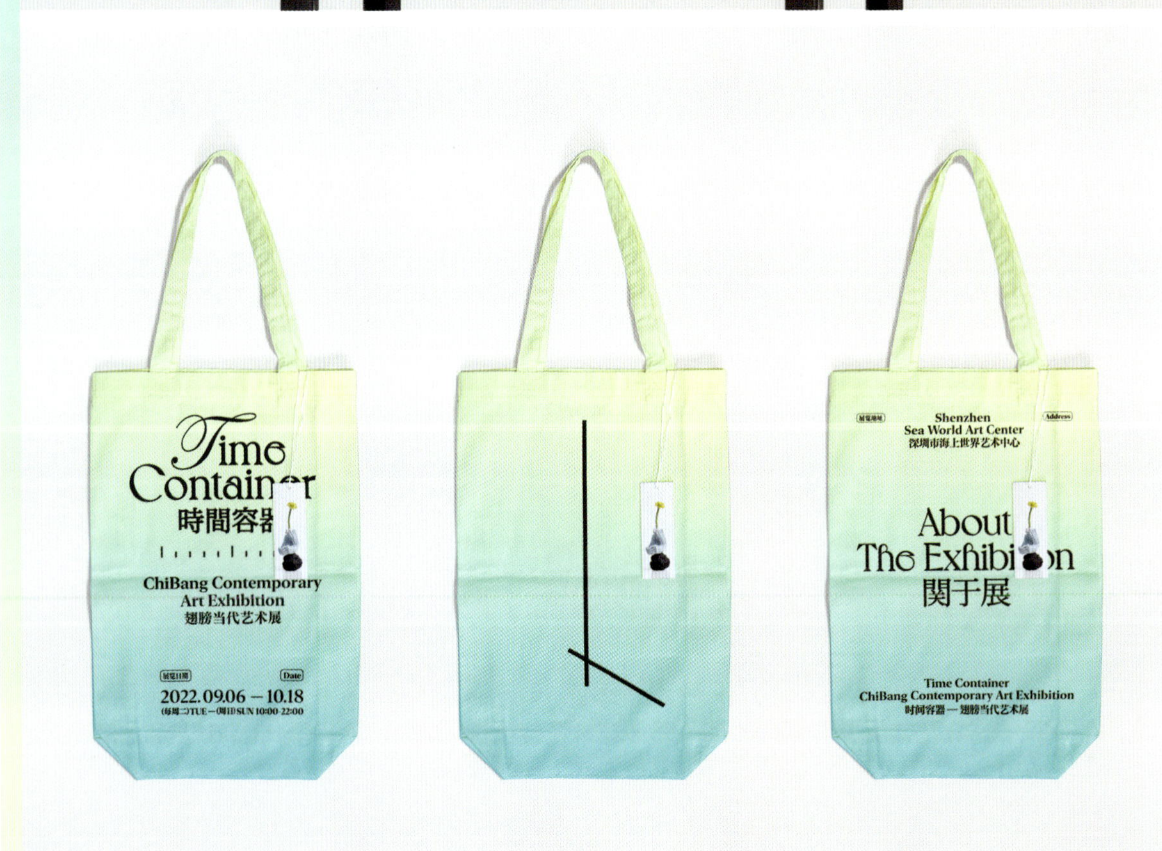
Time
Container
時間容器
ChiBang Contemporary
Art Exhibition
翅膀当代艺术展
Date
2022.09.06 – 10.18
Address
Shenzhen
Sea World Art Center
深圳市海上世界艺术中心
About
The Exhibition
関于展
Time Container
ChiBang Contemporary Art Exhibition
时间容器 — 翅膀当代艺术展

Time Container
時間容器

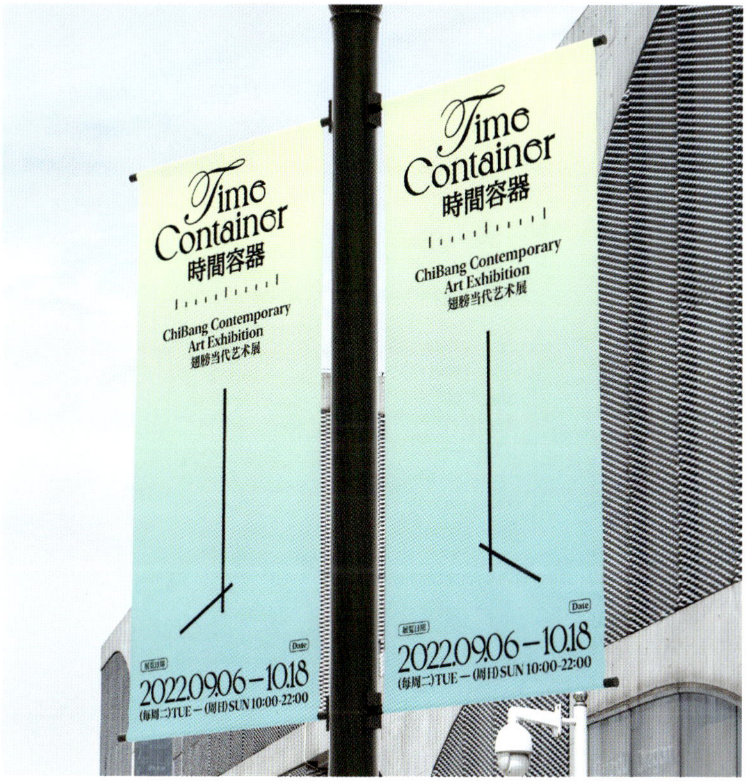
Time Container
時間容器
ChiBang Contemporary Art Exhibition
翅膀当代艺术展
Date
2022.09.06 – 10.18
(每周二)TUE – (周日)SUN 10:00-22:00

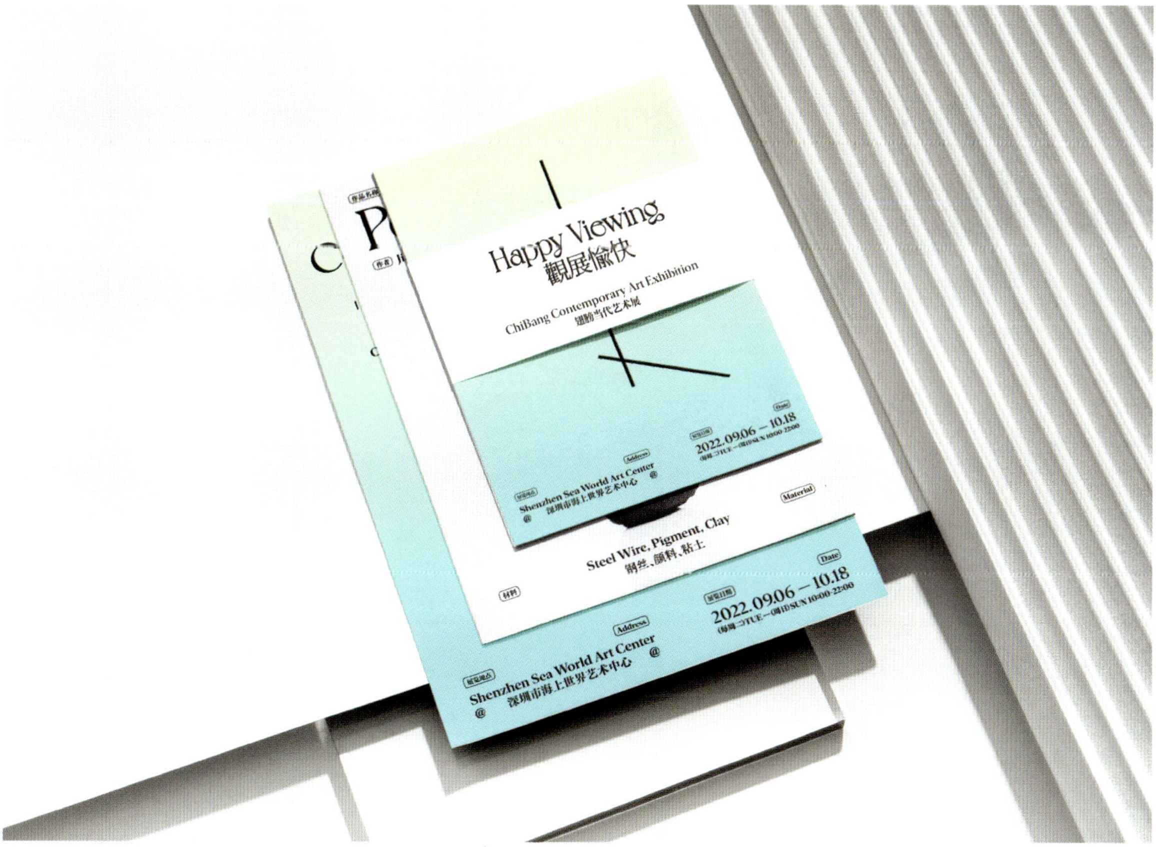
Happy Viewing
觀展愉快
ChiBang Contemporary Art Exhibition
翅膀当代艺术展
Date
2022.09.06 – 10.18
Address
Shenzhen Sea World Art Center
深圳市海上世界艺术中心
Material
Steel Wire, Pigment, Clay
钢丝、颜料、粘土

C46 · M0 · Y100 · K0
C18 · M0 · Y30 · K0

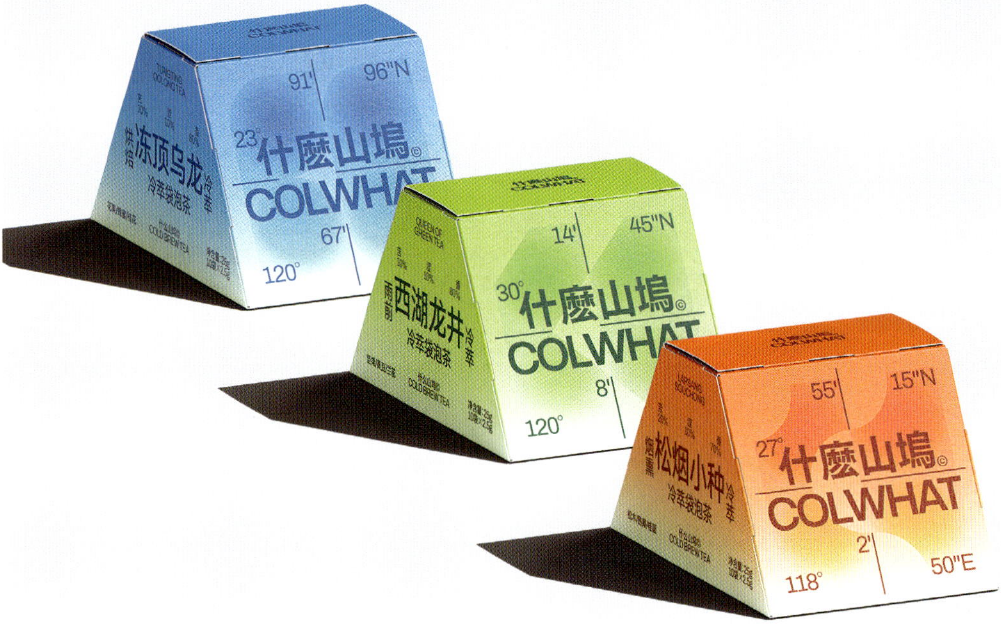

C0 · M70 · Y92 · K0
C18 · M0 · Y30 · K0

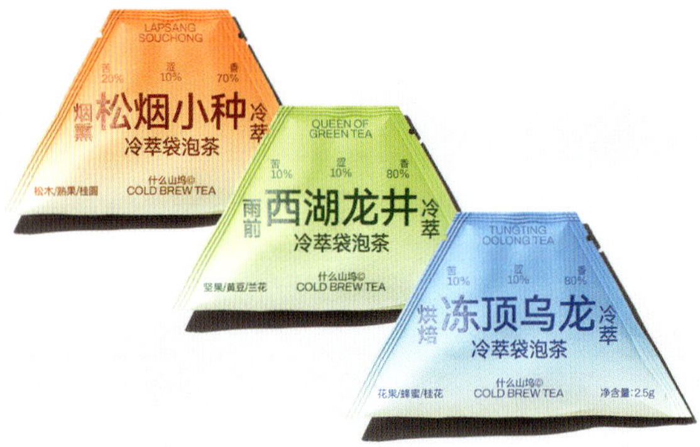

C76 · M19 · Y0 · K0
C18 · M0 · Y30 · K0

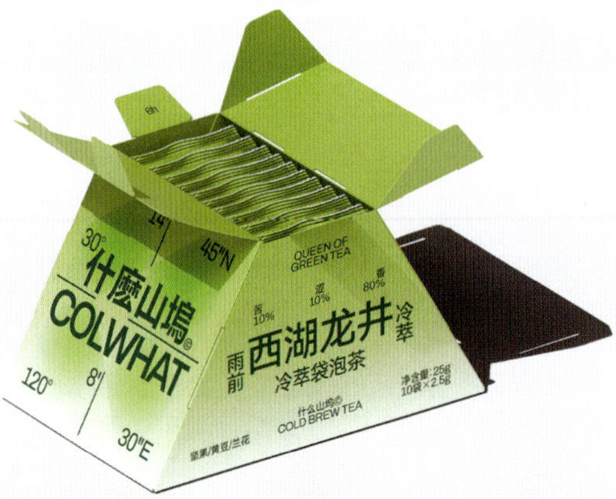

COLWHAT

Colwhat hopes to provide a rich and relaxed user experience while retaining the stability of Eastern tea drinks. Sort out the scenery of the gradually change of the sky colour in the tea mountain, making colour gradually change the core of the brand's visual recognition. Through the application of colour, the audience can quickly identify different flavours and characteristics of the product.

Art Director
Yann

Designer
Xu Ye

Design Studio
TWOPTWO Design

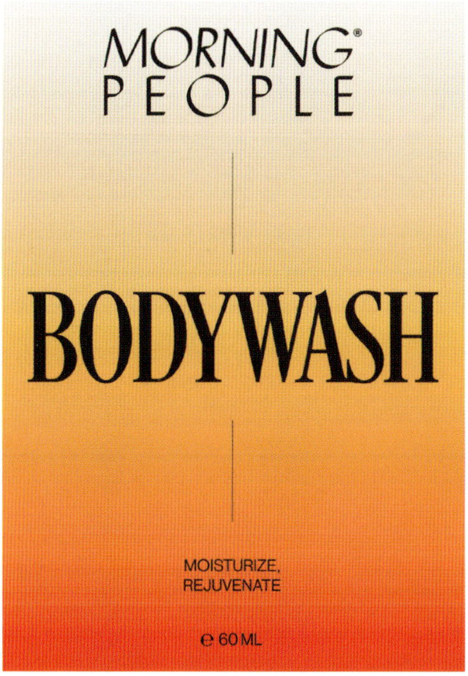

MORNING PEOPLE

Morning People is a clean, sustainable, cruelty-free skincare brand for all humankind, born out of Jasmyn Wilkins' vision to inspire people to find their peace and happiness through something as simple as a self-care routine. Mariam created a bold and minimalistic typographic logo and an equally strong submark that can be used along with it. Through the typographic logo-submark pair, Mariam aimed for a mix of elegance, boldness, and relatability, conveying the idea that *Morning People* is a brand that truly sees and understands its audience.

Designer
Mariam Khalifah

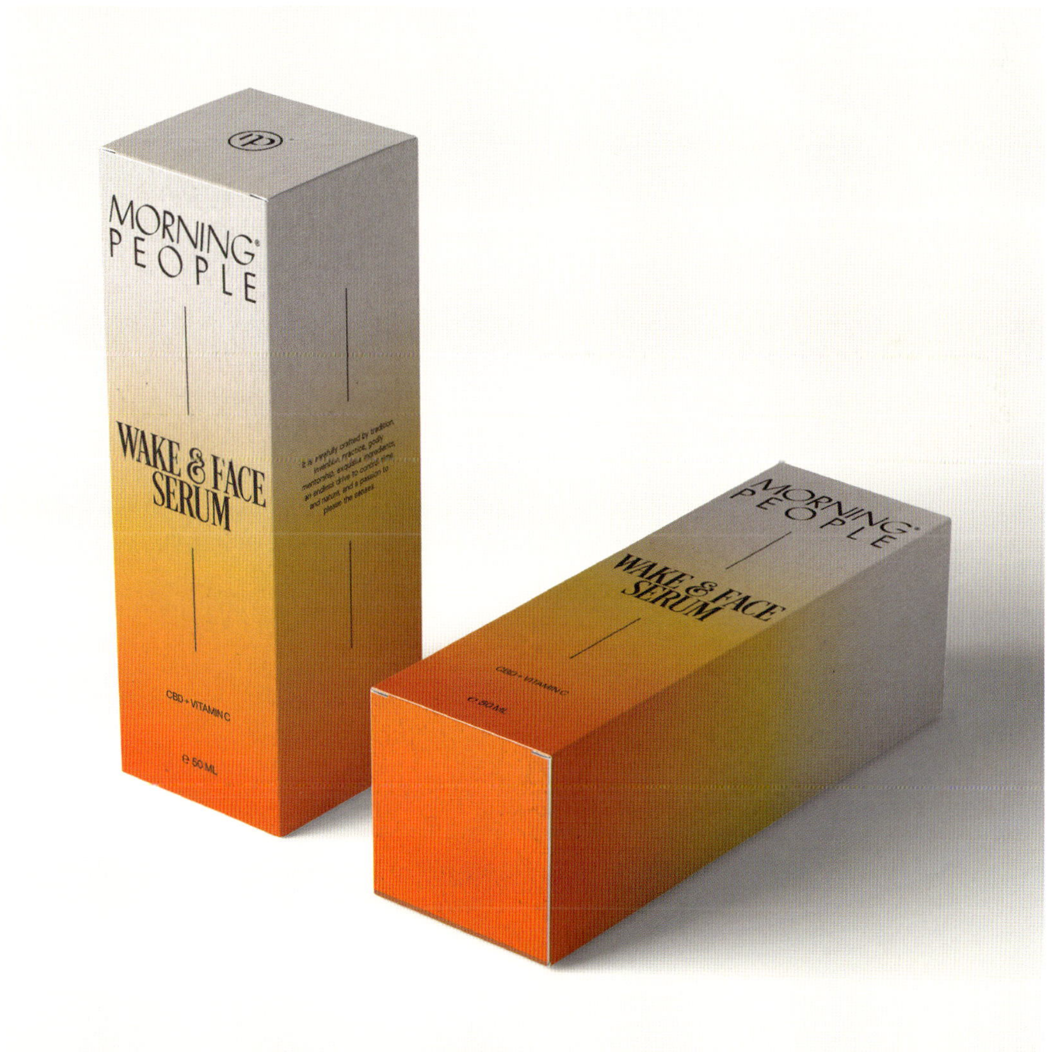

PANTONE 143 C

PANTONE 172 C

C0 · M80 · Y90 · K0

C0 · M30 · Y80 · K0

C0 · M90 · Y50 · K0

C0 · M70 · Y30 · K0

C80 · M50 · Y0 · K0

C70 · M10 · Y0 · K0

SUNRISE-THE SCIENTIST COFFEE

Sunrise is the theme of *The Scientist Coffee*'s new year season, aiming to bid farewell to the difficult 2020 and meet the hopeful 2021. The visual identity design of this season starts from the gradient colour echoing the sunrise, with the intention to arouse the consumer's awareness to resonate with beautiful and hopeful colour forms.

Creative Director & Art Director
Alex

Designer
Alex & Karo

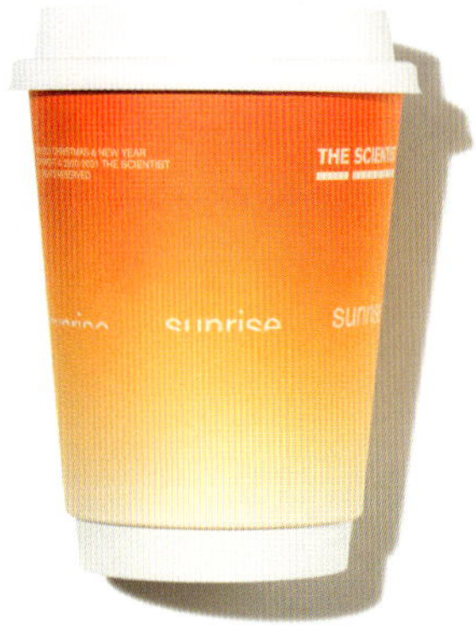

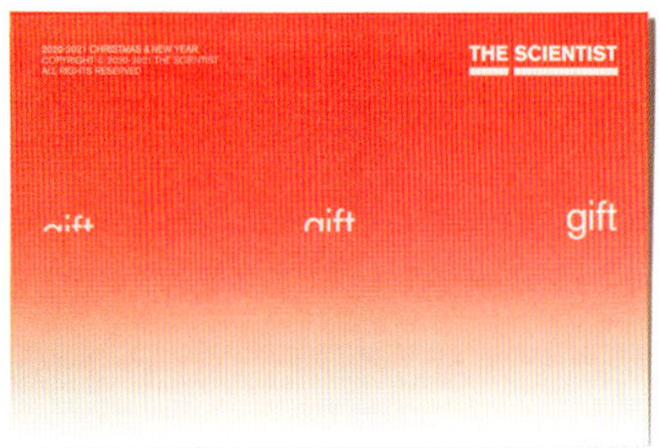

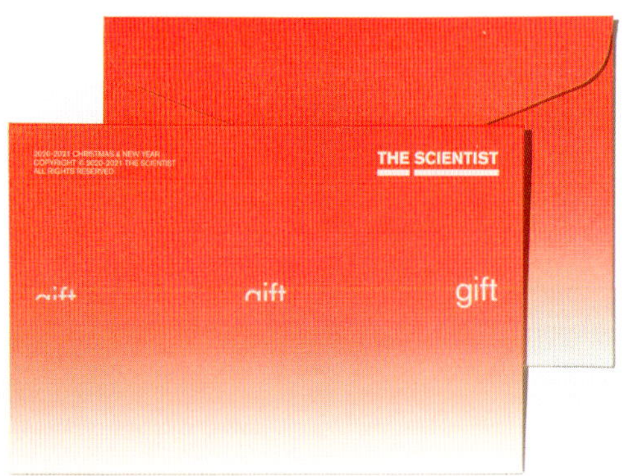

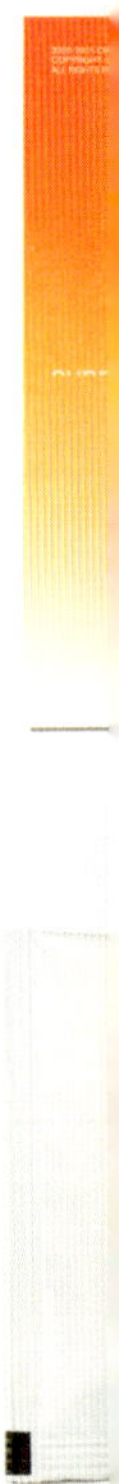

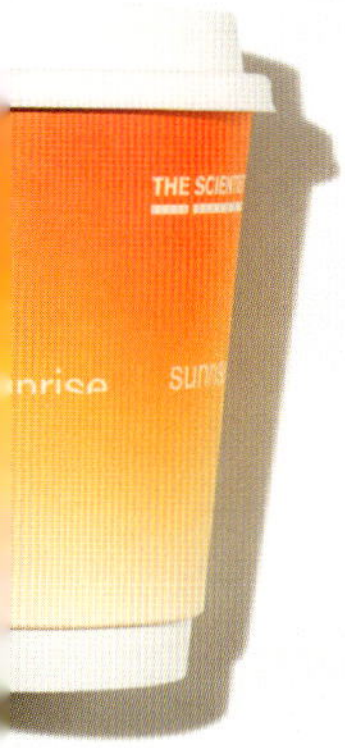

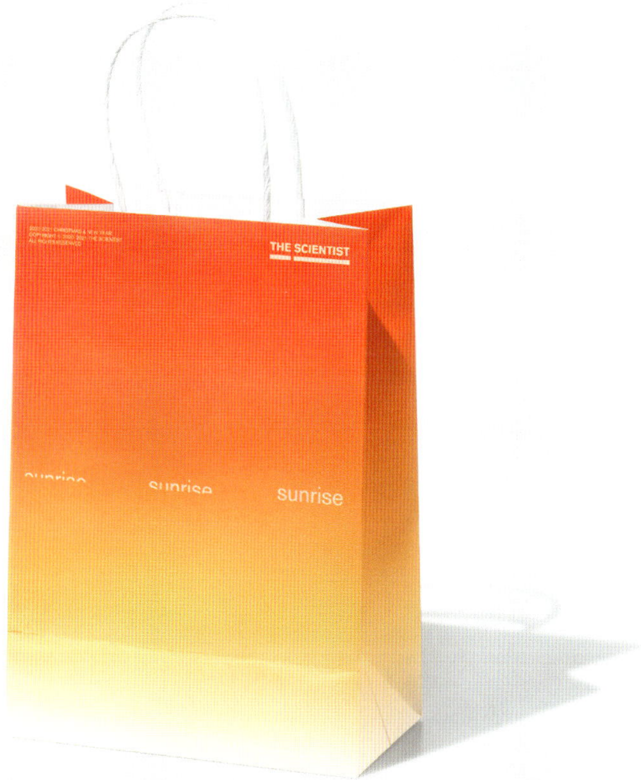
THE SCIENTIST
sunrise

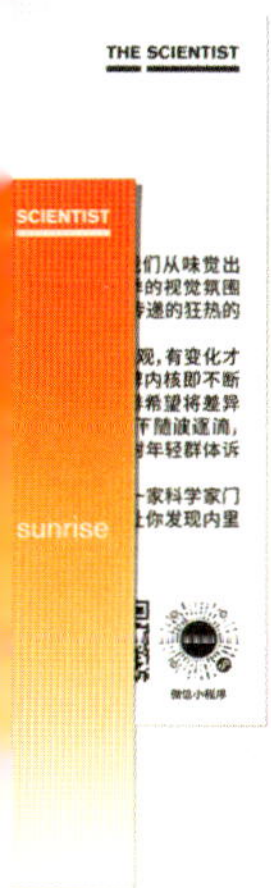
THE SCIENTIST
sunrise

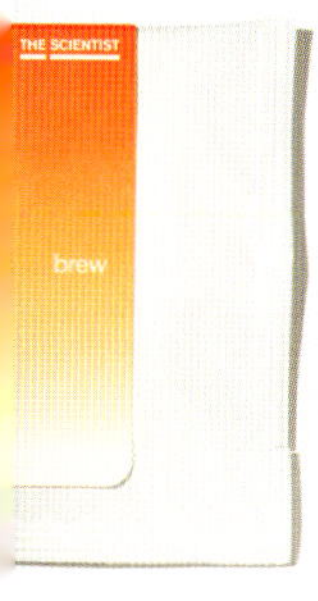
THE SCIENTIST
brew

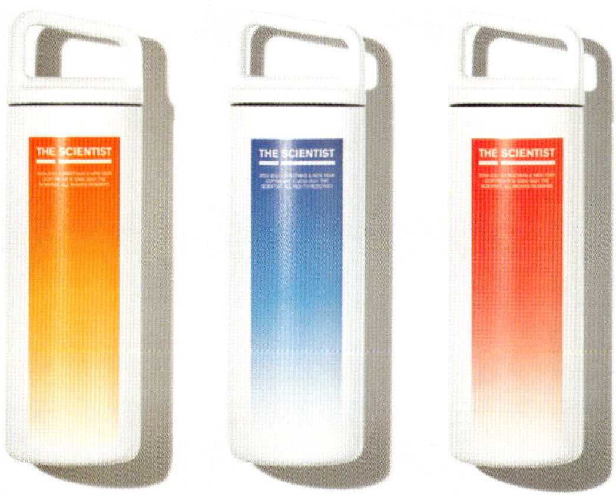
THE SCIENTIST
THE SCIENTIST
THE SCIENTIST

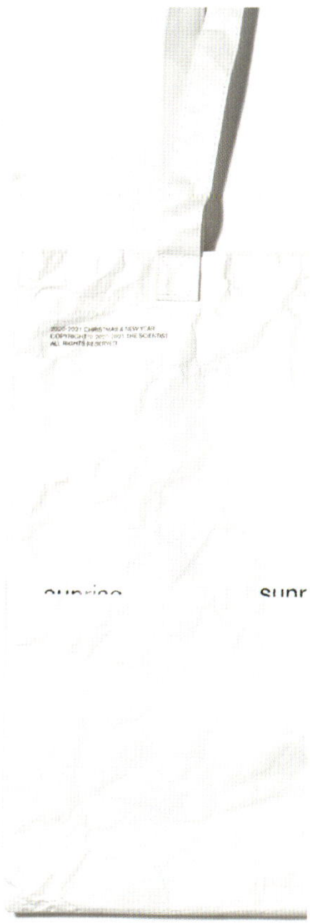

(IN)DESIGN

Graphic design manual made for the Hochschule der Künste Bern, Switzerland. Printed in risography and bound in Druckatelier.

Designer
Anaïs Vidal (anaisvidal.ch), Mattia Marchese (mattiamarchese.com) & Irini Gleglakou (irinigleglakou.ch)

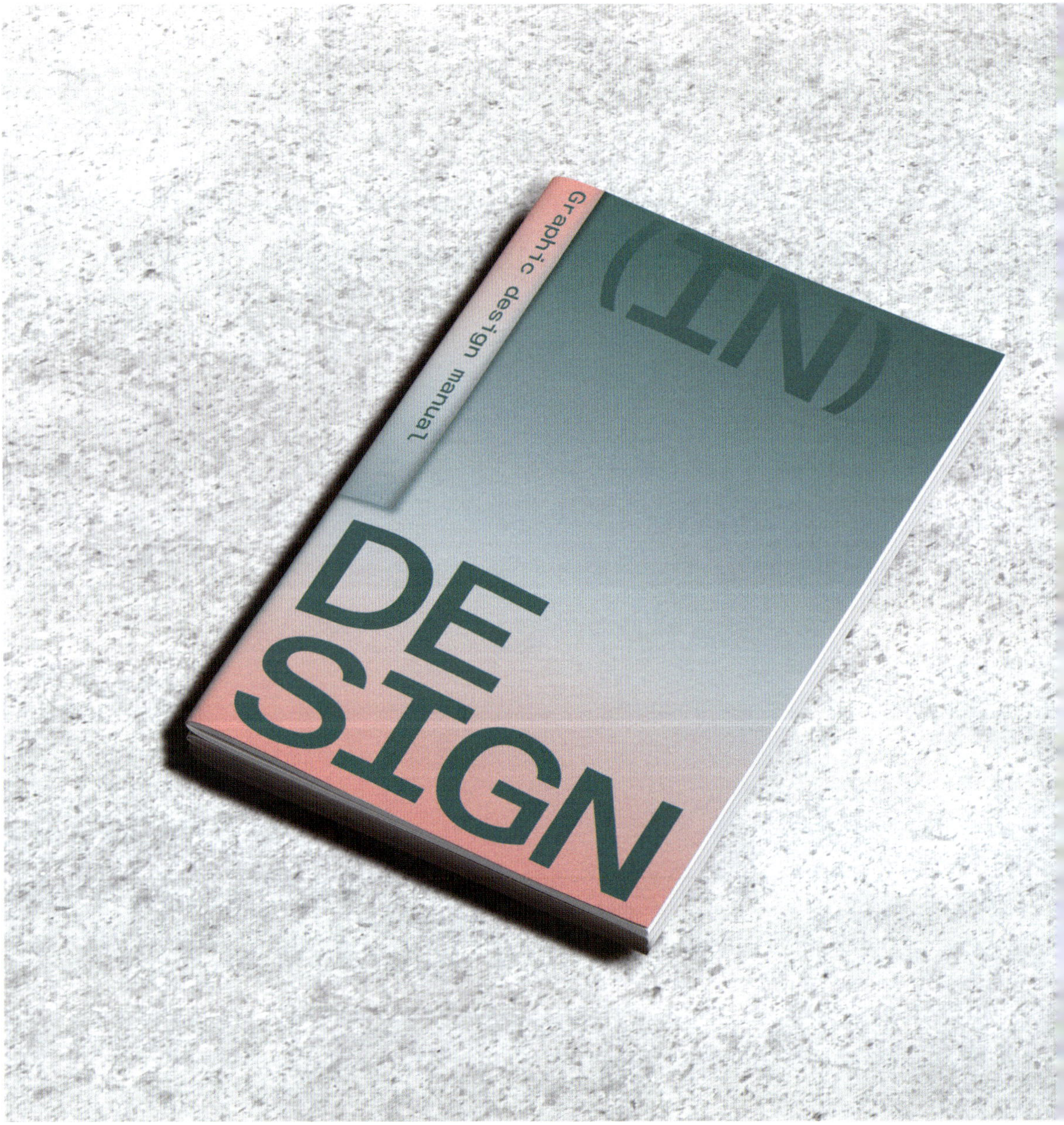

#00838A

#FCAE5F

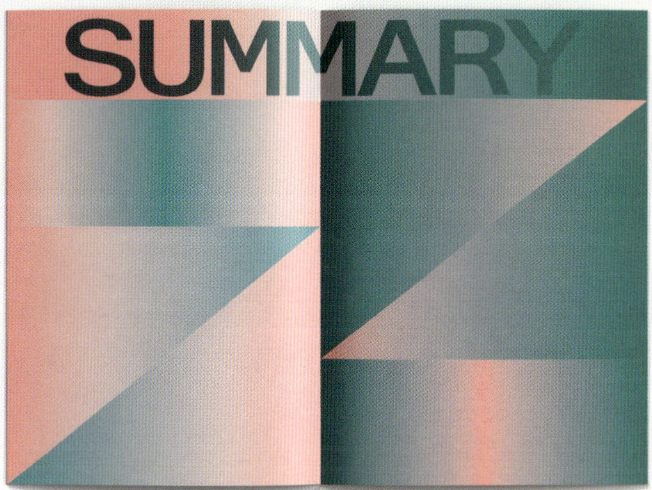
SUMMARY

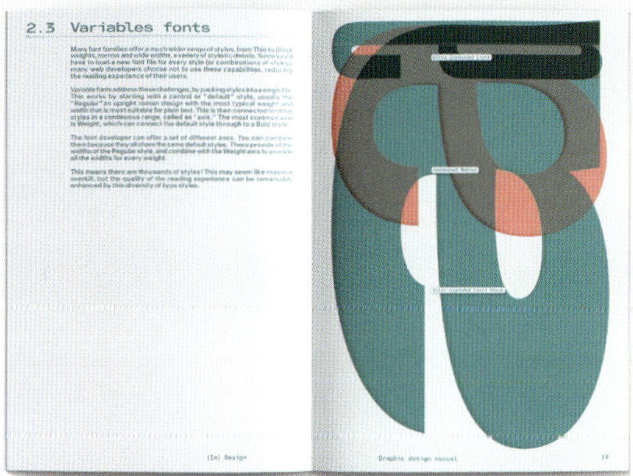
2.3 Variables fonts
(In) Design
Graphic design manual

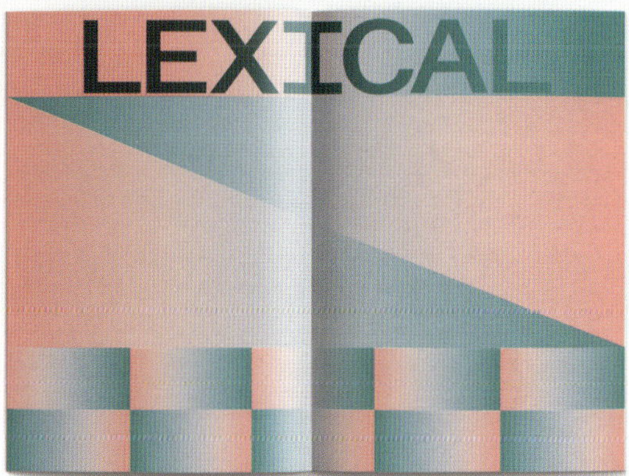
LEXICAL

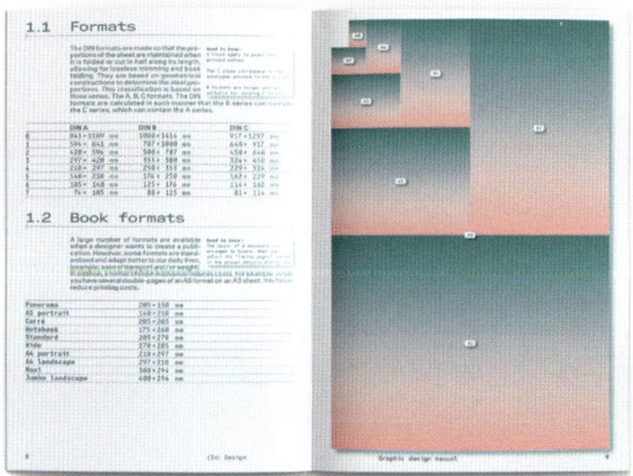
1.1 Formats
1.2 Book formats
(In) Design
Graphic design manual

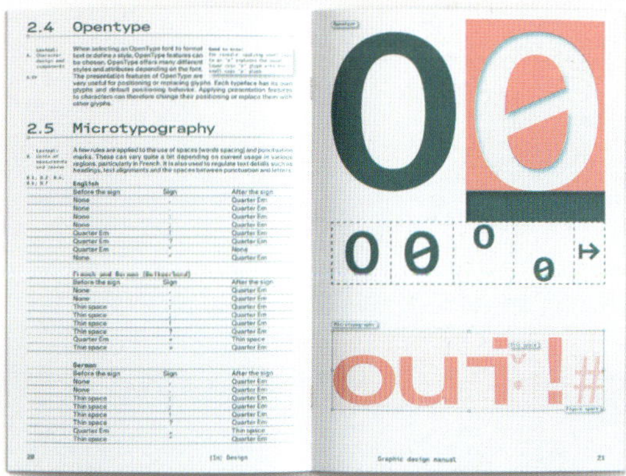
2.4 Opentype
2.5 Microtypography
(In) Design
Graphic design manual

C56 · M0 · Y8 · K0
C66 · M0 · Y49 · K0

C0 · M64 · Y6 · K0
C71 · M6 · Y0 · K0

C60 · M0 · Y82 · K0
C21 · M0 · Y80 · K0

C0 · M67 · Y88 · K0
C0 · M83 · Y49 · K0

C0 · M8 · Y78 · K0
C10 · M48 · Y78 · K0

DESIGNS FOR TRAVEL

Designs for Travel is a collection of design works proposing travel and tourism while highlighting the appeal of land and movement. For the key visuals, Sitoh inc. adopted the theme of moving during travel and the allure of travel, using window frames of trains, airplanes, and ships as motifs to graphically construct the travel scenes. During the key visual shoot, the window frames were made beforehand, and lighting and projectors were placed in the foreground and background to create the impression of distance and height without digital retouching. It graphically presents an expression between reality and fantasy.

Art Director & Designer
Sitoh inc.

Photographer
Shinya Sato

Artist
Kiyoshi Kagiyama (Nitto Soubi)

Retouch
Akio Yamaguchi

Editor
Sayaka Ishii (BNN)

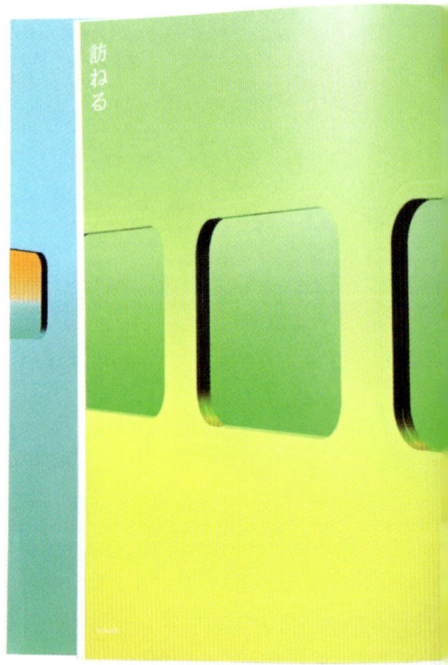

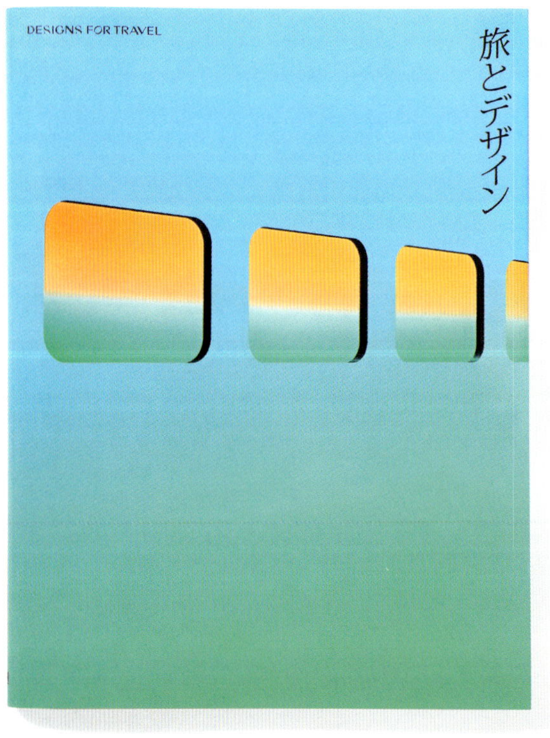

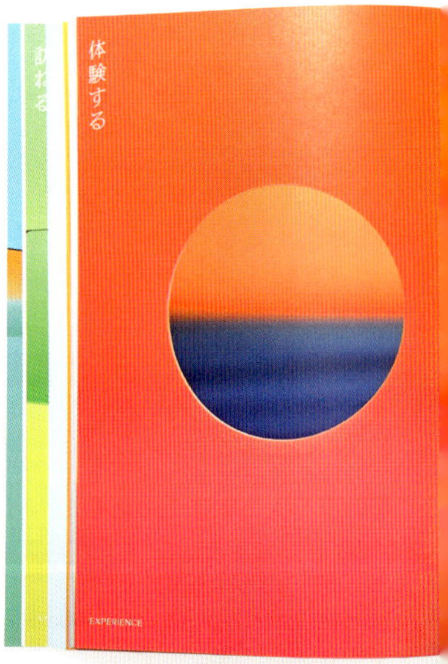

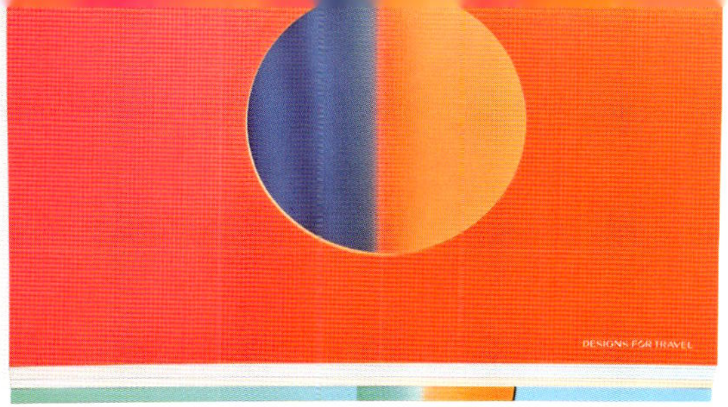

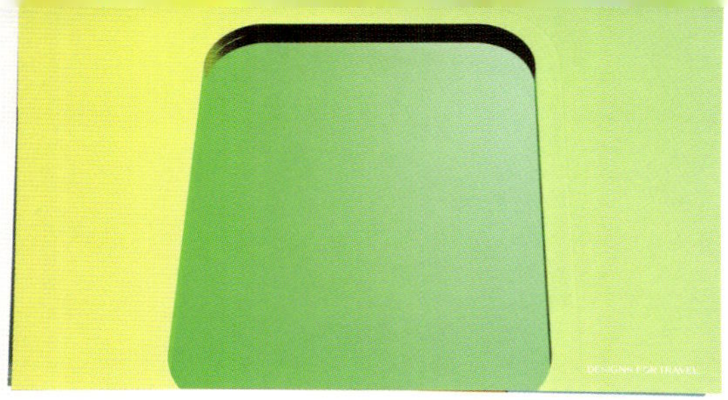

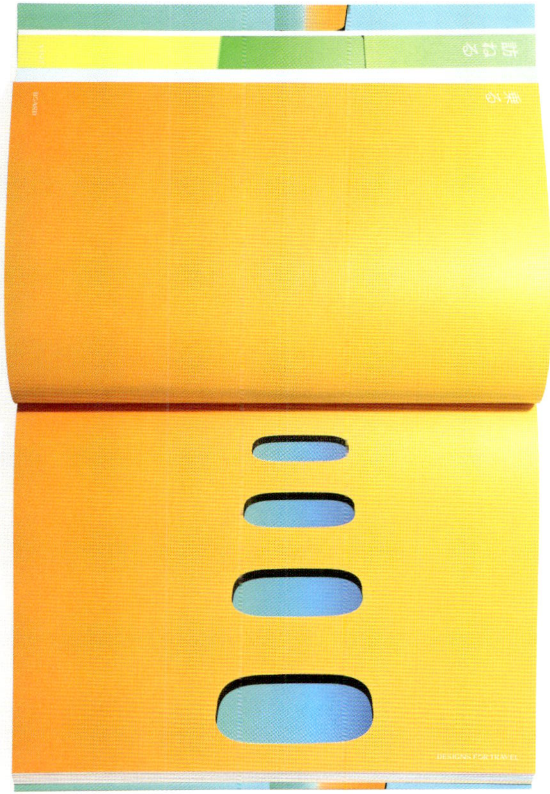

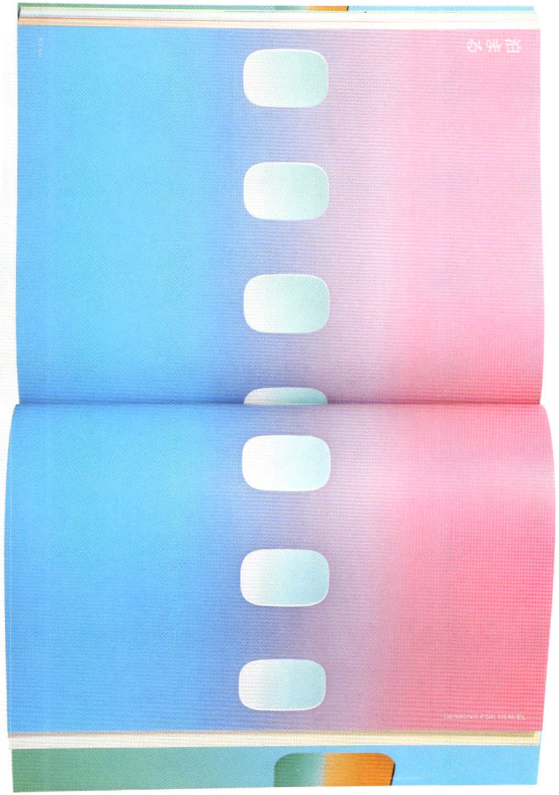

C1 · M89 · Y86 · K0

BLONOTE

Blonote by Daniel Armand Lee (Tablo) compiles transcripts from his radio show into a format resembling a gallery photography series, presented in written form. With improvised sentences, readers can resonate with contemporary life situations. The cover features a sunset sky created using spray-painting techniques.

Art Director & Designer
Manita Songserm

C57 · M0 · Y10 · K0

Pantone 805

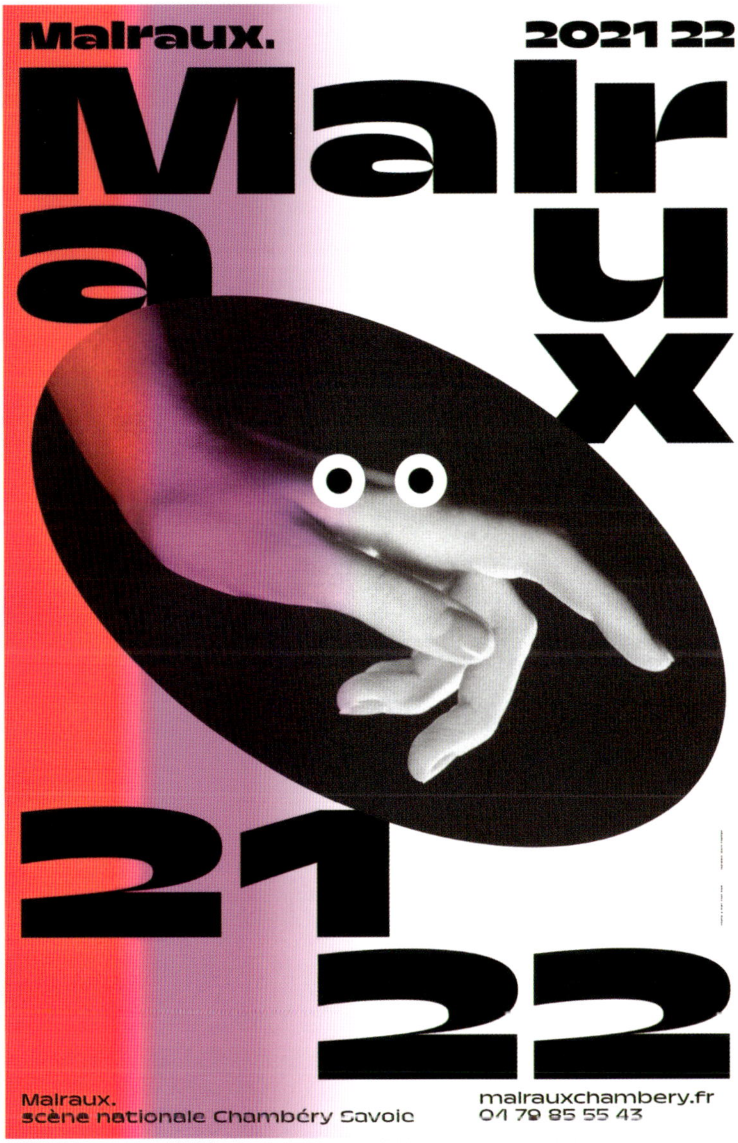

MALRAUX-SCÈNE NATIONALE CHAMBÉRY SAVOIE 2021-2022

Visual identity for the 2021-2022 season of Malraux—National Stage of Chambéry (FR).

DESIGN STUDIO
Brest Brest Brest

PANTONE 806

PANTONE 238 C
PANTONE 155 C

PANTONE 151 C
PANTONE 472 C

PANTONE 7712 C
PANTONE 324 C

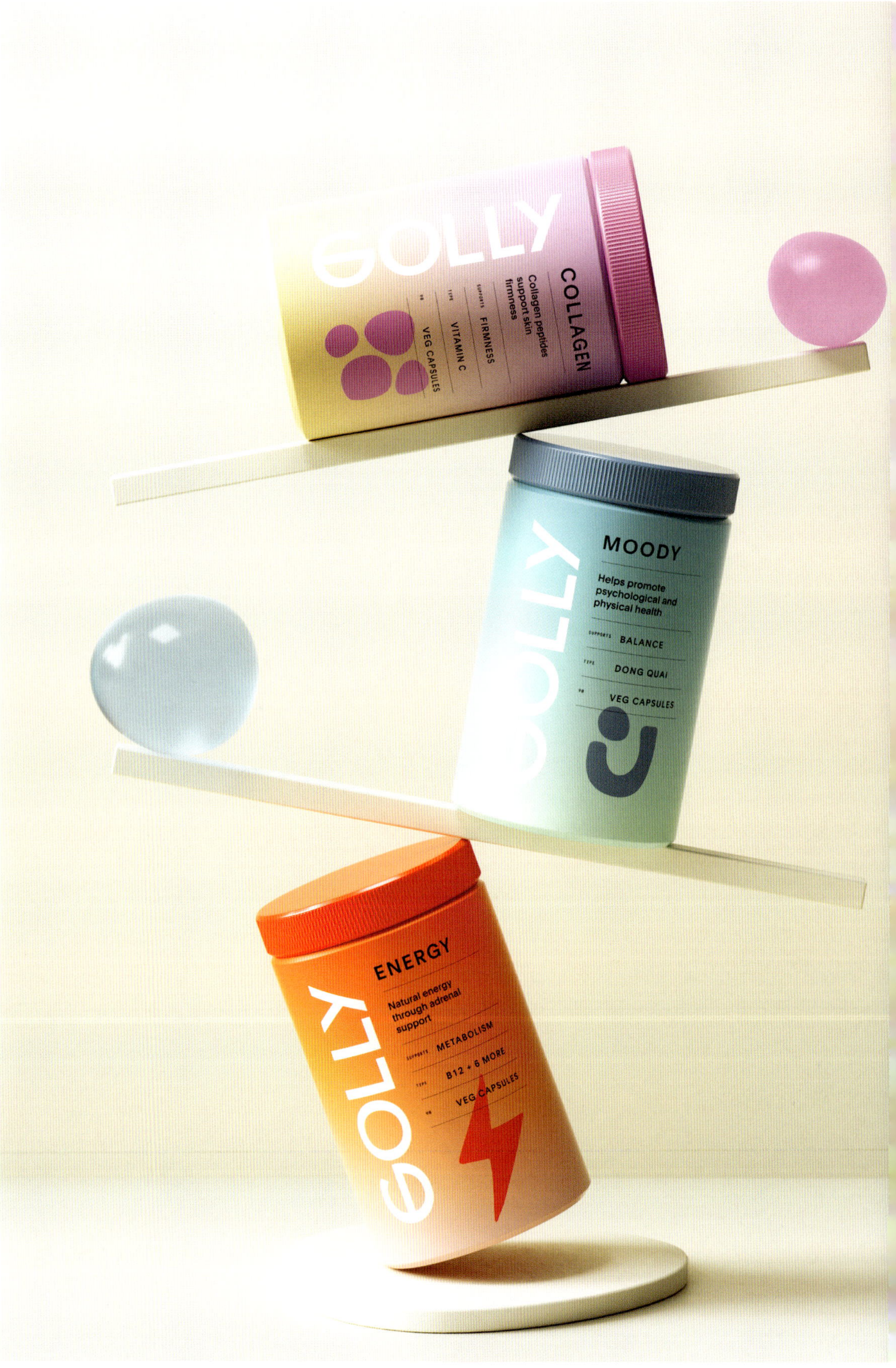

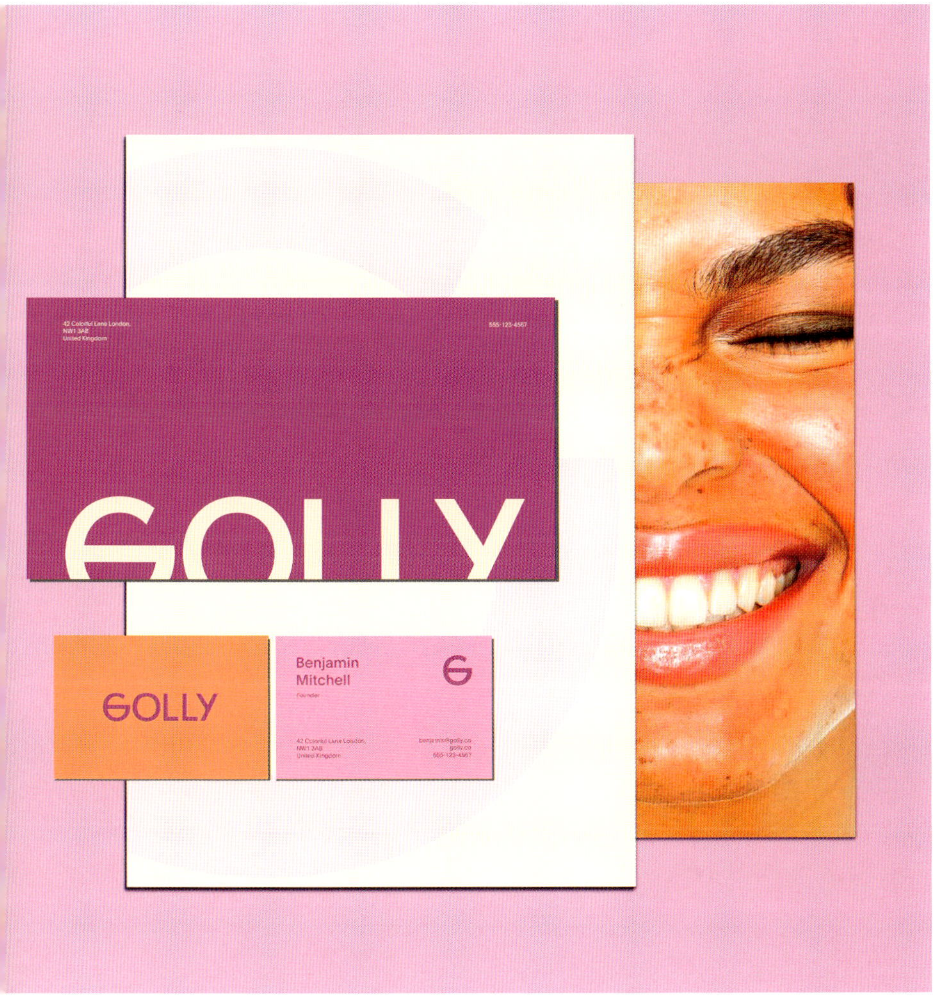

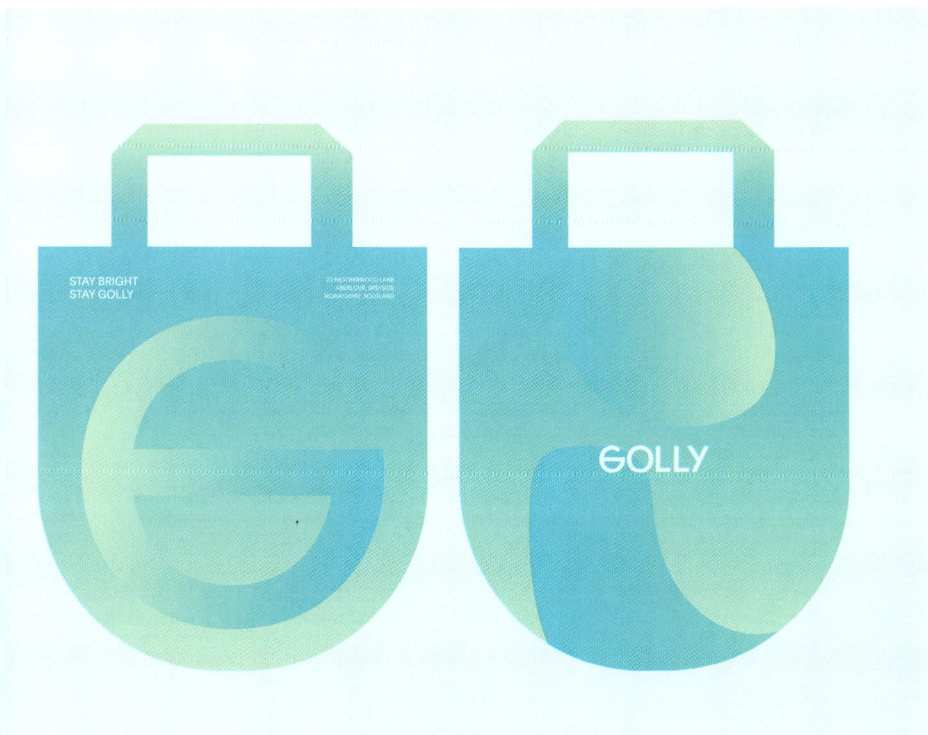

GOLLY

As the branding agency behind *Golly*, their mission was to transform supplement consumption. *Golly*, a UK-based supplement brand, focuses on energy, collagen, and mood support, aiming to make supplements fun and integral to daily life. Vibrant packaging and messaging was used to target Millennials and Gen Z, rejecting the mundane and embracing vitality. They crafted branding and marketing materials to highlight *Golly's* uniqueness, poised to shake the industry with creativity and consumer appeal. *Golly* inspires a new approach to wellness, emphasizing enjoyment and wellness in every product.

Creative Director
Mustafa Akülker

Graphic Designer
Neşe Tongaz,
Ayşe İbiş

Motion Designer
Umut Ulusoy

PANTONE WARM RED

C100 · M0 · Y82 · K0

C100 · M58 · Y0 · K0

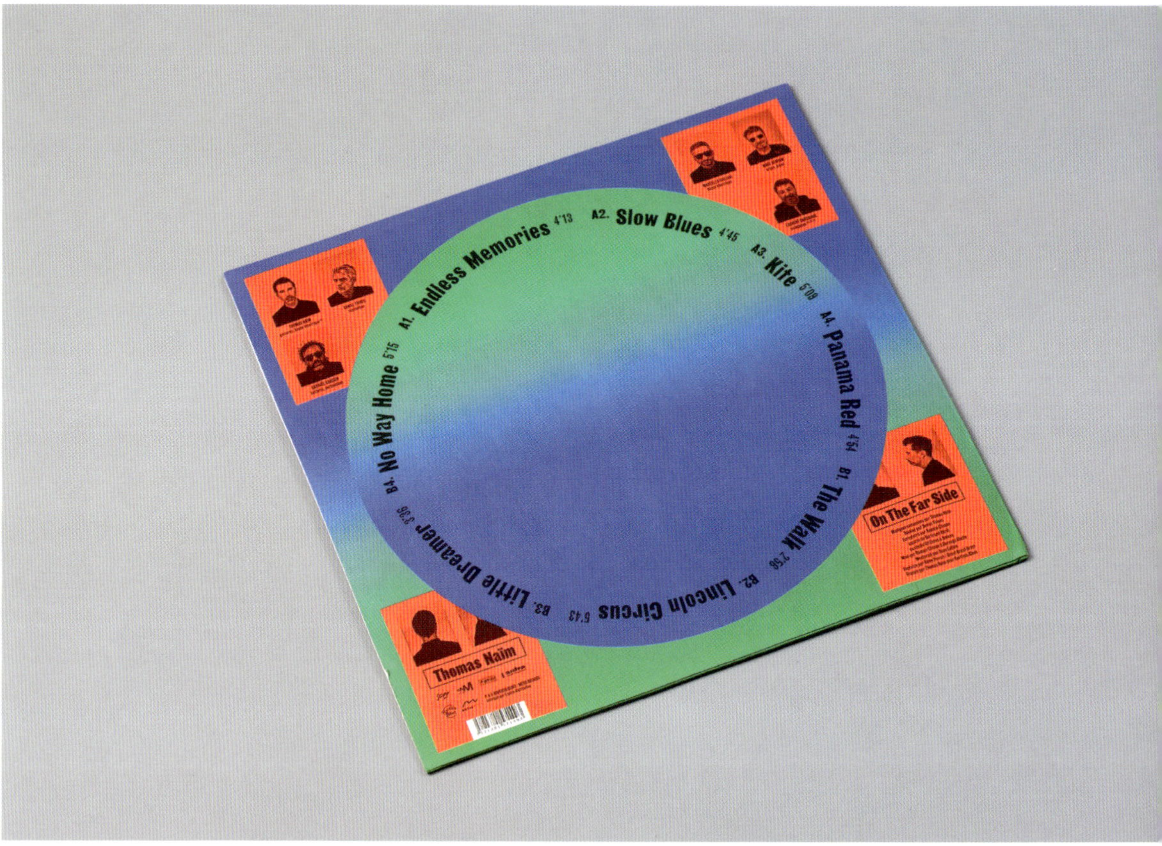

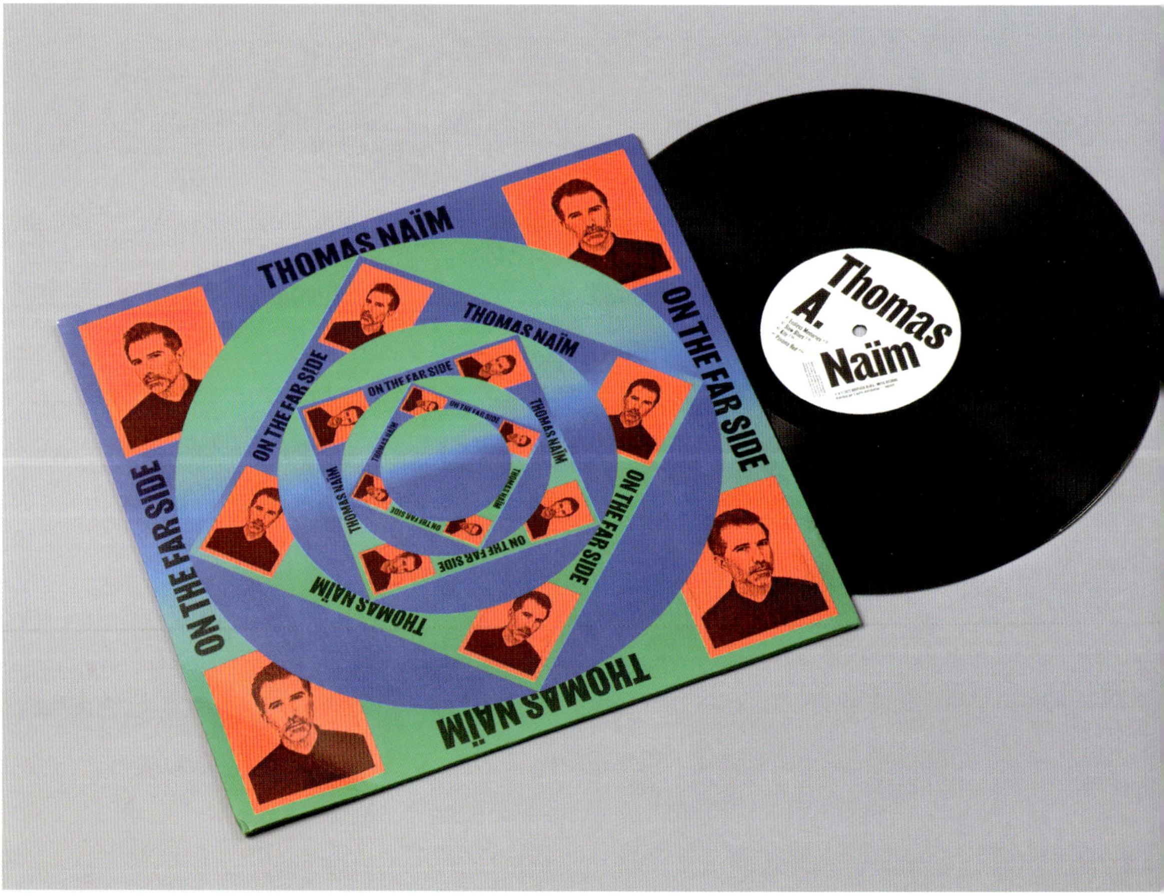

THOMAS NAÏM-
ON THE FAR SIDE

Album cover design
for French guitarist
Thomas Naïm.

Design Studio
Brest Brest Brest

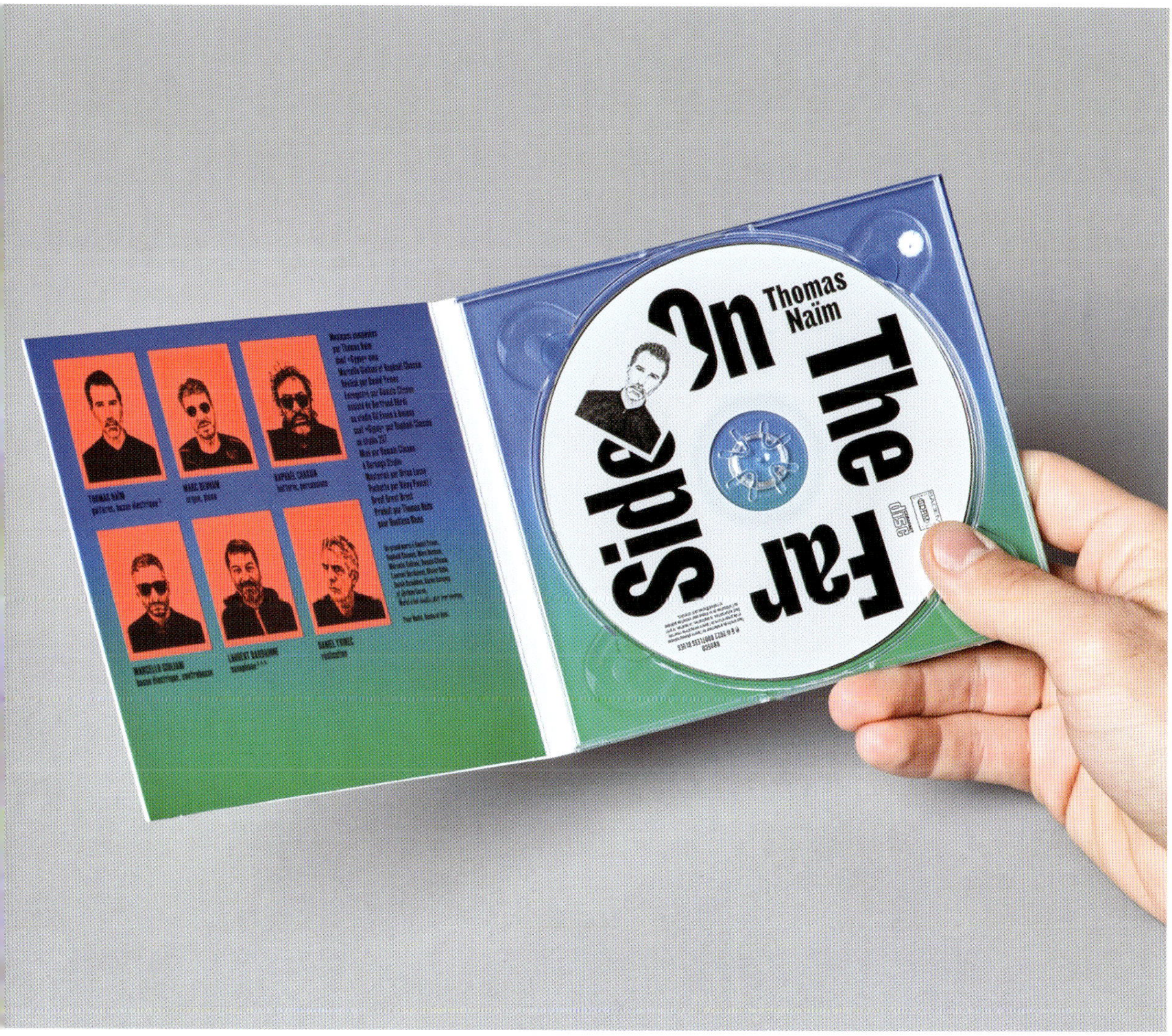

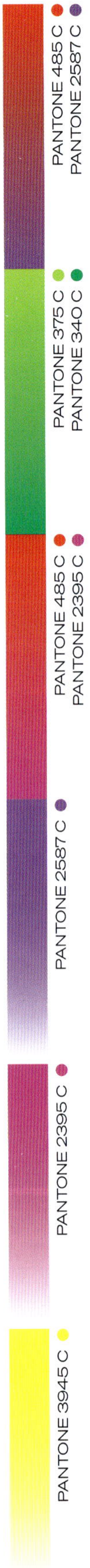
PANTONE 485 C
PANTONE 2587 C
PANTONE 375 C
PANTONE 340 C
PANTONE 485 C
PANTONE 2395 C
PANTONE 2587 C
PANTONE 2395 C
PANTONE 3945 C

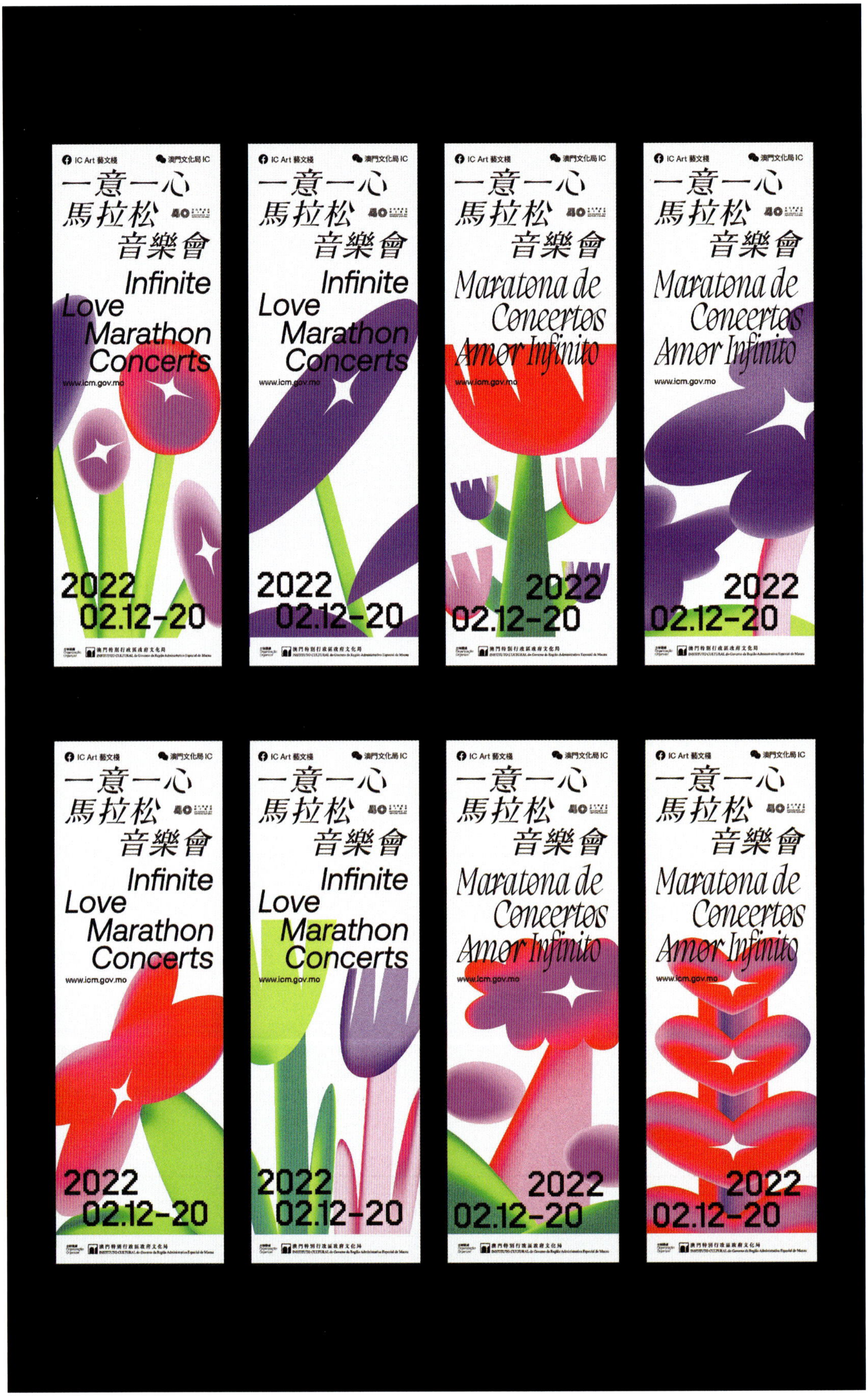
IC Art 藝文棧
澳門文化局 IC
一意一心
馬拉松
音樂會
Infinite
Love
Marathon
Concerts
Maratona de
Concertos
Amor Infinito
www.icm.gov.mo
2022
02.12-20

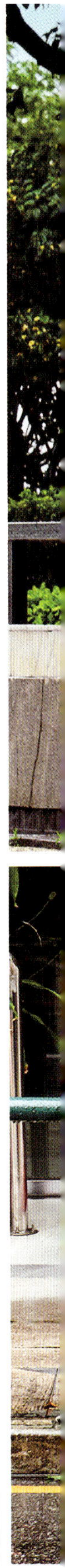

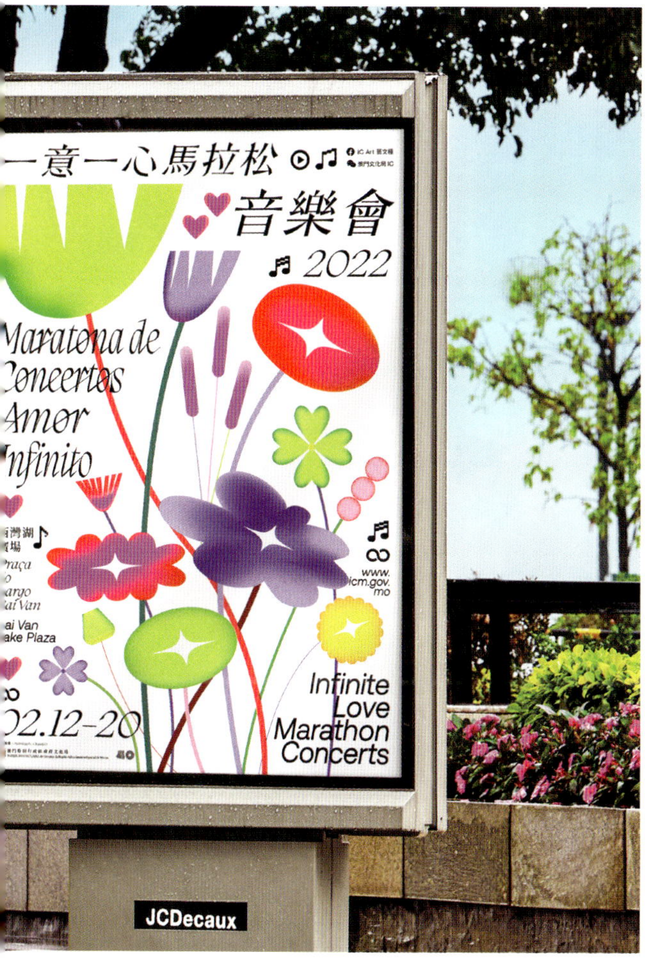

INFINITE LOVE MARATHON CONCERTS

Beautiful flowers can create a romantic atmosphere and bring people a pleasant mood. The theme of the event is "flower", and the overall use of abstract and concise patterns is combined with bright and lively colours to create a picture. The large three-dimensional flower installation looks like flowers blooming in the city, hoping to make participants feel like they are in a garden, enjoying music and a strong festive atmosphere. The arch decoration as the check-in location presents a picture of flying through the sky, which symbolizes the unforgettable love story of the Cowherd and the Weaver Girl.

Design Studio
Untitled Macao

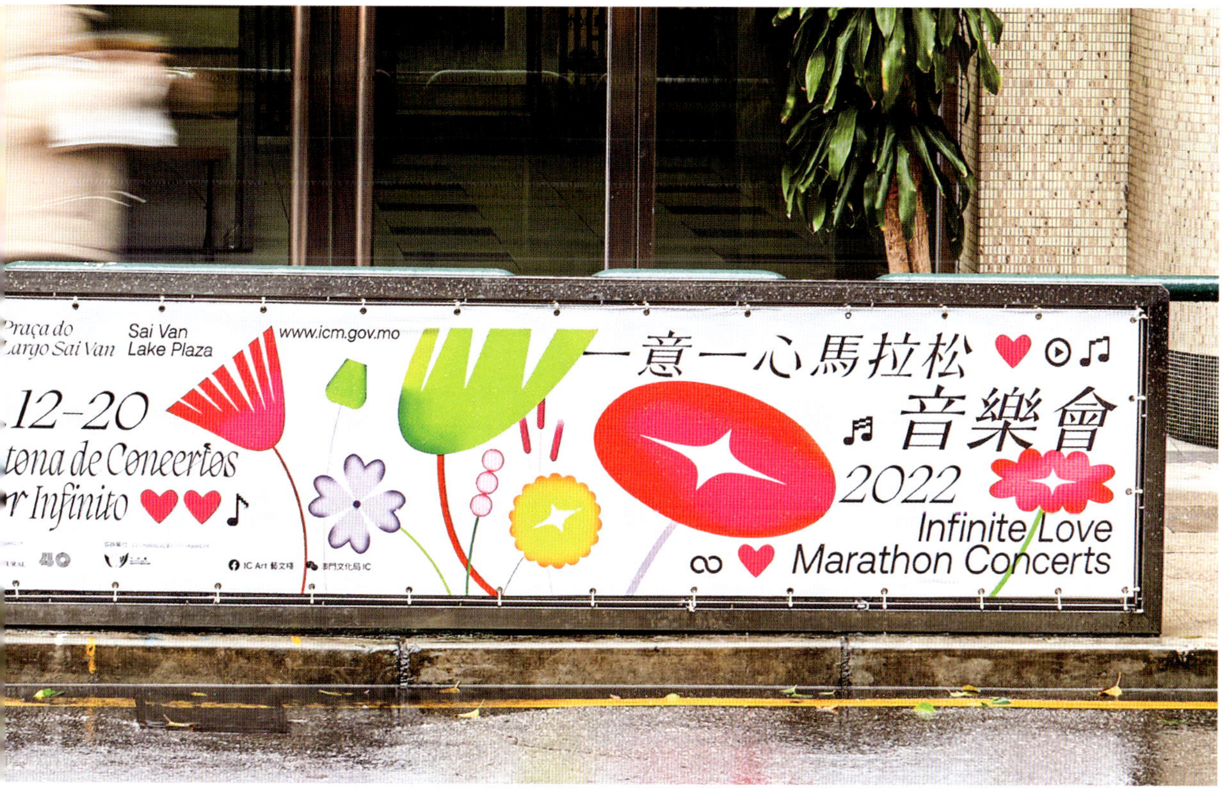

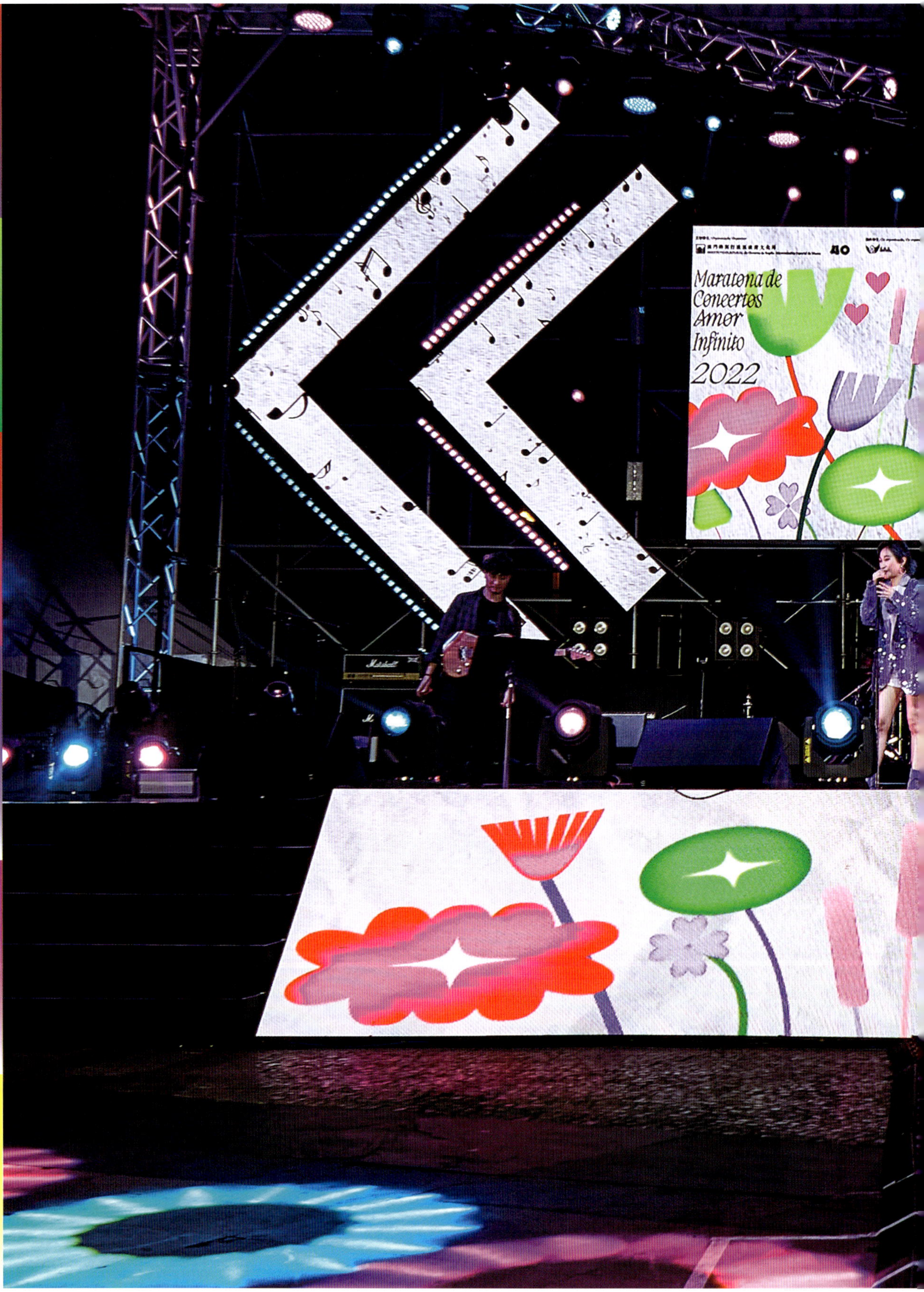
Maratona de
Concertos
Amor
Infinito
2022

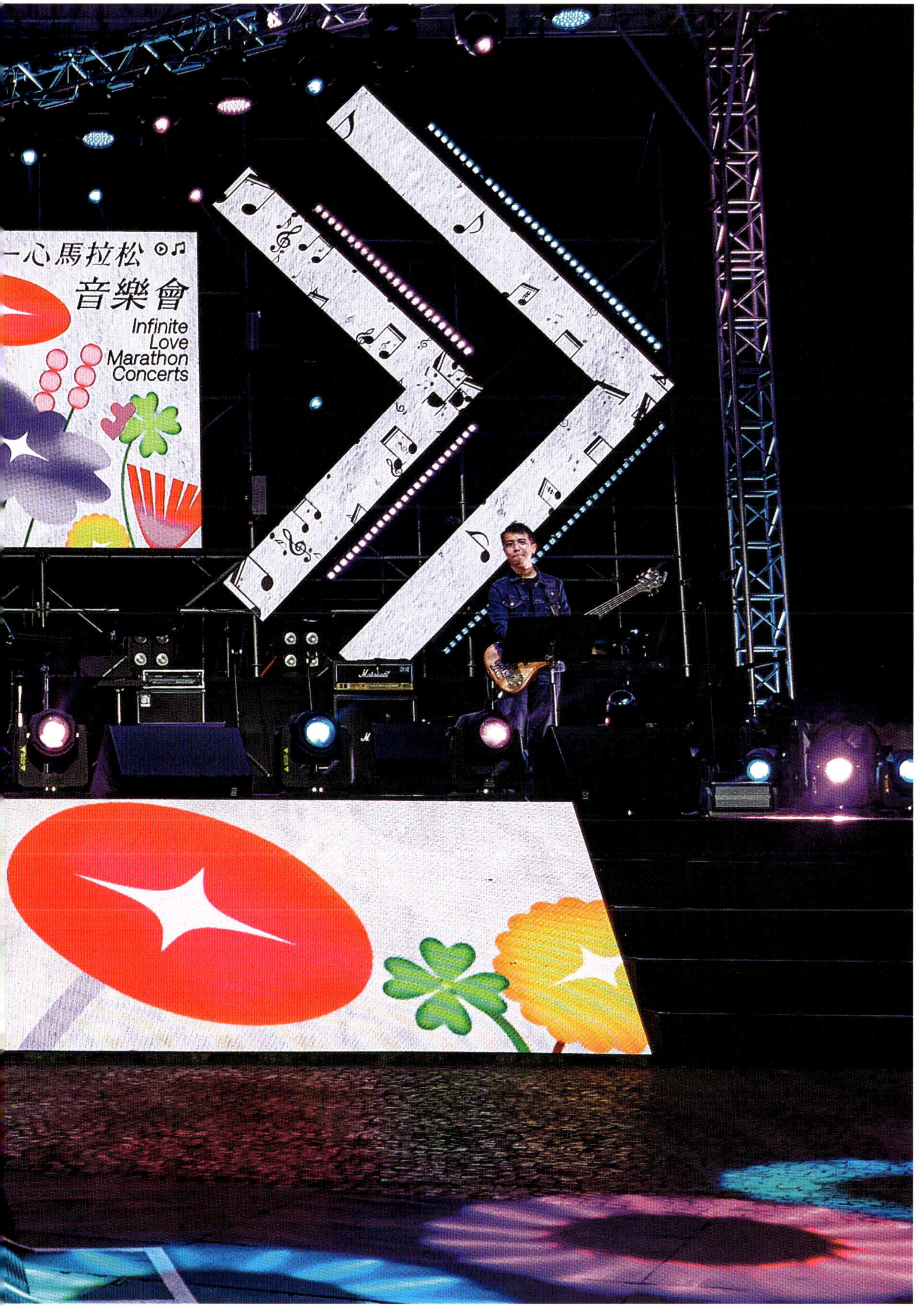
一心馬拉松
音樂會
Infinite
Love
Marathon
Concerts

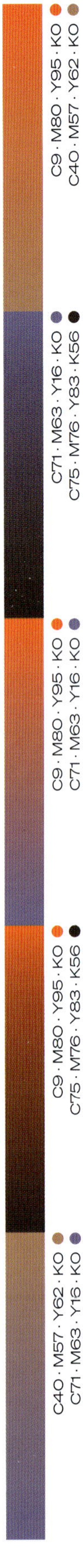
C9 · M80 · Y95 · K0
C40 · M57 · Y62 · K0
C71 · M63 · Y16 · K0
C75 · M76 · Y83 · K56
C9 · M80 · Y95 · K0
C71 · M63 · Y16 · K0
C9 · M80 · Y95 · K0
C75 · M76 · Y83 · K56
C40 · M57 · Y62 · K0
C71 · M63 · Y16 · K0

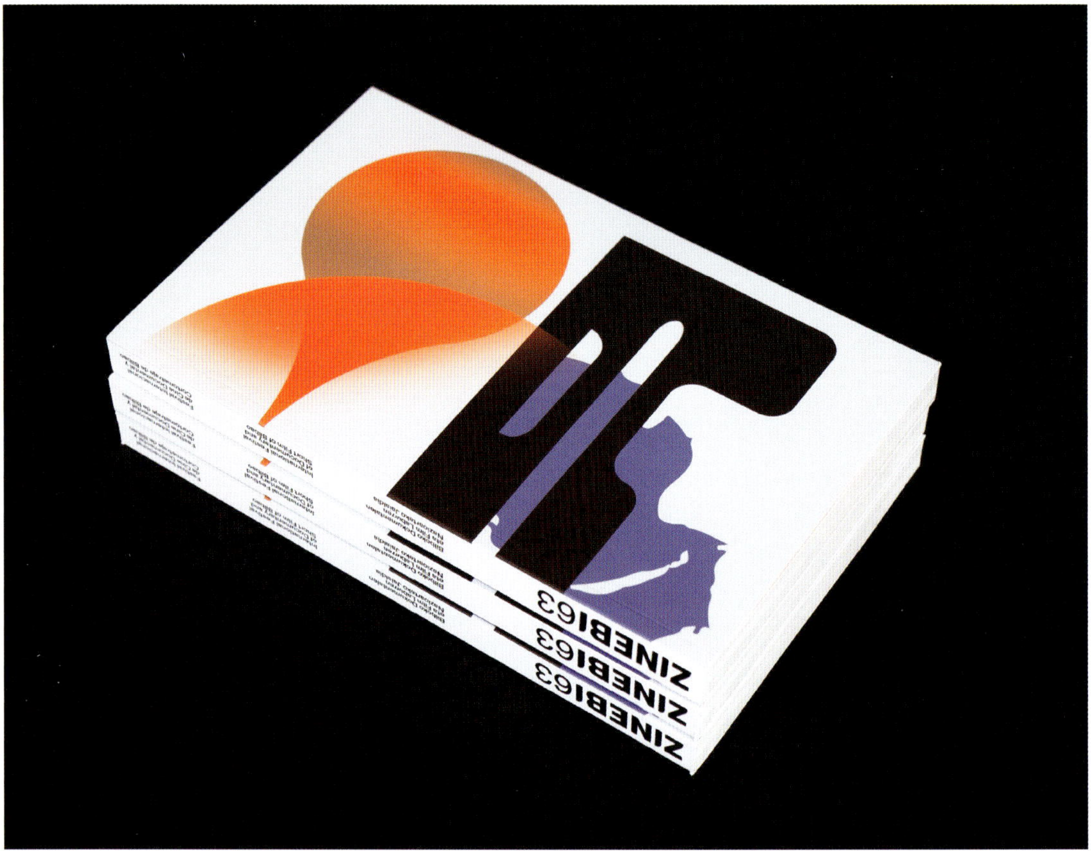
ZINEBI63
ZINEBI63
ZINEBI63

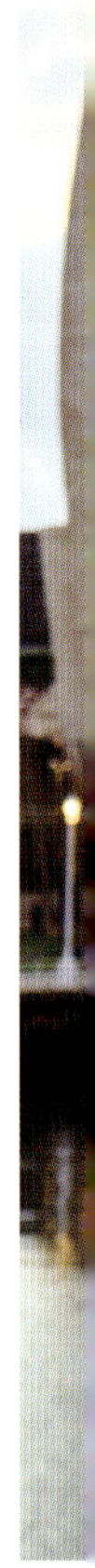

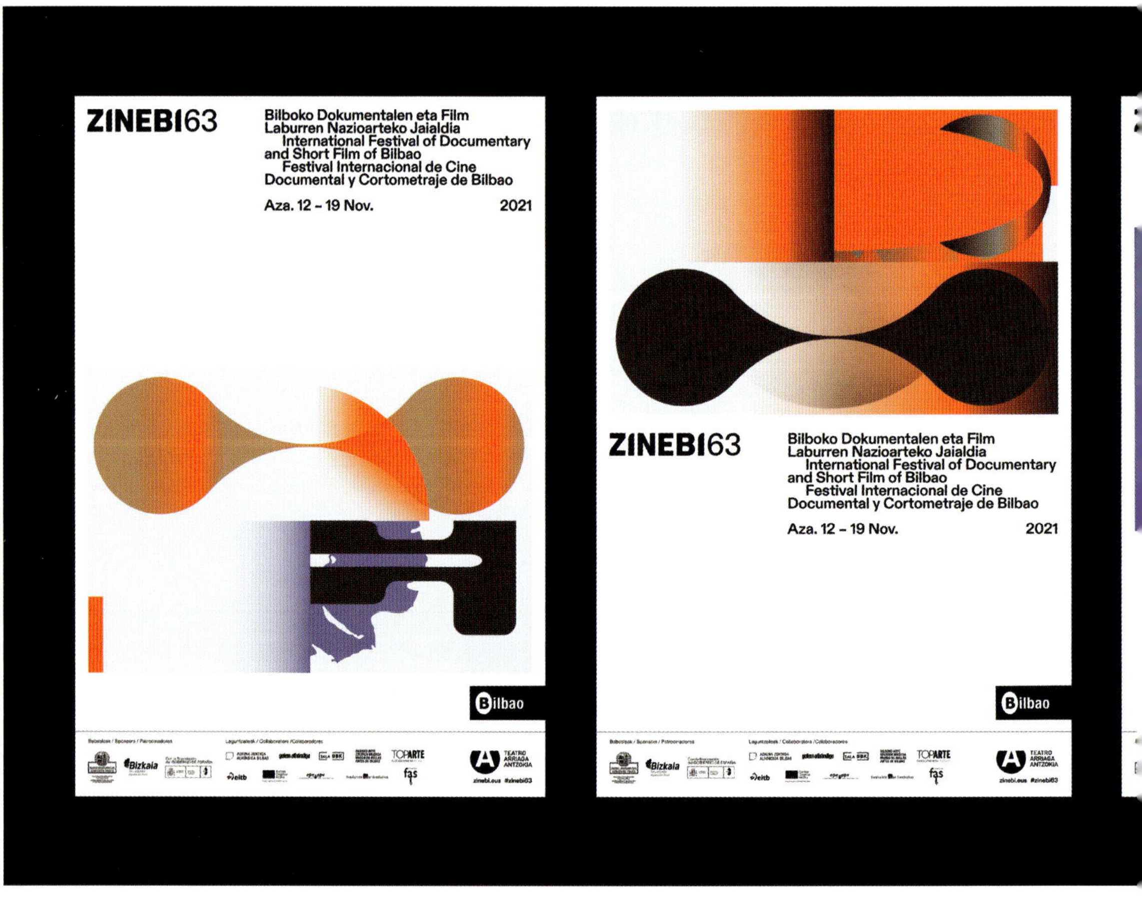
ZINEBI63
Bilboko Dokumentalen eta Film
Laburren Nazioarteko Jaialdia
International Festival of Documentary
and Short Film of Bilbao
Festival Internacional de Cine
Documental y Cortometraje de Bilbao
Aza. 12 – 19 Nov.
2021
Bilbao
ZINEBI63
Bilboko Dokumentalen eta Film
Laburren Nazioarteko Jaialdia
International Festival of Documentary
and Short Film of Bilbao
Festival Internacional de Cine
Documental y Cortometraje de Bilbao
Aza. 12 – 19 Nov.
2021
Bilbao

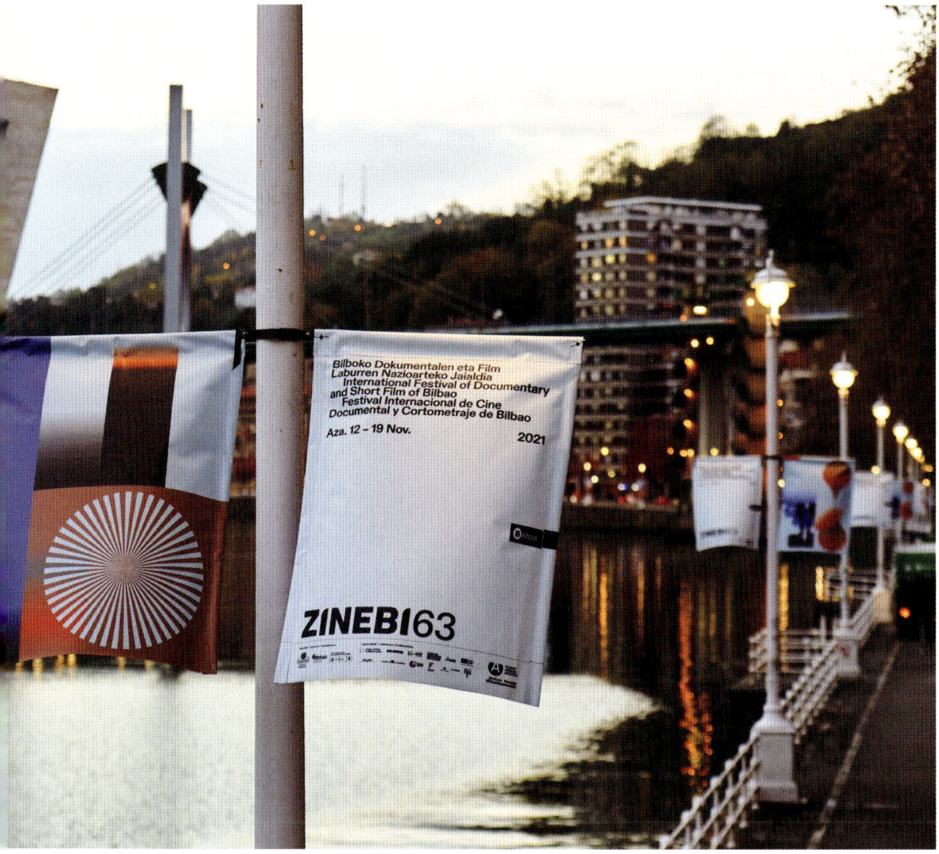

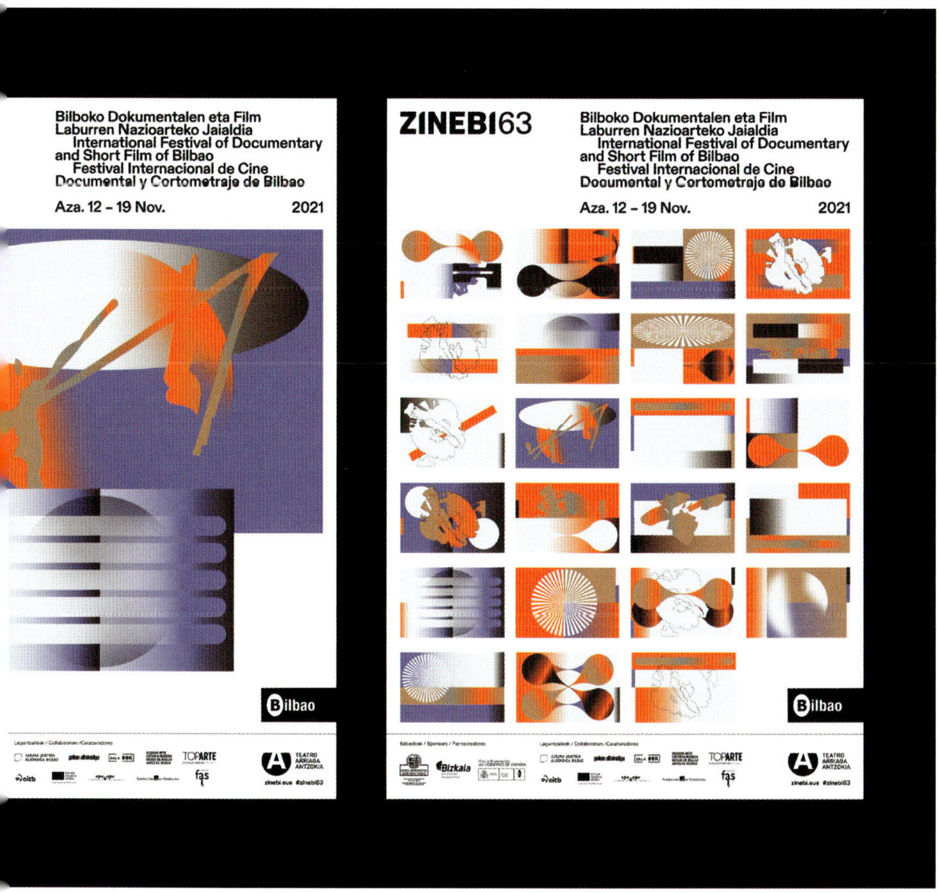

ZINEBI INTERNATIONAL FILM FESTIVAL

"Non-place" is a term coined by the anthropologist Marc Augé to describe those places of transience that are not important enough to be considered as "places" such as hotel rooms, airports or supermarkets. So what if these non-places had identity and were able to generate belonging? Zinebi 63 Film Festival's graphic campaign builds around finding the answer to this question. The designer created a system of infinite flags of the non-places based on generative design, in contrast to the socially constructed single-flag.

Creative Director & Designer
Rebeka Arce Studio

Generative designer & illustrator
Jannis Maroscheck

Type Design
Diatype by Dinamo

Motion designer
Nacho Velasco

Client
Zinebi Film Festival

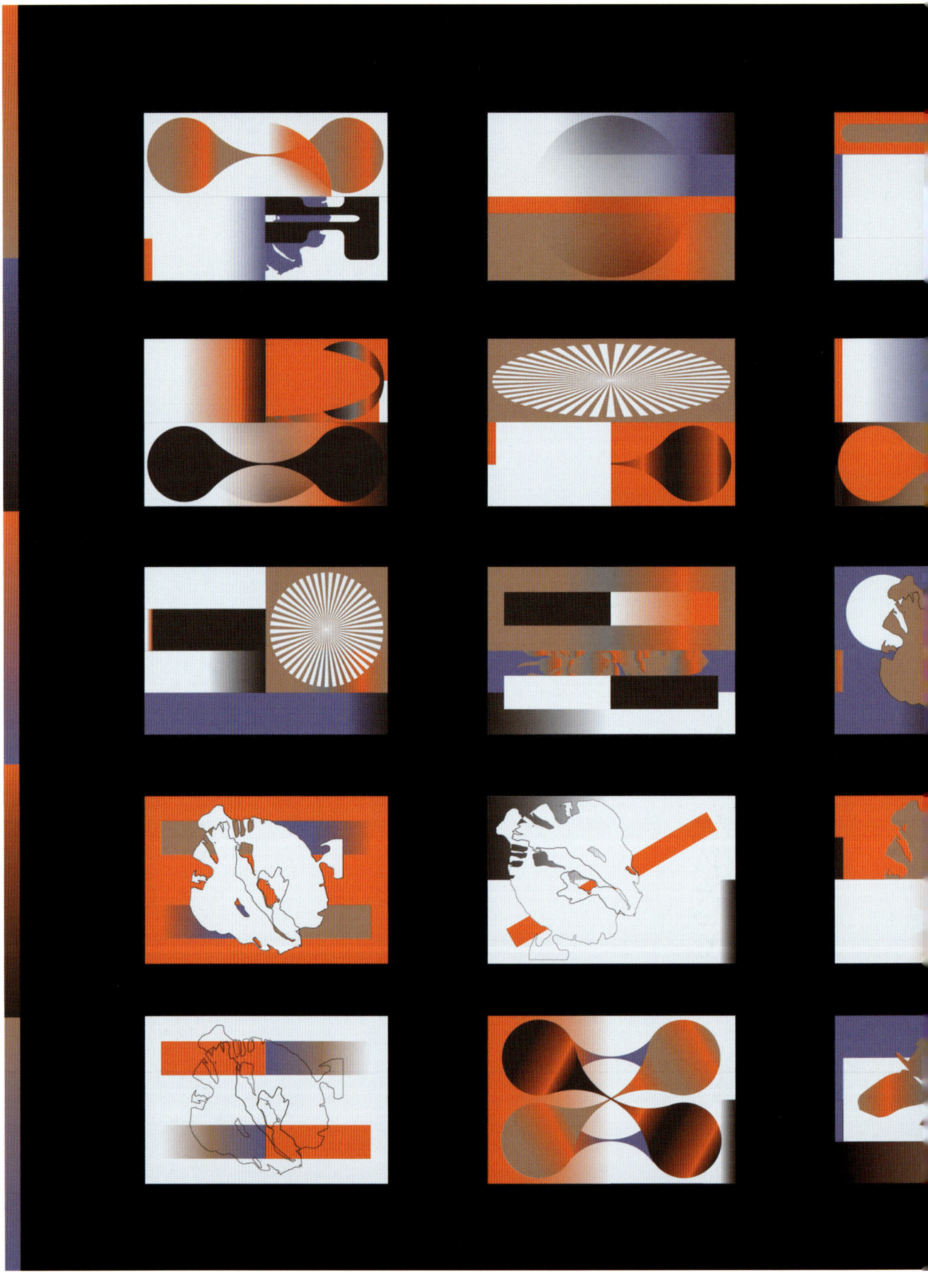

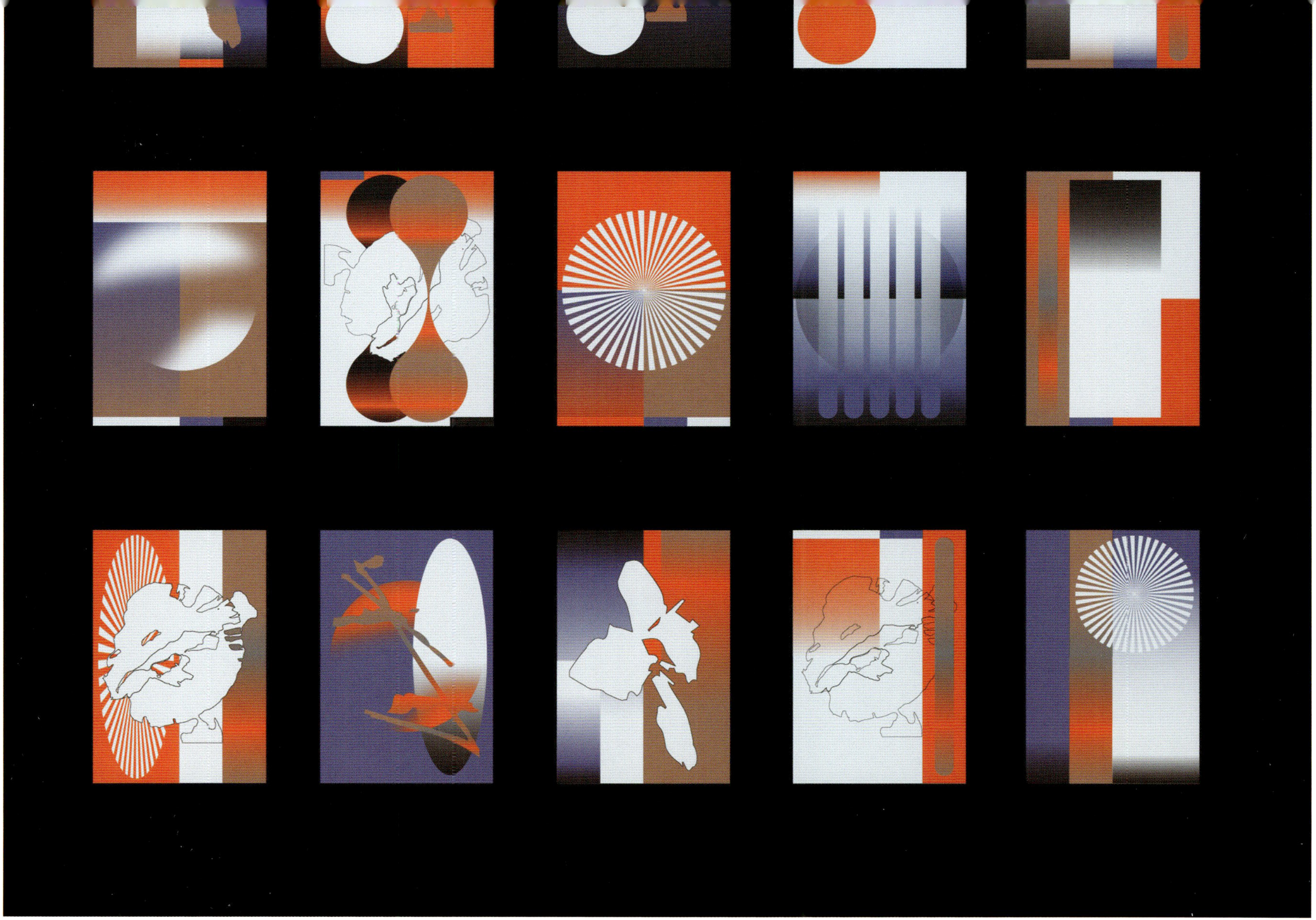

C77 · M81 · Y0 · K0
C12 · M23 · Y0 · K0

C64 · M0 · Y85 · K0
C21 · M0 · Y7 · K0

C15 · M78 · Y5 · K0
C9 · M0 · Y61 · K0

C0 · M83 · Y70 · K0
C0 · M17 · Y60 · K0

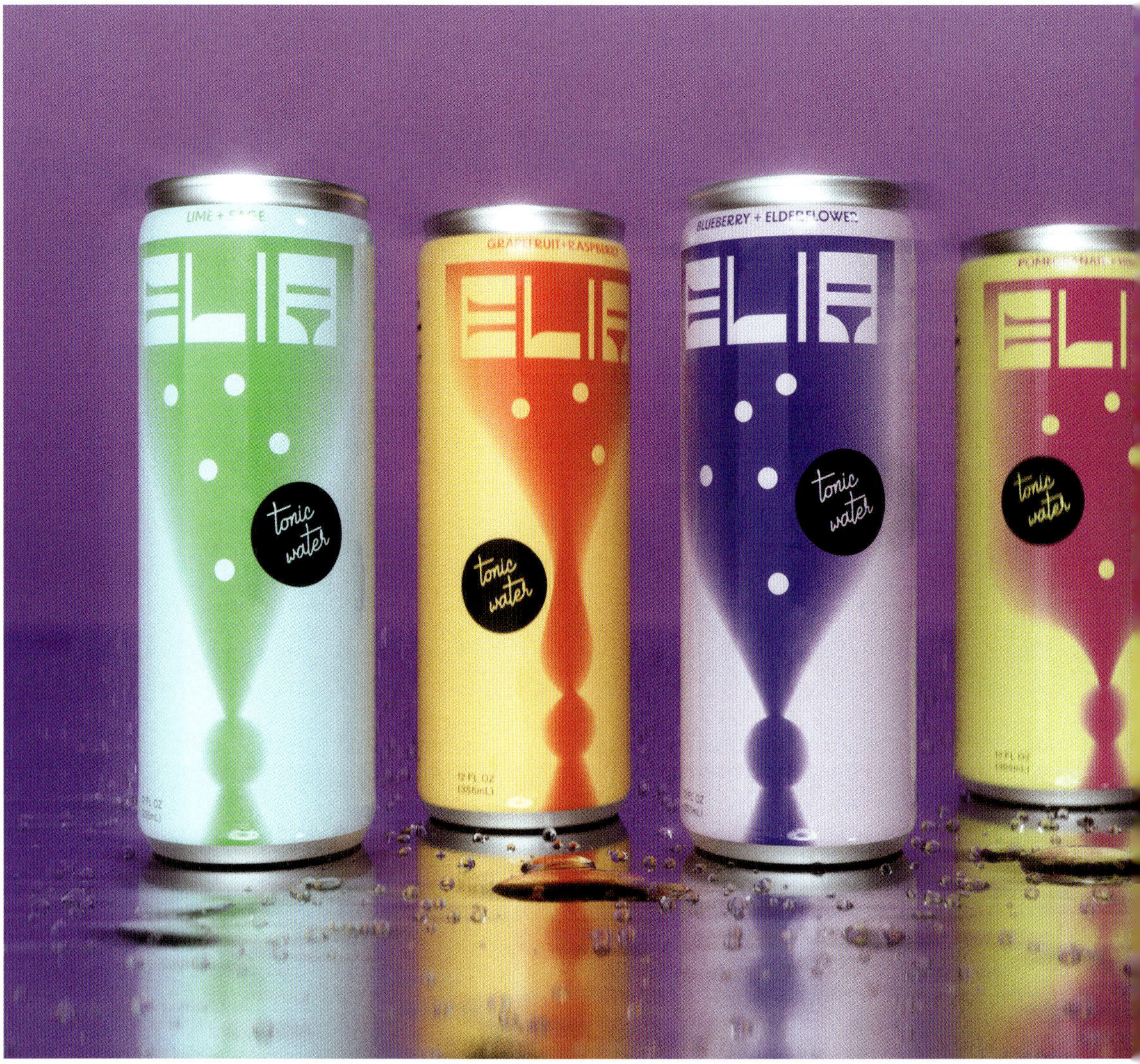

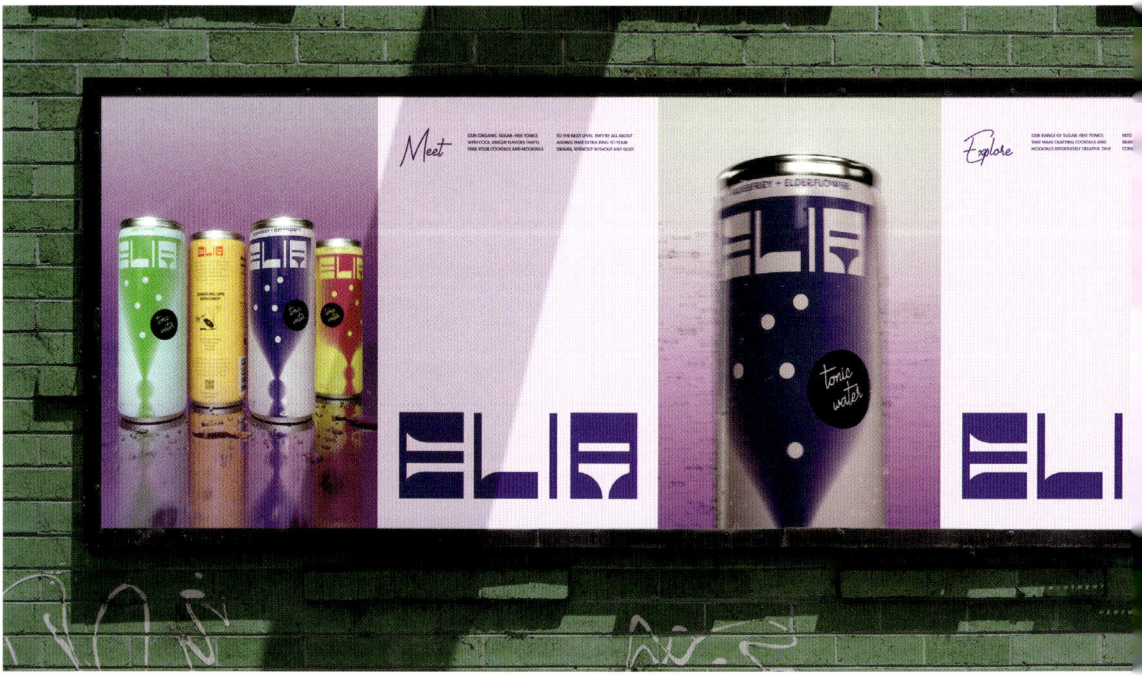

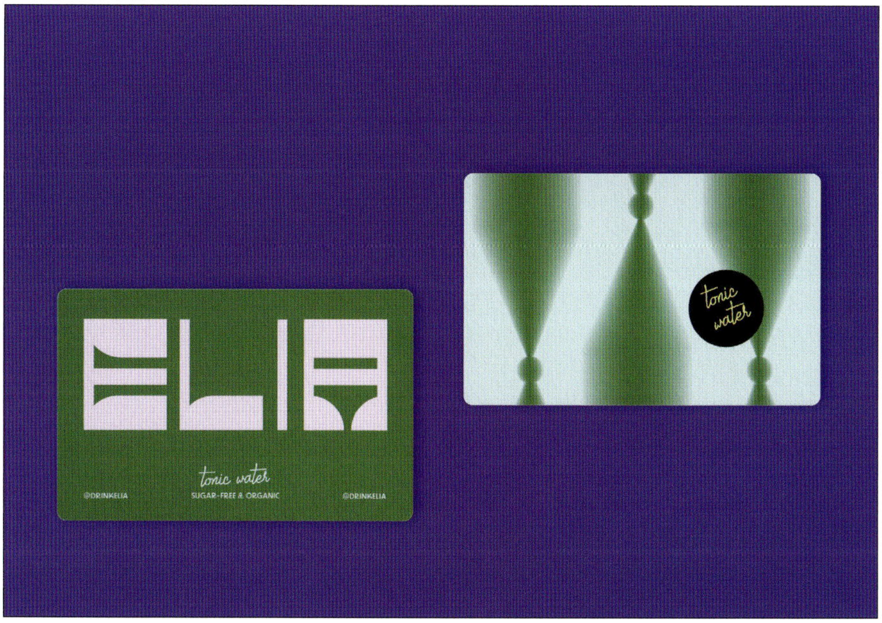

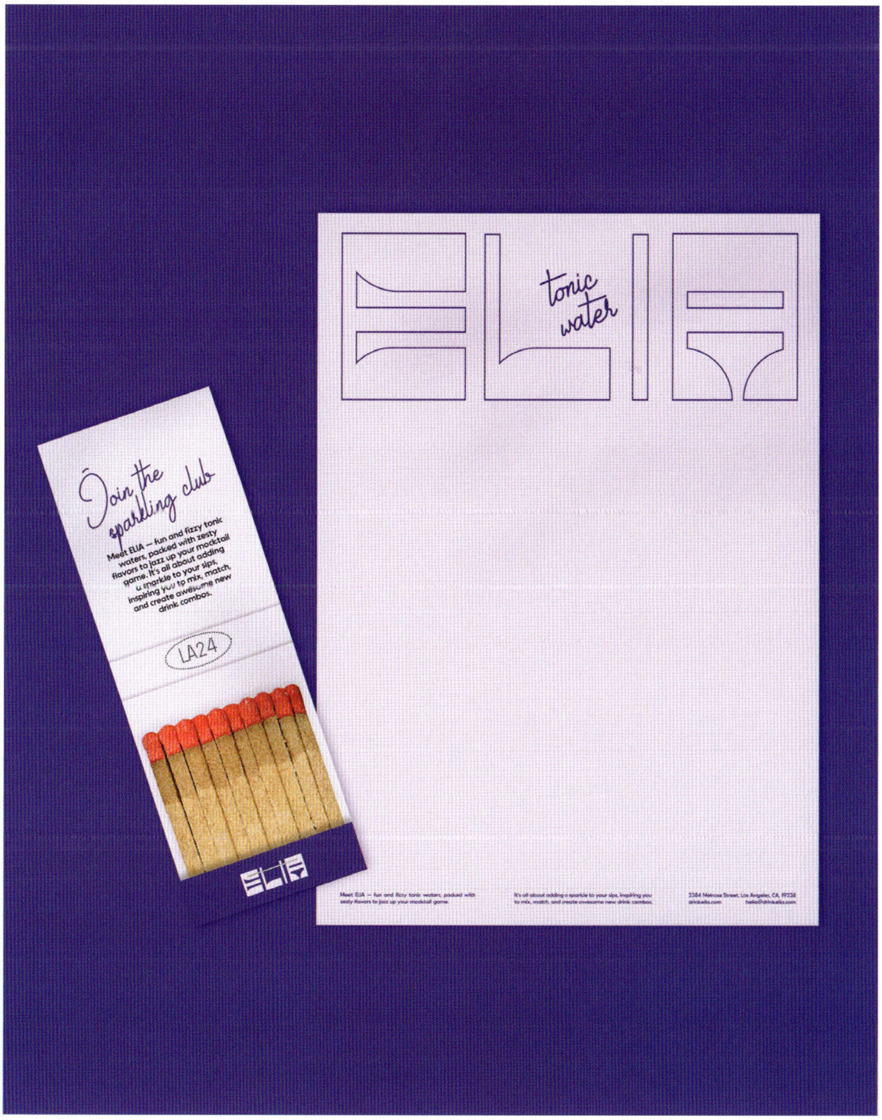

ELIA TONIC WATERS

The identity draws its inspiration from the dynamic essence of bubbles, infused with youthful ease. The designer has crafted a design that's both eye-catching and straightforward with a striking combination of bold typography, unique graphics and vibrant colours. Her goal was to make a product that really pops off the shelf and looks just as good when you open it up for your cocktail party.

Designer
Yuliya Tverdokhlib

C3 · M100 · Y55 · K0

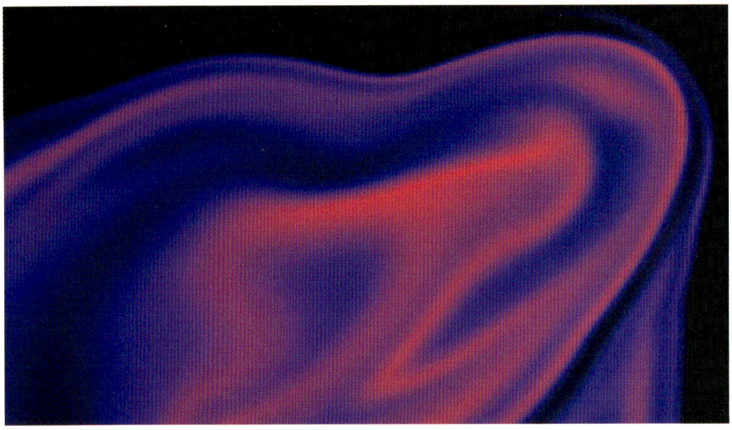

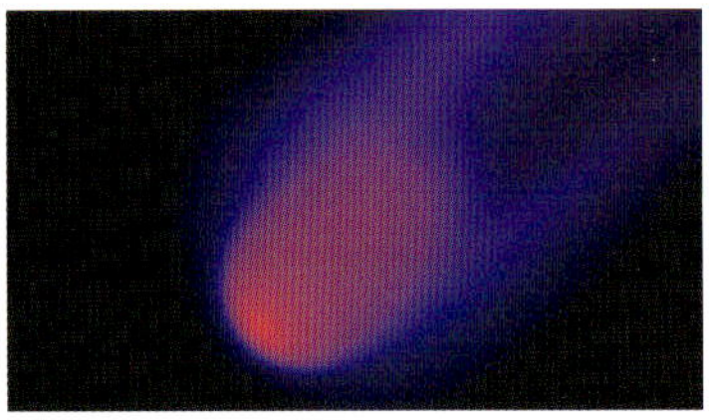

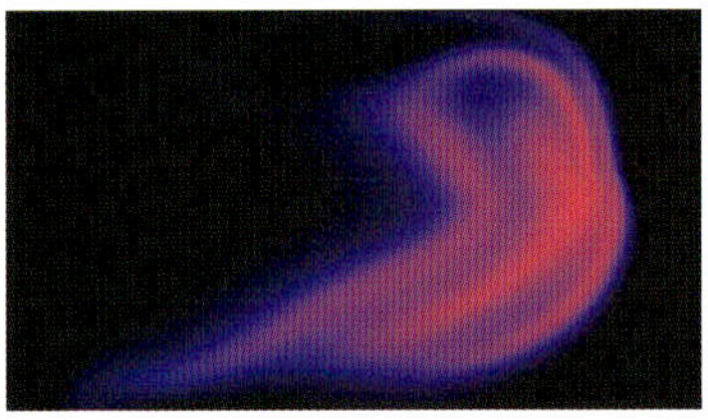

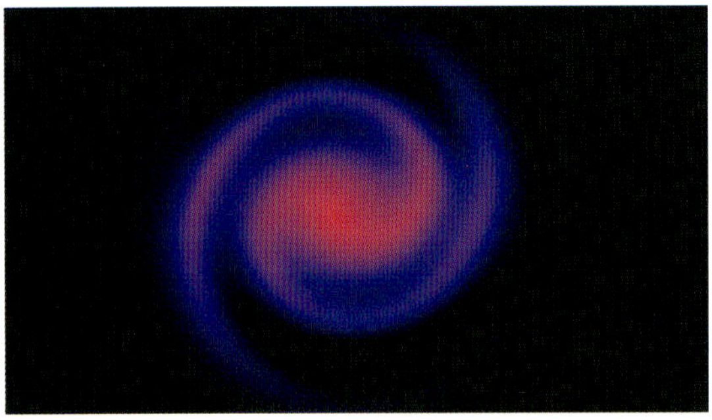

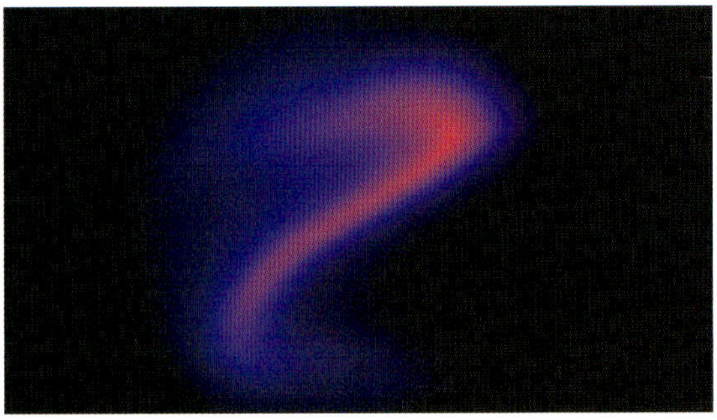

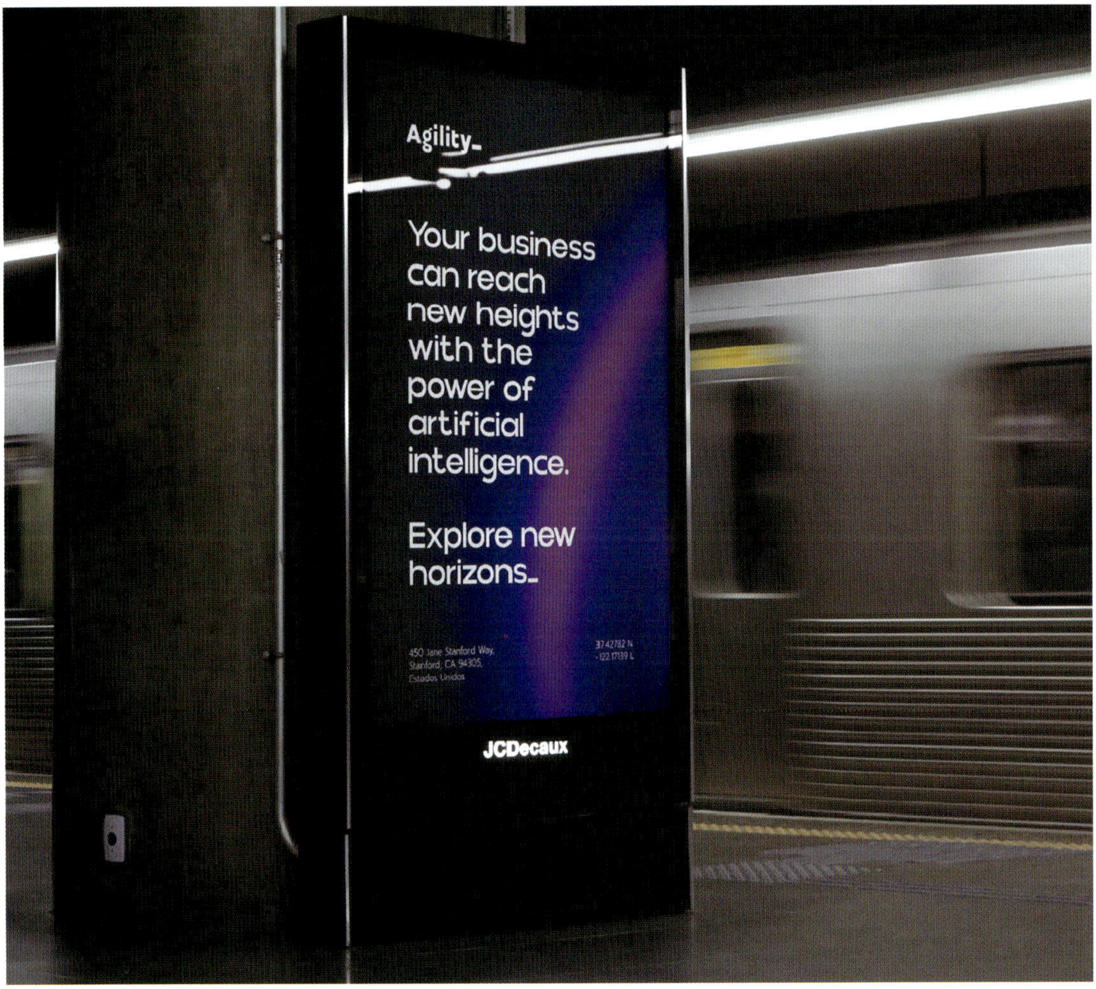

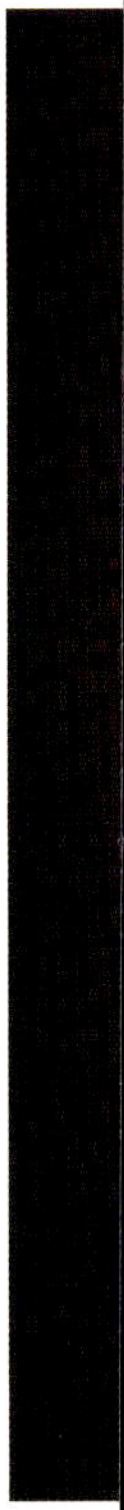

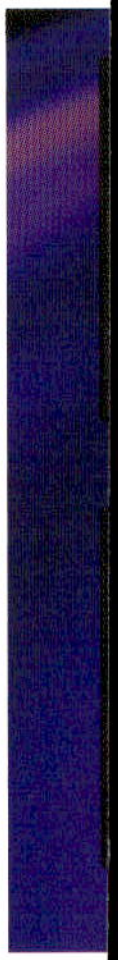

C93 · M98 · Y0 · K0

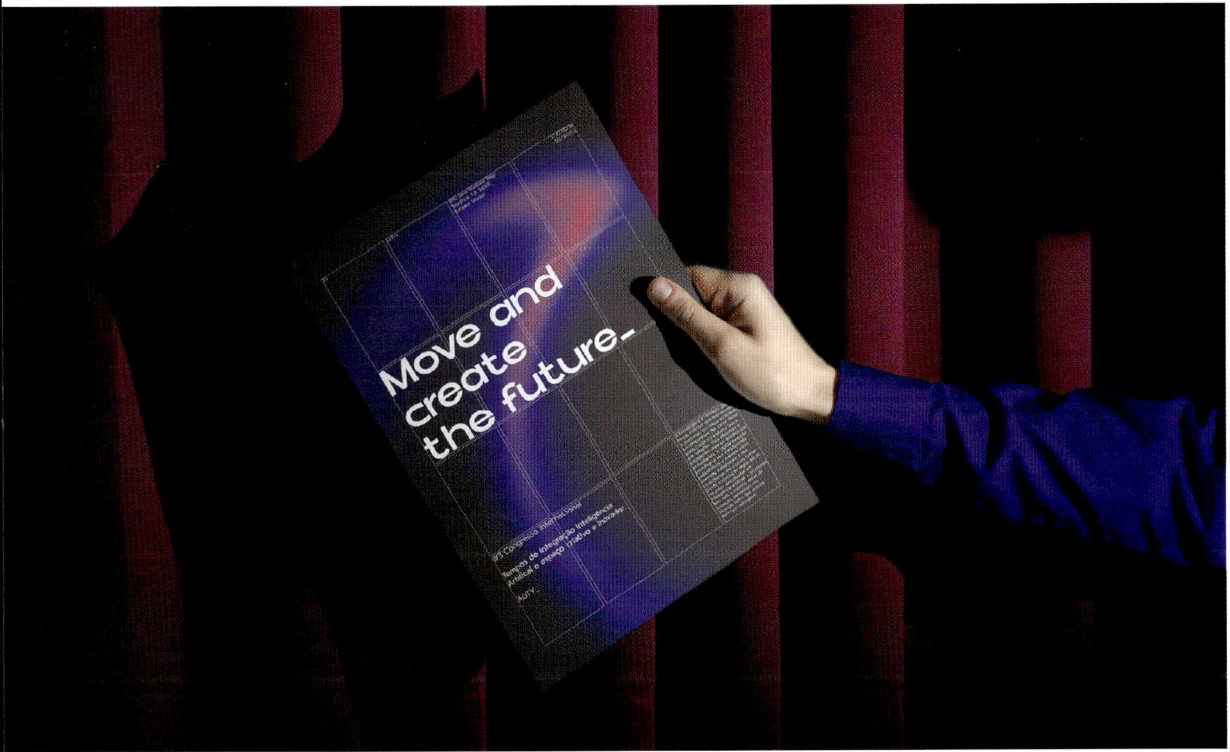

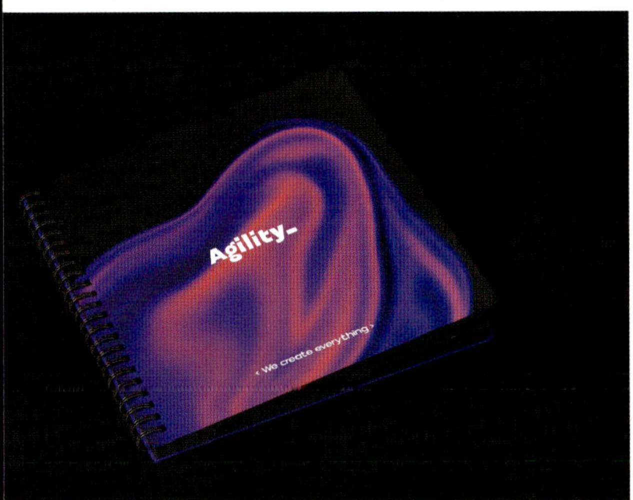

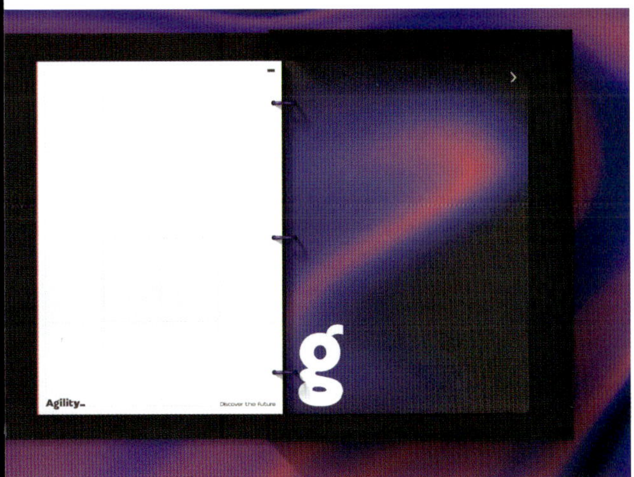

AGILITY TECH STARTUP

Agility is a leader in software development consulting, specializing in artificial intelligence. The designers act as a bridge between vision and reality, between data and solutions. The designer's commitment is to go beyond conventional limits, elevating companies to unprecedented levels of efficiency, innovation, and success. At Agility, they are always looking ahead, not just planning to follow, but to lead tomorrow. They are committed to providing APIs that unlock the true potential of your business's artificial intelligence, offering holistic solutions that exceed their clients' expectations, generating comprehensive and functional solutions. They are building the future now.

Creative Director & Designer
brunolima.design

Animator
pgabrielsouza

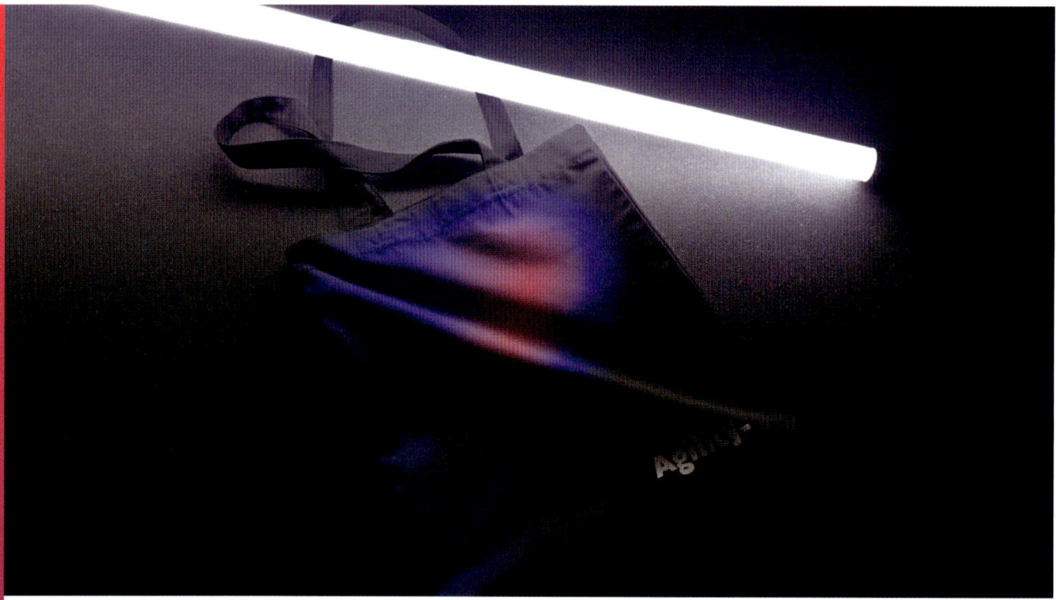
Agility_

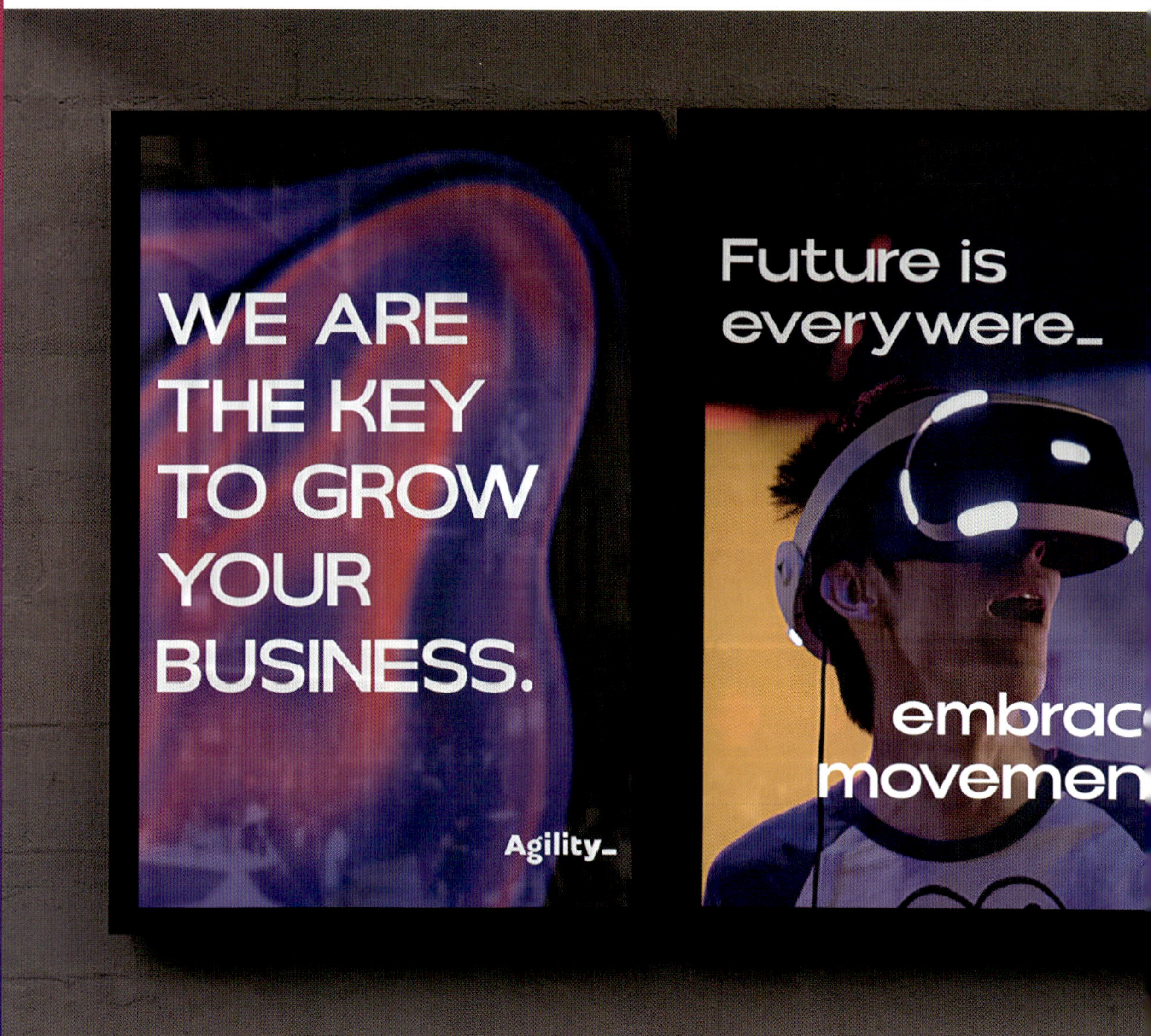
WE ARE
THE KEY
TO GROW
YOUR
BUSINESS.
Agility_
Future is
everywere_
embrac
movemen

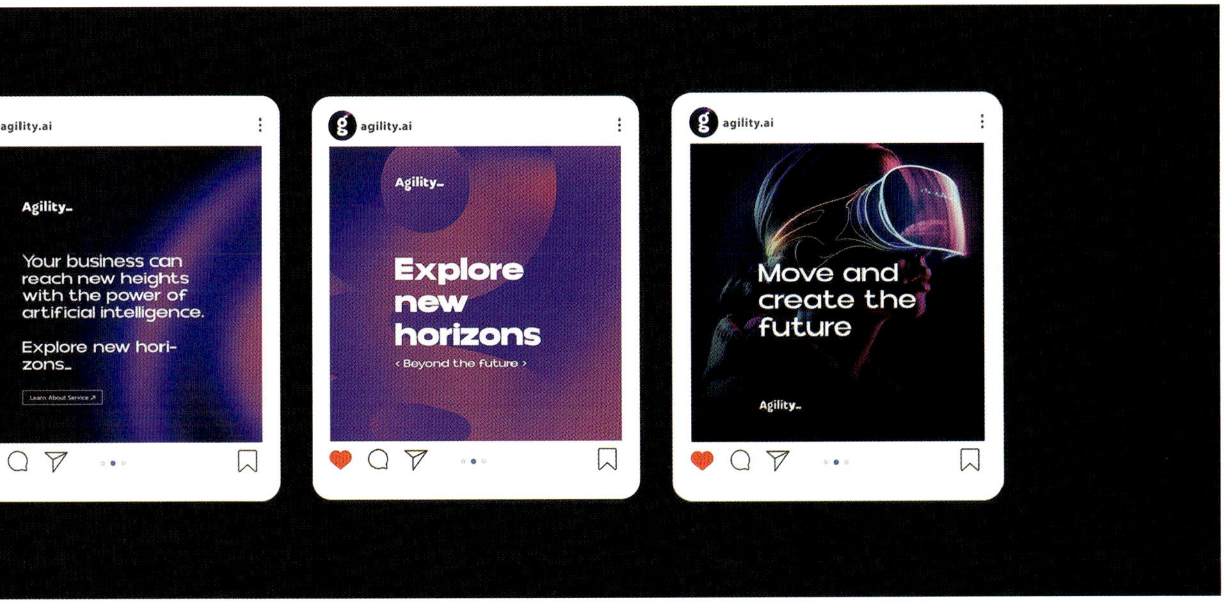
agility.ai
Agility_
Your business can reach new heights with the power of artificial intelligence.
Explore new hori-zons_
agility.ai
Agility_
Explore new horizons
‹ Beyond the future ›
agility.ai
Move and create the future
Agility_

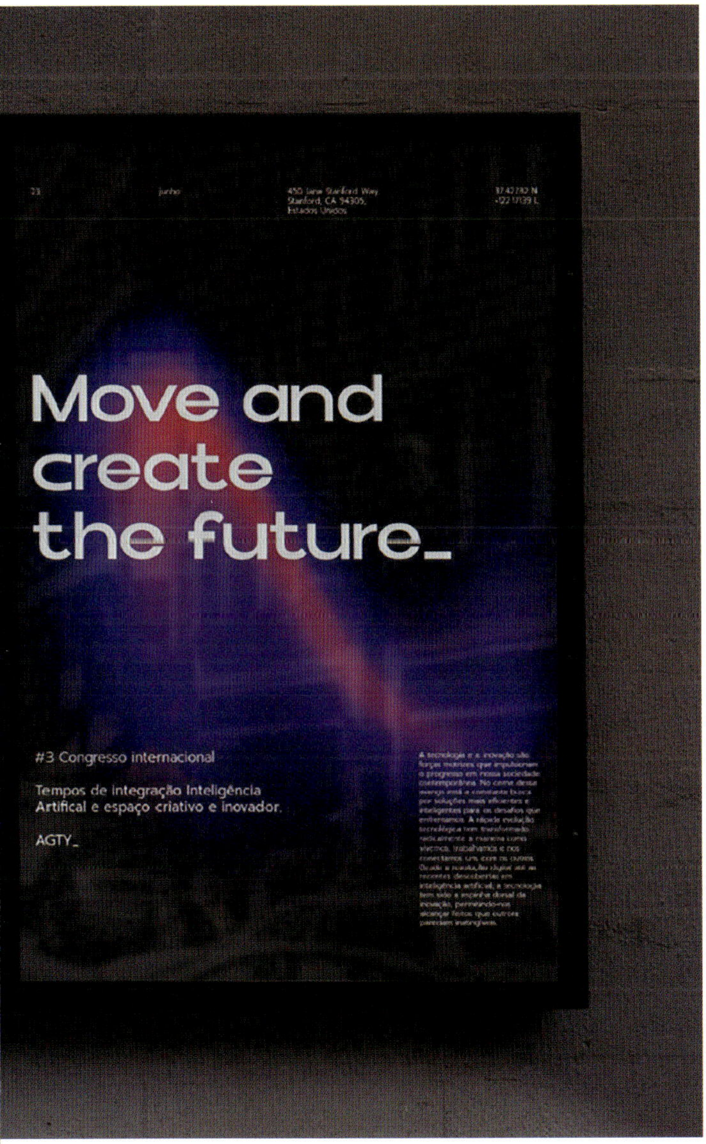
Move and create the future_
#3 Congresso internacional
Tempos de integração Inteligência Artifical e espaço criativo e inovador.
AGTY_

C60 · M100 · Y0 · K0
C0 · M55 · Y0 · K0

C0 · M0 · Y100 · K0
C5 · M0 · Y20 · K0

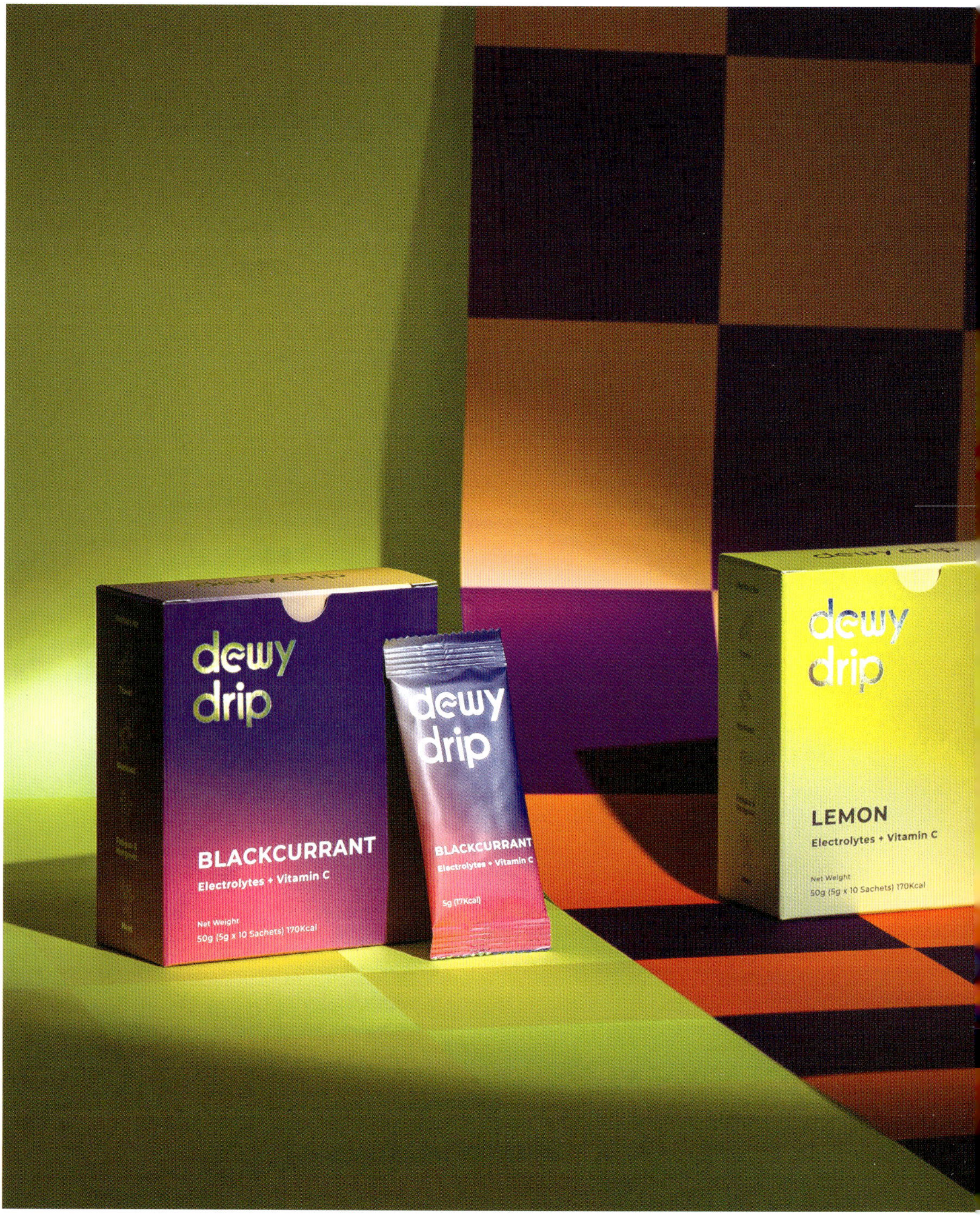

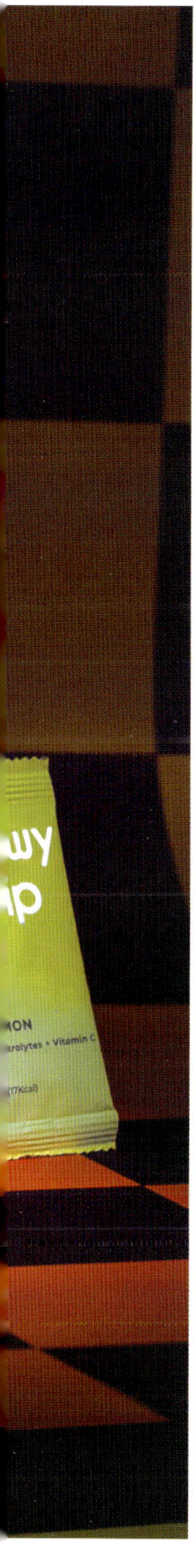

DEWY DRIP

Dewy Drip is a personal brand that focuses on body hydration supplements. To achieve optimal impact, the designers boldly incorporated gradient colour blocks to highlight the product's distinctive features. They made subtle modifications to different structures and even improved the overall shape. The designs and colours for both the box and pouch are consistent, deliberately adding holographic foil for an extra visual effect. They hope consumers will be captivated by their bold design choices, steering clear of the common and mundane directions often seen in health supplement packaging.

Client
Sonder8

Creative Director
Jay Lim

Designer
Michelle Ku

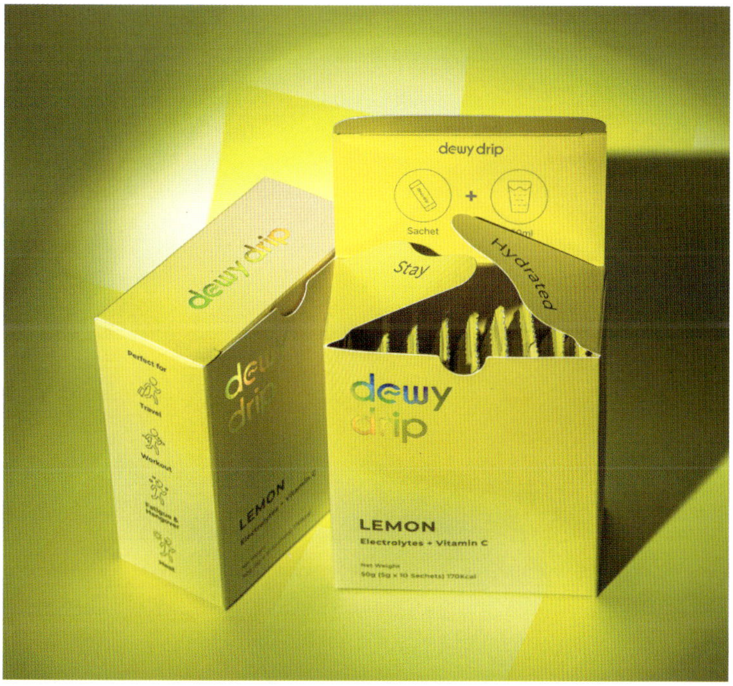

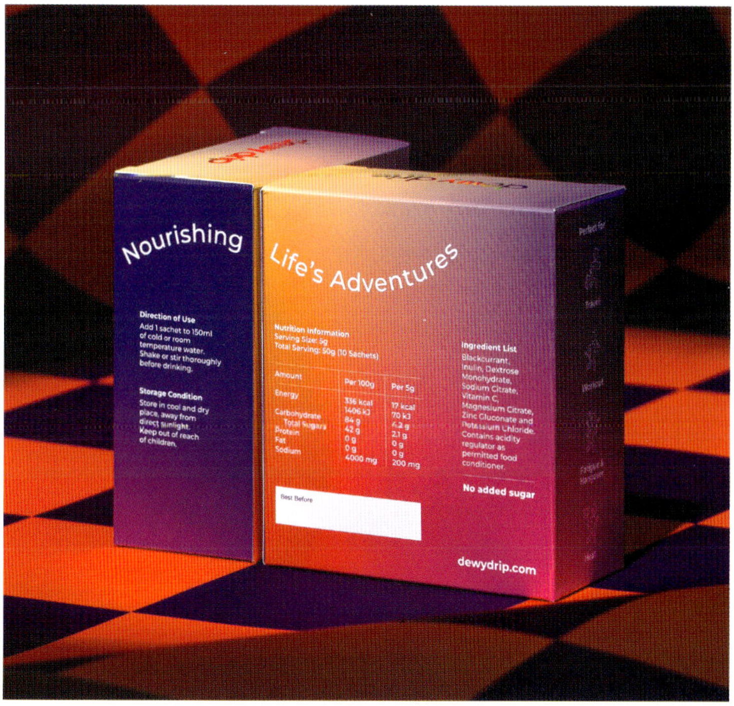

PANTONE 3005 U
PANTONE 637 U

PANTONE 1225 U
PANTONE 2577 U

PANTONE 2268 U
PANTONE 388 U

MUBASHIR

A fusion of faded and solid triangles, the logo embodies the essence of innovation and forward-thinking symbolizing dynamism and modernity. At its core lies a play symbol reminiscent of the iconic triangle play button, symbolizing engagement and interaction. The incorporation of arrows suggests progress and advancement towards the future, echoing Mubashir's commitment to pioneering digital out-of-home advertising solutions.

Design Studio
Baianat

Art Director
Mostafa Wahba

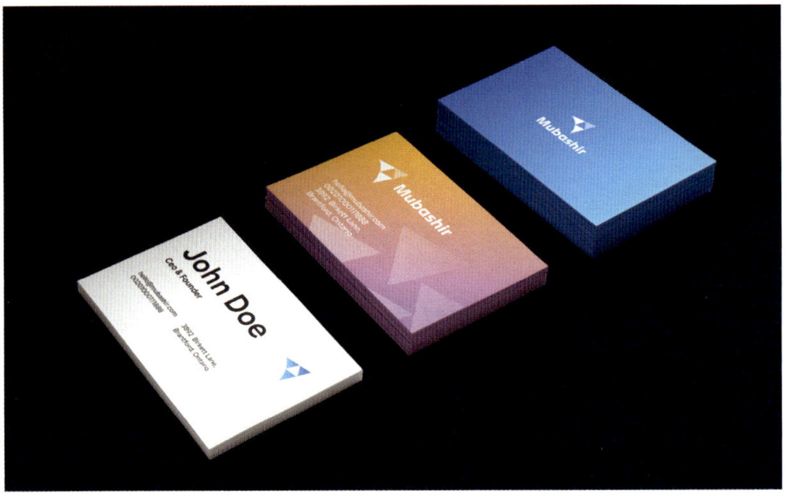

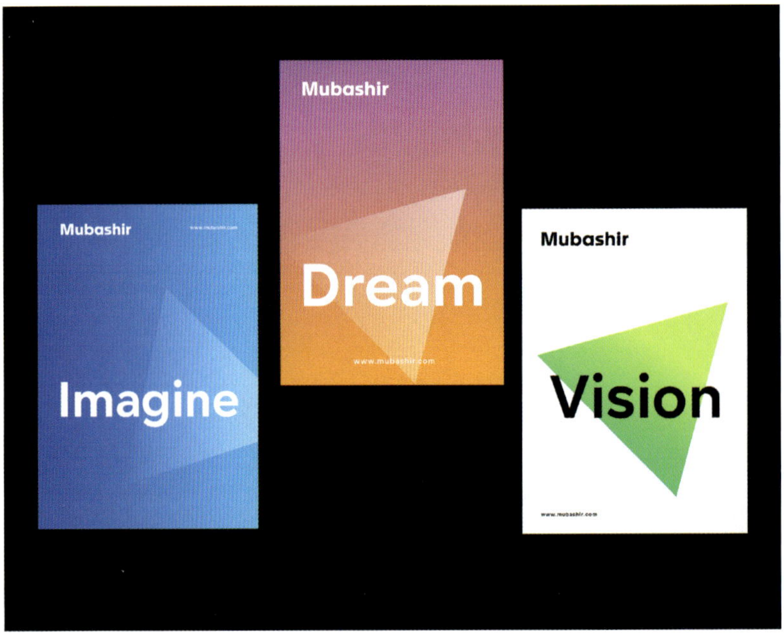

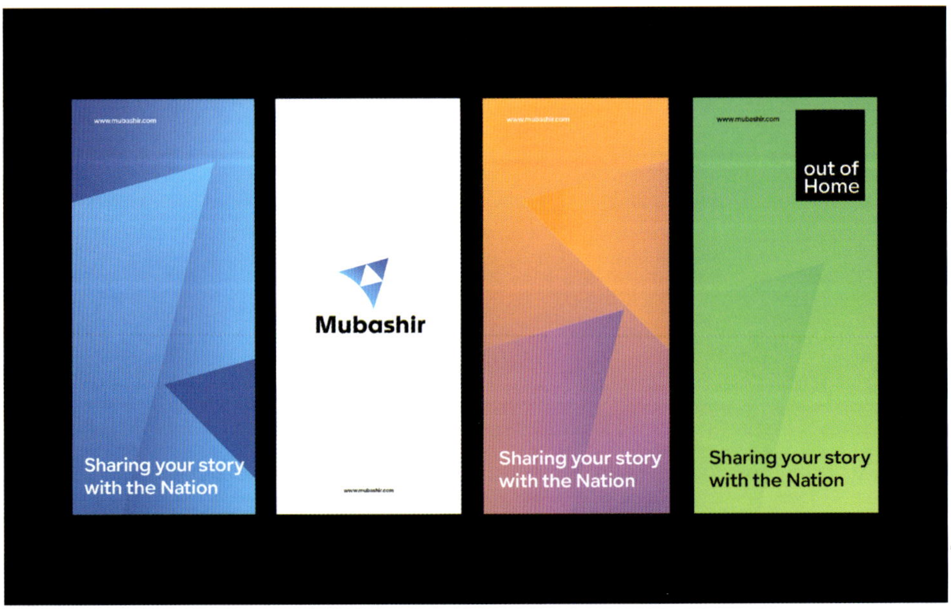

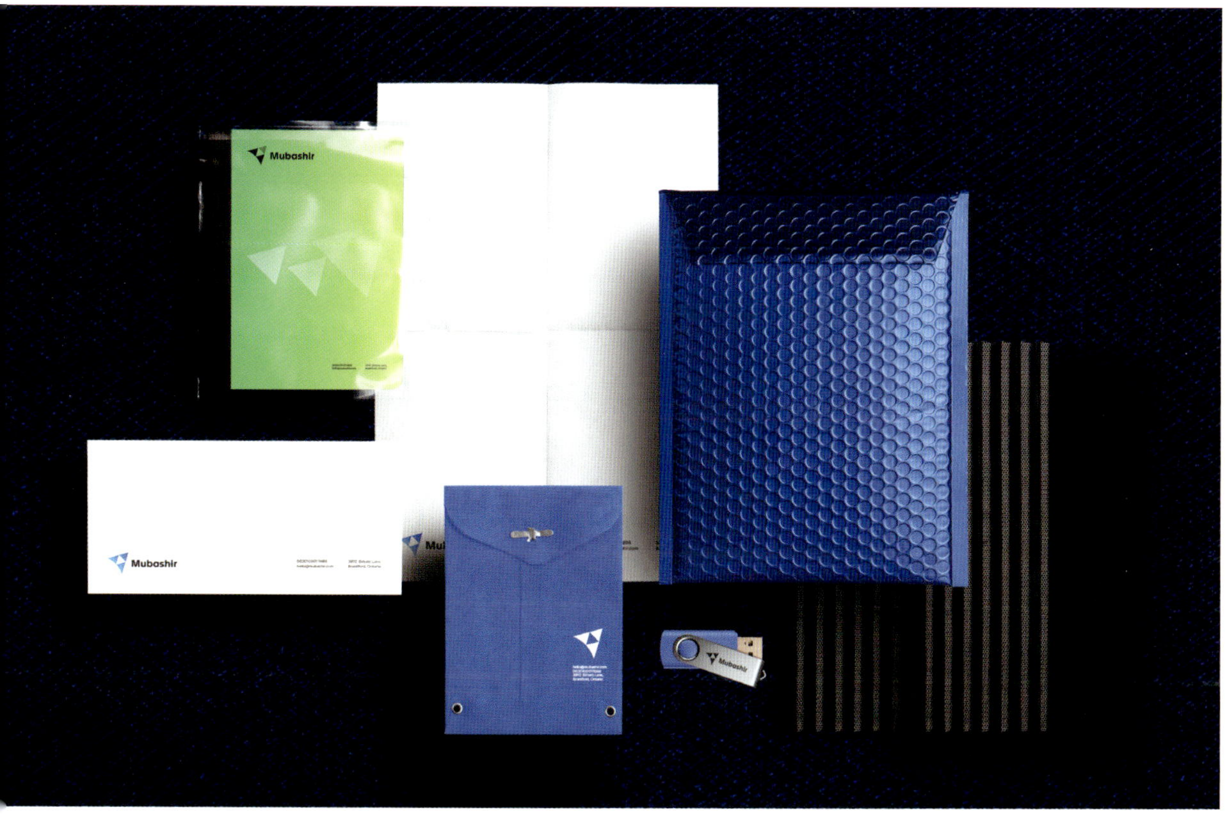
Mubashir
Mubashir

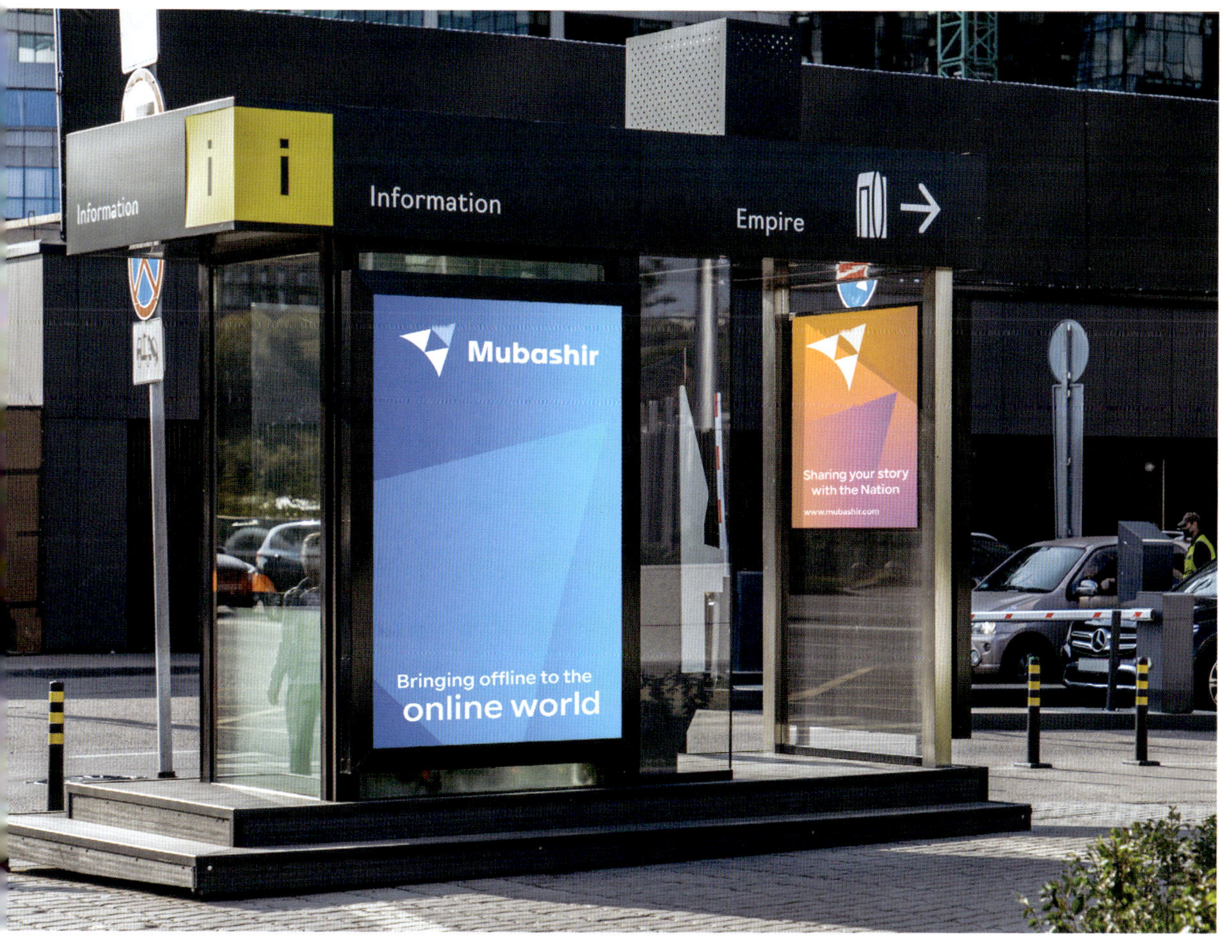
Information
i
i
Information
Empire
Mubashir
Bringing offline to the
online world
Sharing your story
with the Nation
www.mubashir.com

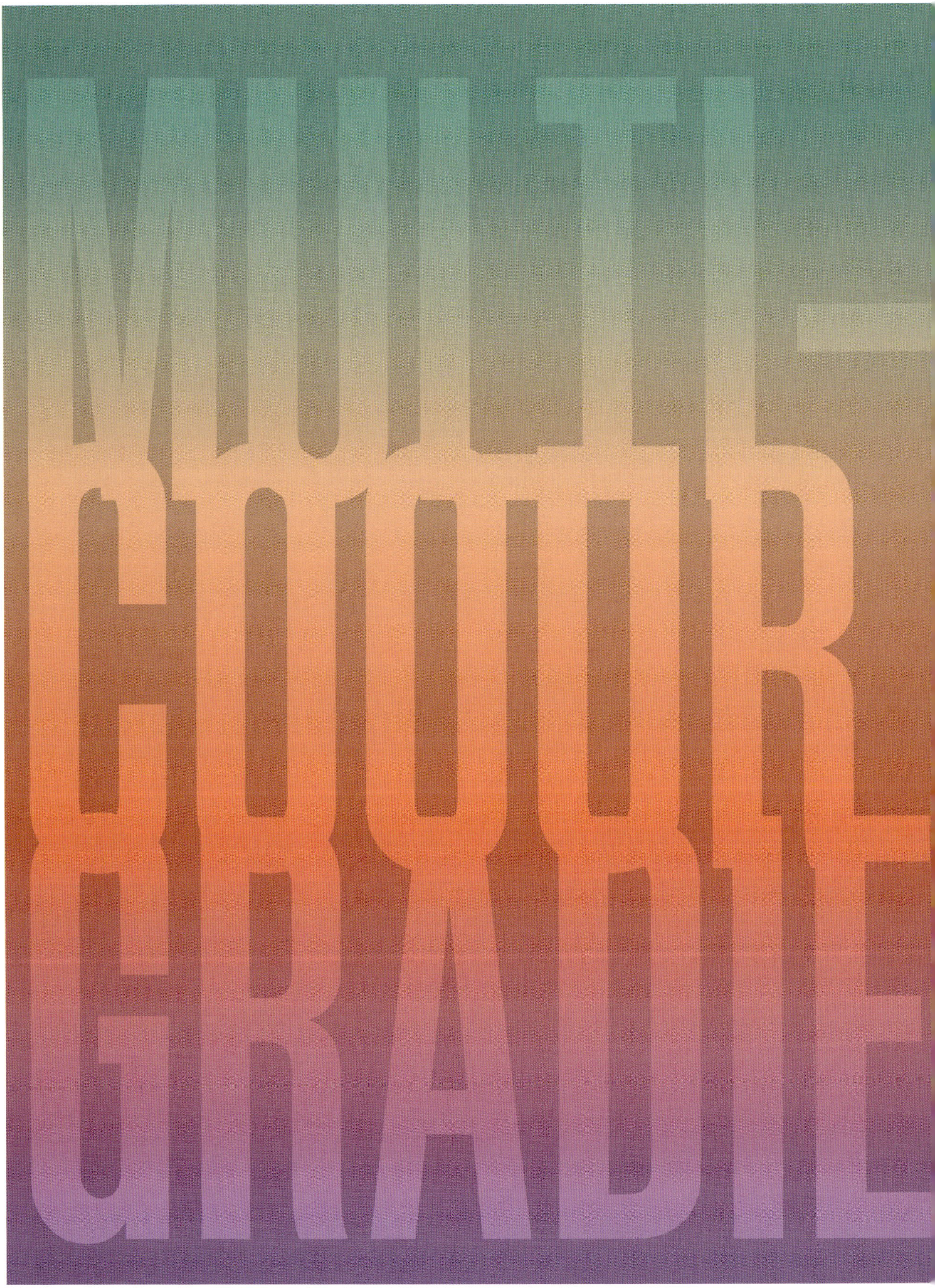

MULTI-
GRADIE

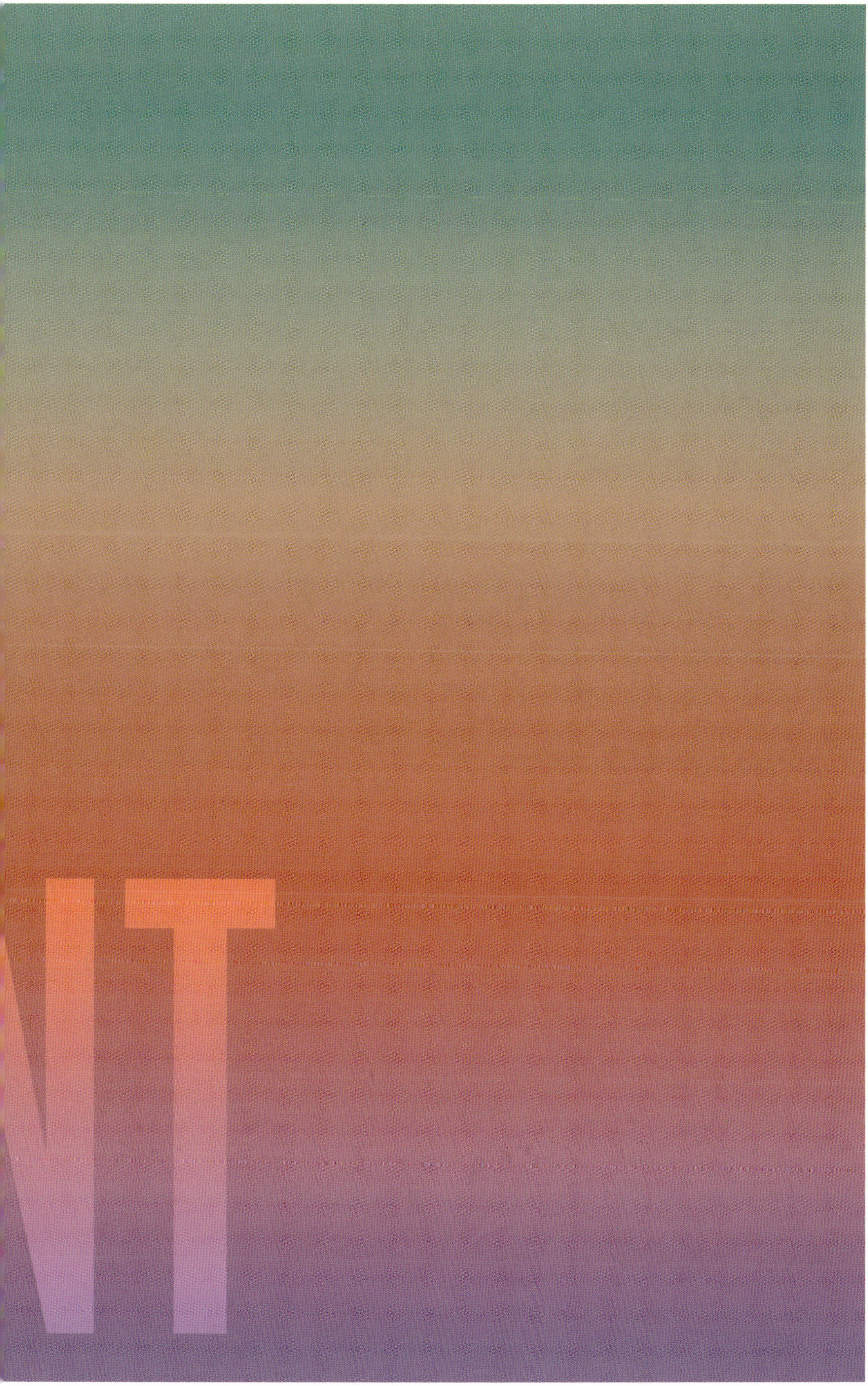

C70 · M19 · Y55 · K1

C9 · M43 · Y57 · K0

C6 · M76 · Y83 · K0

C44 · M63 · Y0 · K0

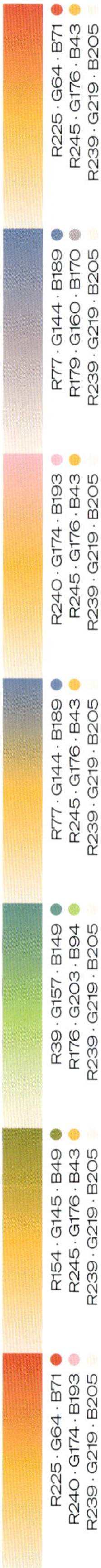

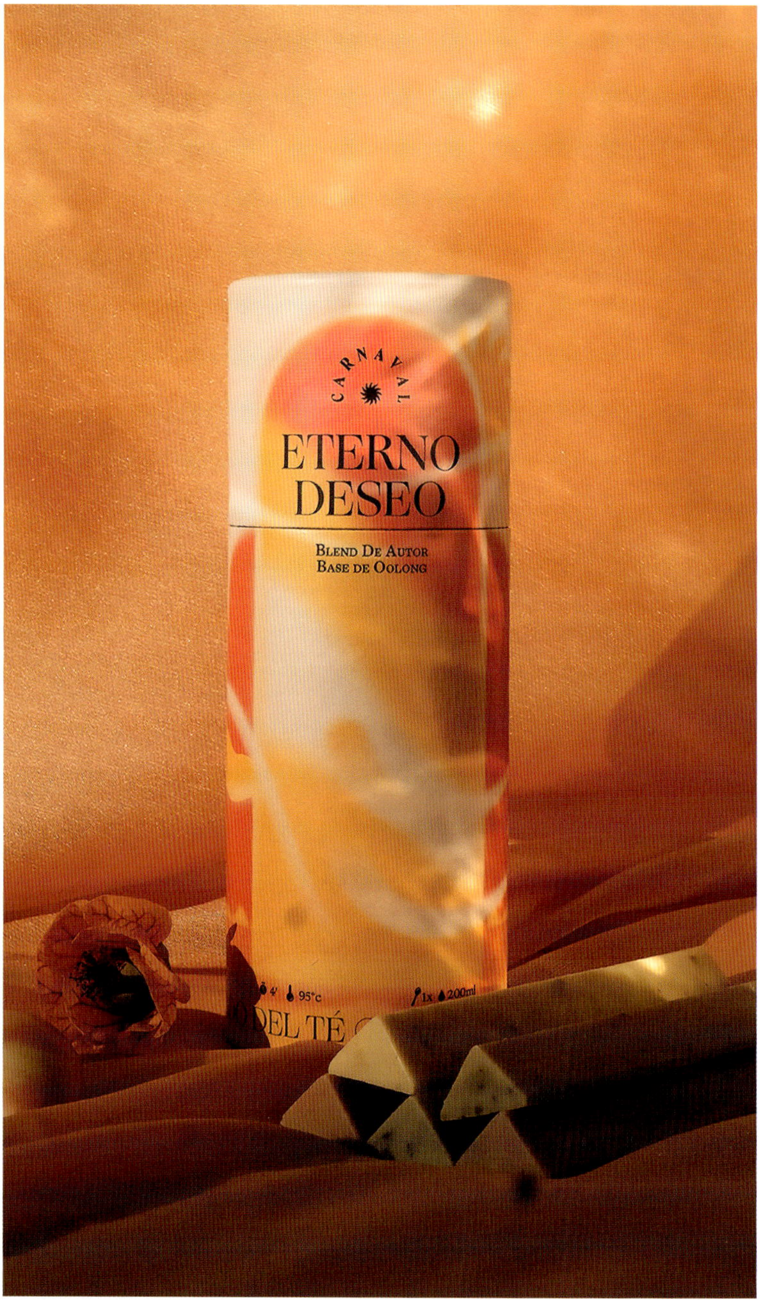

CARNAVAL

Between humans and spirits, *Carnaval* is the portal that connects the physical world and the spiritual world. Invoke *Carnaval, The Other Side Of Tea*. The packaging design hopes to visualize the portal ritual that brings new experiences, combining colours and shapes that come out of the portal. Torres and Lachimia choose the path of sustainability and organic. A ritual from start to finish inspired in the different festivals, flora and fauna ... they go hand in hand with nature, music and art. Packaging design arose from the idea of "portal ", a phenomenon that connects us with new worlds, new pairings, new strands, new herbs, new consumptions, new habits.

Designer
Angello Torres &
Fiorella Lachimia

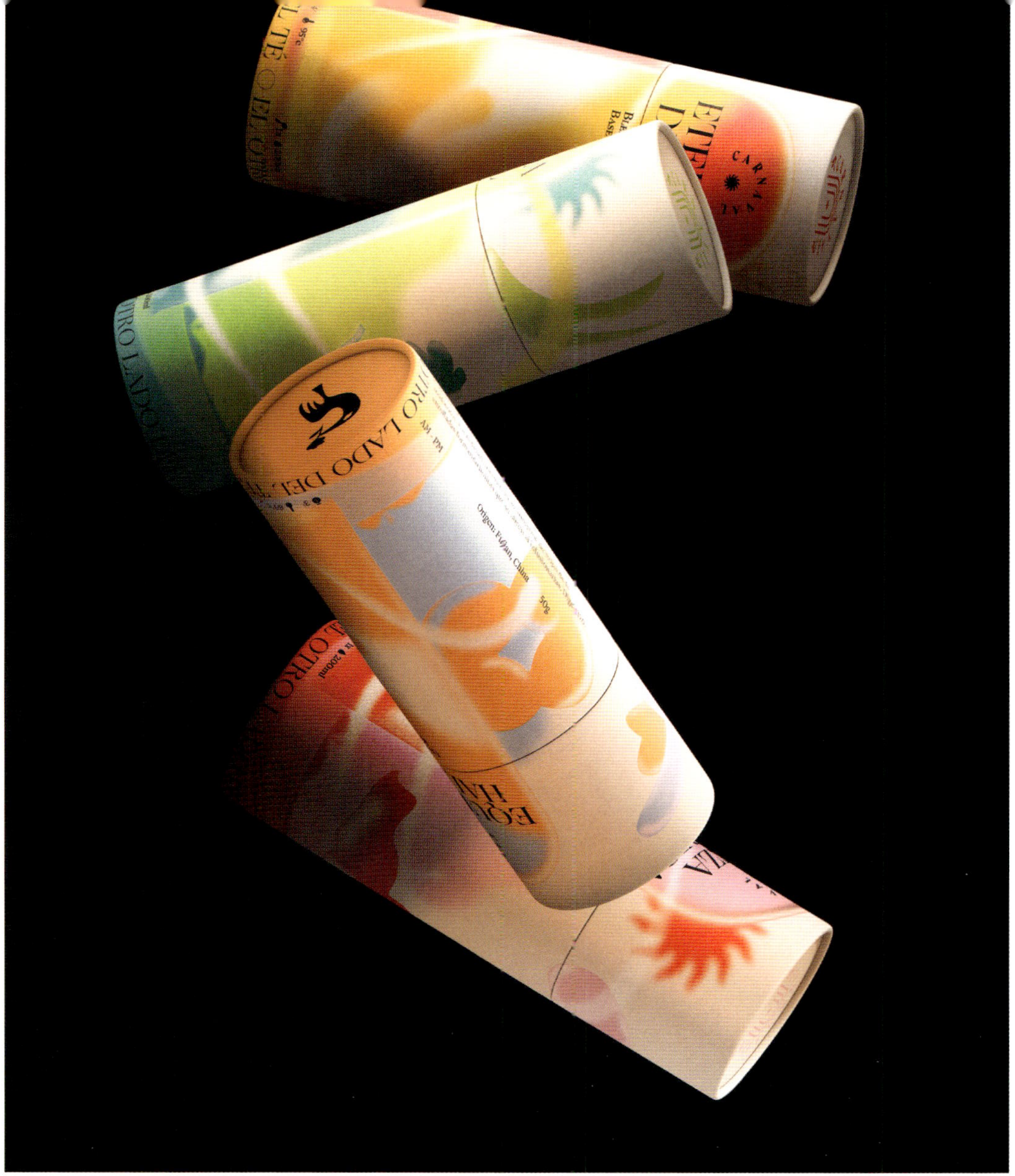

CARNAVAL
Origen: Fujian, China
50g
AM - PM
OTRO LADO DEL

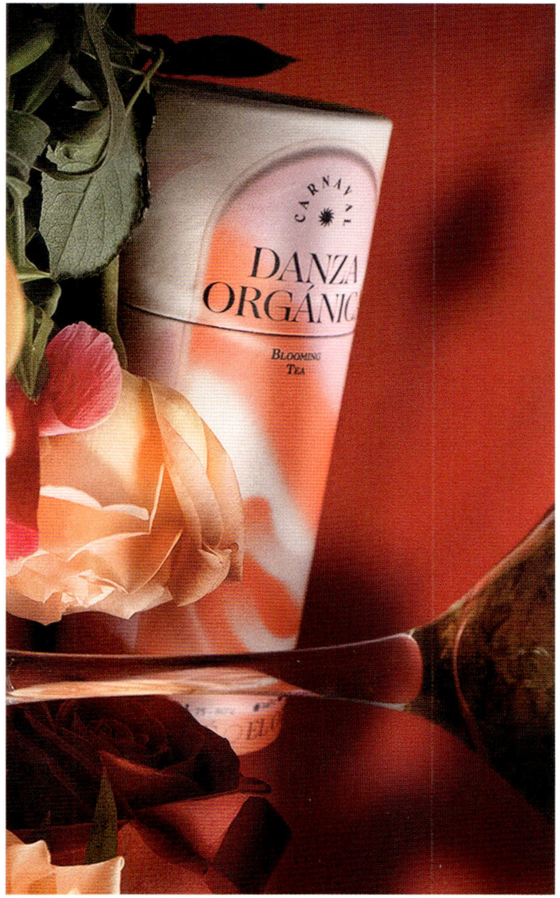

CARNAVAL
DANZA
ORGÁNIC
BLOOMING
TEA

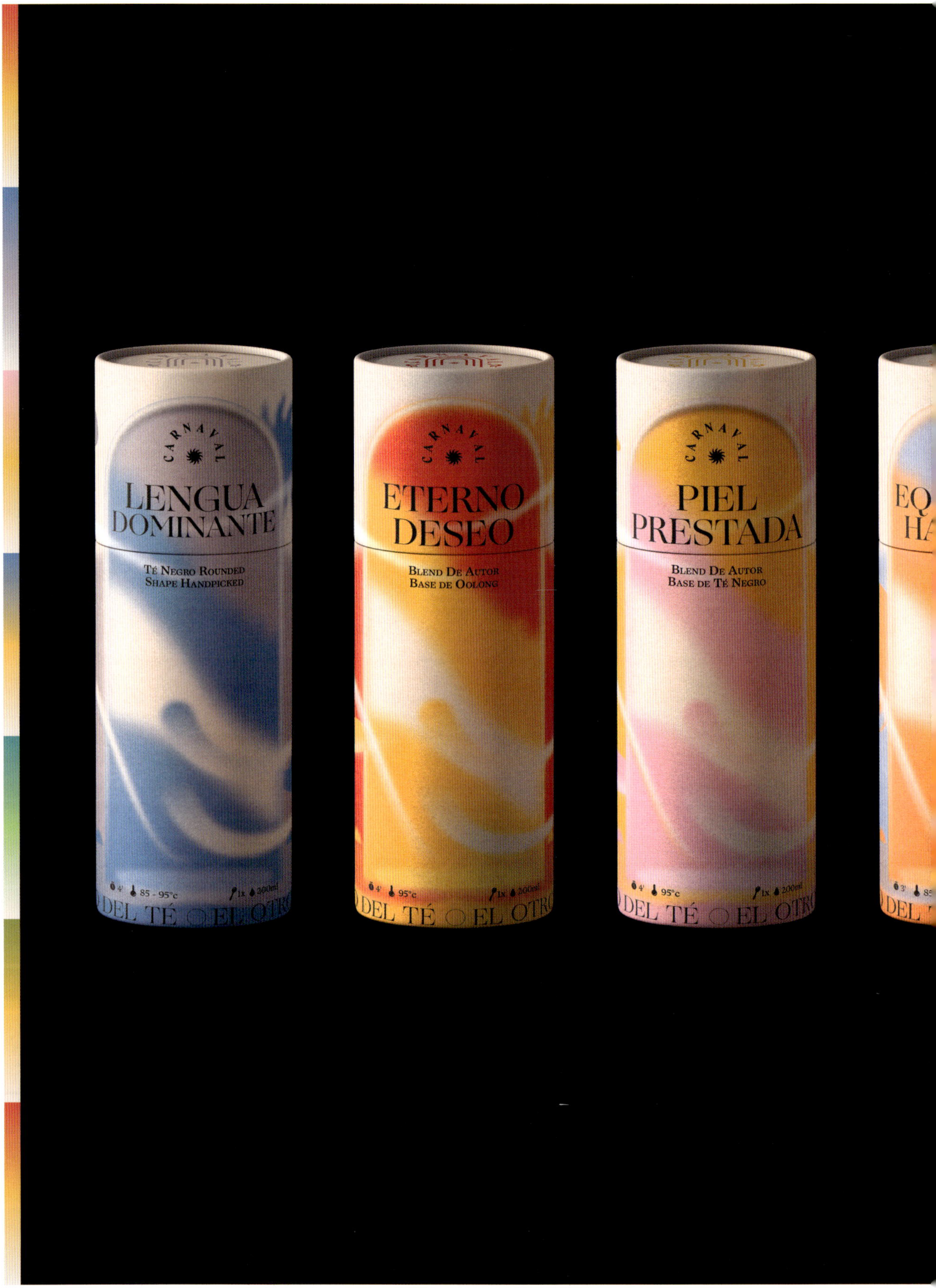
CARNAVAL
LENGUA DOMINANTE
Té Negro Rounded
Shape Handpicked
85 - 95°c
DEL TÉ
CARNAVAL
ETERNO DESEO
Blend De Autor
Base de Oolong
95°c
DEL TÉ
EL OTR
CARNAVAL
PIEL PRESTADA
Blend De Autor
Base de Té Negro
95°c
DEL TÉ
EL OTR

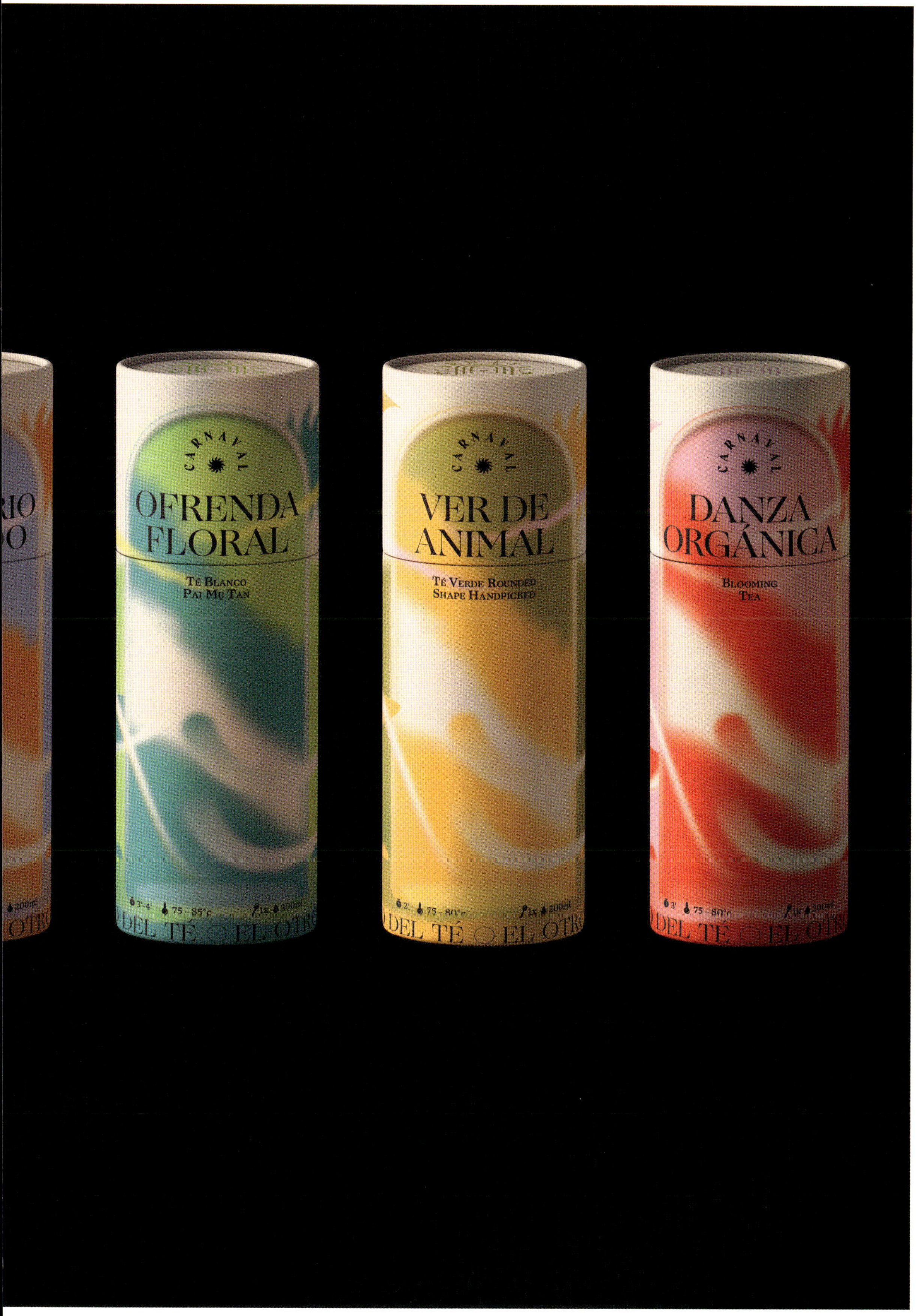
CARNAVAL
OFRENDA
FLORAL
Té Blanco
Pai Mu Tan
CARNAVAL
VER DE
ANIMAL
Té Verde Rounded
Shape Handpicked
CARNAVAL
DANZA
ORGÁNICA
Blooming
Tea

C50 · M50 · Y0 · K0
C0 · M50 · Y5 · K0
C0 · M75 · Y75 · K0

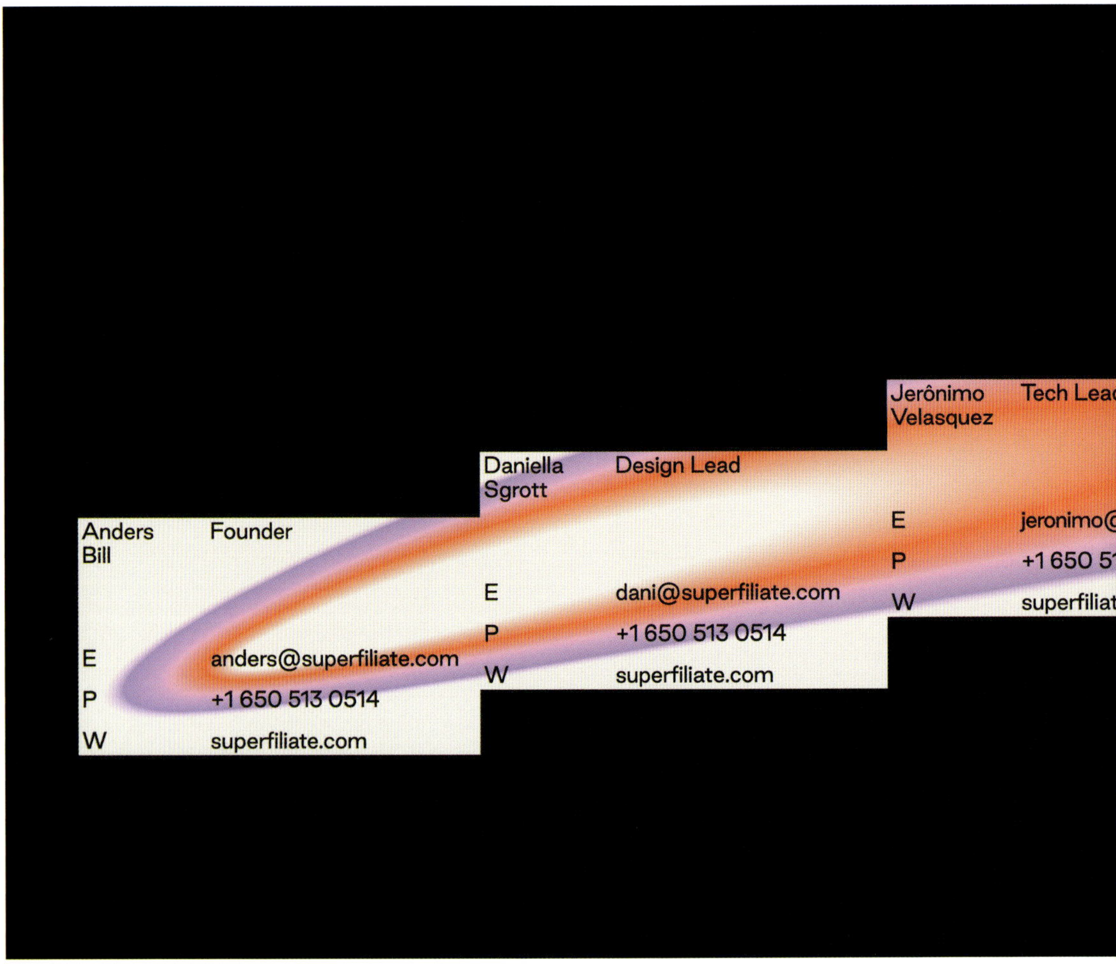

C50 · M50 · Y0 · K0
C64 · M13 · Y1 · K0
C0 · M50 · Y5 · K0

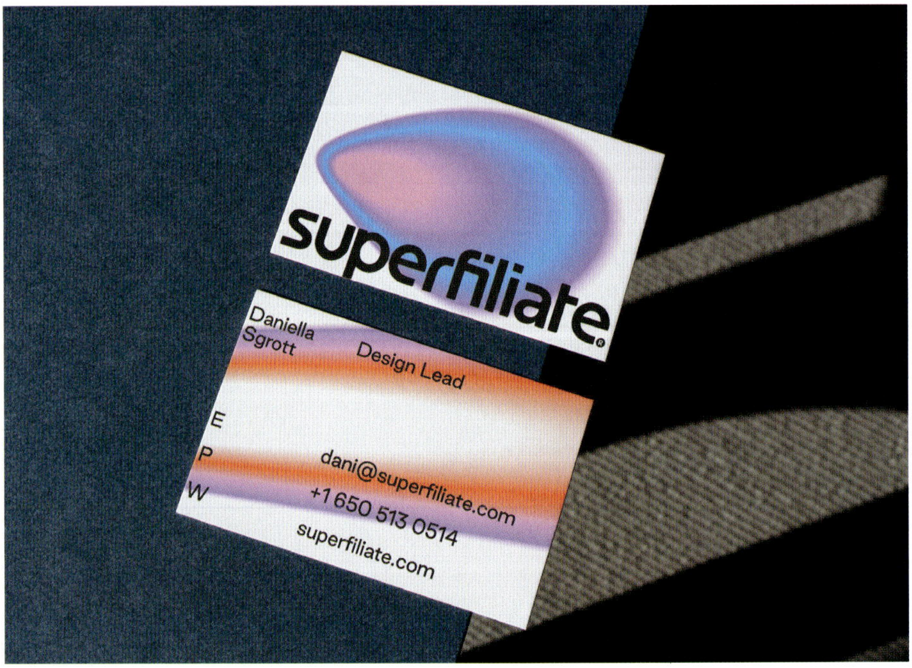

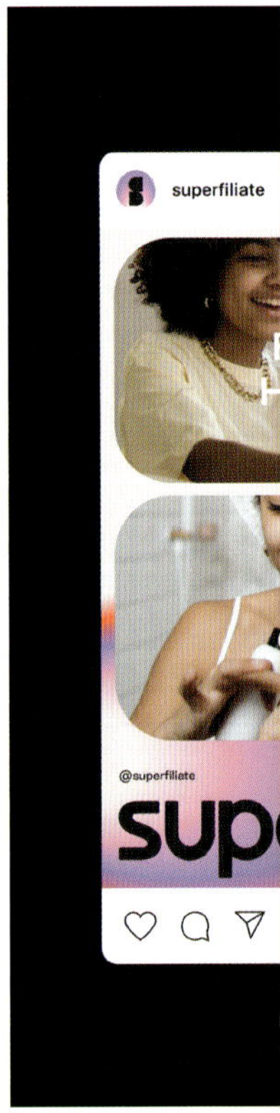

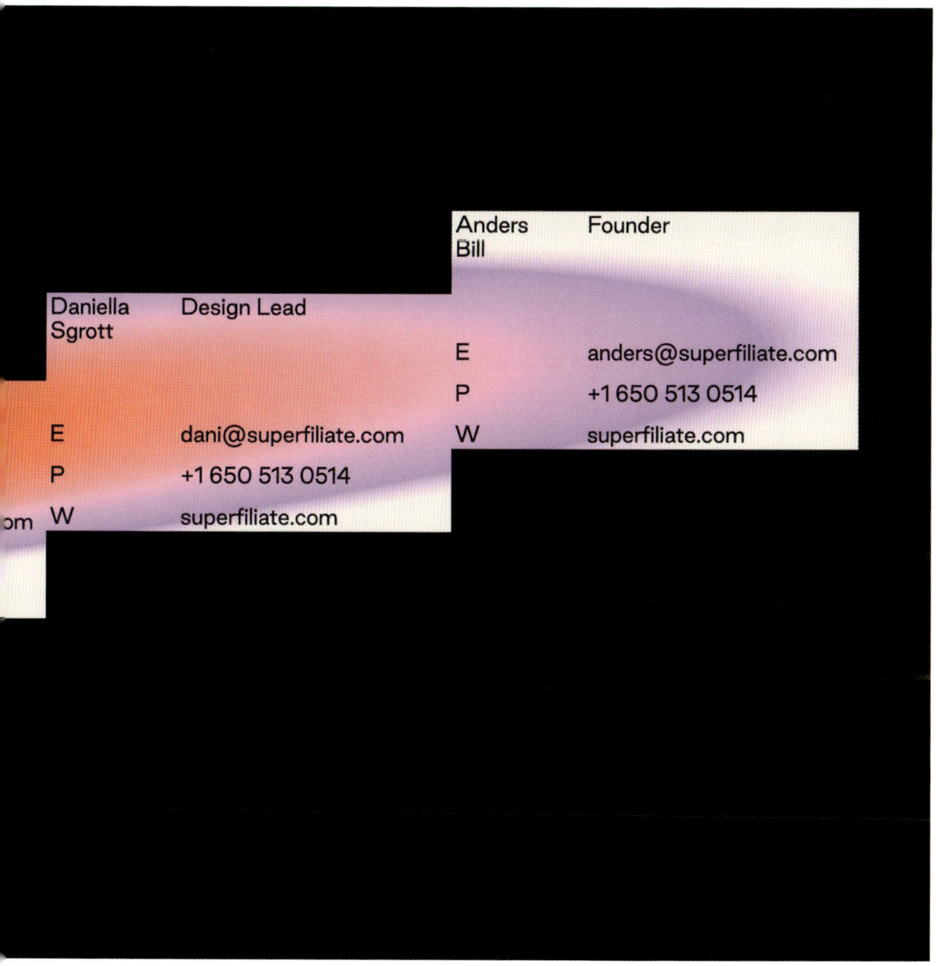

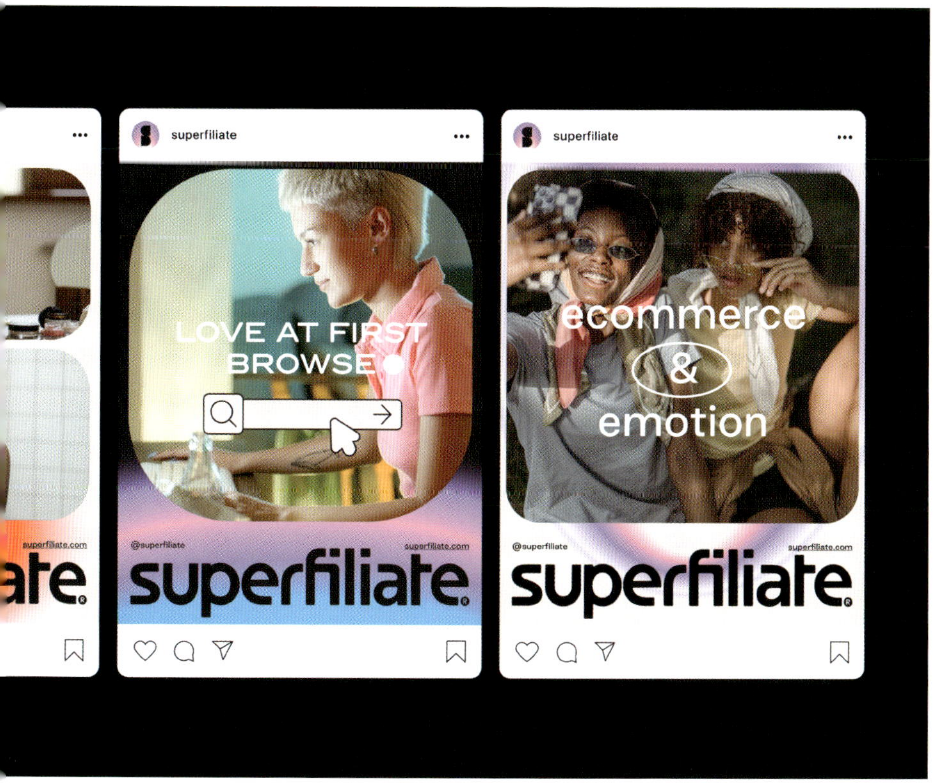

SUPERFILIATE

Superfiliate is a brand that creates personalized shopping experiences that empower customers and creators to share their brand's stories online. This project consisted of developing the whole branding. The starting point for the brand's concept and aesthetics was the idea of making *Superfiliate* warmer and friendlier, transforming their customers into fans and their cold and transactional digital experiences into memorable and funny ones. The work included the visual identity, as well as its communication concept, copywriting, social media, and website.

Design Studio
Bacile* & La Libertad TNC

Art Director & Designer
Nicolás Bacile & Gonzalo Prunesti

Creative Director
Nicolás Bacile, Gonzalo Prunesti & Santiago Guillamondegui

Concept & Copywriter
Santiago Guillamondegui

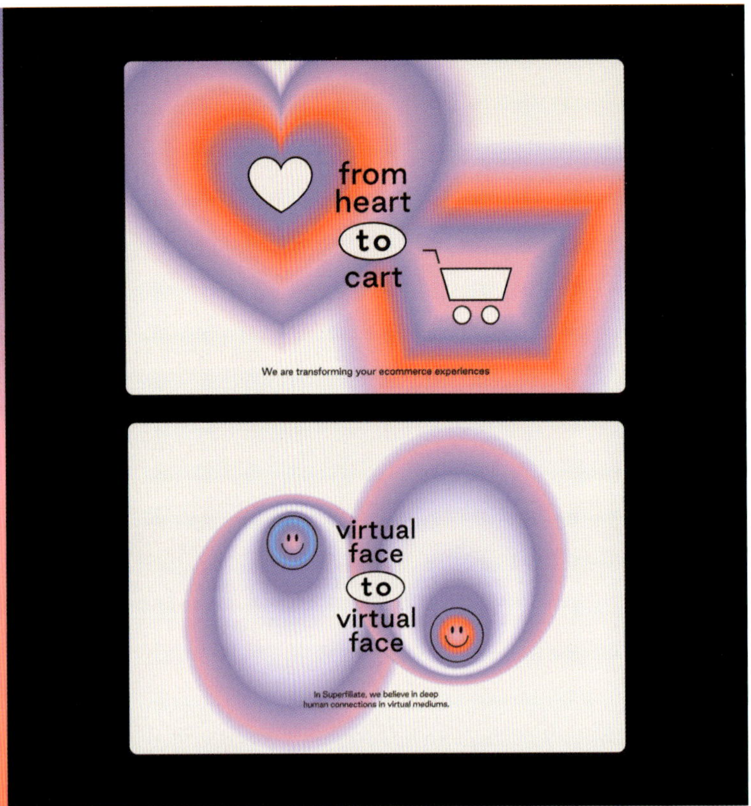
from
heart
to
cart
We are transforming your ecommerce experiences
virtual
face
to
virtual
face
In Superfiliate, we believe in deep
human connections in virtual mediums.

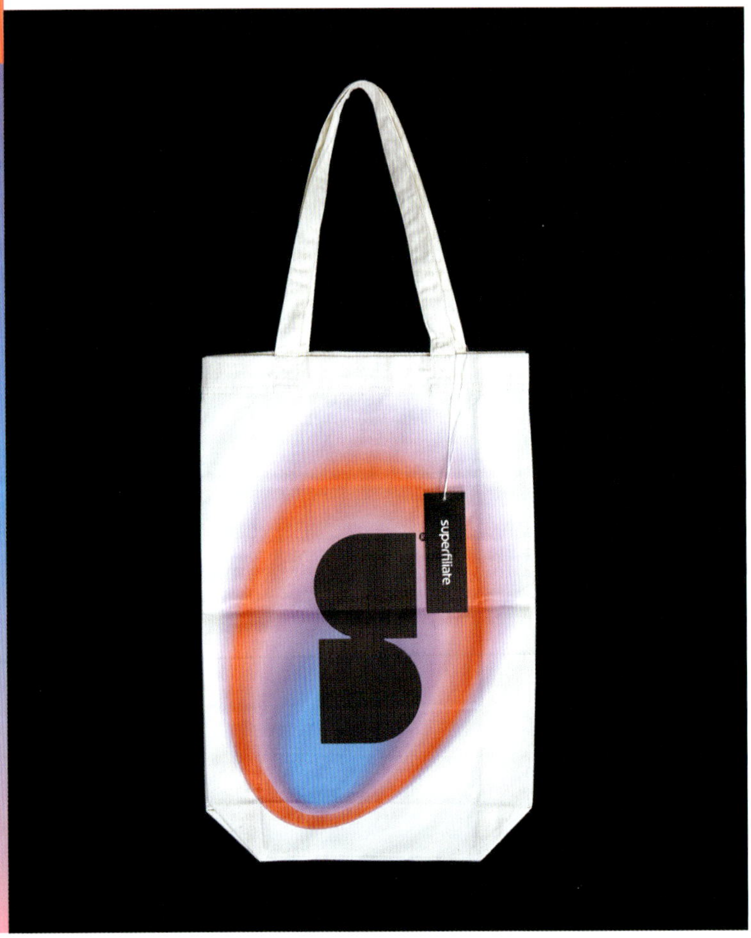
superfiliate

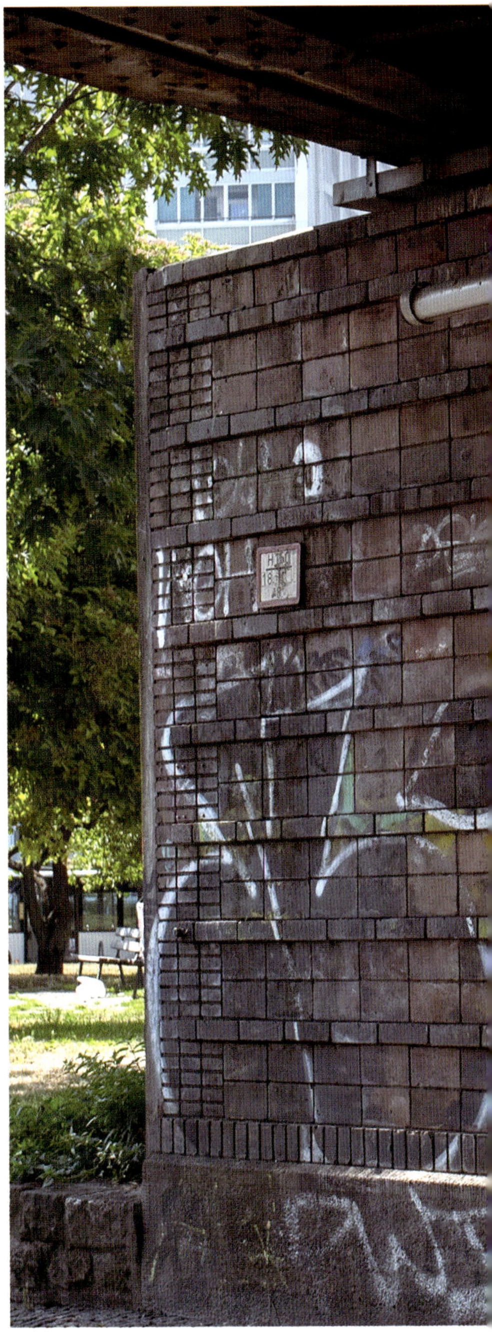

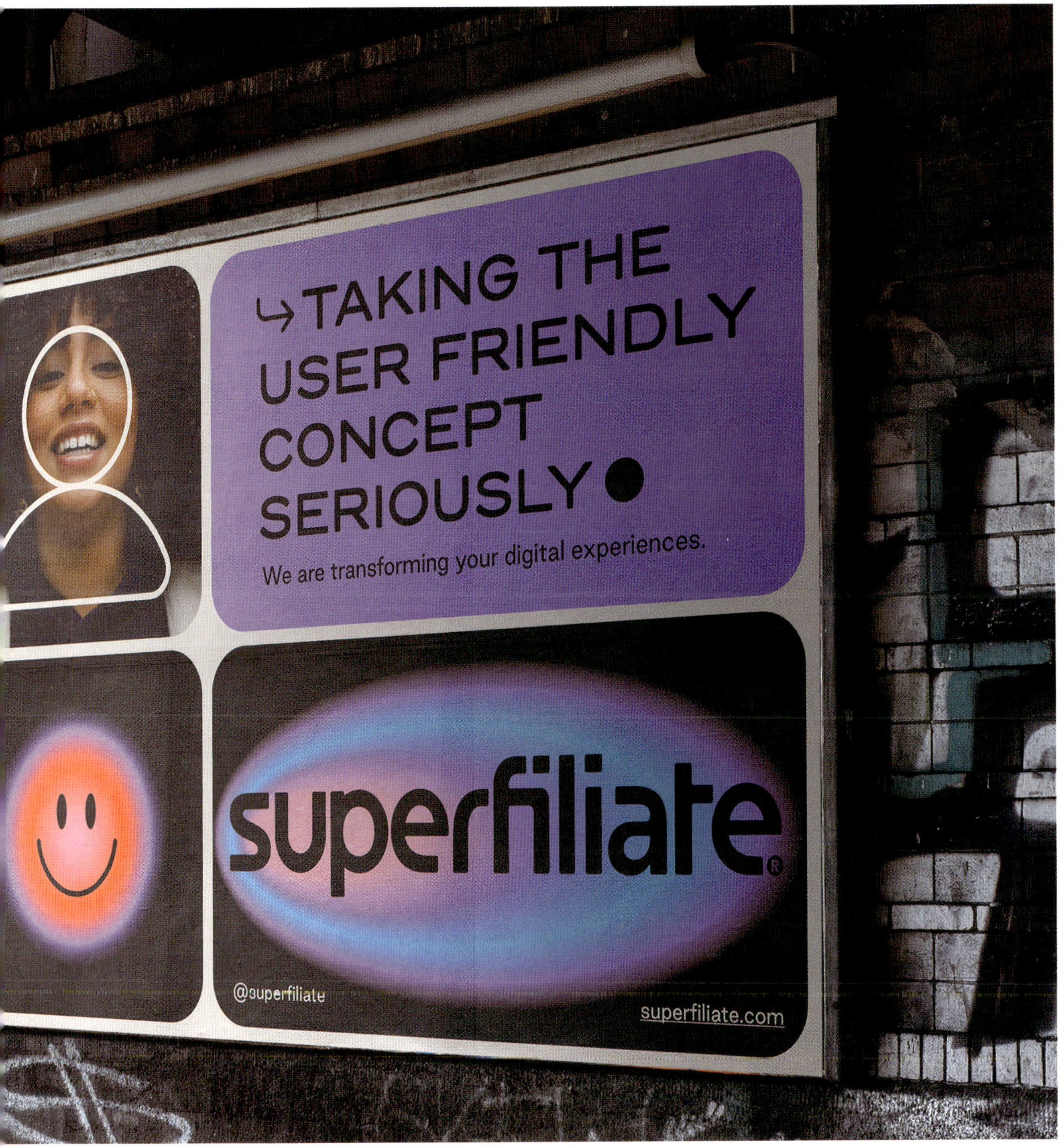
↳TAKING THE
USER FRIENDLY
CONCEPT
SERIOUSLY
We are transforming your digital experiences.
superfiliate®
@superfiliate
superfiliate.com

PANTONE 2935 C

PANTONE 211 C

PANTONE 5544 C

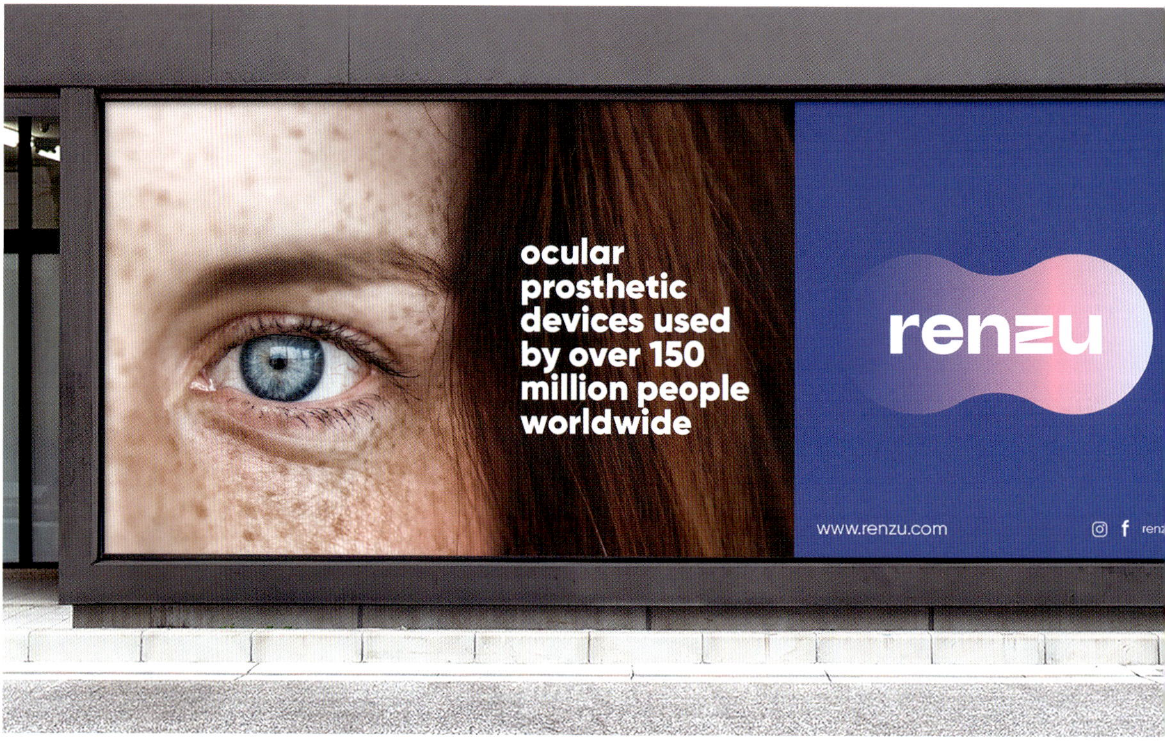

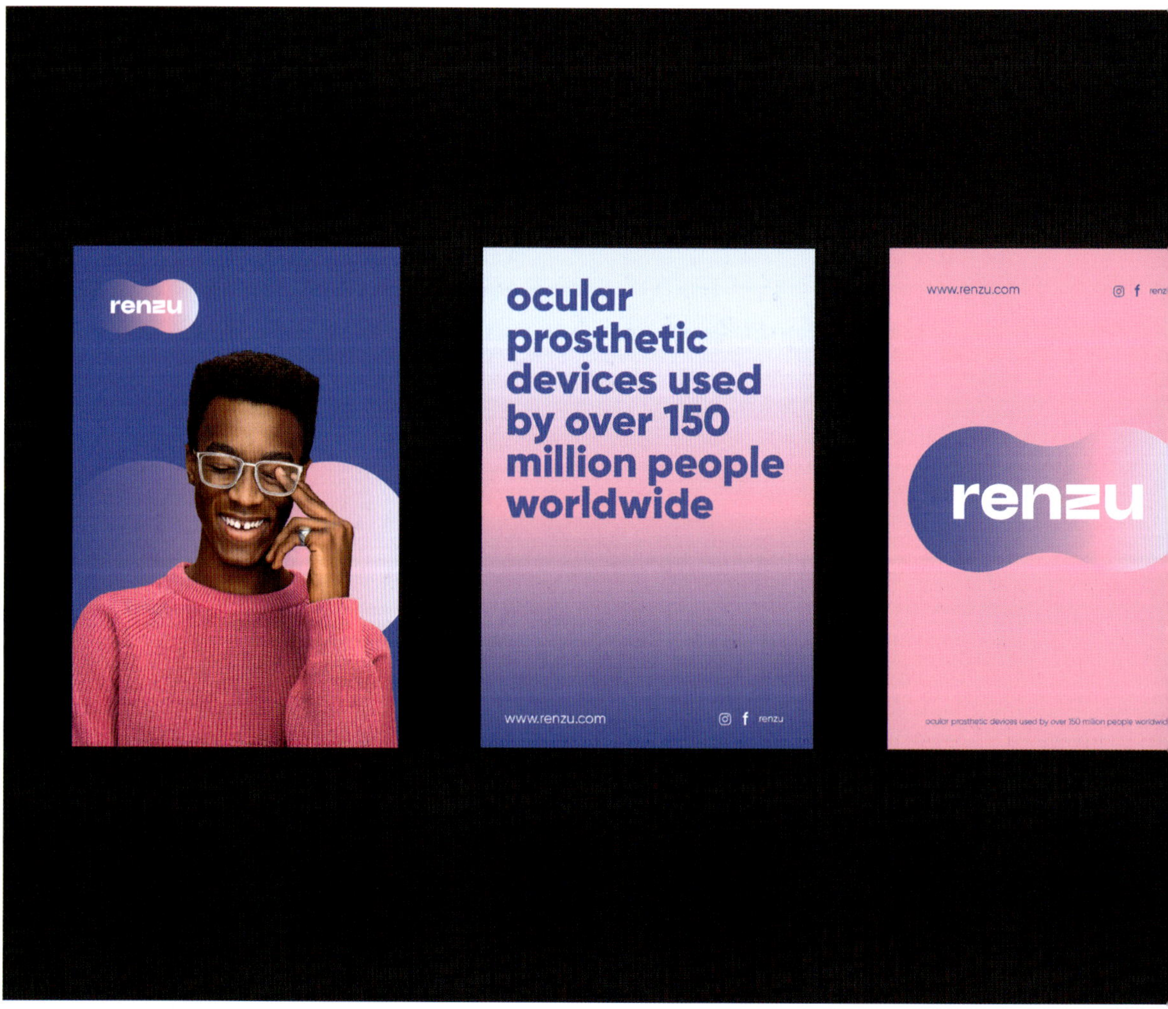

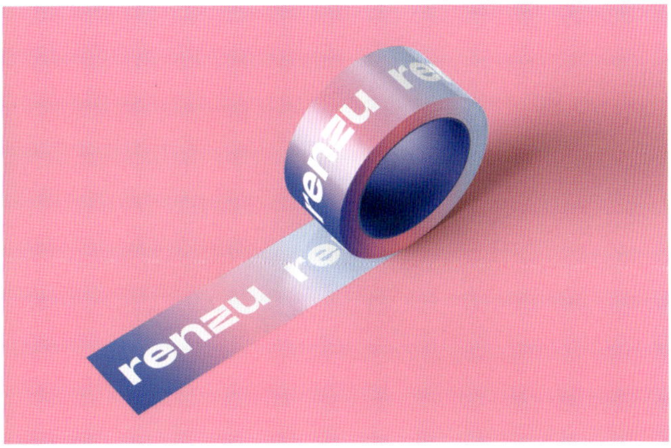

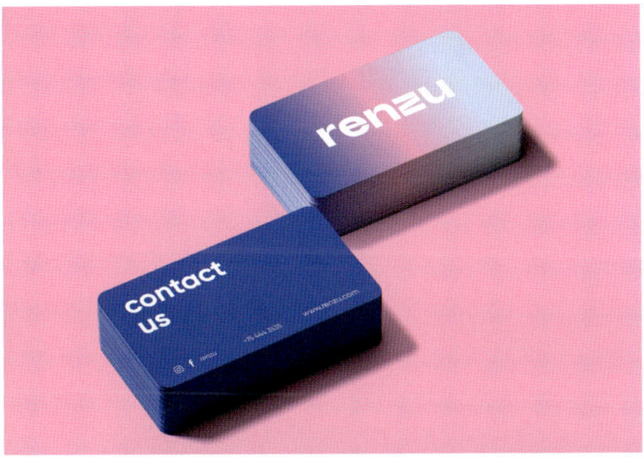

RENZU

Renzu Company is a Japanese manufacturer of liquid for contact lenses and moisturizing eye drops. Logo, identity and packaging were created for the company. The prototype for the logo was the shape of the lens container, and its smooth flowing lines are also supported by the gradient graphics of the corporate identity.

Art Director & Designer
Andrey Lazutkin

Design Studio
Townsfolk Design Bureau

3D Artist & Motion Designer
Nastasia Romanova

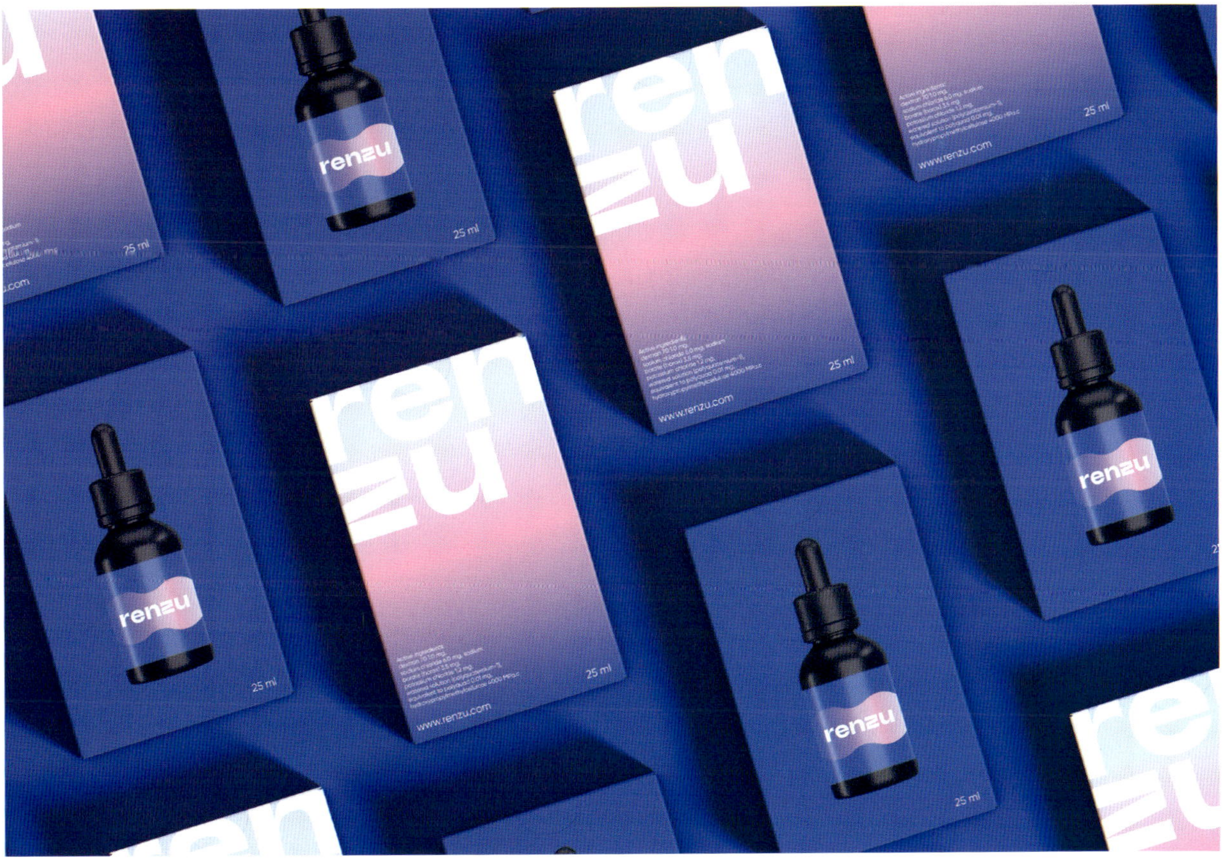

R105 · G7 · B21
R150 · G248 · B235
R81 · G0 · B7
R110 · G234 · B173
R145 · G21 · B81

R172 · G212 · B0
R83 · G43 · B255
R148 · G167 · B177
R229 · G183 · B72
R30 · G72 · B192
R24 · G0 · B96
R231 · G255 · B159
R65 · G44 · B163

R40 · G0 · B183
R52 · G28 · B16
R255 · G255 · B31
R146 · G215 · B84
R101 · G31 · B161
R161 · G135 · B21
R94 · G120 · B233
R24 · G53 · B185

R4 · G0 · B0
R88 · G59 · B113
R157 · G154 · B80
R162 · G193 · B175
R60 · G29 · B47
R195 · G226 · B208
R202 · G227 · B240
R215 · G255 · B71

R0 · G0 · B79
R156 · G208 · B0
R254 · G217 · B243
R143 · G178 · B156
R167 · G196 · B142
R26 · G32 · B117
R112 · G76 · B99
R157 · G175 · B0

R26 · G32 · B117
R155 · G171 · B18
R215 · G241 · B196
R99 · G84 · B234
R40 · G14 · B59
R137 · G161 · B24
R118 · G94 · B232
R12 · G0 · B126

R31 · G56 · B12
R224 · G198 · B243
R162 · G120 · B0
R91 · G133 · B254
R174 · G147 · B198
R65 · G118 · B0
R229 · G223 · B137
R26 · G118 · B0

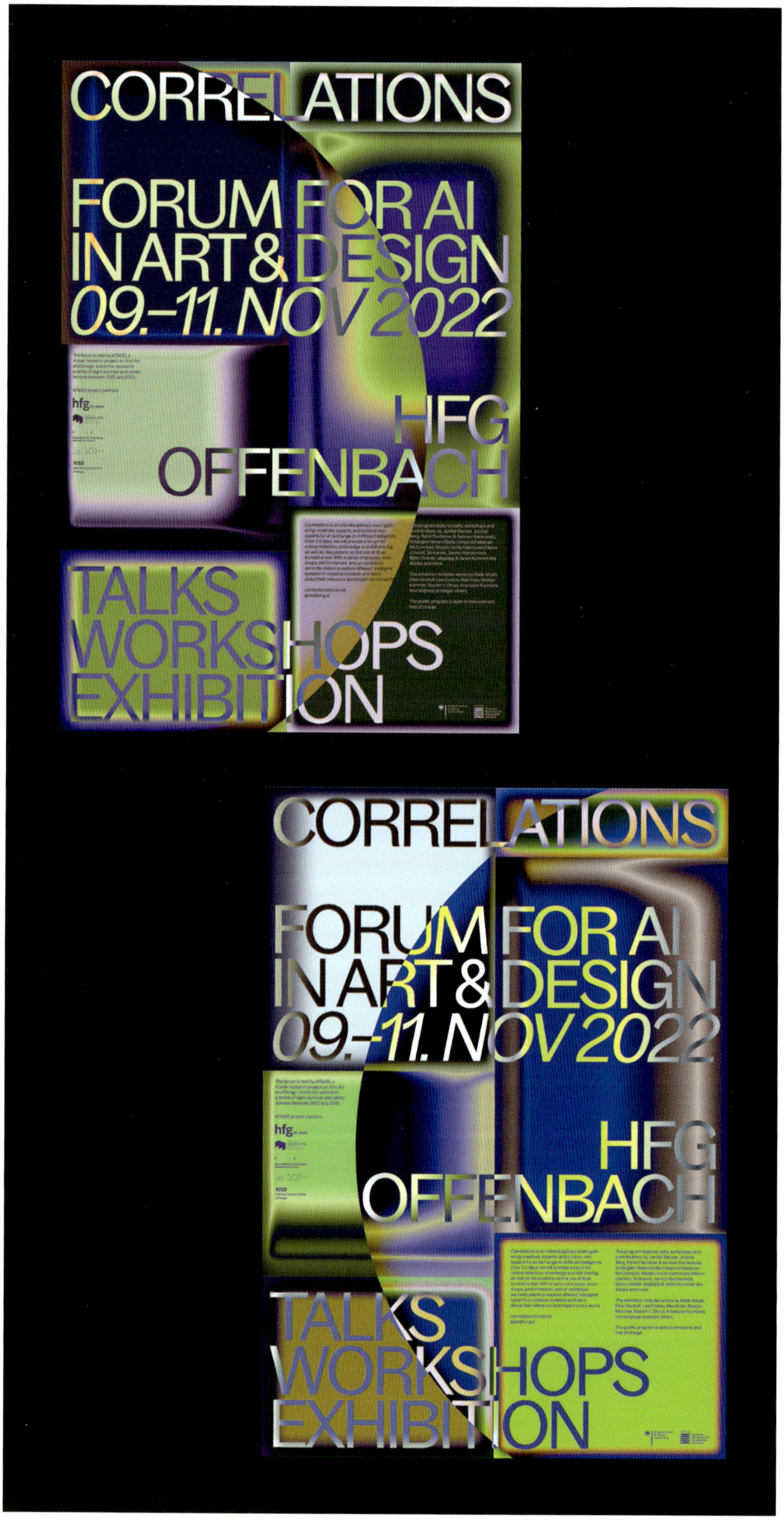

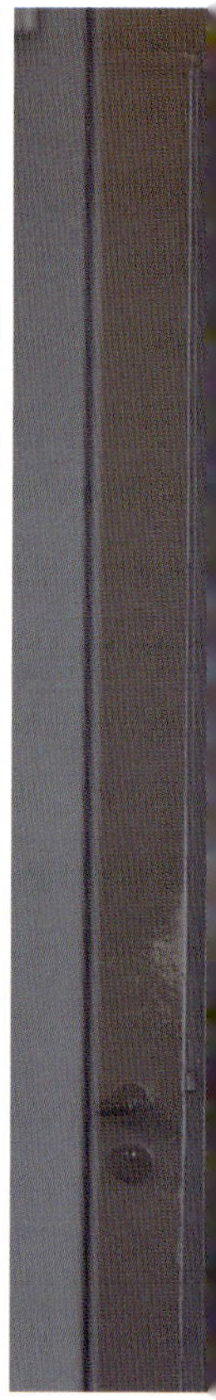

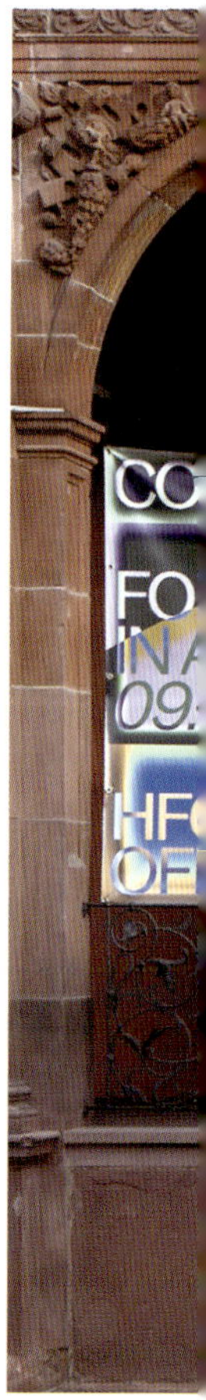

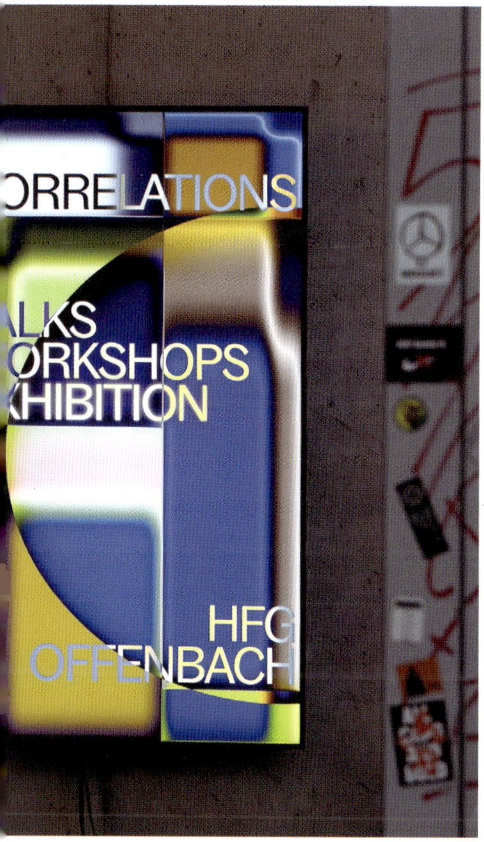

CORRELATIONS VISUAL IDENTITY

"Correlations—Forum for AI in Art and Design" is an interdisciplinary event about artificial intelligence in art and design, which takes place at Hochschule für Gestaltung Offenbach, providing a series of lectures, workshops, performances, and an exhibition. It is part of the joint project "KITeGG—Making AI tangible and comprehensible: Connecting technology and society through design", which is a four-year program that aims to bring artificial intelligence topics and methods into design teaching. The graphic language for "Correlations" consists of many stacked gradient layers with different blend modes that change the initial images and resemble an AI process.

Designer
Laura Hilbert

Motion Designer
Tobias Rauch

Supervision
Catrin Altenbrandt & Adrian Nießler

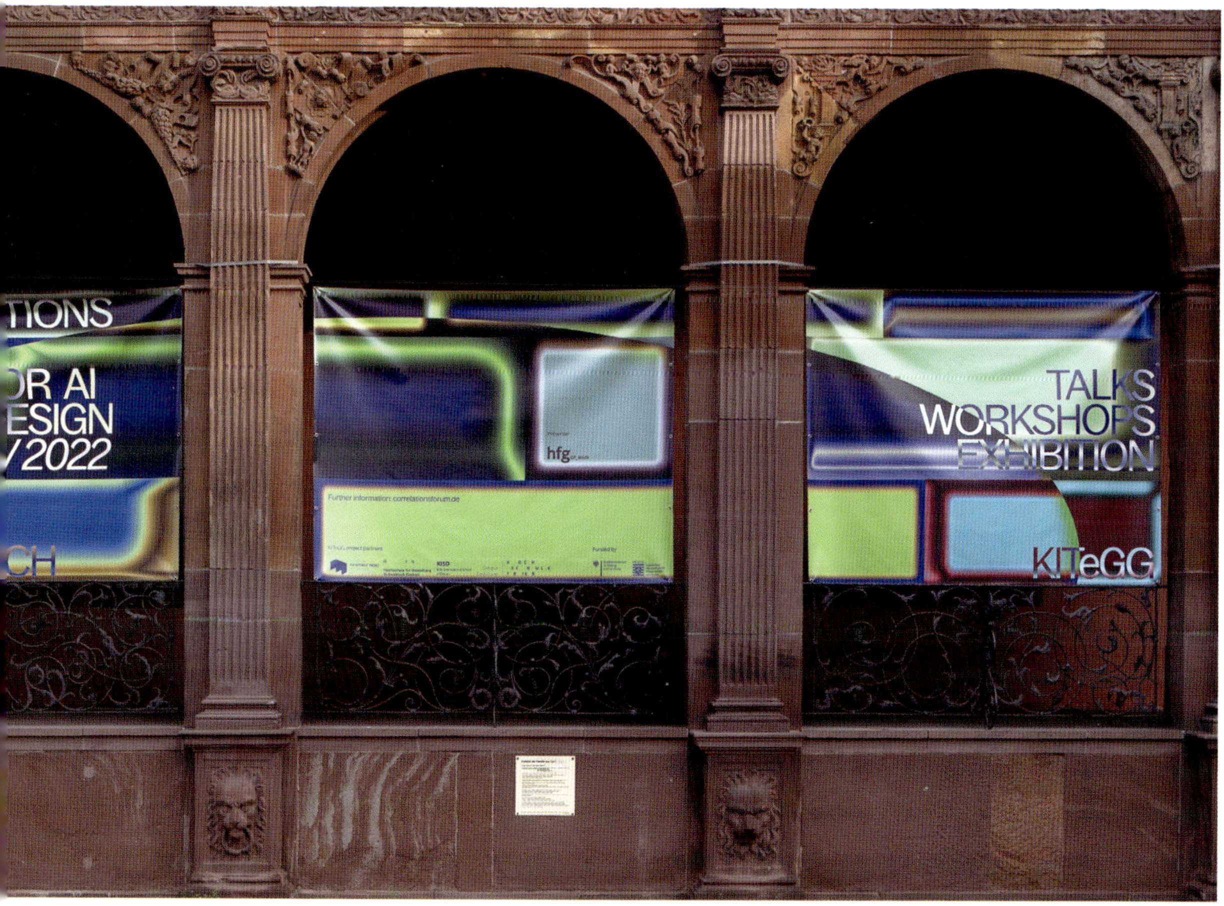

R91 · G161 · B37
R229 · G129 · B252

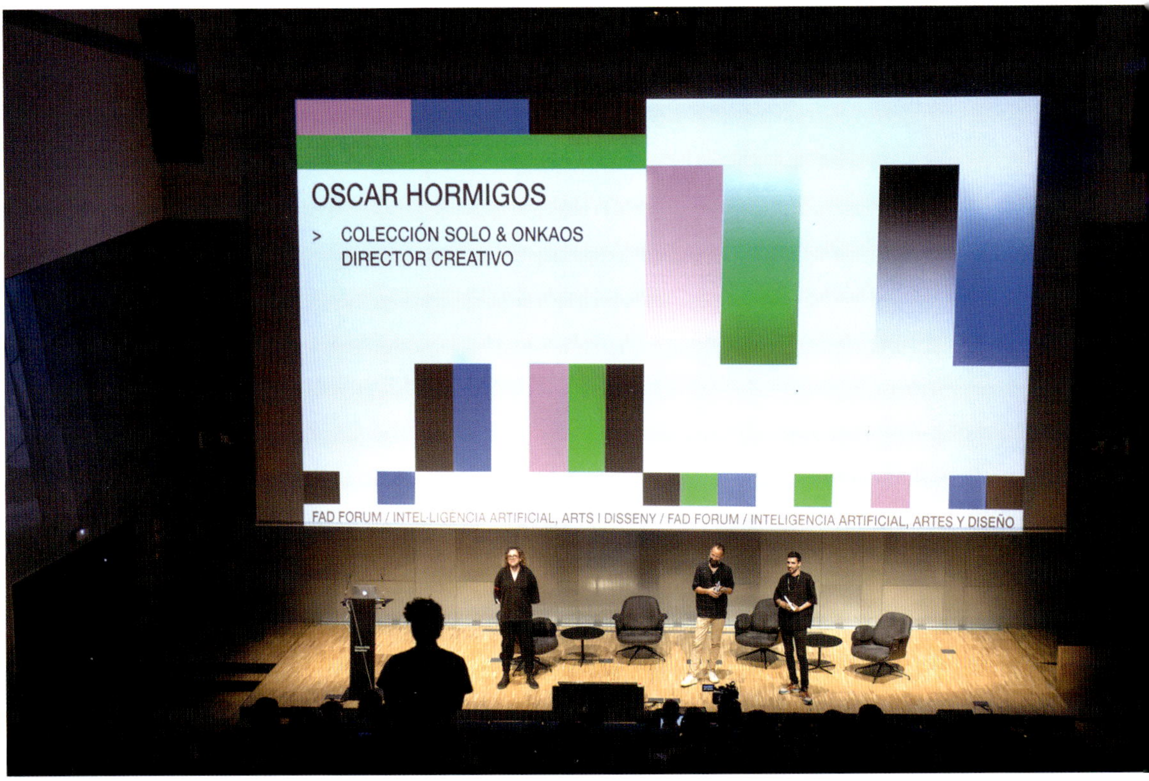

R64 · G112 · B220
R206 · G206 · B208

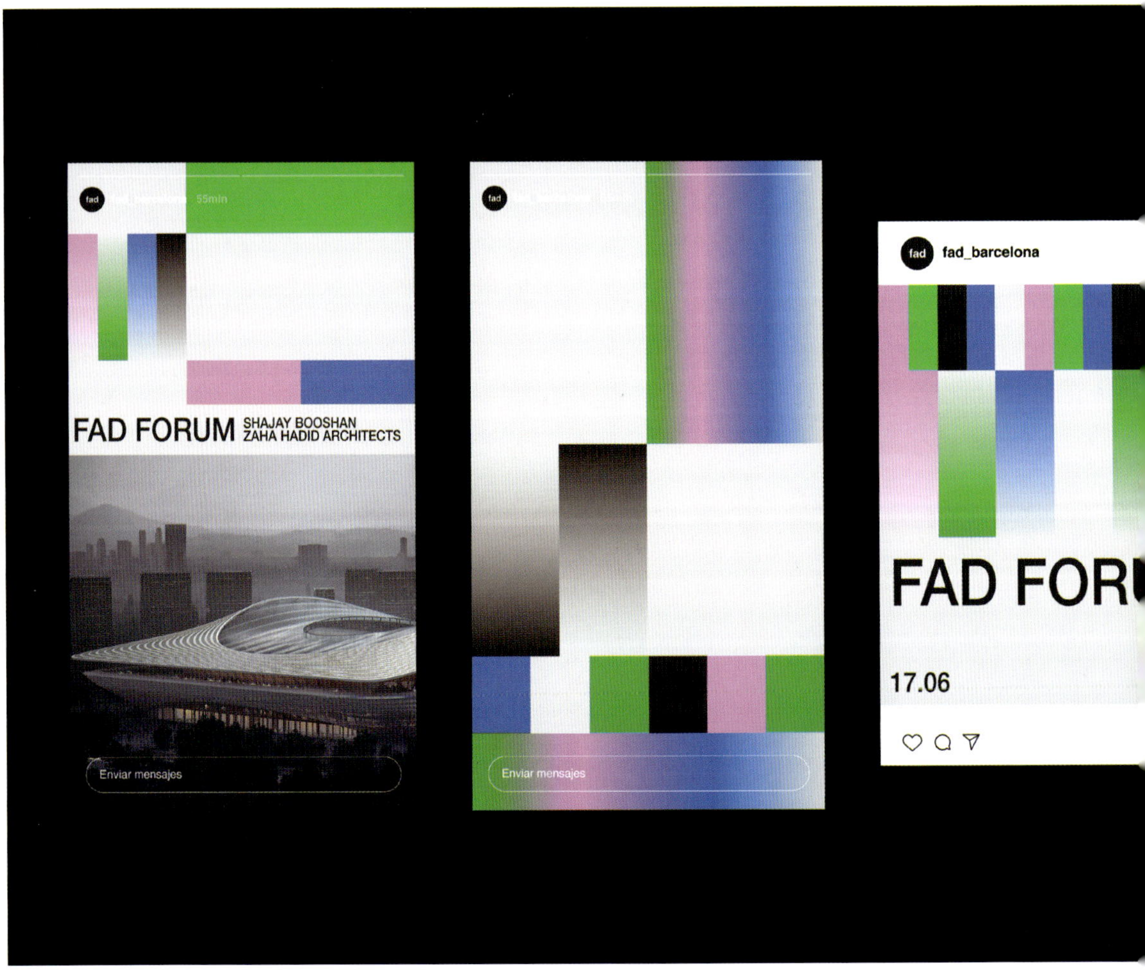

R36 · G36 · B34

FAD FÒRUM 2022

Art direction and communication design for FAD Fòrum 2022 which organizes conferences and workshops where the main topic is artificial intelligence applied to the professional practice of art, design and architecture. The graphic identity must be flexible enough to be used in different formats.

Design Studio
Bakoom Studio

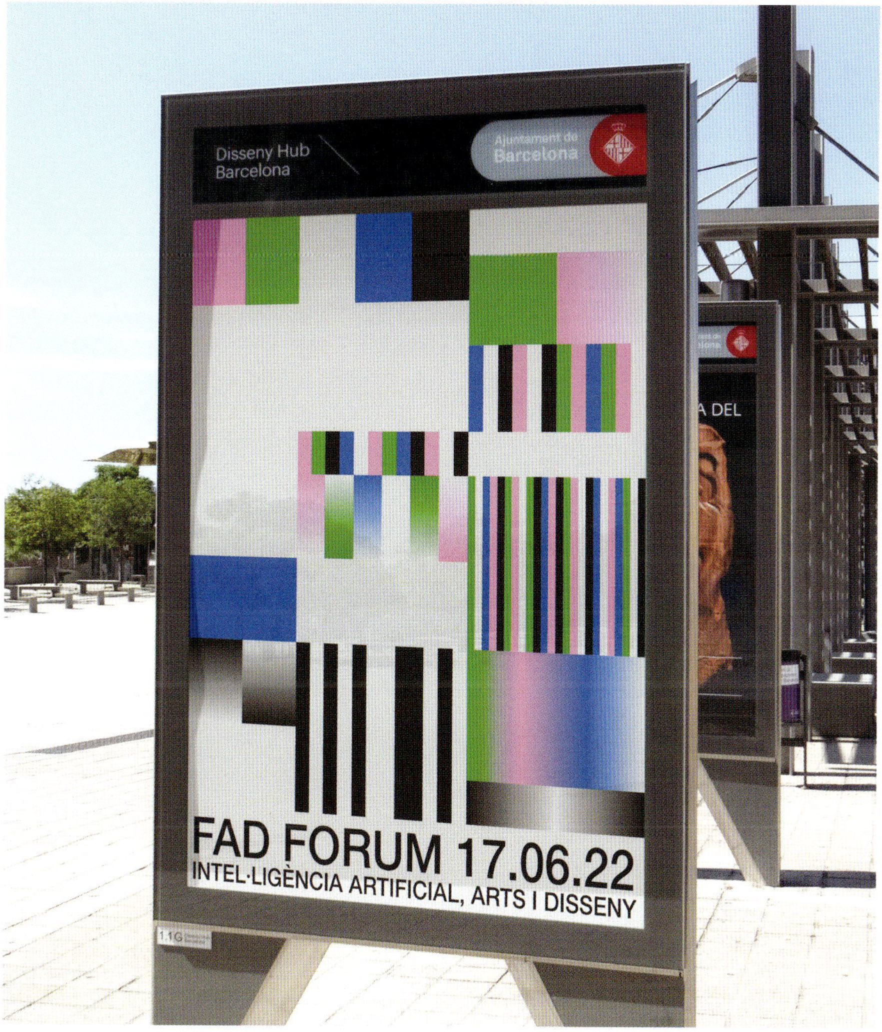

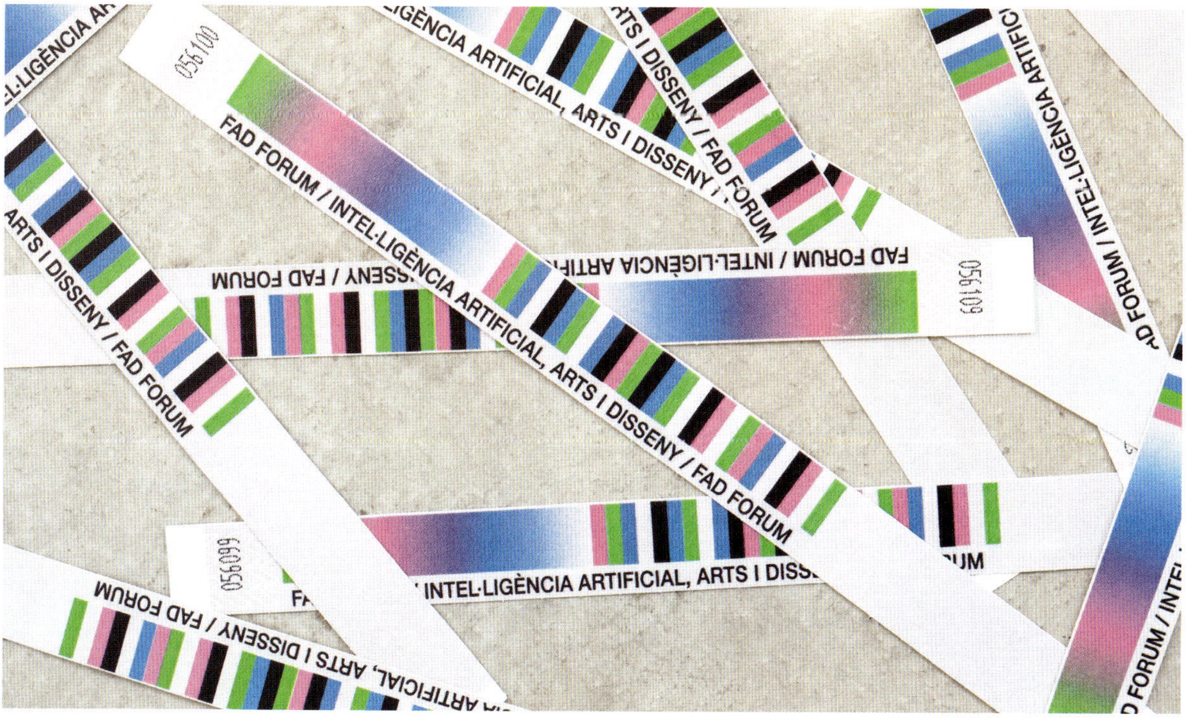

PANTONE 7416C
PANTONE 156 C

PANTONE 7768 C
PANTONE 7456 C

PANTONE 480 C
PANTONE 7552 C

PANTONE 7686 C
PANTONE 5215 C

PANTONE 480 C
PANTONE 7552 C

PANTONE 603 C
PANTONE 708 C

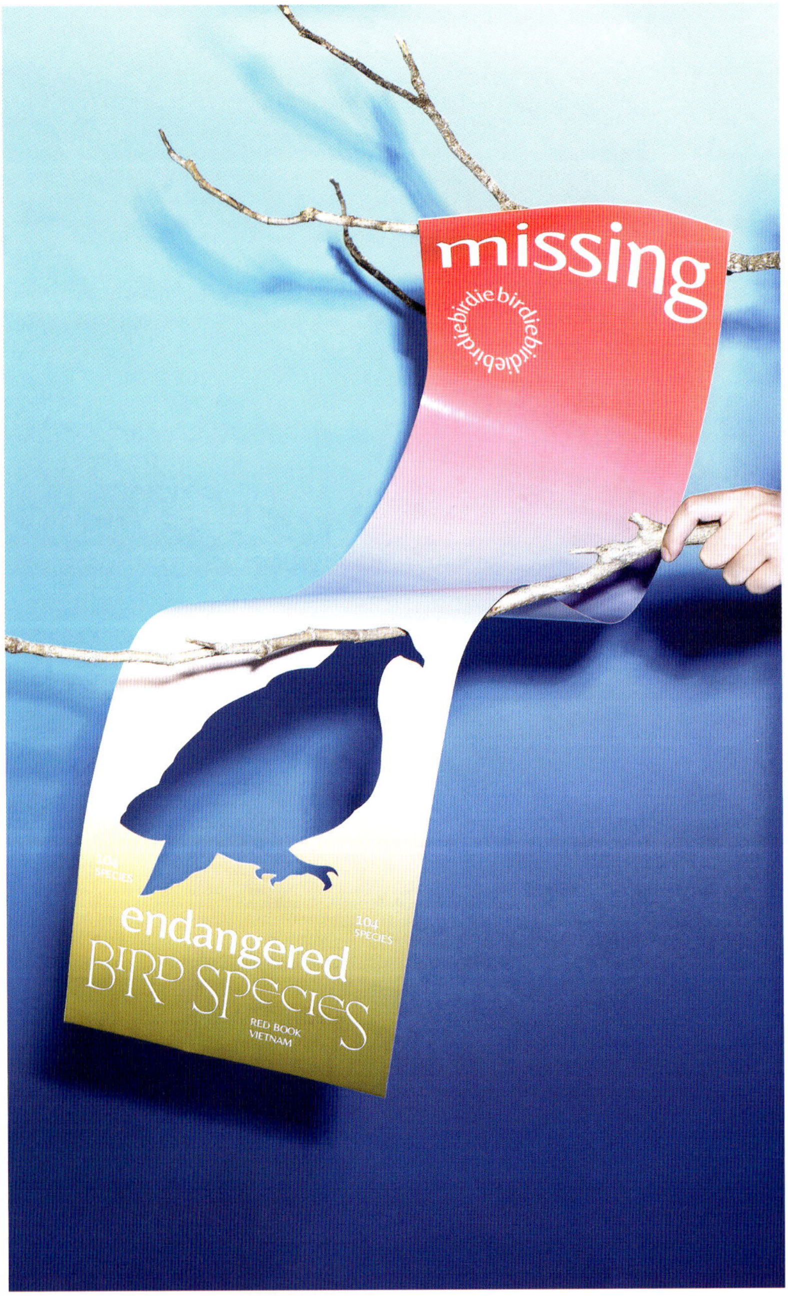

BIRDIE

Birdie is a non-profit dedicated to conserving local birds and habitats. As “Bird’s Buddies”, they raise awareness about endangered birds through birdwatching trips, conservation activities, and an online archive. Using the metaphor of “missing birds”, *Birdie* illustrates the risk of extinction and encourages people to seek lost species. *Birdie’s* logomark, inspired by nature, symbolizes the home for birdies and bird-lovers. Die-cut techniques create a unique identity system, and bird stickers offer a symbolic safe haven. *Birdie’s* mission extends to building green habitats and using dynamic typography to engage the audience.

Design Studio
Layơ Lab

Creative Director
Alex Dang

Client
Birdie

Designer
Truong Thanh
& Danson Vu

Photographer
Thinh Tran

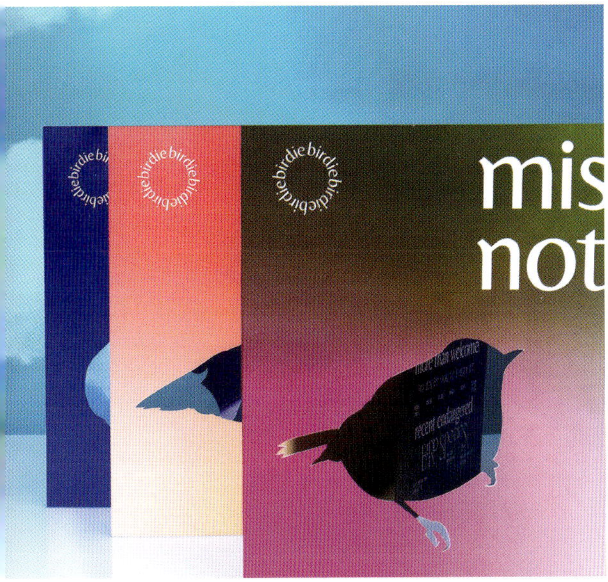
mis
not

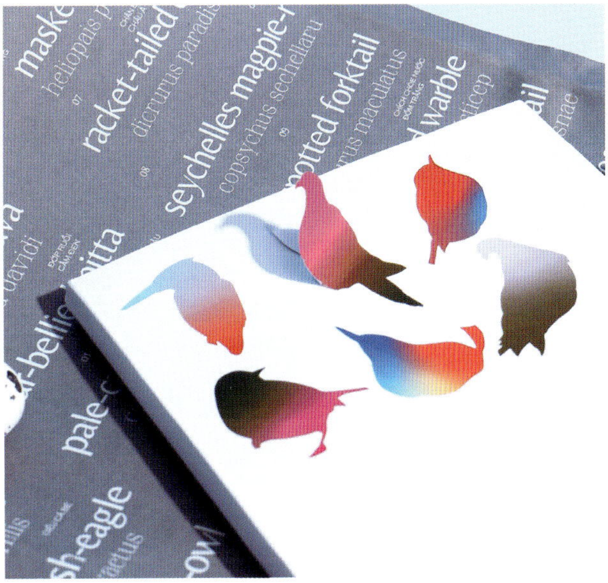
racket-tailed
seychelles magpie-r
potted forktail
pitta
pale-c
sh-eagle

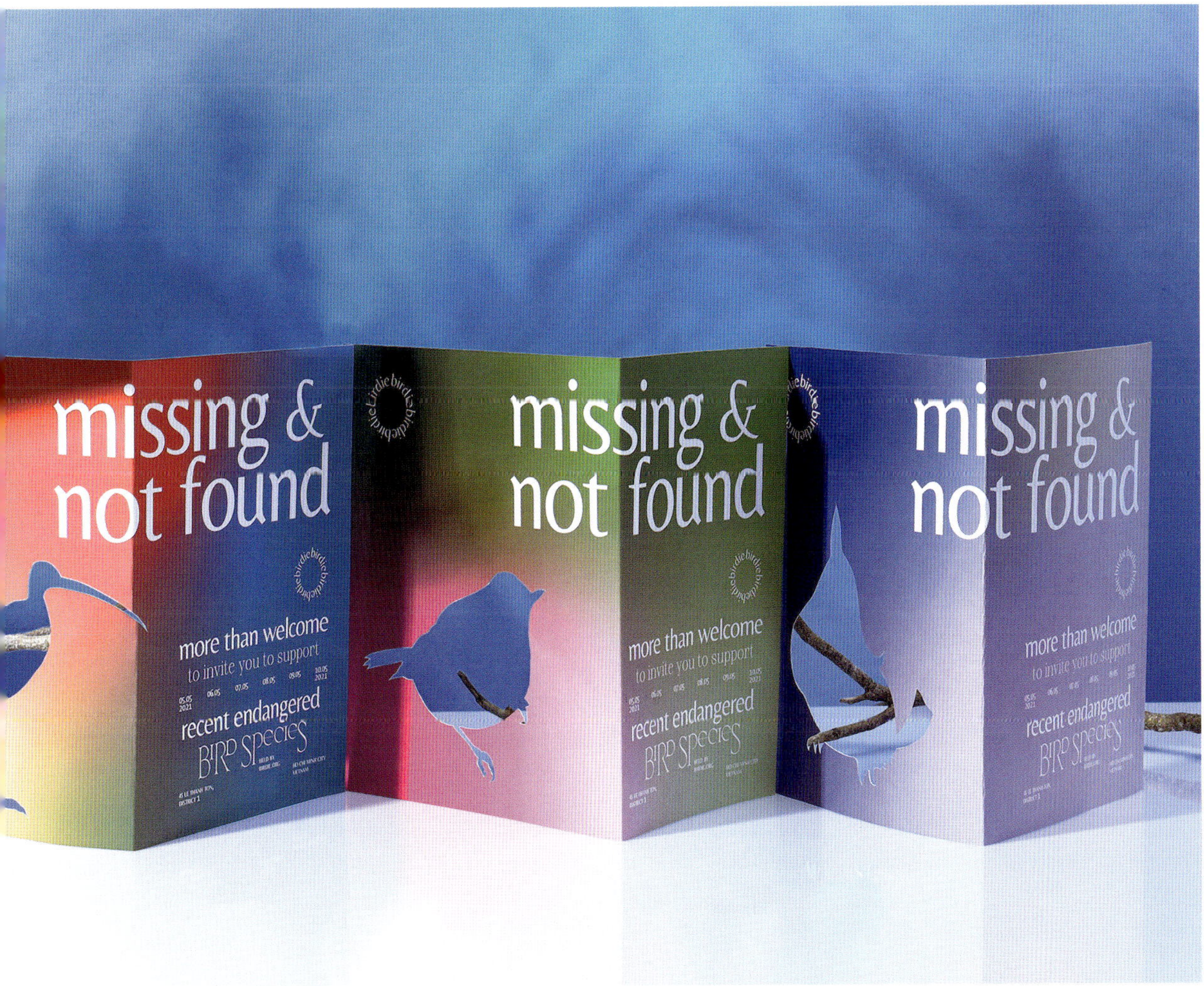
missing &
not found
more than welcome
to invite you to support
recent endangered
BIRD SPECIES
missing &
not found
more than welcome
to invite you to support
recent endangered
BIRD SPECIES
missing &
not found
more than welcome
to invite you to support
recent endangered
BIRD SPECIES

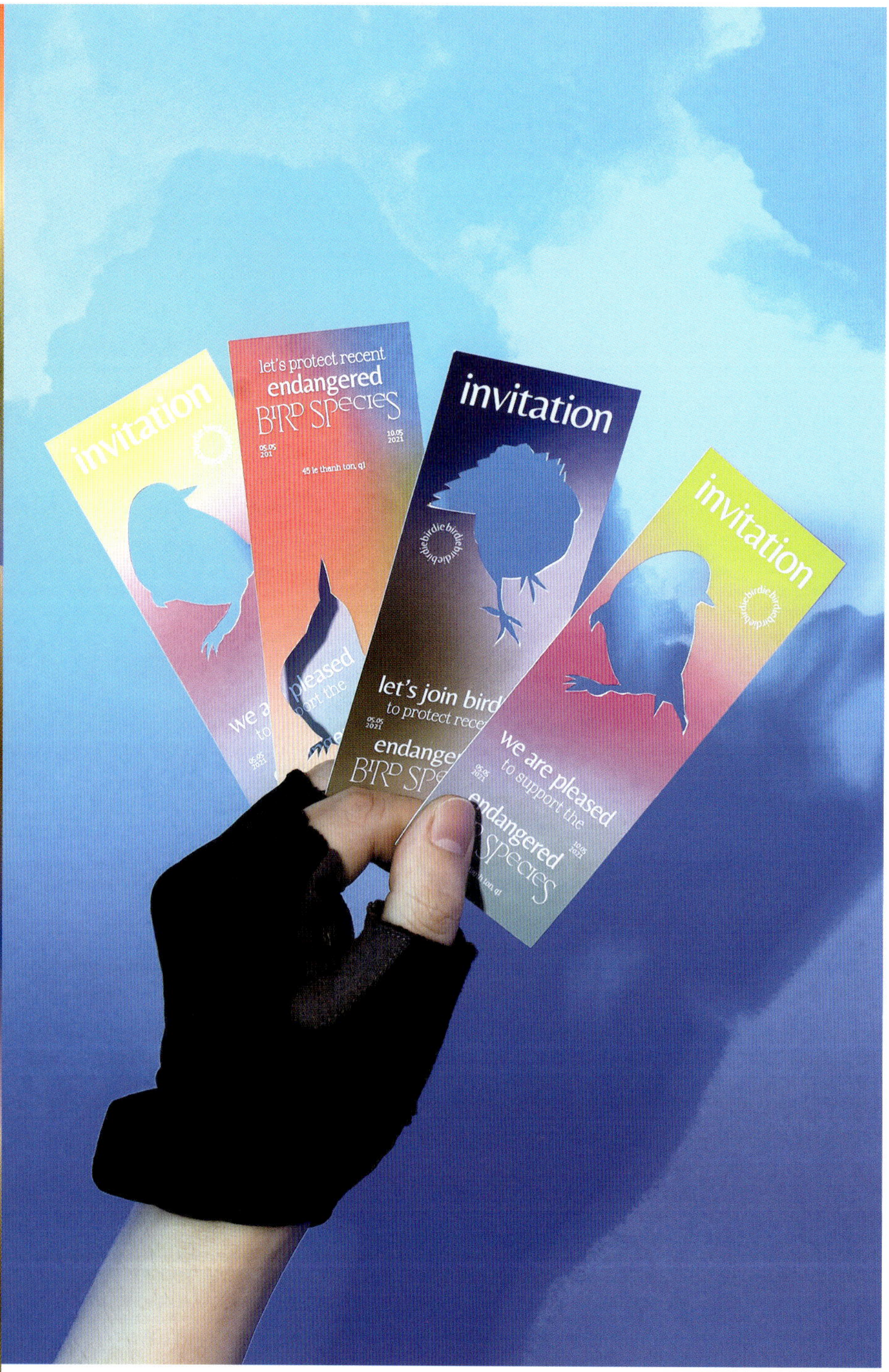
invitation
let's protect recent
endangered
BIRD SPECIES
invitation
let's join bird
to protect rece
invitation
we are pleased
to support the
endangered
species

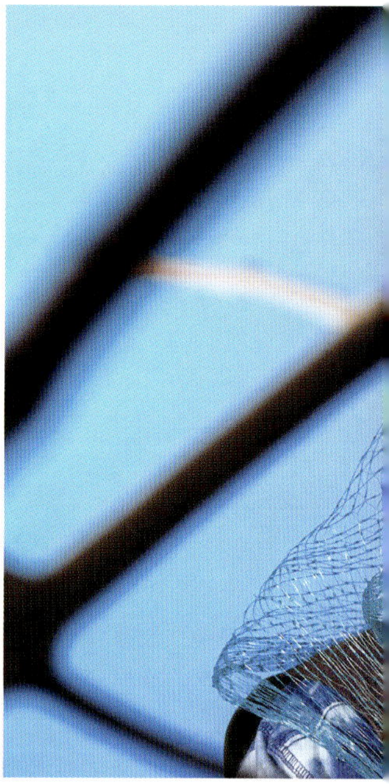

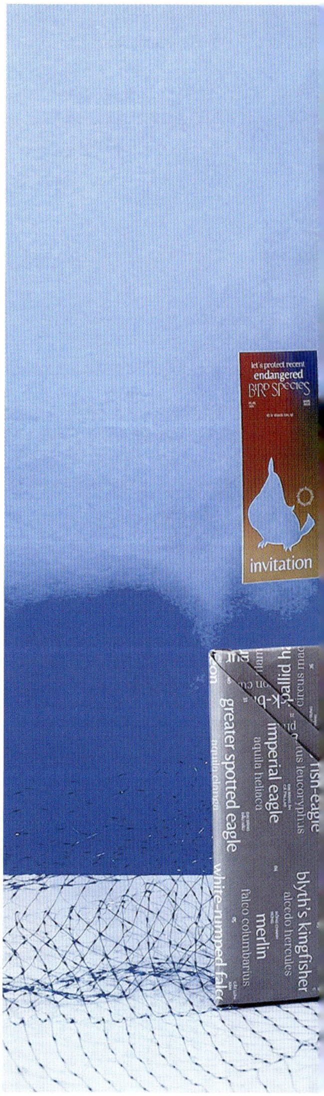
let's protect recent
endangered
BIRD SPECIES
invitation
imperial eagle
aquila heliaca
greater spotted eagle
blyth's kingfisher
alcedo hercules
merlin
falco columbarius

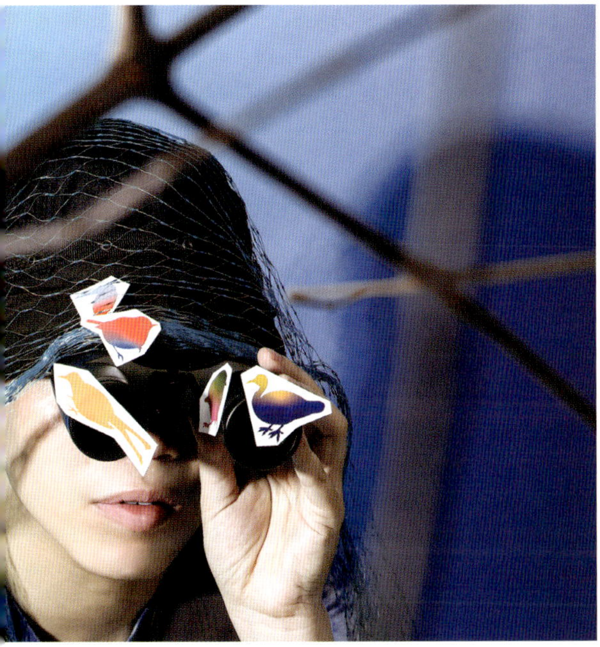

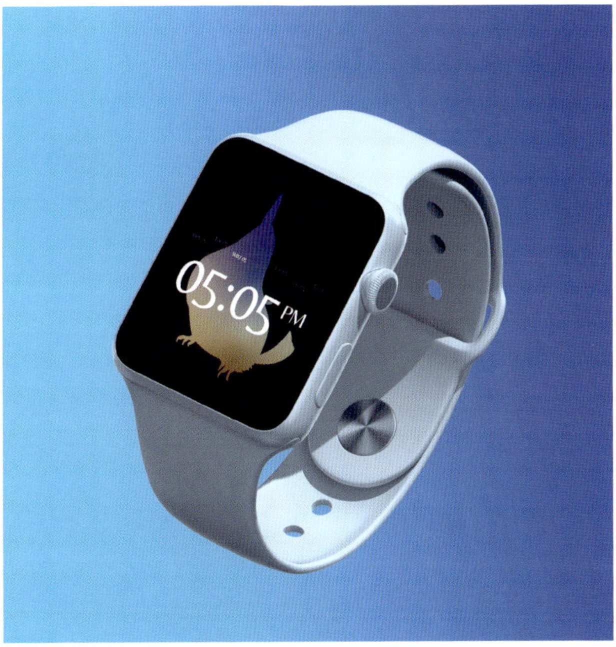
05:05 PM

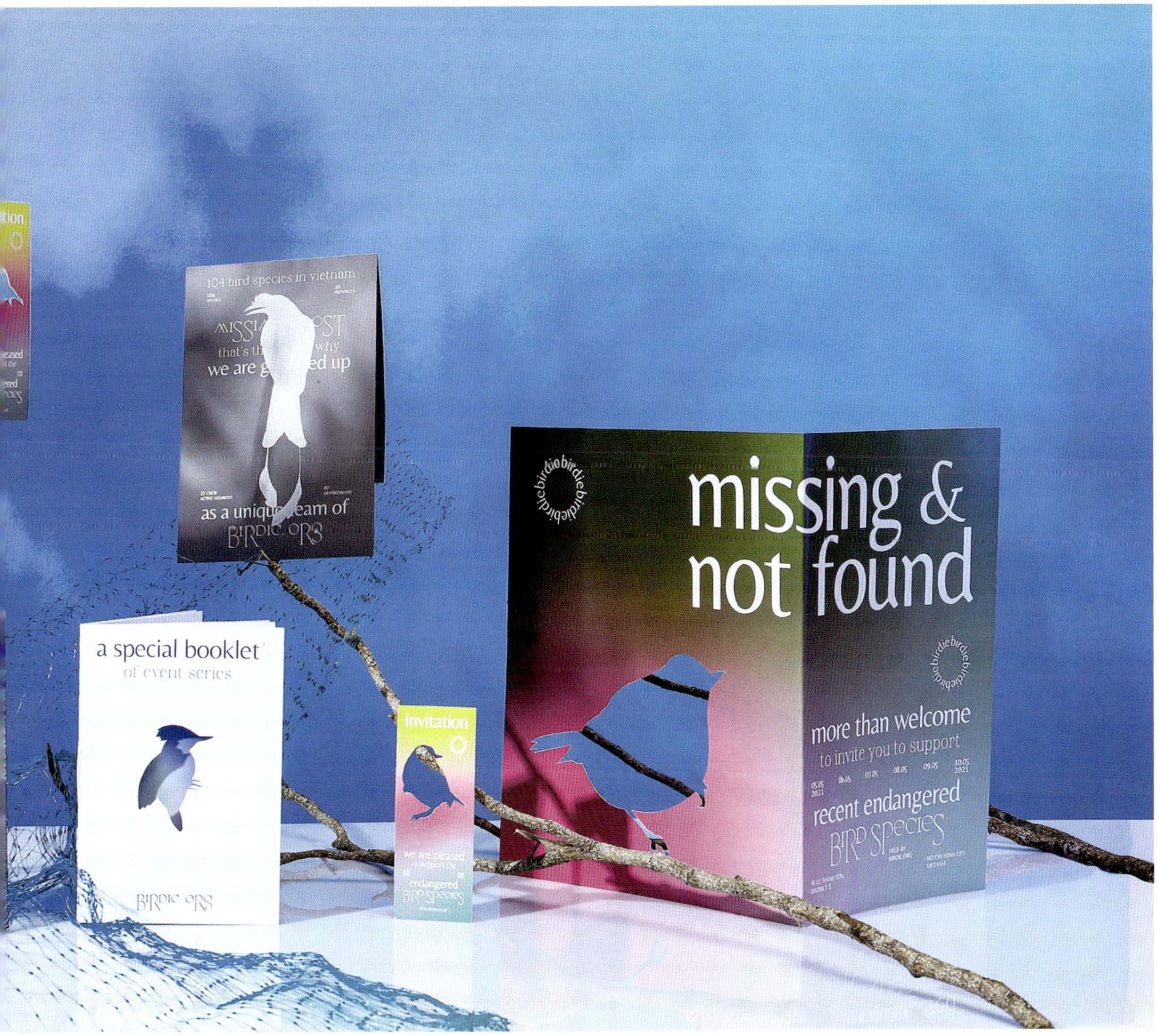
104 bird species in vietnam
as a unique team of
a special booklet
of event series
invitation
missing &
not found
more than welcome
to invite you to support
recent endangered
BIRD SPECIES

C0 · M81 · Y55 · K0
C43 · M56 · Y0 · K0

C90 · M0 · Y54 · K0
C93 · M17 · Y29 · K0

C78 · M72 · Y0 · K0
C0 · M58 · Y66 · K0

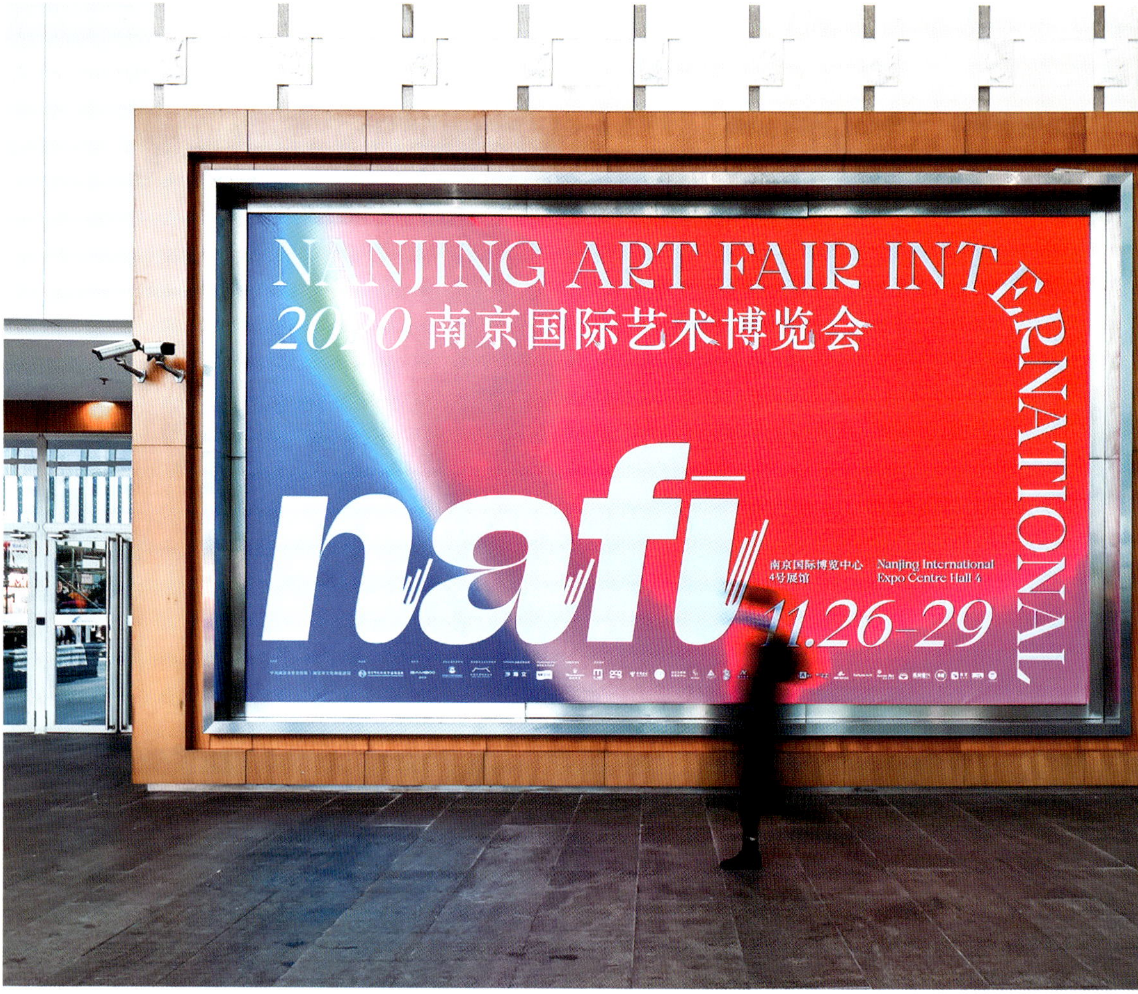

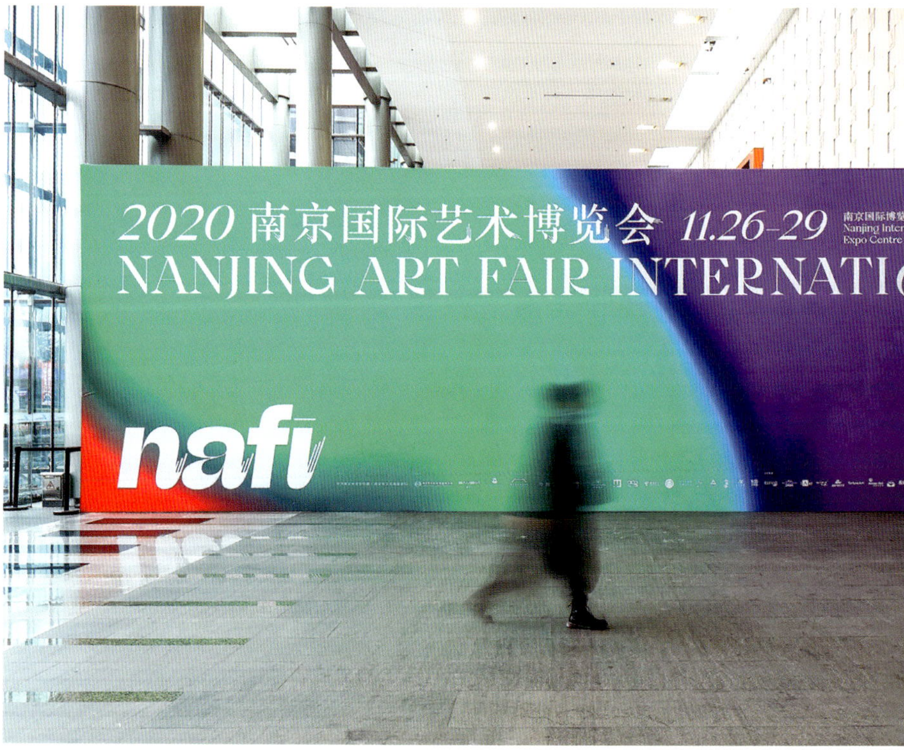

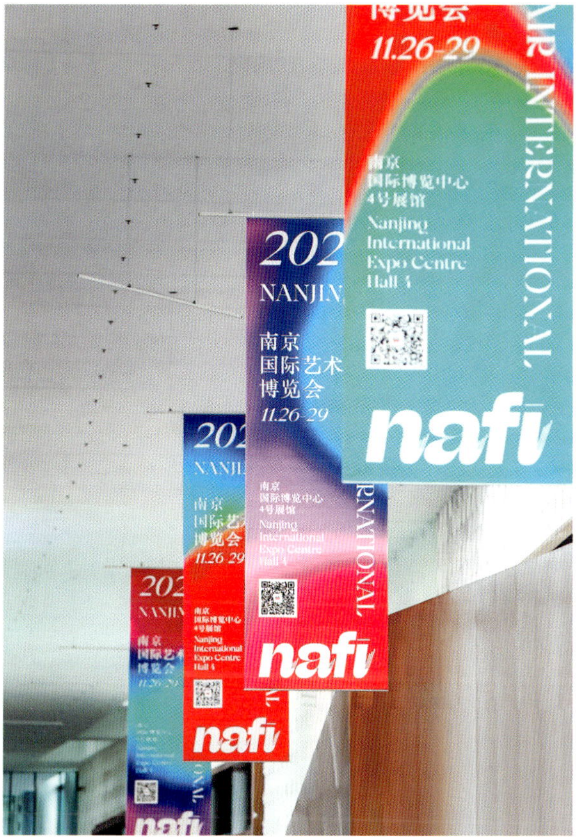

NANJING ART FAIR INTERNATIONAL

The Nanjing Art Fair International 2020 is the first art expo in China with a focus on imagery. Therefore, the main visual design uses different blocks of colour as the background, expressing the expo's collection of diverse and unique art pieces, providing the public with a different artistic experience.

The fusion of these colour blocks highlights the cohesion between the artists, their works, and the audience. The concept of the expo as a bridge between artists and viewers is abstractly outlined with the event name on the colour block background.

Design Studio
Untitled Macao

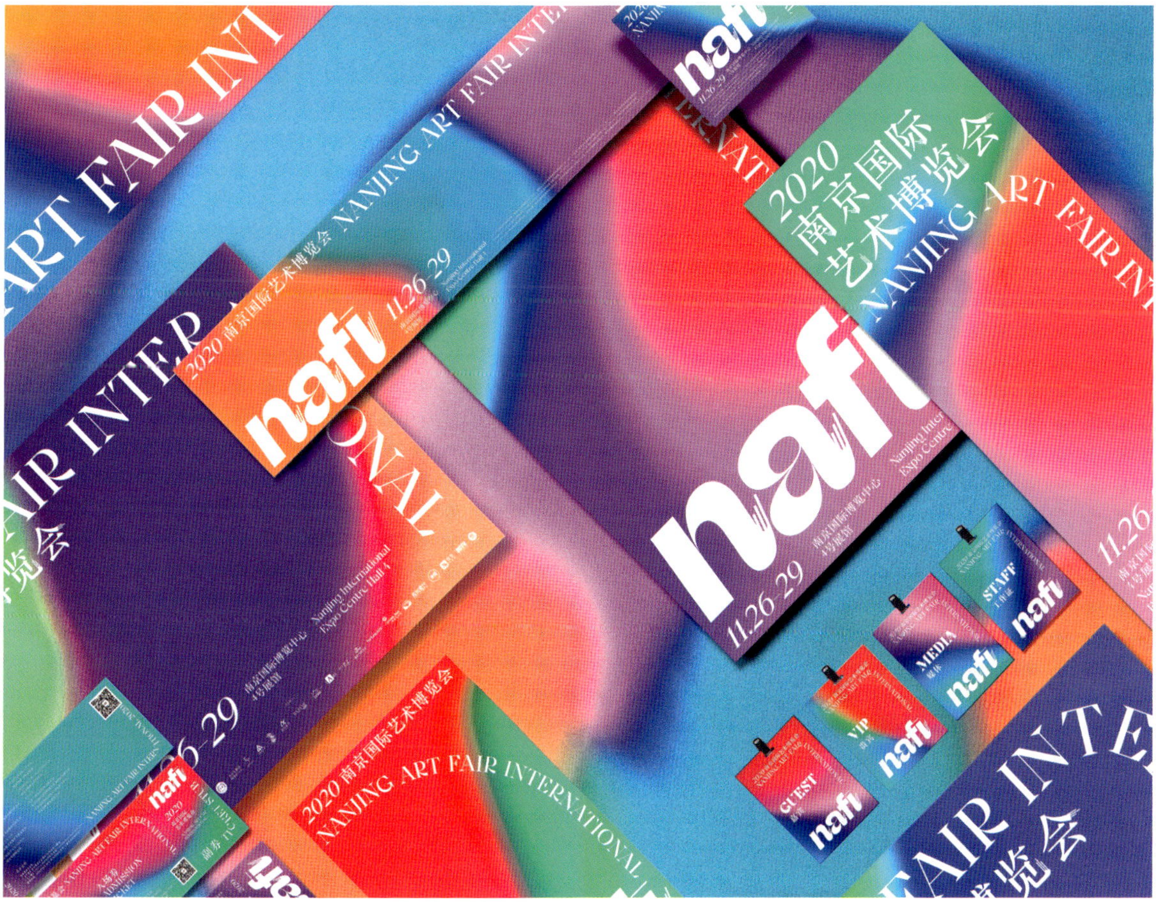

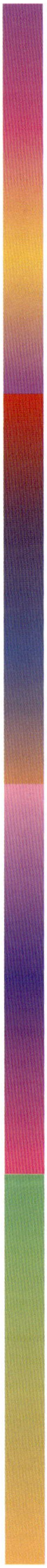

R170 · G89 · B159
R218 · G75 · B142
R236 · G176 · B48
R170 · G89 · B159

R204 · G31 · B36
R105 · G78 · B117
R64 · G107 · B161
R211 · G132 · B105

R232 · G144 · B186
R89 · G72 · B155
R228 · G64 · B144

R104 · G171 · B110
R232 · G161 · B81

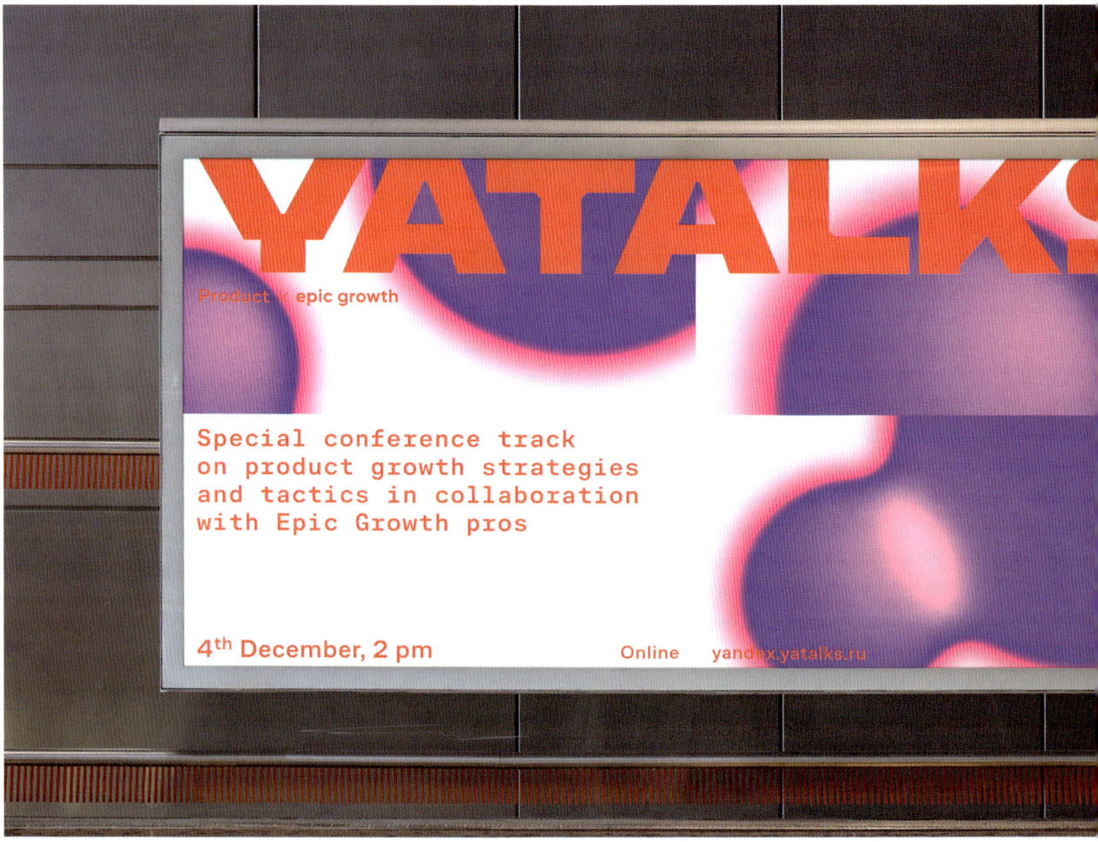

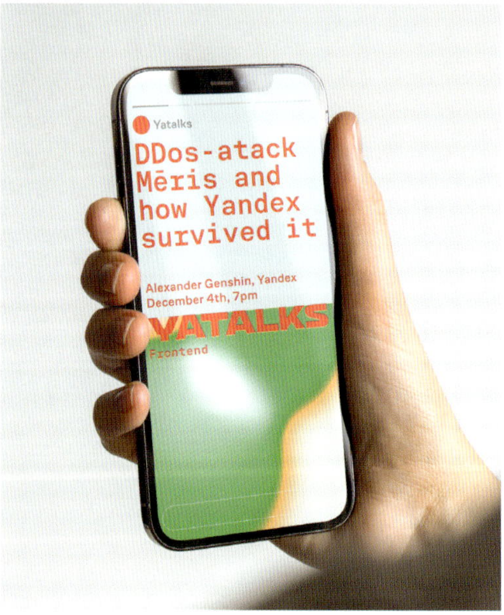

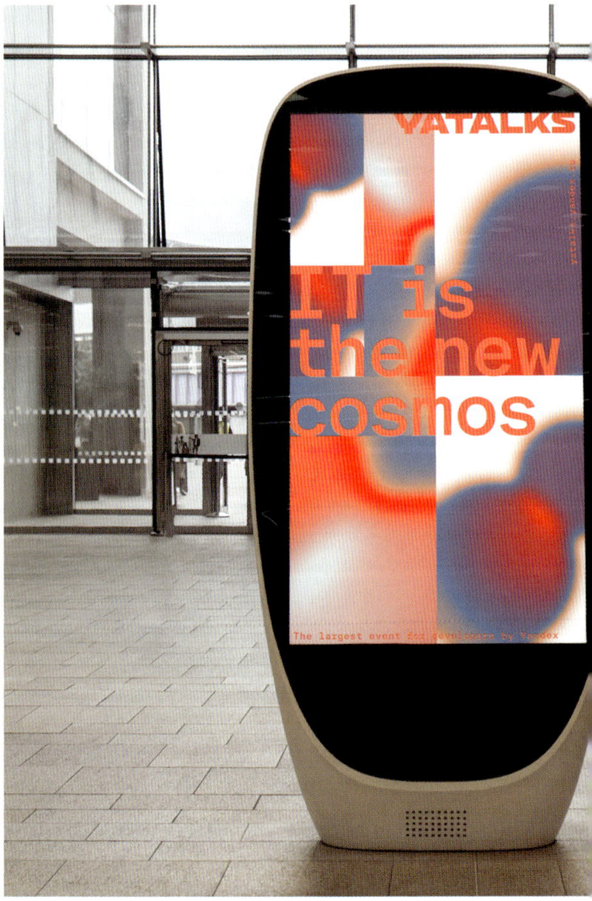

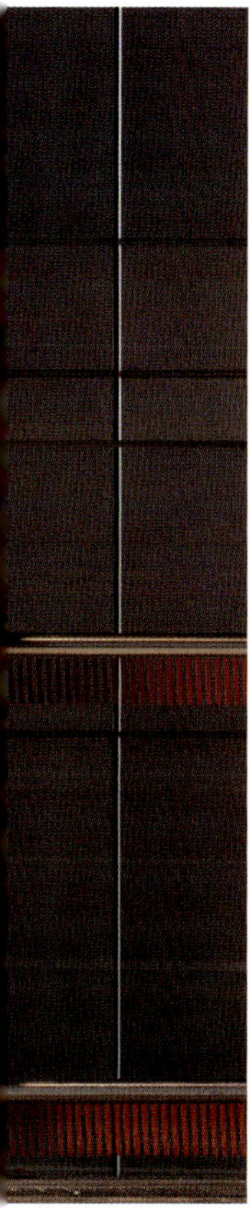

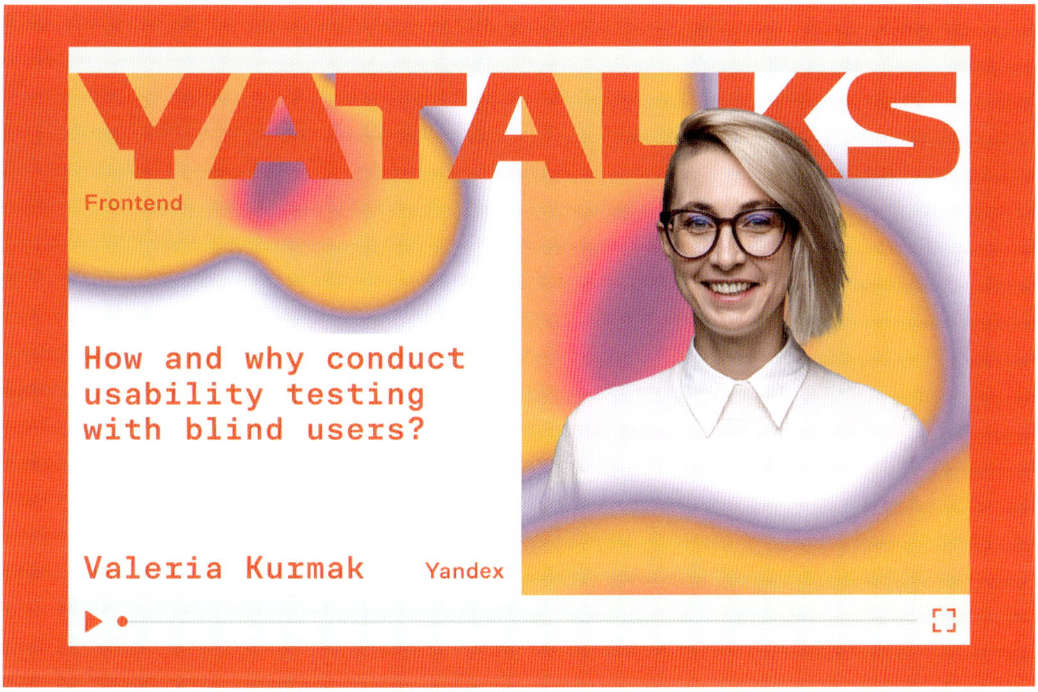

YATALKS CONFERENCE

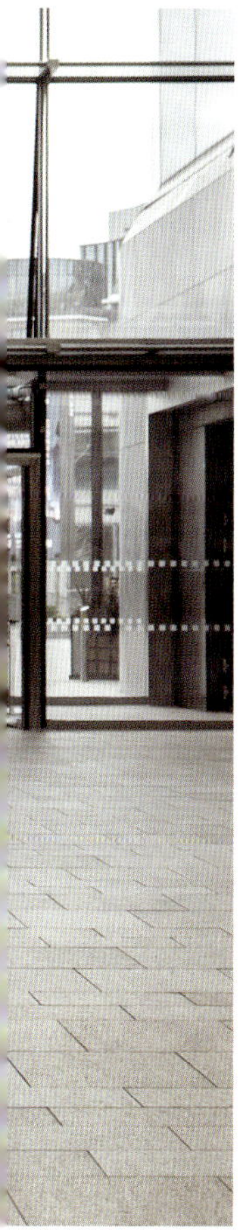

In the 1960s outer space became a collective dream of humankind. Contemporaries of Yuri Gagarin, Neil Armstrong, and generations to follow read and watched science fiction, fantasizing about extraterrestrial journeys. Their dreams have become earthlier since, but the cosmos still remains a synonym of continuous elaboration and progress. "IT is a space for today" became the theme of YaTalks conference 2021 by Yandex, as the general metaphor of the visual identity of this event, uniting nearly 100 experts from leading companies from all over the world to share their views on the IT industry, technology, and digital trends.

Creative Director
Ivan Velichko (Shuka)

Design Director
Anna Katsur (Yandex)

Art Director
Daria Zudina (Shuka) & Sofya Karavaeva (Yandex)

Lead Designer
Evgeny Drozhzhev (Shuka)

Lead Motion Designer
Dmitry Kozlyaev (Shuka)

Designer
Dmitry Kozlyaev (Shuka), Dina Isaeva (Shuka), Rant Blagaya & Masha Larionova (Yandex)

Sound Designer
Simeon Melnikov (Shuka)

Project Manager
Anna Eremina (Shuka), Anna Kuzyutina (Yandex) & Anna Shayakhmetova (Yandex)

Content Director & Writing
Vasily Kolesnik (Shuka)

Producer
Ekaterina Shcherbakova (Shuka)

R255 · G77 · B0

R1 · G222 · B103

R73 · G118 · B213

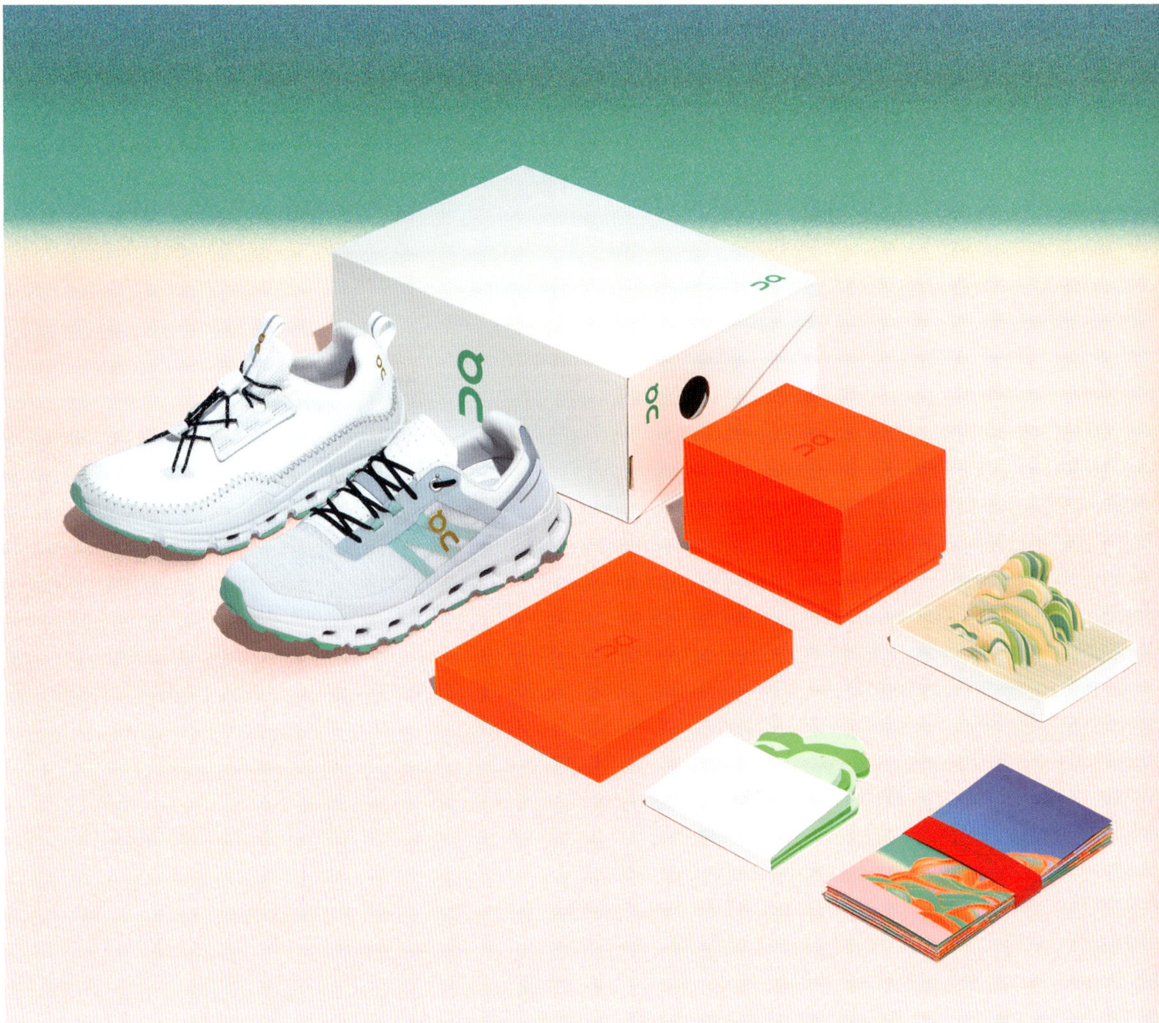

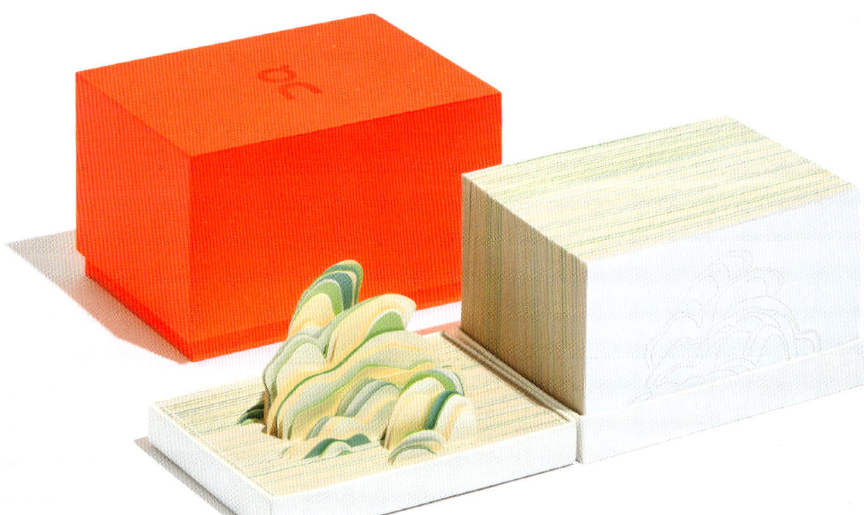

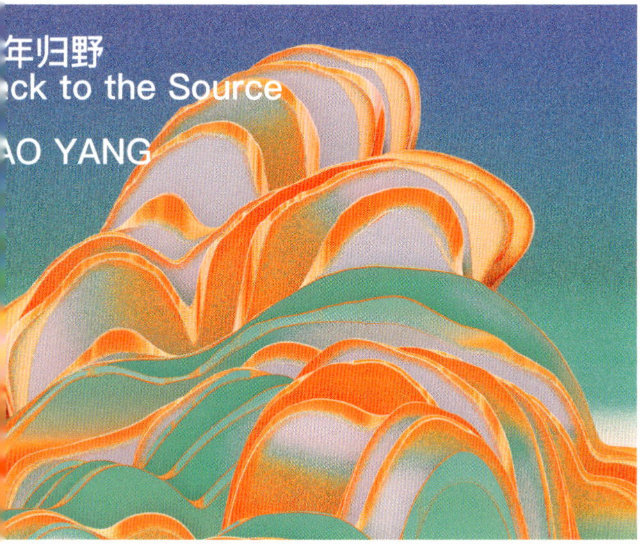

ON—CHINESE NEW YEAR

A collaboration with On Running for the 2023 Chinese New Year celebration, its concept was "Back to the Source" [in the New Year], a nod to the rich artistic and cultural heritage of China and the spirit of the brand. The rabbit form, a classic element in ancient Chinese art, was combined with the flowing, organic shapes of Chinese landscape art to create a piece that is both timeless and contemporary. In addition, the designer used the mountain form as the central visual element, echoing the Swiss landscapes where the On brand was born.

Designer & Motion Designer
Gao Yang

Set Designer
On China

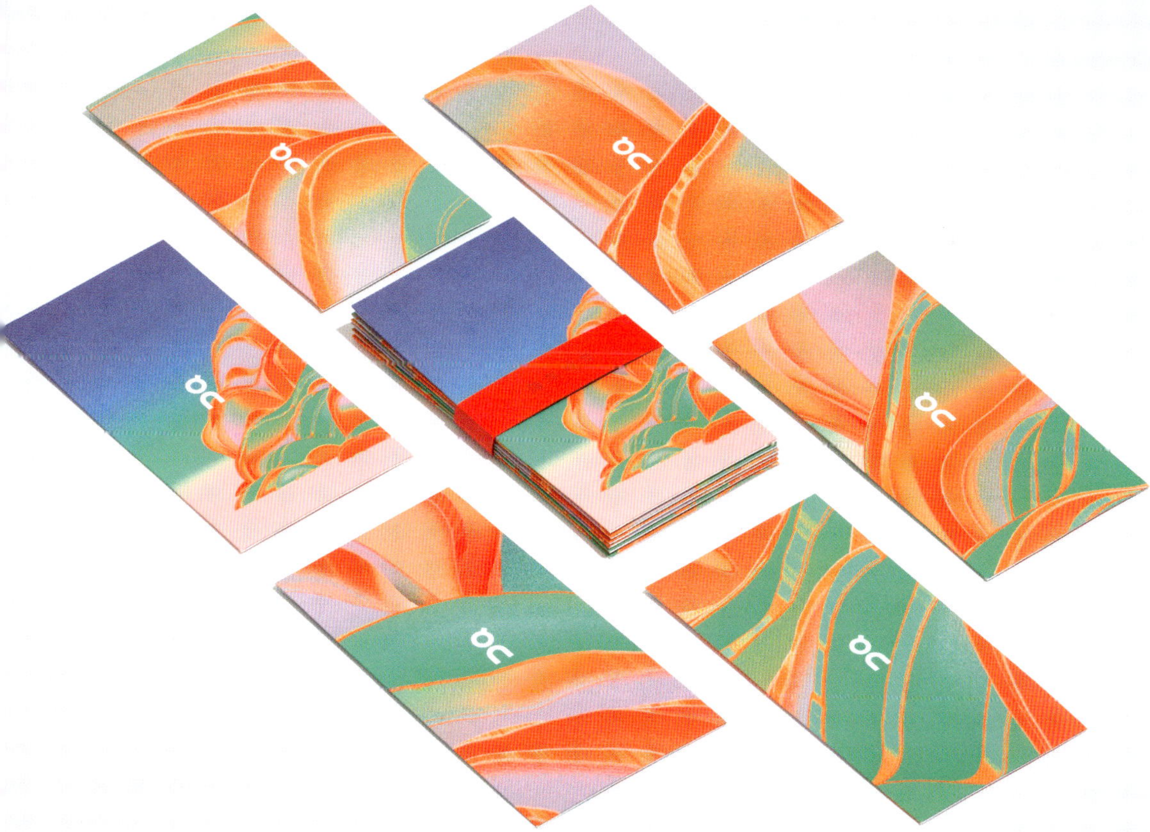

C0 · M66 · Y89 · K0

C2 · M13 · Y0 · K0

C4 · M0 · Y19 · K0

C0 · M0 · Y3 · K0

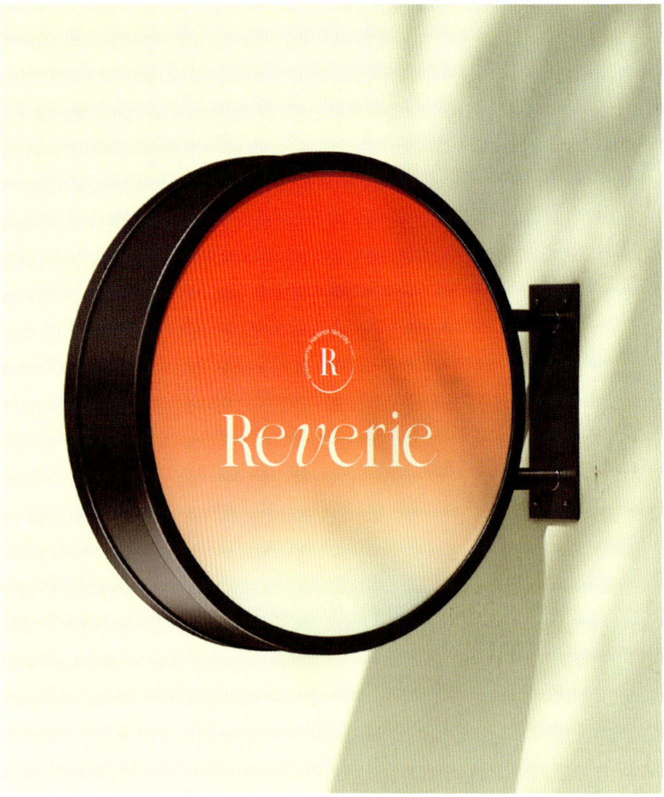

REVERIE

Reverie is a high-end skincare brand that exudes a sense of refined beauty and sophistication. The brand is committed to harnessing the power of nature for skincare production. For the brand identity, the typography should evoke a sense of timelessness, and a clean and minimalist design approach conveys elegance and sophistication for the brand.

Designer
Souvik Paul

Art Director
Souvik Paul

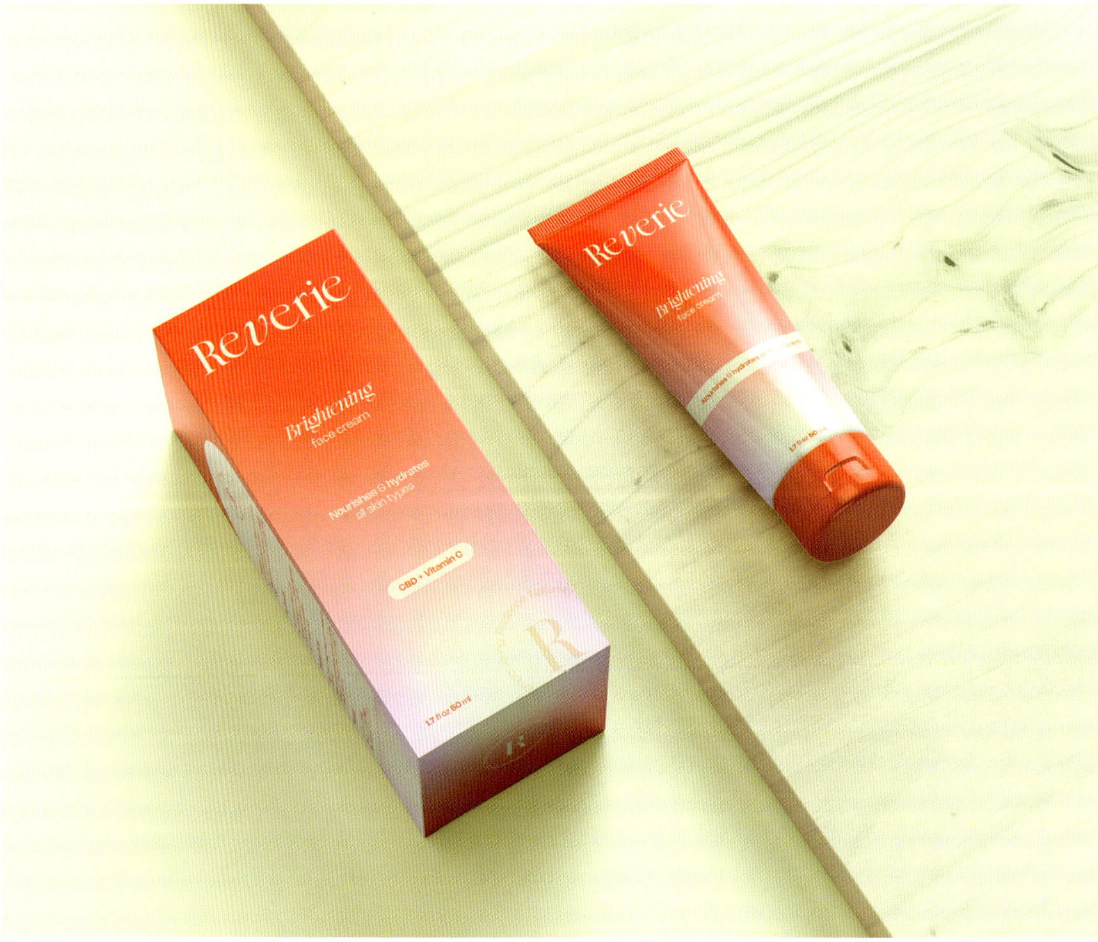

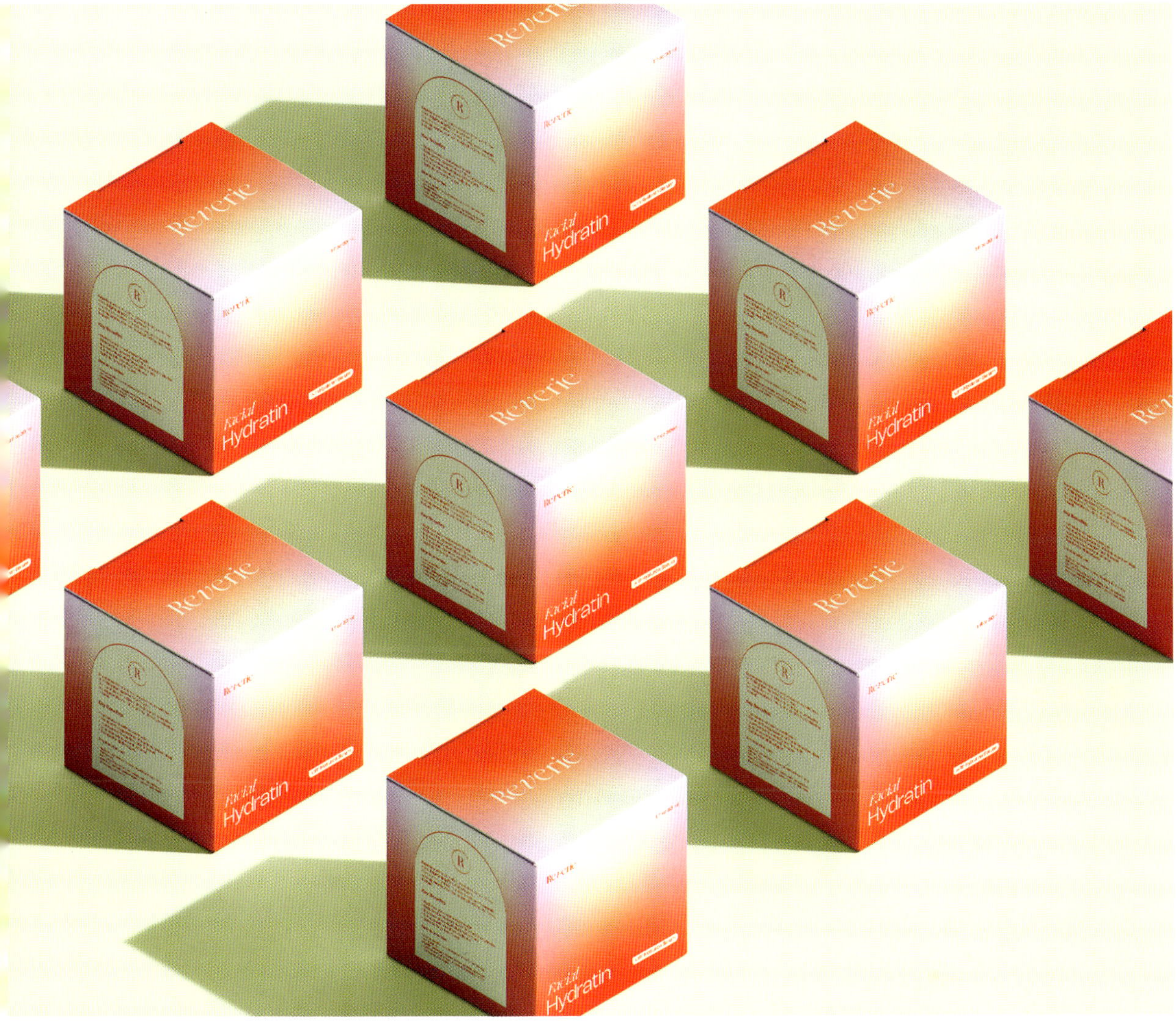
Reverie
Facial
Hydratin

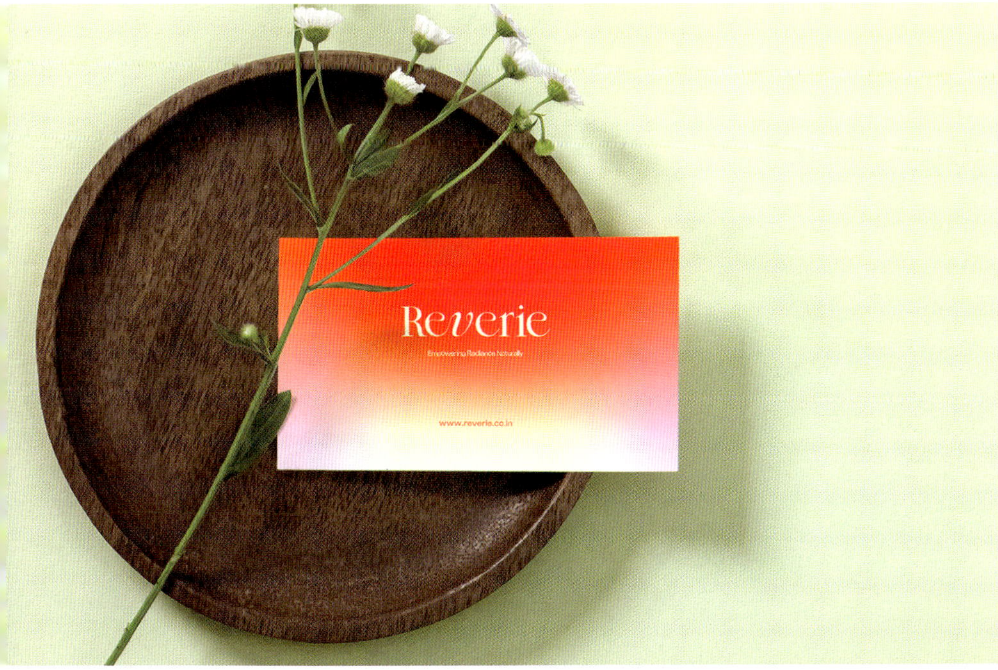
Reverie
Empowering Radiance Naturally
www.reverie.co.in

C78 · M13 · Y76 · K0

C9 · M39 · Y74 · K0

C61 · M9 · Y39 · K0

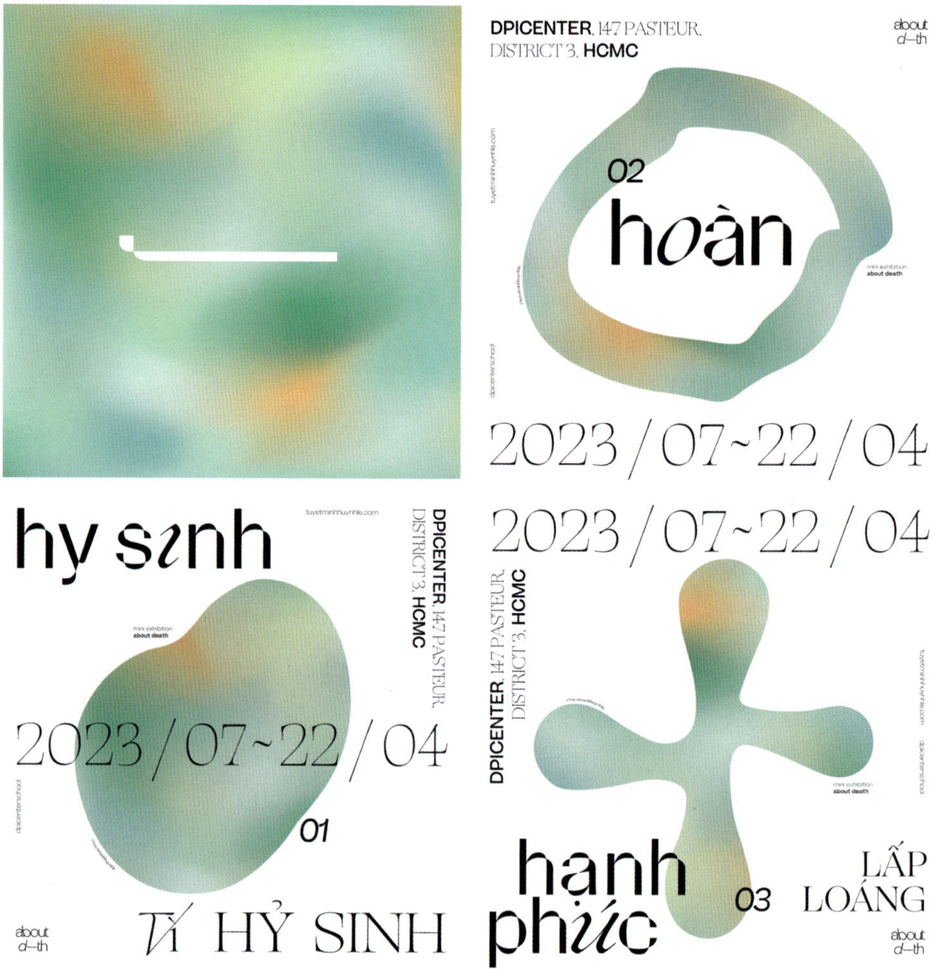

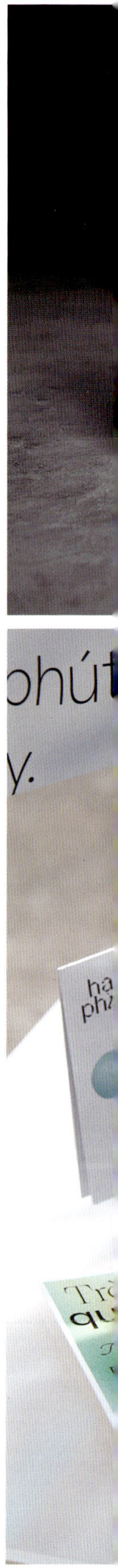

ABOUT DEATH

The "About Death" exhibition invites audiences to explore the concept of death and reflect on its romantic elements for all of us: individuals simultaneously experiencing life and death. The piece visualizes the author's contemplation of death and its inherent beauty. The goal isn't to change your perspective or overcome fear but to converse with yourself.

Art Director & Designer
Tuyet Minh

Supervision
Pham Luu Ngoc Uyen
Tuan Huynh

3D Model Support
Quang Luan

Content Support
Kim Ha Vo

Photographer
Dat Ho Thanh

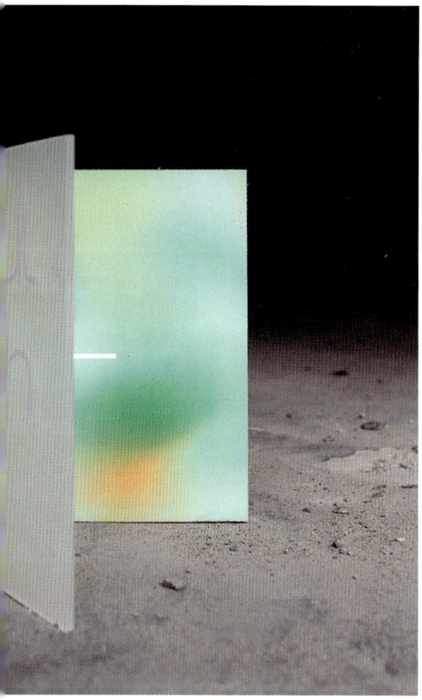

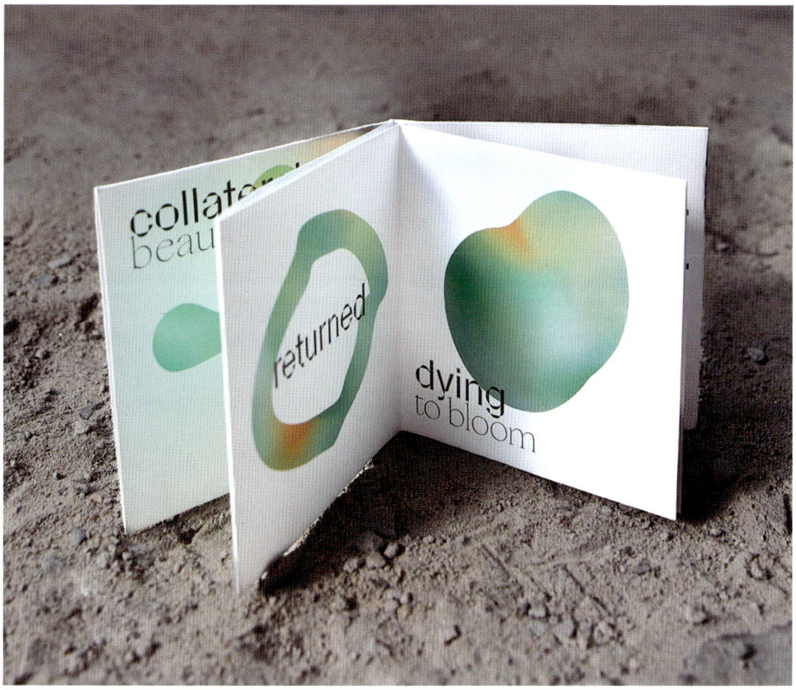
returned
dying
to bloom

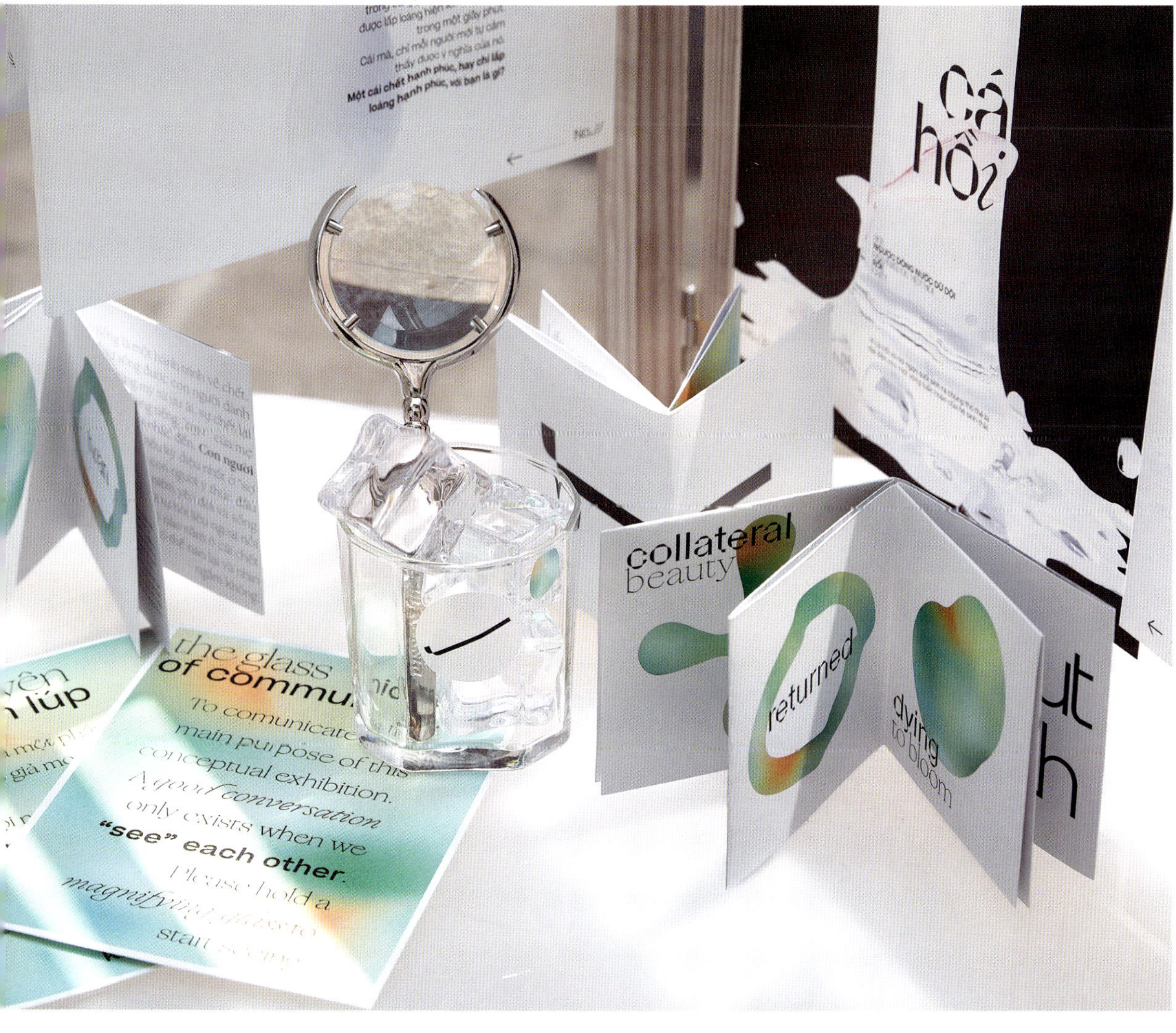
Một cái chết hạnh phúc, hay chỉ lấp loáng hạnh phúc, với bạn là gì?
collateral
beauty
returned
dying
to bloom
main purpose of this
conceptual exhibition.
A good conversation
only exists when we
"see" each other.
Please hold a

C60 · M5 · Y55 · K0
C25 · M0 · Y75 · K0

C0 · M40 · Y85 · K0
C5 · M10 · Y65 · K0

C0 · M90 · Y0 · K0
C0 · M60 · Y0 · K0

C70 · M80 · Y0 · K0
C50 · M40 · Y0 · K0

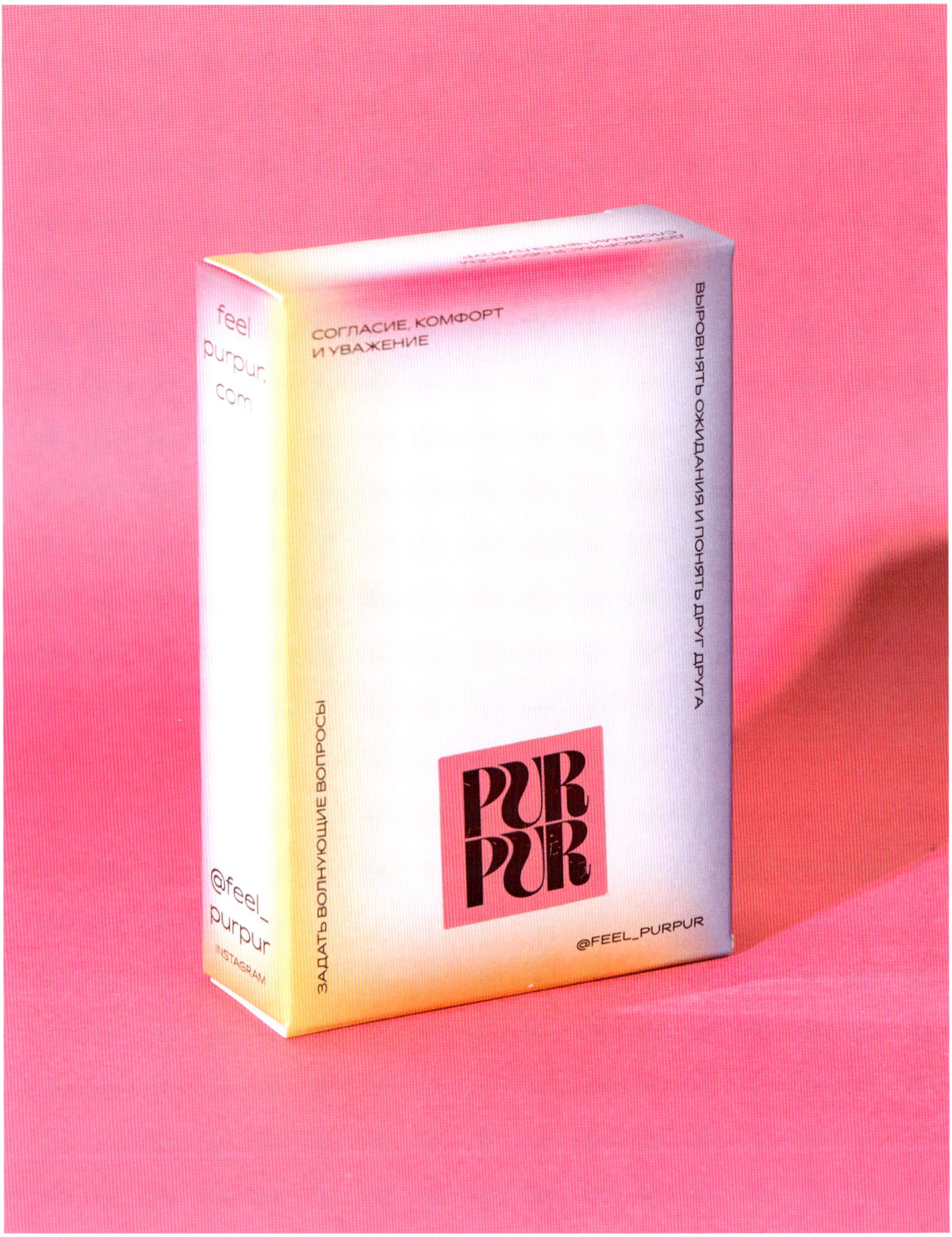

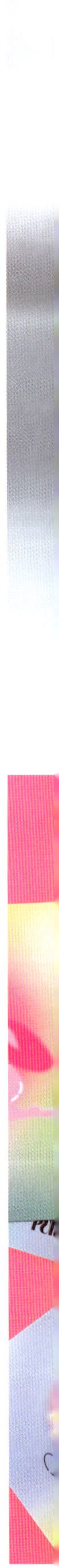

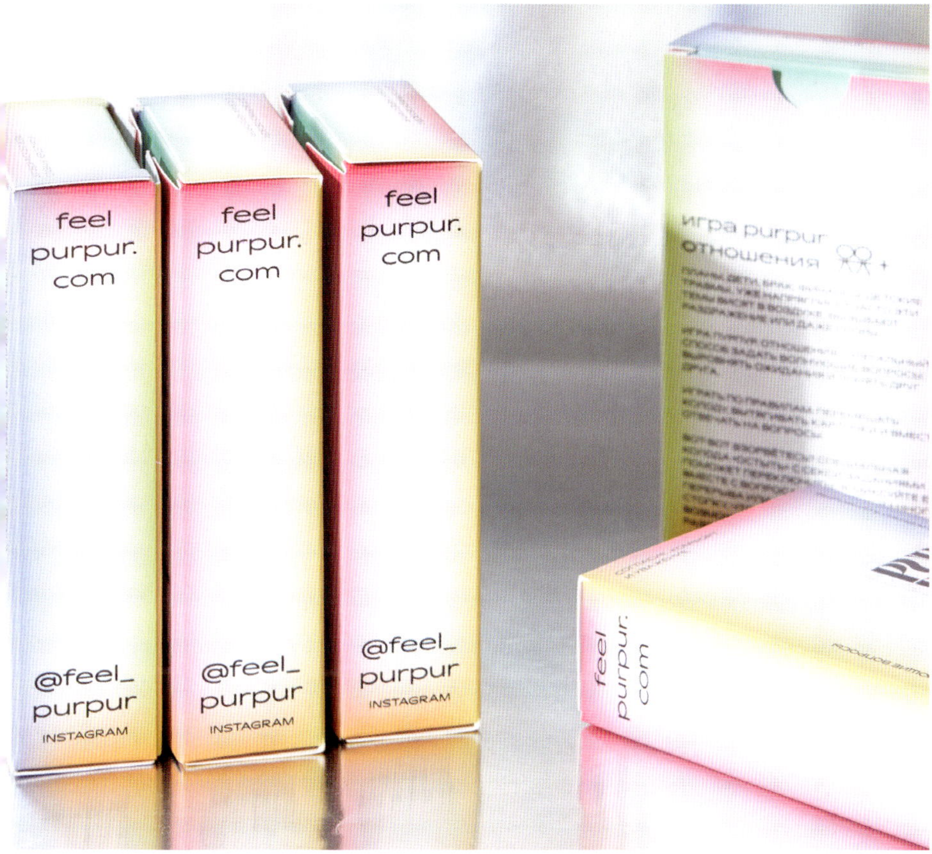

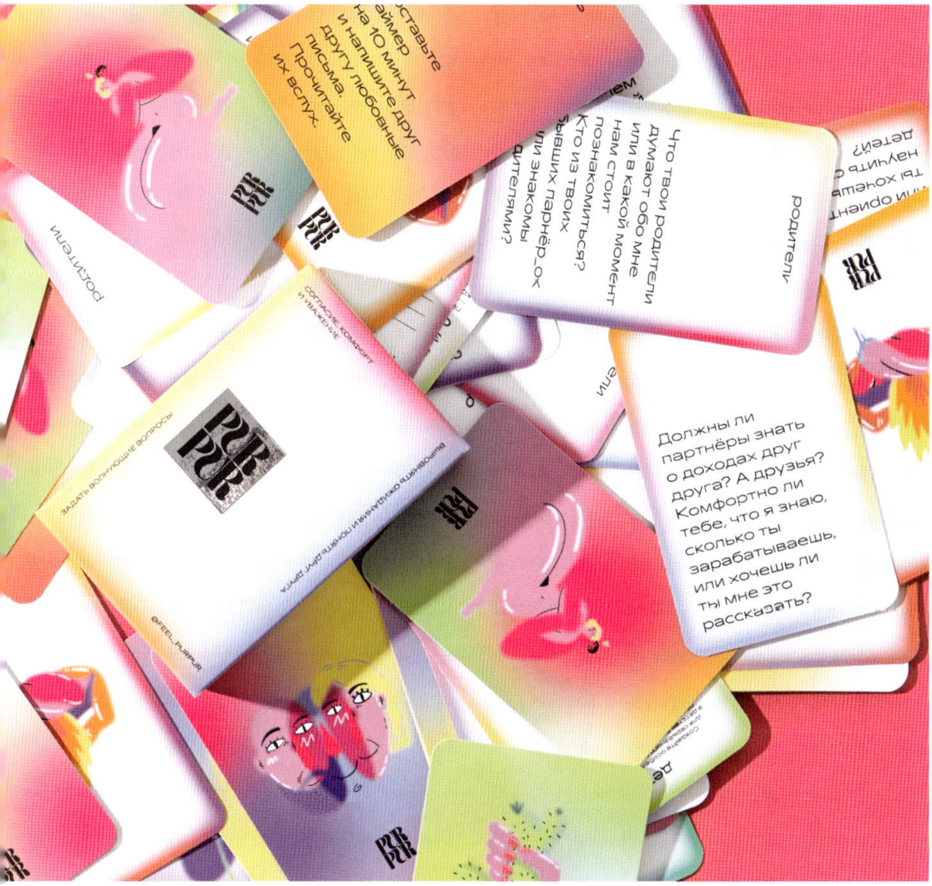

PURPUR GAME RELATIONSHIPS

Life goals, kids, marriage, family budget and childhood traumas. Sounds triggering? Purpur Relationship Game is a green light to discuss painful topics. It helps partners meet expectations, ease the tension and feel more connected to each other. In a playful way, the game invites people to answer deep questions about therapy, sex life, first loss and family planning. They have balanced tough questions with a simple design, like a memory book which brings the joy of sharing.

Brand Development
Anfisa Savchenko & Elena Zaharova

Creative Director
Elena Zaharova

Designer
Polina Zagumenova

Illustrator
Nastasiia Samokhina

Photographer
Lera Braun

Set Design
Polina Zagumenova

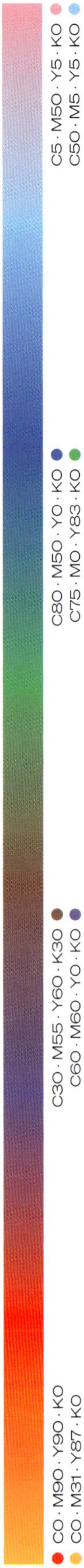
C5 · M50 · Y5 · K0
C50 · M5 · Y5 · K0
C80 · M50 · Y0 · K0
C75 · M0 · Y83 · K0
C30 · M55 · Y60 · K30
C60 · M60 · Y0 · K0
C0 · M90 · Y90 · K0
C0 · M31 · Y87 · K0

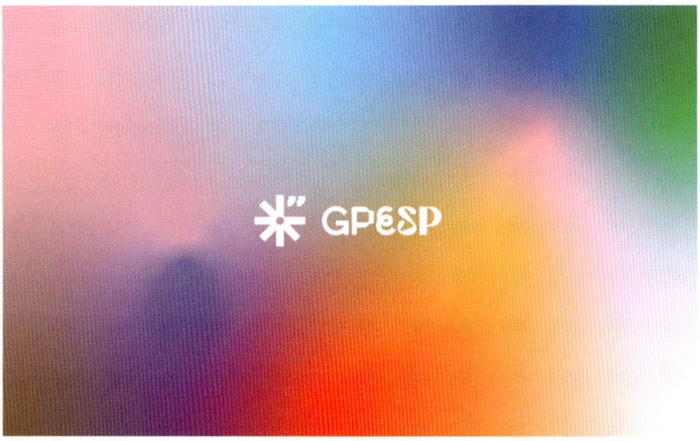
GPESP

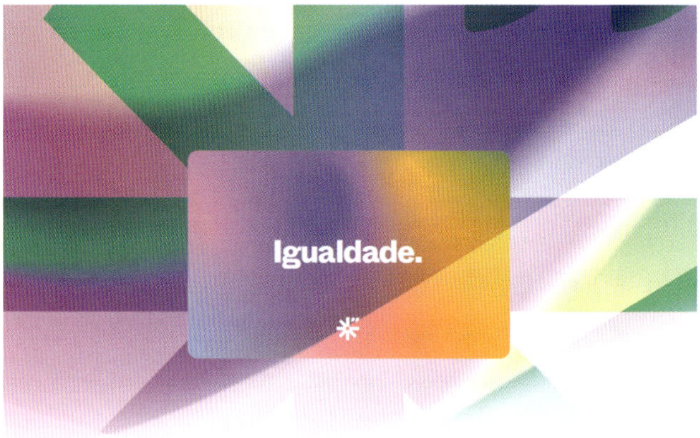
Igualdade.

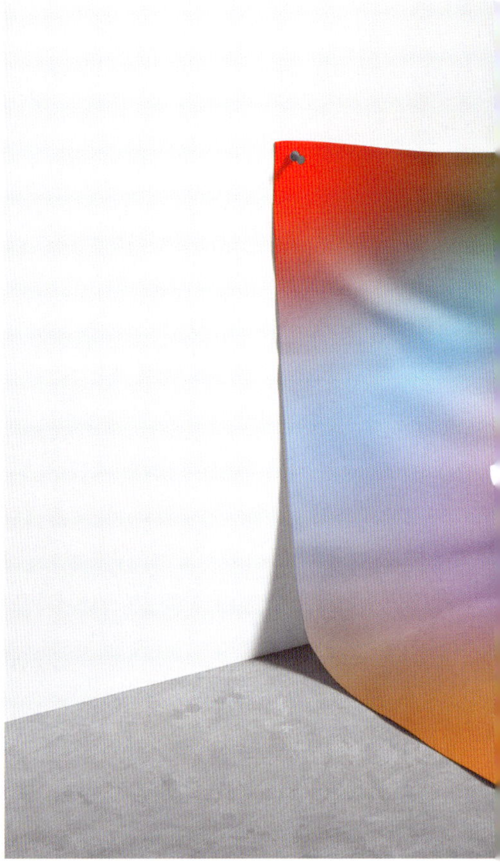

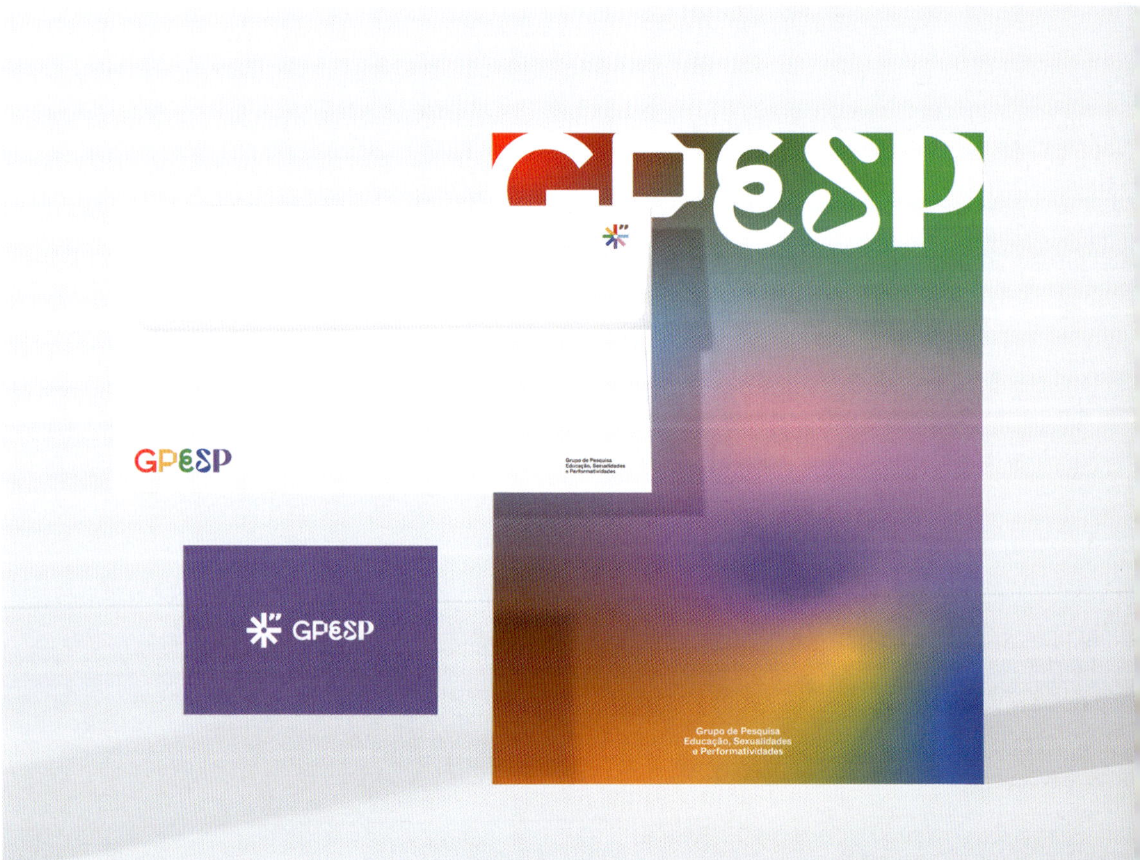
GPESP
GPESP
Grupo de Pesquisa
Educação, Sexualidades
e Performatividades
GPESP
Grupo de Pesquisa
Educação, Sexualidades
e Performatividades

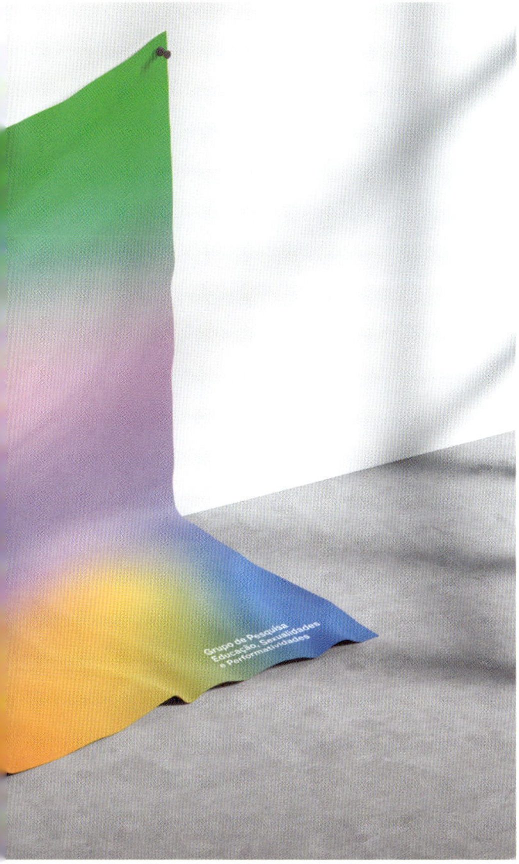

GRUPO DE PESQUISA EDUCAÇÃO, SEXUALIDADES E PERFORMATIVIDADES (GPESP)

GPESP is a formative environment where students and researchers look into social, political, and cultural systems that are present in human identities. The group's goal is to create an inclusive space for LGBTQIAP+ people who want to discover new strategies for creating social impact and paths to a more equitable and more egalitarian society. Folksonomias also used the colours from the LGBTQIAP+ flag for the applications in order to align with the brand's attributes.

Designer
Carlos Gabriel Ferreira

Design Studio
Folksonomias

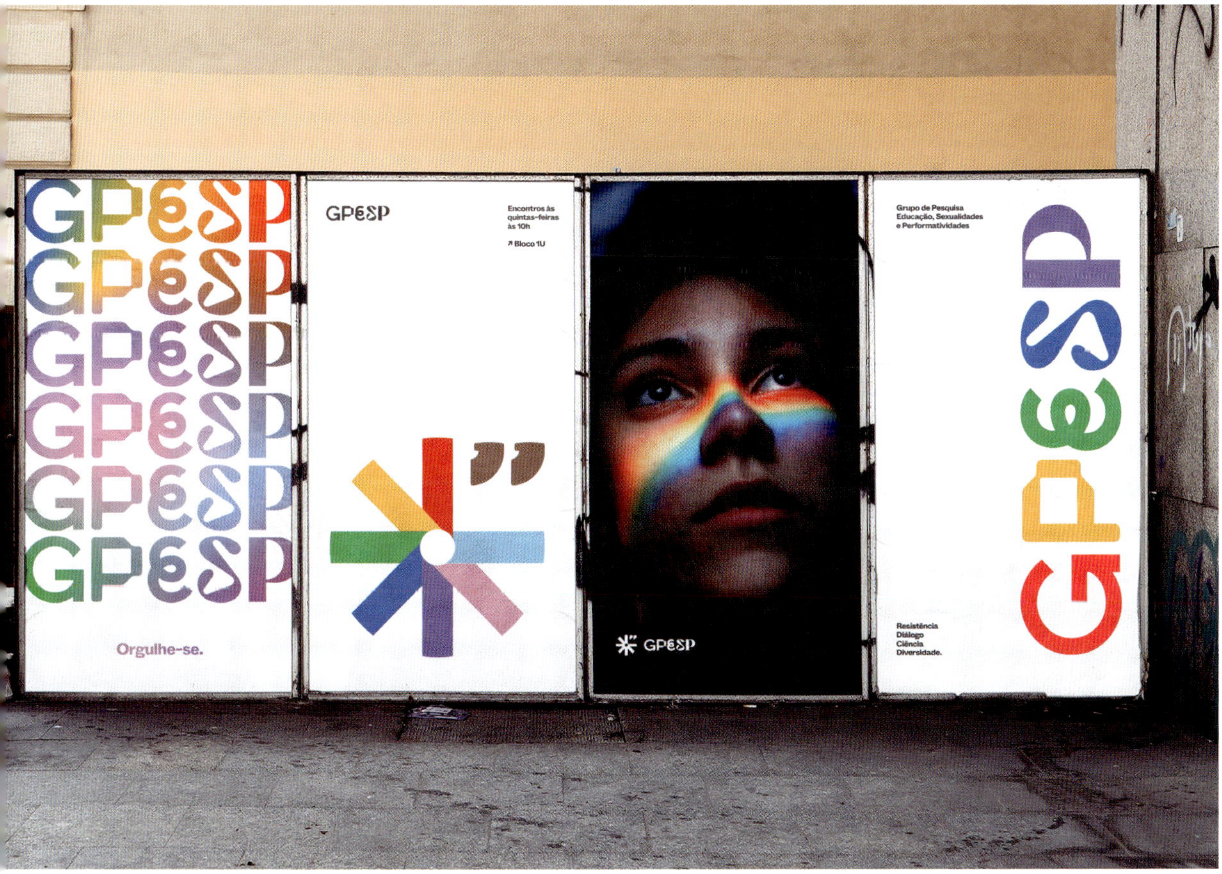

PANTONE 266 C
PANTONE 179 C
PANTONE 1635 C
PANTONE 7401 C

PANTONE 1635 C
PANTONE 555 C
PANTONE 150 C

PANTONE 555 C
PANTONE 7569 C
PANTONE 266 C
PANTONE 179 C

PANTONE 1635 C
PANTONE 264 C
PANTONE 7443 C

PANTONE 555 C
PANTONE 563 C

PANTONE 7569 C
PANTONE 7485 C

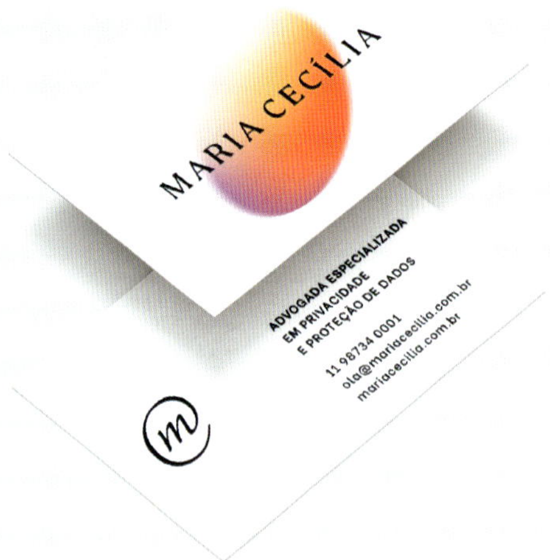

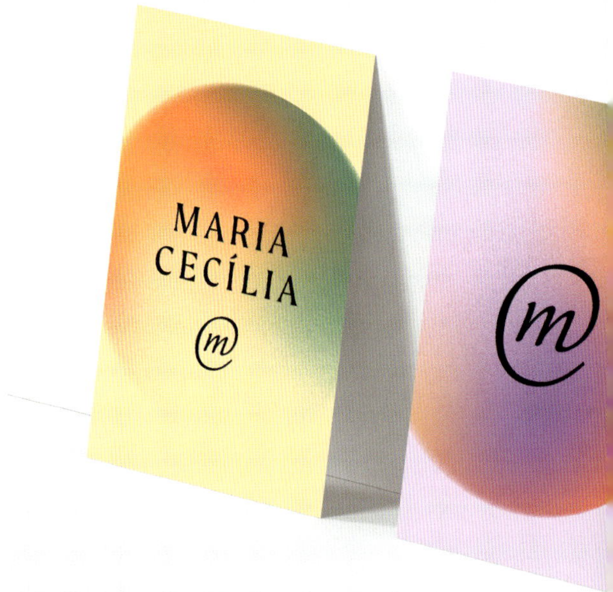

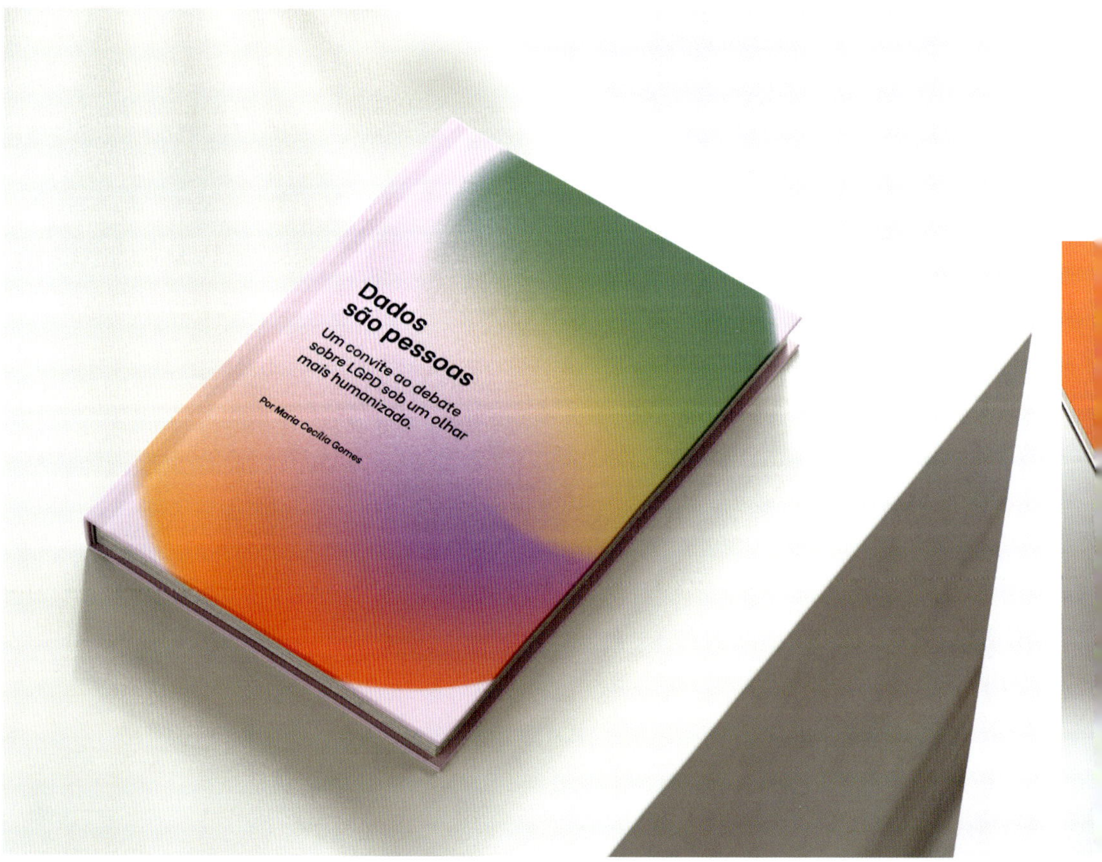

MARIA CECÍLIA

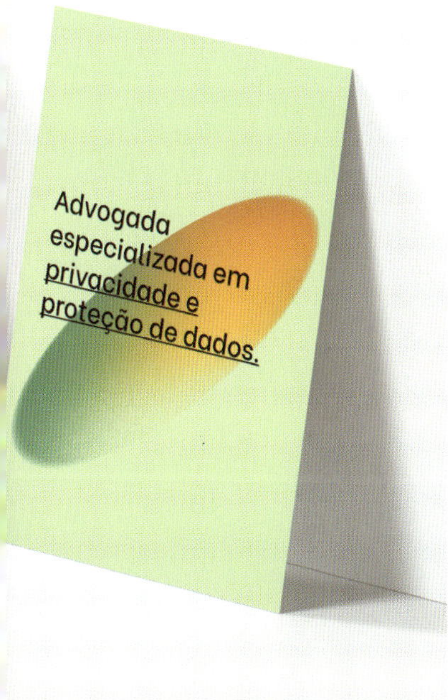

Maria Cecília, a lawyer specializing in privacy and data protection, has an enriching academic and professional trajectory, which allows her to look at the subject from various perspectives. She shares her knowledge through articles, videos, lectures, courses, and consultancy, standing out for her clarity in addressing complex issues and for the dynamic way she has pursued her career. The challenge was to create a visual identity that reflected her legal experience, while simultaneously conveying a young and disruptive approach.

Designer
Amanda Louisi

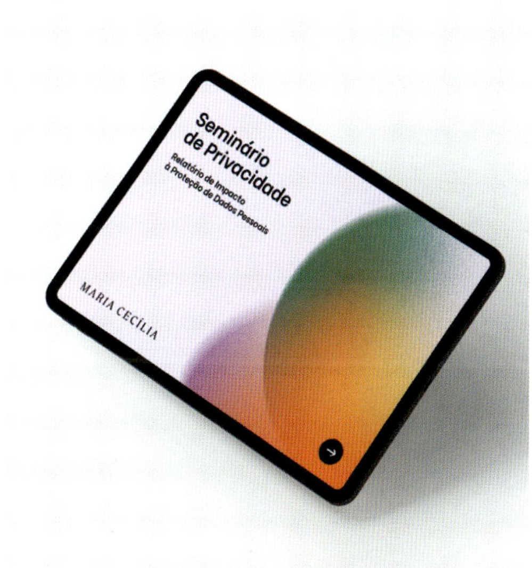

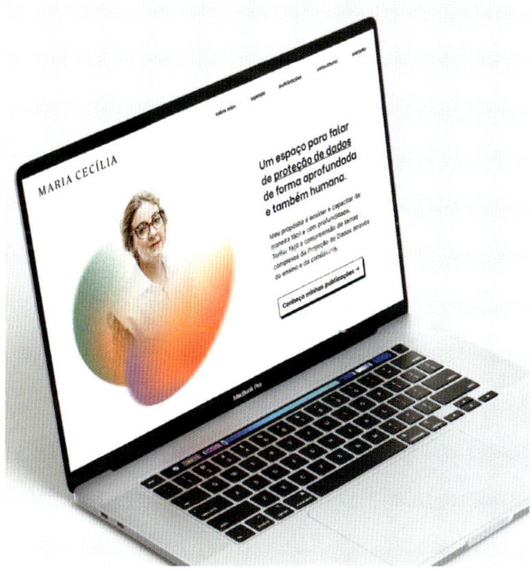

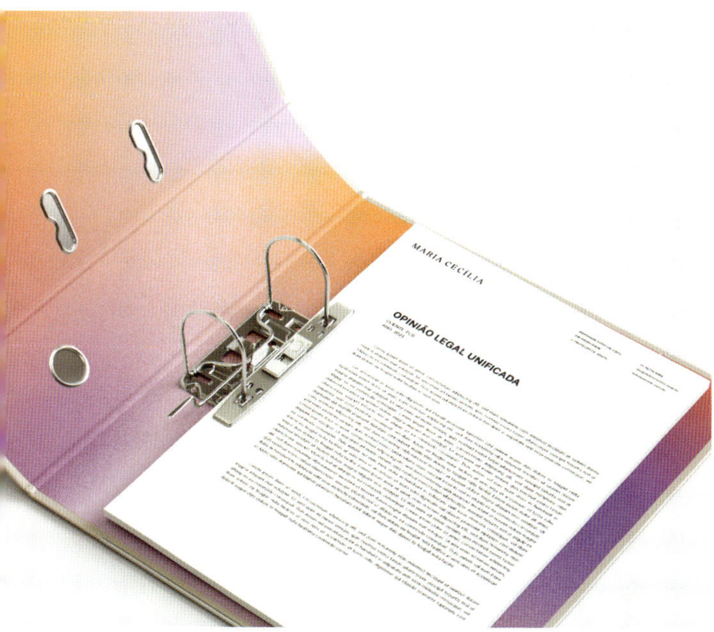

C2 · M84 · Y2 · K0

C70 · M12 · Y0 · K0

C82 · M6 · Y97 · K0

C5 · M98 · Y67 · K0

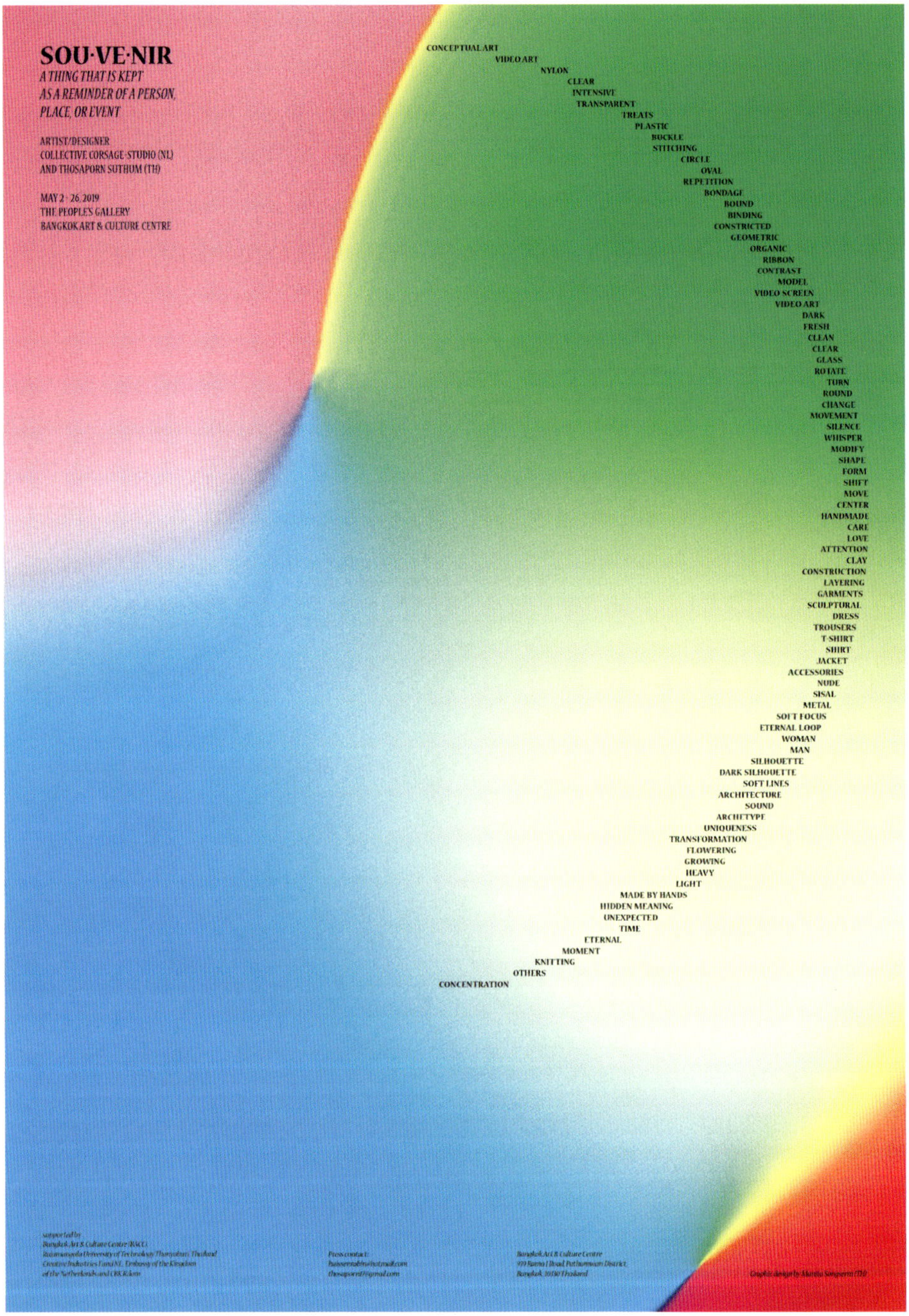

SOU•VE•NIR

The "Sou·ve·nir" exhibition delves into contrasts such as natural versus artificial, geometric versus organic, blackness versus colourfulness, and memory versus matter. It showcases soft sculptures crafted from natural fibres and nylon plastics, complemented by fashion design, video projection, photography, and mixed media artworks.

The poster is designed by distorting forms and colours based on the angle of light.

Art Director & Designer
Manita Songserm

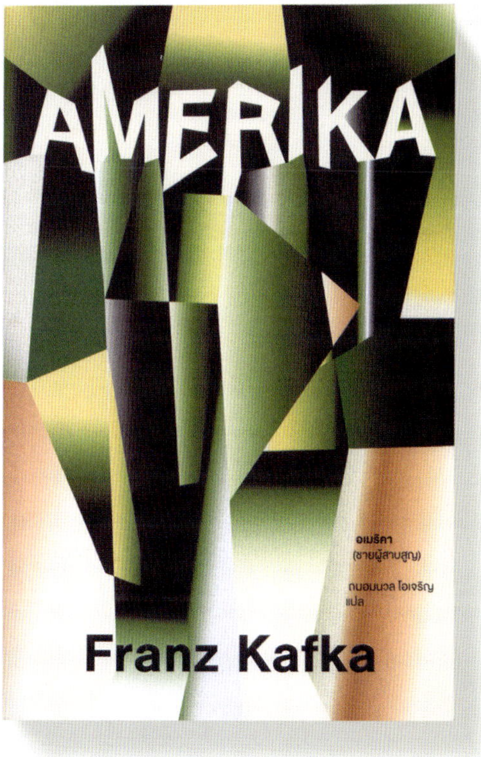

AMERIKA

Amerika tells the story of characters embarking on a journey for fortune in new territories, from Kafka's viewpoint in the 1920s. The cover design, featuring abstract shapes inspired by New York City, reflects a distorted utopian world in Cubist style. Through gradient shifts in colours and images, it symbolizes both the industrial era and futuristic elements of modernity.

Art Director & Designer
Manita Songserm

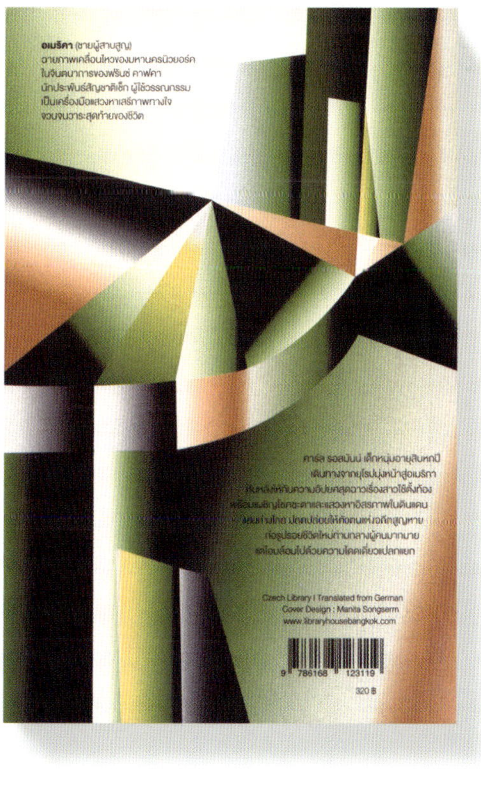

C0 · M0 · Y0 · K100

C58 · M16 · Y100 · K23

C75 · M5 · Y100 · K24

C5 · M17 · Y54 · K7

C19 · M53 · Y78 · K3

PANTONE 459 C

PANTONE 7416 C

PANTONE 698 C

PANTONE 566 C

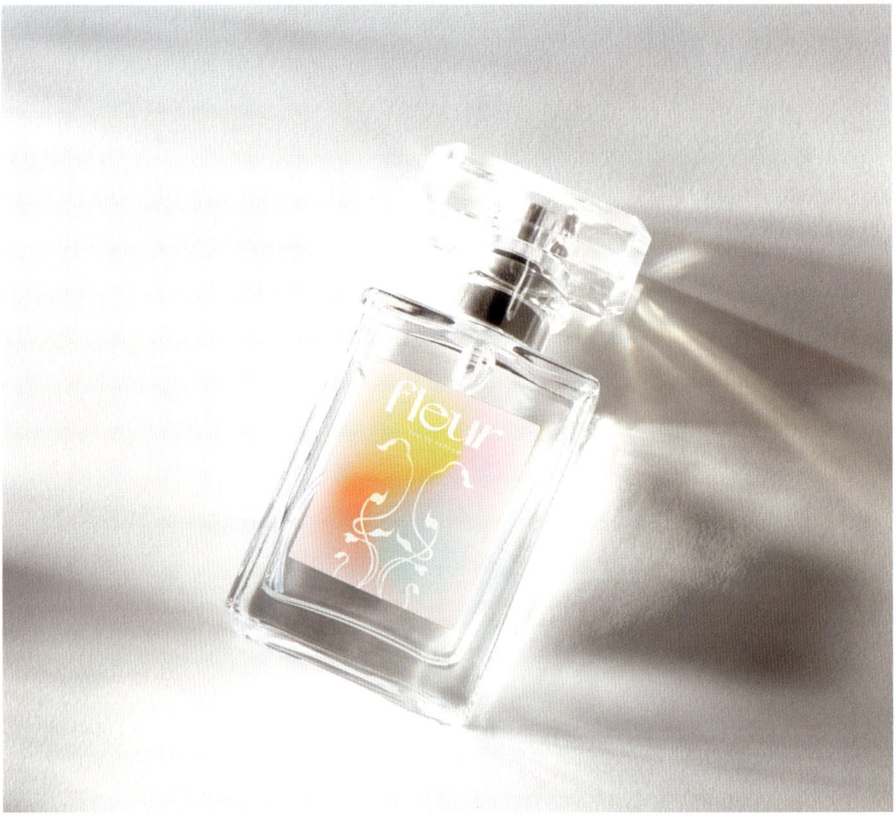

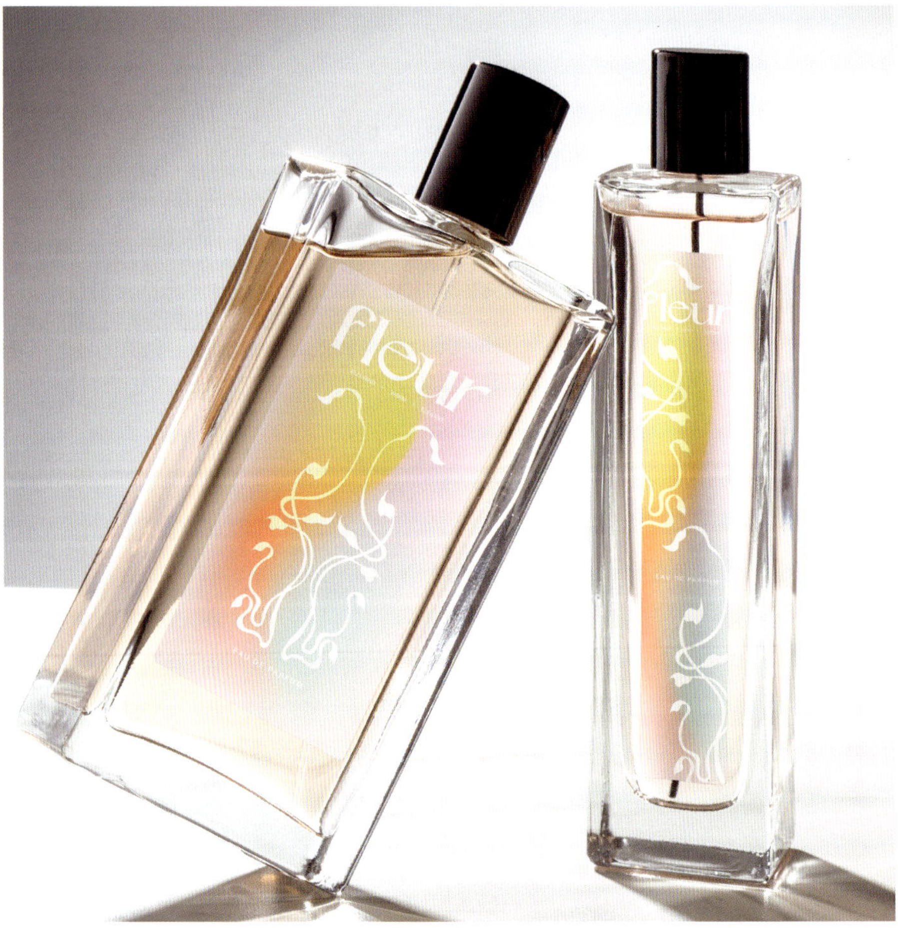

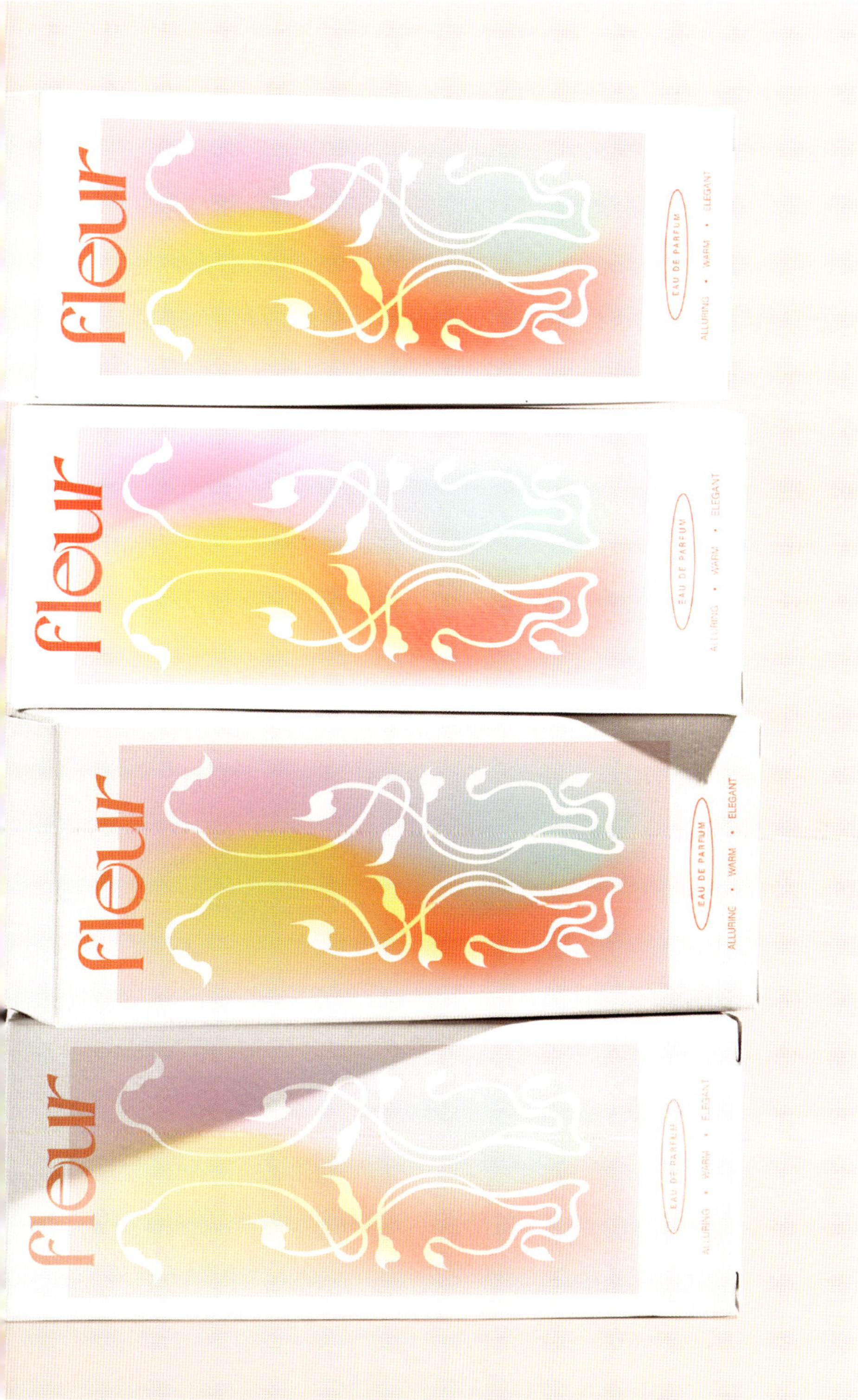

FLEUR

Fleur is a passion project of exquisite fragrances. The design is made to reflect the luxurious and ethereal qualities of their scents. The primary goal is to infuse the brand with feminine accents and soft gradients that evoke a sense of timeless elegance. The essence of femininity was captured through design elements like soft pastels such as blush pink and lavender, and light blues with gradient transitions between colours to add depth and visual interest.

Art Director, Designer & Illustrator
Ashley Isaac

Design Studio
By Ashley Design

C87 · M84 · Y0 · K0
C6 · M25 · Y2 · K0
C7 · M23 · Y77 · K0

C20 · M78 · Y75 · K0
C22 · M27 · Y9 · K0
C58 · M19 · Y23 · K0

C60 · M36 · Y93 · K0
C12 · M24 · Y35 · K0
C8 · M27 · Y83 · K0

C75 · M41 · Y58 · K0
C15 · M15 · Y22 · K0
C11 · M5 · Y83 · K0

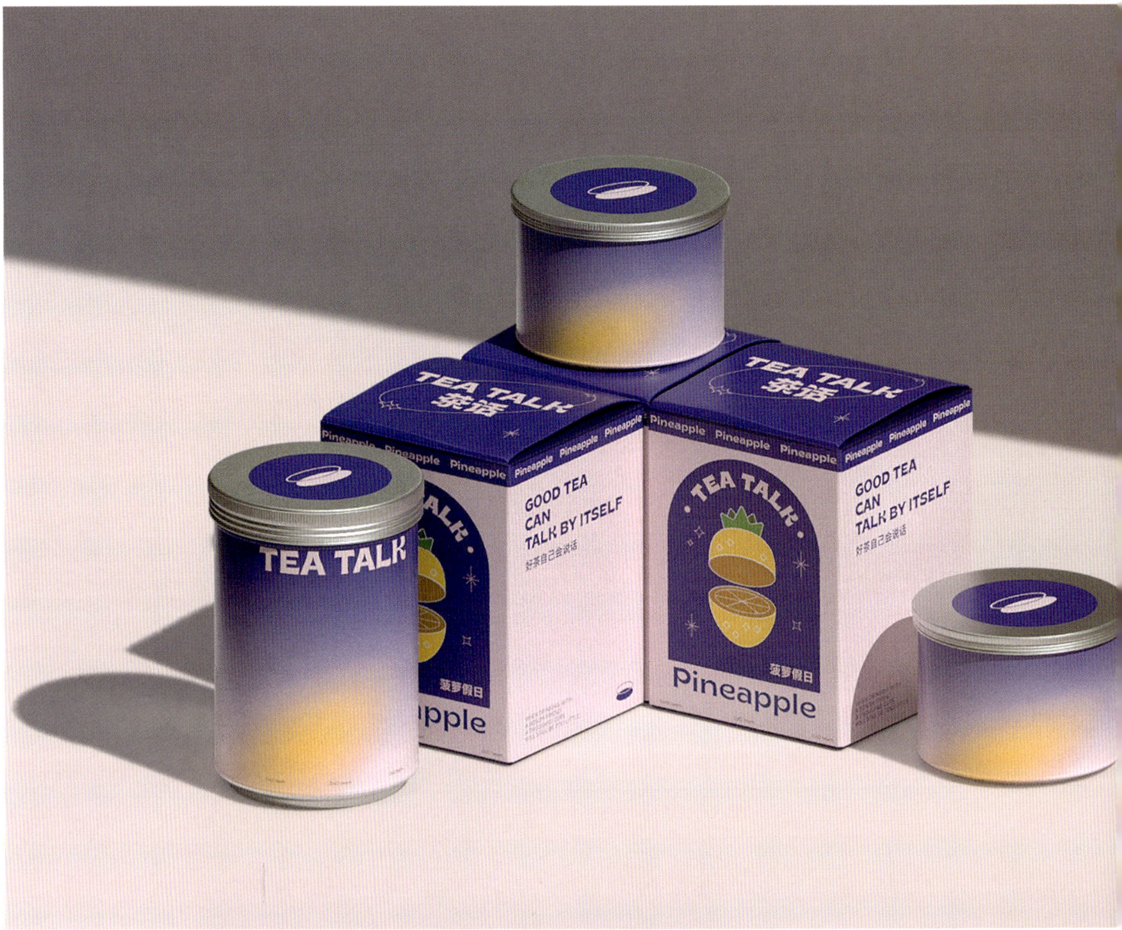

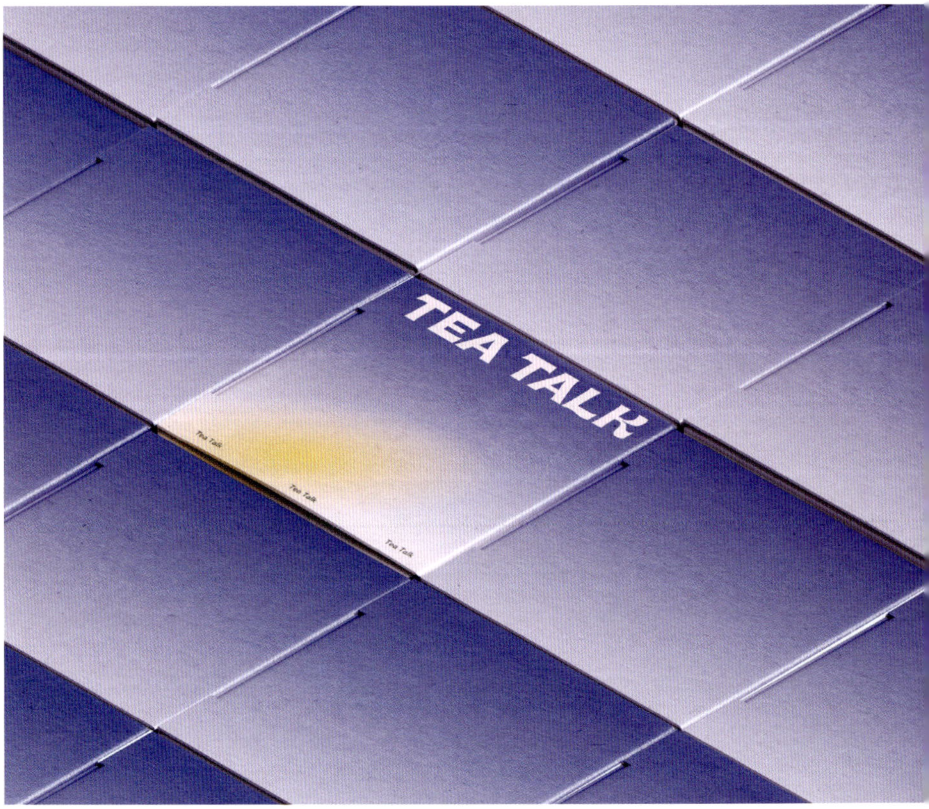

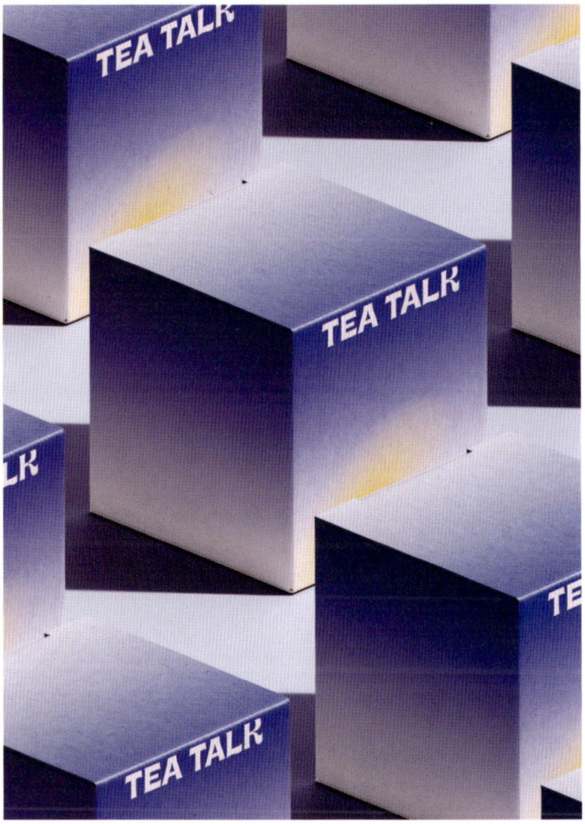

TEA TALK

Tea Talk, as a new tea-based beverage brand, takes "good tea speaks for itself" as its brand concept. Its products also focus on tea drinks and tea beverages. In the future, online retailing will be the main direction of business development. When facing the current market demand for female-oriented tea drinks, *Tea Talk* insists on shaping a unisex brand image concept, using a visual language that meets the emotional demands of young people and conveys aesthetic tendencies to create a high degree of brand differentiation.

Design Studio
DXD studio

Art Director
Carmen Lai

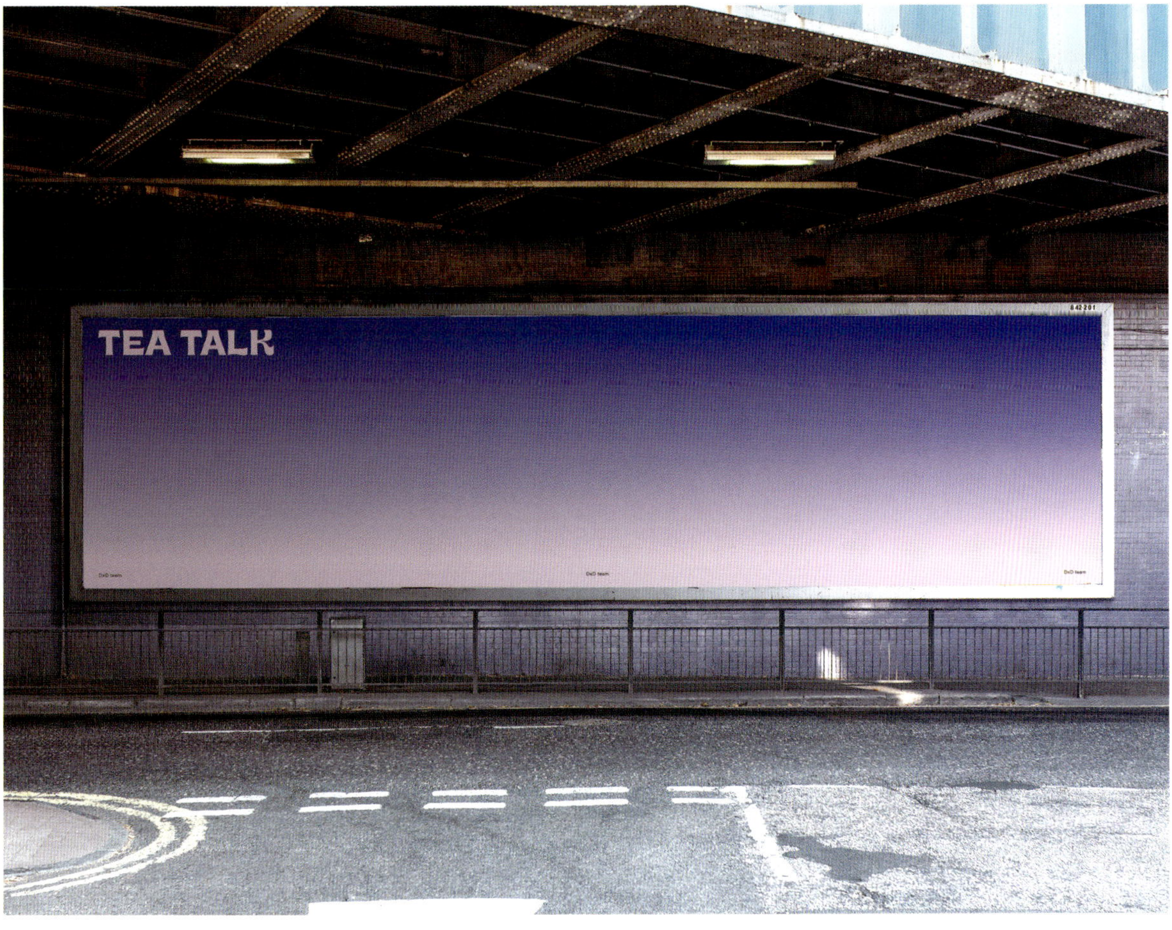

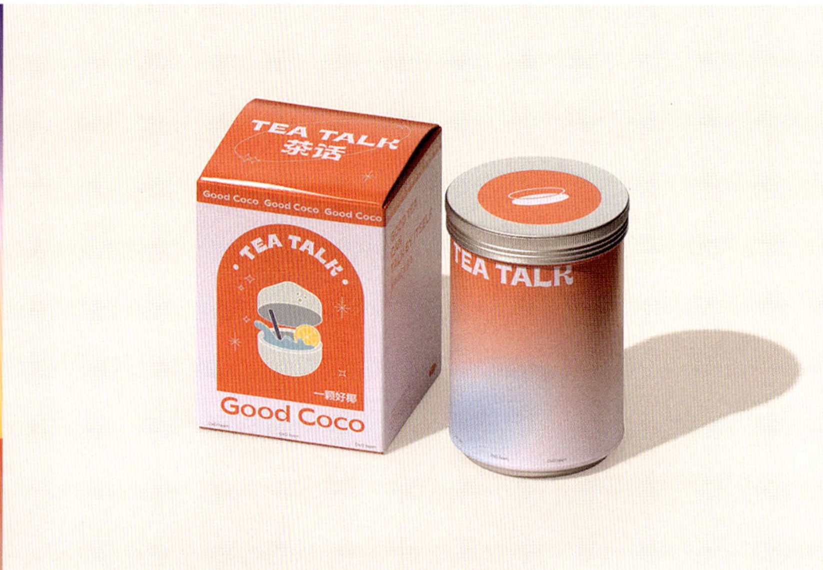
TEA TALK
茶话
Good Coco Good Coco Good Coco
TEA TALK
一颗好椰
Good Coco
TEA TALK

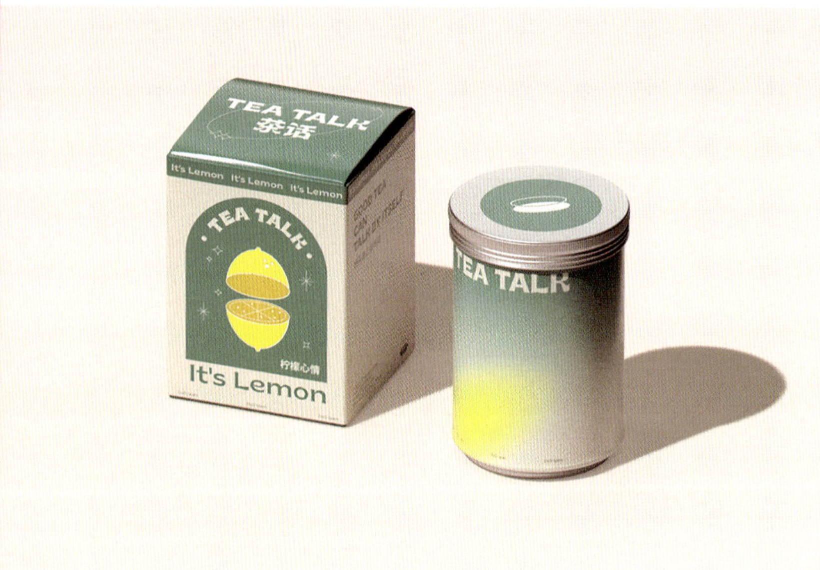
TEA TALK
茶话
It's Lemon It's Lemon It's Lemon
GOOD TEA
CAN
TALK BY ITSELF
TEA TALK
柠檬心情
It's Lemon
TEA TALK

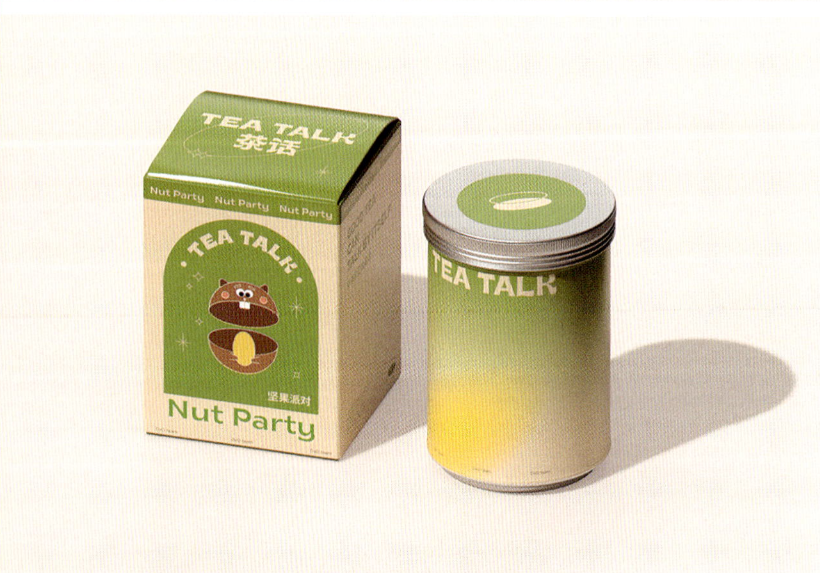
TEA TALK
茶话
Nut Party Nut Party Nut Party
TEA TALK
坚果派对
Nut Party
TEA TALK

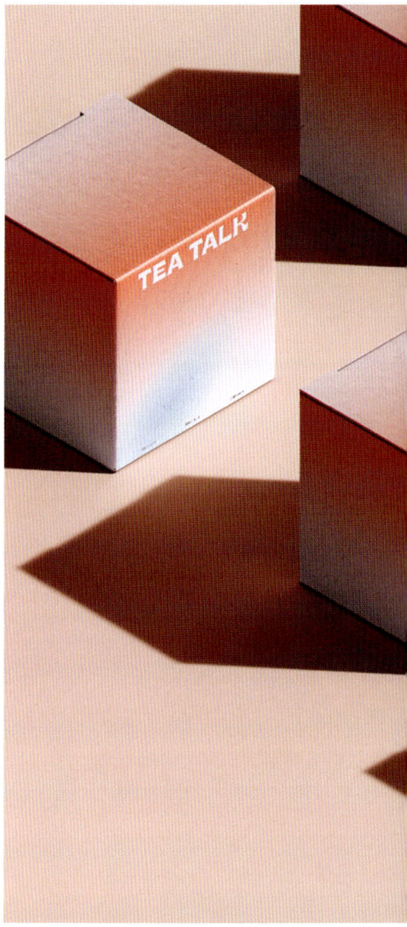
TEA TALK

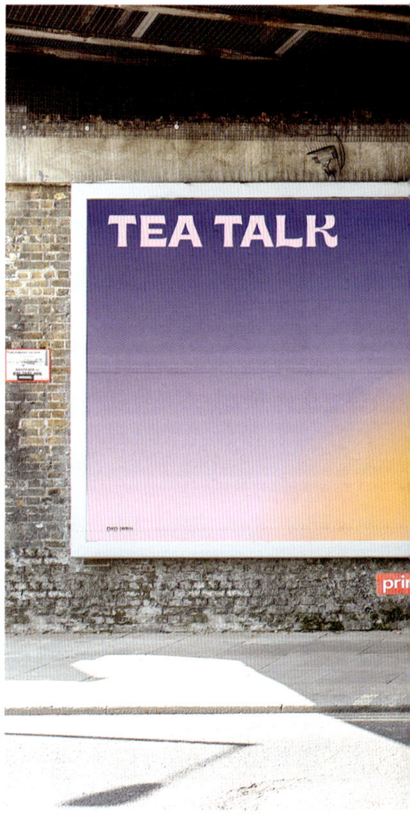
TEA TALK

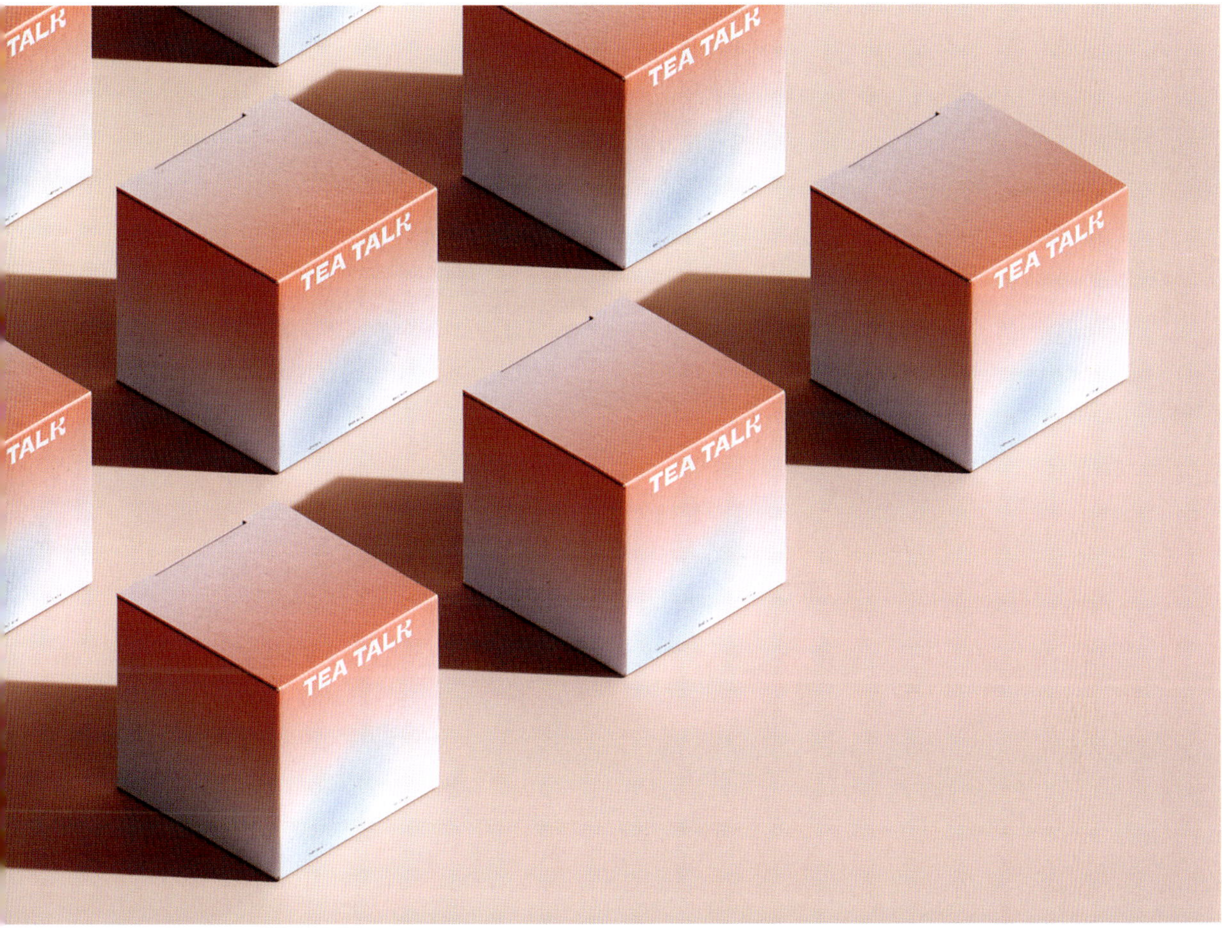
TEA TALK

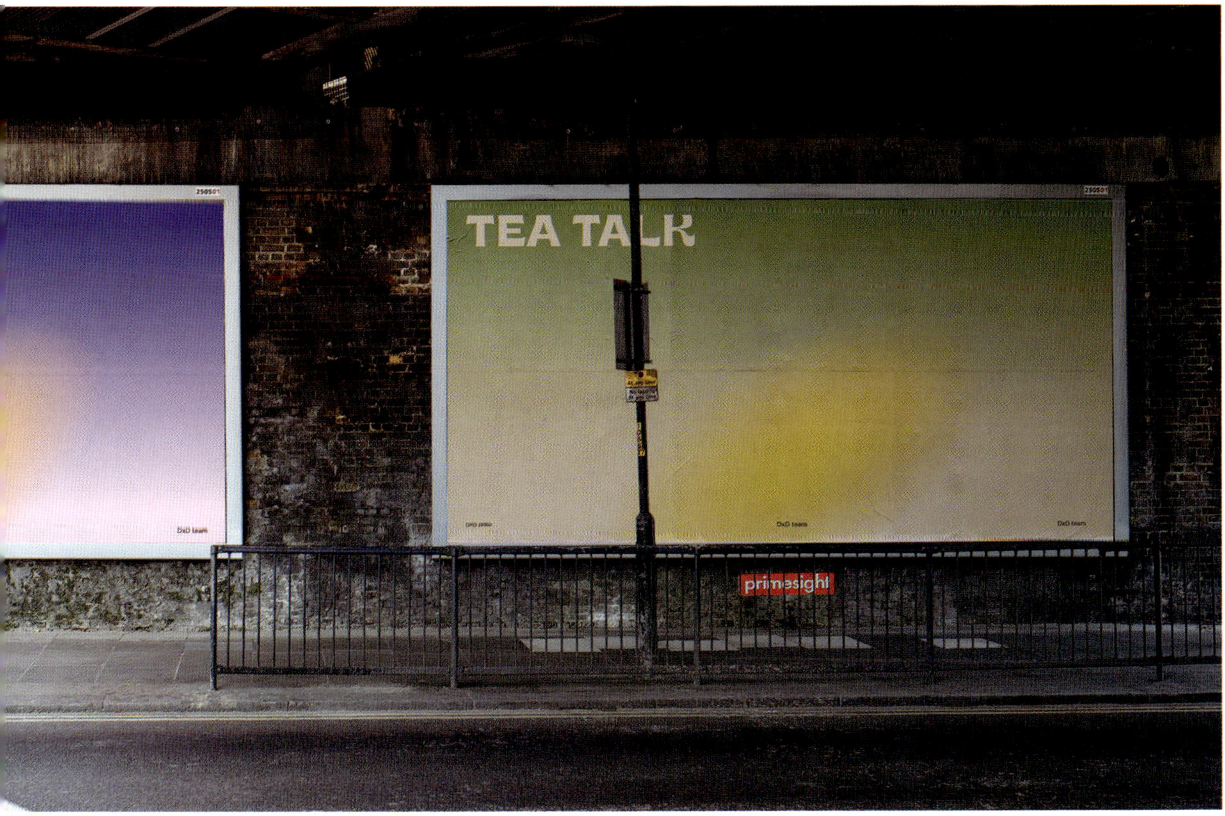
TEA TALK
primesight

C30 · M0 · Y25 · K0
C37 · M0 · Y0 · K0

C25 · M40 · Y0 · K0
C0 · M40 · Y0 · K0

C0 · M40 · Y29 · K0
C0 · M24 · Y42 · K0

C0 · M4 · Y50 · K0

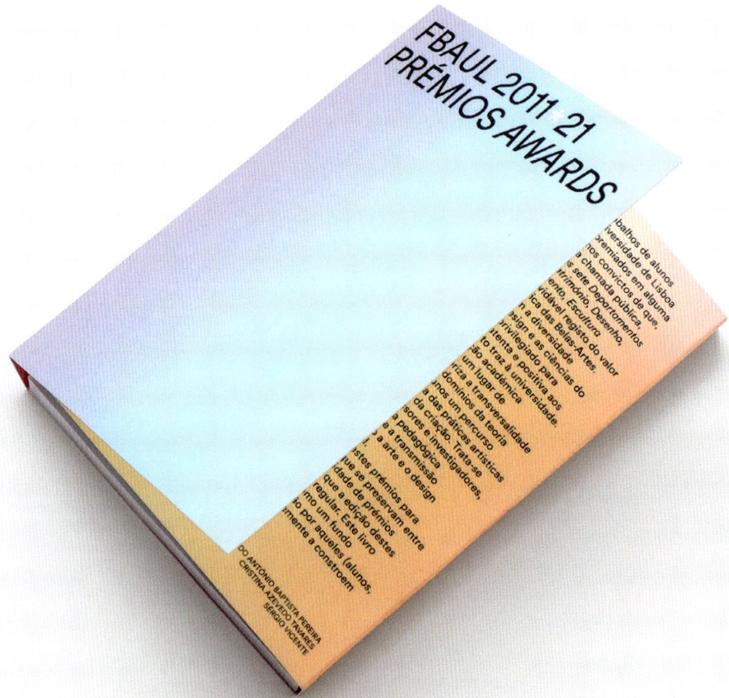

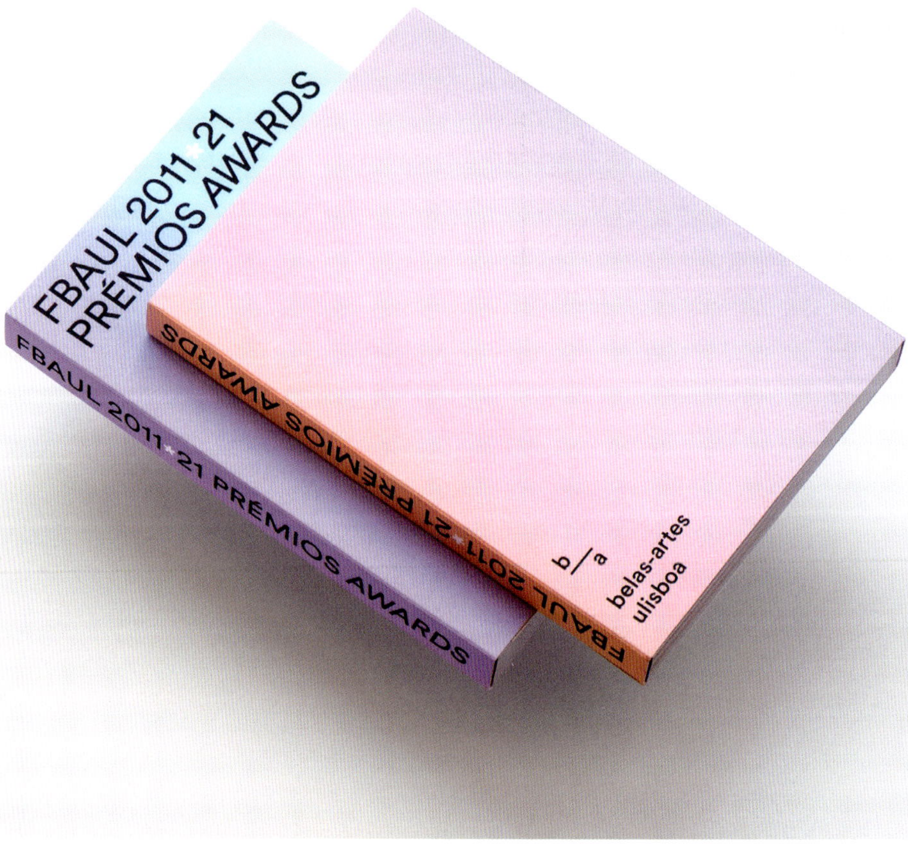

FBAUL 2011-2021 PRÉMIOS/AWARDS

This book is a compilation of awards, scholarships, and other honours awarded to students and alumni of the prestigious Faculdade de Belas-Artes da Universidade de Lisboa (Faculty of Fine Arts of the University of Lisbon) during the decade of 2011-2021. The cover and interior design features gradients of seven colours, each colour representing one school department: art and heritage studies, communication design, drawing, new media art, painting, product design and sculpture.

Designer
Tomás Gouveia

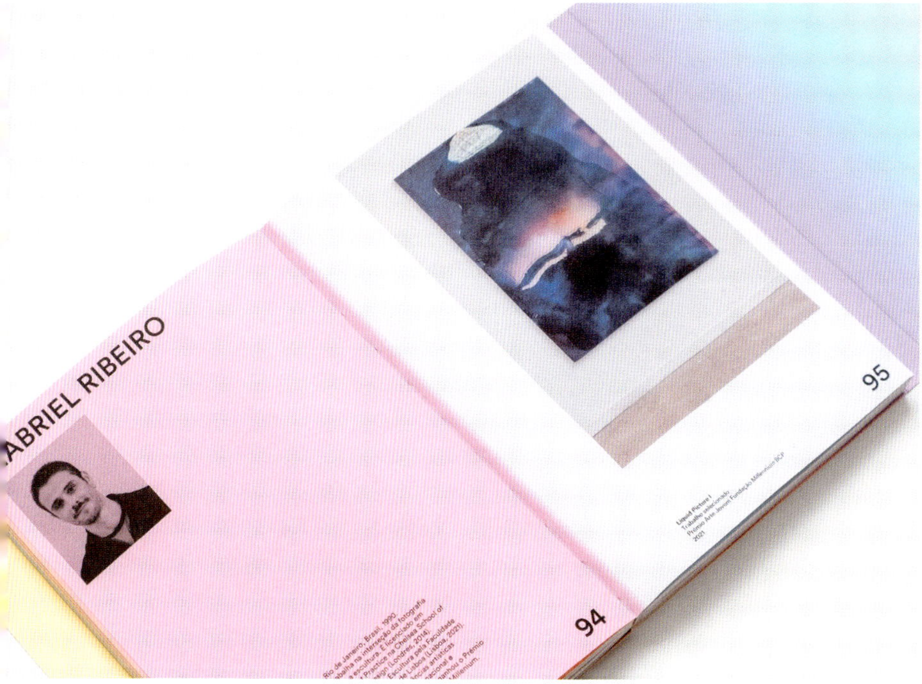

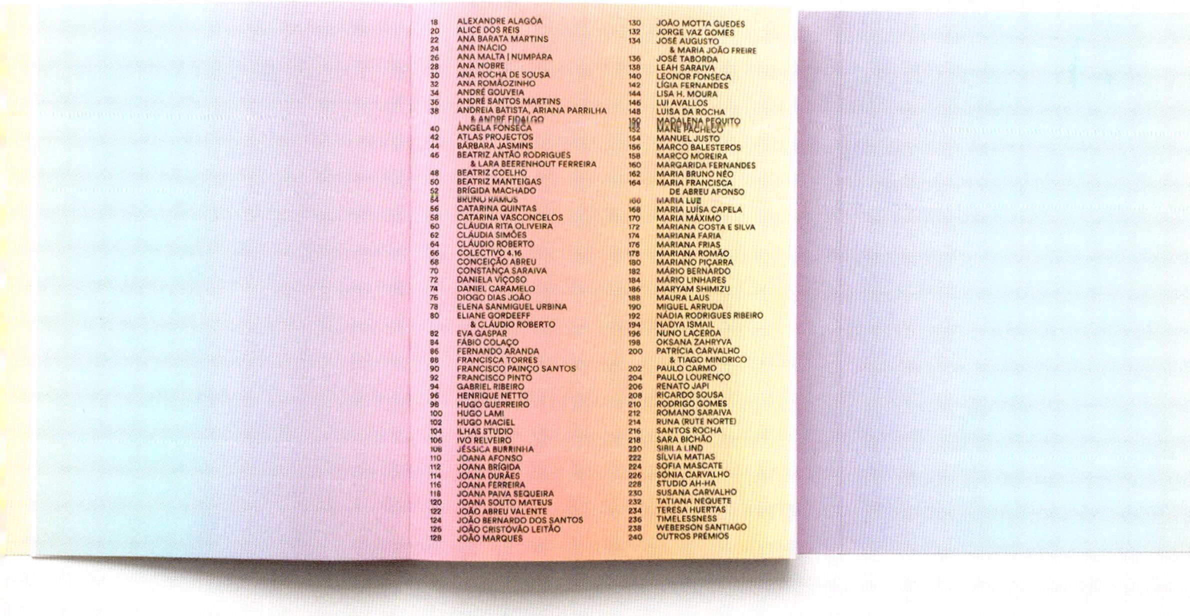

PANTONE WITHE
PANTONE 7730 C

PANTONE 393 C
PANTONE 7416 C

PANTONE BLACK 6 C
PANTONE 167 C

PANTONE 7583 C
PANTONE 7569 C

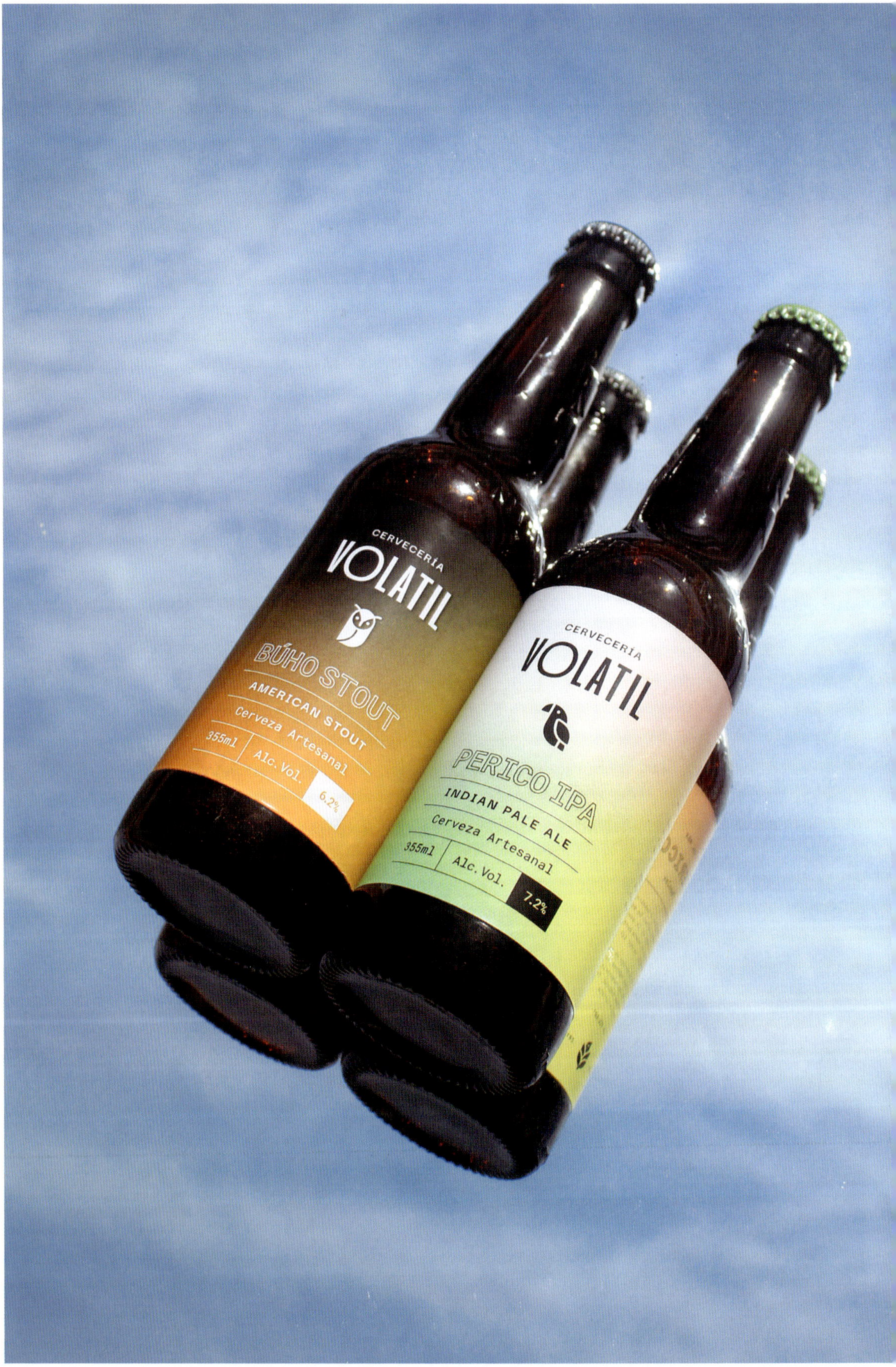

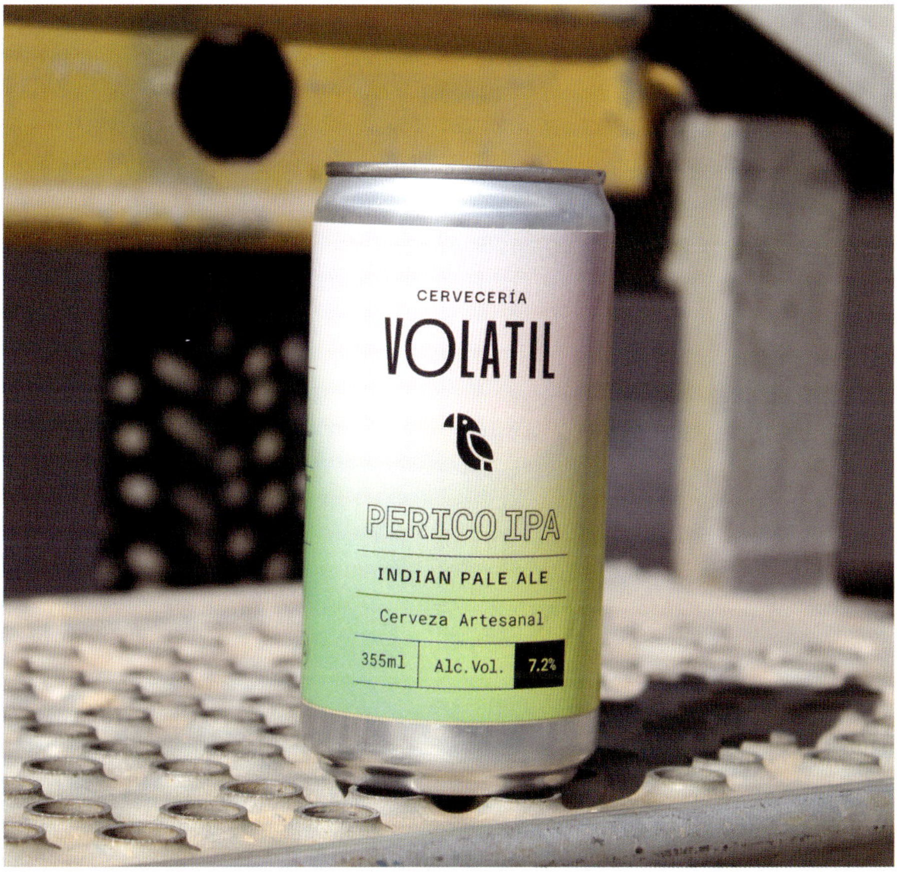

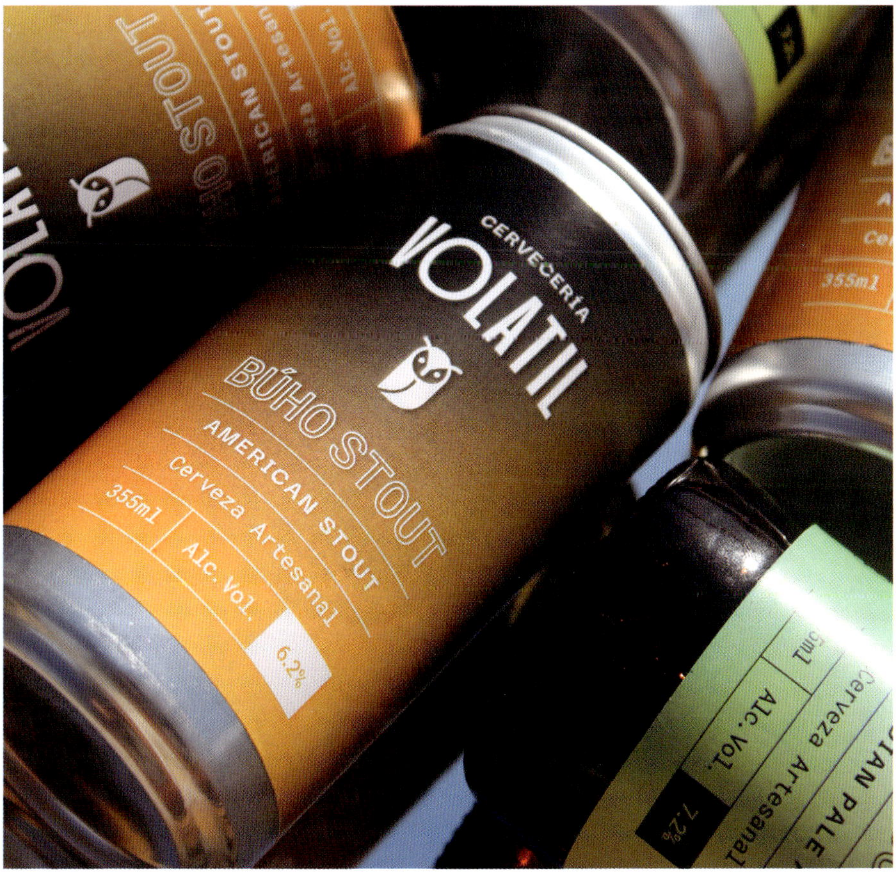

CERVECERIA VOLATIL

Branding and packaging development for *Cerveceria Volatil*, a Mexican brewery established in 2013. The brand, along with its name, takes its inspiration from birds; the isotype of the brand represents the mixture of the hop flower and a bird. The company produces two main beers: *Parrot IPA* and *Owl stout*, each represented by the colour palette present in the plumage of its respective bird, resulting in a gradient system for each beer.

Design Studio
By Cuic

Designer
Enrique Segura Gonzalez

R255 · G101 · B35
R170 · G142 · B247

R1 · G104 · B191
R255 · G154 · B154

R233 · G65 · B92
R231 · G40 · B135
R72 · G28 · B131

R59 · G67 · B149
R73 · G134 · B223
R195 · G255 · B67

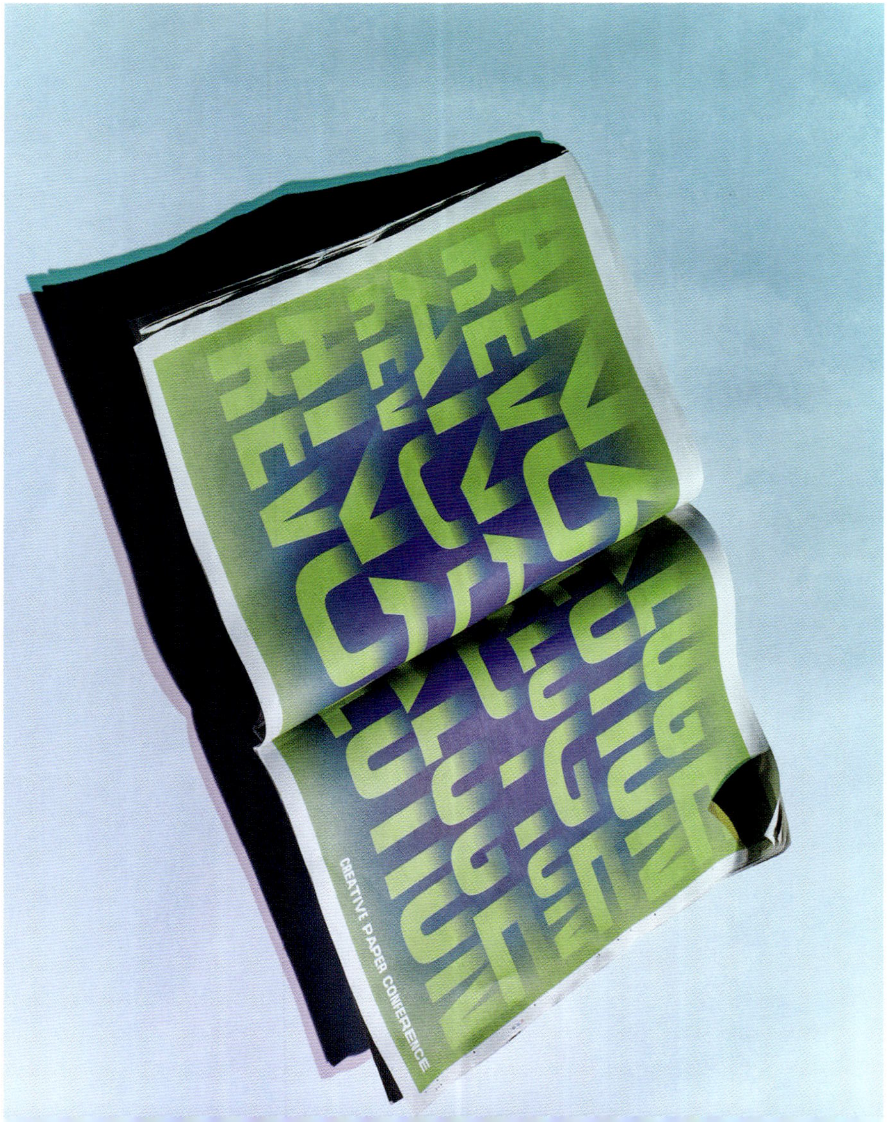

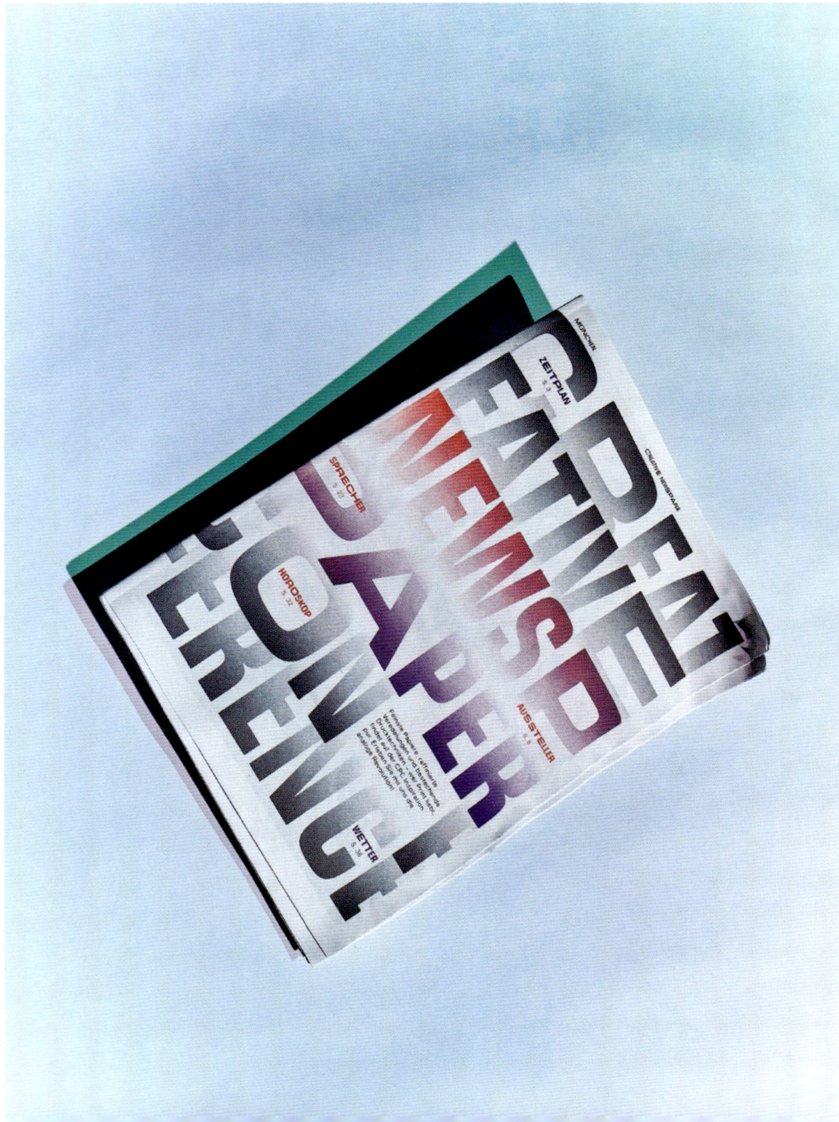

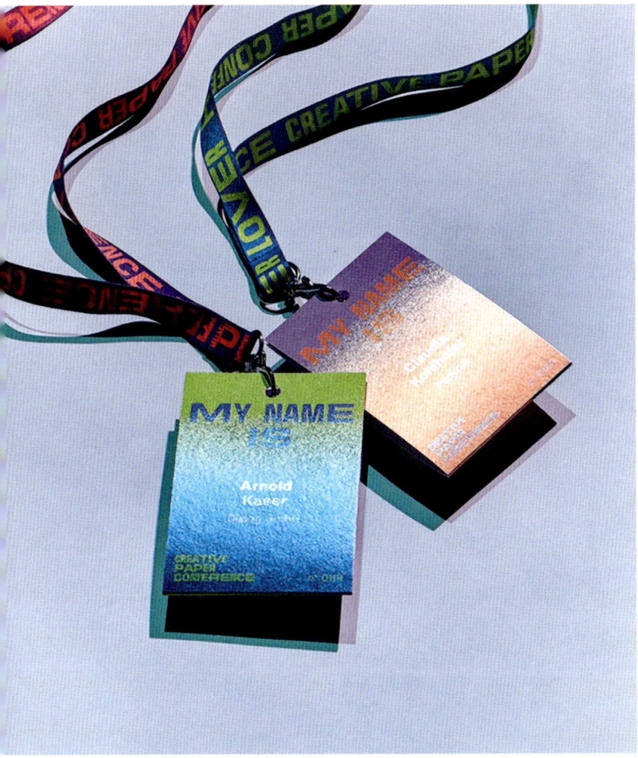

CREATIVE PAPER CONFERENCE

Branding of the "CPC-Creative Paper Conference", which takes place bi-annually in Munich. A lot of elements were created, in print and digital, on stage and off stage. From lanyards to dinner invitations, goodie bags to a newspaper, coasters to name tags, screen design to moving images, everything came to play in Munich. A tangible and highly entertaining experience—in all aspects.

Design Studio
Paperlux Studio

Creative Director
Max Kuehne

Art Director
Elisabeth Pichler

Photographer
Tom Medici

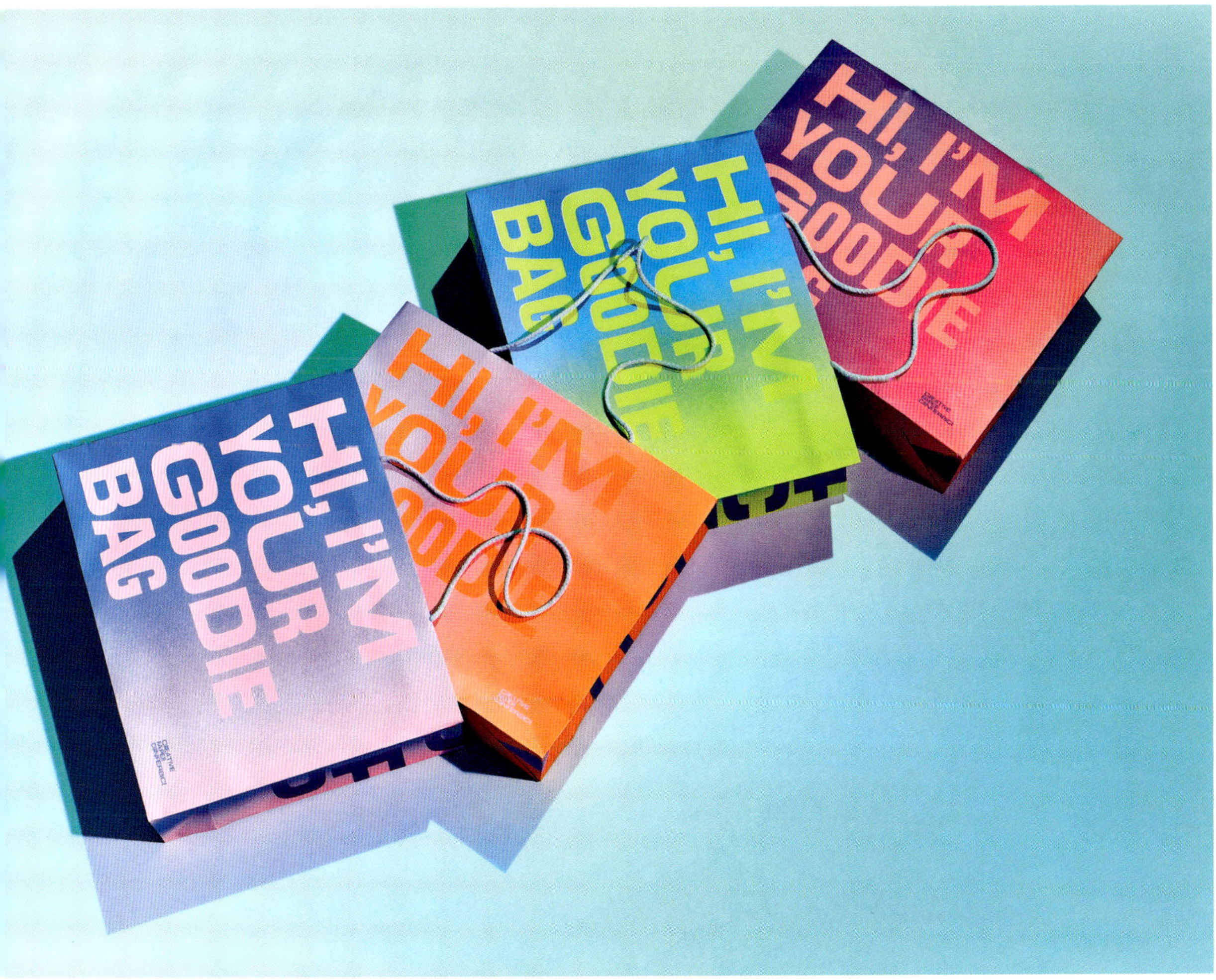

PANTONE 801 C
PANTONE 806 C

PANTONE 802 C
PANTONE 801 C

PANTONE 803 C
PANTONE 801 C

PANTONE 805 C
PANTONE 803 C
PANTONE 802 C

PANTONE 806 C
PANTONE 805 C
PANTONE 803 C

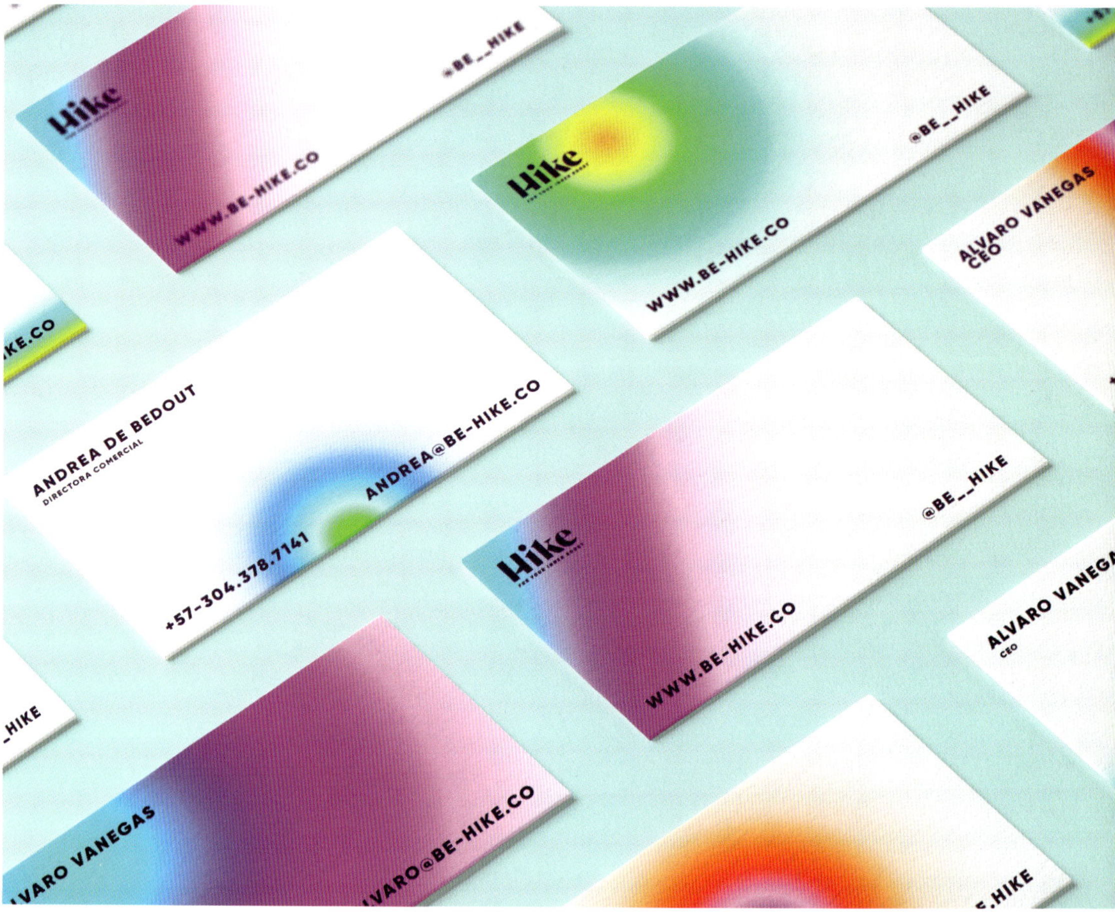

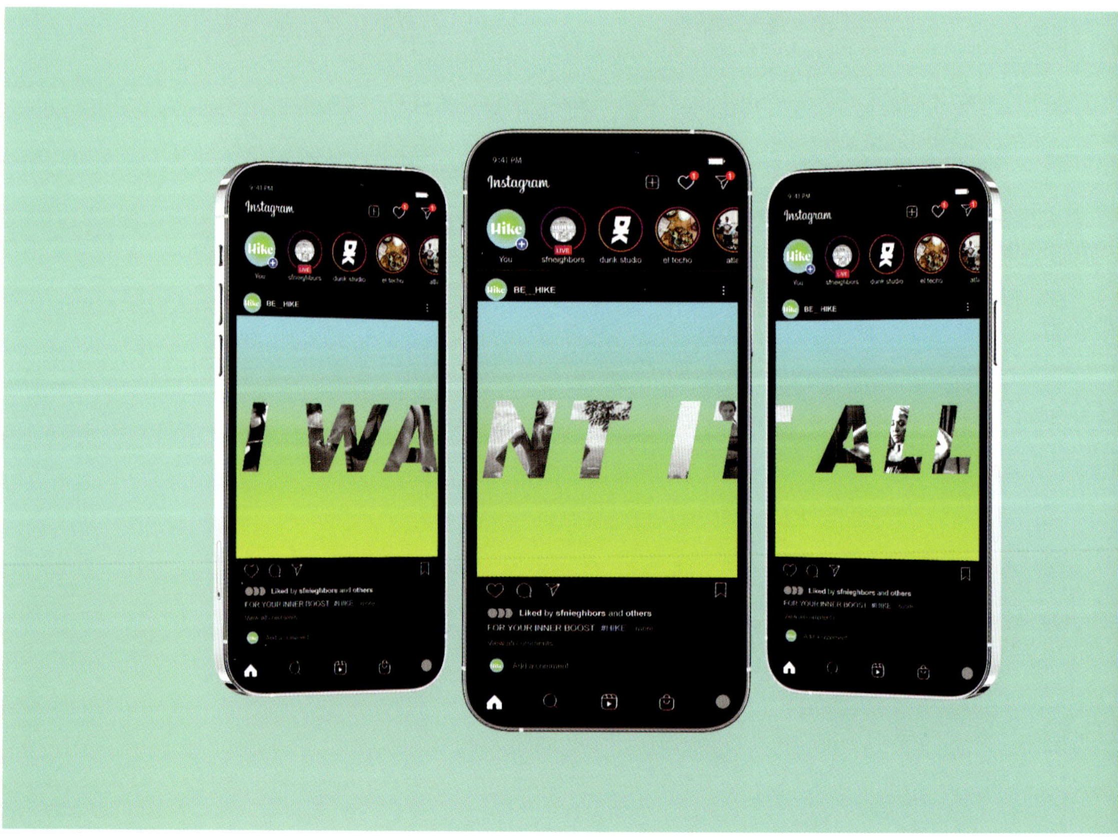

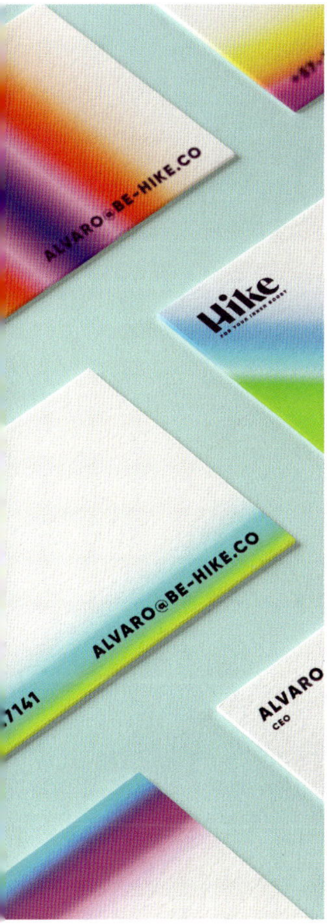

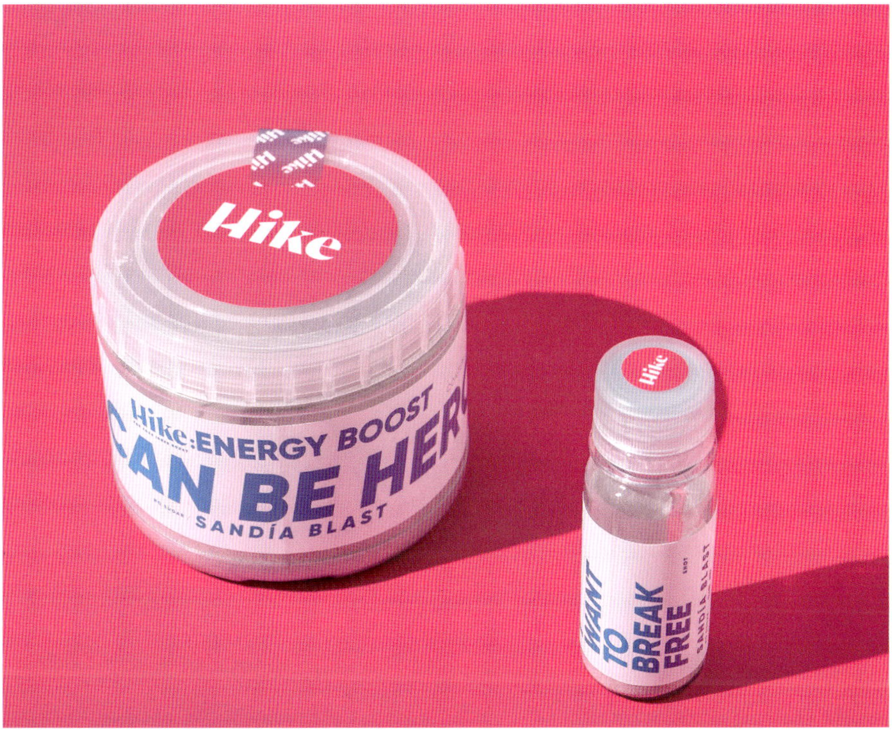

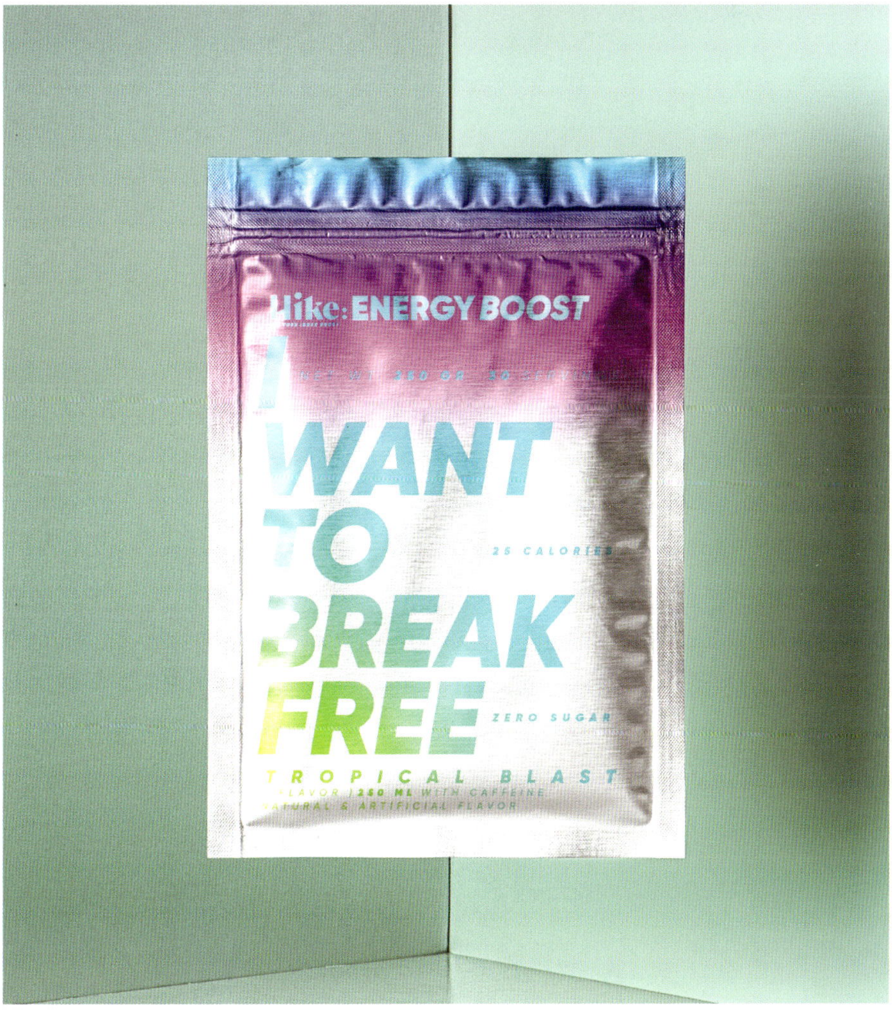

HIKE

This is a brand that inspires, motivates and boost the inner power that exists in each person. Active, dynamic and strong.

Designer
Jose Ortiz (Dunk Studio)

Photographer
Steven Victoria

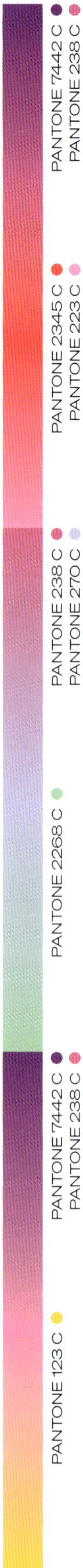

GEOPAGOS

Geopagos is a digital payment platform to boost companies worldwide. In 2021, Papanapa was sought after to revolutionize its global presence. The design solution transformed every aspect of the brand, starting with the logo, presenting a structure that brings a new spelling format (all in lowercase) while balancing human and technological characteristics by combining rounded shapes and sharp angles. Aside from bringing movement to the communication and amplifying the experiences promoted by the company, the extensive colour palette reflects the adaptability that *Geopagos* offers to its partners.

Creative Director
Gustavo Garcia

Designer
Isabella Mello, Lucas Rodrigues & Thiago Bellotti

Design Studio
Papanapa

Motion Designer
Lucas Rodrigues

Positioning & Verbal Identity
Criatexto

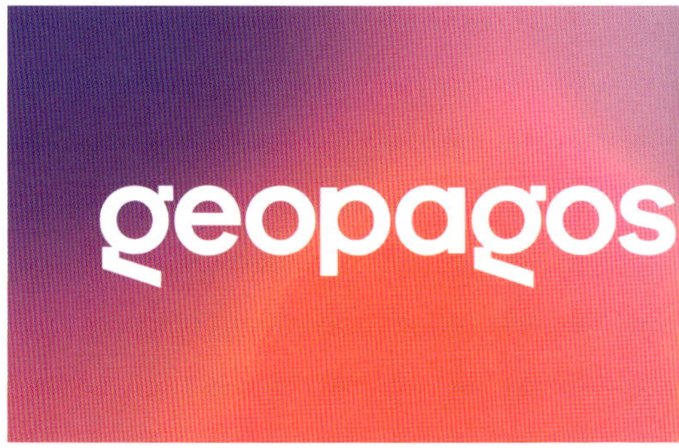

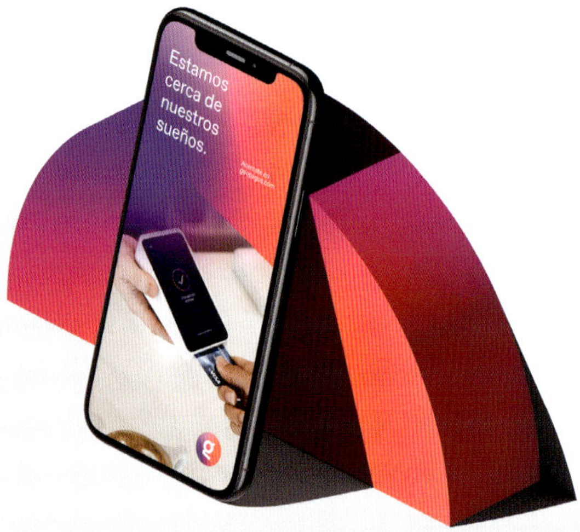

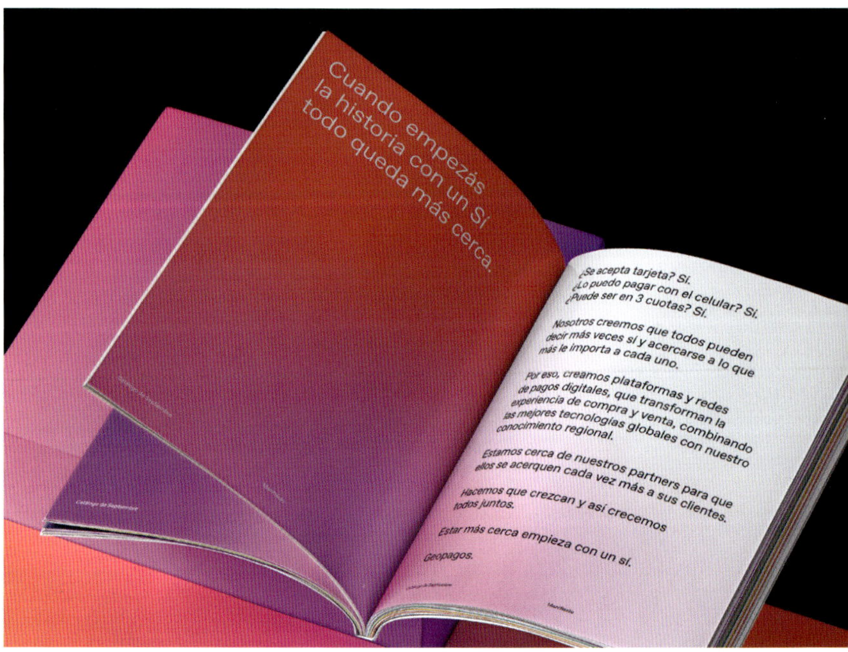

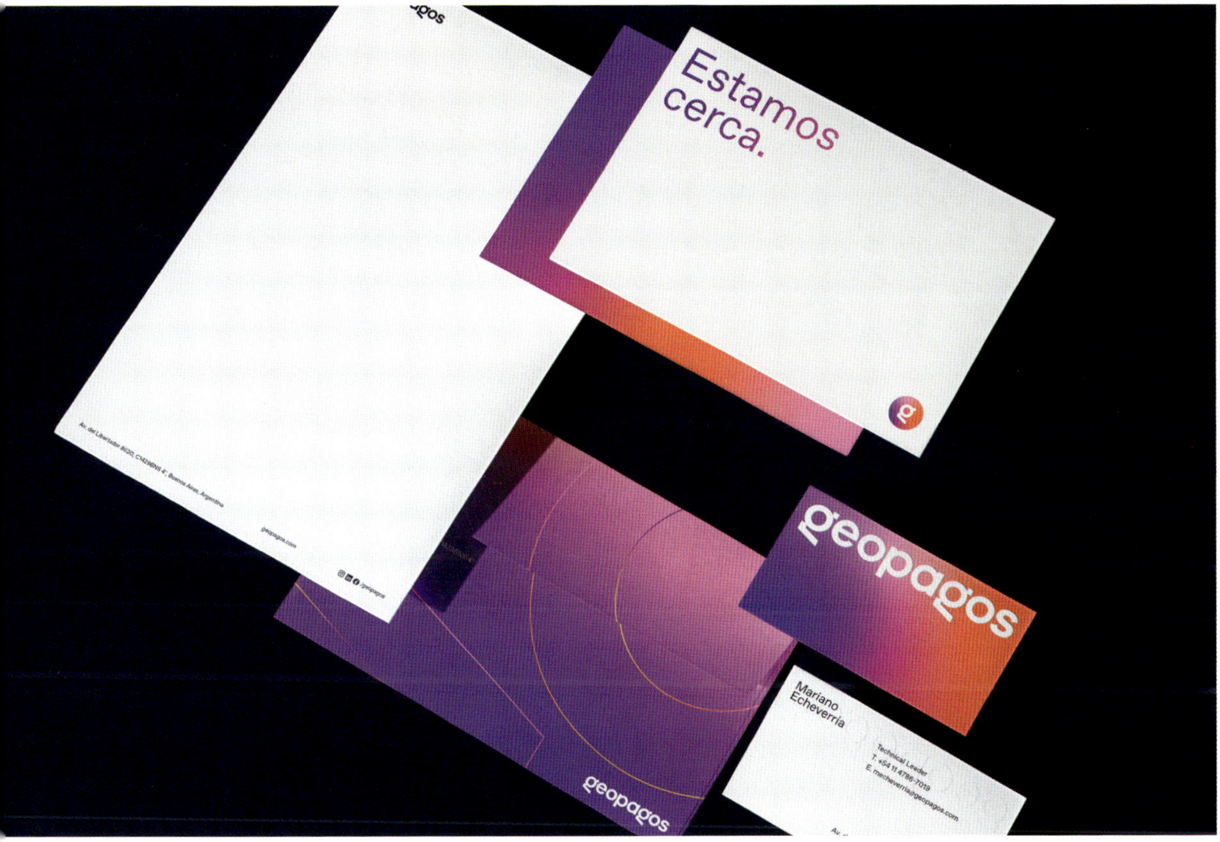
Estamos
cerca.
geopagos
geopagos
Mariano
Echeverria
Technical Leader

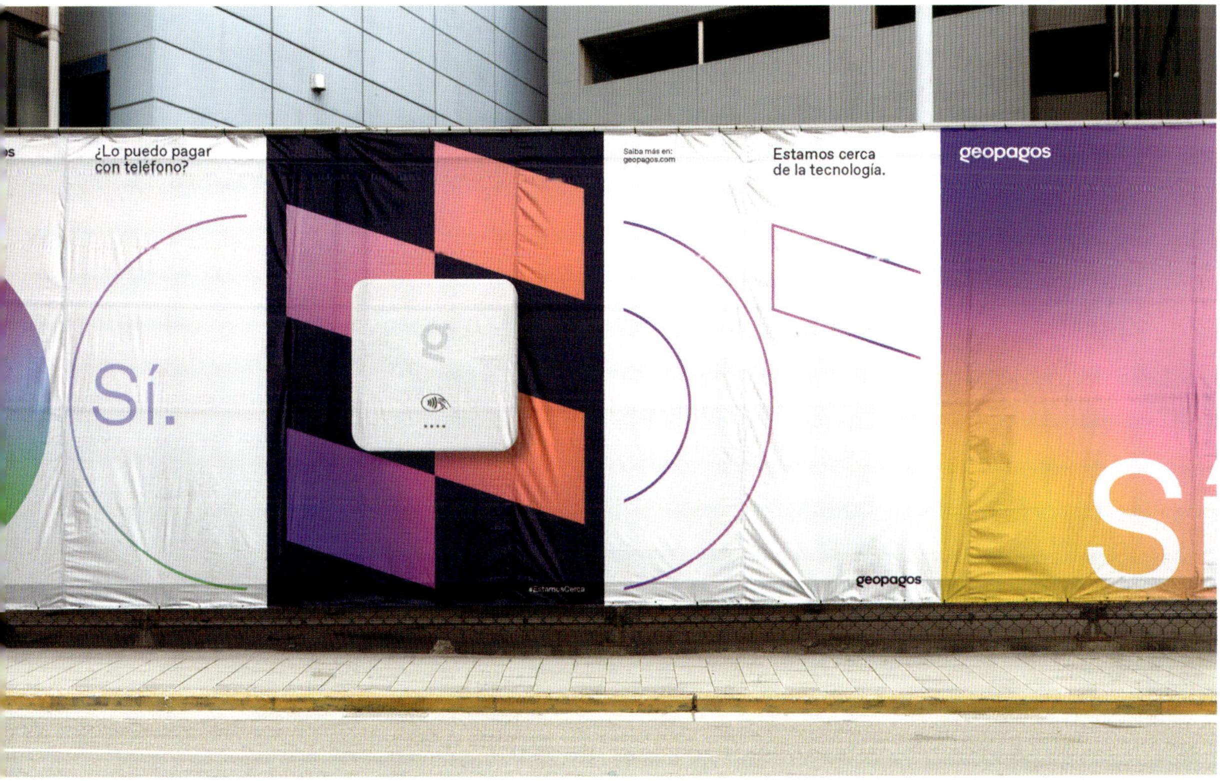
¿Lo puedo pagar
con teléfono?
Sí.
Estamos cerca
de la tecnología.
geopagos
geopagos

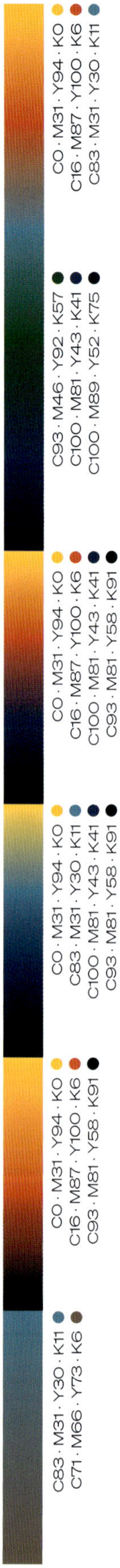
C0 · M31 · Y94 · K0
C16 · M87 · Y100 · K6
C83 · M31 · Y30 · K11
C93 · M46 · Y92 · K57
C100 · M81 · Y43 · K41
C100 · M89 · Y52 · K75
C0 · M31 · Y94 · K0
C16 · M87 · Y100 · K6
C100 · M81 · Y43 · K41
C93 · M81 · Y58 · K91
C0 · M31 · Y94 · K0
C83 · M31 · Y30 · K11
C100 · M81 · Y43 · K41
C93 · M81 · Y58 · K91
C0 · M31 · Y94 · K0
C16 · M87 · Y100 · K6
C93 · M81 · Y58 · K91
C83 · M31 · Y30 · K11
C71 · M66 · Y73 · K6

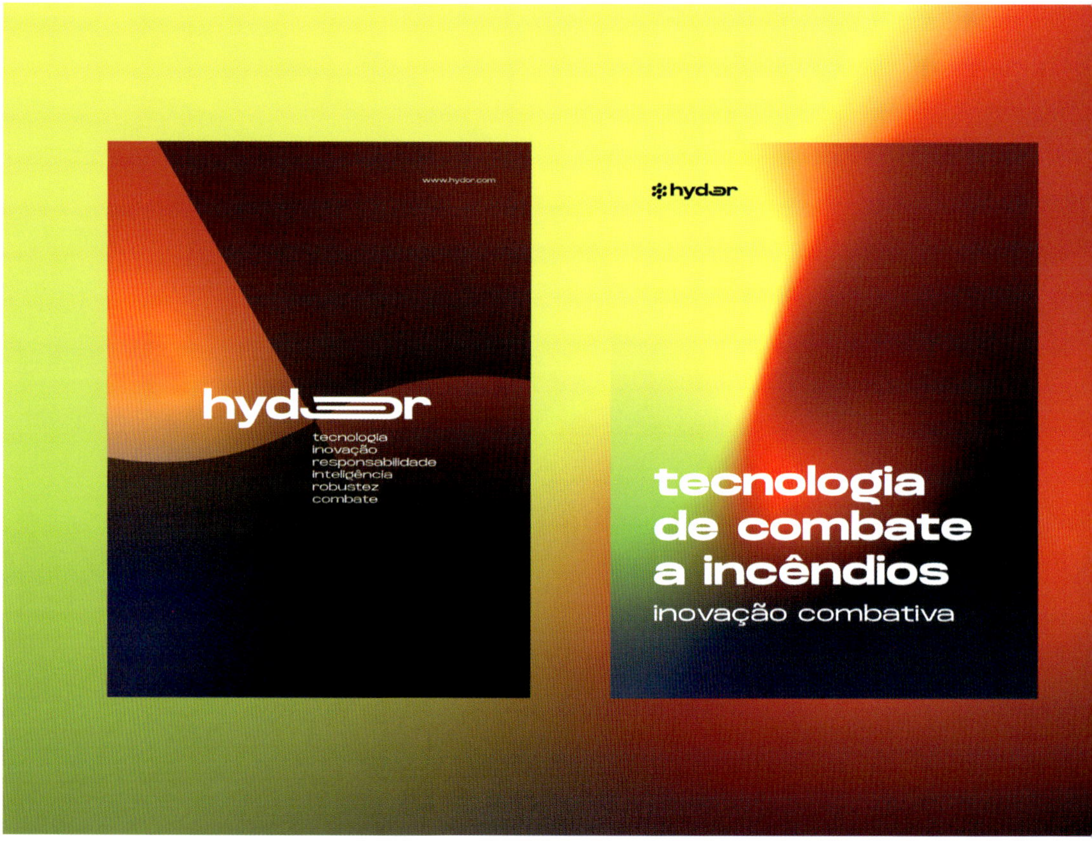
www.hydor.com
hydor
tecnologia
inovação
responsabilidade
inteligência
robustez
combate
hydor
tecnologia de combate a incêndios
inovação combativa

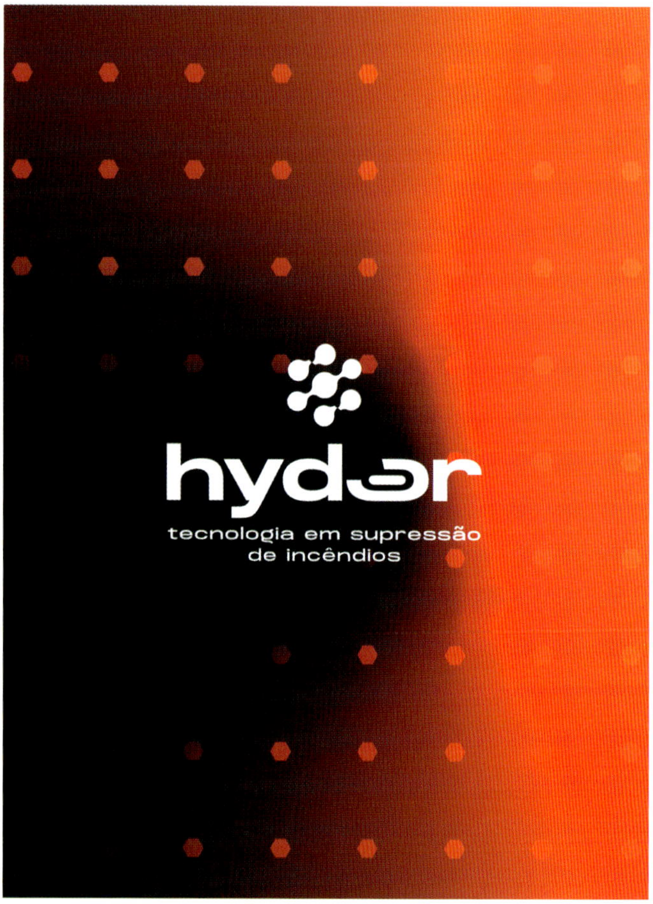
hydor
tecnologia em supressão de incêndios

PANTONE
água
Hydor
PANTONE®
contraste
Hydor

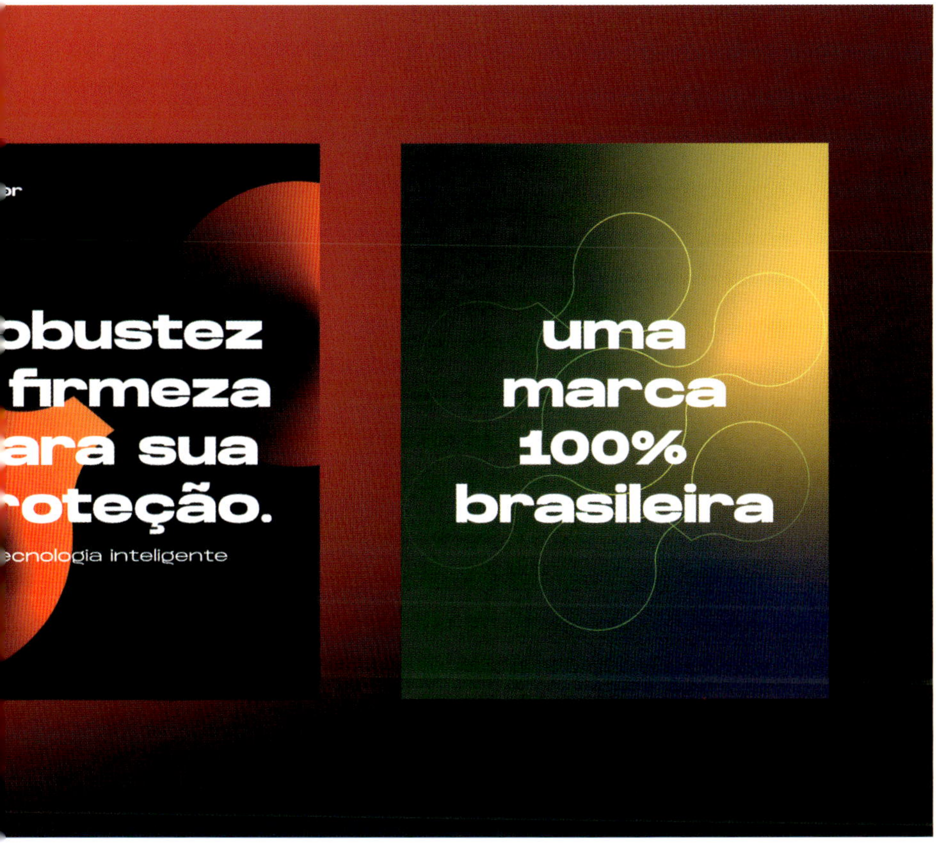

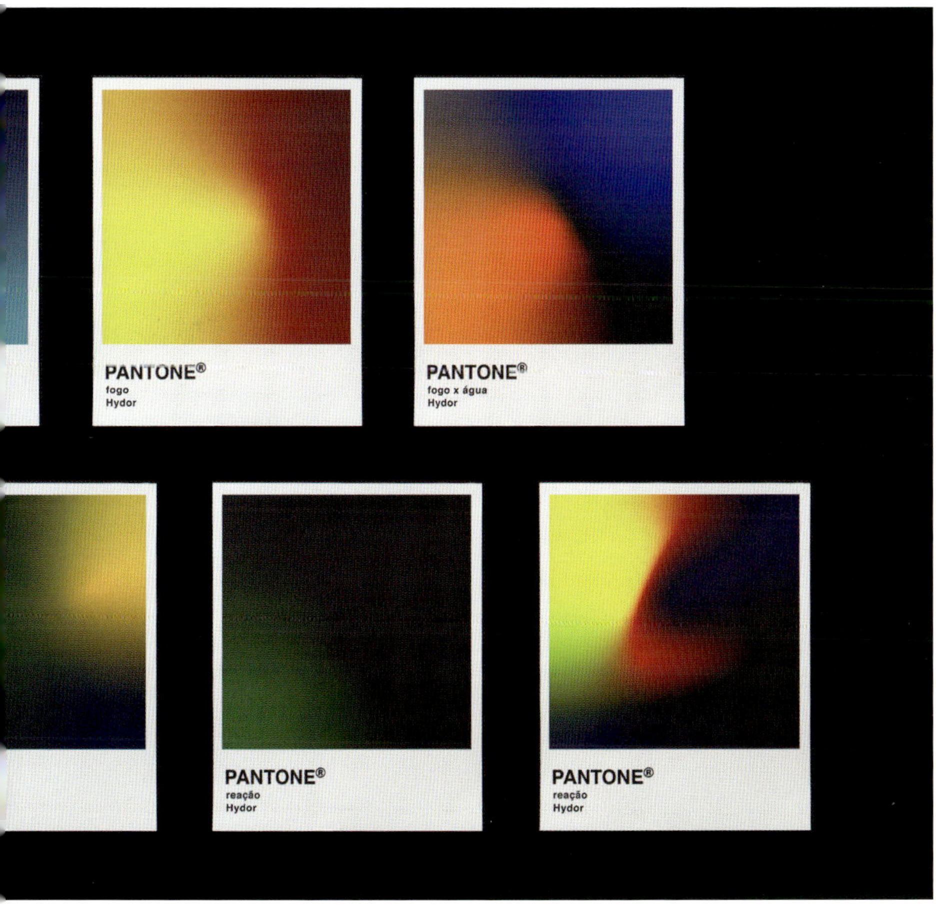

HYDOR-FIRE TECHNOLOGY

The brand project was developed for a new Brazilian company with innovation in fire suppression technologies. *Hydor* values science and engineering in its deepest form, bringing passion to new possibilities and a re-education in the market, making technologies accessible to new Brazilian and foreign companies, generating a network of global changes. Robustness, combat, science, technology, national appreciation, innovation, accessibility, sustainability, and intelligence are our deep values. Protect life on earth at any cost.

Designer
Diana Coe

Assistant Designer
Emanuel Pappis

Brand Book
Marina Hauers

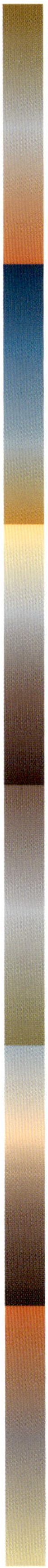

C38 · M57 · Y100 · K25
C34 · M25 · Y27 · KO
C14 · M77 · Y93 · K3

C98 · M72 · Y45 · K38
C86 · M41 · Y29 · K3
C47 · M25 · Y29 · KO
C18 · M56 · Y98 · K3

CO · M20 · Y60 · KO
C34 · M25 · Y27 · KO
C44 · M61 · Y65 · K30
C53 · M71 · Y73 · K69

C44 · M61 · Y65 · K30
C34 · M25 · Y27 · KO
C43 · M46 · Y79 · K18

C47 · M25 · Y29 · KO
C3 · M29 · Y47 · KO
C44 · M61 · Y65 · K30
C53 · M71 · Y73 · K69

C14 · M77 · Y93 · K3
C47 · M47 · Y46 · K9
C17 · M24 · Y56 · KC

JAMES FLOWER

Deep electronic music and vibrant melodic atmospheres, in a mix between nostalgic and warm textured sounds is how *James Flower* describes his music. The first challenge for the team was to develop a brand story to form the basis of the identity. The logo is based on a flower and in the ouroboros symbol, signifying infinity and the cycle of birth and death. The selected colours reference earth tones, inspired by the ever-changing gradients in the sky. This results in a blend of organic and digital visuals that set the mood for *James Flower* soundscapes.

Art Director
Ana Abreu

Designer
Tiago Narciso &
Leticia Ortín

Design Studio
Humana Studio

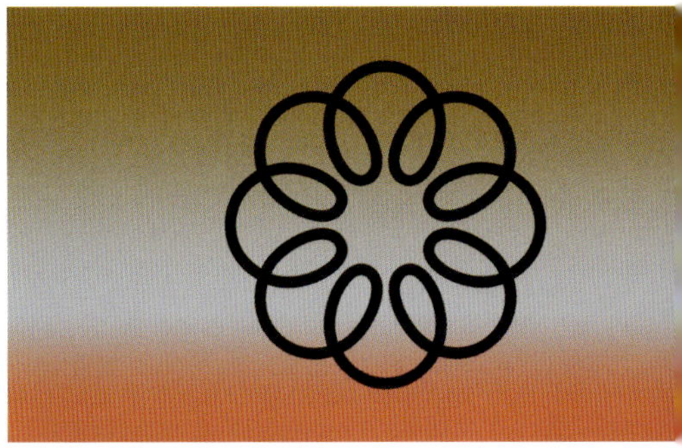

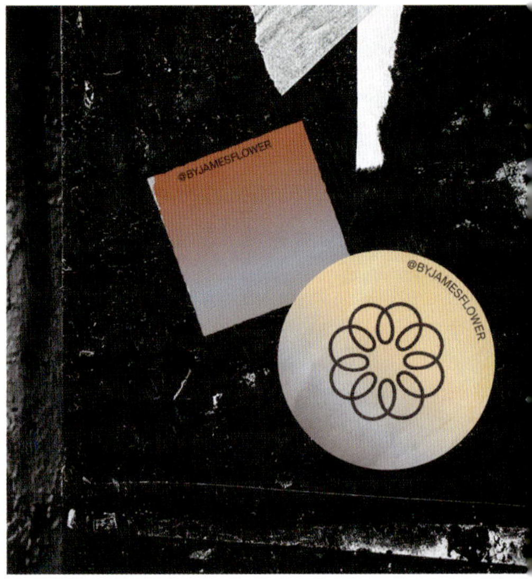

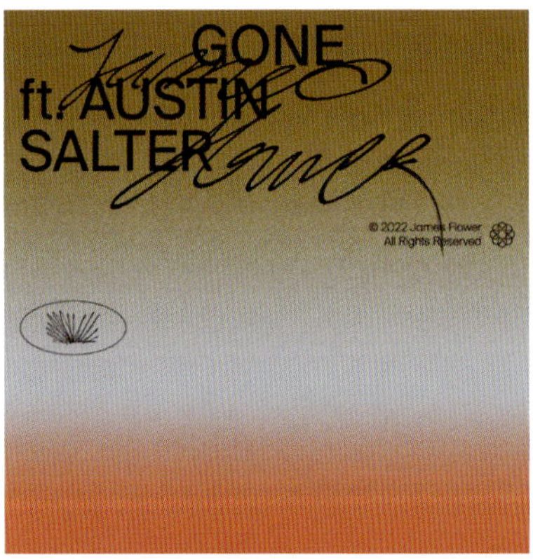

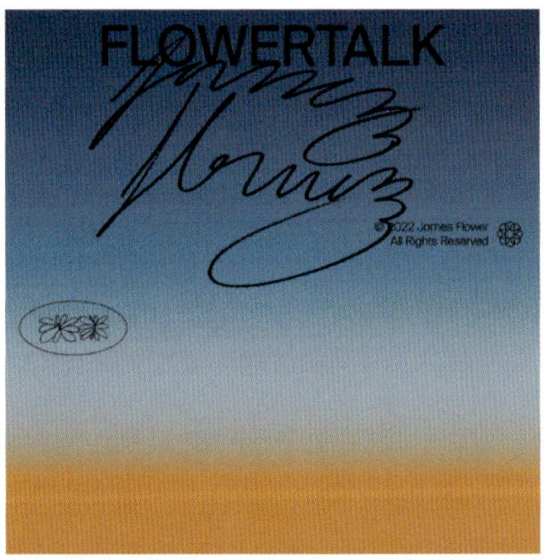

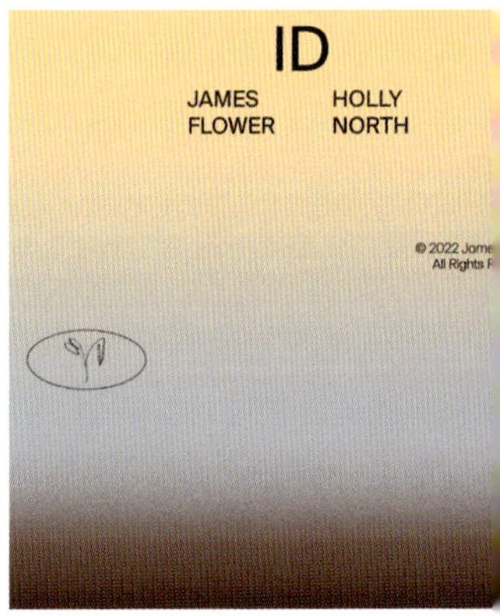

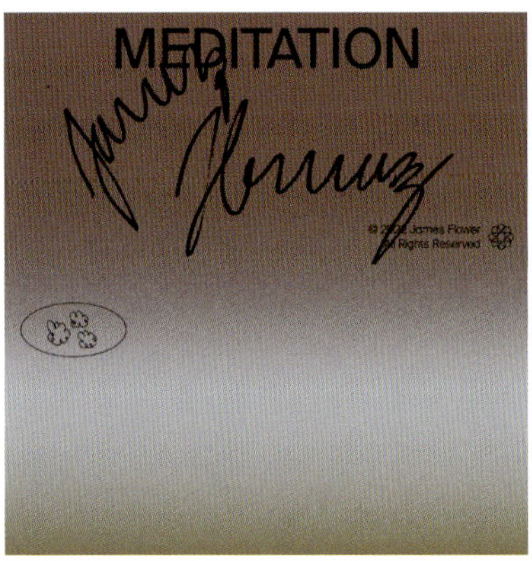

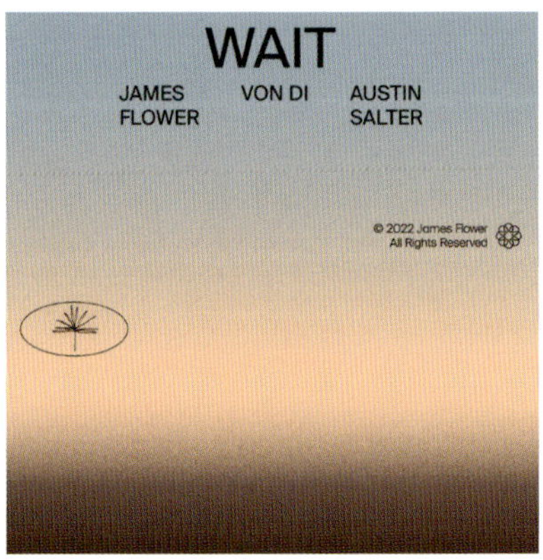

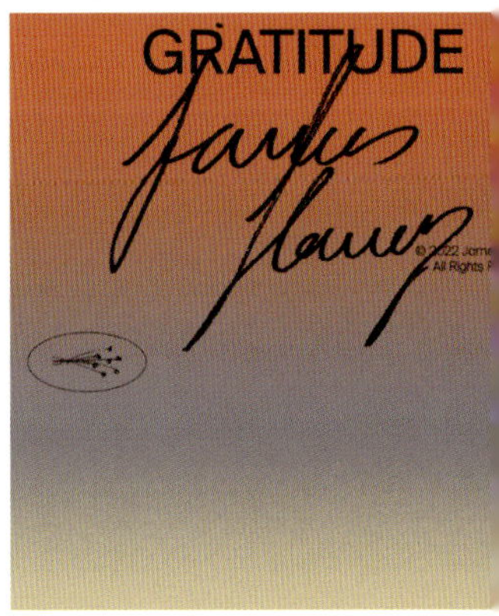

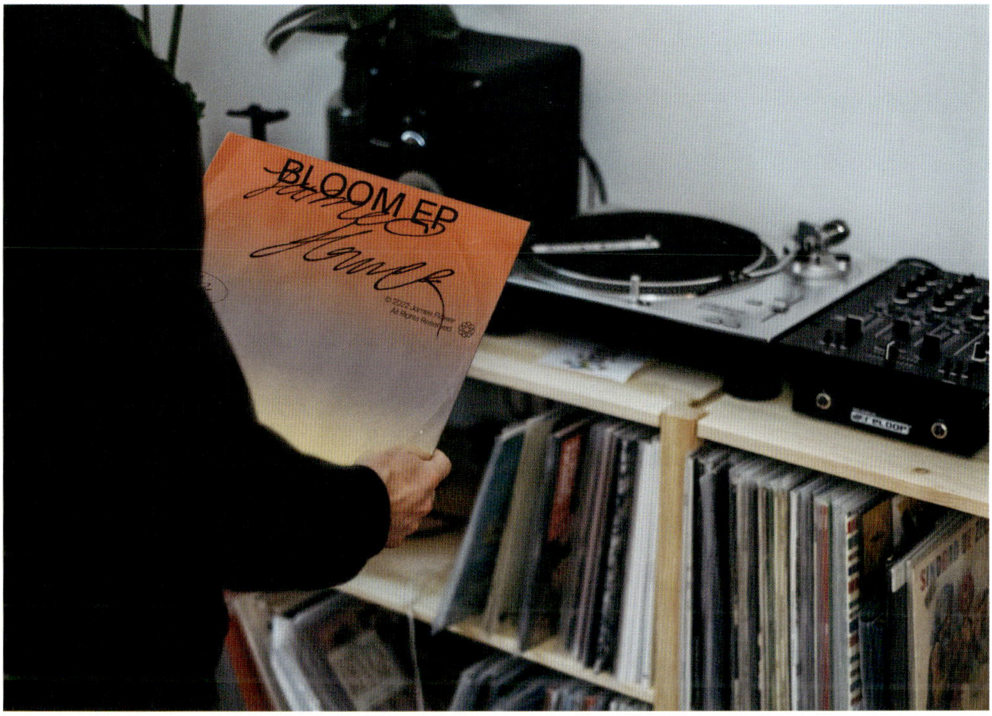
BLOOM EP
© 2022 James Flower
All Rights Reserved

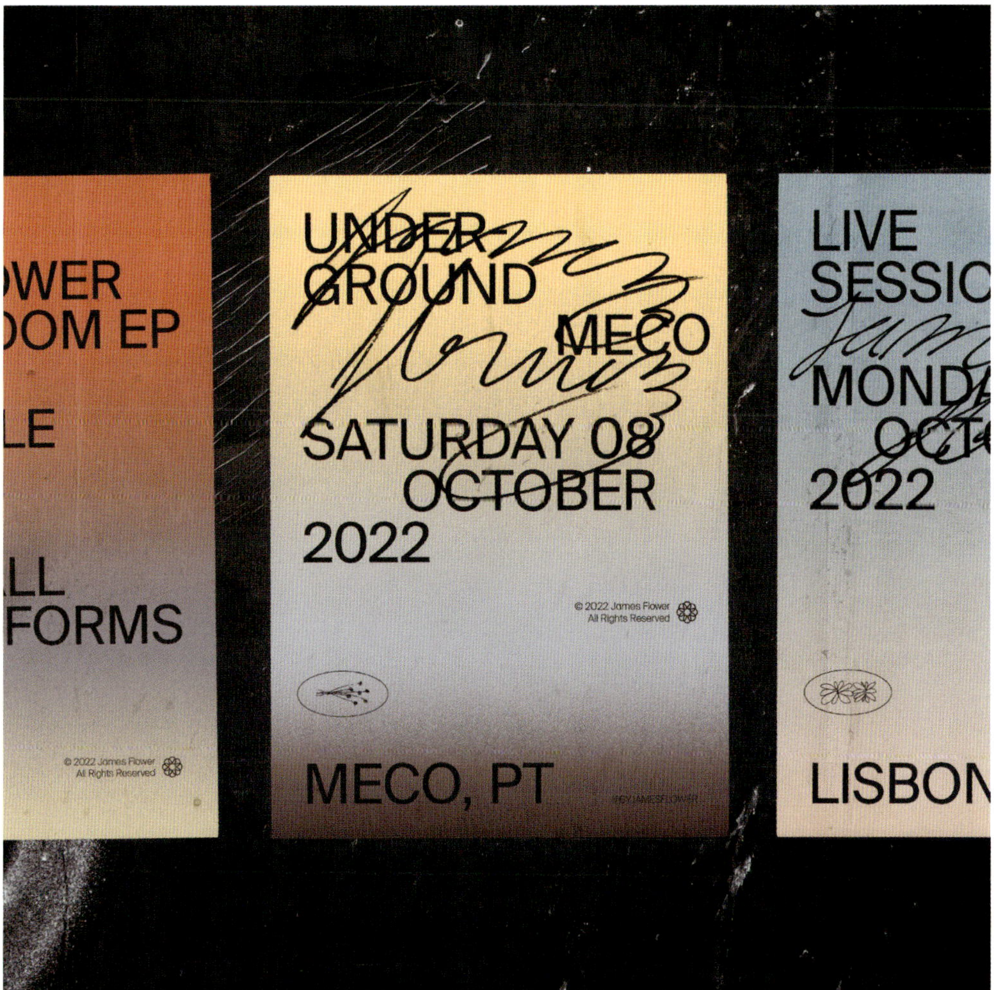
OWER
OOM EP
LE
LL
FORMS
© 2022 James Flower
All Rights Reserved
UNDER-
GROUND
MECO
SATURDAY 08
OCTOBER
2022
© 2022 James Flower
All Rights Reserved
MECO, PT
LIVE
SESSIO
MONDA
OCTO
2022
LISBON

C0 · M100 · Y100 · K0
C0 · M100 · Y0 · K0

C28 · M100 · Y100 · K0
C39 · M100 · Y19 · K0
C61 · M100 · Y35 · K0
C84 · M100 · Y100 · K0
C100 · M100 · Y100 · K0

C52 · M100 · Y44 · K0
C38 · M65 · Y33 · K0
C52 · M71 · Y29 · K0
C73 · M70 · Y39 · K1
C79 · M47 · Y53 · K1

C71 · M100 · Y100 · K0
C49 · M100 · Y100 · K0
C24 · M38 · Y52 · K0
C11 · M34 · Y54 · K0
C4 · M50 · Y78 · K0

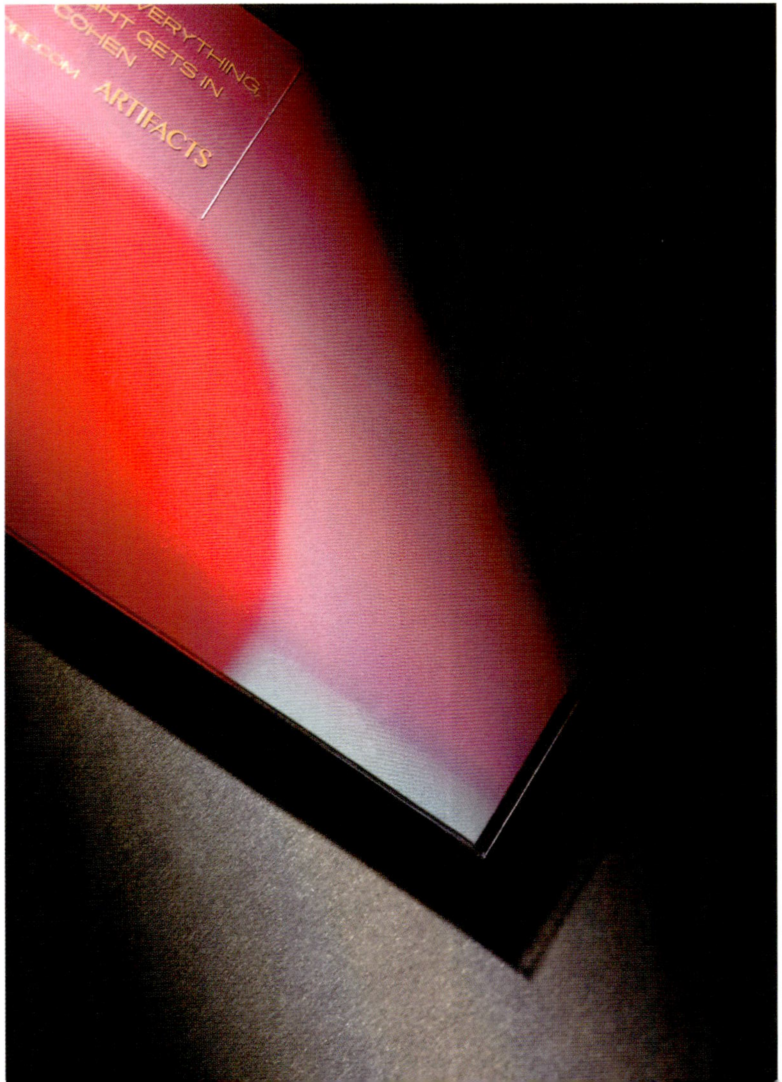

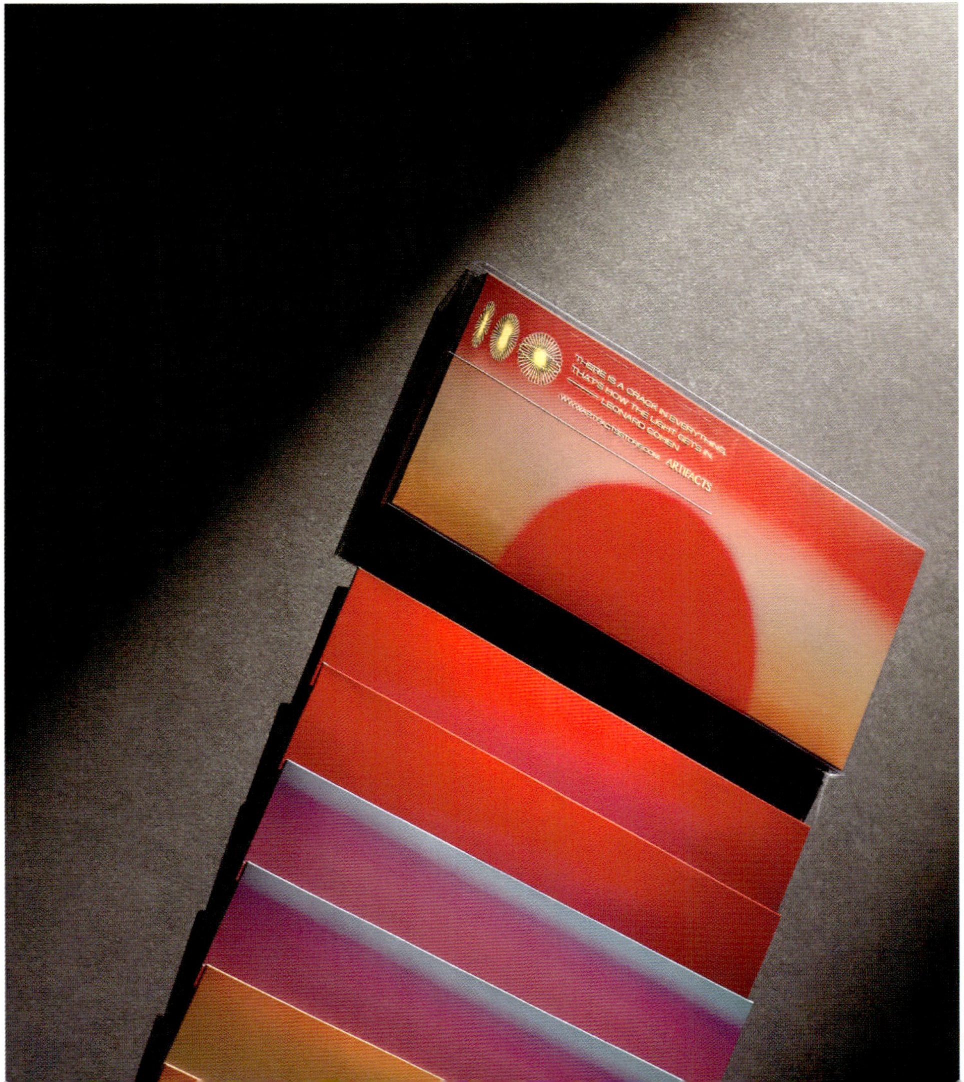

DAWN: RED PACKETS

"Dawn" is a New-Year red envelope design for *Artifacts*. We presented a contemporary image to showcase the moment when the sun appears on the horizon in the morning. Optical illusions and phenomena are achieved by a combination of different printing materials.

Design Studio
Out Of Office

Designer
Liang Chu Ching

Photographer
Lee Tsung Yu

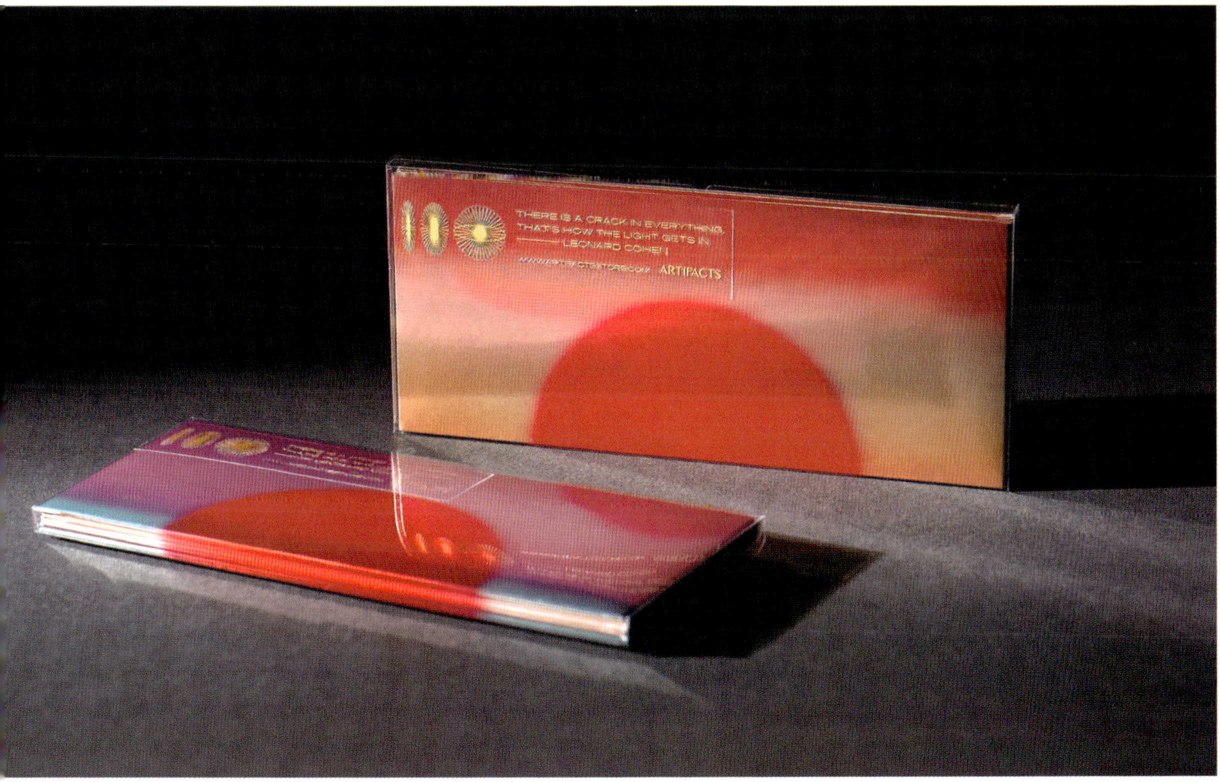

PANTONE 2665 C
PANTONE 2685 C

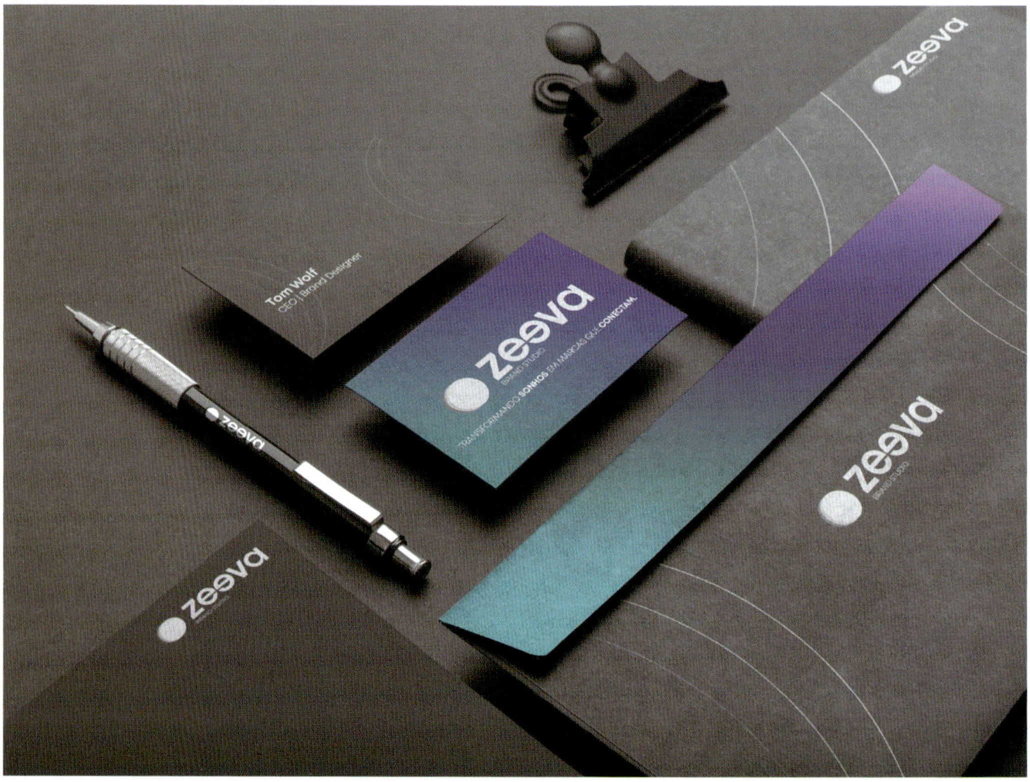

PANTONE 2765 C
PANTONE 316 C

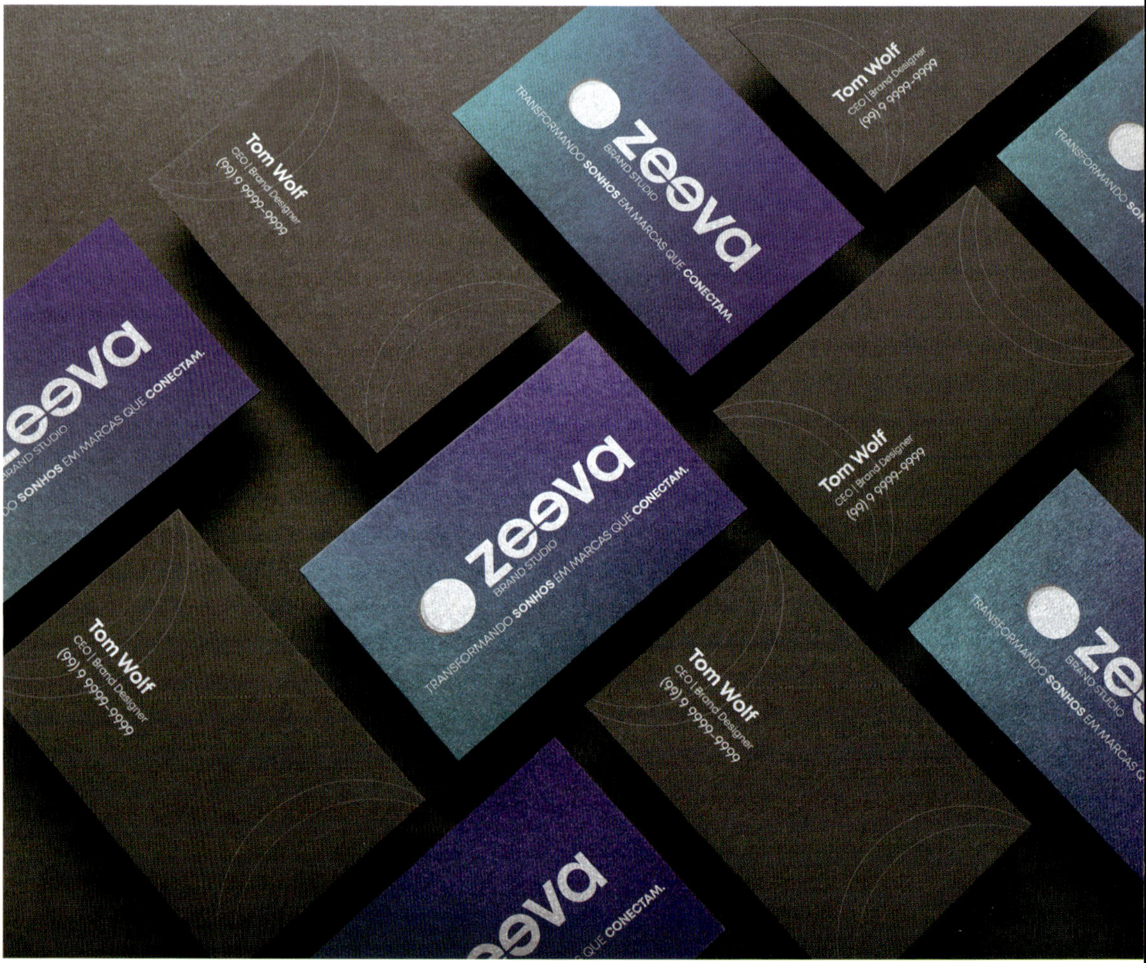

PANTONE 7711 C
PANTONE 3115 C

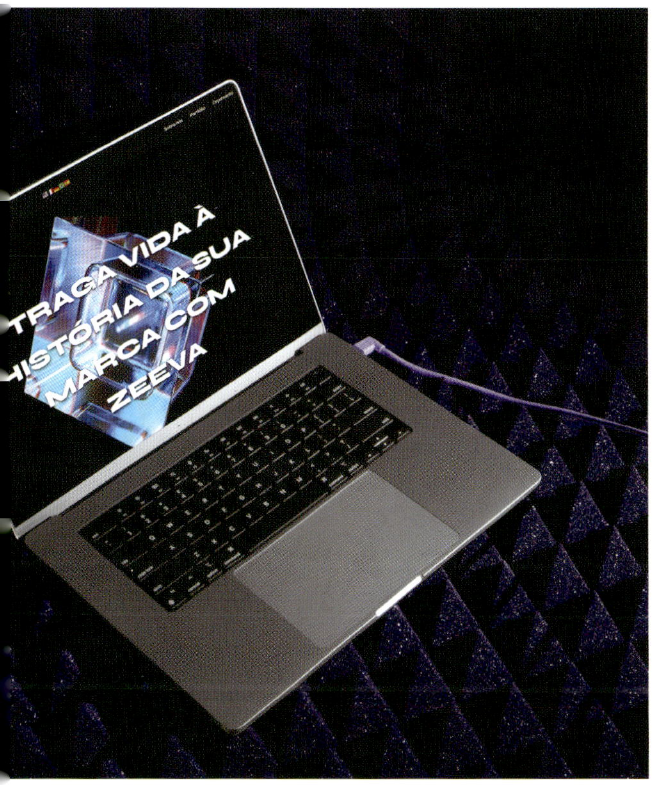

ZEEVA

The project in question is a brand of its own, called *Zeeva Brand Studio*. The biggest challenge was to combine the minimalism characteristic of the works Tom Wolf, the founder, and at the same time bring vibrant and eye-catching colours to represent nature, culture and the elements of the universe. With this challenge, they decided to use gradients, a strong trend in global design, giving more versatility and modernity to the project.

Designer
Tom Wolf

Motion Designer
Ronald Rodrigues

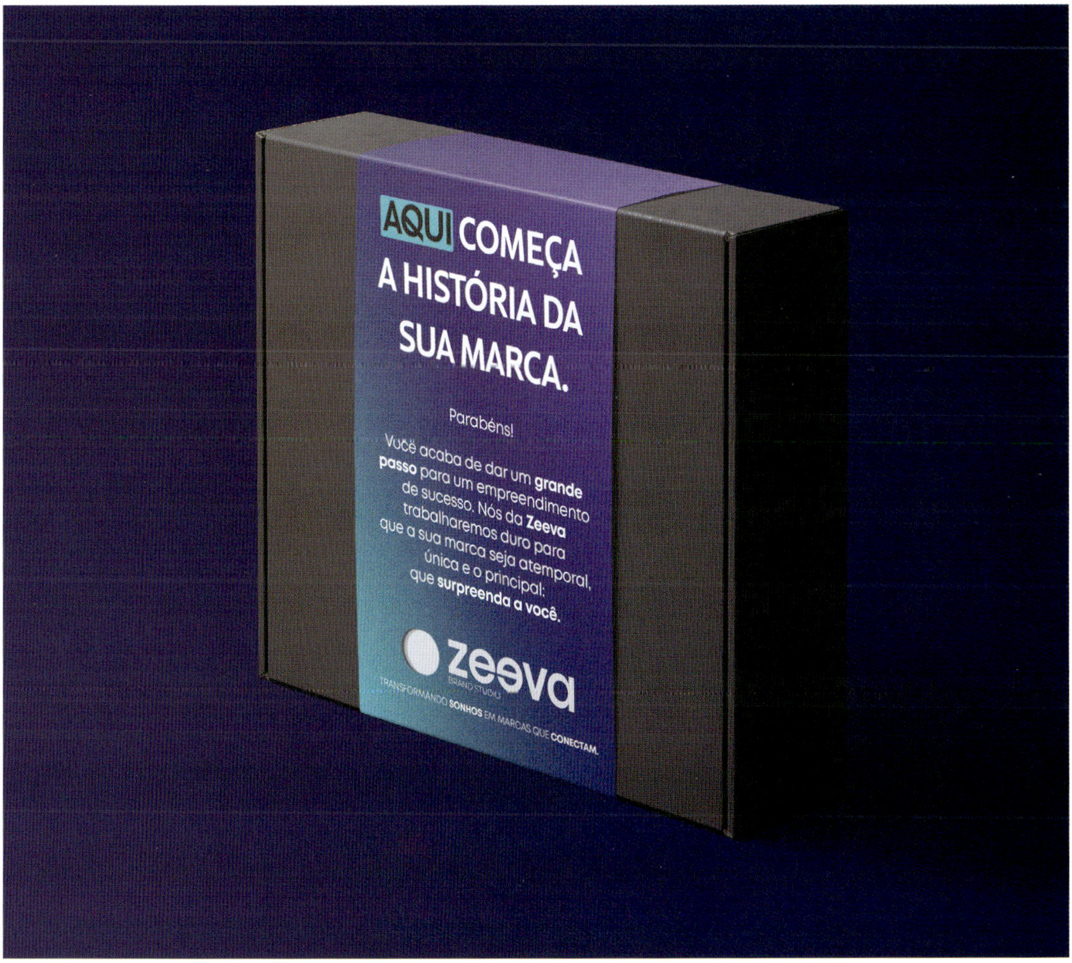

#3C383C
#C6B3B7
#9BAC6D
#AC6C84

#E3BD99
#F7DCB2

#9A5F9B
#D6B1AD
#F5B633

#D62F24
#EC9633

#FAD889
#FCC42E
#F4EFDE

#C0B8CE
#ECBE5A
#75588E

#FBCB18
#FBEBC7
#F9CE76

#B2446F
#F2E0AA
#DC9CBB

#F16F46
#E9A0B5
#EC3027
#FCA425

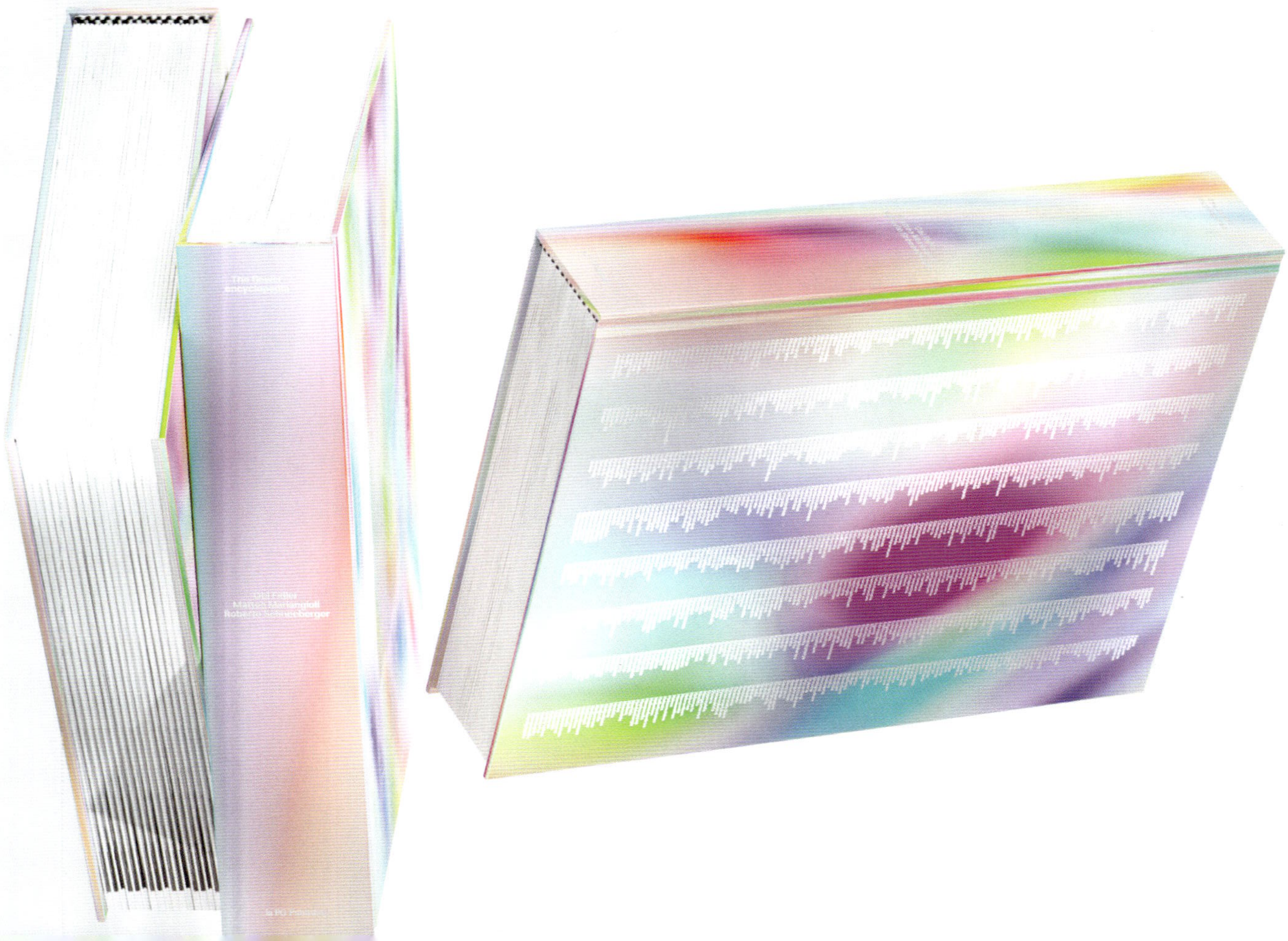

THE FLOWER ENCYCLOPEDIA

The Flower Encyclopedia 2022 is structured by reusing articles extracted from Wikipedia's online platform to provide a comprehensive presentation of information related to flowers, using modern reading methods. The book's effective use of colour is its defining feature. Imagine a beautiful garden with each flower blooming with unique circular gradients. These gradients are created by carefully selecting colour points directly from plant images. The end result is a mesmerizing display of nature's beauty. To provide an accurate scale, a black bar has been added to the outer edge of each page to represent the flower's actual size in comparison to the book.

Art Director, Concept & Designer
Obi Fidler,
Matteo Mariangioli,
Roberto Schneeberger

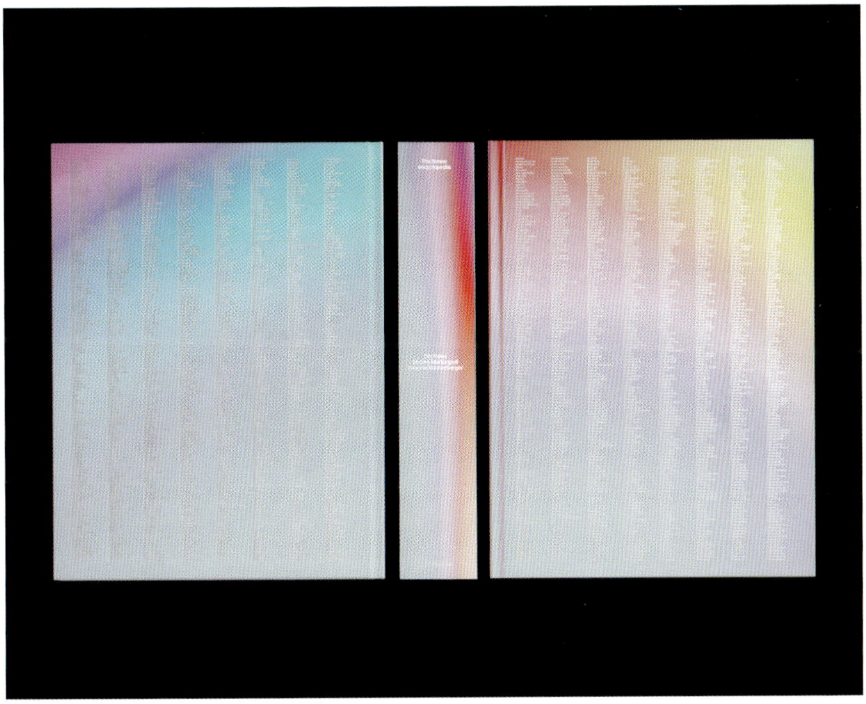

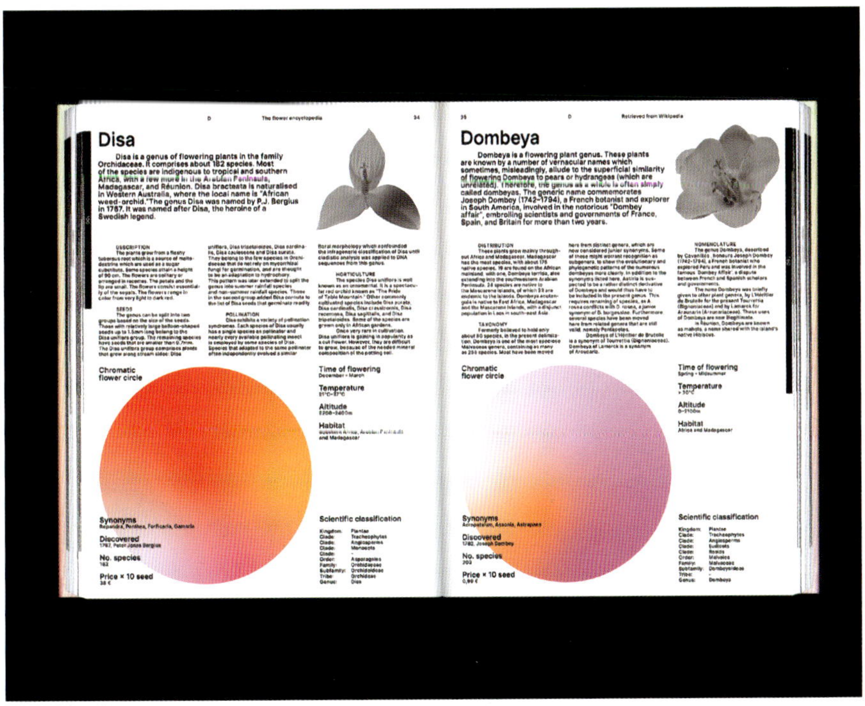

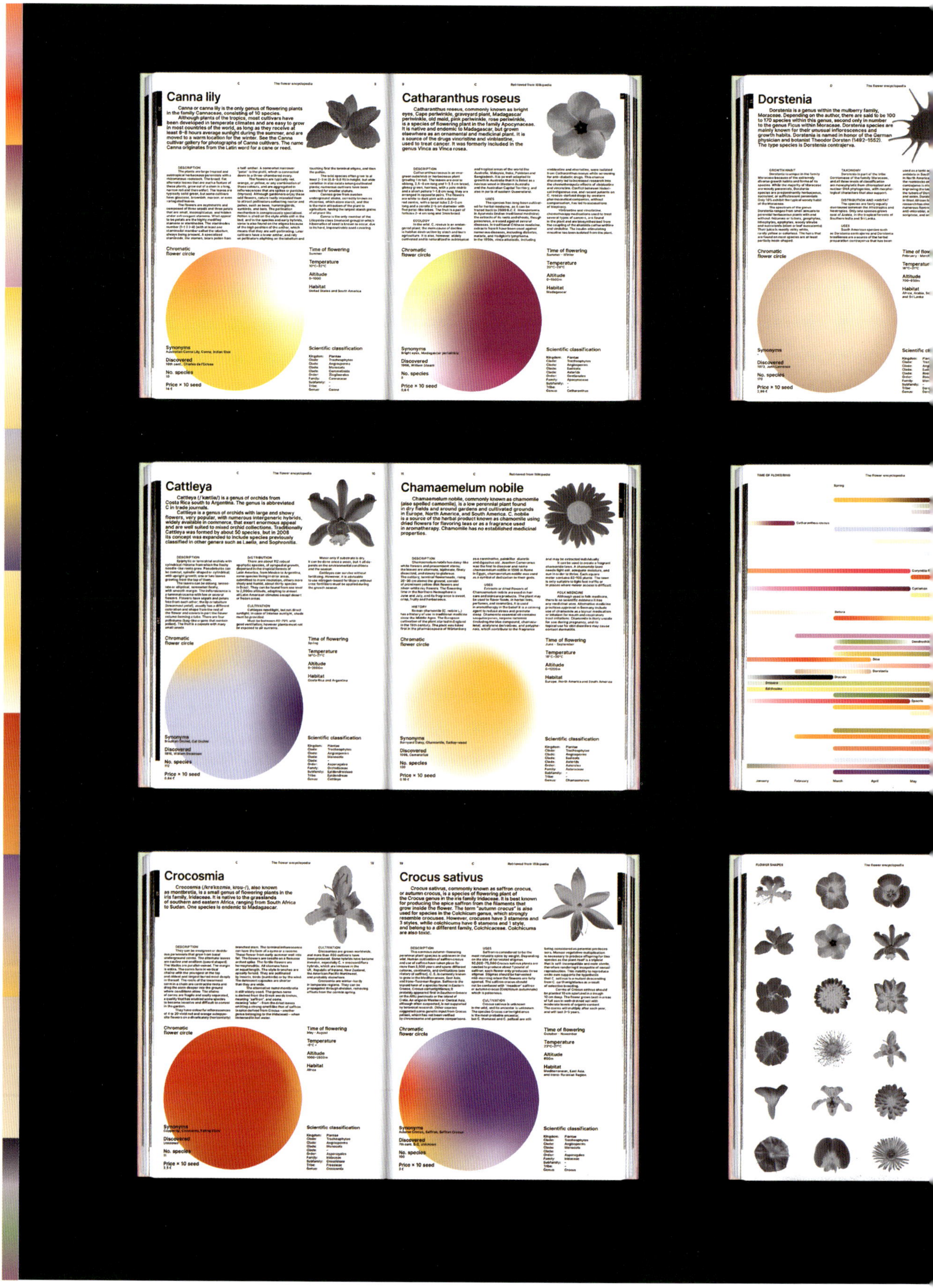
Canna lily
Catharanthus roseus
Dorstenia
Cattleya
Chamaemelum nobile
Crocosmia
Crocus sativus

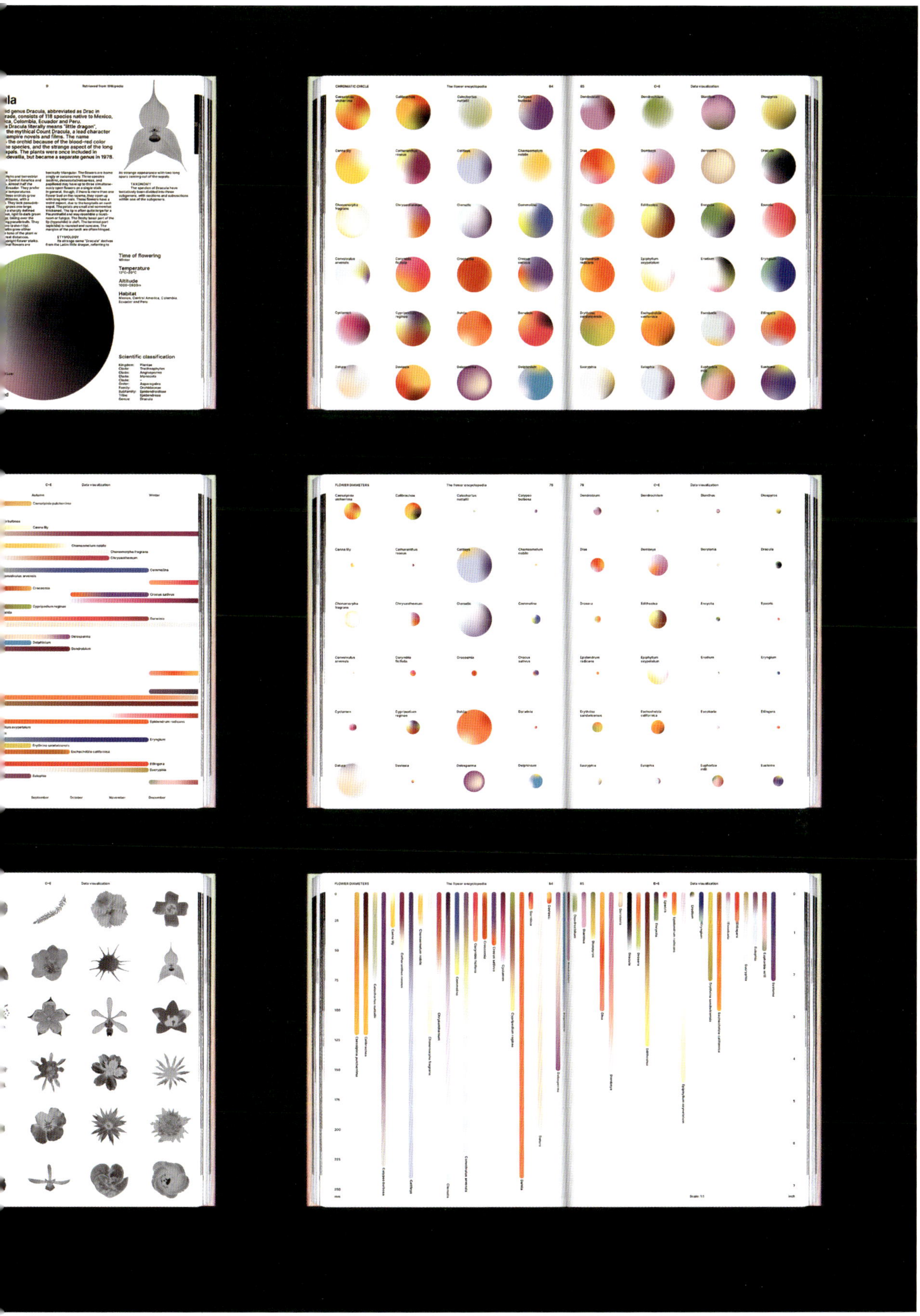

PANTONE 2935 C
PANTONE 294 C

PANTONE 312 C
PANTONE 2025 C

PANTONE 2935 C

PANTONE 312 C

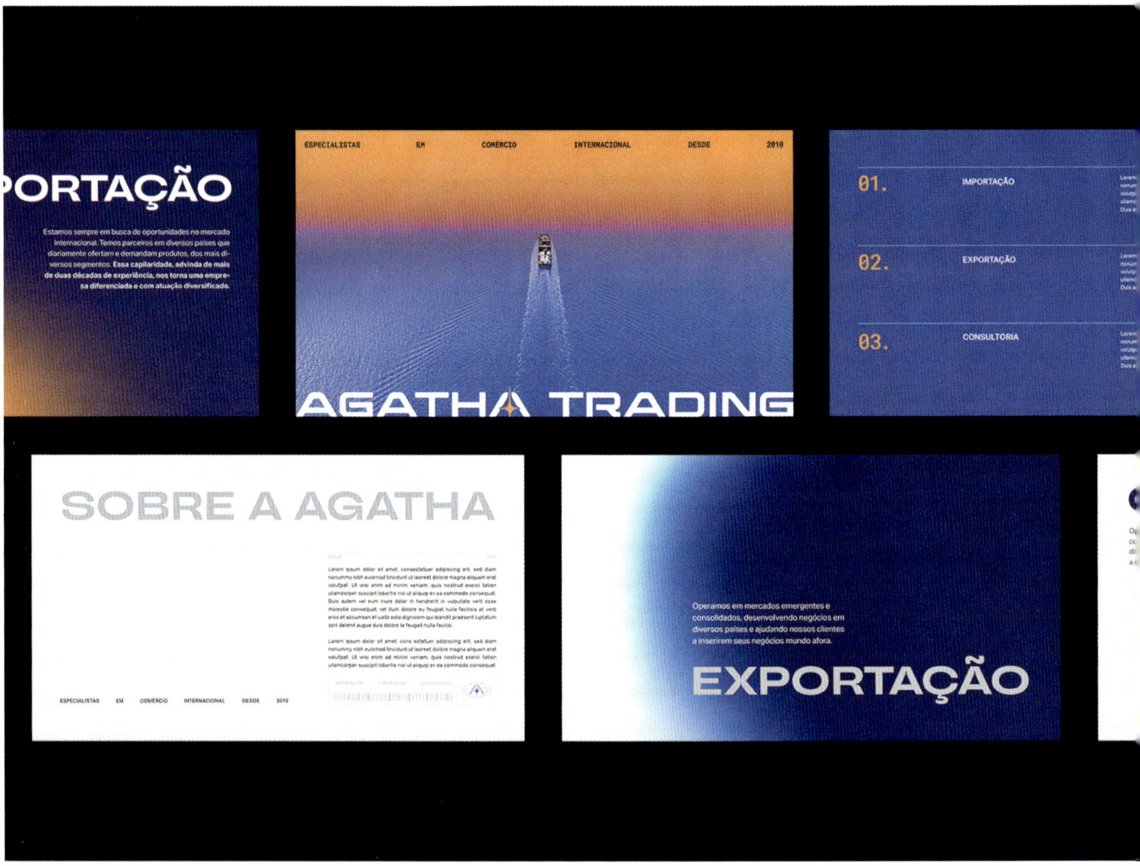

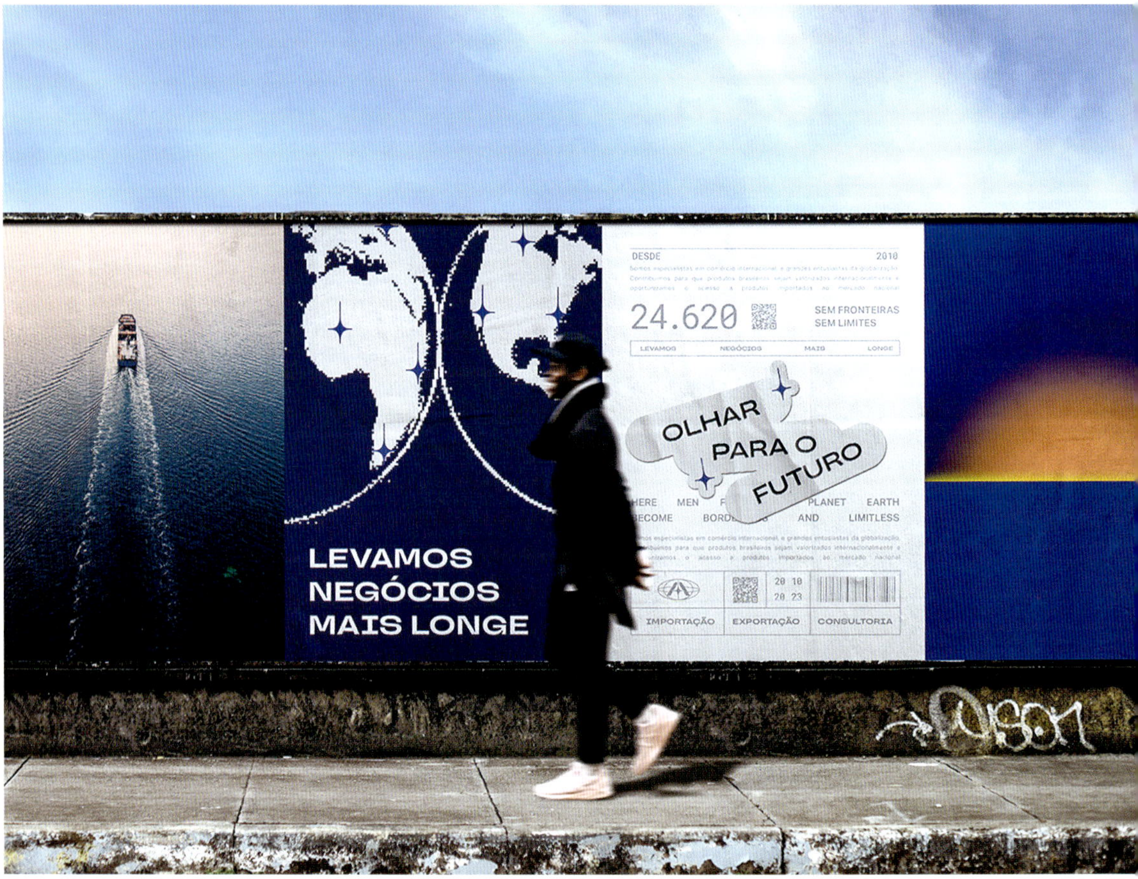

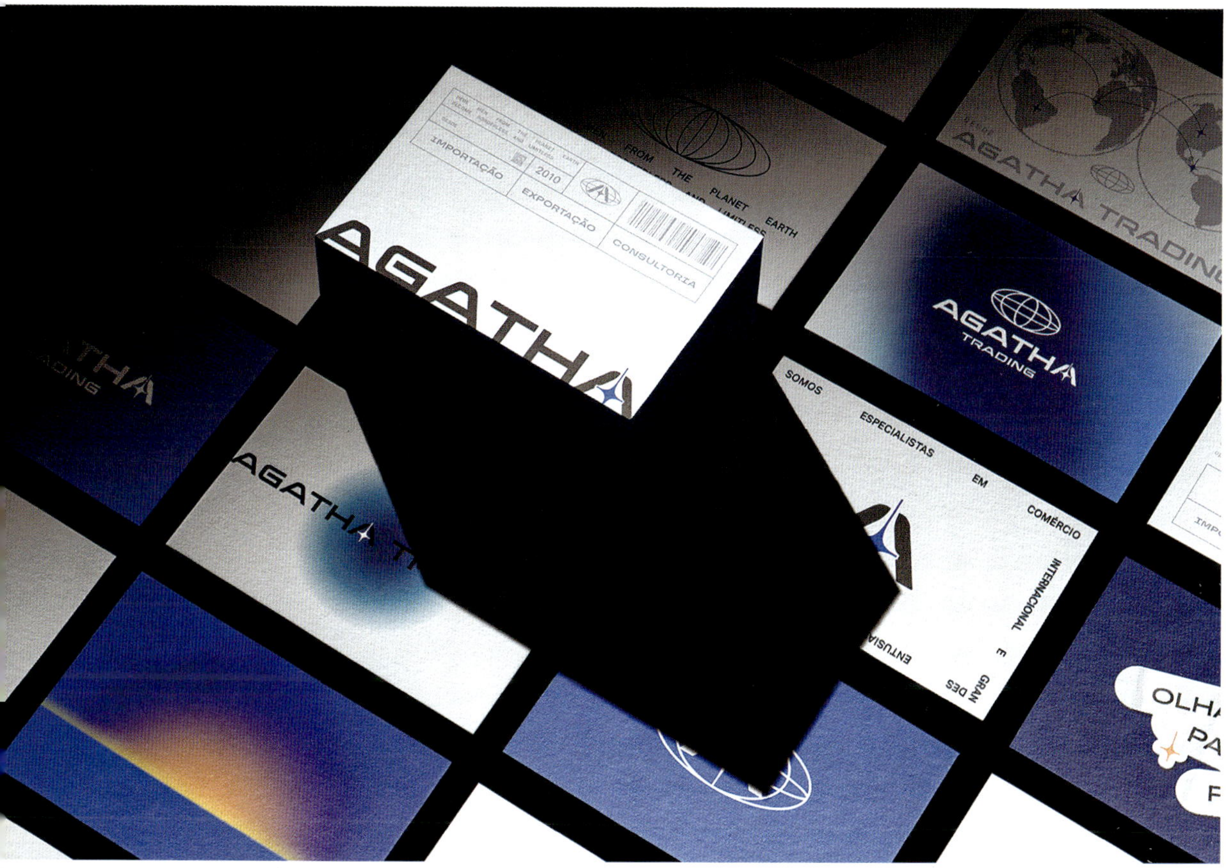

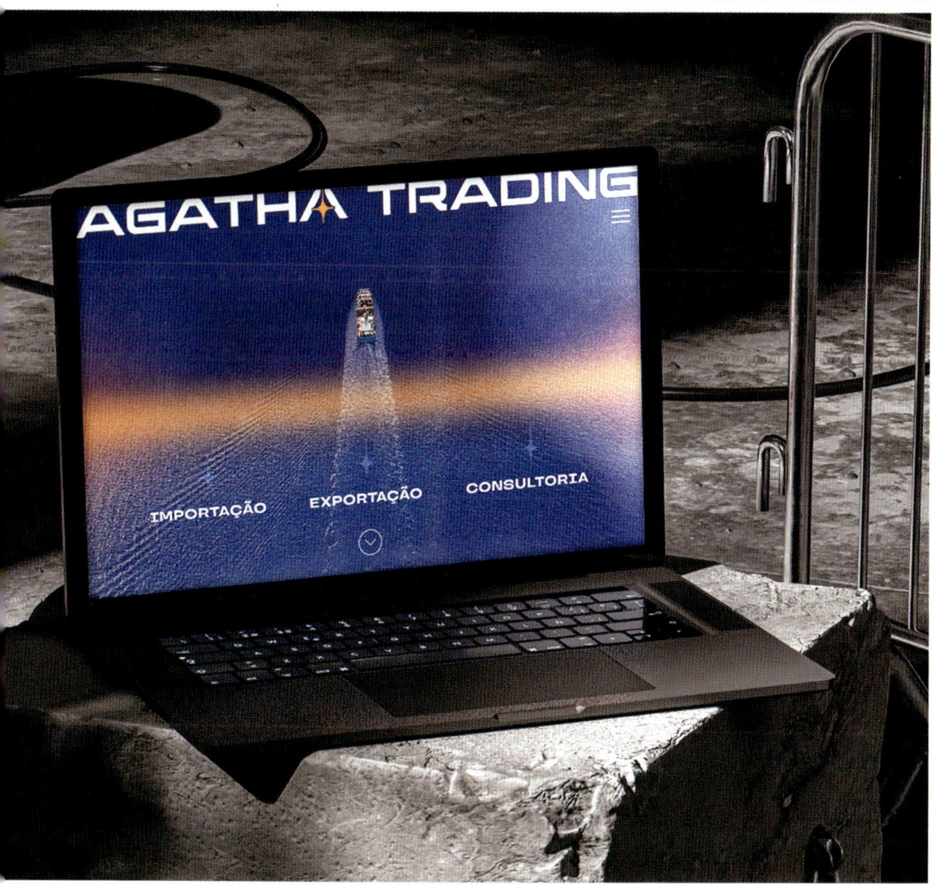

AGATHA TRADING

Agatha Trading, aspiring for a global footprint and a contemporary persona, draws inspiration from the sea and sky. Infused with blue and orange hues symbolizing night and day, this design reflects confidence and adaptability.
It encapsulates *Agatha Trading's* commitment to navigating change while firmly grounded in the present and future.

Design Studio
Mirela Melo Design & Monga Design

PANTONE 285 C
PANTONE BRIGHT RED C
PANTONE 7527 C
PANTONE 7508 C
PANTONE 7473 C

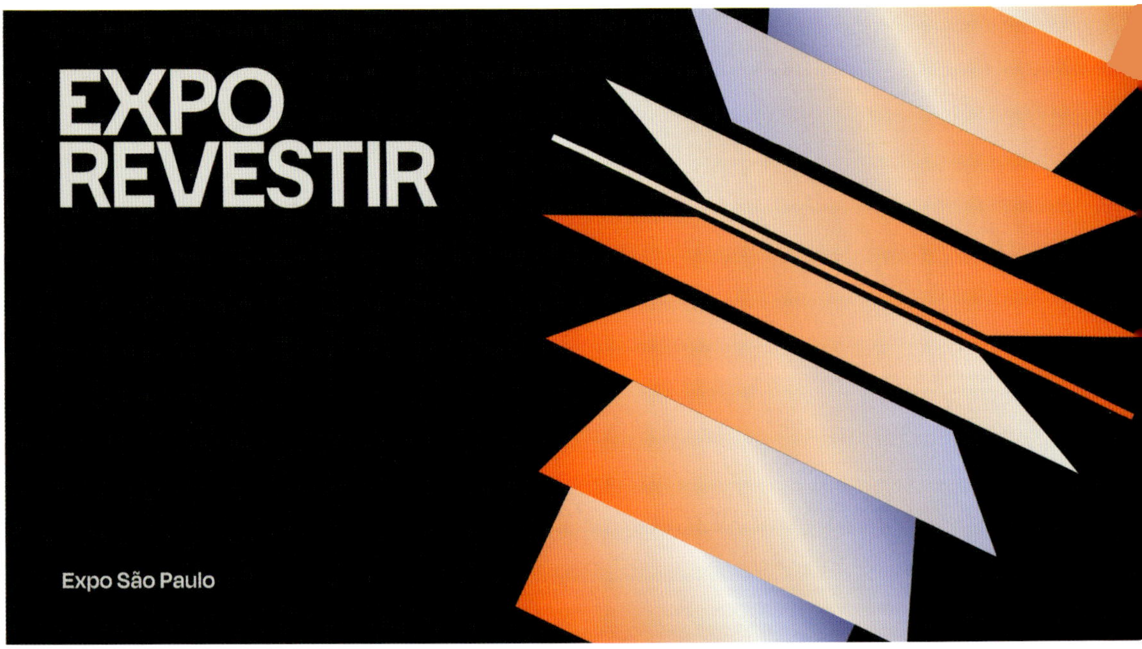

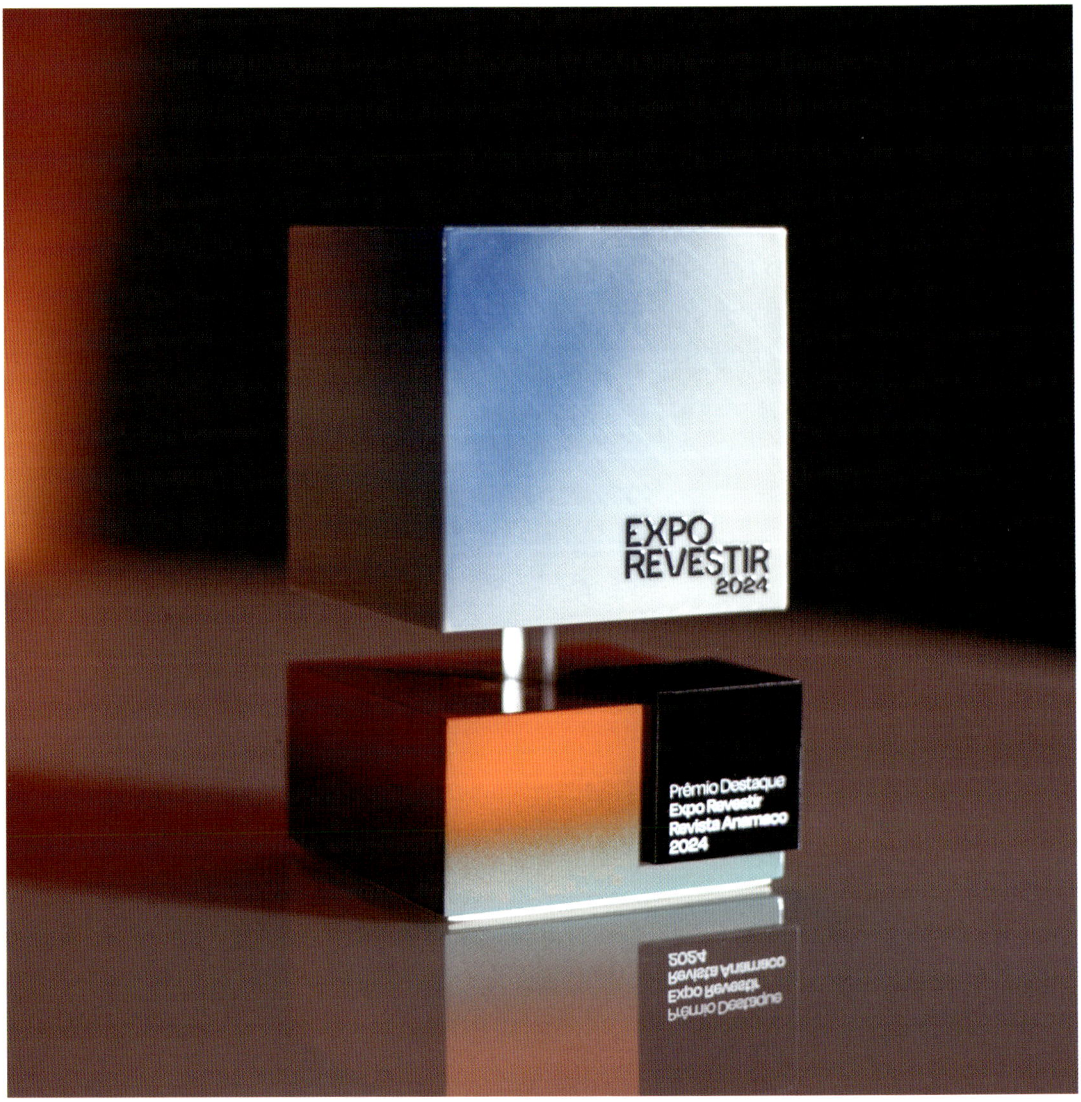

EXPO REVESTIR

"Expo Revestir" is the largest fair for coverings and finishes in Latin America. Estúdio Caxa developed a visual identity composed of abstract graphic elements that evoke images familiar to this audience, such as coverings, texture swatches, material palettes, and three-dimensional objects. These elements also suggest movement, as if ready to connect, reflecting the dynamic nature of the fair—a place for meetings and connections. The colour palette is broad, featuring many colours in gradients and black, ensuring clarity and sophistication in communication during the event.

Design Studio
Caxa

Graphic Designer
Débora Gomes dos Santos, Fabricio Luciano Gonçalves, João Maiolini & Renato Brito Mamede

Planner & Social
Ioná Ricobello

Motion Designer
Paulo Fragatti

Creative Director
Vitor Brito Pereira

Photographer
Raquel Santos

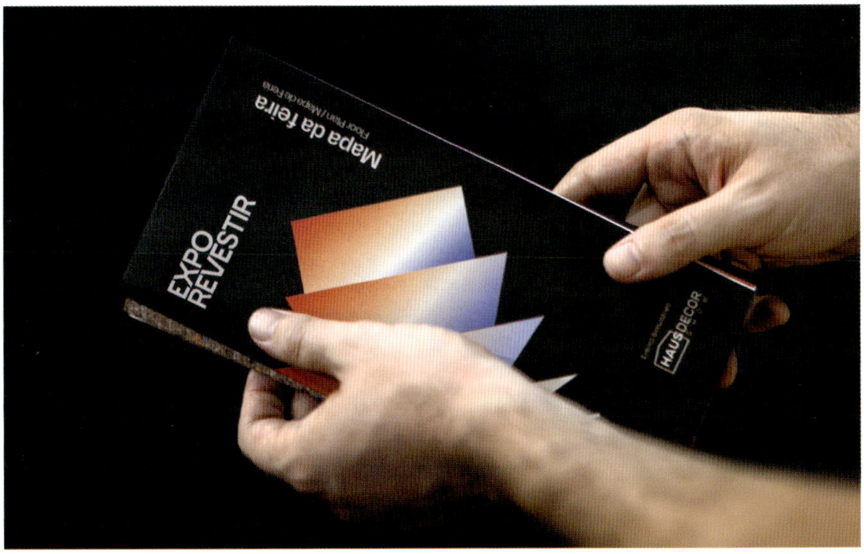

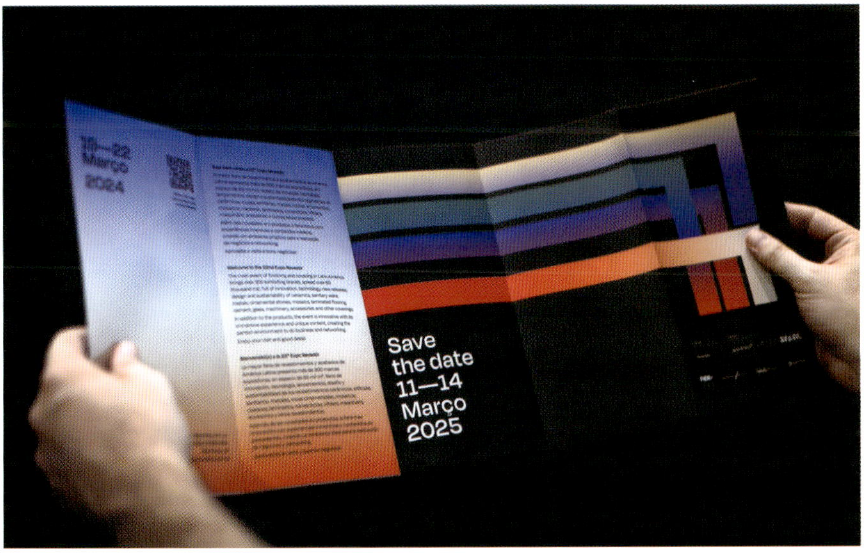

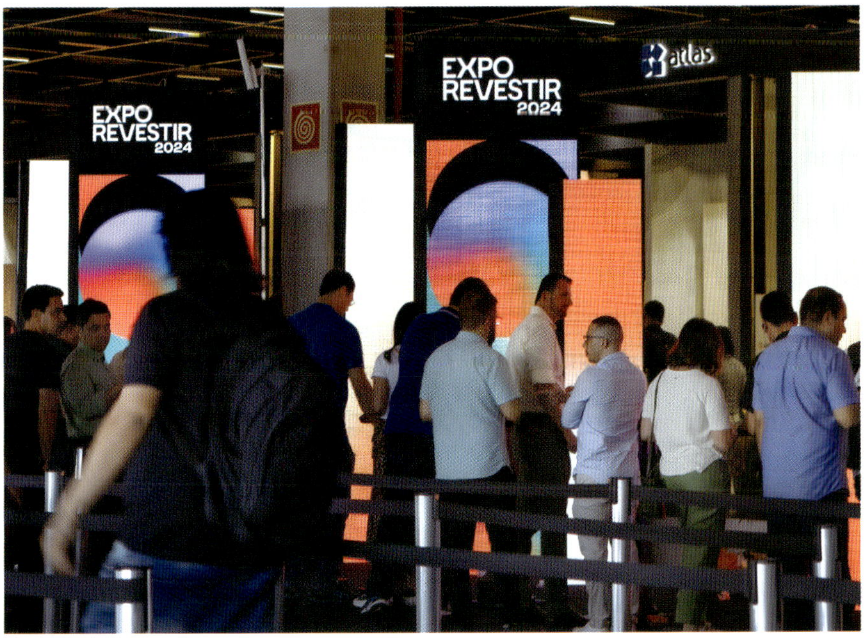

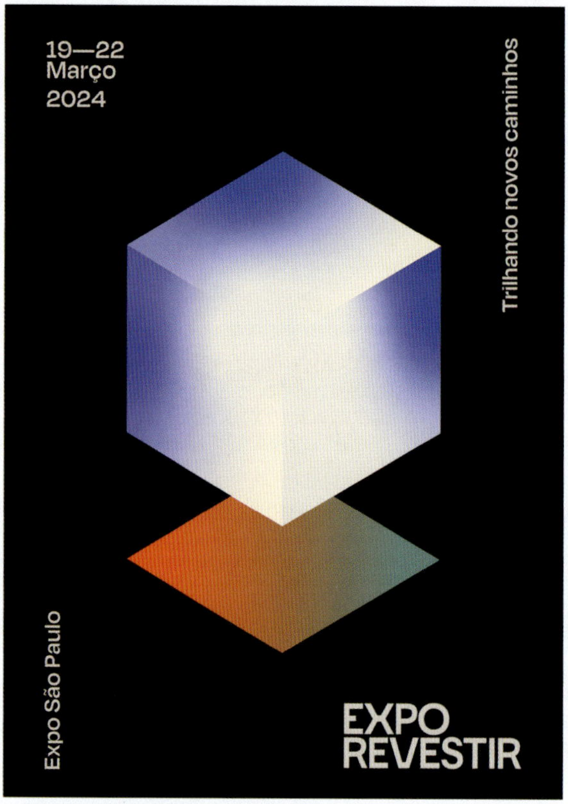
19—22
Março
2024
Trilhando novos caminhos
Expo São Paulo
EXPO
REVESTIR

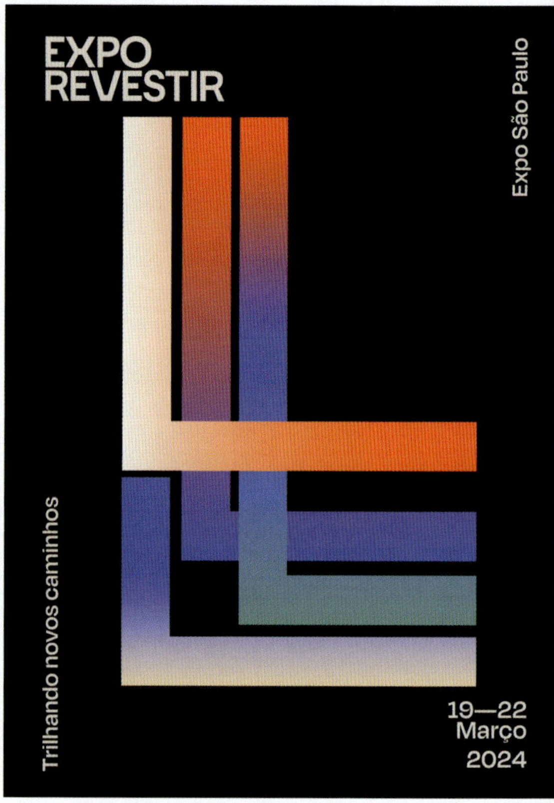
EXPO
REVESTIR
Expo São Paulo
Trilhando novos caminhos
19—22
Março
2024

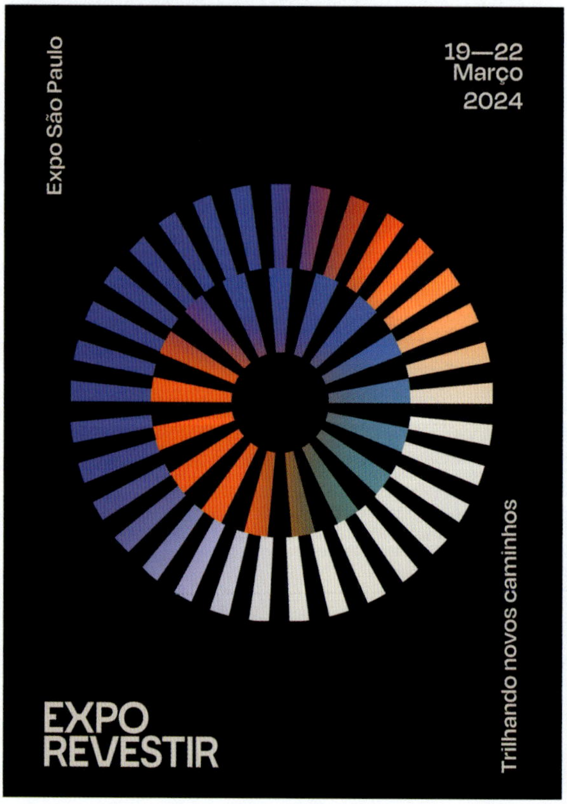
Expo São Paulo
19—22
Março
2024
EXPO
REVESTIR
Trilhando novos caminhos

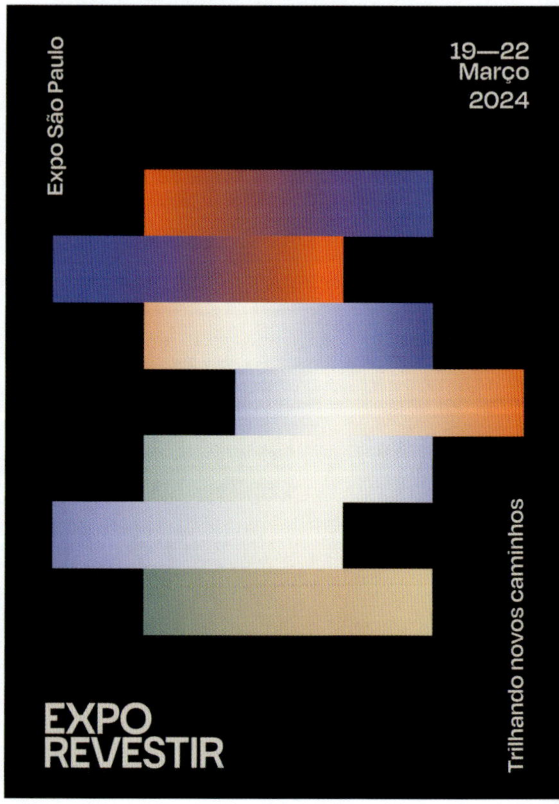
Expo São Paulo
19—22
Março
2024
EXPO
REVESTIR
Trilhando novos caminhos

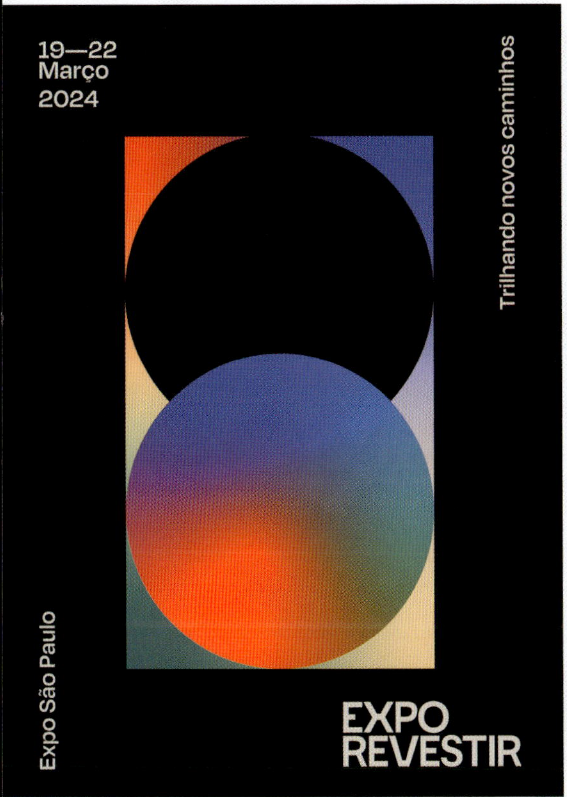
19—22
Março
2024
Trilhando novos caminhos
Expo São Paulo
EXPO
REVESTIR

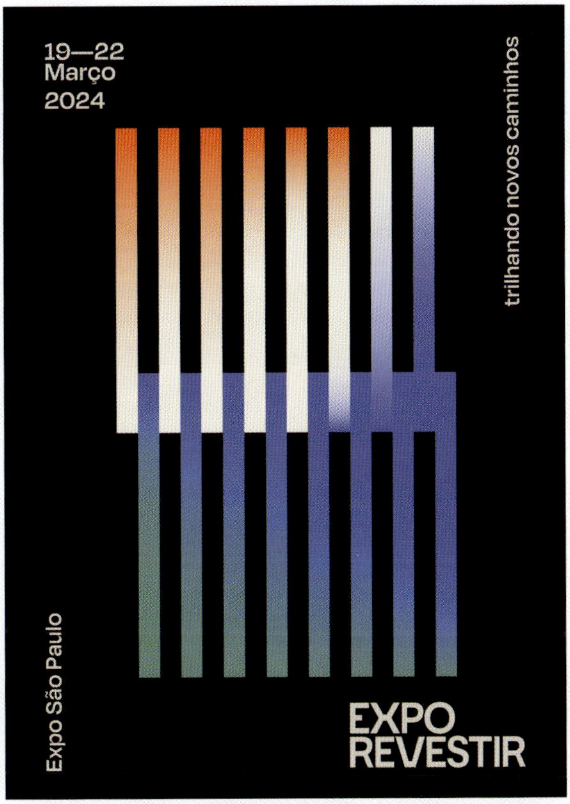
19—22
Março
2024
trilhando novos caminhos
Expo São Paulo
EXPO
REVESTIR

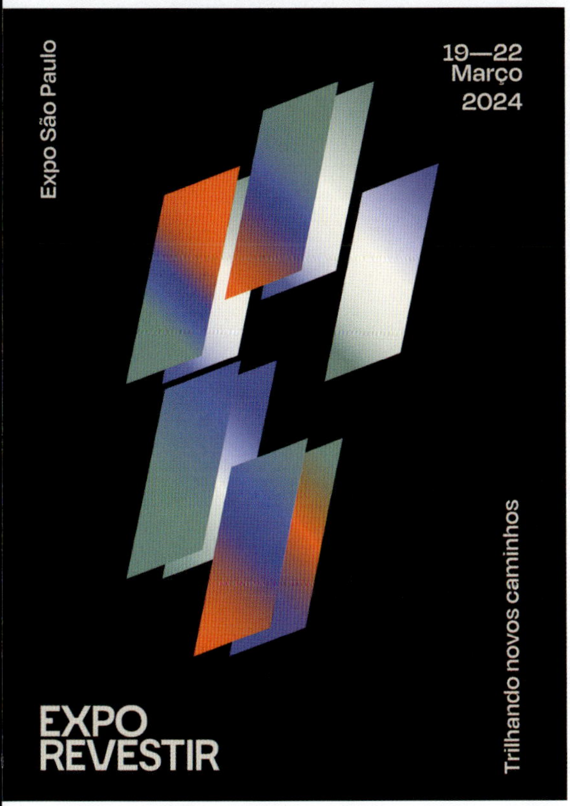
Expo São Paulo
19—22
Março
2024
Trilhando novos caminhos
EXPO
REVESTIR

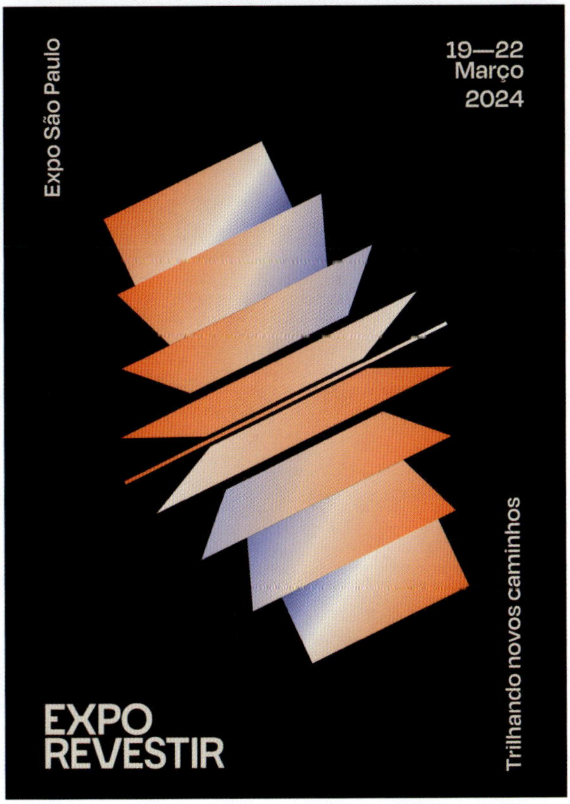
Expo São Paulo
19—22
Março
2024
Trilhando novos caminhos
EXPO
REVESTIR

#FF3366

#CC33FF

#3366FF

#66CCFF

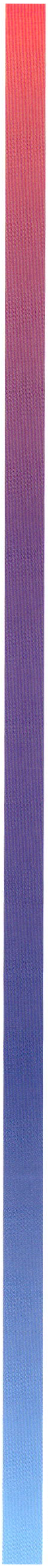

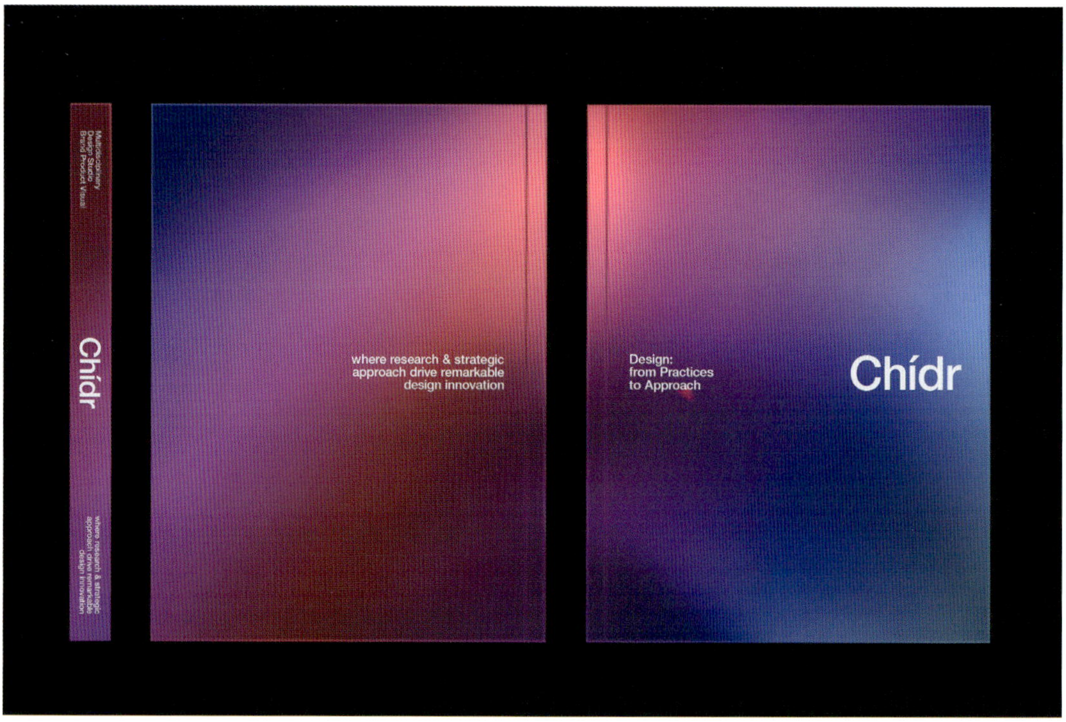

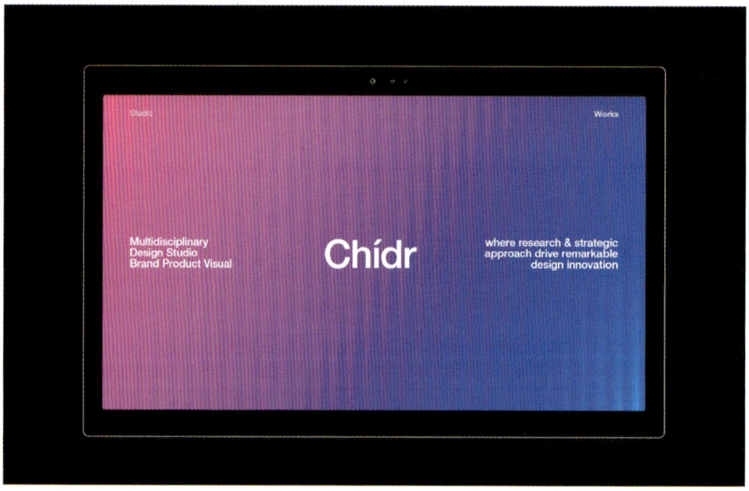

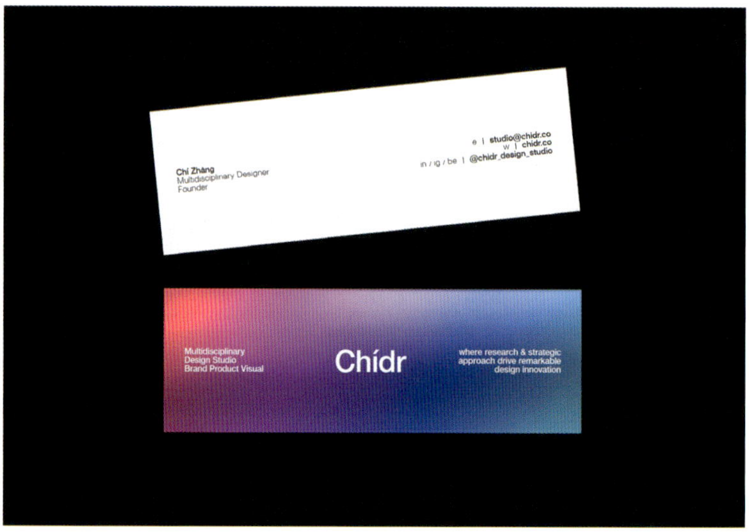

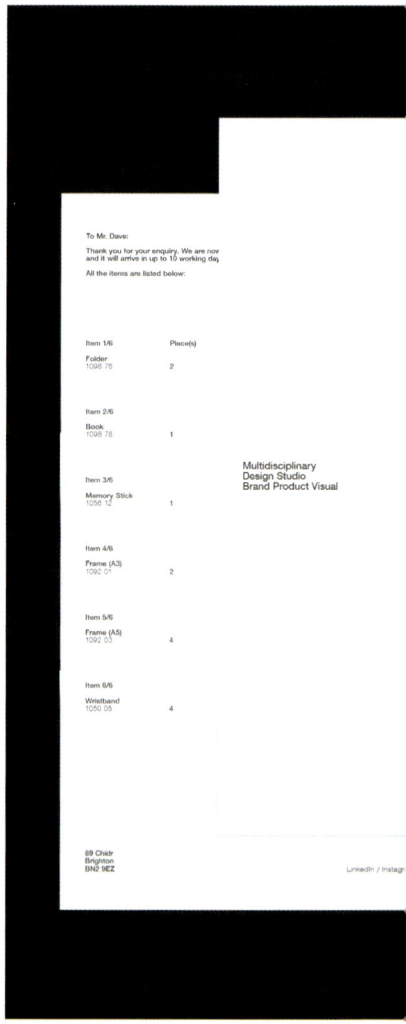

CHÍDR STUDIO

Chídr is a multidisciplinary design studio based in Brighton. At *Chídr*, they craft remarkable designs that spark meaningful connections and brighten everyday life. In 2022, we renewed the studio's identity with a touch of modern elegance, aiming to amplify its voice and influence in our public communication and upcoming initiatives.

Design Studio
Chídr

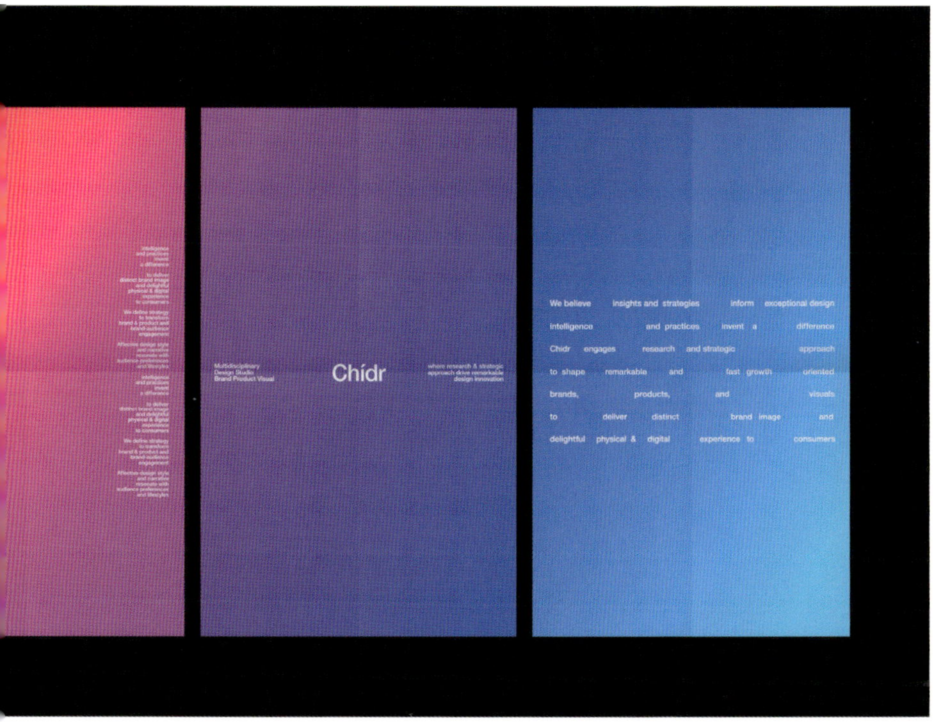

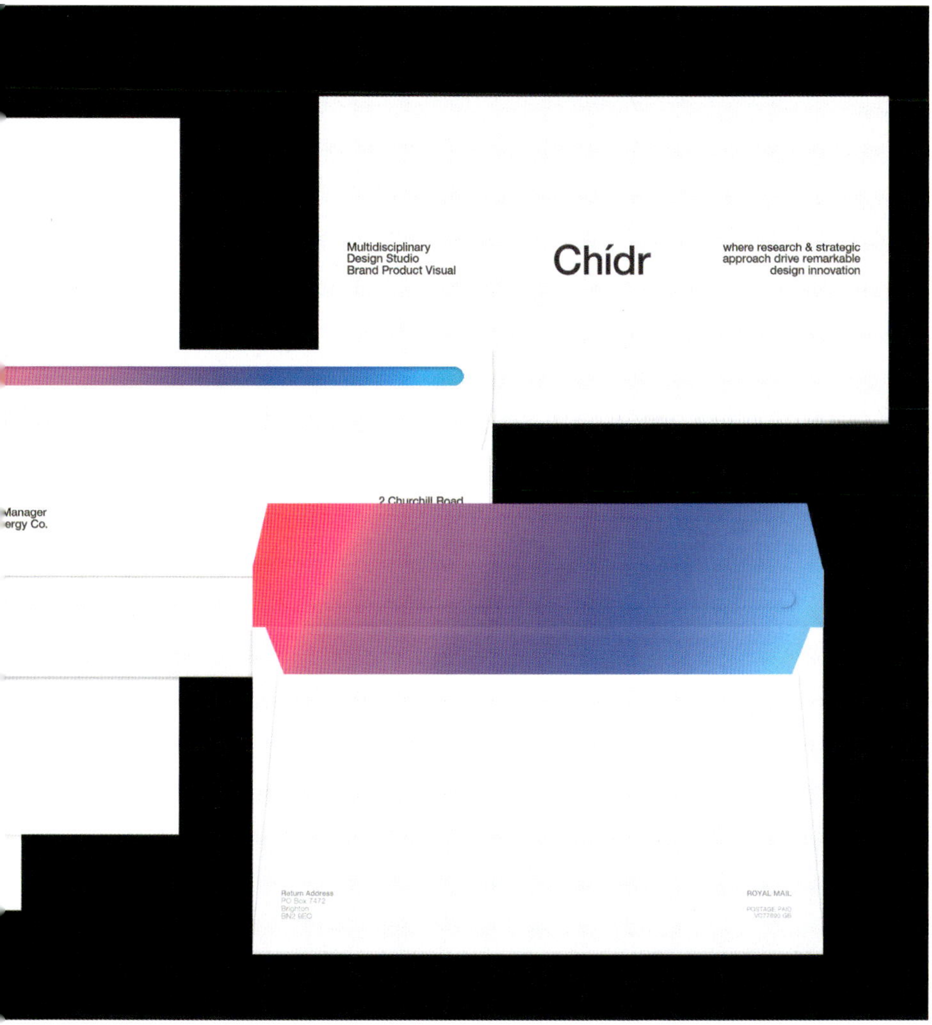

#051F29

#013C52

#005272

#FF93EE

#799FFF

#FF663D

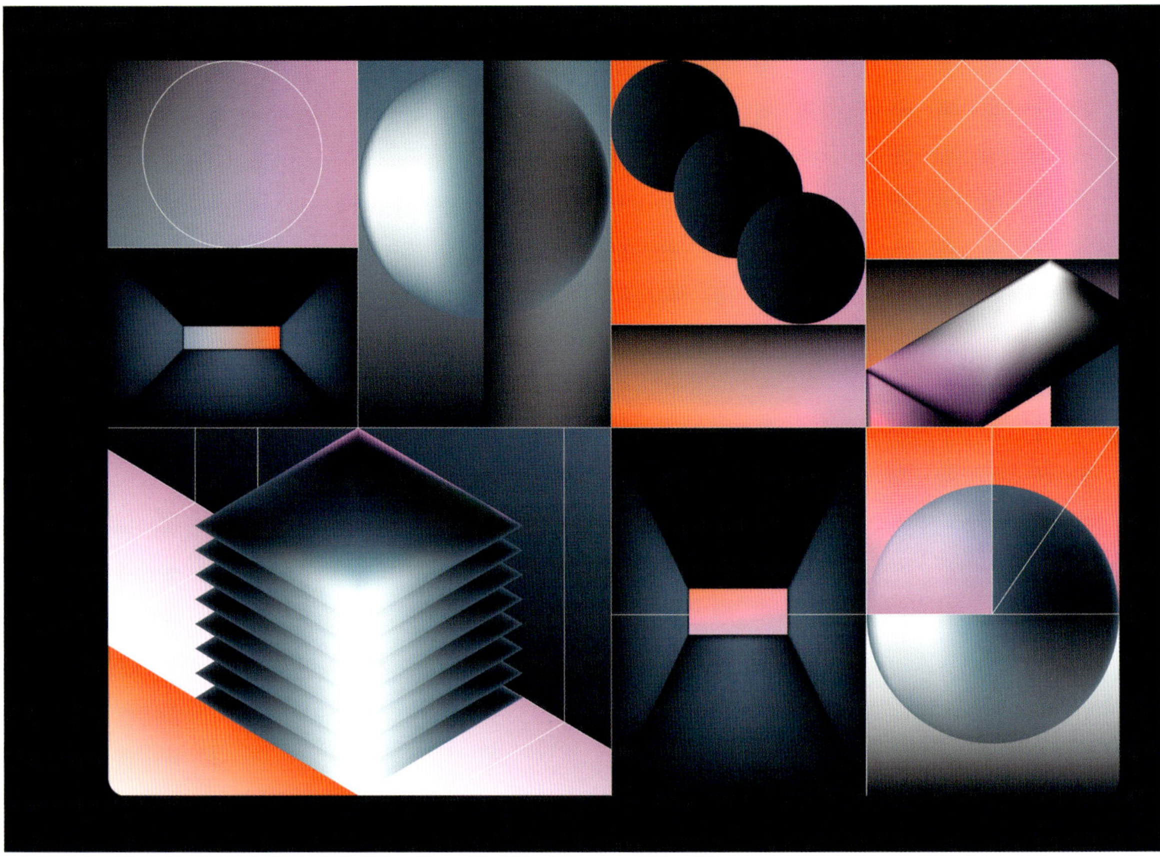

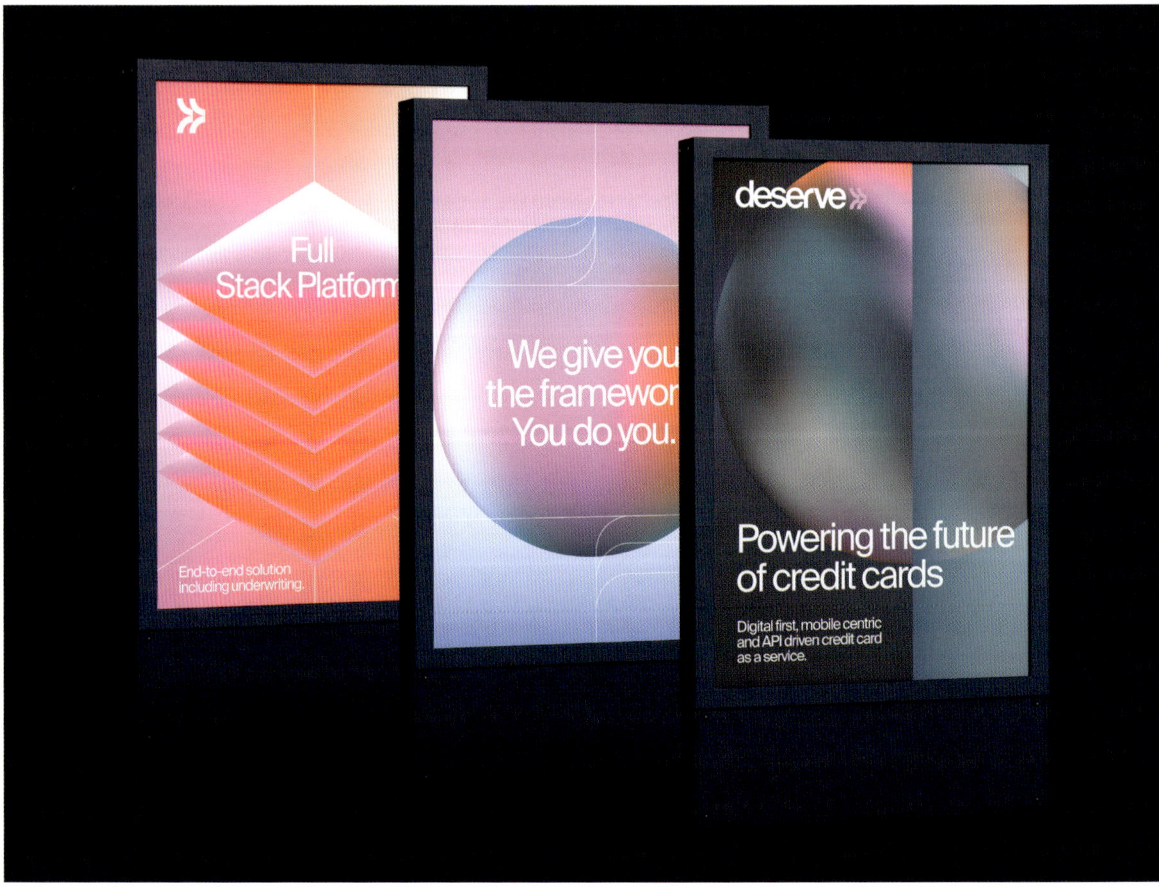

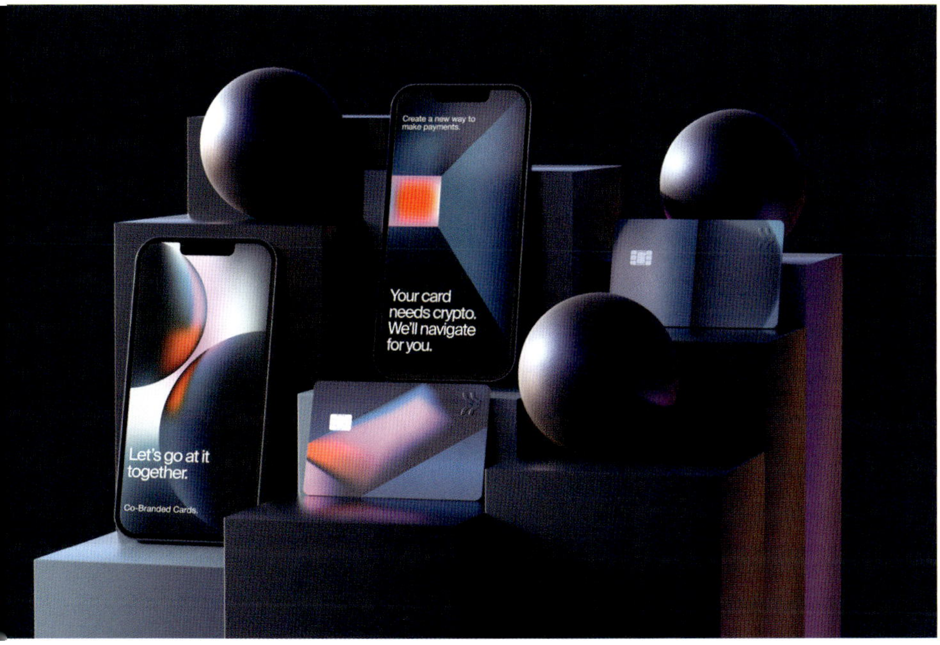

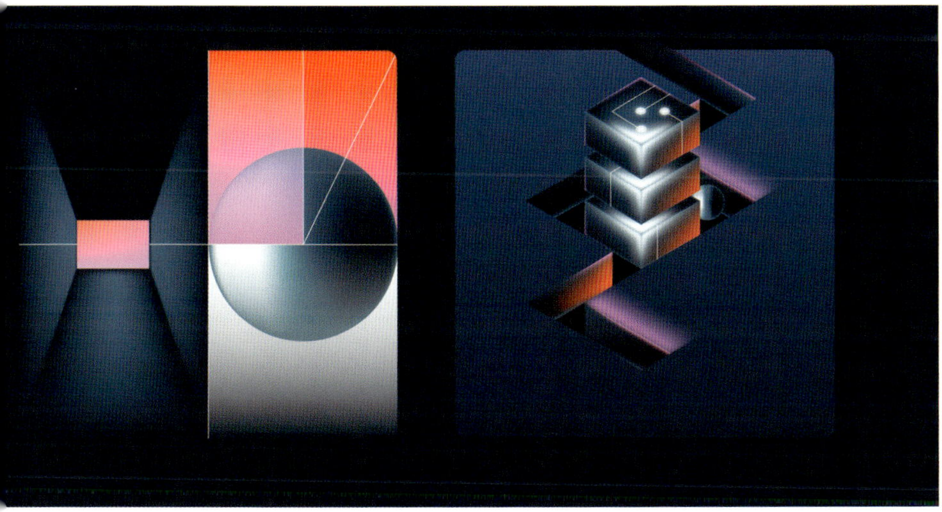

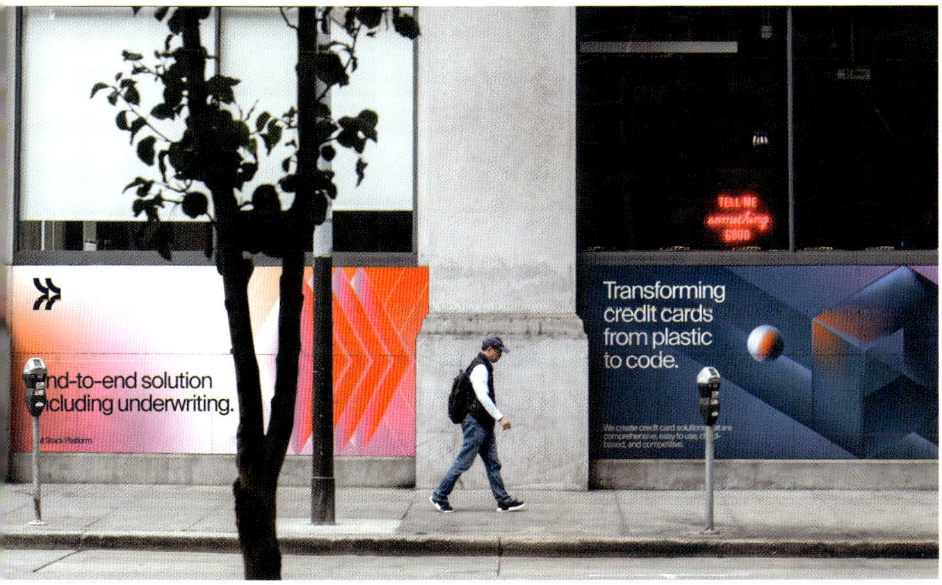

DESERVE

For *Deserve*, a mobile-first credit card platform with $500m in funding, the designer crafted a playful and soulful brand identity from the ground up, creating comprehensive guidelines that enabled their sizable internal team to seamlessly integrate it into their website. Also, they updated all digital interfaces, crafting UX/UI experience for landing pages and marketing websites.

Design Studio
Humbleteam.com

C94 · M58 · Y29 · K14

C72 · M73 · Y56 · K77

C16 · M4 · Y31 · K0

C34 · M78 · Y36 · K24

C9 · M45 · Y65 · K1

ECHOES OF THE CHILD'S MIND-FACE THE DAY

Album cover and digipack design.

Art Director, Designer & Illustrator
Ada Zielinska

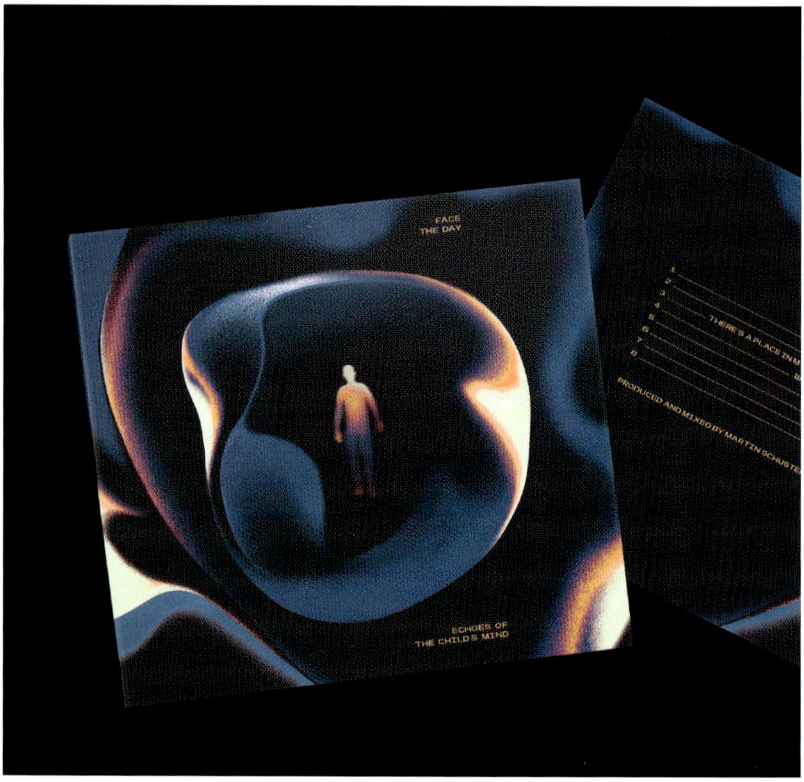

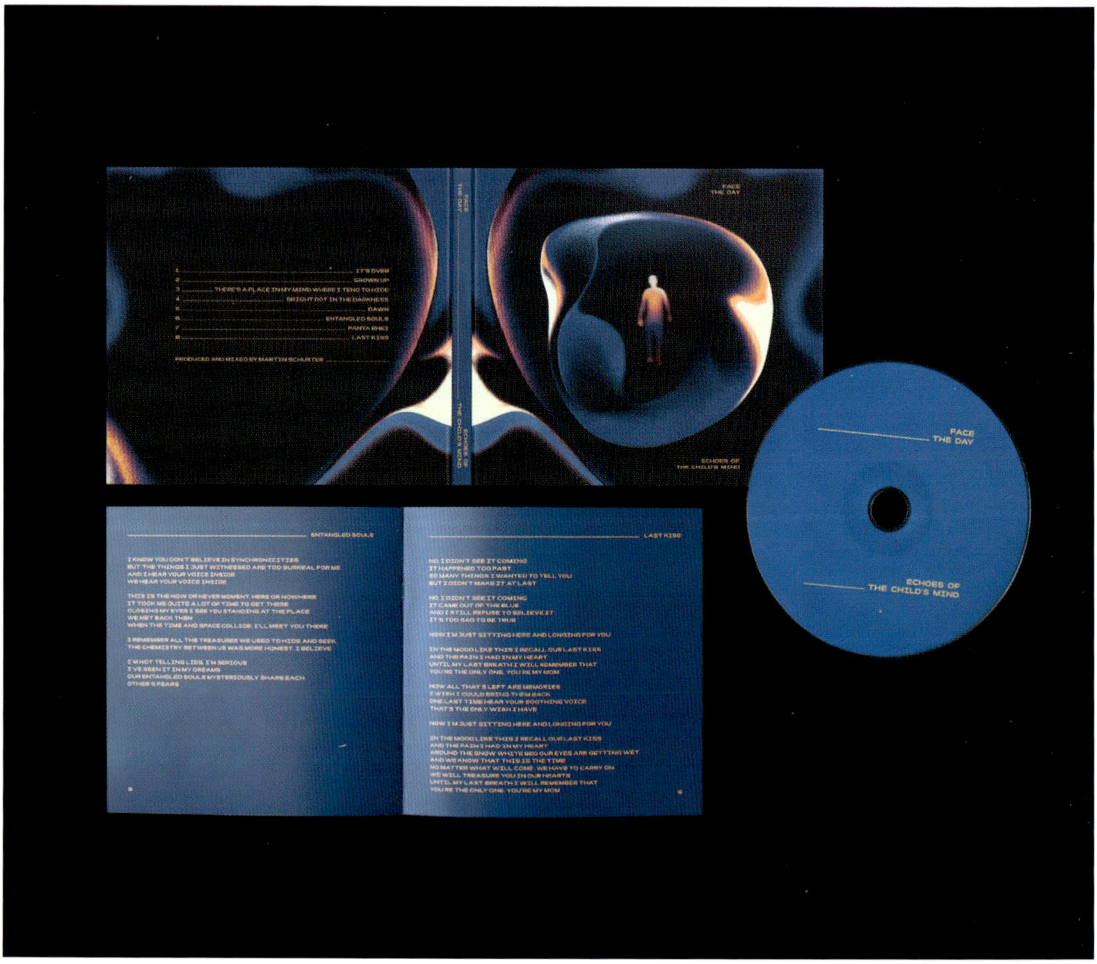

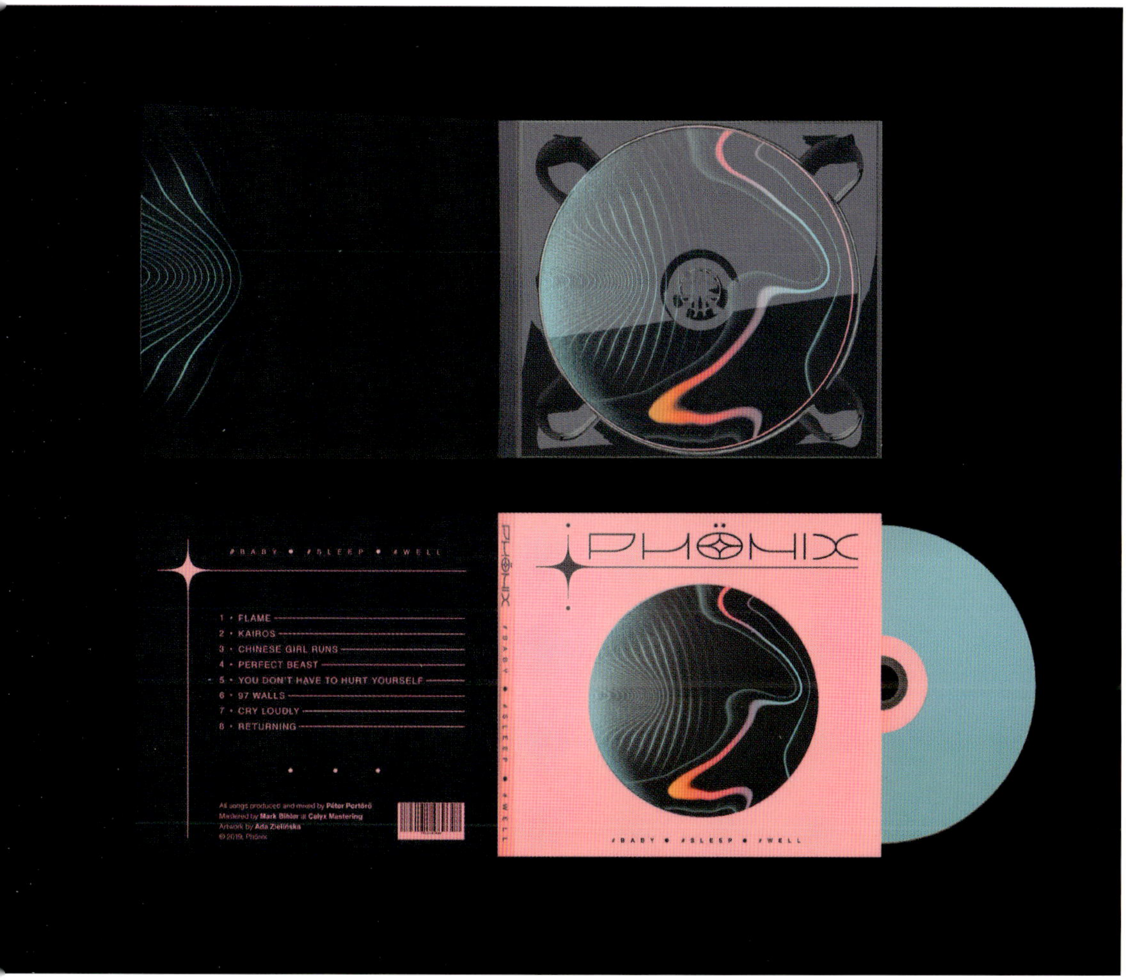

#BABY #SLEEP #WELL-PHÖNIX

Album cover and digipack design.

Art Director, Illustrator, Designer & LOGO Designer
Ada Zielinska

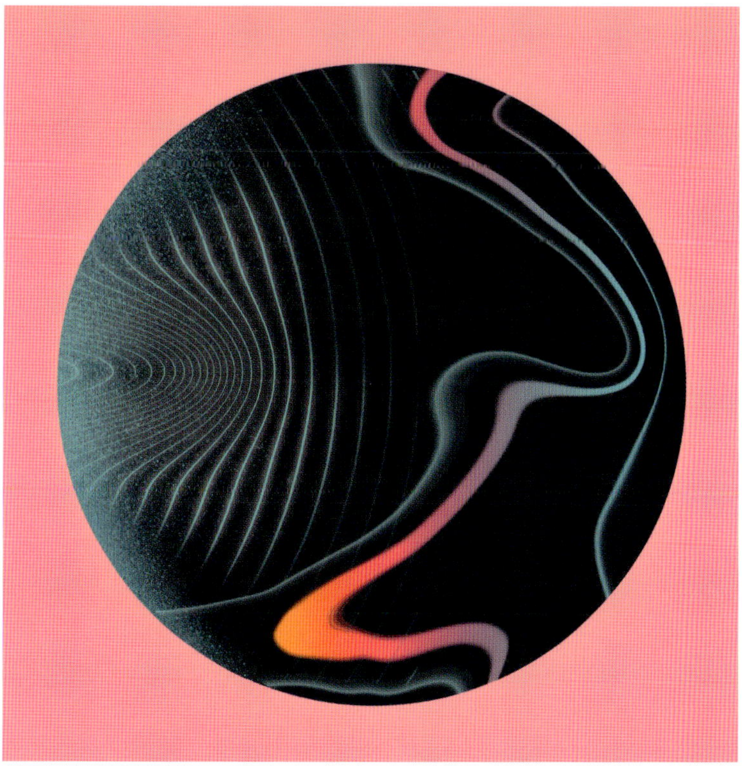

C0 · M90 · Y47 · K0

C1 · M64 · Y89 · K0

C72 · M9 · Y42 · K0

C89 · M77 · Y56 · K80

C0 · M61 · Y21 · K0

PANTONE 487 C

PANTONE 1345 C

PANTONE 3248 C

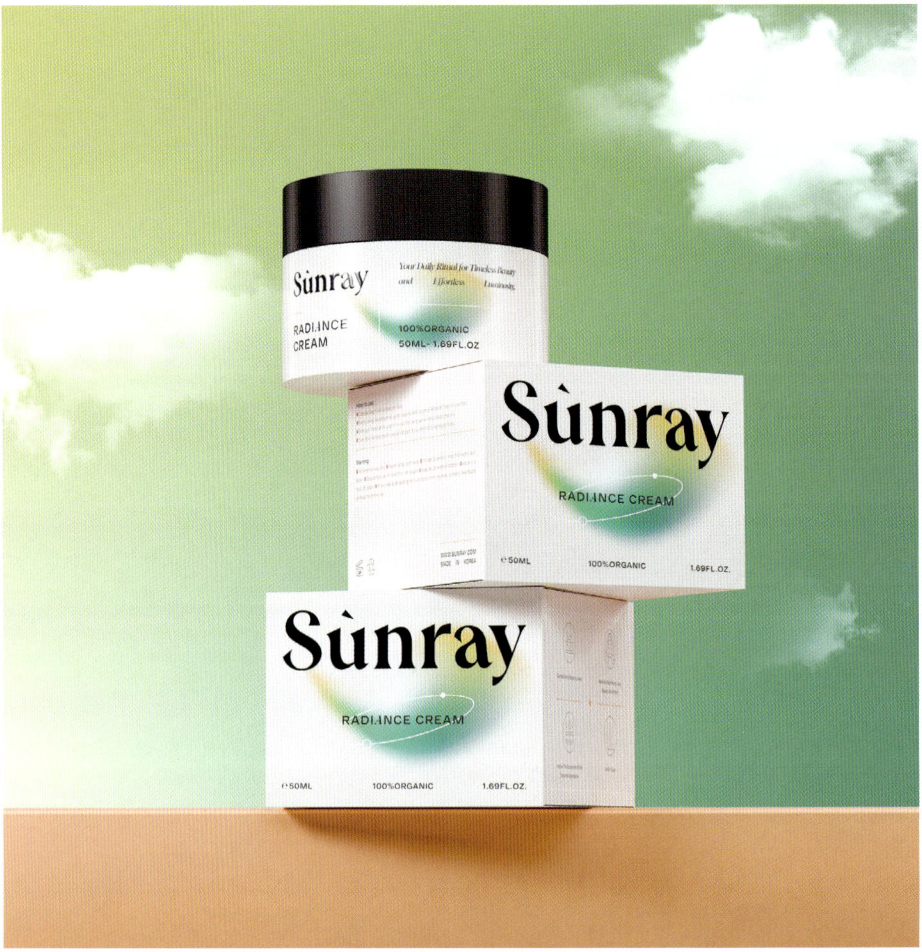

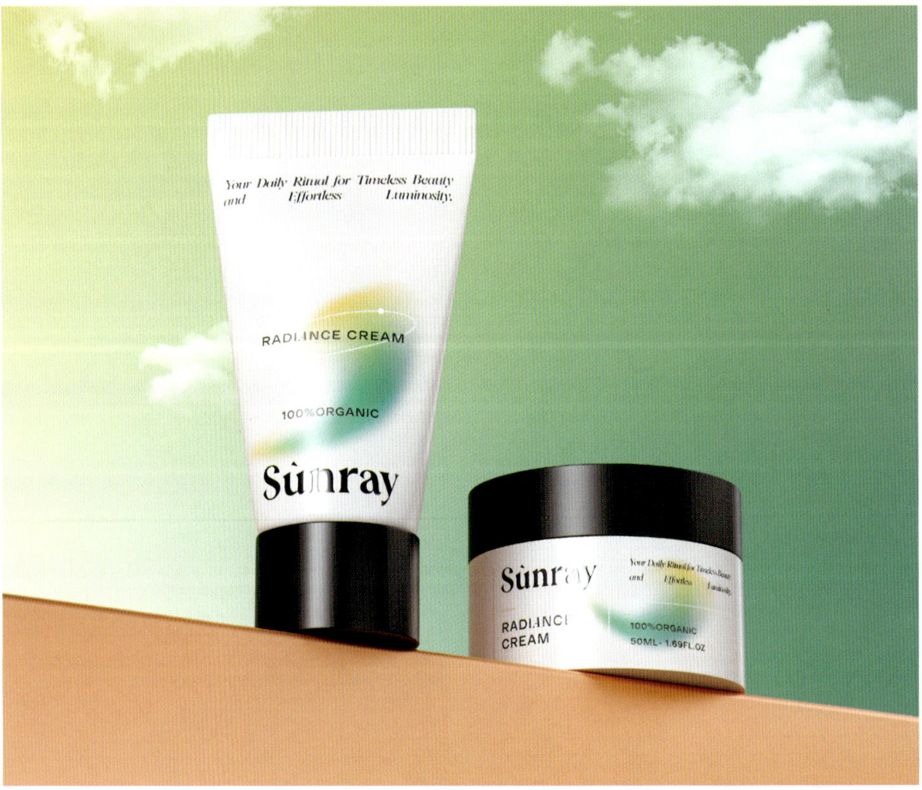

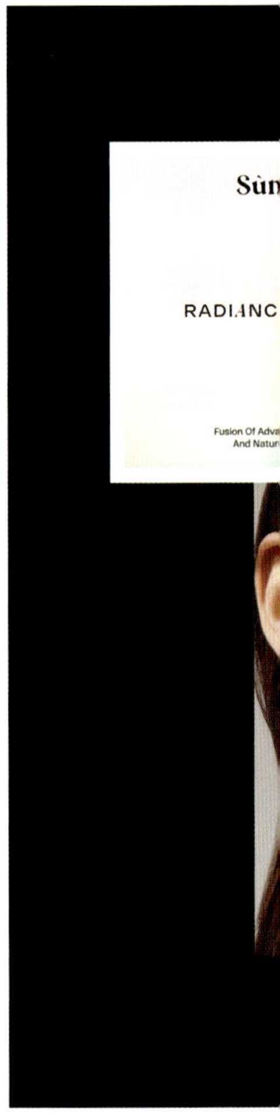

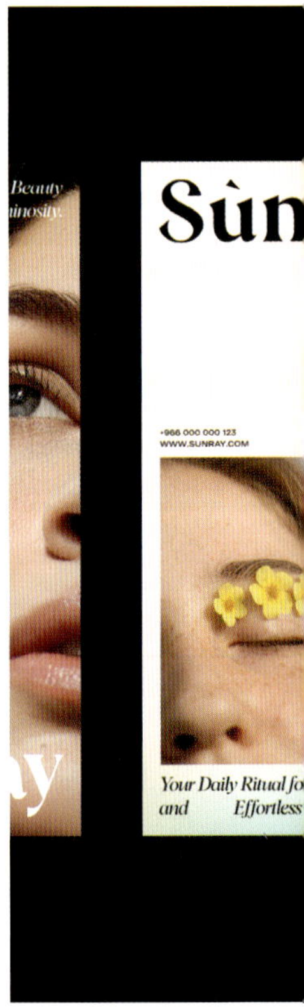

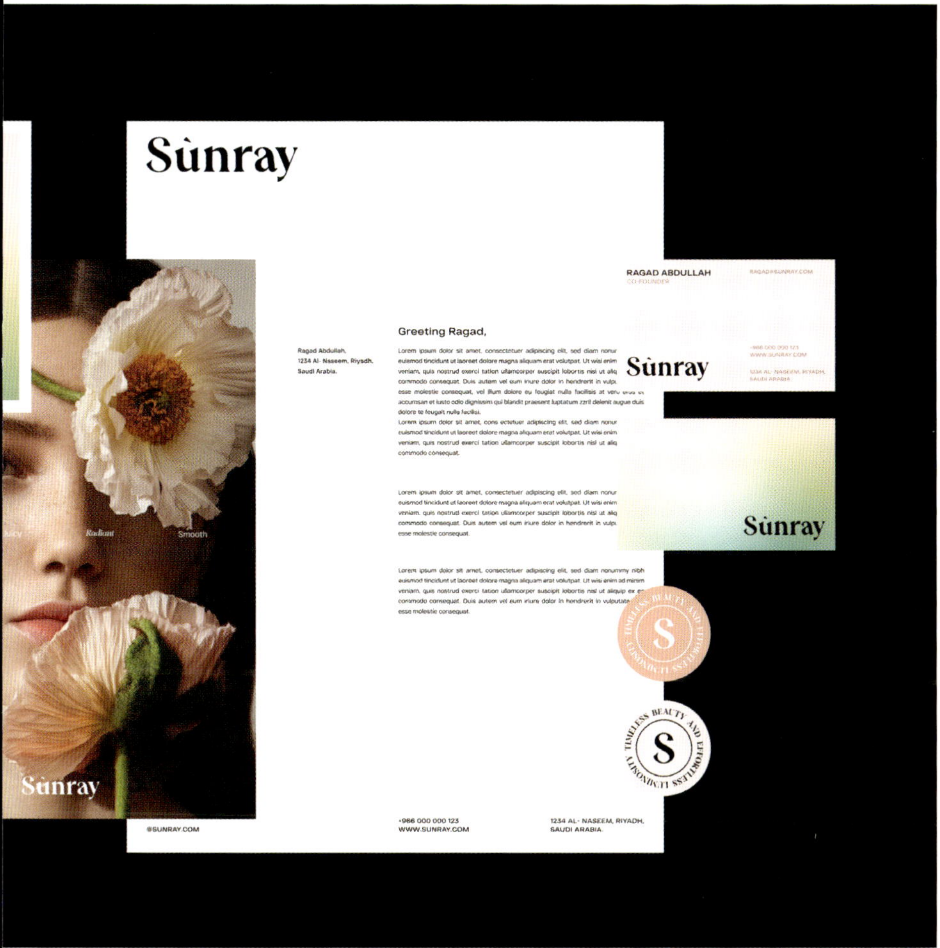

SÙNRAY SKINCARE

Sùnray is not just a skincare brand; it's a philosophy centred around simplicity, effectiveness, and elegance. Their mission is to uncover the inherent beauty within every individual through transformative skincare experiences. Whether it's their commitment to using natural ingredients or their dedication to creating products that promote radiance and vitality, *Sùnray* is more than just skincare—it's a journey toward embracing your natural glow.

Designer
Mahmoud Mahroos

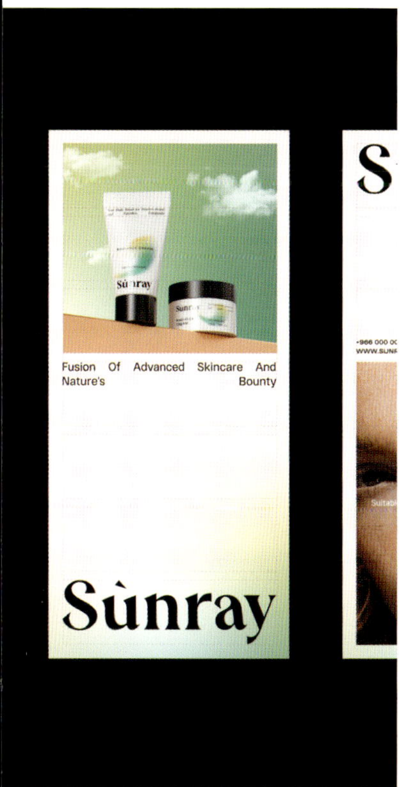

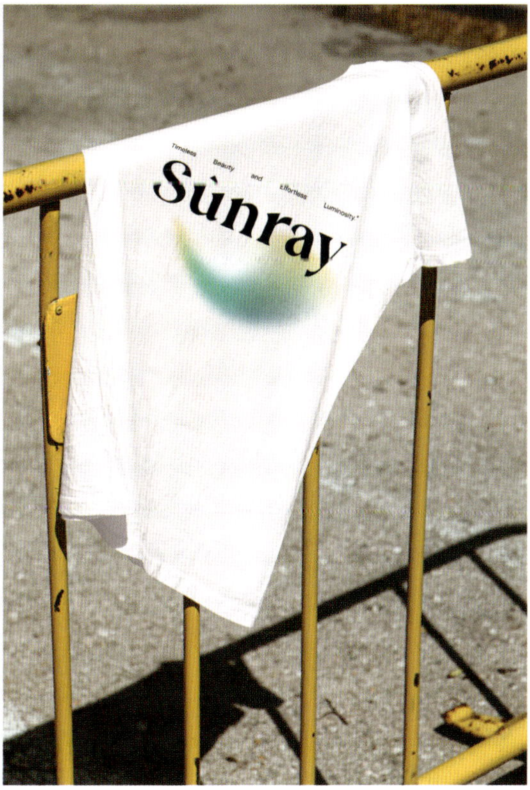

R51 · G255 · B51
R255 · G255 · B0

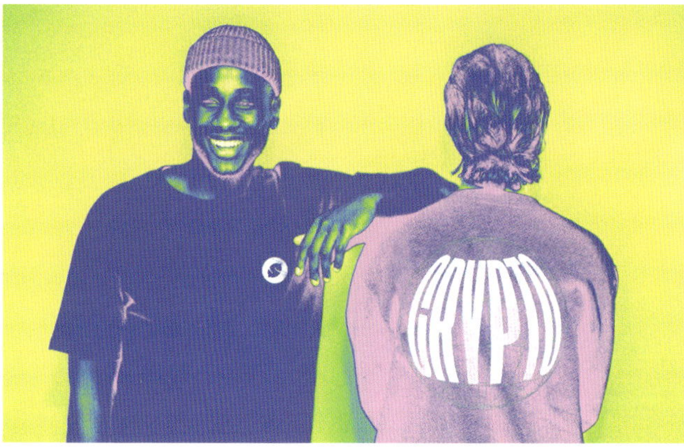

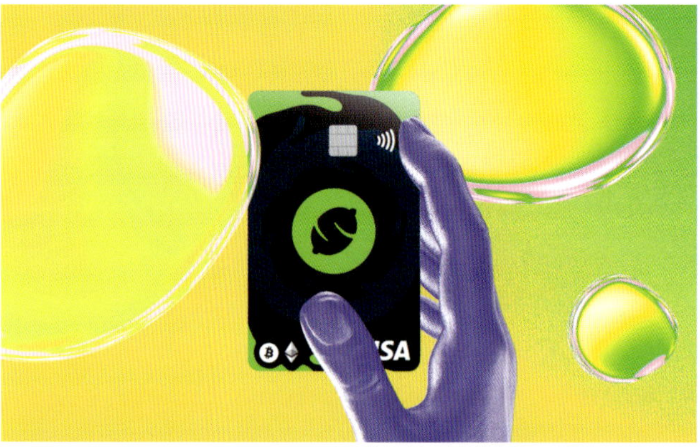

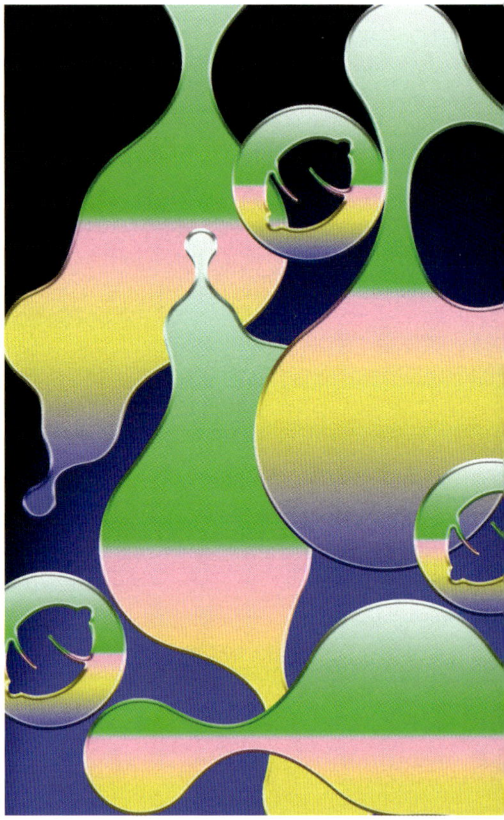

R255 · G153 · B0
R255 · G204 · B255

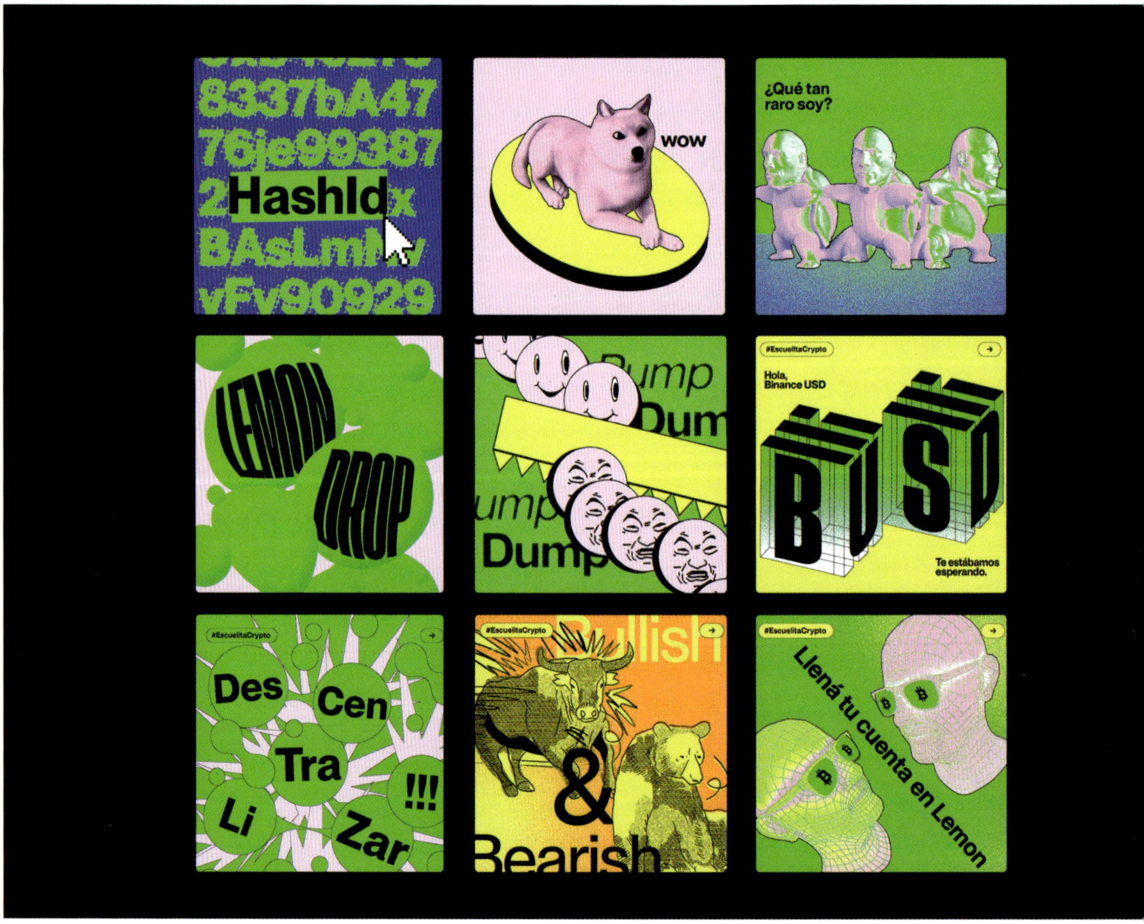

R102 · G102 · B255

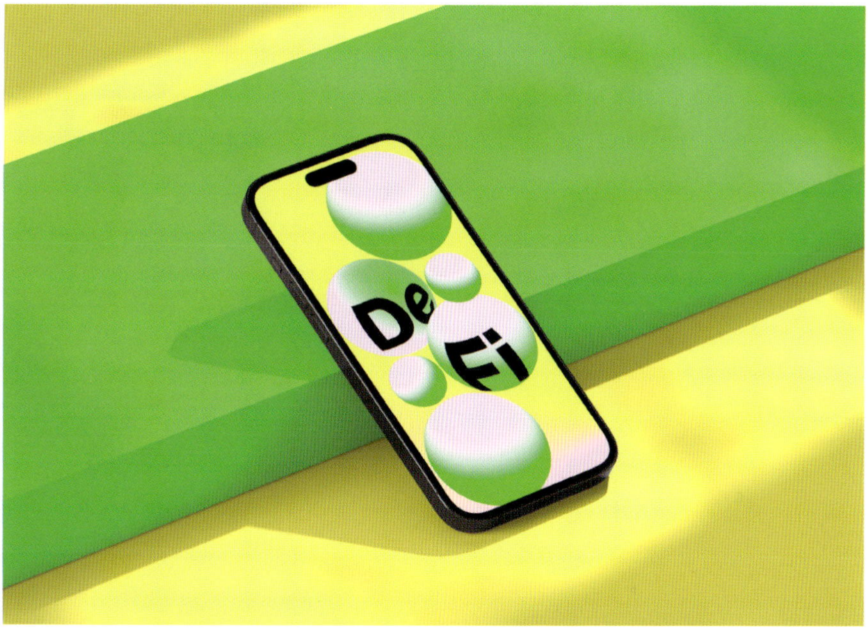

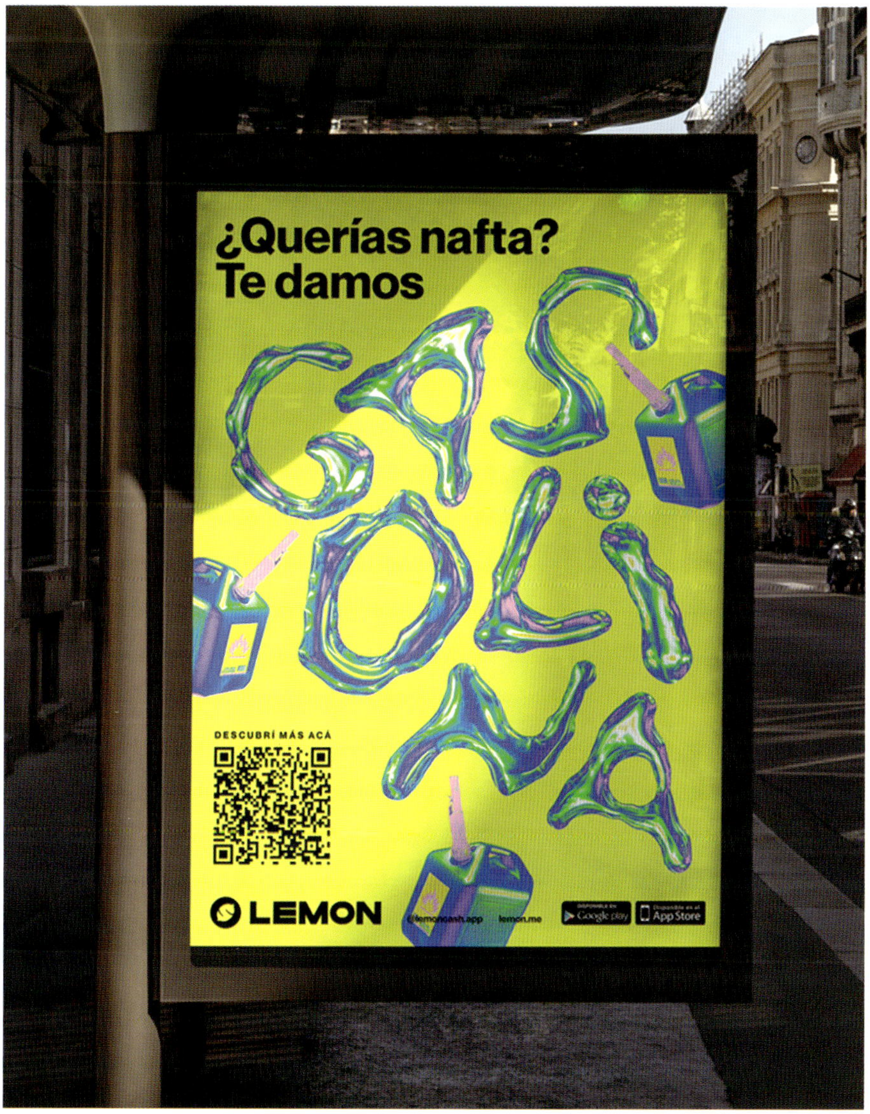

LEMON CASH

Making crypto sexy, pop, and friendly—this was the primary DNA of *Lemon Cash's* new visual identity. *Lemon* aimed to engage with the young audience entering the world of cryptocurrencies through playful and straightforward communication. The designer crafted a "pop" version of the brand, where colours take centre stage, evoking emotions and sensations. Lemon's refreshed visual identity celebrated the brand's core personality in an open, lively, and dynamic way.

Design & Concept
Alexandro Valcarcel

Creative Director
Fernando Oltolina, Juan Martín Muiño

Designer
Fiorella Nucara, Bautista Mantovani, Ailin Pancia, Emmanuel Rehbani & Nicolás Cavazzoli

Original Illustration
Bárbara Gedacht, Fiorella Nucara & Bautista Mantovani

Motion Graphic
Matías Mondillo

3D Artist
Gastón Carballal & Sebastián Cavazzoli

C80 · M42 · Y0 · K0

C19 · M0 · Y72 · K0

C87 · M39 · Y100 · K39

PEAK SOUND

The *Peak Sound* branding project aims to establish the brand as the epitome of audio excellence. Through sleek design and strategic messaging, it communicates *Peak Sound's* commitment to precision, depth, and clarity. The project seeks to elevate the auditory experience across music, movies, and gaming, promising unparalleled fidelity and immersion.

Designer
Sabbir Dzns

Design Studio
ETA* Pixels

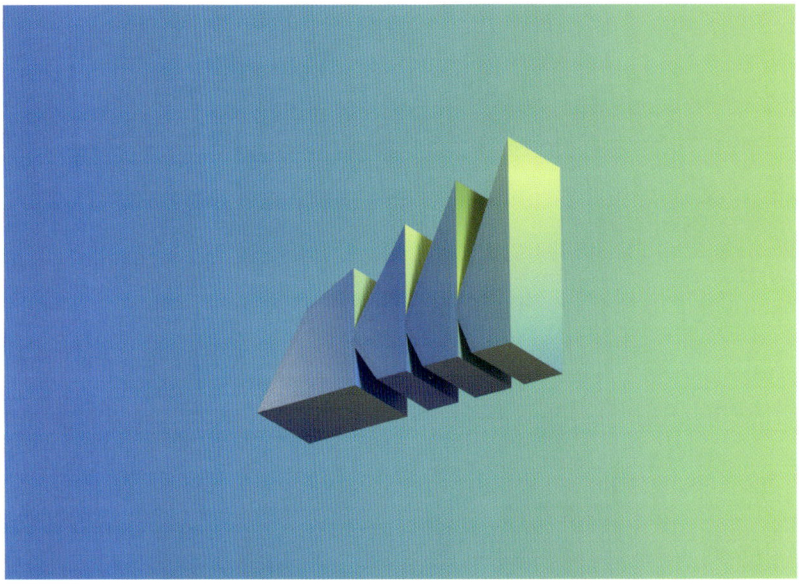

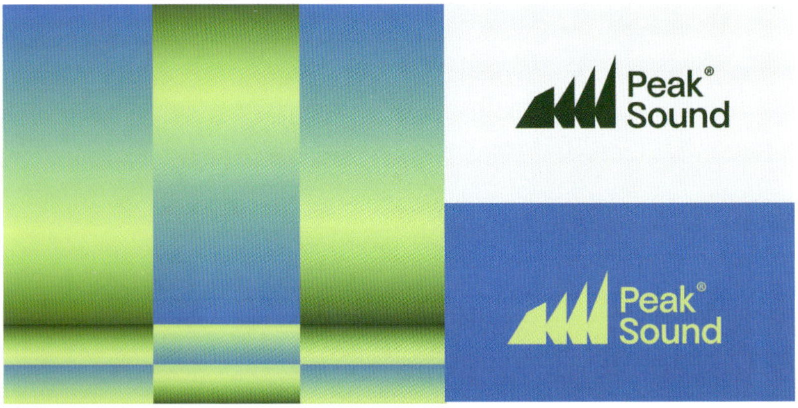

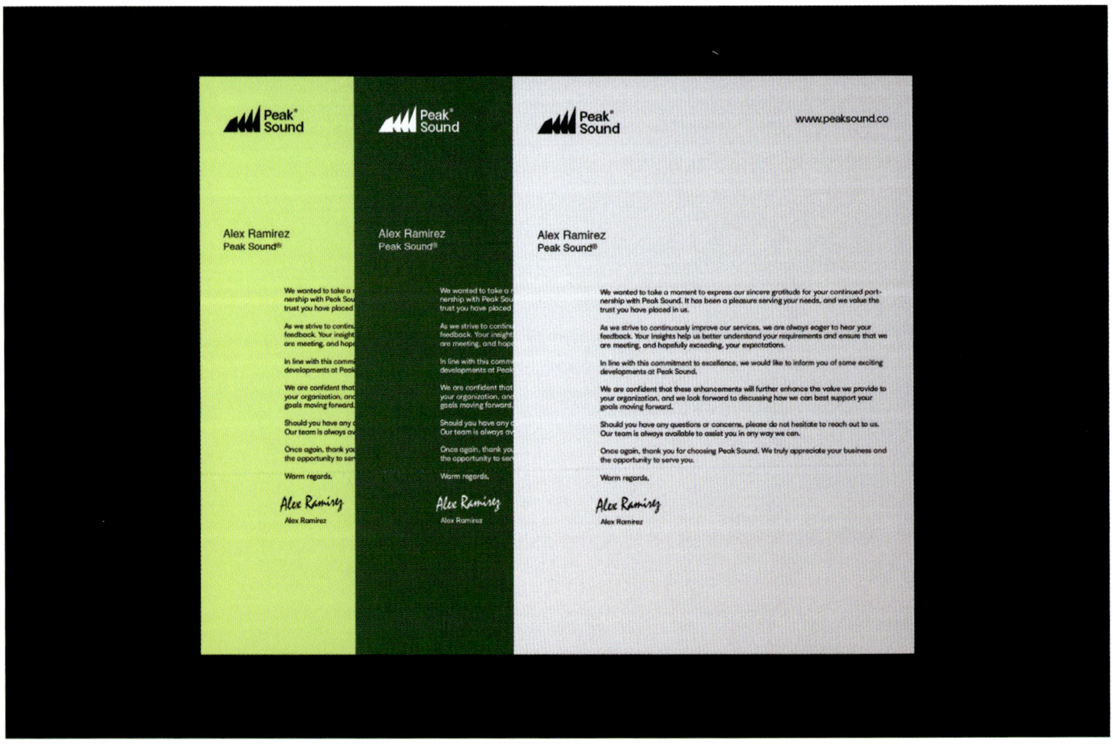

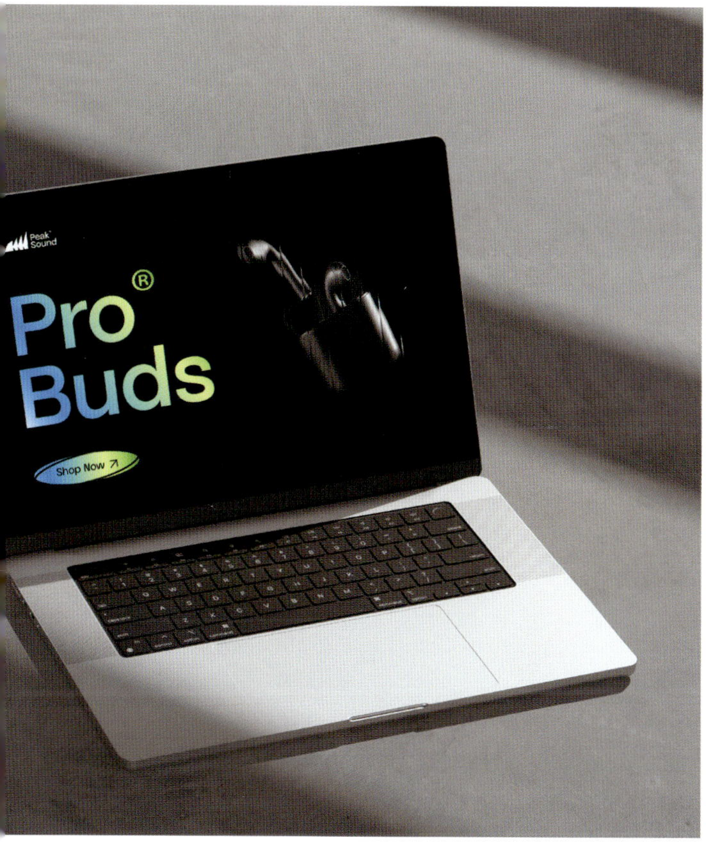
Peak Sound
Pro® Buds
Shop Now ↗

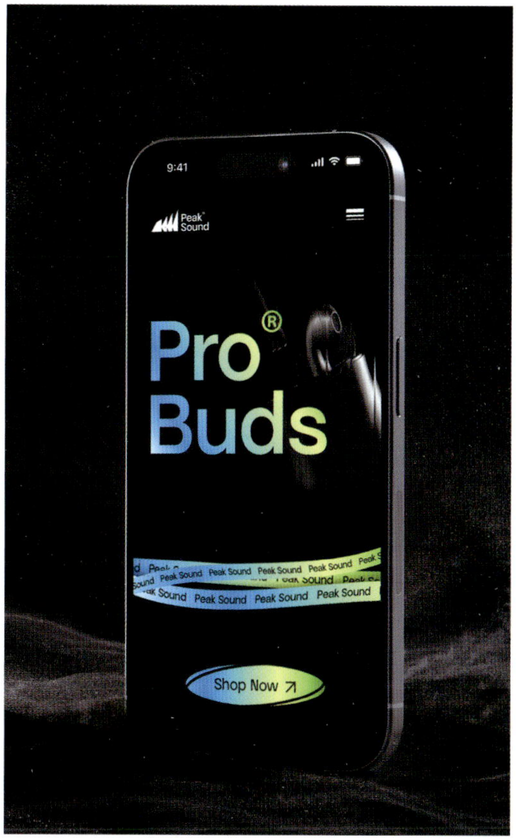
9:41
Peak Sound
Pro® Buds
Peak Sound Peak Sound Peak Sound Peak Sound
Shop Now ↗

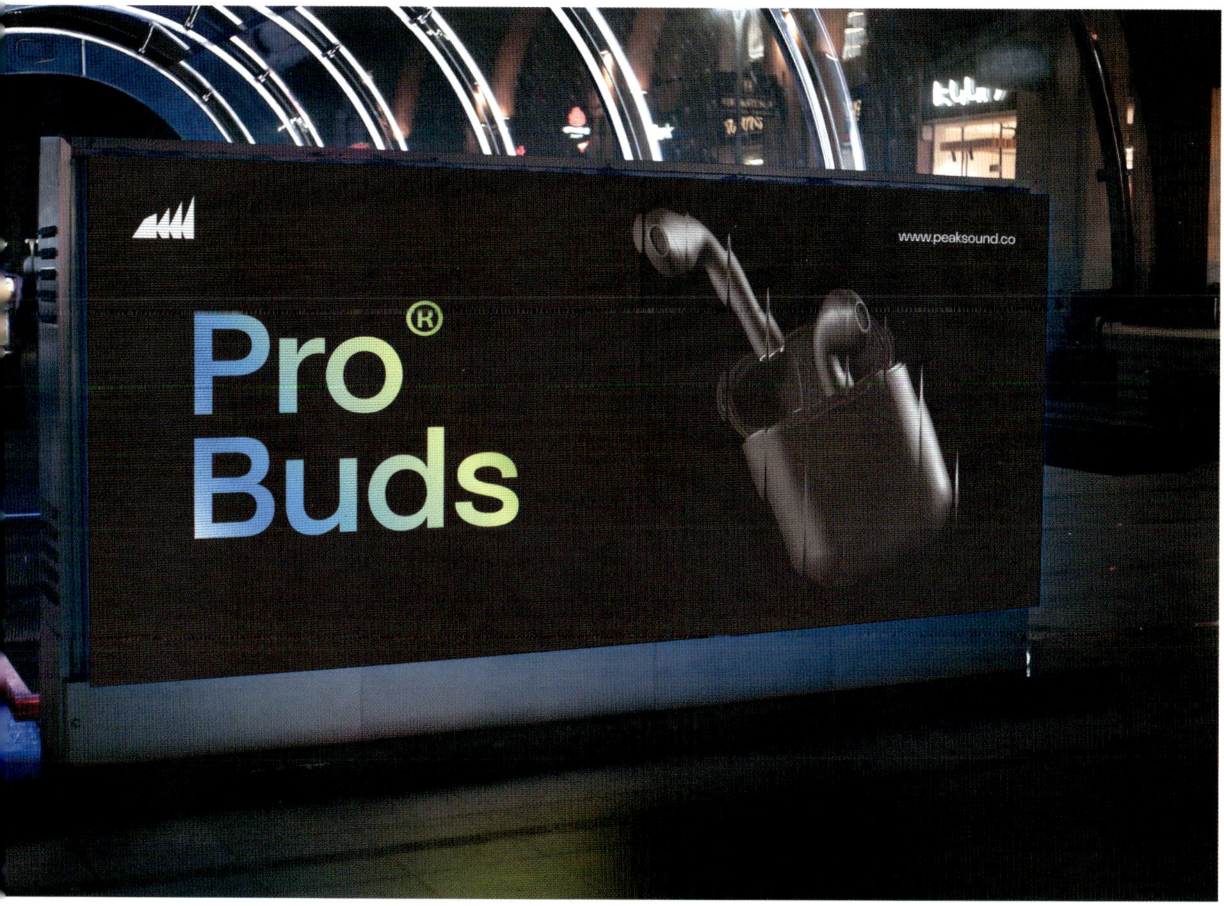
www.peaksound.co
Pro® Buds

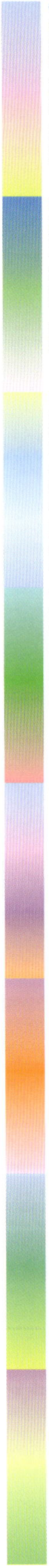

R187 · G211 · B255
R255 · G191 · B240
R255 · G253 · B67

R52 · G170 · B251
R157 · G248 · B120
R252 · G229 · B250

R255 · G254 · B149
R172 · G212 · B255
R218 · G229 · B243
R187 · G211 · B255

R151 · G248 · B235
R16 · G249 · B70
R255 · G158 · B169

R187 · G211 · B255
R247 · G192 · B235
R222 · G138 · B245
R255 · G187 · B106

R251 · G150 · B255
R255 · G160 · B36
R255 · G207 · B255

R187 · G211 · B255
R90 · G248 · B146
R255 · G253 · B67

R251 · G150 · B255
R251 · G249 · B144
R165 · G245 · B112

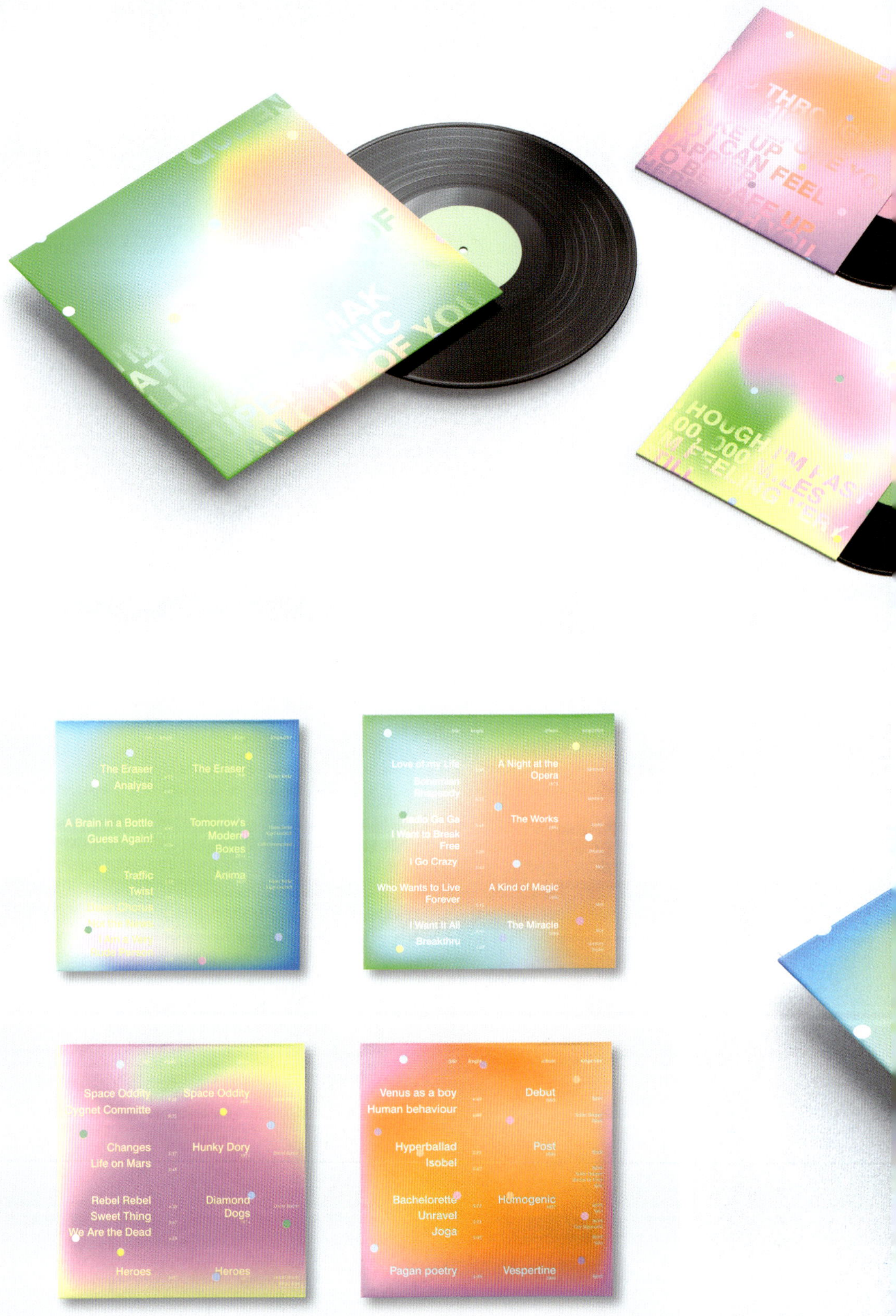

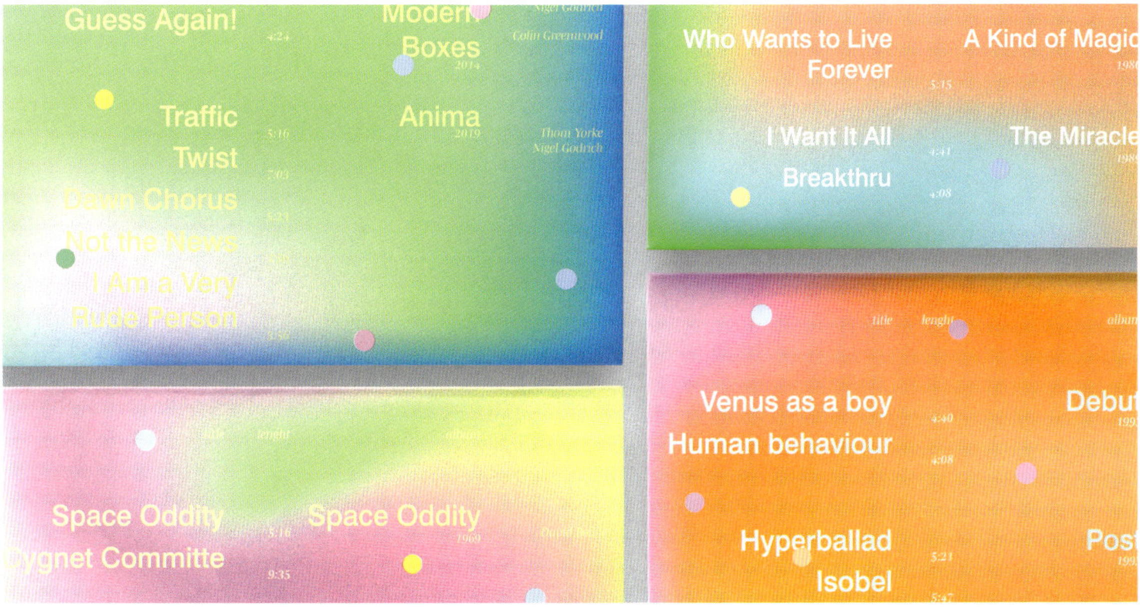

RECORD COLLECTION

For the designer, music plays a pivotal role in her perception of the world. She dedicated this series to her favourite artists: Thom Yorke, Björk, Queen, and David Bowie. In the design, she wanted to reflect on the one hand the elusiveness of its beauty, and on the other hand, the brightness of the impressions that it leaves. The chosen colour scheme for each artist corresponds to her associations with them.

Graphic Designer
Julia Figlovskaya

Art Direction
Svyat Vishnyakov

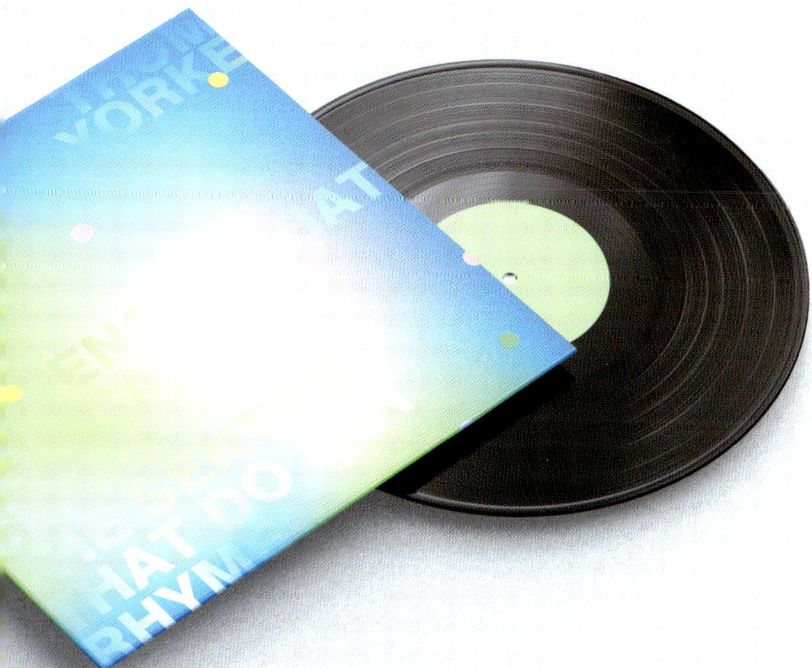

C52 · M2 · Y2 · K0

C100 · M99 · Y18 · K6

C0 · M73 · Y72 · K0

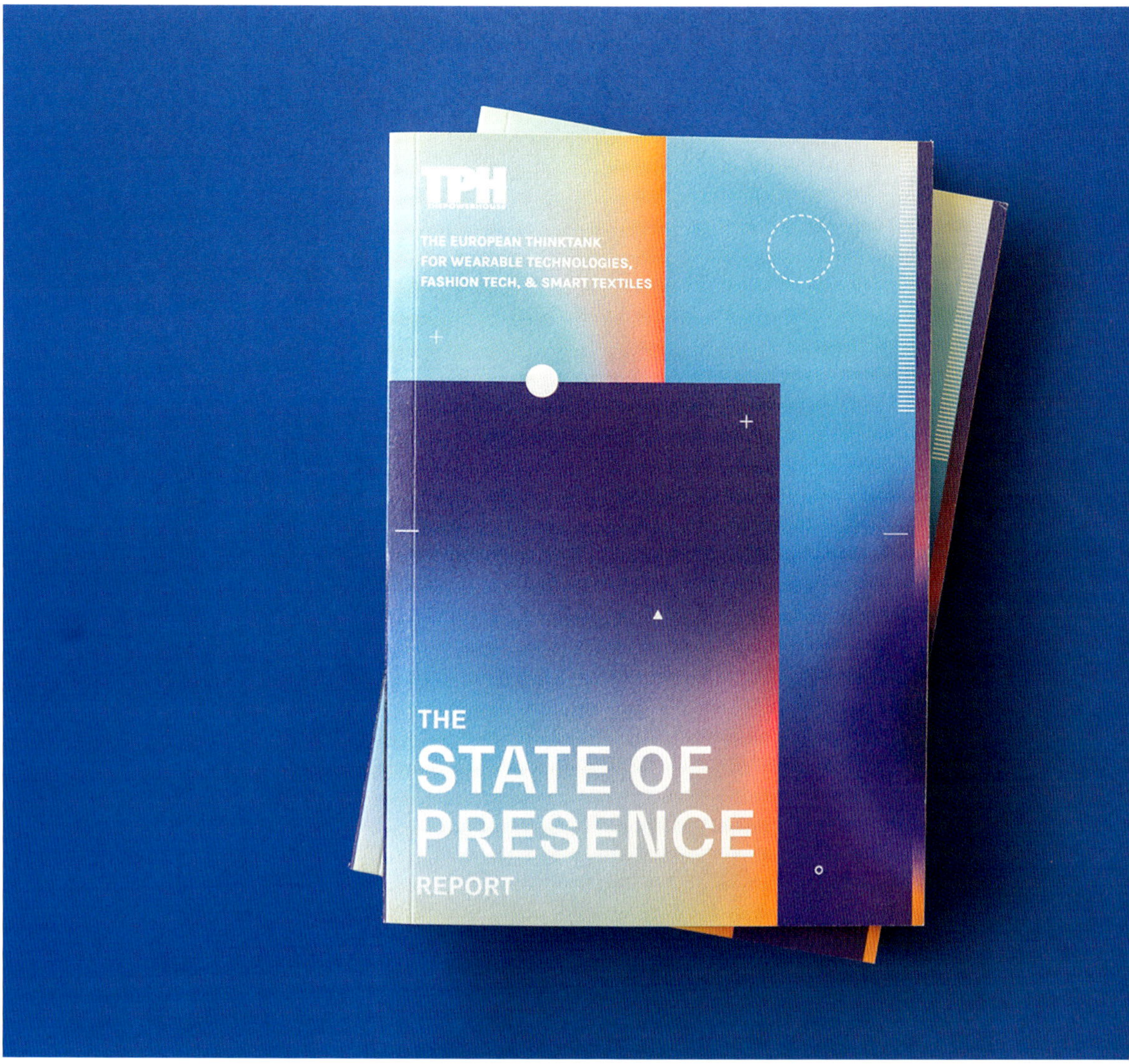

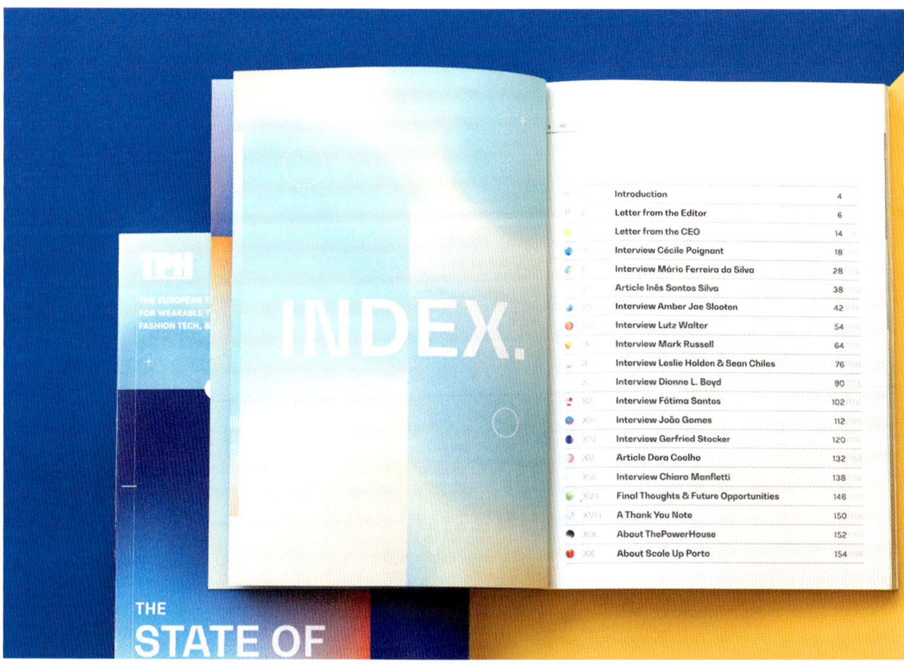

THE STATE OF PRESENCE

Without a doubt, 2020 was a challenging year. In an attempt to better understand what was happening and how we could anticipate future behaviour, O FNDMT (part of ThePowerHouse) put together this report, by interviewing people from different disciplines with innovative and entrepreneurial spirits, to learn how they were dealing with the present crisis, and how they were adapting to face the future. Taking this uncertainty as a starting point, Mano a Mano Club's team chose not to define a colour palette, but instead to give each chapter a gradient with different colours. This 156-page report is filled with bright colours and insightful interviews.

Designer
Mano a Mano Club

Print Producer
Gráfica Maiadouro

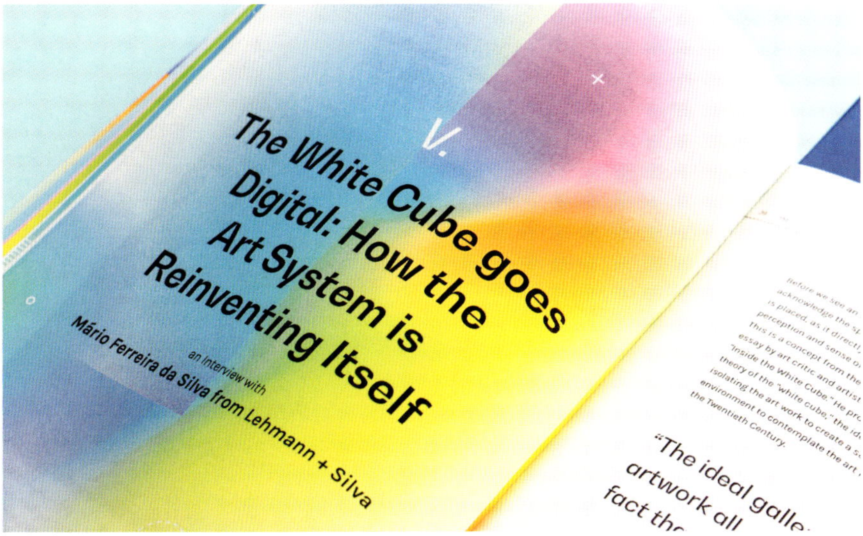

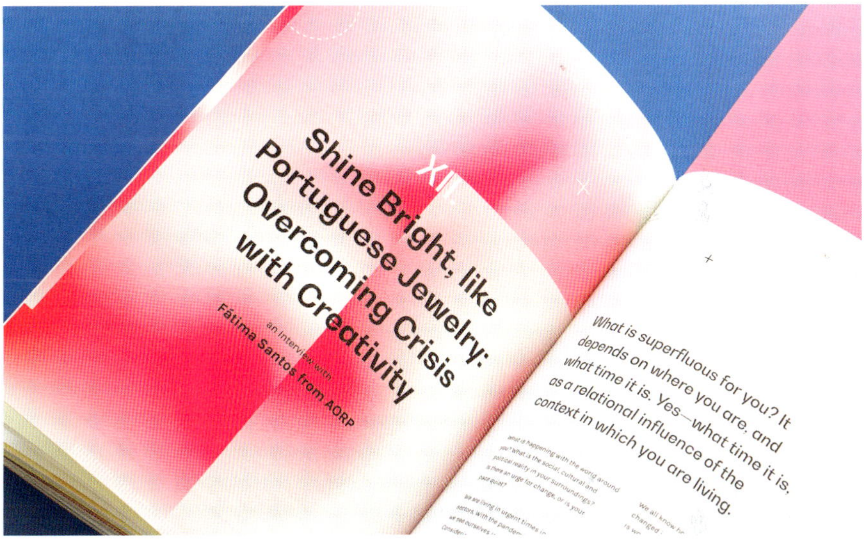

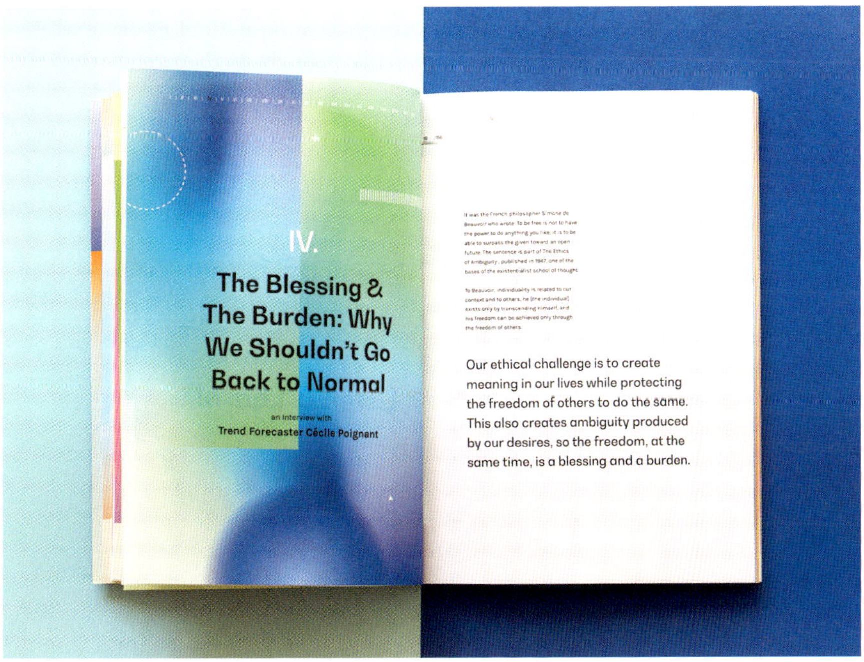

C85 · M30 · Y40 · K0
C80 · M0 · Y40 · K0
C75 · M0 · Y60 · K0

C50 · M0 · Y5 · K0
C15 · M0 · Y90 · K0

C0 · M95 · Y30 · K0
C0 · M55 · Y65 · K0
C5 · M55 · Y0 · K0

C25 · M35 · Y0 · K0
C0 · M20 · Y85 · K0

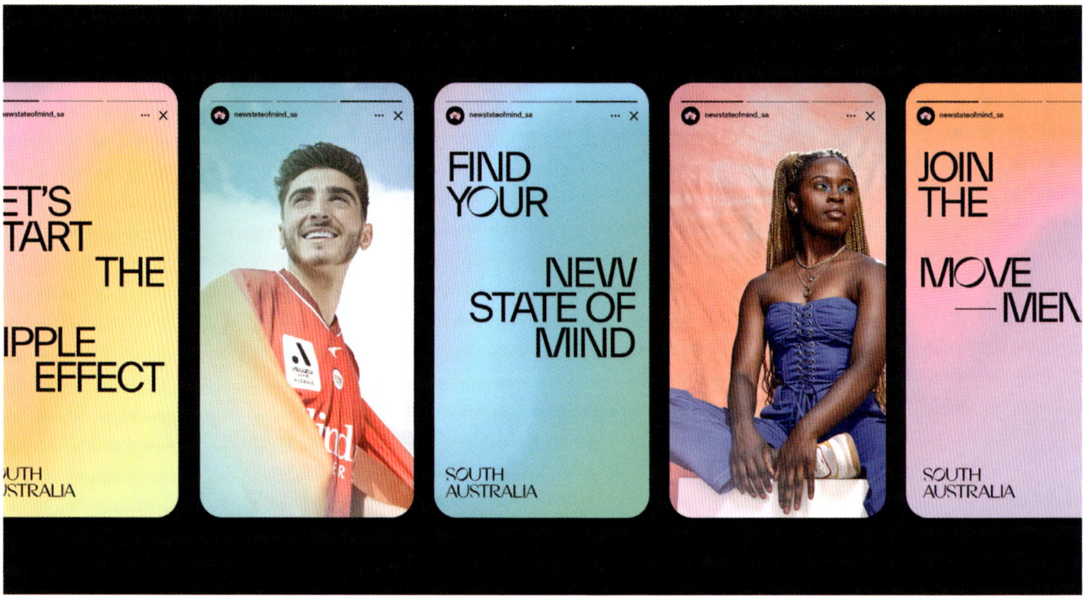

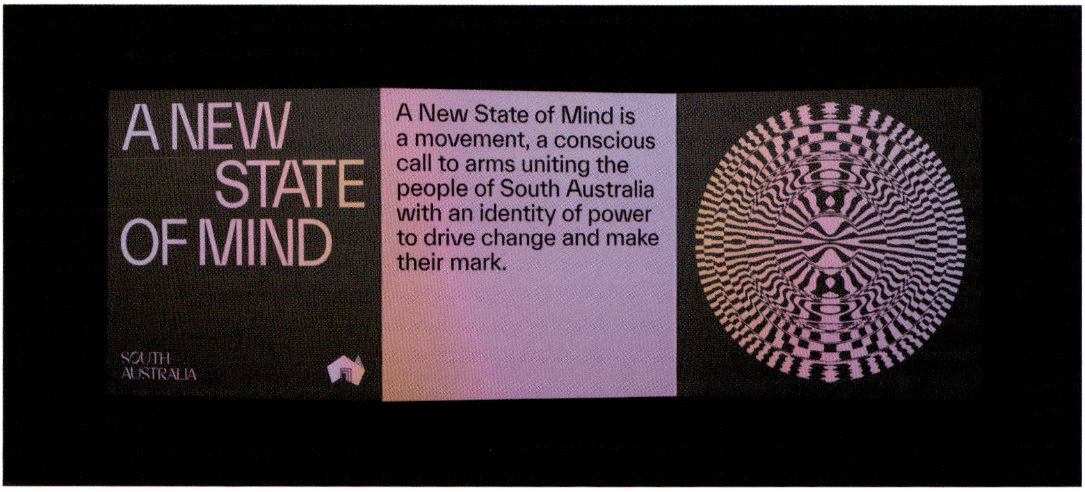

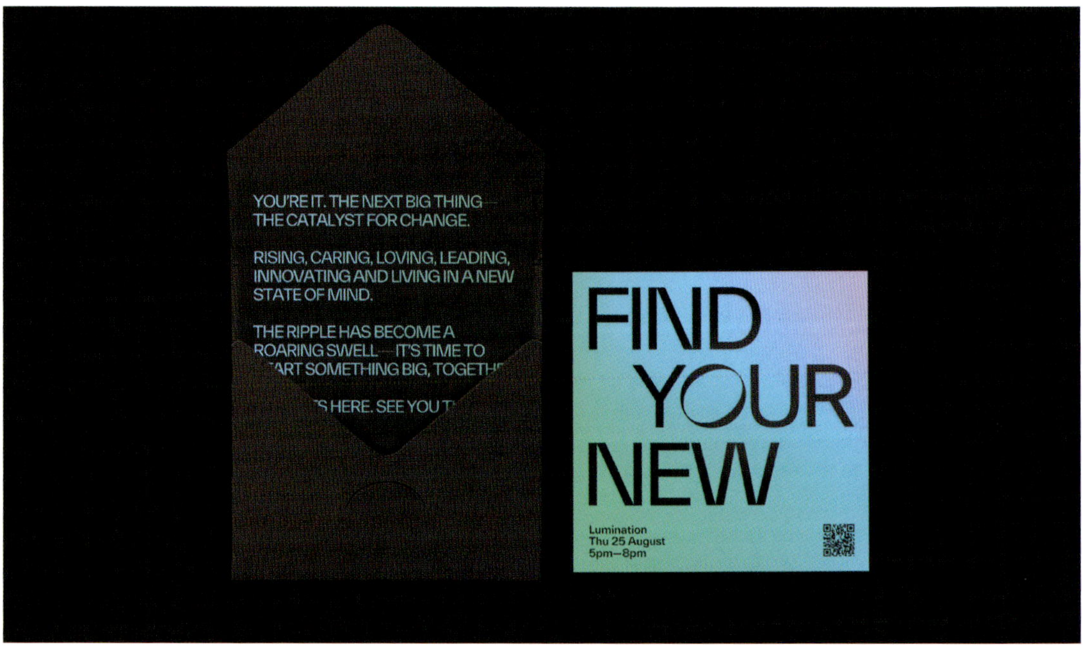

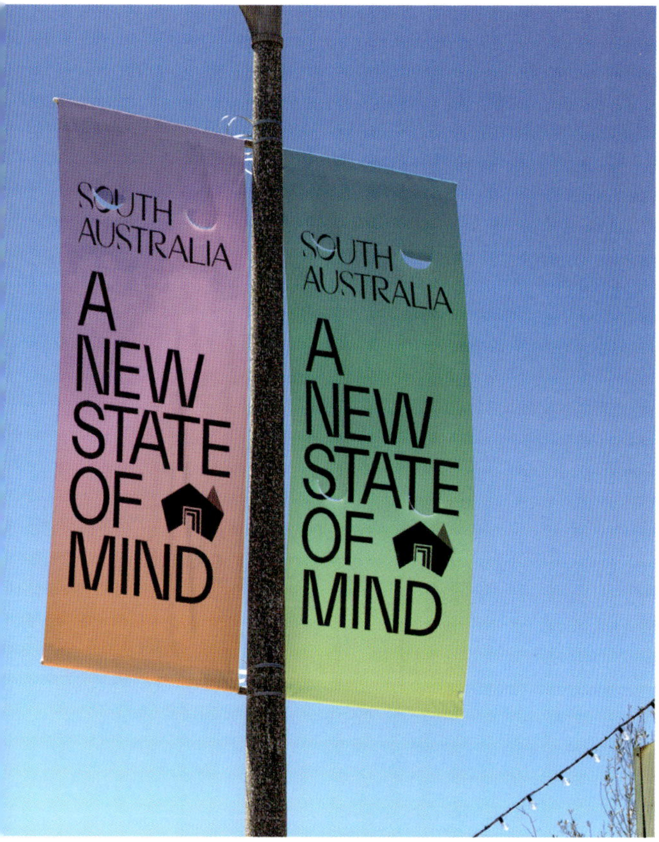

A NEW STATE OF MIND

To shed its "city of churches" image and appeal to young talent, South Australia's government initiated "A New State of Mind", a campaign showcasing the state's progressive, diverse, and innovative character.
Leading the campaign with a dynamic approach, "A New State of Mind" introduces a vibrant and modern visual identity for South Australia, featuring a bold colour palette, dynamic typography, and captivating design elements. This refreshing aesthetic reflects the campaign's deep purpose, sparking a generational shift and forging a compelling narrative for the state.

Senior Strategist
Will Fuller

Creative Director
Michael Gagliardi

Photographer
Josh Geelen &
Ryan Cantwell

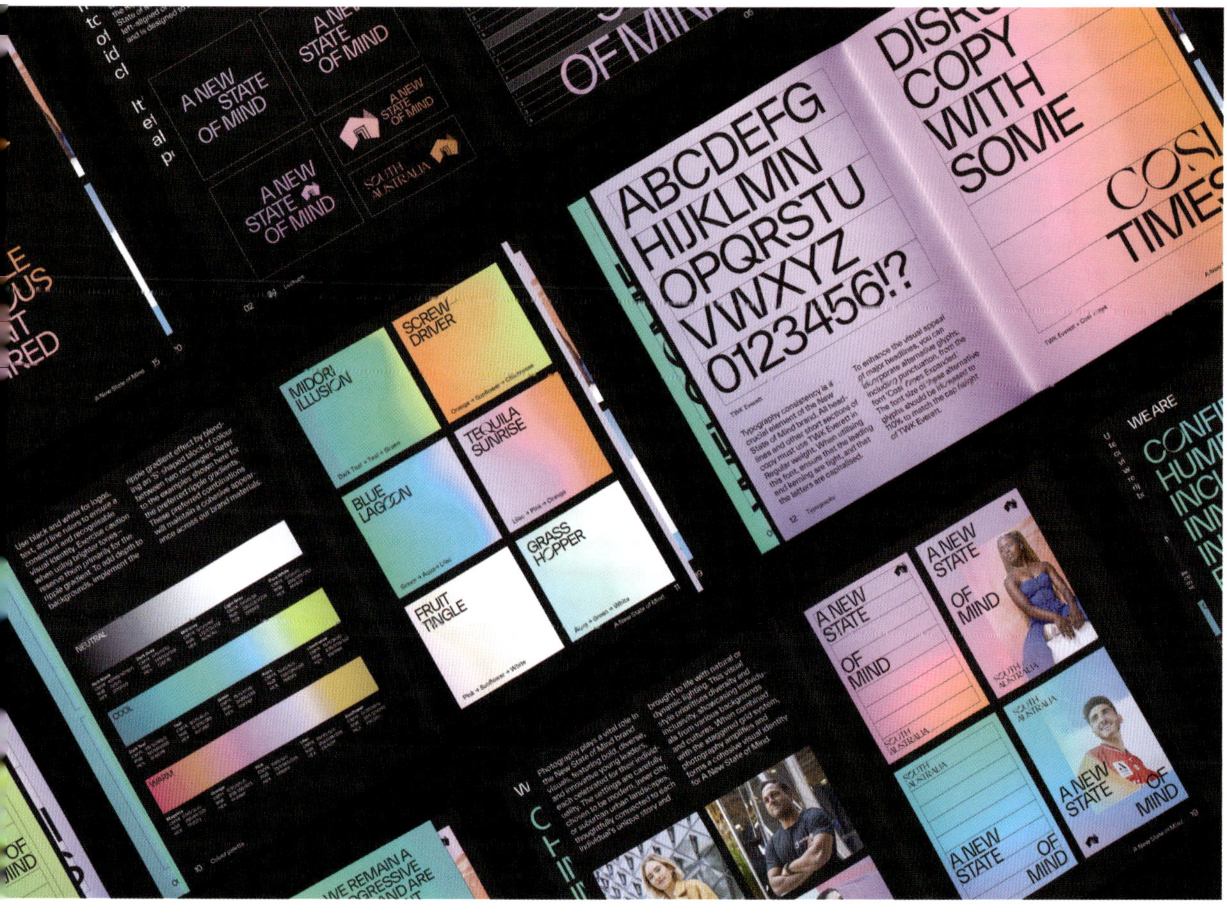

PANTONE 1787 C

PANTONE 1775 C

PANTONE 1215 C

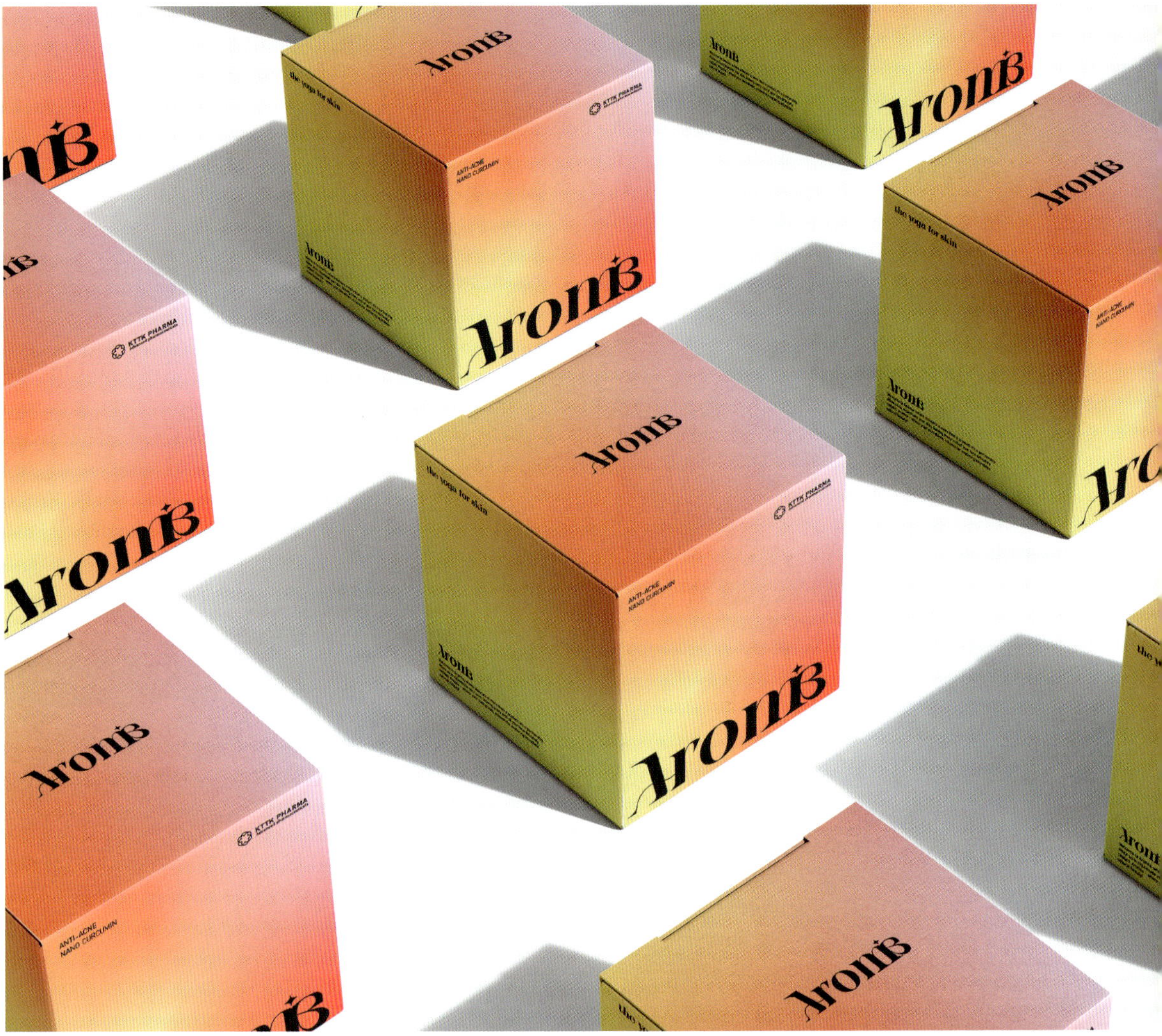

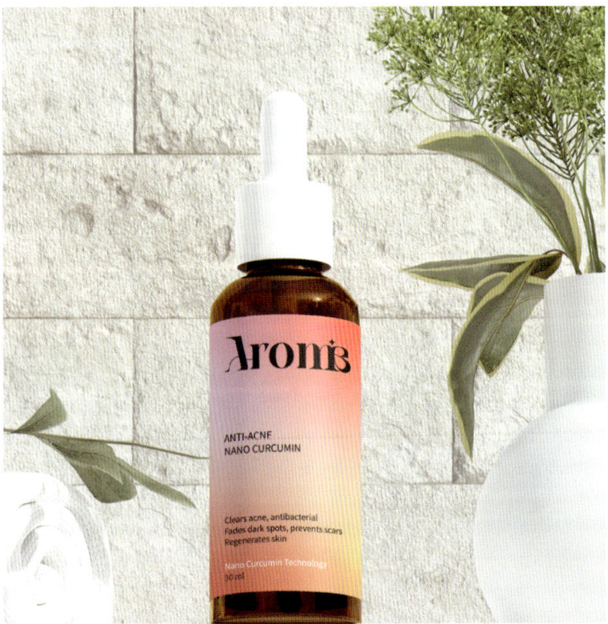

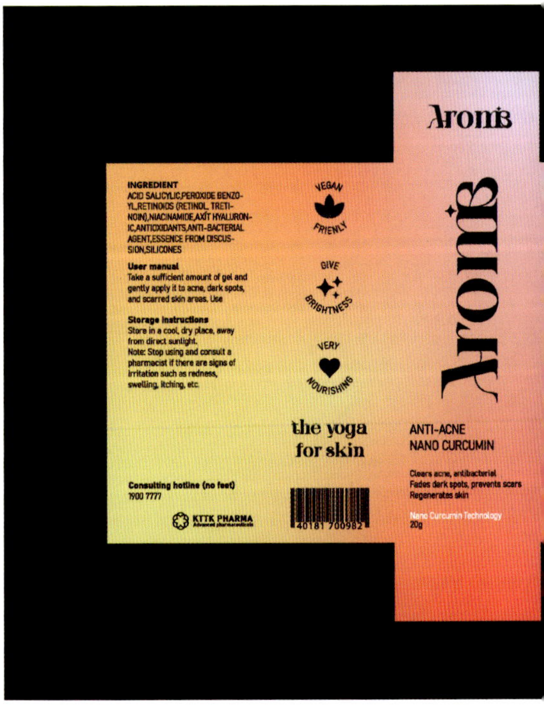

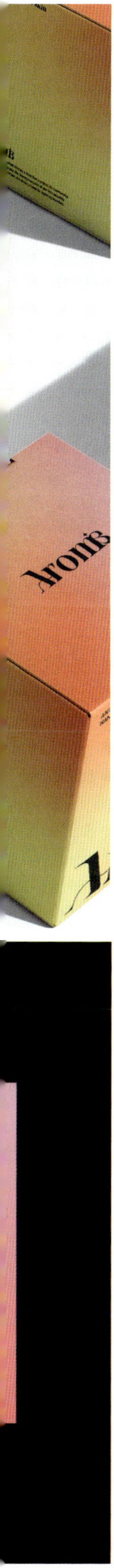

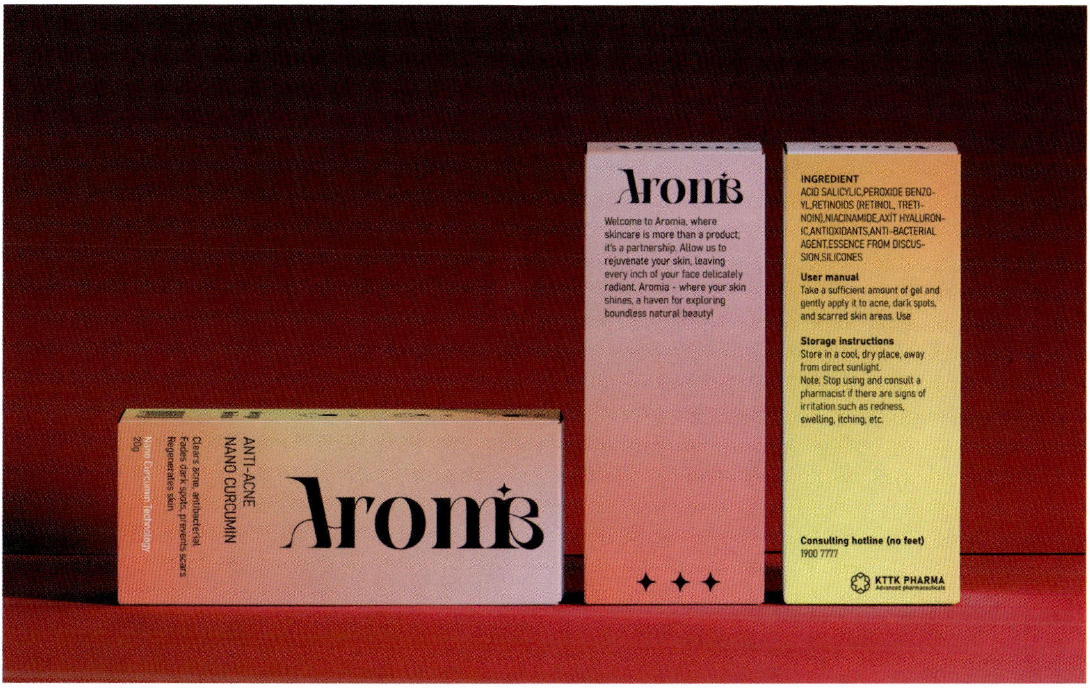

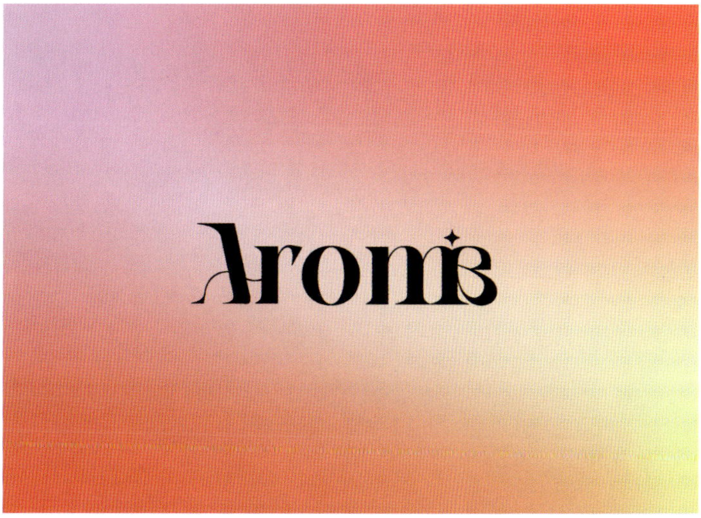

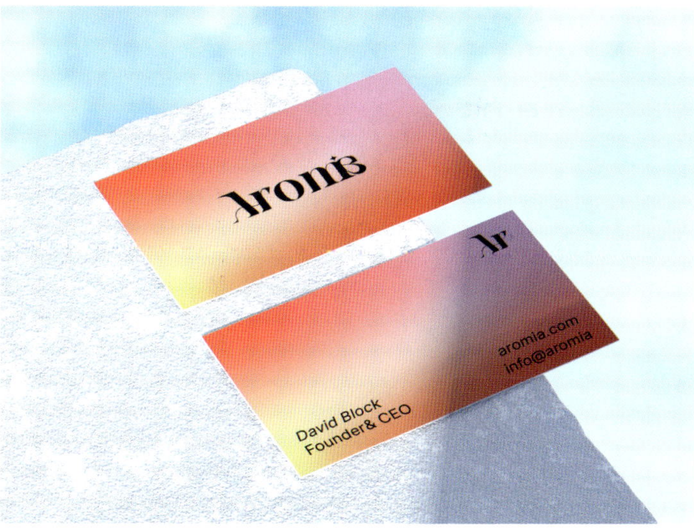

AROMIA

The packaging, with its simple design and sunset-inspired gradient colour, creates a striking and unique ease of use that distinguishes it from existing brands offering products on the market. The gradient colours are selected from the moment of dawn, from the gentleness of the gradually decreasing darkness to the warmth of the golden sunlight, creating a harmonious and charming combination.

Designer
Lực Dương

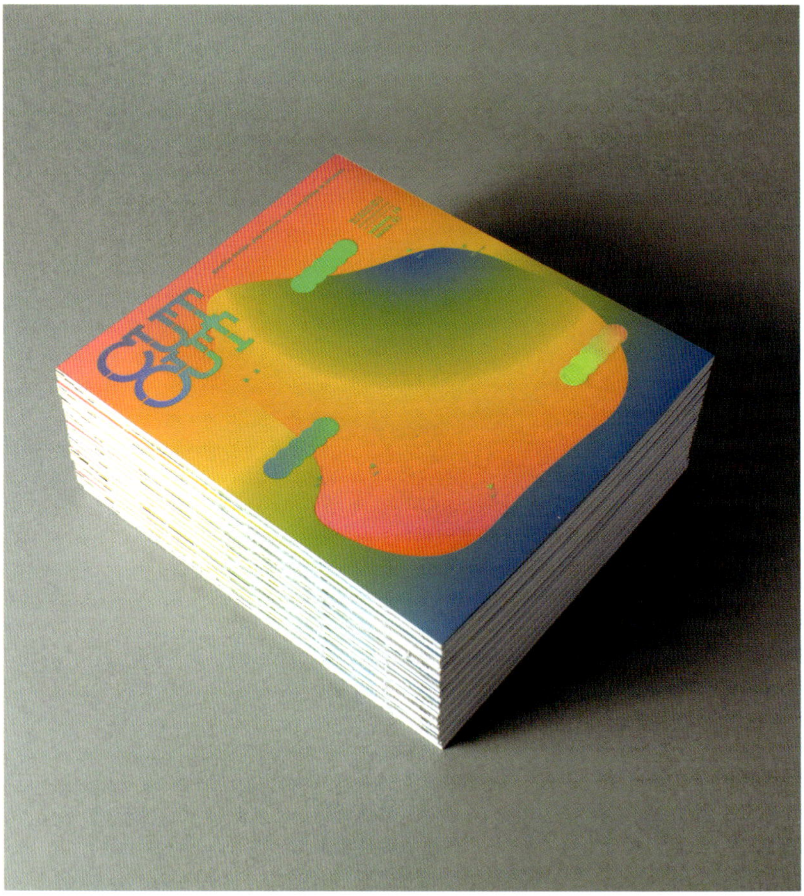

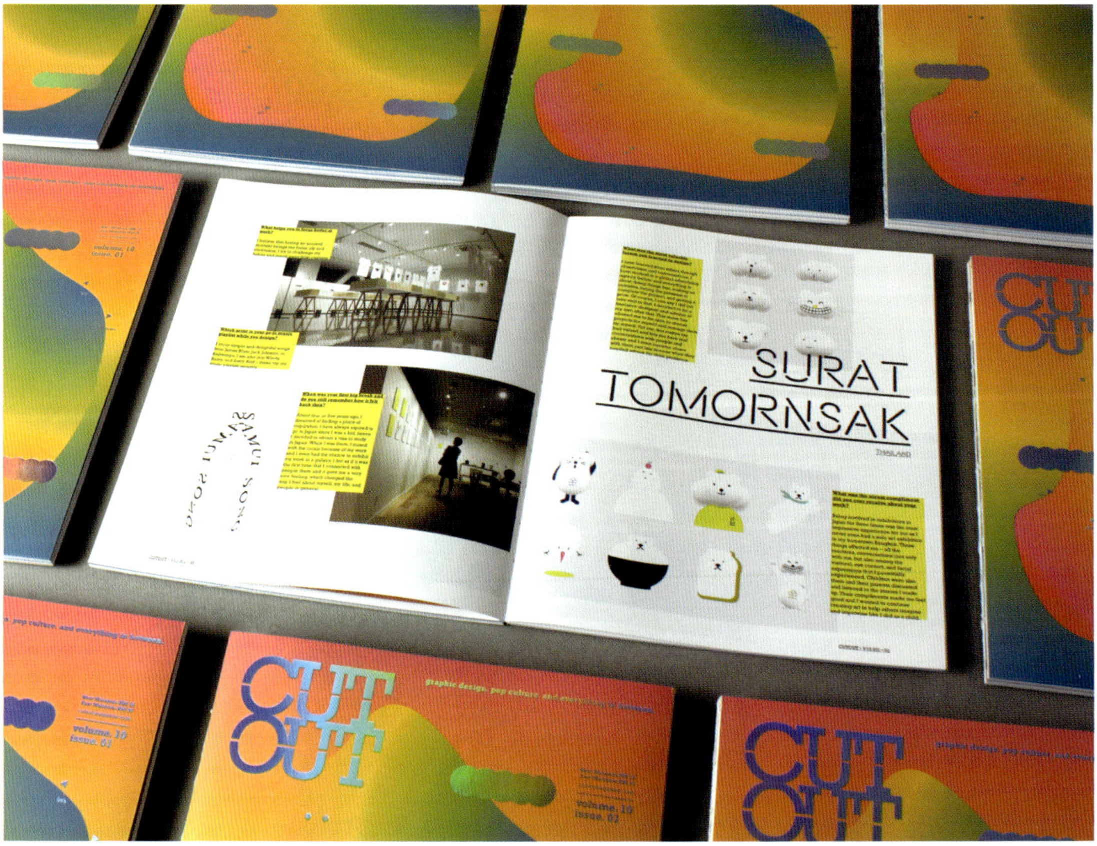

CUTOUT MAGAZINE ISSUE

Malaysia's prolonged lockdown due to COVID-19 spurred *Cutout*'s team to reimagine their approach. Their 26th issue, "Celebration," marks a departure from tradition, featuring pearl and rainbow foil stamping for a unique aesthetic. The exposed spine symbolizes resilience amidst change. The vibrant orange-green palette evokes celebration, while the 84-page spread exudes positivity.

Designer
Jay Lim

C0 · M75 · Y75 · K0

C0 · M40 · Y75 · K0

C0 · M10 · Y60 · K0

C50 · M0 · Y35 · K0

C90 · M20 · Y40 · K0

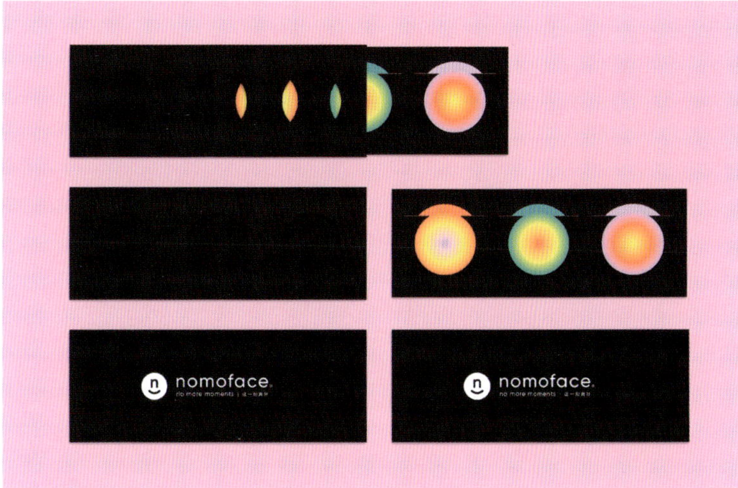

NOMOFACE

Nomoface is an offline physical space for children's photography, fashion styling and activity sharing. It is also a content platform that creates a community of experts to share knowledge and skills of children's growth, and provides in-depth experience activities for families related to sports, art, and travel.

Art Director
Qiongjie Yu

Designer & Type Designer
Xiaomei Liu

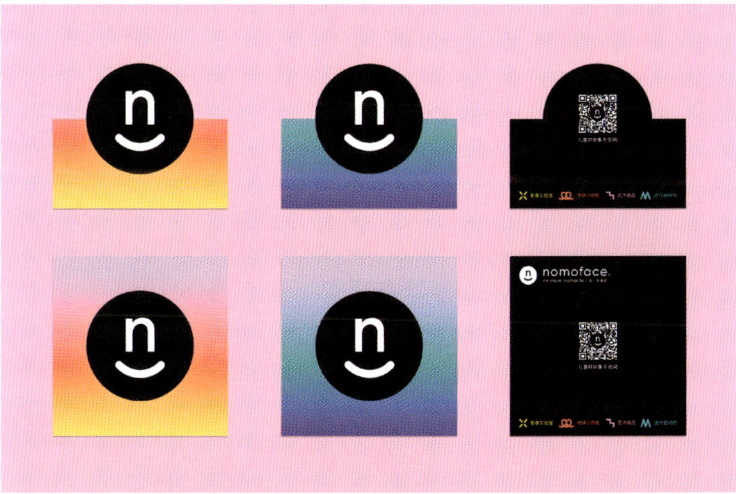

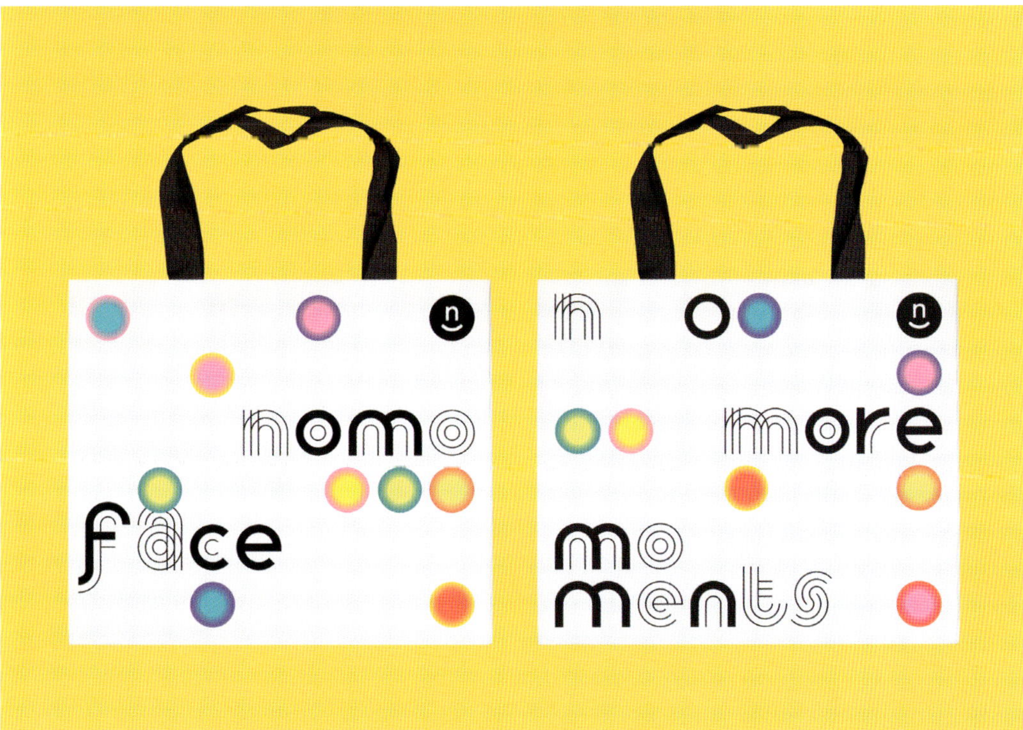

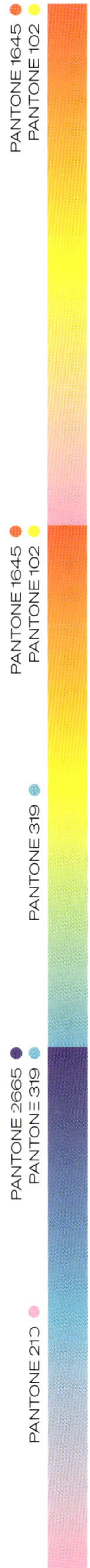

C49 · M25 · Y26 · K0
C40 · M55 · Y100 · K0
C87 · M57 · Y24 · K0

C68 · M58 · Y96 · K22
C88 · M69 · Y100 · K60

C31 · M28 · Y34 · K0
C29 · M77 · Y100 · K0
C54 · M54 · Y67 · K2

C49 · M25 · Y26 · K0
C87 · M57 · Y24 · K0
C93 · M66 · Y88 · K51

C70 · M100 · Y58 · K33
C30 · M70 · Y11 · K0

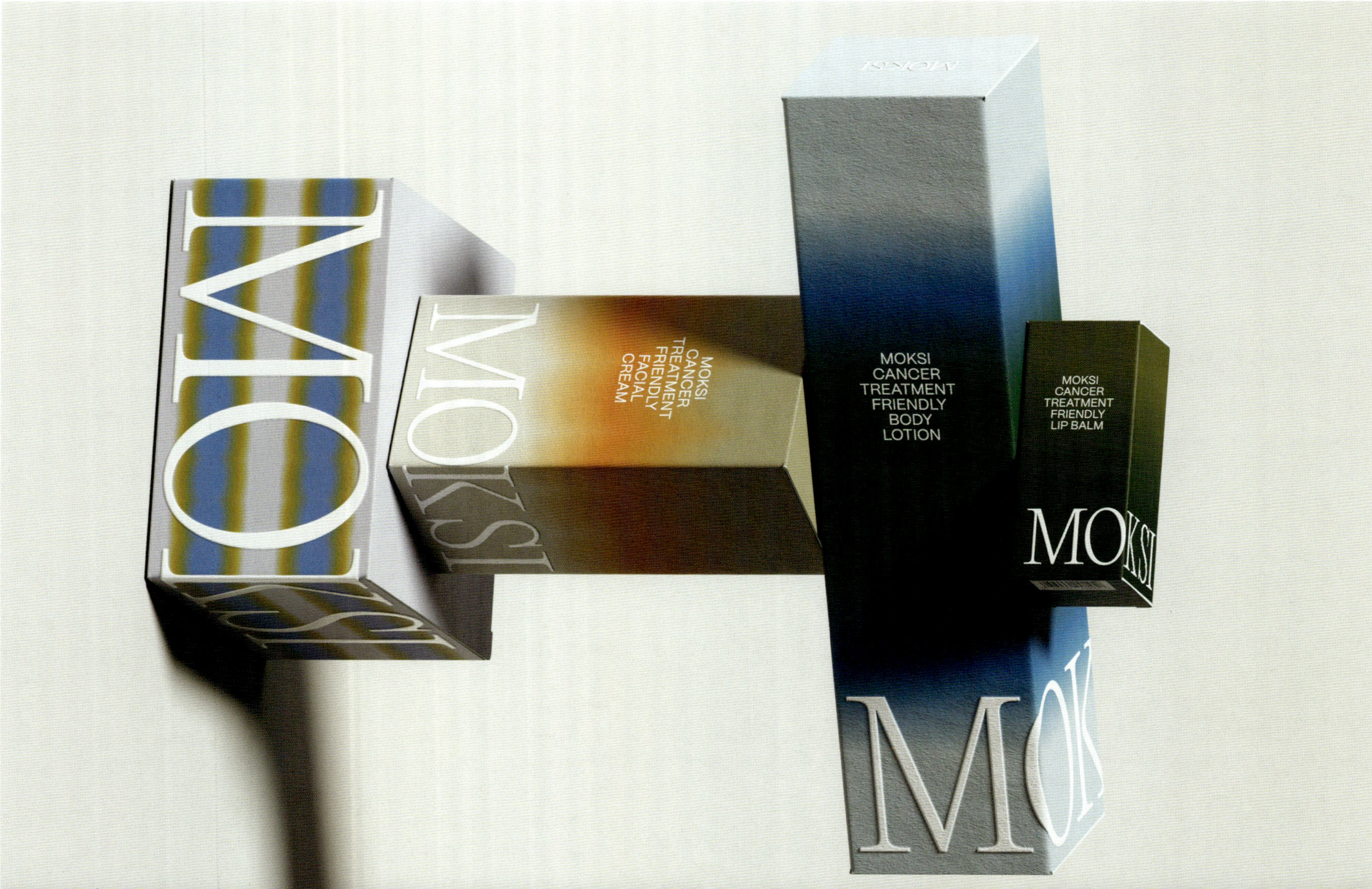

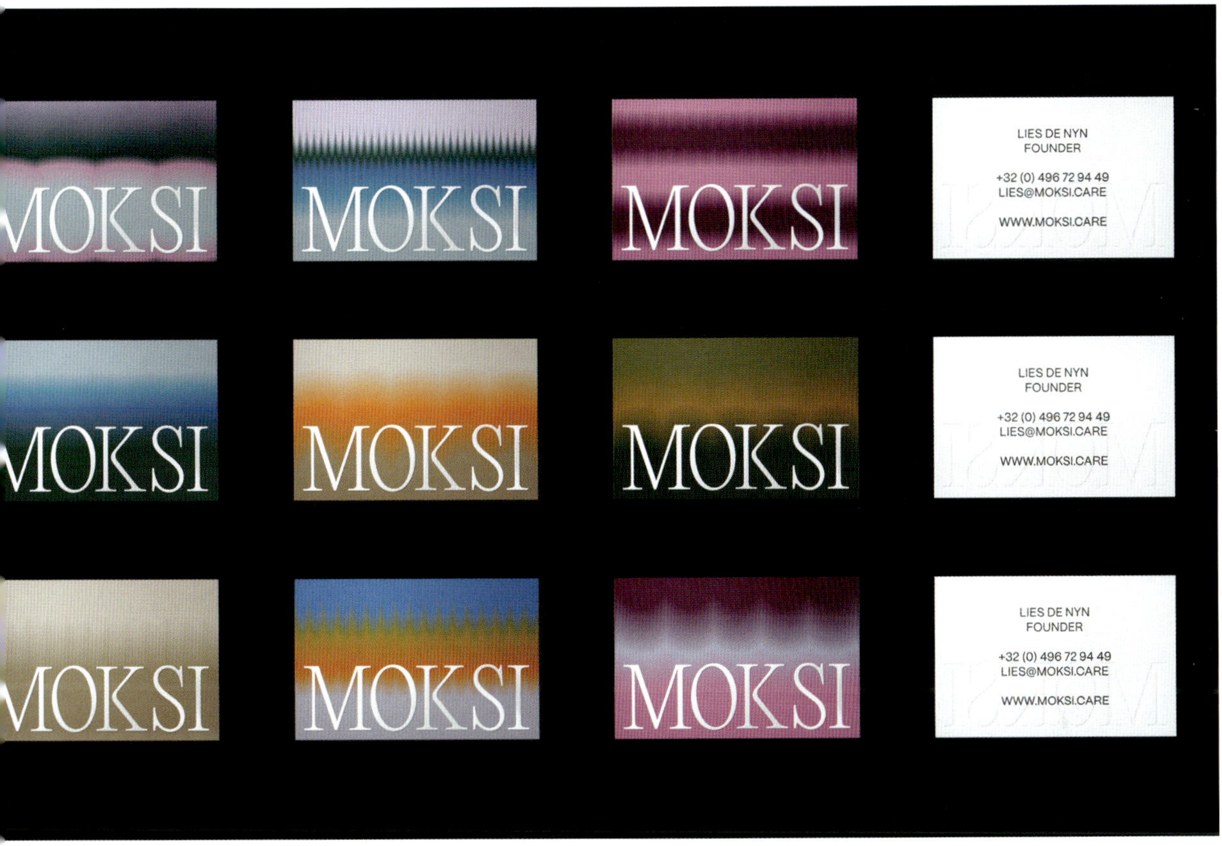

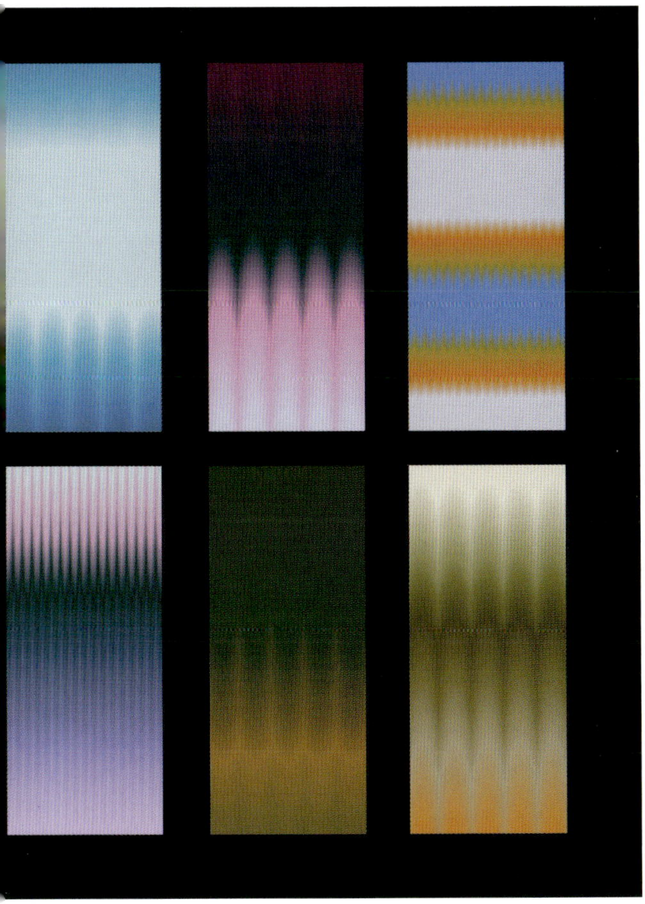

MOKSI

The collaboration with Lies began when the venture started. The name of the brand was originally *Moxie*, and was tweaked to *Moksi* for neutrality and impact, with 'K' being key in the logo design. The designers used fonts from Pangram Pangram, blending modern and classic serifs, with slight modifications to the 'K'. The colour palette is inspired by dawn sky gradients, representing optimism and new beginnings. Clean product design and unique shades for each product enhance user comprehension and differentiation. The gradient tones ensure shelf visibility.

Designer
Jeroen van Den Bogaert, James Kruger, Tarryn Blackwood, Marc Ferrer Vives & Stefanie Evenepoel

Design Studio
FCKLCK

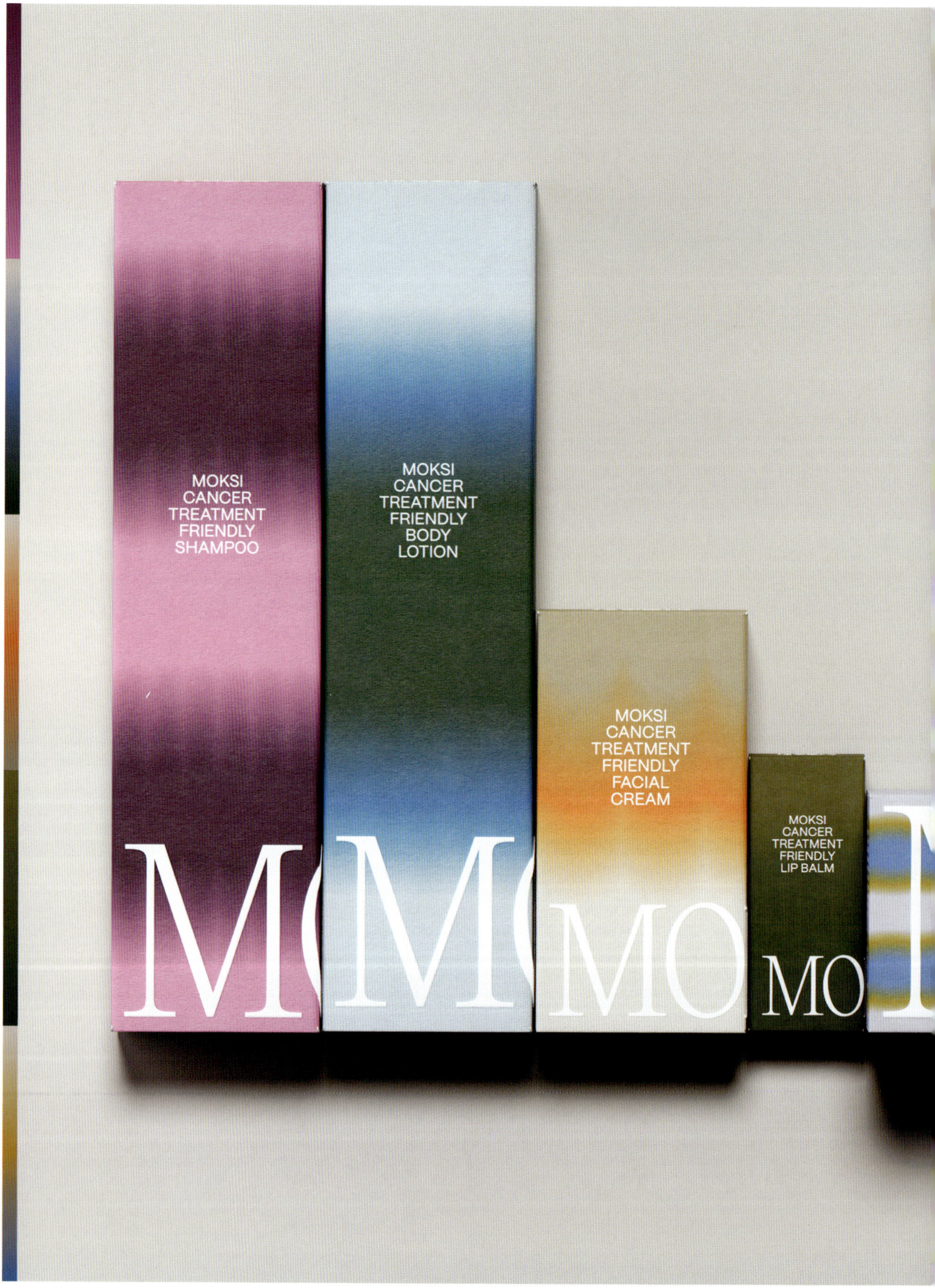
MOKSI
CANCER
TREATMENT
FRIENDLY
SHAMPOO
MOKSI
CANCER
TREATMENT
FRIENDLY
BODY
LOTION
MOKSI
CANCER
TREATMENT
FRIENDLY
FACIAL
CREAM
MOKSI
CANCER
TREATMENT
FRIENDLY
LIP BALM

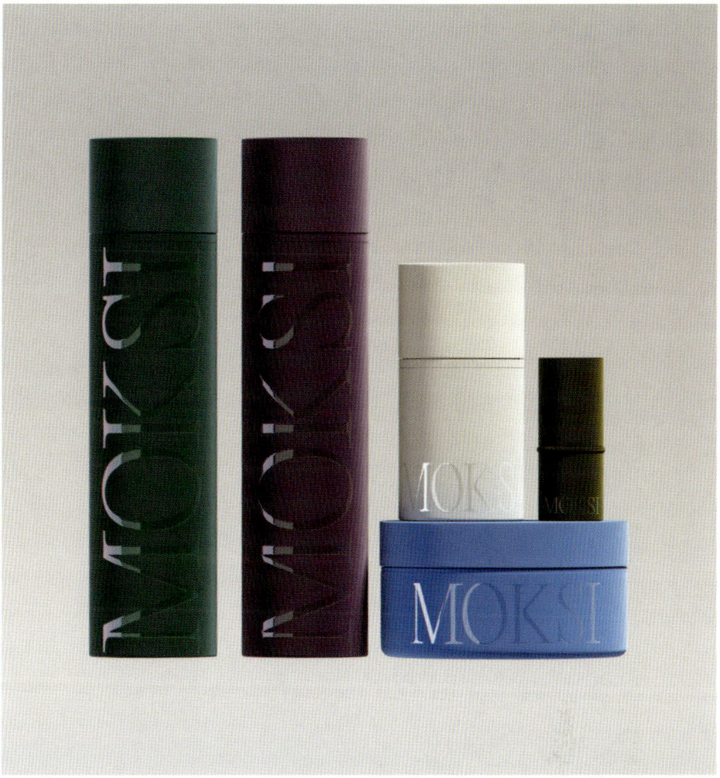
MOKSI
MOKSI
MOKSI
MOKSI

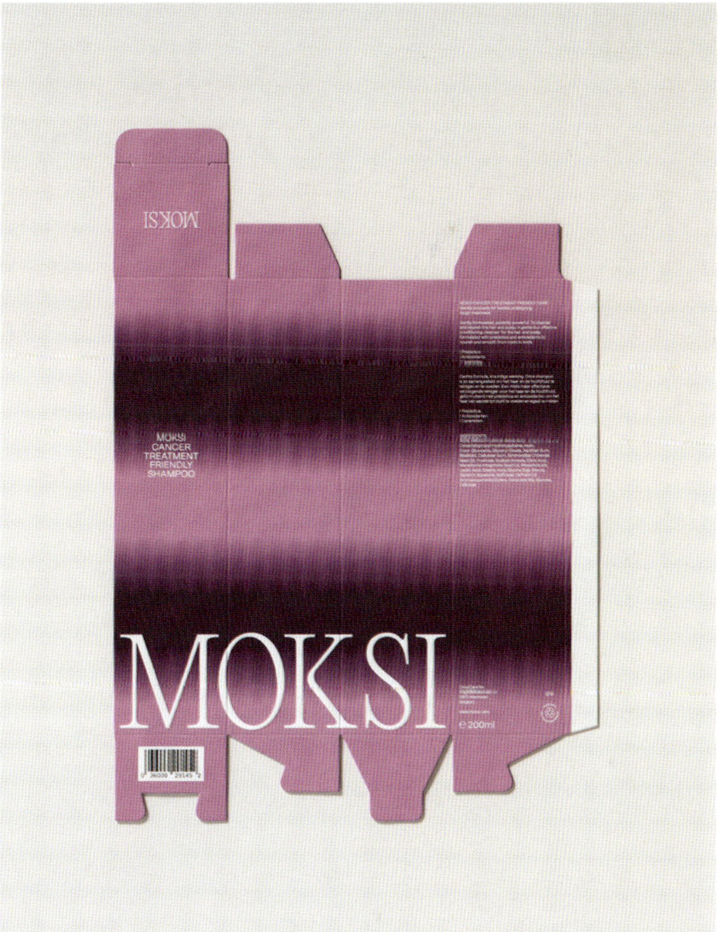
MOKSI
MOKSI
CANCER
TREATMENT
FRIENDLY
SHAMPOO
MOKSI
℮ 200ml

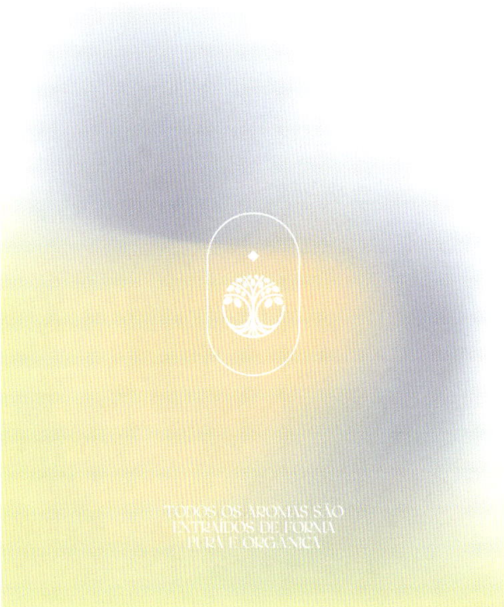

DI GIANNA

Di Gianna is a healthy and natural alternative to assist in addressing daily challenges. The brand believes that the compounds in its products can improve both personal well-being and the ambiance of one's home, leading to the slogan "Feel better, every day." Light, simple, accessible, and 100% natural, the entire visual identity was designed with these attributes in mind, aiming to create a warm brand using various skin tones, complemented by the natural hues of the scents. These elements blend seamlessly to forge a unique personality for this brand.

Naming & Strategist
Alex Monteiro

Designer
Alex Monteiro
& Max Silva

3D Artist
Gonçalo Alves

Client
Di Gianna

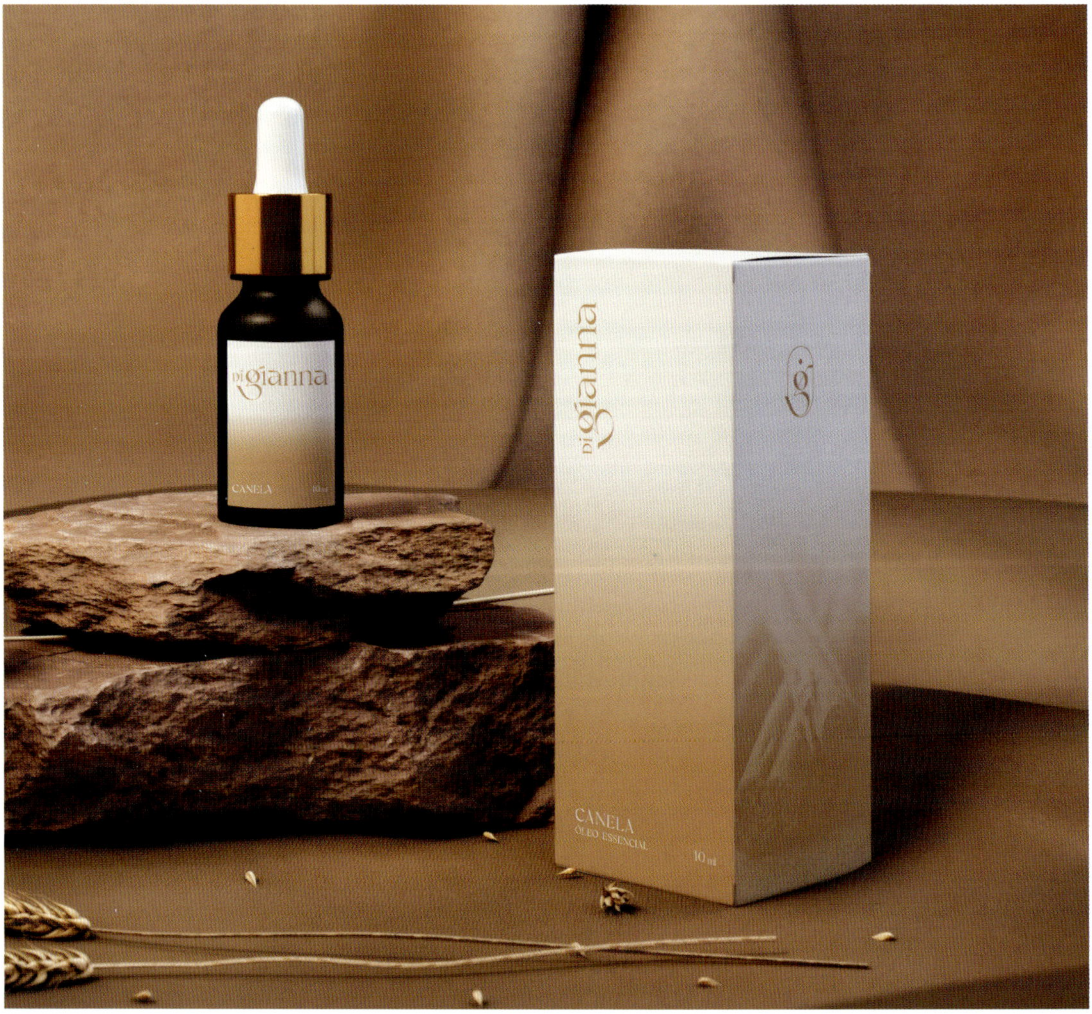

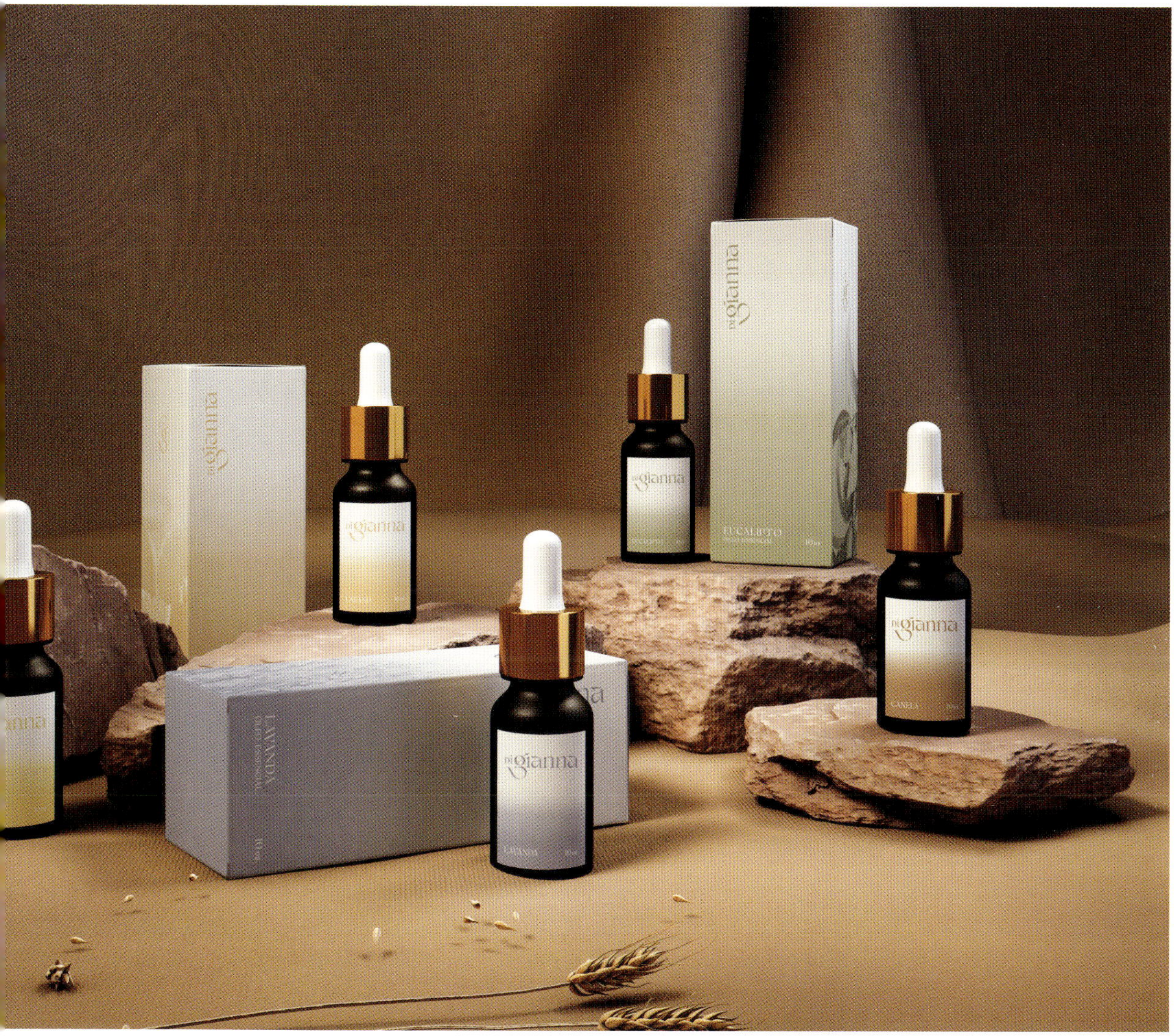
gianna
EUCALIPTO
LAVANDA
CANELA

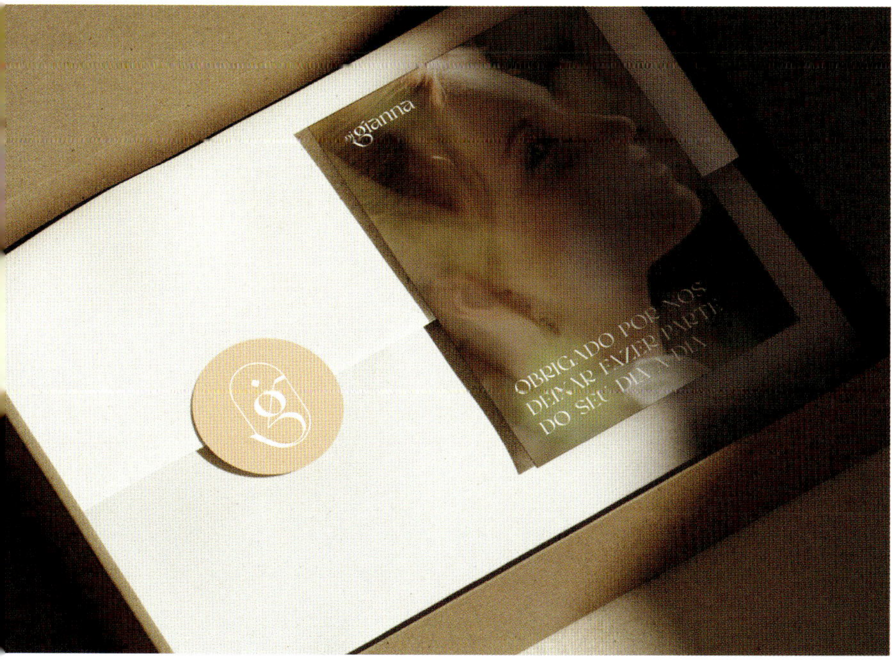
gianna
OBRIGADO POR NOS

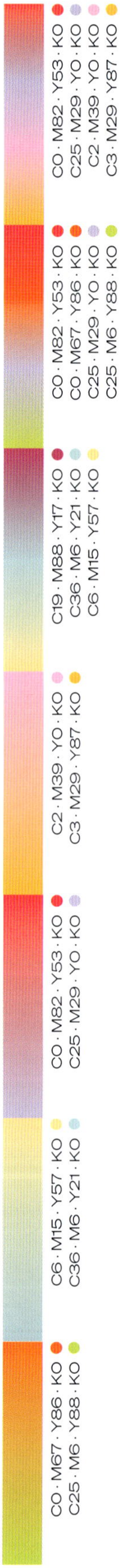

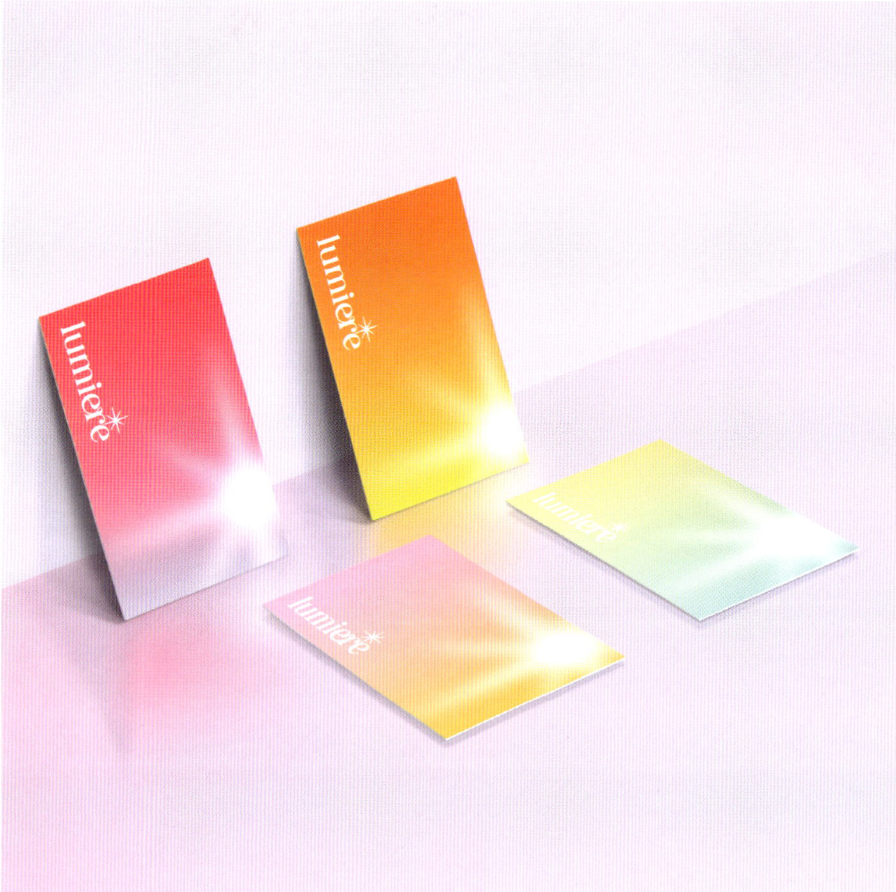

LUMIERE PERFUME

Lumiere perfume is an amber floral fragrance designed specifically for women, embodying elegance and sophistication. The design elements are inspired by the delicate beauty of flowers and the warm, enchanting colours of a sunset, presented in a captivating gradient. For this project, the designer meticulously designed both the box and the label, ensuring that every detail reflects the luxurious and alluring nature of *Lumiere.* The packaging aims to enhance the sensory experience, making the fragrance not just a scent, but a visual and tactile delight as well.

Designer
Huang Waki

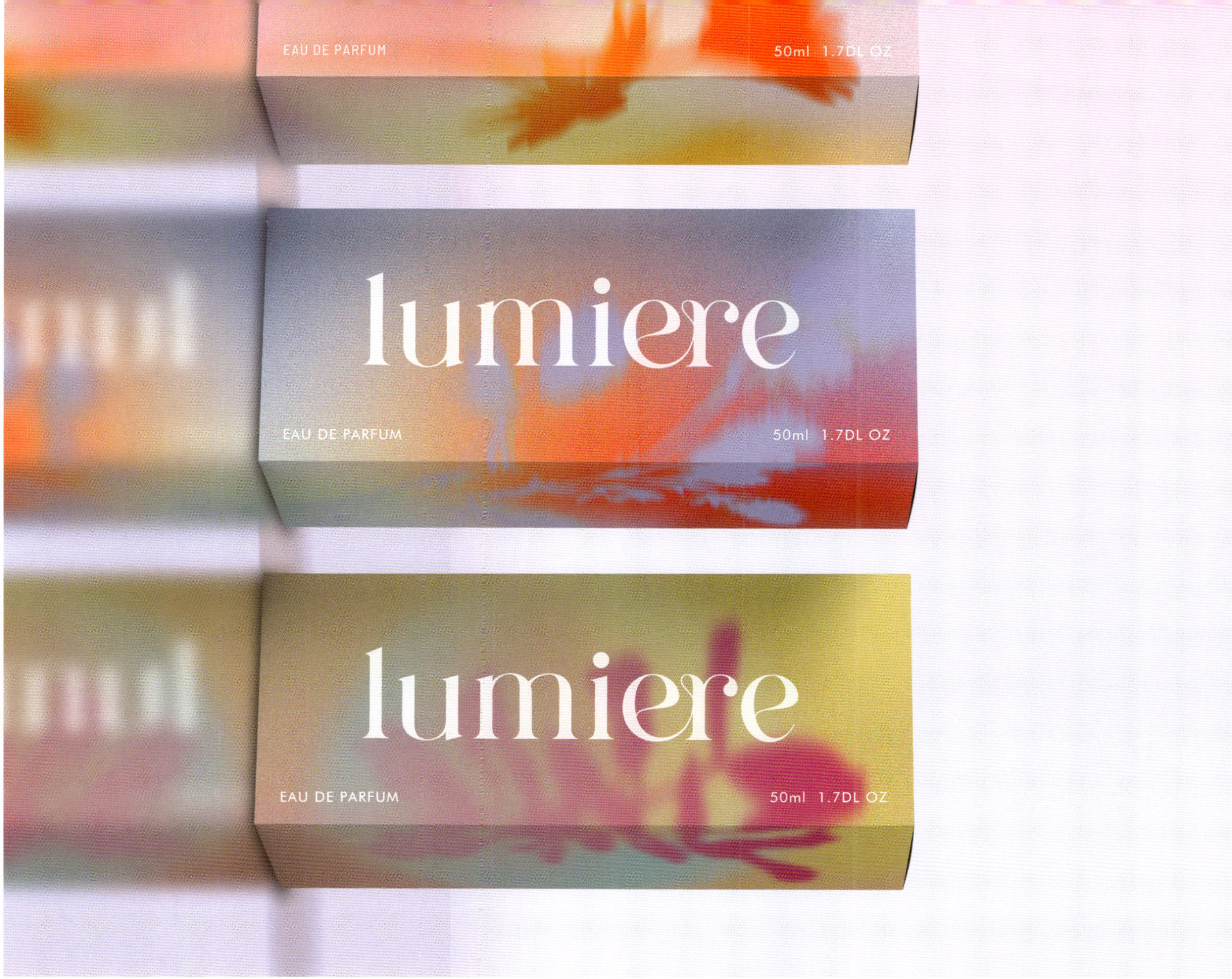
EAU DE PARFUM
50ml 1.7DL OZ
lumiere
EAU DE PARFUM
50ml 1.7DL OZ
lumiere
EAU DE PARFUM
50ml 1.7DL OZ

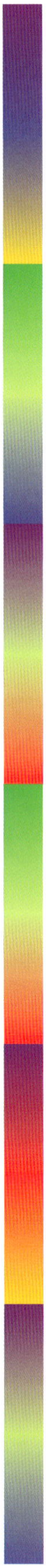

C55 · M80 · Y0 · K0
C76 · M52 · Y0 · K0
C6 · M18 · Y100 · K0

C78 · M0 · Y90 · K0
C27 · M0 · Y70 · K0
C76 · M52 · Y0 · K0

C55 · M80 · Y0 · K0
C27 · M0 · Y70 · K0
C0 · M84 · Y58 · K0

C78 · M0 · Y90 · K0
C27 · M0 · Y70 · K0
C0 · M84 · Y58 · K0

C55 · M80 · Y0 · K0
C0 · M84 · Y58 · K0
C6 · M18 · Y100 · K0

C55 · M80 · Y0 · K0
C27 · M0 · Y70 · K0
C76 · M52 · Y0 · K0

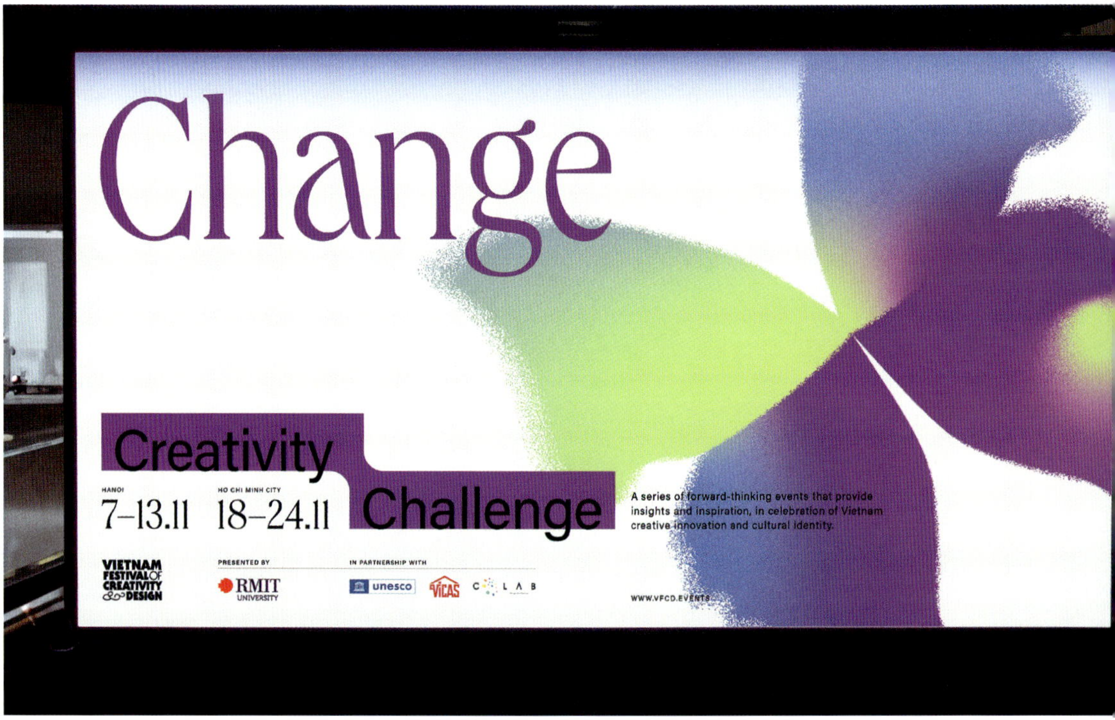

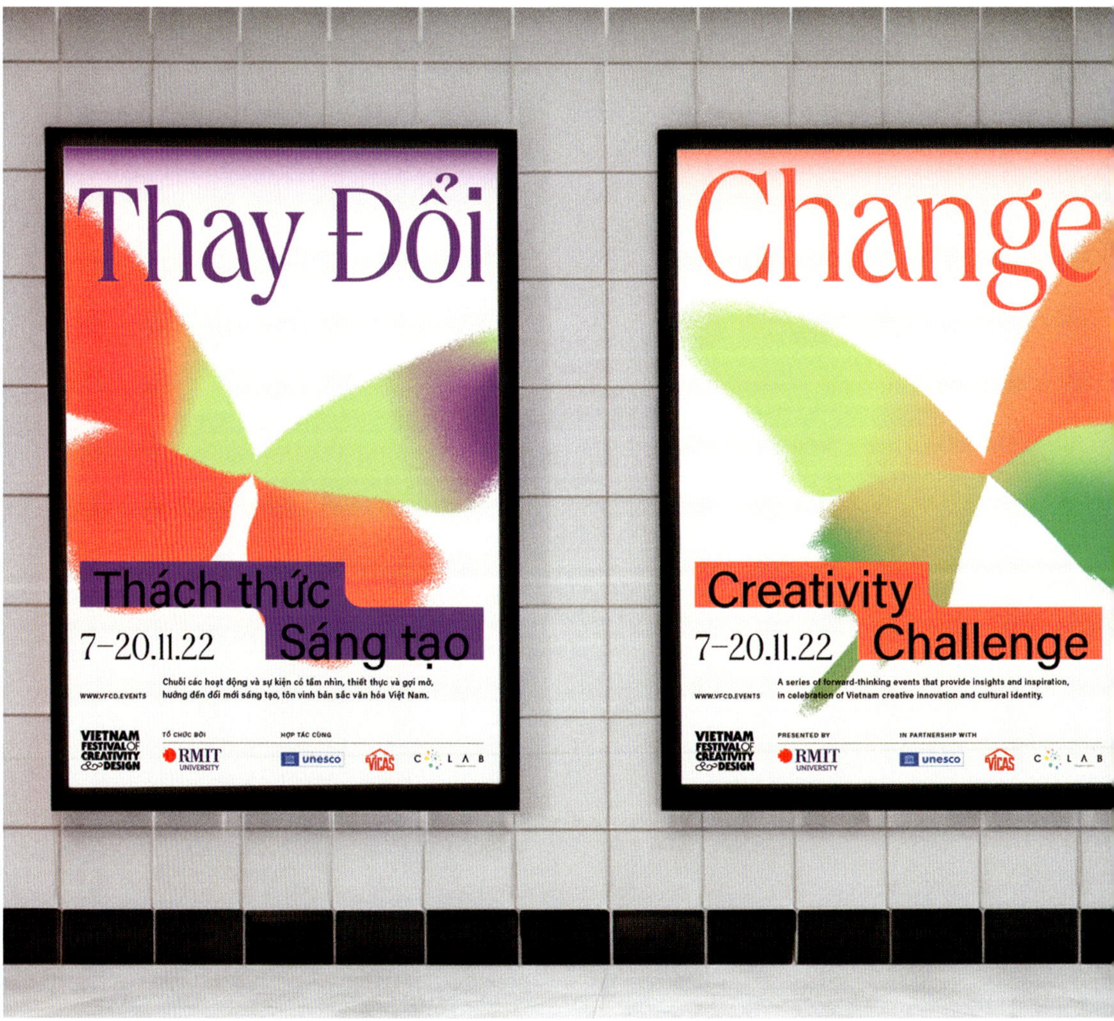

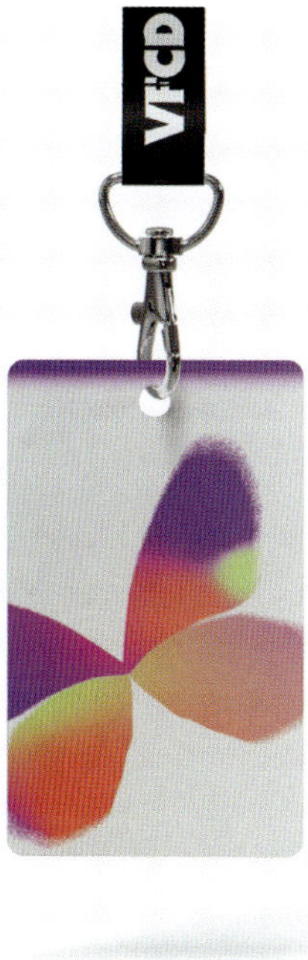

VIETNAM FESTIVAL OF CREATIVITY & DESIGN

The "Vietnam Festival of Creativity & Design (VFCD)" returned for 2022 with the theme "Change: Creativity Challenge." Behalf Studio, as the design partner, interpreted the theme "Change" through the visual metaphor of the butterfly. Embodying change through its morphology, the creature adjusts its shapes, sizes, and colours in perfect harmony with nature, illustrating coexistence with the natural world. The designer utilized a generative engine to showcase the butterfly metaphor's mutations, integrating natural models with abstract colour patterns.

Brand Identity
Behalf Studio

Creative Director
Giang Nguyen

Designer
Minh Nguyen, Anh Nguyen & Chau Nguyen

Creative Coder
Minh Nguyen

Illustrator
Phong Pham

Project Manager
Lam Nong

Producer
Dung Nguyen

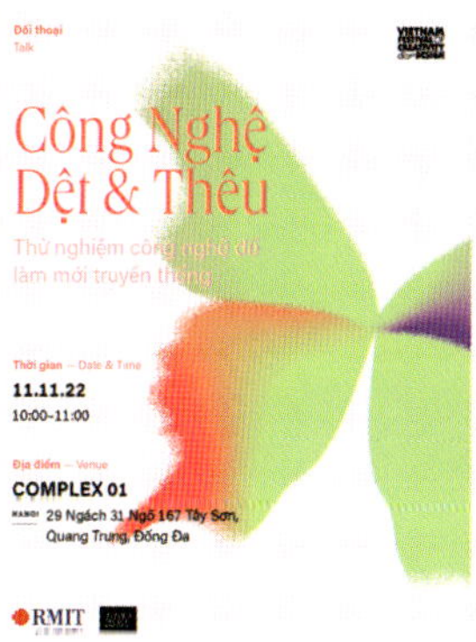

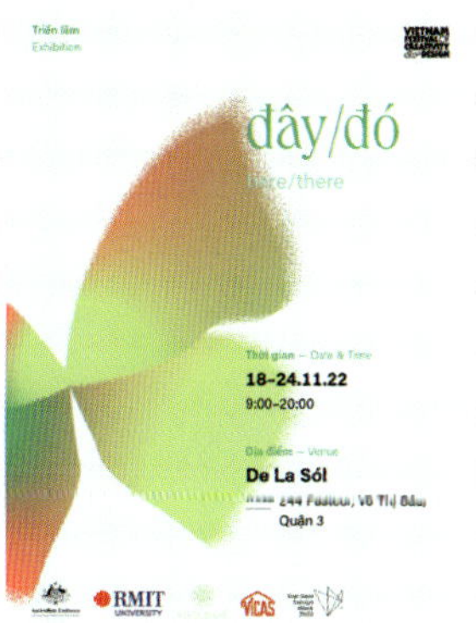

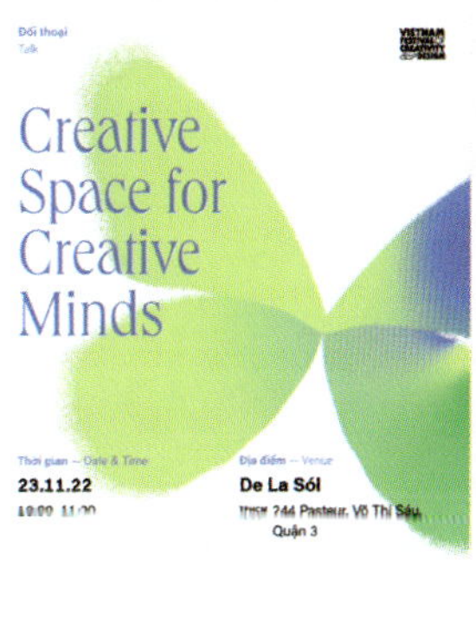

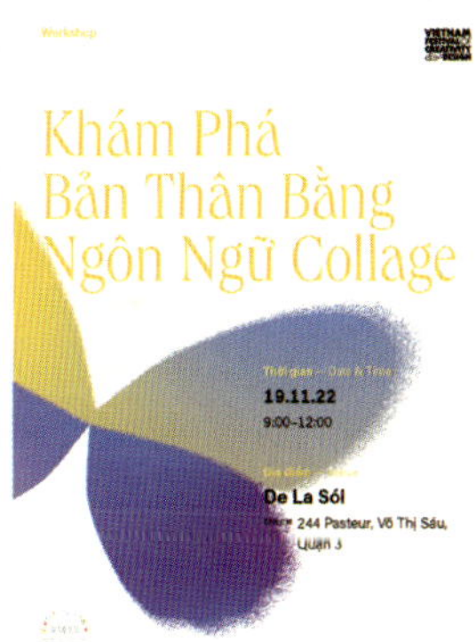

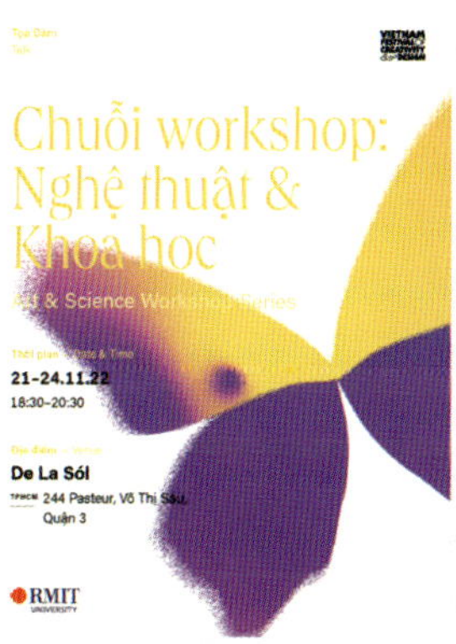

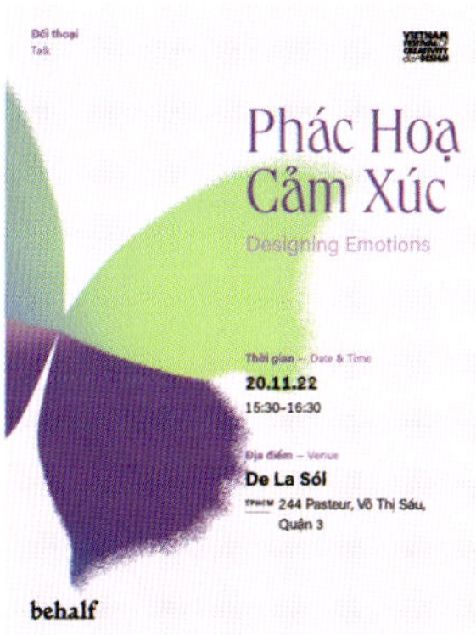

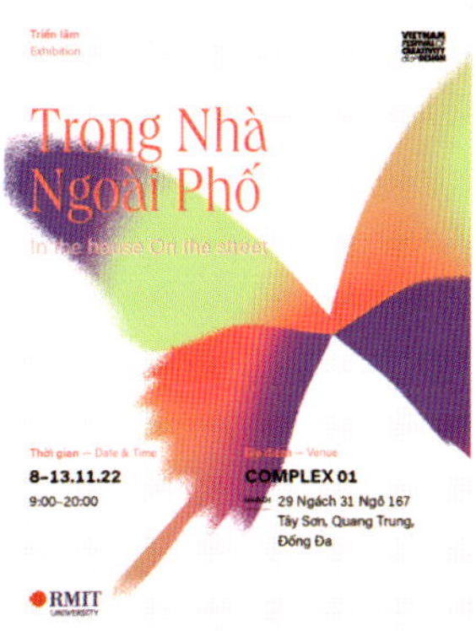

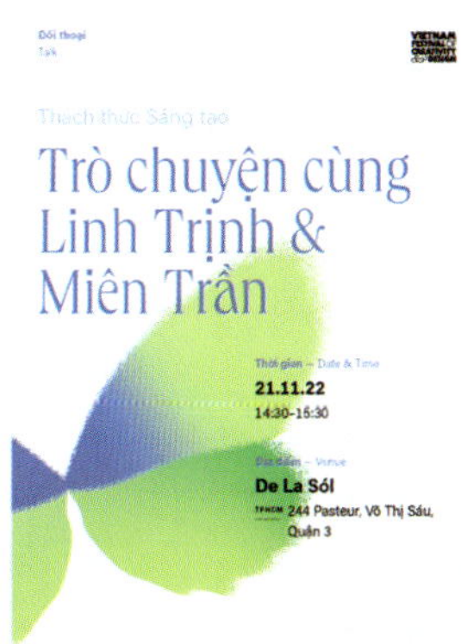

C14 · M7 · Y2 · K0
C42 · M20 · Y0 · K0
C44 · M2 · Y23 · K0

C22 · M2 · Y0 · K0
C15 · M40 · Y0 · K0
C0 · M57 · Y0 · K0

C2 · M24 · Y0 · K0
C38 · M0 · Y71 · K0
C40 · M20 · Y0 · K0

C38 · M3 · Y0 · K0
C39 · M0 · Y84 · K0
C64 · M0 · Y33 · K0

C3 · M17 · Y0 · K0
C0 · M49 · Y54 · K0
C42 · M0 · Y100 · K0

C7 · M13 · Y52 · K0
C36 · M14 · Y0 · K0
C56 · M0 · Y51 · K0

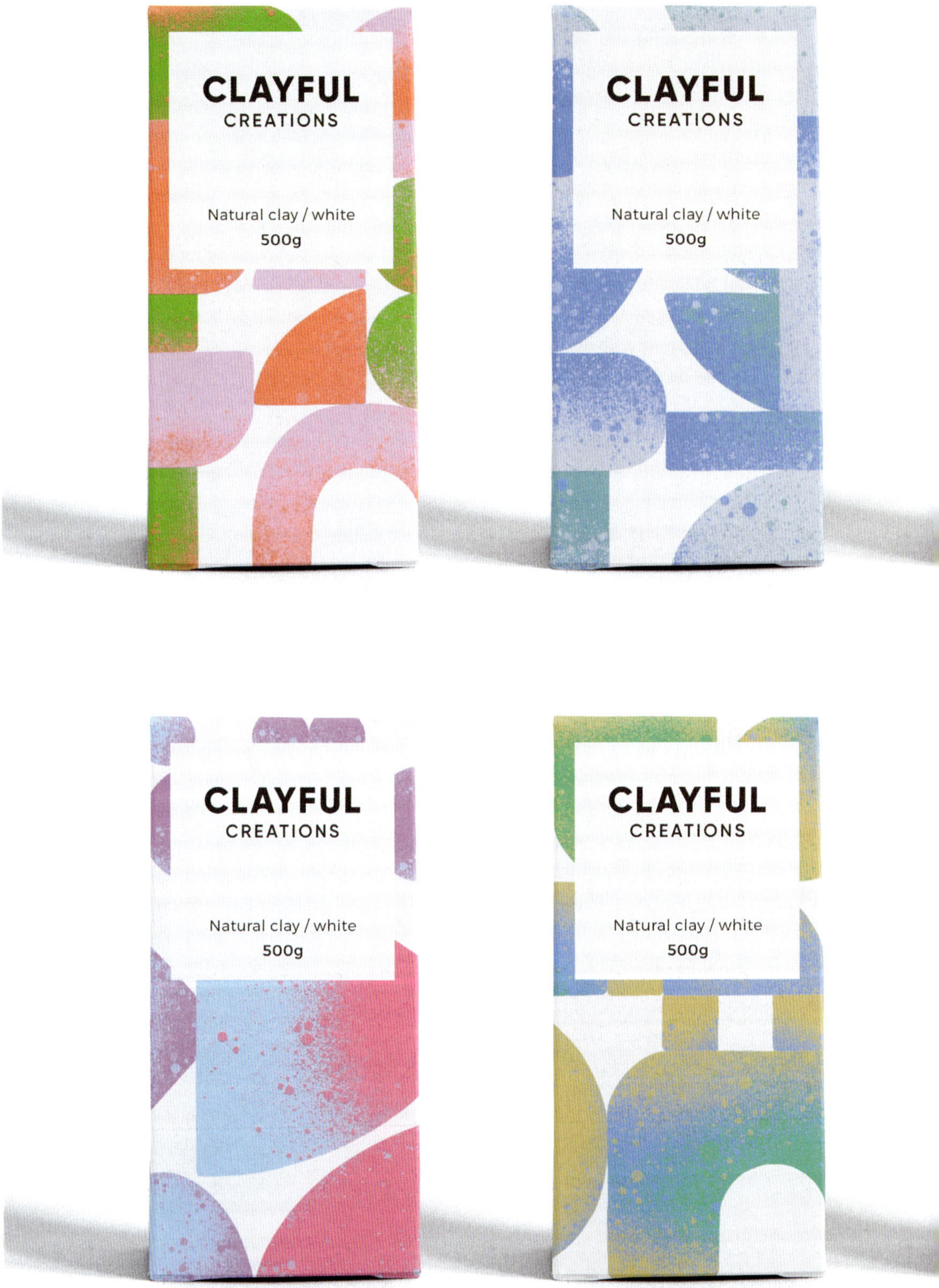

CLAYFUL CREATIONS

Concept packaging for *Clayful Creations* pottery studio. The goal was to create hand-crafted patterns for clay packaging, conveying a modern approach to pottery making.

Illustrator & Designer
Elmira Gokoryan

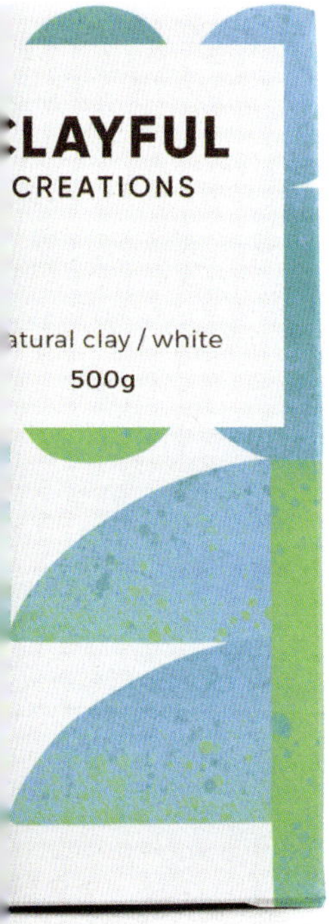

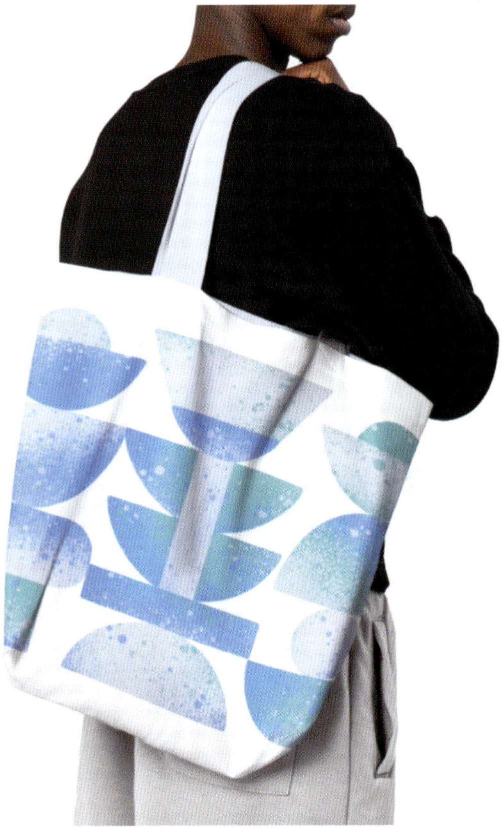

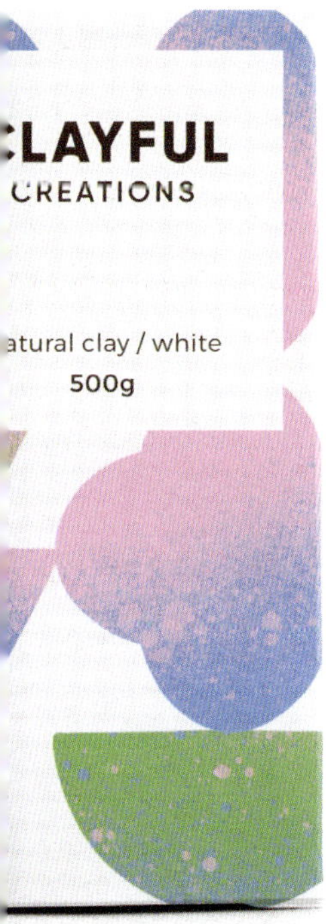

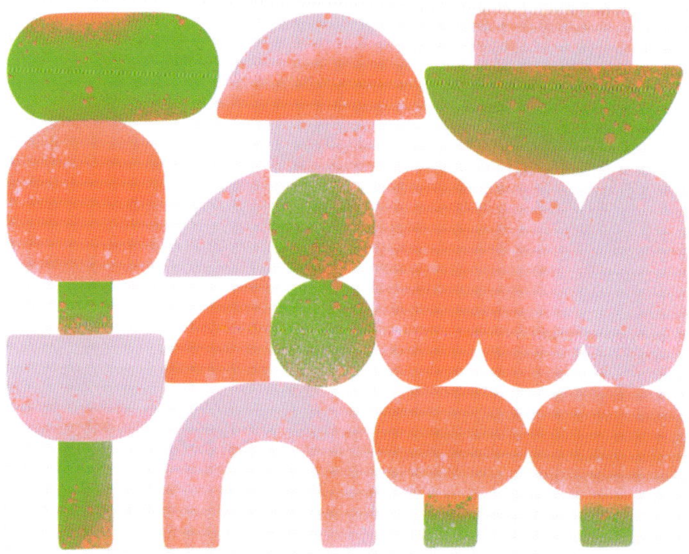

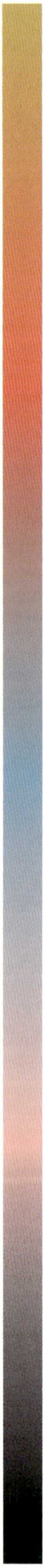

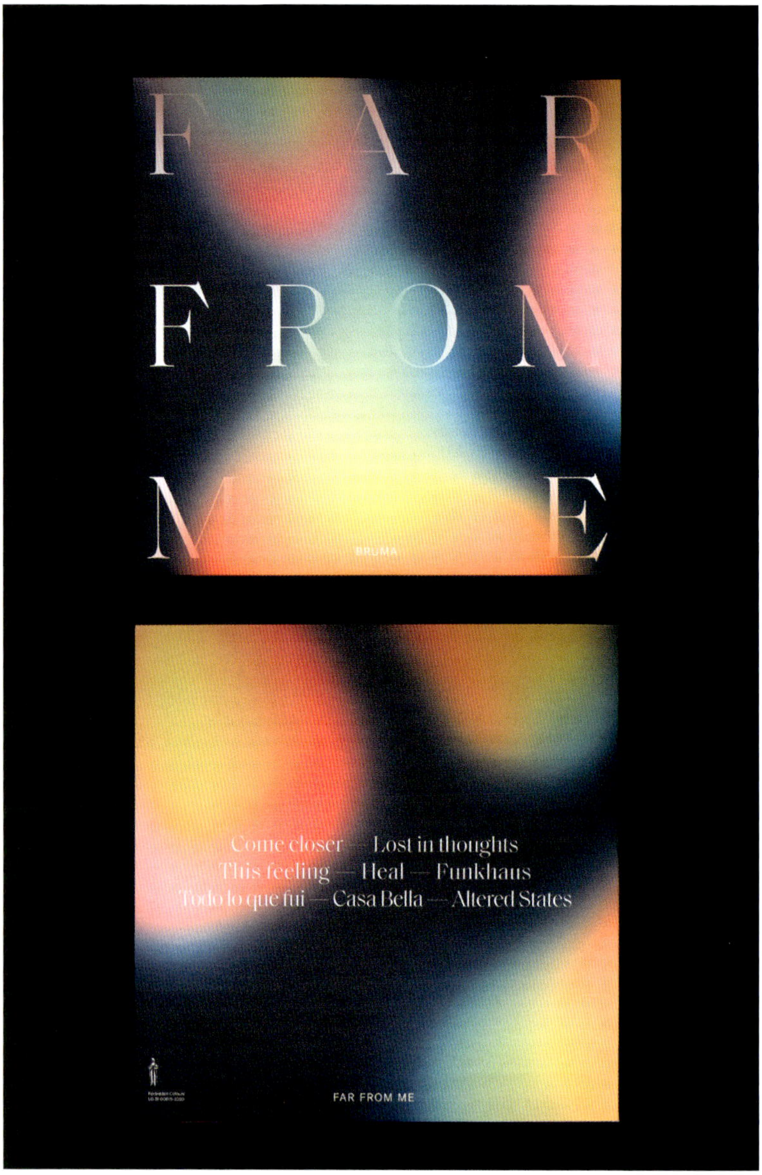

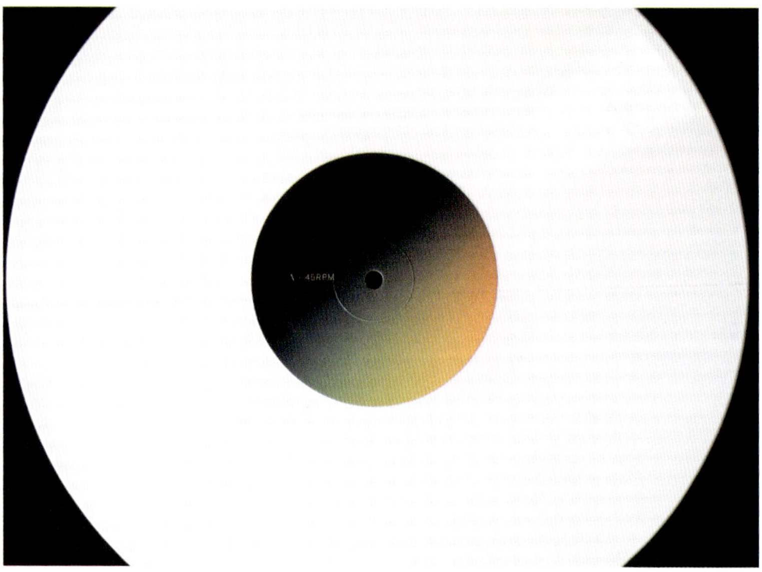

BRUMA: *FAR FROM ME* ARTWORK

The studio was commissioned by Madrid-based electronic artist Bruma to art direct and design his first studio album *Far From Me*. The artwork is based on blurry gradients inspired by a Finnish scientific study that correlates body temperature with different types of emotions, where scientists worked to induce a range of emotions by exposing more than 700 participants to a variety of videos and stories. Then, using pictures of human bodies, people were asked to map out areas that felt different after viewing each piece of material. The researchers were surprised to discover that all the participants held incredibly similar answers, even across different cultures.

Creative Direction & Design Studio
Rebeka Arce

Photography
Rebeka Arce Studio

Client
Forbidden Colours Record Label, Bruma

PANTONE 2089 C

PANTONE 2736 C

PANTONE 298 C

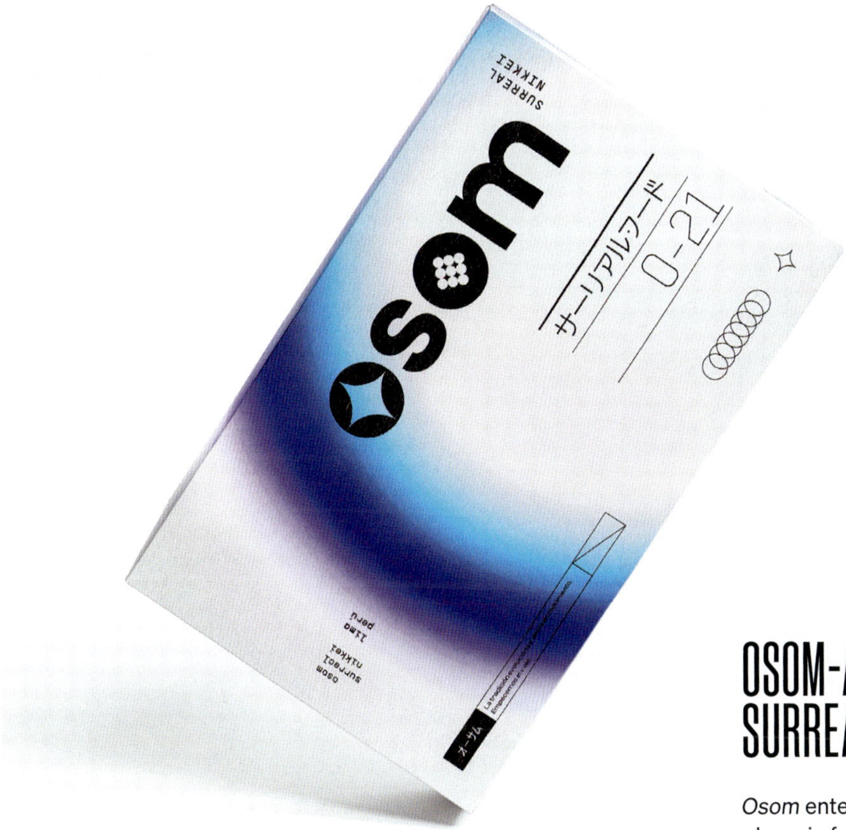

OSOM–A GUIDE TO SURREAL JAPAN

Osom enters as a new player in food delivery services with a fresh way of understanding Japanese and Nikkei cuisine. For the visual identity, the designers were inspired by the eclectic side of Japan and its city lights. As a team, they dreamt of traveling to this imaginary place. Elements such as plane tickets, airport flipboard fonts, and a gradient palette made them daydream of what it would be like to eat out in the streets of Tokyo from home.

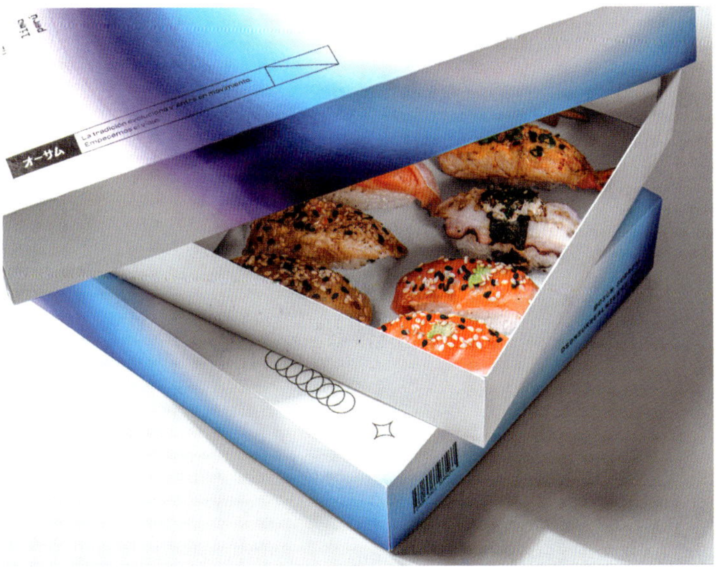

Art Director
Paloma Nieri & Andrea Zorrilla Loo

Copywriter
Kaori Hirakata

Designer
Belén Diaz

Photographer
Cristina Hara

C0 · M4 · Y50 · K0
C0 · M24 · Y42 · K0
C0 · M40 · Y29 · K0
C0 · M40 · Y0 · K0
C25 · M40 · Y0 · K0
C37 · M0 · Y0 · K0
C30 · M0 · Y25 · K0

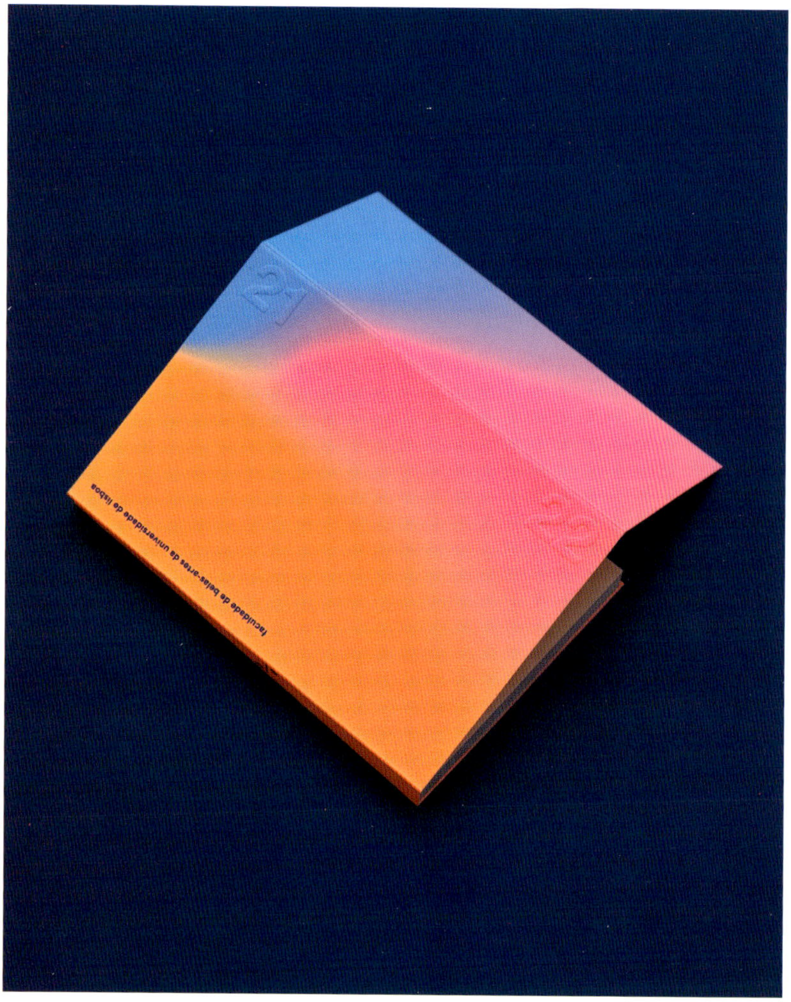

BELAS-ARTES ULISBOA PLANNER NOTEBOOK

The Belas-Artes ULisboa planner notebook for 2022 was designed to help the school's students and professionals stay organized, productive and creative throughout the year. The monthly calendar provides plenty of space for notes and appointments, making it easy to keep track of important dates and deadlines. The planner cover was designed with a fluid and dynamic gradient, using bold and vibrant colours, while the interior pages are clean and elegant with yellow binding lines.

Designer
Tomás Gouveia

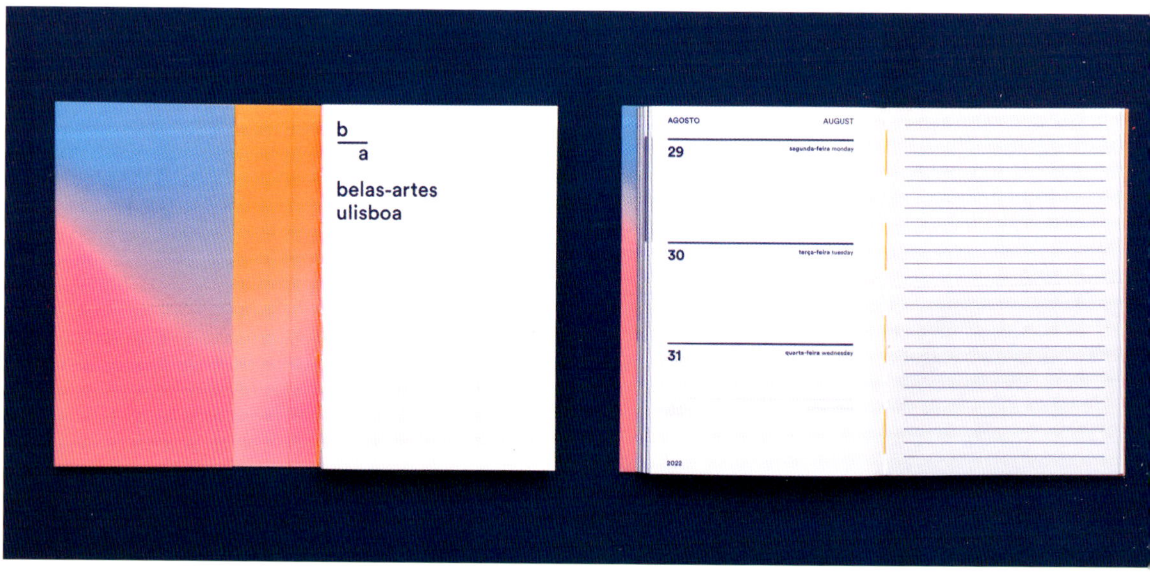

INDEX

Ada Zielinska

www.behance.net/adazielinska
www.instagram.com/zielinska.ada

Ada Zielinska is engaged in the broad field of graphics and illustration, seamlessly blending modernity with the nostalgia of the 70s and 80s in her works. She openly expresses her fondness for analog techniques and incorporates them whenever the opportunity arises. A lecturer at the Academy of Fine Arts in Gdańsk, she has collaborated with brands and institutions such as Adobe, Netflix, Levi's, Spotify, Domestika, CD Projekt RED, *Fast Company* Magazine, *New Scientist* Magazine, the National Museum in Gdańsk, and others.

P216-217

Alexandre Monteiro

www.alexmonteiro.pt

Alex Monteiro specializes in strategic brand design. For over a decade, he has explored a range of fields, from design to audiovisuals, and ventured from creative direction to entrepreneurship. His journey has led to collaborations with a variety of companies and agencies, both locally and internationally, aiding many brands in their growth and market impact.

P238-239

Amanda Louisi

www.amandalouisi.com.br

Amanda Louisi is a graphic designer focused on brand identity, with over 15 years of experience. Her graphic style is most known by the rich colour range, fluid shapes and gradients. She has worked with clients worldwide and the main branding offices in Brazil.

P174-175

Ana Noversa e Inês Vieira

www.manoamanoclub.com

P226-227

Andrea Flemma

www.andreaflemma.com

Andrea Flemma is an Italian freelance brand designer who helps agencies and companies create visual identities that can endure over the years, maintaining a forward-looking perspective, without betraying the past and the heritage of European design.

P072

Angello Torres

www.angellotorres.com

Angello Torresstudio is specialized in digital solutions and graphic identities. From brand identity, UI design to poster, they insist "More is More".

P142-145

Ashley Isaac

www.instagram.com/byashleydesign/

Ashley, the creative force behind By Ashley Design, is a Trinidadian-based brand designer with an unwavering passion for infusing bold colours and typography into the world of visual identity. Ashley embraces bold colour palettes, drawing inspiration from the lively hues of the Caribbean, to create designs that captivate attention and tell a compelling story. Her portfolio is a kaleidoscope of diverse projects, each exuding a unique charm and personality.

P178-179

Atto

www.atto.si

Atto is a visual design and communication studio born in Milan in 2013 through the partnership of two professional graphic designers. They design graphics, both on paper and in the digital world, draw artwork for books and catalogues, imagine identities for cultural entities and businesses. They love research and are committed to self-publishing, love processes, materials and techniques of printing.

P021

BACILE* & La Libertad TNC

www.bacile.com.ar
www.lalibertad.com.ar

BACILE* & La Libertad TNC is a branding, advertisement, and motion graphics studio born in Córdoba, Argentina. From the minds of Gonzalo Prunesti, Santiago Guillamondegui, and Nicolás Bacile, three creative directors obsessed with adding value to brands through creativity and design.

P146-149

Baianat

www.baianat.com

Baianat, Inc. is a multidisciplinary cultural company with a customer-centric mentality working across business, design, development, and technology.

P138-139

Bakoom Studio

www.bakoom.com

Bakoom Studio is a brand and design studio based in Barcelona with a strong focus on creating significant and aesthetic solutions for their clients.

P154-155

Behalf Studio

www.onbehalfof.studio

Behalf is a creative hideout of prudent thinkers and a well-kept secret based in Saigon, Vietnam. They provide creative solutions spanning across different fields of branding, graphic design, digital design, and the yet-to-be-discovered. Their work is fueled by concept, driven by research, stirred by intuition, and ignited by fearless experimentation. There is no common recipe for innovation and every project is an opportunity to pose unique questions.

P242-243

Brandtown Studio

www.brandtown.studio

Brandtown is a branding studio based in Chile since 2019. They were born with the purpose of giving life to brands that tell stories that transcend and establish genuine emotional connections with people. They do not create decorative brands, but create concepts and visual worlds that speak for themselves and go beyond aesthetics.

P080-081

Brest Brest Brest

www.brestbrestbrest.fr

Founded in 2009 and led by Arnaud Jarsaillon, Rémy Poncet and Loris Pernoux, the members of Brest Brest Brest collective work exclusively in fields dedicated to culture and arts. They imagine posters that are bigger than they are. They design album covers for musicians and labels. They are fond of two-colour printing and direct tone overprints. They dismantle samples of popular imagery for fun. They exhibit their work, and are also musicians (Cowbones / Chevalrex). They are irrevocably tending towards more simplicity. They are doing well.

P020, 073, 095, 117, 120-121

Bruno Lima

www.brunolima.design

Bruno Lima is the creative director of LIMA BRANDS. He creates strategic brands that convey the values, dreams, mission and vision of clients in order to connect them with their audience.

P132-135

Carlos Gabriel Ferreira

www.behance.net/carlosgabrielf

Carlos Gabriel Ferreira is a Brazilian graphic designer and communicologist who loves creating visual identities for cultural projects—also available for illustrating, branding and new ways of creating with art direction. Graduated from the Federal University of Uberlândia with a Bachelor's degree in social communication and a Master's degree in technologies, communication, and education.

P172-173

CB Design

www.behance.net/cb625

CB Design is a graphic design studio founded in 2016 by Jackie Price. Nestled in Shenzhen, China, they offer a range of design services with a focus on branding and visual identity. Their team consists of passionate designers who are dedicated to the art of design and take pride in being designers. They believe in collaboration and mutual respect for ideas to create outstanding results. Their slogan "Let's create something awesome together!" reflects their dedication to work closely with their clients to bring their visions to life.

P104-107

Chia-Lin Wu

www.behance.net/ChiaLinWu

Taiwan graphic designer, undertaking a variety of books, editorial binding, editing and layout, exhibition visuals and other graphic projects. Her works have won the Silver Award of the Golden Pin Design Award, the Golden Butterfly Award, shortlisted for the 34th Golden Melody Award for the best album binding design, and is also included in Asia-Pacific Design. She specializes in the use of design to reconstruct poetic meaning and translate from text, and collects fingerprints of creation through printing and paper materials.

P056-058

Chídr Design Studio

www.chidr.co

Chídr is a multidisciplinary creative agency based in Brighton, United Kingdom, with expertise encompassing branding and communication, product innovation and experience, visual and packaging design. Chídr believes in the transformative capacities of insight, strategy, intelligence and practice. Their mission is to elevate and empower businesses and organizations through transformative design and strategy, fostering profound connections between brands and customers.

P212-213

Diana Coe

www.dianacoedesign.com

Diana Coe, 29, autistic (TEA) and high ability (AHSD), graduated from visual communication of ESPM Rj. Brand designer (emotional for unconventional companies) and brand strategist.

P194-195

DXD Studio

www.behance.net/dxdstudio

DXD is a design and innovation studio. They specialize in creating connections between brands and young consumers, providing brand and packaging design, e-commerce visuals and photography services to our clients. Becoming a team that is loved by everyone and creating brands that influence the younger generation is what DXD is working towards.

P180-183

Elmira Gokoryan

www.behance.net/elmirag

Graphic Designer and Illustrator.

P244-245

Enrique Segura González

www.instagram.com/bycuic

Mexican senior designer based in Barcelona, self-taught designer focused on branding since 2019 with studies in architecture and art direction.

P186-187

Estudio Albino

www.estudioalbino.com

Estudio Albino is a creative studio specialized in the development of distinctive branding, solid graphic identity systems, art direction, creative direction and packaging experiences. They explore ways to tell stories and create strategies; finding beauty as a means to transform those ideas into concepts that adapt to any expression.

P086-087

Estúdio Caxa

www.estudiocaxa.com.br

Estúdio Caxa is the result of the creative union between Vitor Brito Pereira and Renato Brito Mamede. They are cousins who grew up together and always had illustration as a hobby. Driven by the desire to make graphic material a fundamental part of problem-solving, Caxa focuses on developing visual identity, key visual, packaging, illustration and lettering, always seeking to create concepts that balance visual experimentation with practical ideas to meet the needs of each project.

P208-211

Estudio Paloma

www.estudiopaloma.pe

Creative studio specialized in creating tasty brands. Based in Lima, Peru.

P054-055, 247

FCKLCK

www.fcklck.studio

FCKLCK is a small, independent studio led by three senior-level creative industry veterans. Being so lean, they work in a streamlined and agile way. All three founders get hands-on with every project and client. Between them, they comfortably cover every flavour of creative brief from concept to execution.

P234-237

Feng Lei

www.behance.net/leifeng2

Graphic designer, director of One By One Lab, Member of SGDA. His works have been selected or awarded by GDC, Award360* 100 of the Year, Tokyo TDC, HKDA Hong Kong Global Design Awards, GDFS Scottish Graphic Design Festival, etc.

P028-031

Forma

www.forma.co

Forma is a graphic design and illustration studio based in Barcelona. Their goal is to assist people, companies and institutions in creating or enhancing their visual identity. Forma approaches every project with a focus on generating innovative ideas and embrace a clean and bold aesthetic in their work. By combining creativity and simplicity, Forma delivers designs that leave a lasting impact.

P042-045, 059

Gao Yang

www.behance.net/wqxnc

Designer and digital artist, often using digital tools and visual language to create works. He designs with a unique perspective on Chinese ancient and modern intertwined cultural concepts, fascinating for exploring the human-centred side of science. His work *Mountains & Rivers* was exhibited in TX Huaihai mall and included in *BranD* Magazine. The rest of his works have been exhibited in Taikoo Hui of Shanghai and Sanlitun of Beijing. *Inorganic Flowers* was selected for the DEMO Festival and exhibited at the Design Museum Den Bosch.

P164-165

Guangzhou Sense Design

www.behance.net/krisbird9

Guangzhou Sense Design is a design agency that fuses innovative creativity with visual arts. The studio has rich market experience in the fields of creativity, design, marketing and new retail. They provide their clients with services of brand planning, brand design, product packaging design and e-commerce design. They focus on the integrated brand experience, including visual communication, brand language system construction, marketing and promotion, providing design and consulting services to clients in different fields. They are committed to combining creativity, craftsmanship and technology on the ground, so as to create a pioneering brand that cannot be ignored.

P082-083

HDU^{23} Lab

www.hdu23lab.com

HDU^{23} Lab is a small graphic design studio located in Wuxi, China. The studio provides graphic design services for branding, visual identity, posters, product packaging and other areas, mainly covering industries of retail, light food catering and internet. They also regularly conduct design practice for independent projects. They insist on finding new perspectives, exploring the possibilities of design form and its inevitability in content and context, and making accurate and distinctive visual expressions. Their works have been professionally recognized regionally and internationally many times.

P018-019, 110-111

Hoooly Design

www.hooolydesign.com

An emerging visual design studio of China, providing brand integration and cultural visual design for cultural organizations and commercial clients. The studio has been honored with a number of international top awards such as the German Red Dot Design Award (including three Red Dot Best of Best), iF Design Award, New York TDC, Tokyo TDC, and Golden Dot Design Award.

P026-027

Huang Waki

www.behance.net/wa_huang

Huang Waki is a designer from Hong Kong who studied design at Hong Kong Polytechnic University and Atelier Chardon Savard in Paris. Her passion for design has been evident since childhood, driving her to explore various aspects of the field with enthusiasm and creativity. Huang Waki is particularly drawn to modern, innovative, and playful designs. She loves to incorporate a vibrant palette of colours in her work, constantly experimenting with new styles and techniques. Her approach to design reflects a dynamic and forward-thinking mindset, making her work both distinctive and influential in the industry.

P240-241

Humana Studio

www.humanastudio.com

Humana Studio is the work of Ana Abreu and Tiago Narciso. They do brand artistic direction, identity design, and print collaterals for people who don't mind being different.

P196-197

Humbleteam

www.humbleteam.com

Humbleteam helps tech companies create successful digital products through design and branding.

P214-215

Huynh Le Tuyet Minh

www.huynhletuyetminh.com

Minh is a graphic designer and an architect based in Ho Chi Minh City, Vietnam. She came from an architecture background with over 4 years of hands-on graphic designing and art directing experiences for various projects from culture, fashion, and interior to technology.

P168-169

Ianca Alves

www.iancaalves.com

Ianca is 25 years old and always been passionate about art in general. She has been a designer since 2016 inspired by her father who is also a graphic designer. Today she specializes in visual identity and her main objective is to help companies develop brands that stand out and are capable of transmitting their message in a unique and attractive way.

P066-067

Irini Gleglakou

www.irinigleglakou.ch

Irini Gleglakou is a graphic designer based in Switzerland. Her work focuses on creating visually captivating imagery through dynamic graphic solutions and cutting-edge concepts, redefining the boundaries of design.

P078-079, 112-113

Jose Ortiz

www.dunk.studio

Graphic Designer with over 20 years working with branding, art direction on diverse fields such as food and drink, design and architecture, fashion and beauty, hospitality and leisure, publishing, professional services, entertainment and culture.

P190-191

Julia Figlovskaya

www.figlovskaya.com/

P224-225

Keresztény Lilla

www.behance.net/lillakereszteny

Lilla is a Hungarian graphic designer. She got her Master's degree in 2022, and during her studies she made this zine. Besides graphic design, she does illustration, 3D design, publications, animation and web design. In 2023, she was lucky enough to win the website of the year award in Hungary. Currently she works for a creative agency as a UX-UI designer, most of the time designing web applications.

P068-069

La Flower Gang

www.instagram.com/la.flowergang

The Flower Gang is a young and creative collective consisting of Obi Fidler, Matteo Mariangioli, and Roberto Schneeberger. They first crossed paths during their master's degree courses in Communication and Publishing Design at the ISIA in Urbino. Since then, they've come together to bring their unique talents to the world of graphic design and photography. With their diverse backgrounds, they're able to take on all sorts of projects, from print to digital, type design to 3D rendering, and even more complex tasks like publishing and identity systems.

P202-205

Laura Hilbert

www.laurahilbert.de

Laura Hilbert is a German graphic designer who likes to explore the bridge between analog and digital design, creating visual and often tactile experiments across a range of digital and physical mediums. Her work includes projects like visual identity, posters, books, and websites and shows her strong love for typography and colour.

P152-153

Layơ Lab

www.layolab.com

Layơ is an inviting creative haven, where the power of design unfolds inspiring brand stories. Experience the world where visionary thinking meets purposeful design, as Layơ Lab sparks inspiration, empowers brands, and opens doors to endless possibilities. Based in Ho Chi Minh City, they are enthusiastic about collaborating with their clients to develop exceptional, unique, and appealing graphic solutions. Together, they create authentic, relevant, and trustworthy brands.

P038-041, 156-159

Lực Dương

www.behance.net/lucduong

Duong Cong Luc is a creative graphic designer and digital art enthusiast. She creates unique and attractive graphic solutions for her projects. With a diversity of skills and styles, she is confident to meet all of her customers' design needs from logos, to brand identities and more. Her mission is to turn physical ideas into visual reality. She believes that every project is an opportunity for you to develop.

P230-231

Lung-Hao Chiang

www.behance.net/st60701

Involved in visual, copywriting, planning, commercial space. Loves FMCG, especially food and beverage.

P062-063

Luzia Hein

www.luziahein.com

Luzia Hein is a graphic designer and art director based in Hamburg, Germany. Her work is characterized by a reduced design language and a passion for bright colour combinations. In 2019, her work was honoured by the German Design Council with the Newcomer Prize at the German Design Awards.

P088-089

Mahmoud Mahroos

www.behance.net/mimahroos

Mahmoud Mahroos knows himself as a graphic designer specializing in branding and logo design. He is passionate about art, corporate identity, logos, stories, and technology. He loves to help people define their brand story to be more than just visuals because he believes that every brand has its own story that needs to be told.

P218-219

Manel Font. FONT (STUDIO)

www.manelfont.com

FONT (STUDIO) was founded in 2021 by Manel Font. After 20 years of experience in the design world, as a partner of Luna and Natural studios, he decided to found his own studio. FONT believes in the transformative power of design and art, trying to bring our vision through innovation, aesthetics and commitment. The solidity in the concept is the door to good design. They love to give identity to people, brands and products, so that they connect with different audiences.

P094

Manita Songserm

manita-s.tumblr.com

Manita Songserm (born in 1990) is a Bangkok-based graphic designer and a member of AGI inducted in 2019 whose fixation flashes upon communication between art and graphic design. Been collaborating with Bangkok Art and Culture Centre (Bacc) on an exhibition department since 2013, she has conflated the muse of experimental medium with her oeuvre as a meeting of multi shades of artists spur the inspiring wave. Her iconic work is perceived through typo-eccentric book cover design and personal art for Typewriter project.

P116, 176-177

Mariam Khalifah

www.mariamkhalifah.com

Mariam is an art director and brand designer based in Cairo, Egypt. As an art director and brand designer with over 6 years of experience, her expertise lies in branding, art direction, editorial, and packaging design, enabling her to create truly distinctive and memorable visual identities. She has assisted numerous brands and motivated entrepreneurs in bringing their stories to life by integrating design, strategy, research, and marketing into cohesive visual systems.

P109

Marka Works

www.markaworks.com

Marka Works is an award-winning branding agency specialized in branding, packaging, web and 3D. Founded by award-winning creative director and multi-disciplinary graphic designer, Mustafa Akillker. They work with brands and startups worldwide. They help brands stand out through powerful, elegant visual designs. They offer unique branding experiences for their partners and make them a success.

P118-119

Minkyun Seo

www.behance.net/alsrbstj793012

A graphic designer in Seoul. Working for branded industry.

P052-053

Mirela Melo Design

www.mirelamelo.com

Mirela Melo Design, featured three times on Behance, specializes in crafting visually compelling brand identities. With a global approach, they transcend borders, bringing innovation and creativity to diverse projects worldwide.

P046-047, 206-207

Monograf

www.monograf.studio

Monograf is a branding and design studio with experience in art direction and advertising. They believe in the importance of the concept and visual communication in each project, finding inspiration in art, music, stories and everything that connects them. They know that creating projects with a simple language makes it easier for people in a visually saturated world.

P102-103

Mr. Studio

www.mrstudio.me

Mr. Studio is a design company. Their design process is information collecting through comprehensive research and close cooperation with clients and partners.

P070-071

OD Lab

www.behance.net/ODL

ODL is an innovative design agency founded in Chengdu, China. They are always curious about new fields and media, integrating commercial and aesthetic values, providing professional, accurate and suitable solutions for clients in different fields, conveying new visual language and culture, and creating unique brand values; they provide brand identity, visual image, creative strategy, art direction and graphic design services for clients in different fields.

P048-051

Olivier Segers

www.segers.agency

Olivier has over 10 years of experience in brand creation, digital product design, and typography design. He has worked for a range of brands from Europe, the United States, Africa, and Australia. His portfolio is hugely diverse, having worked with a range of clients from Silicon Valley start-ups to legacy brands.

P036-037

OUT OF OFFICE

www.outofoffice.tw

Design studio that creates happenings for ongoing, collaborative dialogue and design.

P198-199

Panna Eszenyi

www.behance.net/pannaeszenyi

Panna Eszenyi is a graphic design student at Media and Design Institute, who is in her second year of MA. Designing and illustration have always been her passion since she was little. Her favourite projects to make are editorials, illustrations, print design, and she recently started learning 3D design. She loves to experiment with different kinds of layouts, colour combinations and typography.

P074-075

Papanapa

www.papanapa.com

Papanapa is an independent branding studio based in São Paulo, Brazil. In the space between the unknown and exploration, they thrust bold brands into transformation.

P192-193

Paperlux Studio

www.paperlux.com

Paperlux Studio is responsible for a wide range of design services since 2006. Corporate design, visual identity, product and packaging design are brought to fruition on a shared journey. They consult, design and craft in our vocation as intuitive curators, open-minded travellers and visionaries of instinctive awareness.

P188-189

Play Studio

www.play.studio

Play studio was founded on the belief that original, impactful work is best made by using processes that do not feel like work. They explore and experiment. Collaborate with ease. And lead with curiosity. Then they use what we learn to build brands that resonate deep into the future. Headquartered in San Francisco and designing across all time zones. They apply this ethos to every brand, campaign, experience, and product we shape.

P100-101

Polar, Ltda.

www.polar.ltda

Polar is a place where what is identified around people, brands and spaces is designed. With both a studio and shop, Polar brings together professionals from different specialties who see projects as a means to provoke new perspectives.

P034-035

Polina Zagumenova

www.instagram.com/polinazagumenova

Graphic designer and art director with 8 years of experience in art direction, branding, package design and photo styling. Graduated from the British Higher School of Art and Design and worked with dozens of brands from cosmetics to web3 wallets. Her works got awards at such festivals as Pentawards, Dieline and ADCE, ADCR.

P170-171

Rebeka Arce Studio

www.byarce.com

Rebeka Arce is a multidisciplinary designer and lecturer based in New York. She founded her creative studio in 2013 working for brands such as RedBull, Sony Pictures, Netflix, Vodafone, Columbia Records, Schweppes and Thyssen-Bornemisza National Museum, among others. With over 13 years of experience in the design industry, she teaches at IE University and IED Madrid, and has been part of DNA Paris Awards and ADG Laus Awards Jury. Her work has been awarded in Laus Awards, Vimeo Staff Pick, Los Angeles Fashion Film Festival and has been recognized by AIGA, Computer Arts, Creative Boom, Ètapes, Huck and Type01.

P126-129, 246

Sabbir Ahmed

www.behance.net/sabbirdzns

Individual Designer.

P222-223

Sean Kane

www.Seankanedesign.com

Sean, a highly respected graphic designer with over a decade of experience, is driven by a minimalist philosophy, crafting authentic and timeless brands that deeply resonate with audiences. Since founding his studio in 2012, he has lent his expertise to esteemed brands, building a reputation as a preeminent bespoke typographer whose typefaces have elevated international brands.

P228-229

Shuka

www.shuka.design

Brand transformation bureau established in Moscow in 2003, based in Western Europe, Asia and Australia. Shuka has more than 30 professionals in strategy, creative, digital, and graphic design. The bureau has been awarded various European prizes and featured in numerous international publications. The managing partners Anastasia Butrym, Ivan Velichko, and Ivan Vasin participated in the Brand New Conference in New York, they were on a jury board of the ADCE Awards, headed the British Higher School of Design, and hold their own course.

P162-163

Sitoh Inc.

www.sitoh.co.jp/

Sitoh inc. is a Tokyo-based design consulting firm that focuses on communication designs. They are dedicated to extracting the context that maximizes a company's philosophy and principles and building up a corporate stance that embodies its worldview through creativity.

P114-115

Souvik Paul

www.behance.net/souvikpaul_

A passionate graphic designer with a fresh perspective and a creative spirit that's ready to take flight. For him, design is not just what he does; it's a part of who he is. He sees the world through a lens of aesthetics and innovation, always seeking the perfect balance between form and function. Whether it's creating visually stunning branding or compelling marketing materials, he thrives on turning ideas into captivating visual stories.

P166-167

Studio Born

www.studioborn.co

Studio Born is an independent design studio based in Miami and Istanbul, with a focus on branding, packaging, and graphic design. It was founded by the design duo Ebru Sile Goksel and Ipek Eris Ugurlu, who united their creative forces in early 2017. Studio Born's passion is all about transforming good ideas into good design. They see their brands as their good friends and their work as inspiring memories. Thriving on a powerful identity, they all share one good journey.

P096-097

Teresa Chylińska-Kur

www.behance.net/teresa_chylinskakur

The designer brings 15 years of expertise in graphic design to the table, having successfully navigated roles as both a freelancer and a valued member of design teams. Her background includes extensive interaction with clients and proficient project management, handling tasks from initial sketching through to the completion of final versions, print production, and online implementation of designs. As a distinctive touch, she often incorporates patterns as integral elements in her graphic design projects.

P090-091

The Brand Side

www.brandside.studio

The Brand Side is a creative studio specializing in brand design, based in Buenos Aires, Argentina, and Lima, Peru. Established in 2023 by Juan Martín Muiño, Alexandro "Alex" Valcarcel, and Fernando Oltolina, it offers expertise in design, branding, communication strategy, creativity, and various other "sides", blending multiple creative disciplines such as 3D design, motion graphics, and illustration. With a particular emphasis on crafting new brands from scratch, TBS strives for a balance between concept, imagery, and innovation.

P220-221

The Lab Saigon

www.thelabsaigon.com

The Lab Saigon is the full-service creative and design studio, with an expertise in combined branding and interior architecture projects across industries.

P022-025, 064-065

Third Paragraph

www.thirdparagraph.co

The founder and creative director of Third Paragraph, William Tsao, focuses his attention on publication design, leveraging his expertise in paper and print techniques to craft designs that are both subtle and powerful, imbued with a poetic aesthetic. Recognized with many famous awards, including the British D&AD Awards, Tokyo TDC Awards, New York ADC Awards, and Taiwan Golden Pin Awards.

P084-085

Tomás Gouveia

www.tomasgouveia.com

Tomás Gouveia is a Portuguese designer specialized in editorial design and branding, based in Lisbon. Works since 2010 within the arts and culture sector—from institutions to individual clients—designing visual identities and publications for a variety of projects and exhibitions. His work is featured on several websites and publications.

P184-185, 248

Townsfolk Design Bureau

www.behance.net/townsfolk

Townsfolk is an association of creative professionals whose main goal is to develop unique design solutions for improving visual culture in an urban setting and creating meaningful brands. They develop complex projects related to branding, strategy, creativity and 3D visualization of interior solutions.

P150-151

Transwhite Studio

www.transwhite.cn

Founded in 2011 in Hangzhou, China, Transwhite Studio is an experimental and multifaceted visual design agency that focuses on graphic design and expands into exhibitions, events, experiments, and cross-border collaborations, providing a full range of design services to clients in the commercial and cultural fields.

P233

TSUBAKI Studio

www.behance.net/tsubakistudio

TSUBAKI is a Japanese word for camellia, the flower associated with good luck. Sharing this spirit with everybody, Tsubaki has grown leaps and bounds in the span of 15 years with 18 international awards under its belt. Set up in 2007 by Jay Lim and Vivian Toh, the dynamic duo are known for their expertise in graphic design, visual communication and commitment to details with a core focus on brand management, packaging design, graphic design, and creative writing. Their clients are forward-thinking companies and those that are eager to leave a footprint in their business niche through design.

P136-137, 232

TWOPTWO Design

www.behance.net/1365421834b513

A graphic design team organized as a partnership. The team's work revolves around a wide range of client sectors and design types. They provide creative ideas, brand design, visual identity, product packaging, logo design and motion graphics. They believe that the essence of brand design is the connection and transmission of emotions; graphic design is not only in the plane, but also in the communication.

P108

UNTITLED MACAO

www.untitledmacao.com

UNTITLED MACAO is a design studio founded by Au Chon Hin in 2017. They are keen on branding, visual identity, web design, wayfinding and signage system design. The studio is highly recognized by the design industry and media for its forward thinking and bold visions. Throughout the years, the company has successfully created outstanding high-quality design solutions which have been recognized by multiple renowned international committees and awards, including the ADC Annual Award (Silver and Bronze Cubes), The One Show Awards (Merit), Young Guns 17 Award, D&AD Awards 2022, Tokyo TDC Annual Awards (TDC Prize), Taipei Design Award (Silver Prize), Macau Design Award (Grand Prize and Brand Identity Gold Award) etc.

P122-125, 160-161

Veronika Papadopoulou

www.behance.net/veronikapapadopoulou

An award-winning design practice founded with the aspiration to create meaningful, playful and multi-layered design. Their work aims to realise each project with a focus on its content; producing bespoke designs and staying truthful to the medium and its unique substance. They research, they experiment, they change, and above all they constantly evolve.

P092-093

VIW Design

www.viw.design

VIW Design is a creative design collective working in Seoul, London, Beijing. Their name, VIW (Vapor-Ice-Water), represents the fluidity of their design methodology, adapting and transforming to meet the unique needs of each project.

P098-099

XXD Design

www.xxddesign.com

XXD DESIGN LAB is a young visual design company established in Shenzhen in 2021, founded by Xiao Qiyuan and Xu Yuchun. XXD specializes in the field of new consumer brands with experimental and exploratory thinking. Also the studio assists clients in creating unique market value through conceptual innovation and new visual experiences, providing design services such as brand design, visual identity, product packaging, and graphic illustration. Its work have won more than 30 top domestic and international design awards, including the German Red Dot Award, the Pentawards Silver Award, the Muse Platinum Award, the Tokyo TDC, the Korea K-Design Awards, the GDC Awards, etc.

P032-033

YAGA Studio

www.yagastudio.tv/

YAGA Studio is an innovative design team specializing in CGI digital art and visual integration. They combine surreal techniques and diverse methods to create refreshing visual experiences and creativity. They have been honoured with prestigious design awards such as the Telly Awards, Golden Pin Design Award, and New York Design Award. Their services include brand visual planning, animation, video production, graphic design, and character design. Collaborating with brands such as Taipei City Government, Shin Kong Bank, Cathay United Bank, GMA Golden Melody Awards, VOGUE, SONY MUSIC, BenQ, ASUS, and more.

P060-061

Yuliya Tverdokhlib

www.yuliya.tv

Graphic Designer with passion for visual storytelling. Creates bold and remarkable brand experiences to form meaningful bonds between the brand and the audience.

P130-131

Zeeva Brand Studio

www.zeeva.com.br

Zeeva is a Brazilian brand creation studio founded by Tom Wolf, a brand designer with 3 years of experience in the business. Their studio's creations draw inspiration from nature, culture, and art to craft creative, sophisticated, and original solutions. At Zeeva, they always aim to create brands that are timeless, impactful, and express the essence of each client.

P200-201

ACKNOW–LEDGMENTS

We would like to express our gratitude to all of the studios, artists and designers for their generous contribution of images, ideas, and concepts. We are also very grateful to many other people whose names do not appear in the credits, but who have made specific contributions and provided support. Without them, the successful compilation of this book would not have been possible. Special thanks to all of the contributors for sharing their innovation and creativity with all of our readers around the world.